DISRUPTED DECADES

The Civil War
and Reconstruction Years

ROBERT H. JONES

DISRUPTED DECADES

The Civil War and Reconstruction Years

Cartography by Bernhard H. Wagner

CHARLES SCRIBNER'S SONS
New York

Poems by John Greenleaf Whittier reprinted from
The Complete Poems of John Greenleaf Whittier
by permission of Houghton Mifflin Company.
Pictures for Part I are reproduced from
Ballou's Pictorial, April 19, 1856, and from
Picturesque Holyoke, courtesy New York Public
Library; for Part II from *Harper's Weekly*,
November 12, 1859, courtesy James Truslow
Adams, *Album of American History*; for Part III
from *Harper's Weekly*, April 12, 1862, courtesy
James Truslow Adams, *Album of American History*;
for Part IV from W. C. Bryant and S. H. Gay,
Popular History of the United-States, 1876.

1 3 5 7 9 11 13 15 17 19 c/c 20 18 16 14 12 10 8 6 4 2
1 3 5 7 9 11 13 15 17 19 c/p 20 18 16 14 12 10 8 6 4 2

Printed in the United States of America
Library of Congress Catalog Card Number 79–162758
SBN 684–12580–3 (cloth)
SBN 684–12579–x (paper)

To Rob and Judy

Contents

Preface

For most Americans the era of the Civil War is still very much alive, even though more than a century has passed since the last gun boomed and the final bugle call faded. Civil War battlefields have become great tourist attractions, and the number of enthusiasts who collect all sorts of memorabilia from books and pamphlets to Minié balls are as numerous as ever. The motion picture, television, and publishing industries continue to supply this audience with both fictionalized and documentary accounts that romanticize the era for each new generation. Historians cannot yet approach the period without emotion; they still explore its pathways and argue their cases from a variety of different viewpoints. So attractive a topic has the period been for authors that over 40,000 volumes have been written about this single episode in American history. The heritage of the time includes a nostalgia for the Confederacy's "lost cause," a folk-hero status for men like Abraham Lincoln and Robert E. Lee, a reverence for the Union that freed the slaves and preserved the nation, and respect for thousands of soldiers who valiantly gave their lives.

Conservative estimates place the number of Union and Confederate dead at 529,332, nearly as many as those who perished in all of the other wars of the United States (648,585). The number of wounded nearly equals that for America's other wars, 1,077,213 to 1,094,639.* No other war in the nation's history was so destructive of manpower, and the casualties are all the more awesome when it is remembered they were attained without machine guns (the Union used very few Gatling guns), repeating cannon, tanks, flame throwers, aircraft (except for an observation balloon or two), radio communications, or atomic bombs. Just grim infantrymen armed for the most part with single-shot weapons killing other determined infantrymen similarly armed. To suggest the extent of the war's trauma on the United States, other statistics might also be used. For example, a part of the dollar cost of the Civil War as of 1968 was the more than $8,500,000,000 paid out in pensions to Union war veterans and their dependents. (Confederate veterans did not qualify for federal pensions until 1959 when the question was largely academic.) The current annual Civil War pension cost is in the neighborhood of $3,000,000. Efforts to compute other aspects of the dollar cost bring even more astronomical figures.

The casualty figures and war costs are mentioned only to illustrate the extent of the "national schizophrenia," as novelist James Street called it, and to point out that it was a horrible and costly episode in American history, not the romantic and glamorous one so often portrayed in the mass media. National schizophrenia might also apply in a way to American historians, who, even more than a hundred years later, are far from united in their interpretations of the Civil War; nor has the perspective of time dimmed the emotionalism with which they react. Thomas J. Pressly observed in *Americans Interpret Their Civil War* how Allan Nevins' *Ordeal of the Union* was censured by Southern historians for its Northern bias, and by certain Northern historians for being too harsh on the abolitionists. Pressly said that he had come to think "that historians are not so much agreed as they sometimes like to think they are in describing the 'facts' of an historical situation," which may go a long way to explain the difference in the meaning historians attach to a single event or movement.

---

* The figures for the Confederacy and Vietnam are estimated. The Civil War total could well reach over 600,000 dead, and the figure for the wounded could easily equal 1,100,000.

Regarding the causes of the war, for example, historians have asked if it was caused by Machiavellian maneuvers of sinister Southerners or malevolent Northerners? Did Northern and Southern politicians fumble their way to war? Had some weakness in American democracy appeared? Was the true reason genuine concern for the "rights" of sovereign states as opposed to the cancerous spread of national power? Could it have been an inevitable clash of dynamic industrialism and maturing agrarianism for control of federal economic and political power? Was the vivid contrast of social systems, of sectional culture, at fault? Had the moral question of slavery become so demanding? Was it a psychological blending of motives that drove men, North and South, to such a fever pitch of hatred?

Gifted historians have proposed and documented all of these, and more. Willingly or unwillingly, a common denominator appears in each interpretation. Pressly cautiously observed that "the institution of slavery has consistently occupied a place in many . . . interpretations of the causes of the Civil War." In fact, historians, consciously or unconsciously, have constructed sophisticated arguments about the way in which slavery most effectively brought the war on, and it is a fascinating game in which economic, constitutional, political, cultural, and moral issues are brought into play. This diversity in interpretation in no way stops with the causes of the American Civil War.

Almost every war-related issue has similar historical conflicts raging about it, from the first shot through the beginnings of reconstruction. Postwar reconstruction historiography is in ferment, bringing new disagreements, new perspectives, and new light to that once-neglected period. The scholar searching for a consensus is hard put to find one, and that perhaps is as it should be; otherwise history would be colorless and sterile. Lee Benson, in *Toward the Scientific Study of History*, comments "small wonder that of the making of 'new' interpretations [of history] there is no end." He points to the diversity of the nation and the differences in the backgrounds, approaches, and impressions of historians that partially serve to explain the "lack of consensus." He sees the lack of consensus as ahistorical and proposes a solution in his book. By Benson's terms, this volume is not by any means a scientific history either, since it rests on the author's background, approach, and impressions as do the works of most others. This is not to deny that Benson's criticisms of the way in which historians have or have not approached history are not worthy of attention.

Purpose and Organization

This volume then is not a definitive study of the period. Neither is it intended to be a summary of the latest scholarly interpretations. Its purpose is to provide the general reader or the undergraduate student with an approach to the period that is neither so detailed as to appeal only to the sophistication of graduate students or mature scholars, nor so limited as to be little more than an outline. Hopefully the initiate will seek to become acquainted with other viewpoints and will sample the variety of scholarly literature available.

The book divides roughly into four unequal parts. The first is an attempt to sketch some aspects of Northern and Southern society with emphasis on their differences rather than similarities. American society, North and South, had a great deal in common in the antebellum period, including, for instance, common racist attitudes, a healthy suspicion of federal encroachment in state affairs, an optimistic desire for material progress (if not always defined the same way in each section), an urge for expansion (although the reasons sometimes differed), and an abiding faith in the basic principles of American government (despite sectional disagreement on details). Both sections were alike in their outspokenness on political and social issues, and both subscribed to American-style laissez-faire, believing the government should aid but not regulate the economy. Most readers can add to this list and perhaps quarrel with the above suggestions as well.

The second part of the book deals primarily with the political aspects of the coming of the war. It should not be interpreted as excluding other areas of sectional disagreement, especially economic and social, but it is so structured because the economic and social issues so often met in the political arena. It was there that many Americans believed the nation's problems either would or should be solved, and certainly politics was the most visible highway along which were fought the sectional battles that led to war.

The third part of the volume considers various phases of the war itself, the effect on the homefronts, wartime politics, wartime diplomacy (primarily Northern), and military operations and strategy. The chapters on military history have been structured within the framework of "theaters of operations" rather than chronology. Events in the Eastern theater make up one chapter, the Western theater another, the Trans-Mississippi West a third, and the naval war a fourth. This arrangement provides a clearer look at overall strategy and avoids the confusion of skipping from one theater to another as would occur in a chronological treatment. Neither type of organization is perfect, but since the armies in each theater faced different problems and often operated independently of the others, this method was adopted. A conscious effort has been made to include affairs in the Trans-Mississippi West, for although operations there did not change the outcome of the war, the war itself had an impact on the West, and it should not be left for summary treatment in Western history accounts.

The last part of the volume concerns itself with reconstruction, again largely from a Northern political point of view. This too was not done with a view that social and economic aspects should be omitted, but rather for less satisfactory reasons of convenience and compactness. The focus is primarily on the war-related phases of the national scene, to the neglect of other factors that mark the period as an economic, political, and social introduction to the twentieth century. Throughout the volume, little specific attention has been paid to the political or social history of the individual states, which provides a rich and rewarding study in itself but which is necessarily beyond the scope of this volume.

Acknowledgments

The author owes a great deal to many students of his who have at one time or another studied aspects of the era in detail especially in seminars at Case Western Reserve University, but also at Kent State. He owes a debt as well to those doctoral candidates whose dissertations have either extended or will explore aspects of his own study. As much is owed to undergraduates in recent years at Case Western Reserve and the University of Akron who allowed the author to test out some of the material in this volume in class and whose criticisms are reflected herein.

Similar obligations are due various colleagues who read parts of the manuscript, such as Professors Jerome Mushkat and Warren

Kuehl of the University of Akron, and others who encouraged the production of the manuscript, such as my friends in the history department at Case Western Reserve. Kent State University provided me with a summer research grant over a decade ago that launched the work, and Case Western Reserve allowed me a sabbatical that helped bring the work to conclusion. Professor Arthur Bestor, Jr., of the University of Washington, graciously allowed me to paraphrase extensively from his copyrighted article "State Sovereignty and Slavery" that first appeared in the *Journal of the Illinois State Historical Society* in the summer of 1961. Professor Bestor taught at the University of Illinois when I studied there, and I was privileged to be one of his assistants for a time. I owe a great deal indirectly to the late Professor Fred A. Shannon who directed my Civil War studies many years ago.

Elsie Kearns, college editor at Scribners, put a good deal of work into the manuscript, and the encouragement of Roger Billings and Charles Boak (now retired) at Scribners also was welcome. The patience of my wife and children for the last couple of years was more than appreciated. In the acknowledgments to another book recently, an author remarked (tongue in cheek?) that tradition required him to absolve his critics "from responsibility for all errors." Though he respected the tradition "as a matter of principle," he saw "no reason to absolve them." Bowing to the same tradition, I must admit that the errors in this volume *are* all mine, including any bias that readers may find. As much as I would like to implicate others, that is not possible.

Stow, Ohio
July, 1972

DISRUPTED
DECADES

The Civil War
and Reconstruction Years

PART ONE

THE HOME
OF THE FREE ──────
AND THE SLAVE

*The most formidable evil threatening the future of the
United States is the presence of blacks on their soil. . . .
I see that slavery is in retreat, but the prejudice from
which it arose is immovable. . . . [It] seems stronger
in those states that have abolished slavery. . . . In the
South . . . customs are more tolerant and gentle. . . .*

*It is odd to watch with what feverish ardor the Americans
pursue prosperity and how they are ever tormented by the
shadowy suspicion that they may not have chosen the
shortest route to get to it.*

ALEXIS DE TOCQUEVILLE,
Democracy in America

1
Away Down South in Dixie

"Away, away, away down South in Dixie," chorused Dan Bryant's Minstrels in 1859 at the premiere of "Dixie Land" in New Orleans. Written by Ohio Yankee Daniel Decatur Emmett, "Dixie" was soon a favorite theme in the South. Along with Stephen Foster, who wrote for E. P. Christy's minstrels, these song writers produced tune after tune of nostalgia and romance about life in the old South. "Dixie" and "Old Black Joe," for example, evoked scenes of happy black men and women performing on the old plantation.

That South, that happy land below the Mason-Dixon line where sunshine bathed endless fields of white cotton, where kindly old "Massas" sat on shaded verandas sipping mint juleps, was nearly always a land of plantations, slaves, and a few poor whites. In song and story, the region emerged as a sentimental and romantic land where deep-throated black voices filled the air with music as they bent to their tasks, a place where romantic cotton planters' sons endlessly romanced hundreds of Jeannies with vapory, light brown tresses.

Stylized and unreal, such a South existed only in the imagination of the song writers, or in the minds of those who sought to escape reality, the same people who in post-Civil War times dreamt longingly of the "good old days." Historians have struggled for decades to lay to rest this romantic myth of the "Plantation South," yet the phantom still appears from time to time in the mass media of popular culture, as often as not accompanied by one of the old minstrel tunes.

Structure of Southern Society

In 1860, about 12,000,000 Americans lived in the South.* Nearly one-third of these were black slaves held in bondage by about 2,000,000 slave owners. Another 250,000 blacks lived a life of circumscribed freedom, primarily as farmers or workers in the towns. Of the slaveholders only about 8,000 owned 50 to 100 slaves or more and might have fitted into the "plantation South" myth. By far the largest number of slaveholders kept 9 or fewer slaves and did not suit the myth at all. Neither did the 6,000,000 nonslaveholding whites, who made up half the population of the antebellum South. Although a few of the white farmers, herders, and workers tucked away among the sandy hills—whom historian Frank L. Owsley called the "Plain Folk of the Old South"—suffered poverty, most white nonslaveholders energetically pursued many occupations, from farming to law.

Numbering a third less than in the Northern states and inhabiting a larger geographic area, the South's population was more widely diffused than the North's. The South attracted fewer immigrants, who shunned competition with slave labor and who generally lacked the experience and capital necessary for the production of Southern agricultural staples. As a result, Southern whites remained preponderantly Protestant Anglo-Saxon in origin and cultural outlook, in contrast to a more heterogeneous Northern population. The institution of slavery dominated Southern society. Although another 250,000 or so black Americans lived in the North, only in the South did another race exist in such large numbers.

From the third decade of the nineteenth century on, the institution of slavery in the American South came under constant at-

* For purposes of this comparison, the South includes Delaware, Maryland, Virginia, District of Columbia, North and South Carolina, Georgia, Florida, Kentucky, Tennessee, Alabama, Mississippi, Arkansas, Louisiana, Missouri, and Texas.

tack, not only from Northern abolitionists but also from foreigners. Britain had abolished slavery throughout its empire, and most Latin Americans and Europeans had rejected it. Yet, though the tide of world opinion swirled against the South, criticism seemed only to make white Southerners stand more firmly together, lest they be dragged down into a sea of blackness by the undertow.

The Planters

In Southern society, the major planters flourished at the apex of the social pyramid. They owned the largest plantations, the most slaves, and often the largest debts. According to Southern agricultural lore, an efficient plantation unit numbered about a thousand acres, worked by 50 to 100 slaves. Using that yardstick, about 8,000 Southern planters qualified as major planters in 1850.

When Charles Mackay, a former editor of the *Illustrated London News*, visited General James Gadsden's Pimlico Plantation in South Carolina in 1858, he observed that "the mansion . . . gave little promise of the comfort and elegance to be found within." On another plantation, the house fit the description of "an old farm house, where the white folks lived." Still others were pictured as "long, log, story-and-a-half structures, verandaed in front and rear, with an open hall in the middle. . . ." Even these were "generally surrounded with beautiful trees and shrubbery . . . making even the rudest log building look romantic." The planter's home usually sat in front of a group of satellite buildings, housing the kitchen, stables, other utility buildings, and the slave cabins.

However, more opulent plantations did flourish. William H. Russell, a military correspondent for the London *Times*, sampled the hospitality of planter John Burnside at Houmas Plantation in March, 1861. Located about sixty miles north of New Orleans, Burnside raised sugar, not cotton. Russell recorded his impression in his diary.

Alighting from his journey up river, Russell climbed a high bank to a road edged with a white picket fence that extended as far as he could see. Through a gateway, he discovered a tree-lined avenue adjoining a red brick walk. Proceeding, he came upon a white house surrounded by a carefully manicured lawn. Colorful climbing flowers clung to the six white Doric pillars that spanned the front, providing shade and fragrance to those who lounged on the first or second floor verandas. The house itself, surrounded on three sides by the imposing columns and the porches they enclosed, rose in impressive neo-Greek style to a widow's walk around the square cupola that crowned the structure.

The journalist thought the lands even more impressive than the house. His enthusiasm overwhelmed his limited agricultural knowledge as he recorded his belief that the soil would support cultivation without fertilizer for a hundred years. Russell looked across 6,000 acres of corn and sugar cane, the fields flat as a table top. He could see some slave cottages, plantation offices, and sugar mills rising "like large public edifices in the distance." All together, Russell discovered, the plantation contained 40,000 acres, 18,000 of which remained to be cleared, drained, and cultivated. Russell did not speculate on the number of slaves that his host used to operate the plantation.

Magnificent establishments such as the Houmas Plantation, Melrose Plantation near Natchez, Mississippi, Gainswood Plantation in Alabama, the Anchorage in South Carolina, and, of course, Mount Vernon in Virginia, tended to give visitors to the South the idea that there were only two classes: those who lived on the plantations, and the poor whites who scratched out a mean living on the poorer lands. Studies of the South based on the impressions of travelers helped create and sustain the myth of the "Plantation South."

There were actually many "Souths," only one of which represented the major planter whose measure could not be taken merely by the number of acres he cultivated. Very large landholdings had endured in other parts of the country, from the time of the Spanish grandees in the Southwest and the Patroons of the Hudson River Valley. Spreads of 70,000 acres in Illinois, 100,000 acres in Kansas, and Spanish grants of over 300,000 acres in California could be found even in the post-Civil War period. The typical plantation of the antebellum South was generally smaller in acreage than the Northern and Western estates, though more numerous. Incomplete statistics indicate there were in the pre-Civil War period about 700 of the 1,000-acre, 50–100 slave plantations in Alabama, and perhaps 900 in Georgia. A few planters owned more than one plantation of this size; a very few owned plantations that were much larger.

Southern planters and farmers concentrated upon staple crops of cotton, sugar, tobacco, rice, and indigo for sale on the world market. The agrarian South grew large amounts of corn and other food crops, and raised hogs and cattle as well, but these products were largely for home or local consumption and not for the world market. The emphasis upon marketing staple crops is a feature of the commercial nature of Southern agriculture and the colonial nature of its economy; it partly explains the South's close ties with England and Europe.

Long before 1860 the major planter's life style had become the Southern model. Surrounded with many of life's luxuries, living on large estates with household slaves to take care of their personal needs and field hands to tend to their economic ones, they made every effort to live grandly and to partake of education and politics. They were the envy of most Southern whites and some blacks as well. Yet this aristocracy rose from common origins, often from an indentured servant heritage, and not from old English families who had migrated to the new world, as they frequently intimated.

By 1860, many of the Cavalier Virginians had migrated westward to the Gulf states and were joined by newcomers to their ranks, the recently affluent cotton growers of the Southwest. The same class lines existed as in the old Atlantic Coast South, but the classes were more fluid in the younger states. The ambitious farmer-turned-planter had little difficulty rising on the social scale. Among the Southern aristocracy, old or new, the planter's social and political leadership was more secure than the influence enjoyed by the Northeastern factory owner or businessman in his community. Yet the major planters could not have maintained their position of leadership without the support of the great majority of Southern whites. Slavery bonded all Southern whites together, making them all feel a part of the ruling class.

The second-rank planters who owned from 10 to 50 slaves emulated the major planter in many ways. There were in 1850 about 84,000 such individuals. Often they had as much, or nearly as much, acreage as the larger planters but were in the process of improving it, of draining the swamps or clearing the forests. They were "on the make": they exploited the richness of the soil for all it was worth and put the profits back into their businesses. They enjoyed less leisure than the major planters. They worked in the fields, often alongside their slaves, and few of them employed overseers. As their economic condition improved, they upgraded their style of living.

They built a new house or clapboarded and expanded the log one. They purchased more slaves and worked them hard at clearing and planting.

Other Agrarians

Nonetheless, a third group included most of the slaveholders in the South—over 154,000 in 1850—all those who held nine slaves or fewer. About 60 percent of this group owned farms ranging in size from 50 to 300 acres. Over 60 percent of the nonslaveholding farmers of the South operated farms of about the same size as the small planter. Owsley notes a couple of farmers in Bolivar County, Mississippi, who had 200 and 450 acres under cultivation respectively, both producing large cotton and corn crops and keeping much valuable livestock. He speculated that they found it more profitable to hire slaves from other planters than to own slaves themselves.

In the Appalachian highlands and the sandy pine woods dwelt yet another group of Southern whites often referred to as Southern Highlanders. A rule of thumb that geographers and the United States census takers in 1850 and 1860 used to judge the migrations of farmers was that the farmers tended to move westward into areas as nearly like those they left as possible. In other words, migration westward ran almost parallel from the starting place. The reason, of course, was a farmer's familarity with a soil type, a crop (or crops), and methods of raising specific crops successfully. Grain farmers of the southeastern uplands settled the southwestern uplands and southern portions of the Old Northwest. Tobacco and cotton farmers moved into the middle and lower reaches of the Gulf states. The herdsmen, forced off the lower grasslands, moved into the grasslands of the pine belt and grassy hills and valleys of the highlands. These folks, who preferred the life of the hunter or herdsman to that of the farmer or planter, were then driven into the highlands and pine woods as the agrarians preempted the better lowland soils. They built rough cabins, often cleared several acres and grew vegetables and perhaps some cotton or tobacco as well. They made most of their furniture by hand.

To casual travelers, they seemed an isolated, sometimes shiftless lot. Yet they were proud of their isolation, and they were not nearly so shiftless as passersby thought. Their few cleared acres and rude cabins made them appear to be poor farmers, but the casual observer often missed the significant part of the highland economy: the herds of cattle and hogs nearly concealed in the great forests and the highlander's much-used rifles and trap lines. Owsley classifies these people as frontiersmen and calls their regions the "inner frontiers." The facts support his contention, for large reaches of mountain country and pine forests from Georgia to Arkansas remained in the public domain until the 1870s.

A newspaper reporter traveling through the pine woods of Mississippi before the Civil War was impressed with the "thousands" of cattle raised there. He described the luxuriant grasses and the abundance of other game, including wild turkeys. Others made the same observation, often noting how good the land appeared for pasturage but not for cultivation. So many cattle grazed in the lush pine forests of Florida in the decades before the Civil War that Florida was second only to Texas in the per capita value of herds.

The Southern white highlanders not only prized their physical isolation from society, but they also clung to old customs and beliefs, including a strong nationalism that contrasted with notions of states' rights frequently heard elsewhere in the South. The isolated, slaveless, nationalistic highlanders refused to reconcile themselves politically or ideologically to their neighbors. Eastern Tennessee and western Virginia, for example, remained bastions of Union sentiment during the war.

About 500,000 Southerners of yet another class, often simply labeled "poor whites," inhabited the South in 1860. They stood just above blacks on the South's social scale, and often below them on the economic scale. An indolent, unpretentious, poverty-stricken group, they shared the pine woods and the highlands with the herdsmen, or they could be found on the edges of towns, or indeed in almost any corner of any Southern state, barely subsisting on neglected or unproductive lands. They lived primarily by hunting, fishing, or stealing, and occasionally produced a few garden vegetables. The contemptuous term, "poor white trash," distinguished them from other whites who happened to be respectably poor.

The source of this poor white class is not clear, but the fact that almost every frontier in American history had similar elements suggests that they might have been by-passed by the Southern frontier and driven to less desirable areas by migrants with greater zeal. The effects of an inadequate diet and disease, especially malaria and hookworm, partly explained their chronic lack of ambition and energy. When the advance of medicine controlled the diseases by the turn of the twentieth century, the class virtually vanished.

Thus, except for the highlanders and poor whites, the smaller planters and nonslaveholding farmers composed the bulk of the white population in the South. Very much like their Northwestern counterparts, they engaged in general farming to a greater degree than did the planters. By 1850, nonslaveholding white farmers were increasing more rapidly as a group than slaveholders. Yet they still differed little from the slaveholder in their racial attitudes, and were dogmatic and persistent in their support of slavery. Many aspired to become planters, or at least to keep blacks from owning land and competing for the soil; indeed, they were often more fanatical on the slave question than were the planters.

Business and Professional Society

Although primarily a rural land, the South in 1860 had a lively urban population that included merchants and manufacturers centered in 20 cities with over 10,000 population each, the largest of which were Baltimore and New Orleans. By contrast, the Northern states boasted some 78 cities with over 10,000 population each, although both Baltimore and New Orleans ranked among the 10 largest cities in the United States. By 1860, the South had more than $96,000,000 invested in about 20,000 factories. Nearly 110,000 factory workers were turning out products worth approximately $155,000,000 annually. But with only a few exceptions, most of the Southern manufacturing enterprises were dwarfed by their Northeastern counterparts. Many of the laborers toiled in the plants only a portion of their time, for many of the factories still operated on the old domestic or putting-out system. As in other rural areas of the United States, flour milling was a major industry, along with textile manufacturing and iron making.

Though Southern industry had made a creditable beginning, it lagged far behind the North. Statistics for Southern industry compared with New England alone illustrate the point: nearly equal in numbers of facilities, New Englanders invested two and a half times the capital, produced annual products three times greater in gross value and employed four times as many workers.

The Southern businessmen who acted as commission agents, or brokers, for the planters occupied an extremely important position.

They made their living by freighting, storing, and selling cotton and tobacco, by purchasing abroad for the planter, and by supplying credit to him, making a commission on each transaction. Planters frequently remained indebted to commission agents for extended periods of time, with future crops pledged as security. The agents were staunch supporters of the Southern economic system since it provided their livelihood, and since many of them owned plantations of their own, they were deeply involved in the system socially as well.

The professional classes of the South were not unlike professional classes anywhere else, except that their prosperity depended upon the success of the planters. The doctors, lawyers, journalists, and career military officers—economically and socially tied into the planter economy—generally shared the planter's point of view. This was reinforced by the younger sons of the gentry who chose professional careers; the custom of primogeniture prevailed—that is, inheritance by the eldest son only—although such laws had long been abolished. The professions provided a socially acceptable career for these young men, much more acceptable than business which they considered a demeaning, money-grubbing life beneath them. Thus the professional men were often natural allies of the planter class; in turn, the planters found it useful to have astute and clever lawyers serve their interests in politics and talented editors advertise their philosophies. When the Civil War broke out, the planters quickly took advantage of the Southern boys who had attended the academy at West Point or Southern military schools such as The Citadel or Virginia Military Institute.

Free Black Society

The word "free," in reference to Southern black Americans who were not slaves, was misleading, for it really meant "nonslave." They had been freed by former masters legally, had bought their way out of slavery from masters who allowed it, or had been born to manumitted slaves. But their "freedom" won them no assured status in the South, and any misstep might very well remand them to slavery. Most of the 250,000 free blacks lived in Virginia and Maryland, but clusters could also be found in Louisiana, particularly around New Orleans, in North Carolina, and in the border states of Kentucky, Tennessee, and Missouri.

Free Southern blacks in most communities held unskilled jobs, working usually as farm hands or day laborers. Some were trained as artisans and followed trades such as carpentry or shoemaking. A very few became wealthy, like Thomy Lafon, a New Orleans tycoon who amassed a fortune of over $500,000. Although that sort of success was an exception to the rule, historian John Hope Franklin noted that Maryland blacks paid taxes on property valued at over $1,000,000 in 1860, while in the same year free blacks in Virginia owned over 60,000 acres of farm land and claimed urban holdings valued at nearly $500,000.

Some free blacks became slaveholders themselves. Carter G. Woodson, a pioneer black historian, reported that 4,071 free blacks held 13,446 slaves in 1830. The largest concentrations of black slaveholders were around New Orleans (753 owners with 2,351 slaves), Richmond, and in Maryland. In South Carolina 2 blacks owned 84 slaves each; near Richmond 1 black slaveholder kept 45 slaves; in North Carolina 2 blacks held 44 slaves each. Generally, however, black owners kept only 1 or 2 slaves, usually their wives and children.

Even though white society resisted black economic advancement in the South, and in parts of the North as well, Franklin has shown that free blacks were remarkably successful in finding both unskilled and skilled work, considering the hostile legislation that barred them from certain jobs or discriminated against them in other ways and considering the frequent attempts at intimidation by their white competitors. Rights taken for granted by whites were usually denied free blacks; Southern states did not accord blacks citizenship and forbade them to assemble without white supervision or to move freely from one area to another. All Southern states required free blacks to carry passes or certificates of freedom at all times; if apprehended without a pass, the black was presumed to be a slave.

In fact, Southern white society made every effort to circumscribe the life of the free black. As a result, a black community sprang up, with its own institutions, resembling in many ways a shadow image of Southern white society. There was little communication between the two. Franklin notes how miscegenation laws created family situations for free blacks that were often misunderstood by white society, such as marriage with slaves, or legal or illegal relationships with whites or Indians; how they imitated white recreation, social and fraternal societies, built their own churches, and often overcame Southern reluctance to educate them. Southern whites felt uneasy over the free black man, for he was not only an economic competitor but, worse, a dangerous example for the black slave, and therefore a threat to slavery itself.

The structure of Southern society, with its fixed classes and its base of slavery, did not change much in the eighty-five years after the American Revolution. With the widespread use of the cotton gin, cotton supplanted tobacco as the chief crop, and a cotton planter group of the New South overtook the Virginians and Carolinians as political and economic leaders. In this way the Industrial Revolution touched the system. As the cotton culture spread, slavery became more important than ever to Southern planters, and the numbers of slaves increased markedly. Yet the structure of Southern society remained much as it had been in colonial times.

White Southern Culture

According to the Census of 1850, the illiteracy rate among the South's native-born white population ran over 20 percent, as compared with 3 percent in the Old Northwest and about 0.5 percent in New England. Southern scholars estimated that in parts of the South as much as one-third of the white population could neither read nor write. One reason for the high level of illiteracy was the rudimentary stage of free public elementary education in the South. Urban areas, such as New Orleans, Louisville, Charleston, and Mobile operated public elementary school systems, and solid beginnings had been made in the states of North Carolina and Kentucky. Louisiana had a system planned, but not implemented. Charity schools for orphans existed, but they were not a viable public school system. The rural nature of the country, resistance to the necessary tax burden, and a distrust of education in general stood in the way of the development of an adequate elementary school system across the South, just as the same conditions affected portions of the rural North.

Wealthy Southerners hired tutors for their sons, but even that practice had declined in the immediate antebellum period. Paradoxically, more academies of the secondary school or college preparatory type were located in the South than in the North: nearly 3,000. The Old Northwest had 2,000, and New England, 1,000. The South also supported a number of colleges and universities, including the University of Alabama, Auburn, Baylor, the University of Delaware, Duke, Emory, the University of Florida, Georgetown, the University of Georgia, the University of Louisville, the University of North Carolina, Roanoke College, the University of Tennessee, Transylvania University, Tulane, and the University of Virginia, or their antecedents. With its emphasis on the academy and the college, the South's educational structure served the upper classes, not the masses.

In spite of illiteracy, Southern newspapers multiplied rapidly during the 1850s. They stressed national and foreign affairs, neglected local news, were highly partisan politically and usually more outspoken than most Northern papers. Their editorial opinions provided the basis for lively discussion at Southern gathering places, thus reaching even many of the illiterates.

Although Southerners launched many magazines, few stood the test of time and competition. *De Bow's Review* survived for thirty-four years from 1846 to 1880, one of the most durable, while the *Southern Literary Messenger* was one of the most outstanding. Southerners seemed to prefer British periodicals like *Blackwood's* or Northern publications like *Harper's Magazine* and *Atlantic Monthly*.

Acceptance of native Southern literature by Southern whites either in magazine or book form was further hindered by the absence of urban cultural centers and publishing houses, as well as a rural attitude (not confined to the South) that regarded literature and the arts as decorative, inessential and not practical. Another negative factor was the concentration on the defense of slavery, especially between 1830 and 1860, that absorbed most literary creativity. The absence of freedom of thought on the subject tended to stifle creative thinking.

Given the situation, it was surprising that the South produced as many literary works as it did. The two main Southern literary trends in the antebellum period were romanticism, expressed largely in novels and poetry, and realism, revealed primarily in Southern humor. *Swallow Barn*, romanticized sketches of Virginia plantation life, was published by John Pendleton Kennedy in 1830. Kennedy was a Whig, President Fillmore's secretary of the navy, and a friend of Washington Irving, whose influence permeates the volume. In *Horseshoe Robinson* (1835), an historical romance in a Revolutionary War setting, Kennedy painted a cavalier, aristocratic picture of Southern society, where friendly relations always persisted between master and slave; his Southern women were always refined and romantic, and family tradition came foremost. Kennedy used actual historical situations to frame his romances and showed a fine grasp of the Old South's history. But when the disaster of war struck in 1861, Kennedy remained a Union supporter.

One of the brightest lights on the Southern literary scene shone from Charleston, in the person of William Gilmore Simms. Drug clerk become lawyer, a man without land or slaves and very little schooling, Simms married a planter's daughter and thus found the time and environment in which to write. He produced over thirty works, in which he glorified South Carolina, apologized for slavery, and popularized secession, but he never quite won the plaudits he sought from fellow Southerners. His tale of the South Carolina frontier, *The Yemassee* (1834), was probably the best known of his works at the time. Stylistically influenced by James Fenimore Cooper, the book enjoyed success in the North and in Britain as well. His melodramatic novels of the American Revolution, of which *The Partisan* was one, represented Simms at his best and also drew comparisons with Cooper.

Edgar Allan Poe, the transplanted Northerner from Boston who disliked New England, edited the *Southern Literary Messenger* for two years in the mid-1830s. This talented critic chided New England writers for their alleged literary monopoly and took the abolitionists to task as well; yet for the most part social problems and the realities of life failed to concern him, obsessed as he was with the unusual and morbid. His talent never freed him from poverty and alcohol, though neither clouded his talent.

Often regarded as vulgar, Southern humorists flourished in the tradition of Mark Twain. Augustus Baldwin Longstreet—whose career included not only being an editor and author, but also a judge, preacher, and college president—wrote humorous sketches of Georgia frontier life. *Georgia Scenes* (1835) drew together items earlier published in Longstreet's newspaper, the Augusta *States Rights Sentinel*. The editor of the Montgomery *Journal*, Johnson J. Hooper, wrote *Some Adventures of Captain Simon Suggs* (1845), an imaginary scoundrel who roamed the Alabama frontier. Thomas B. Thorpe, a tall-tale-teller of the Southwest, wrote preposterous stories about Davy Crockett, the mythical Mike Fink, Texan "Big Foot" Wallace, and a fine story about "The Big Bear of Arkansas." Joseph G.

Baldwin, in the *Flush Times in Alabama and Mississippi* (1853), described speculation in the South prior to the Panic of 1837.

Novelists Nathaniel Beverly Tucker and William Alexander Caruthers, M.D., of Virginia, and poets Hugh Swinton Legare, Henry Timrod, and Paul Hamilton Hayne were among other Southern writers who also enjoyed renown. Yet when placed in perspective with other contemporary American authors like Irving, Cooper, William Cullen Bryant, Herman Melville, Ralph Waldo Emerson, Henry Thoreau, Henry Wadsworth Longfellow, Oliver Wendell Holmes, Nathaniel Hawthorne, James Russell Lowell, Francis Parkman, Theodore Parker, and Horace Greeley, they were considerably less than imposing.

Much the same situation held true for Southern leaders in science. Although the natural sciences flourished at the universities of Virginia, Louisville, and Transylvania, and although some Southern states, such as North Carolina, undertook geological surveys of their areas, few outstanding scientists emerged. Among the best known to Americans and the world was the Virginian, Matthew Fontaine Maury, the pioneer in the science of oceanography whose *Physical Geography of the Sea* (1855) became the classic work on the subject. Southern historians often claim John James Audubon, the ornithologist, as one of their own. Probably born in Haiti and educated in France, he returned to the Audubon home near Philadelphia in 1803. He later moved South first to Kentucky and then to New Orleans, where he earned a reputation as a fine portrait painter. Audubon's studies of birds led to publication of the classic *Birds of America* (1838), a giant folio with hand-colored engravings of about five hundred species in their natural surroundings. Published in a limited edition, it was his major work.

As the waves of humanitarian reformism swept over the United States after 1830, the South joined the North in those movements that appealed to the section. However, Southerners escaped the feminist crusades, much of the communitarianism of the social utopias, and obviously the most serious disruptions of the abolitionists. But temperance reform, perhaps a splash-off from the ocean of religious evangelicalism that had drenched the South periodically ever since the Great Revival erupted in Kentucky around 1800, took hold in the South. Southerners formed branches of Northern temperance organizations, and published at least one temperance newspaper of wide circulation. Like their Northern counterparts, temperance parties fought hard battles in the 1850s on the municipal and state levels. Southerners also undertook reform of their criminal codes and penal systems. New England's Dorothea Dix traveled throughout the South unmasking the wretched treatment of the mentally ill. Speaking before state legislatures much as she had earlier in Massachusetts, she was singularly successful: every Southern state but Florida had built asylums by 1860.

White Southern Political Thought

Southern political leadership, long in possession of the Virginia dynasty, shifted to representatives of the cotton states of the newer South by 1860. As late as 1832, Virginia legislators had discussed the abolition of slavery in their state, but neither Virginians nor the question appealed to rank-and-file Southerners for very long. The new South, west of the Appalachian Mountains, deeply resented abolitionist attacks that threatened the very structure of their society. They chose to place their trust in cotton state leaders.

This group absorbed the philosophy of John C. Calhoun of South Carolina, and the constitutional maxims of Georgian Alexander Stephens, both of whom championed the kind of local autonomy that the cotton magnates and their followers believed essential for the protection of their way of life within the United States. Though Calhoun died in 1850, his influence on a generation of cotton state politicians was immense, and though Stephens' constitutional logic led him to oppose secession, he served as vice president of the Confederacy and in later years rationalized the cause of the rupture. The views of the two leaders reinforced each other and formed the basis of practical action by cotton politicians throughout the decades preceding the Civil War.

Calhoun told Southerners that slavery was "a good—a positive good." He compared Southern slavery with the "wage slavery" practiced by businessmen in the North and Europe and concluded that the Southern slave fared better than the Northern or European factory worker. A native of South Carolina, Calhoun was educated at Yale and read law in Connecticut. At the age of twenty-nine he entered politics and spent the next forty years of his life at it. He had been a "War Hawk" in 1812, and as a nationalist and tariff advocate shared Henry Clay's enthusiasm for the "American System."

Calhoun followed the traditional Federalist path until 1828.

That was the year of the Tariff of Abominations, and as the views of his section changed on the subject of tariffs, so did Calhoun's. Tariffs protected Northern industry, but the resultant rise in consumer prices discriminated against Southerners, who were heavy purchasers of both Northern and foreign goods. Moreover, Southern cotton was a major export, and Southerners feared possible foreign discrimination because of Northern tariffs on foreign goods. They also considered the tariff to be an indirect tax on themselves, since it raised the cost of their imports. The opposition to a tax that favored Northern industry at Southern expense made political sense to Calhoun, who led an attempt to nullify the tariff in 1831.

Unsuccessful in nullification, Calhoun strove to construct a system of political philosophy that would protect Southern interests against the encroachments of a federal government which was coming more and more under the control of Northern business and political combinations. He salvaged the concept of states' rights from Jefferson and combined it with Hamilton's concept of a balanced government. He rejected the notion that a national majority was democratic or that the Constitution's checks and balances protected all Americans from capricious legislation.

Discarding also the idea that men were created both free and equal, Calhoun viewed society as composed of classes: hence Richard Hofstadter's sobriquet, "The Marx of the Master Class." Calhoun predicted that the clash of economic interests would destroy the United States unless planters and industrialists as a class united to preserve the Union from any combination of wage earners and slaves.

In the end, Calhoun proposed a scheme that included the erection of constitutional barriers designed to shelter Southerners from the dictates of Northern majorities. The United States, he argued, could operate with a system of "concurrent majorities." That way, each section would have a veto over national policy even if that policy were determined by a national majority. Calhoun speculated that perhaps even regional presidents, one from the North and one from the South, might best serve the "concurrent majorities."

Basing his theory on a broadened democracy, Calhoun, actually attacked the foundations of democracy as it developed in the United States; he wanted to check a democratically expressed national will with a device for protecting any section that might find itself in a minority position. In effect, he exalted local autonomy at the expense of national policy. The position appealed to a South that was dropping behind the North in both political power and population and thus felt the need of perpetuating its sectional parity in Congress. Only with Congressional power could the South protect its peculiar institution against a Northern majority.

Alexander Stephens was not a political philosopher like Calhoun, but a constitutional lawyer. Self-taught, fearless, courageous, he hated pretense and pomposity and championed the Georgia farmer over the planter. Born in poverty in 1812, a slight man who was chronically ill, Stephens proved tough enough to live for seventy-one years. He used his constitutional expertise to support his own opinions and those of his fellow Georgians. Along with them, he exalted the sovereignty of Georgia and opposed the centralization of power by the federal government. Like Calhoun, he supported local autonomy over national control, but unlike Calhoun, he found his answers in the Constitution.

Stephens was convinced that state sovereignty had existed before the Constitution, that it had been carefully preserved by the Constitution-makers, that it had never been surrendered, and that it was the law of the land until destroyed by the Civil War. To Stephens, freedom was only as effective as the level of protection built into the Constitution for the citizens of a state. In the preservation of state sovereignty he found freedom, and loved the Constitution and the Union for it. He defended the Constitution meticulously, yet he could not imagine changing and adapting the document as national conditions changed. Woe to those opponents who found elasticity in the words of the Founding Fathers, especially on the subject of state sovereignty. To Stephens and his fellow Georgians, local autonomy was not an abstract principle but an everyday reality sanctioned by the law.

His reverence for the Constitution he knew led Stephens to oppose secession energetically, but as secession became inevitable, his love of Georgia overcame his resistance. Stephens then labored to construct a Confederate Constitution that in his mind offered at least as great a degree of local autonomy as the one the Confederacy had discarded. As vice president of the Confederacy, he carefully guarded constitutional liberty. He opposed Jefferson Davis whenever he felt Davis sought to circumscribe powers that rightly belonged to the states, as in the suspension of habeas corpus and the imposition of martial law. It seemed inconsistent to him to have seceded in defense of constitutional rights and then attempt to circumscribe free speech. In 1,400 well-documented pages, the Georgian leader made a strong case for state sovereignty after the war in his *Constitutional View of the Late War between the States.*

Stephens' attitude toward slavery also reflected his environment. To him, slavery was sanctioned in the Bible and was not an evil. Men were not equal. Like his fellow Georgians, he was not concerned over the moral aspects of the question. Stephens' position on both the Constitution and slavery were inflexible, and he was impervious to changes in either institution brought about by economics and politics.

Such views were sanctioned morally and politically by the writings of men like Professor Thomas R. Dew, of the College of William and Mary, and George Fitzhugh, a lawyer and planter. Conversely, the works of these men expressed widely held Southern opinions that they merely distilled and systematized. Dew summed up his case in *The Proslavery Argument*, published in 1852.

According to Dew, slavery was good for the slave since he represented an inferior race which needed the guidance of its superiors. Slavery was healthy for Southern society because, as a system, it provided a way for everyone to live together harmoniously. Slavery was good for the nation since the nation depended upon Southern prosperity, and slavery fostered Southern prosperity. As a clincher, slavery was good because the Bible sanctioned it.

In *Sociology for the South* (1854) and *Cannibals All! Or Slaves Without Masters* (1857) Fitzhugh examined the "happy" state of the slave as contrasted to the wretched lot of the British and Northern wage earner, drawing examples from the typical romantic plantation myth. If these works of Dew and Fitzhugh were intended as responses to *Uncle Tom's Cabin* (1852), Harriet Beecher Stowe's dramatic attack on slavery, they failed to measure up to the challenge. As expressions of white Southern thought on slavery, they reflected and reinforced the Southern viewpoint.

As Southern society propagandized for and strove to protect its unique qualities, it responded to Northern economic and social pressures. In turn, these Northern pressures represented that section's efforts to propagandize for and protect its own rapidly evolving economic and social life. Even in its defense of slavery, the South's motives were not unlike the North's. Local autonomy meant a great deal to many Northerners as well as Southerners, for many Americans feared the increasing power of the federal government. Attitudes and opinions on questions of taxation, education, and racial prejudice showed a striking similarity among Americans on both sides of the Mason-Dixon line, especially in rural areas. The one great division between the sections was the institution of slavery, which accentuated and distorted other differences.

2
Old Times There
Are Not Forgotten

The world had known slavery for thousands of years before that day in 1619, when the first Africans set foot in Virginia. Slavery had varied in form and nature from time to time and place to place since the dawn of recorded history. Among ancient peoples, it was associated with conquest and subjugation, and occasionally with debt. Persians, Egyptians, Hebrews, and all Middle Easterners were familiar with it. The Greeks built their city-states on a slave economy, and the Romans emulated them. Christians hedged on the subject; but by the late Middle Ages slavery had nearly disappeared in Western Europe, although it persisted in Eastern Europe. Islam accepted slavery, and the institution became standard in Moslem lands. It continued into the present century as a way of life in the Orient. In Africa, in Ghana, Melle, Songhay, and elsewhere, slavery also endured.

In the fifteenth century, however, a revolution occurred in

slavery as Portuguese explorers under the direction of Prince Henry the Navigator imported black Africans as slaves into Portugal and Spain. Because the trade turned out to be so lucrative, the words "slave" and "black African" became synonymous. So many Africans found their unwilling way to Portugal that the ethnology of the nation was changed. Yet it was in the New World, not Europe, where African slavery became both widespread and profitable.

The first black men in the New World were not slaves, but the Christianized free descendants of Portuguese and Spanish blacks who accompanied the first explorers and settlers into the Americas. They came with Columbus, with Cortes, with Pizarro, and with Balboa. One from De Soto's expedition remained to settle among the Indians. Estevanico, a black Spaniard, explored New Mexico and Arizona. This Europeanized wave of free black men soon gave way to another and much larger wave of unfree, reluctant black men and women direct from Africa. In the West Indies and continental lowlands, the Spaniards found Indian slavery inefficient and unsuitable and soon replaced them with blacks. Thousands arrived, particularly for work on the sugar plantations.

Slavery in Colonial Days

Then in 1619—"before the Mayflower"—a Dutch warship sailed unannounced into Jamestown harbor with a cargo of African slaves, perhaps hijacked from a Spanish slaver at sea. The captain traded twenty slaves for food, and the first chapter in the history of forced black migration to the English North American colonies began. These first transplanted Africans in Virginia were not legally slaves, but entered servitude on the same basis as white bondsmen. According to legend, two of them, Antony and Isabella, brought forth a child in 1624, perhaps the first black baby born in the English colonies. The lad bore the name of William Tucker, after a local planter.

The production of staple crops as well as the plantation economy made black slavery as useful in the Southern English colonies of North America as in the West Indies and South America. The Portuguese, the Spanish, the Dutch, the French, and the English all joined in the slave trade. After initial English failures to establish a successful African slave trading company, the Royal African Company, chartered in 1672, became the most prosperous slave venture in the world, with the greater portion of their trade outside of British North America.

The Southern colonies on the British North American mainland continually required agricultural labor, and had already turned to the indenture system as a partial solution. Migrants who served under terms of indenture included many who desired to emigrate to America but who had not the means and who had sold themselves into service in order to pay for their passage. But many others came unwillingly. Paupers and other prisoners from Britain's jails served out their sentences as indentured servants, as did on occasion dissenters and other political prisoners. Unscrupulous shippers kidnapped children and other unfortunates from the docks of London and sold them into service in America. At first Africans were treated very much like whites, for laws in the southern mainland colonies did not recognize slavery until the middle of the seventeenth century.

Indentured servitude, however, failed to satisfy the demand for labor. Not only were such servants expensive, but after being carefully trained in the arts of agriculture for a few years, they became competitors as their term of service ended. English planters had no more success with the use of Indians than the Spanish had. But black Africans were different. After 1640 most of those imported had no indenture contracts, and others were lifetime indentures. In the 1660s in Virginia and Maryland blacks legally became slaves, and the same condition followed in other Southern colonies.

Black African labor had many advantages. It was cheaper than indentured labor and more easily available. It would not emerge trained to compete within a few years. It was black and highly visible, and could not escape by blending in with the white population. Plantation owners easily rationalized the use of humans as slaves because the black Africans were so different culturally, were not Christians, and were so necessary to the economy.

The legalization of slavery did not remand those blacks who were free into bondage, but it did bring with it social regulations that affected even the free blacks. Intermarriage with whites was forbidden, and black children became slave or free depending upon the status of the mother. As the number of slaves increased and as conspiracies against the whites were uncovered, a new flood of laws were passed designed to keep slaves under control by prescribing penalties for offenses against whites. Before the end of the seventeenth century slave codes were in force throughout the Southern colonies.

Slavery was not confined to the South. Slaves worked on the farms in the Hudson River Valley during the Dutch period, and reputedly found the Dutch more sympathetic masters than the English, who soon instituted slave codes akin to those in the South. Slavery grew slowly in New Jersey and Pennsylvania, where the Quakers opposed it, placed tariffs on the importation of slaves, and generally kept it to a minimum. By the late 1730s, slaves had been introduced into Massachusetts, where shippers sought to compete in the slave trade; even so, Massachusetts listed only 5,200 blacks by 1776, and not all of those were slaves. Connecticut apparently had a larger black population, perhaps 6,500, while blacks in Rhode Island numbered about half the Connecticut total at the time of the Revolution. New Hampshire listed fewer than 700. All together, colonial New England had fewer than 20,000. Blacks had greater educational opportunities in New England than in the South, for both the Puritans and the Quakers proved eager to educate and Christianize them. By 1776 the total number of slaves in the English colonies approached 500,000.

The growing colonial slave system faced definite opposition, albeit widely ineffective. In the eighteenth century, the humanitarian concerns of the Enlightenment led to an outpouring of democratic sentiment complete with attacks on the slave trade and on the institution itself. The onset of the American Revolution with its demands for independence put the question of slavery in a new context. Could white American "freedom fighters" deny black Americans their freedom, especially when those same blacks had fought alongside the whites? Crispus Attucks, for one, a black seaman who had escaped from a Massachusetts master, had died in the famous Boston Massacre. Jefferson attacked the slave trade and Britain's reluctance to allow the colonists to end it. In 1775 the Continental Congress banned the slave trade, though the action was taken mainly in retaliation against Britain's Intolerable Acts. That same Congress struck Jefferson's assault on the slave trade from the Declaration of Independence, where Jefferson had lodged it among other indictments of the king.

Blacks nevertheless took up arms against Britain, beginning with the battles at Lexington and Concord. Peter Salem became an American hero at the Battle of Bunker Hill, where, according to legend, he killed the British officer Major Pitcairn. Even so, the Continental Army was initially instructed not to enlist blacks, an order that was reversed only when the British apparently made an effort to recruit and free them. A number of slaves gained their freedom by escaping to British lines. The British practice led most of the states to enlist both free and slave blacks, with the exception in the end of Georgia and South Carolina. For slaves, service in the army meant emancipation, and about 5,000 blacks fought with the 300,000 or so Americans who took up arms for independence.

Slavery After the Revolution

Although some masters attempted to re-enslave blacks who had borne arms, the movement was a feeble one. Antislavery organizations strongly opposed them, and the social aspects of their revolutionary inspiration usually won out. In the postrevolutionary era the antislavery societies concerned themselves with bringing an end to the slave trade, deporting blacks, and eventually abolishing slavery. They were influential as Pennsylvania, Massachusetts, Connecticut, Rhode Island, New York, and New Jersey took steps to end slavery at the state level. Virginia and North Carolina enacted laws to make it simpler for masters to free slaves if they chose. In 1787 the Northwest Ordinance forbade slavery altogether in that new territory.

However, nowhere in the South did antislavery groups achieve complete success. Slaves represented a much larger capital investment for the Southern owner, and the growing emphasis on cotton renewed the economic viability of slavery. As a result, the Constitution drafted in 1787 specifically recognized the institution of slavery by counting a portion of the slaves in determining representation, and by postponing the end of the slave trade until 1808. Most important, the document provided for the return of escaped slaves. A conservative reaction had set in, and the impetus given to emancipation by the Revolutionary War had come to an end.

The impact of the Industrial Revolution in America bears a fair share of the blame for the reversal. The mills of Europe, England, and New England were nearly insatiable in their demand for raw cotton, and once Eli Whitney had solved the technical problem of separating the fiber from the seeds with his cotton gin in 1793, the potential profit of the plant soared. Cotton quickly replaced to-bacco, sugar, and rice as an important staple. The volume of talk about emancipation dwindled accordingly in America.

At the same time, British humanitarians successfully outlawed the slave trade and gradually brought about the end of the institu-tion throughout the empire. Most of the South American nations, either when they won their independence from Spain or soon there-after, also prohibited slavery. Thus as the institution received a new lease on life in the United States in the early nineteenth century, it began to disappear elsewhere in the western world.

Although three-fourths of the white population in the Southern states owned no slaves, the institution clearly dominated the politi-cal and economic thinking of the section and shaped the social sys-tem. After the American Revolution, as cotton culture took over, each state soon passed its version of the infamous "slave codes" to regulate the conduct of the slaves. These laws, designed to protect slaves as property, also protected white Southerners from slaves and gave slaveowners legal means of getting the most work possible from their chattel.

Though the black codes differed in the various states, they typ-ically provided that a slave could not leave the plantation without his master's assent, that slaves could not assemble unless a white was present, that slaves could not use white law courts, that slaves could not own property (except personal property in some cases) or carry firearms. Usually it was illegal to teach slaves to read or write; and provisions permitting slave marriages were omitted. The codes were tightened up following each slave insurrection, although they were never uniformly enforced. Many slaves learned to read and write in spite of the laws; and many owners were reluctant to take their slave problems to court.

Slave Revolt and Resistance

Slave insurrections proved that black Americans seethed under their bondage. White Southerners grew up on stories of slave re-volts, and each new tale struck terror into their hearts. The most terrible revolt of all, that led by François Dominique Toussaint L'Ouverture in Haiti, was told and retold as the ultimate disaster—that revolution began with the burning of plantations and the slaughter of whites, and concluded with the island free of both slavery and foreign control. The horror stories continued around the revolts of Gabriel Prosser, Denmark Vesey, and Nat Turner.

In the summer of 1800, Prosser, fascinated by the Old Testament, nearly realized his dream of creating a black state in Virginia. He planned an attack upon Richmond and other Virginia cities, which, if successful, would make him king; if not successful, he aimed to continue his war guerrilla-style in the mountains. Carefully stockpiling weapons, he chose midnight, August 30, as the time. However, Prosser's plan was betrayed to the whites, who called out the militia. Unaware his scheme had been discovered and delayed by a raging storm, Prosser and thirty-four of his men were captured by the soldiers, subsequently convicted by a court, and hanged.

Coincidentally, in the year of Prosser's failure, Denmark Vesey purchased his freedom from his master in Charleston, South Carolina. Vesey worked as a carpenter, and was well-known and even feared by other blacks in the area. He had been the property of a slave trader, and knew slavery in its most vicious form. Determined to help his fellow blacks in bondage, he turned down an offer to migrate to Africa. Hatred for the system had smouldered in this hot-tempered man for twenty-two years, until by late 1821 he had an organization and a plan to liberate slaves around Charleston. For much of 1822 he prepared for the great uprising set to begin on July 16, when around 9,000 slaves were to seize military objectives and kill whites. By May, the authorities had word that Vesey planned a rebellion, but his care in selecting lieutenants and his caution in confiding to each only a portion of the plan made it difficult for white investigators to determine its exact outlines. Nevertheless, shortly before the appointed time of insurrection, the militia arrested Vesey and other leaders, brought them to trial, and saw them hanged. Though Vesey's plot failed, as had Prosser's, the thought of it tormented the white community.

Nat Turner was born the year Prosser died. A fanatic who dreamt of vengeance and preached ruthlessness, Turner believed he had been chosen by God to free his race. Like Prosser, he found the essence of insurrection in the Bible, in prayer, and in visions. On August 21, 1831, he outlined his plan to his followers. That same night they went house to house killing all whites, beginning with Turner's master, as they hacked their way through Southampton

County, Virginia, toward Jerusalem, the county seat. Seven men armed with hatchets and axes had set out, but before the end their numbers had grown to seventy. Their bloody spree claimed fifty-seven victims before several thousand armed men hunted them down. Vengeful whites slaughtered many innocent blacks in their panicky two-day campaign, but Turner eluded capture for nearly two months. Over a dozen of his followers who had escaped immediate death were summarily hanged, and Turner, called "The Prophet" by some, went to the gallows on November 11 that year.

If the white South trembled at the mere possibility of Prosser's and Vesey's succeeding, they were terrified at Turner's momentary victory. Carolinians hanged slaves just on rumor of an uprising, and across the South, whites became more vigilant than ever. One conservative historian counted 17 slave uprisings in colonial America, 44 more between 1789 and 1849 in the Southern states, and another 12 in the 1850s. Another historian discovered 250 slave revolts or conspiracies within the continental United States. Although it was difficult to distinguish between rumor and fact in the case of an alleged conspiracy or uprising, there was no doubt that Southerners grew increasingly alarmed after Turner's uprising and were openly afraid by the 1850s.

With the rise of the Republican party, and its participation in the political campaigns of 1856 and 1860, new rumors of insurrections rippled through the South. Southerners attributed slave uneasiness to the activities of white abolitionist agents like John Brown. Even so, between Nat Turner and the Civil War no uprising of a magnitude comparable to Turner's raid occurred—partly because of increased white vigilance, black fear of indiscriminate white retaliation, and a stiffening of already tight slave codes.

A slave's life of resistance seldom led to large outbreaks of violence. Rather, his opposition took more subtle forms. Often it was not a consciously expressed desire for freedom, but a simple reaction against the conditions of his life—malingering bespoke quiet, perhaps unrecognized hostility. Certainly the slave had little interest in his master's business, and no concern in doing more than the minimum work necessary to avoid punishment. If their hours were lengthened, slaves tended to slow down even more or "accidentally" damage tools or other property, or become simply more careless. For the owner, this necessitated closer supervision of the workers, who in turn sought new ways to counter the keen scrutiny.

Some slaves ran away, but the number of fugitives was relatively few since masters obviously took care to prevent escape. Even so, thousands attempted flight every year. Most of these were black males under thirty, and most left alone or with one or two friends. Mass escapes were very rare. Running away proved to be largely a summer activity, for warm weather meant one could sleep comfortably under the stars and forage for food more easily. Slaves often ran away for specific reasons rather than any general dissatisfaction with bondage. Perhaps it was because of a new master who worked him too hard, or fear of punishment for some real or imagined misdeed, or separation from his family.

Fugitives seldom remained at large for long. They were either soon captured and returned or returned of their own accord within a few weeks. Naively, runaways often believed they could remain in the South, hopefully by obtaining a "free pass" in some way. The very few who sought guaranteed freedom at least tried to get out of the South, and of those, even fewer made it. They faced a long, dangerous, and uncertain journey, but enough were successful to keep Southerners alert and to provide Northerners with evidence that slaves did in fact cherish freedom.

As troublesome as successful escapes were the crimes that mirrored the slaves' distaste for the system or for a particular master. Punishment was often more harsh than that meted out to whites for comparable crimes. Petty theft was a virtually universal problem, and items disappeared regularly from the house—food, jewelry, knickknacks, anything. Slaves ate stolen chickens, hogs, and corn. They might trade stolen items to other blacks or to whites in return for luxuries like liquor, tobacco, or money.

According to Southern accounts, arson loomed as a serious problem. Slaves retaliated against harsh treatment by burning a newly picked cotton crop, a barn, or some other building. Masters also worried about potential murder and mayhem, for the institution was rooted in violence, from the very first cruel wrenching of the slave from his African home to his lifelong contest with the system itself. Slaveowners met violence with violence, lest the system collapse. Without brute force, without the whip and the gun, the institution could not have survived.

Discipline and Regulation

The slaveowner exercised considerable latitude in fixing penalties for disobedience. Except for major offenses, slave crimes were the owner's responsibility, and so he made his own law, conducted his own trials, and set his own penalties. Some owners, more apt in psychology than others, enforced the rules with little physical coercion; others depended upon the lash. Slaves had to be taught their limits and obligations, and owners usually attempted to impress them with the consequences of white power. It appeared easier to use fear as a deterrent than to convince slaves that their well-being depended upon that of their master and his plantation.

The rules of the plantation varied from place to place, but all had certain common characteristics. On small units, the master personally supervised his slaves at work, guarded his storehouse, cellar, and livestock, and kept close watch over the slave quarters. Overseers assumed those responsibilities on larger units. Slaves generally were required to observe a curfew, to obtain a pass for any journey off the plantation, and to secure permits to sell goods; they were discouraged from fighting among themselves and from consuming liquor in their quarters, and were prohibited from using abusive language or fighting with whites. Slaves were forbidden to marry free blacks, and discouraged from marrying slaves owned by another master.

To help enforce discipline, masters sought cooperation from selected slaves, and so encouraged status division among them. He set his house servants, trained workmen, and drivers (who assisted him or the overseer in the field) apart from their brothers by according them special privileges, better food and clothing, better living conditions, and the like, so long as they remained loyal and helped him enforce his rules.

Some owners also preached the Christian gospel to their slaves in order to keep them docile. Slaves learned that the Bible sanctioned slavery and made an offense against the owner an offense against God. Owners took care to use the Scriptures judiciously, for too great a familiarity with the Good Book might produce another Prosser or Turner. But because some slaves learned to read, and because both black preachers and churches existed, many slaves in fact knew a great deal about Christian teachings.

Rewards and incentives provided another method of control. A little money, even a dollar, might motivate a slow hand and influence others. Slaves might be allotted a small bit of land of their own to work, in order to supplement their diet and perhaps produce a surplus for trade. They might be encouraged to raise their own chickens or produce their own handicrafts for sale. Masters might distribute rewards at the end of the year or at Christmas, consisting of extra rations, sweets, coffee, tobacco, cloth, or money for those who had worked unusually hard. Other rewards included profit sharing, extra days off, parties, and so on. The revocation of privileges and the suspension of rewards was punishment in itself for disobedience or poor performance.

Other punishment was used for more serious crimes, and the slaves knew as certainly as they knew anything that chastisement followed on the heels of misbehavior. Slaves might be put on short rations or placed in isolation. If they were chronic offenders, they might even be sold and thus banished from the plantation forever. Some owners put their slaves in stocks or irons. Nearly every owner used a whip and ordered a set number of lashes for specific offenses. Remembering that a slave marked with scars brought a reduced price on the market, owners used whips that hurt but did not cut, such as leather straps rather than rawhide. Though not unknown by the nineteenth century, branding and mutilation were less frequent practices than in colonial days.

Runaways merited special punishment. Slaves from the Upper South who seemed even potential runaways were often sold into the Deep South where their chances of escape were remote. Masters terrified their slaves with horror stories of slave life in the rice paddies and sugar fields of Georgia and Louisiana, lest the slaves be tempted to flee. Should a slave escape, he was tracked with packs of dogs that sometimes were urged to maul the fugitive as part of his punishment.

Major offenses such as rape or murder committed by the slave against a white—the reverse was not a crime—had to be tried in a state court. More often than not, however, such an offense landed the slave in the hands of a mob, and if he were fortunate, he might be lynched rather than burnt at the stake or mutilated. Courts seldom punished lynch mobs.

Slave Society

One of the best descriptions of slave life by a white man was written by Kenneth Stampp,* who managed to put himself in the slave's position with reasonable accuracy. Slave life on the plantation looked far different to the slave on the inside than to white society. Family life, for example, endured under very difficult circumstances. Because slave marriages had no standing in law, members could be sold or otherwise disposed of at the whim of a master. Family ties were also weakened since black women were rewarded for their fertility and might well choose or be forced into alliances that would provide her with many children and whatever compensation the owner would provide. Further, although the law prohibited marriages between whites and blacks, no law could prevent sexual contacts between them. Many such matches were casual affairs, such as a white boy proving his manhood or a master attracted to a particularly nubile slave girl, but some liaisons developed into long-term relationships. More than one white wife found herself replaced in bed as her husband took a black mistress. Far less frequently it worked the other way, with a white woman entertaining a black lover or bearing a mulatto child. In that case, the double standard prevailed, for the miscreant white woman would be ostracized by white society, while white men encountered no blame. Miscegenation was apparently quite common at all levels of white Southern society, according to historian Frederick L. Olmsted.

As a result, Southern society included a steadily growing, racially mixed group. By 1860 at least 500,000 Southern blacks were classified as mulattoes by the census takers. The accuracy of the count is open to question as very light persons escaped detection while darker ones were listed as "Negro" despite one or more white ancestors. It was not uncommon for a master to manumit his mulatto children.

Not only masters and their sons fraternized with slave women, but also overseers and white nonslaveholders. Frequently such affairs, even if sanctioned by an owner, brewed trouble in the black community and disrupted family relationships. The slave husband

* Kenneth M. Stampp, *The Peculiar Institution, Slavery in the Ante-Bellum South* (New York: Alfred A. Knopf, 1956).

whose wife cohabited with a white was placed in a terrible dilemma, as was the slave who won the heart of a white man's black mistress. Contrary to the white point of view, many black women did not consider intercourse with a white man as an honor, and viewed miscegenation as little more than rape. Under the circumstances, fatherhood meant little. Quite often a black husband was referred to as a specific woman's man, who happened to live in her cabin.

Not only was slave marriage an uncertain institution, but most black women on the plantation had to turn child-rearing over to a nursery shortly after the birth of their babies and get back into the fields to work. For the most part, the children were raised by one called an "Aunty" in an environment apart from the family for the better part of each day. As black youngsters grew husky enough to perform tasks, they were assigned jobs. They began with light work around the age of six, and moved into the regular heavy routine by the time they were ten or eleven.

In the plantation community, the slaves close to the master usually asserted their superiority over the field hands. House servants mimicked the ways of their master and mistress. A favored "Mammy" acted as governess and nurse for the white children. Elderly slaves usually demanded and got the respect of the younger ones. While such persons had an assured status, they were not always the true leaders of the plantation blacks. A field hand with a strong personality, or a bent for religion, or above-average intelligence, or unusual strength, or a venerated old-timer could very well influence the entire group.

In the field, the task system, often used in rice culture, and the gang system, common to cotton, sugar, and tobacco raising, were the two most common methods of assigning slave labor. The task system provided the slave with a particular job for the day, and when he finished it, the rest of the day was his. Under the gang system the overseer or master divided his slaves into teams, each with a driver, and they worked as long as the master decreed.

Hours of idleness, hours without significant white interference formed a special part of life on the plantation for the slave. They especially looked forward to Saturday nights, Sunday, holidays, and festive occasions when they could dress up and "party" and enjoy welcome relief from the dull routine. Holiday life included hunting, fishing, gambling, singing, dancing, and attending prayer meetings and church.

A religious life that allowed them active participation and promised them a better life in the afterworld was attractive to many slaves, so most took religion seriously. Generally their African faiths faded within a generation, often supplanted by a lively and emotional form of Protestant revivalism. Frequently plantation whites and blacks attended prayer and camp meetings together, sharing in the social and religious experiences.

Especially active, Baptists and Methodists successfully courted the blacks, bringing most of those who joined churches into their fold. The Presbyterians came in a poor third, while the Episcopalians or Anglicans, who had held the white Old South for so long, failed in their appeal. Although Northern free blacks had their own churches, the laws against assembly kept Southern blacks from doing so before the Civil War. Slaves went to white churches or listened to white preachers on special occasions. While this tended to inhibit their religious development, most Southern blacks still learned about Christianity in this manner. Slaves preferred their own religious meetings, either held in secret or with the knowledge of a master who ignored the law. Without white restraints, they felt freer to interpret the Gospel in a way that suited them.

Southern Agriculture

Neither the methods of Southern agriculture nor the plantation existed because of slavery. The plantation evolved prior to the spread of slavery and existed long after the system had died. Despite this, the horror of slavery became a pillar supporting the production of the great staples that characterized Southern agriculture. Cotton, sugar, rice, and tobacco were the cash crops, but by no means were they the only ones, for many Southerners practiced general farming. Contrary to the traditional view, diversification was usually practiced on the larger estates where owners raised as much of the food consumed as possible; smaller farmers were economically compelled to try to be self-sufficient. Tennessee, Kentucky, and Virginia ranked first, second, and third as corn-producing states in 1840, with North Carolina, Alabama, and Georgia close behind in sixth, eighth, and tenth places. As late as 1860 the South produced half the nation's corn crop. Only the prairie West produced more wheat than Maryland, Virginia, Kentucky, and Tennessee in the 1850s. In 1860 the South raised more livestock of every kind except sheep than any other section.

But it was the staples, especially cotton, that were most important in Dixie before the Civil War. Cotton was raised on large and small units from the Carolinas to Texas, and from Tennessee to the Gulf. Planted in the spring, cultivated all summer, and picked in the fall, it was ginned and baled on the plantation or farm, and hauled to a river town for sale, where the commission agents took over.

Like cotton, tobacco was a crop for both large planters and small farmers, also starting in colonial times in Maryland, Virginia, and North Carolina, and spreading after the Revolution into Kentucky, Tennessee, and Missouri. Tobacco required close constant care, what with "worming and suckering," and was economical with slave labor only when slaves were inexpensive. Coastal Georgia and South Carolina provided the irrigation and climate for rice, but cultivation was tedious, harvesting complicated, and milling machinery expensive. Louisiana and east Texas were best suited for sugar, but like rice, because of the necessary refining process, it remained the concern of the wealthy planter.

Planters needed a constant supply of land, for they ravished the soil for quick returns. The westward movement of Southern agriculture, not unlike that of Northern farmers, resulted in part from the search for profit that helped bring about the exhaustion of the soil. As the planters moved ever west, so did slavery. As more and more land was developed, the demand for slaves soared and the price of a slave rose rapidly. Planters found that crude slave labor was well suited to farming staples. Capital investment became so high that abolition, if adopted, threatened to reduce Southerners to poverty.

Production of cotton nearly doubled each decade from 1800 on, with fewer than 500,000 bales (each bale weighing 500 pounds) in 1820 to more than 2,000,000 bales in 1850, and over 4,500,000 bales in 1859. Cotton exports, valued at $72,000,000 in 1850 topped $191,000,000 by 1860, and accounted for about 60 percent of all United States exports. The commanding export position and national financial return from cotton clearly explained the Southern boast, "Cotton is king!"

Tobacco production fluctuated in the nineteenth century, but the decade of the 1850s registered a rise from 199,700,000 pounds in 1849 to over 434,000,000 pounds in 1859, worth about $17,000,000 in that last year. The value of the rice crop held fairly steady throughout the 1850s at about $2,000,000 annually. Production of sugar averaged about 150,000 tons yearly during the 1850s, peaking at 247,000 tons in 1853. By any measure, cotton outstripped them all; slavery contributed mightily to the wealth of the South and as a result to the wealth of the nation.

The Slave Trade

The slave trade within the United States fell for the most part to professional slave traders. As slavery moved westward with the expansion of the plantation system, slave traders transported their human products from the Old South to the new, sometimes by ship, but often on foot over Southern highways. Slave commerce between the states technically came under the jurisdiction of the federal government, but for all practical purposes regulation was left to the states. Most Southern states, except for Arkansas, Florida, Missouri, and Texas, at one time or another forbade the importation of slaves for trade or speculation, but generally such laws were of short duration. By the 1850s only Delaware forbade the slave trade, and no state prohibited the breakup of slave families. Even domestic slave trading was a brutal and degrading business, with little improvement over its transoceanic origins. Trading flourished because of the continuing demand for slaves, but because of the ramifications of the brutal system, genteel whites treated the slave traders as pariahs.

Southwestern cities like New Orleans were depots for the sale of slaves. Olmsted described a slave auction that took place around 1850 where the prospective customers examined the slaves' "respective merits, by feeling their arms, looking into their mouths, and investigating the quality of their fingers." He interviewed one black woman on sale with her three daughters, aged three months, two and three years. He discovered she had had seven children, that her husband lived in another county ("my heart was a'most broke" to part with him), and that her master had put her up for sale in order to raise money for more land. Though the bidding rose to $890, the auctioneer refused to sell "the lot" for so little. A male slave was ordered to disrobe and stood naked for the customers' inspection, but once more the auctioneer failed to get the price he sought and refused to sell. At another auction Olmsted watched a husky boy of seven sold for $630.

As both the demand for and the price of slaves increased in the nineteenth century, a persistent but clandestine trade in African slaves took place. Federal law had outlawed the trade in 1808, but even federal law on top of state prohibitions had failed to end the practice. The embargo on American sea trade in the last years of Jefferson's administration and the subsequent War of 1812 had frustrated those Americans who planned to evade the law, but only for a few years. The illegal trade had blossomed as soon as the war ended.

In the years following the War of 1812, an estimated 10,000 to 20,000 African imports arrived; the panic of 1819 slowed demand, and the mood of give-and-take surrounding the Missouri Compromise in 1820 resulted in a law that defined slave trading as piracy, a capital offense. That law had some effect at first, until it became clear that the courts had little desire to hang kidnappers of blacks. So the American trade revived, climaxing again in the 1850s. And the American traders enjoyed a technological advantage in their constant contest with the naval patrols, both British and American. American clippers "were the greyhounds of the sea," reported Daniel P. Mannix and Malcolm Cowley in *Black Cargoes*,* while naval patrols relied upon well armed, but slow "veterans of the wars against Napoleon."

Nearly every administration in Washington condemned the slave trade and called for better enforcement, to no avail. By the mid-1850s some Southerners openly advocated a legal renewal of the practice. South Carolina Governor James H. Adams in 1856 appealed to the South Carolina legislature for support in repealing the federal prohibition. The Northern states received thousands of emigrants from Europe each year which enabled them to settle the West, he argued, while the South had not blacks enough to compete. In Congress, a representative from Georgia, with support from other Southern members, spoke seriously for reopening the slave trade. The Southern Commercial Convention at Vicksburg in 1859,

* Daniel P. Mannix in collaboration with Malcolm Cowley, *Black Cargoes, A History of the Atlantic Slave Trade, 1518–1865* (New York: The Viking Press, 1962). Quotation from the Viking Compass Edition (1965), pp. 199, 200.

after heated debate, passed a resolution calling for repeal of the federal ban on the slave trade.

The Vicksburg convention proved, however, that many Southerners just as vigorously opposed renewal of the trade. During the fiery debate on the issue, a dozen moderates walked out and the Tennessee delegation voted solidly against it, while Virginia, Maryland, Kentucky, and North Carolina abstained. Resistance to the movement was greatest in the border states, whose slaveholders feared that importation of African blacks would devalue their investment. Elsewhere in the South, even in the cotton belt, some planters opposed renewal of the trade for humane reasons. Nevertheless, the tide of newspapers editorials, speeches, pamphlets, and other propaganda supported the trade.

Yet those who advocated repeal of the federal laws were only a powerful minority, for even after secession the Confederate Constitution forbade the trade. Practical reasons bolstered this moral position. Just as the North walked softly so as not to frighten the border states from the Union during that confused winter of 1860–61, so did the leaders of the new Confederacy hope to attract border-state support. Confederate chiefs desired British recognition as well, and feared they would not get it if they permitted the trade. Advocates of a renewed slave trade bided their time, for they felt the separate states of the Confederacy could always reopen the trade in the future.

The law itself was so laxly enforced that repeal was not really necessary. In 1859 Senator Stephen A. Douglas complained that "there had been more Slaves imported into the southern States, during the last year, than had ever been imported before in any one year, even when the . . . trade was legal." Douglas claimed fifteen thousand or more had arrived, and said he saw some of them at both Vicksburg and Memphis.

Denmark had led the way in abolishing the slave trade in her colonies after 1802. Britain followed in 1807, forbidding slave vessels from clearing British ports in the same year and British possessions the next year, making the slave trade a felony in 1811, and abolishing slavery in the empire in 1833. From then on, the British for all practical purposes were out of the business. Sweden and the Netherlands followed Britain in 1813 and 1814. So did Portugal, Spain, and France, all before 1818, all at Britain's insistence.

Optimistic Englishmen believed that their great navy could

easily shut off the illegal trade by patrolling Africa, and foolishly thought the rest of the world would appreciate their efforts. So, in 1807 the British slave patrol originated as two antique naval vessels were dispatched to the Guinea Coast of Africa. Unable to achieve their objective alone, they were joined by other ships in 1810. Disappointed that these efforts had not stamped out slavery, the Society for the Abolition of the Slave Trade mounted a renewed campaign, and in 1833 Parliament abolished slavery in all British possessions. Still the law alone failed them; in 1840 a spokesman for the Society lamented to Parliament: "the traffic [in slaves] has not been extinguished, but [has] . . . increased."

Cuba had become a tremendous market, with many slaves being re-exported to the American South. Brazil was also a great market, ignoring an 1829 treaty prohibiting the introduction of slaves. And the cotton growers of the American South, as they struggled to meet ever-increasing demands for the fiber brought on by increasing mechanization of the mills of England and New England, blinked at illegality in their search for ever more and cheaper labor.

The British negotiated treaties with other nations (Portugal, Spain, the Netherlands, Sweden, and France) that allowed her to search their vessels, but the United States refused to sign. High-handed British searches and seizures of American ships during the Revolution and the War of 1812 came back to haunt the British lion as slavers of any nationality escaped by hoisting the American flag. Crusty John Quincy Adams, who had resisted being a party to any treaty which allowed British search of American vessels, nonetheless opposed the slave trade. In 1820 the United States organized a patrol squadron of its own, dispatching four naval vessels to Africa. One of these, the *Cyane*, had been captured from the British in the late war and probably had been assigned to African duty to nettle the British. The American squadron soon discovered what the British had been up against, as obviously American-owned slavers took shelter under the Spanish and other flags with whom the United States had no treaty. Not very successful, the American squadron was withdrawn in 1823. In 1824 and later, in the early 1830s, the British tried without success to get the United States to be a party to new search treaties. Slavers on the African coast again flew the stars and stripes.

In 1839 the *Amistad* mutiny took place. The *Amistad* had put out of Havana with a slave cargo when the slaves rebelled, took over the ship, and eventually wound up off Long Island. Taken by the United States navy, the ship was sold for salvage, but the mutineers were held in response to a demand from Spain that they be returned to Cuba to stand trial for mutiny and murder. Abolitionists fought their case all the way to the Supreme Court in 1841, and succeeded in preventing the extradition of the mutineers to Cuba, although they were returned to Africa. The Spanish claimed an indemnity, which Congress debated up to the eve of the Civil War, but never paid.

Two years later, in 1841, the *Creole* was captured by mutiny as she sailed from Virginia for New Orleans with over a hundred slaves aboard. The mutineers sailed her to Nassau, the Bahamas, where British law protected them. Relations between Britain and the United States deteriorated as Britain refused to surrender them. A solution to British-American tension came with the Webster-Ashburton Treaty of 1842, which not only dealt with the Maine boundary with Canada but also stipulated that both nations would maintain viable African slave patrols.

Though the treaty called for both Britain and the United States to support squadrons of "not less than eighty guns . . . each," in 1843 the United States dispatched two vessels with thirty guns. America's naval force off Africa never included more than seven warships, and usually only about five. The British slave patrol always was at least a dozen ships strong, and customarily numbered about twenty. Unfortunately also, the American naval base was at Cape Verde, roughly a thousand miles from the slave trade centers on the west coast of Africa. Not only was the American squadron small and far from the scene of action, but its commander, Matthew C. Perry, was far from enthusiastic about apprehending slavers, even when British officers reported their activities to him. In the end, the squadron reported a few captures. The American navy would not board a ship flying a foreign flag since the United States would not allow foreigners to board her ships; slaves actually had to be found on board, it was not enough for a suspect to be merely outfitted for the slave trade. So once again American traders flew foreign flags or dumped their human cargoes overboard. John Quincy Adams, in 1844, declared he was ashamed of his government for its "false and treacherous pretense of co-operating with Great Britain for the suppression" of the slave trade.

By 1850 the United States kept five ships on the African slave patrol, and the *Perry*, under the command of Andrew H. Foote, cruised off the Angola coast with some success. Foote cooperated with the British more fully than any other American had. Yet along other African slave coasts, the British continued to complain that they seldom saw an American naval vessel. Meanwhile, though the trade with Brazil slackened, that with Cuba continued to thrive, and in addition Americans boldly landed slaves in the Gulf states. American slavers were sailing large clippers built for the China trade, some of which, like the *Martha*, would hold 1800 slaves and could easily outrun the patrols. Moreover, appropriations for the American African patrol were never increased by a reluctant Congress.

Ships such as the *Wanderer*, former flag ship of the New York Yacht Club and perhaps the fastest sailer afloat, hoodwinked the British African patrol in 1858, landing 600 blacks on the coast of Georgia; the ship then brazened its way past the fort guarding the mouth of the Savannah River, and landed the remainder of its cargo, 150 slaves, at a plantation upstream. Though eventually apprehended, the *Wanderer* was rescued by its owners and made still another trip to Africa. The *Rebecca*, a speedy clipper out of Baltimore, outsailed a British steam frigate to complete a successful journey to Cuba in November 1859, while the clipper *Thomas Watson* sailed unhindered to carry over 800 slaves to Cuba in December 1860. The *Nightingale*, out of Salem, Massachusetts, carried on slave trade in the late 1850s until the *Saratoga* captured her off the African coast on April 21, 1861.

Although reports in Southern newspapers told of slaves being brought ashore one place or another in the Confederacy as late as December 1861, it was the capture of the *Erie* and its captain, Nathaniel Gordon, that signalled the end of American participation in the slave trade. The *Erie* was intercepted off Africa with a cargo of 890 slaves by the U.S.S. *Mohican* in August 1860. The cargo was put ashore in Liberia, the *Erie* convoyed to New York. After Gordon's first trial ended with a hung jury, a second trial in November 1861 sentenced him to die. He was hanged on February 21, 1862, the only execution of its kind under the law that made slave trading piracy in the United States.

Perhaps American and foreign abolitionists, reacting to the horror of the illicit trade in the 1850s, had finally brought enough pressure to bear on the government in the election year of 1860 when the *Erie* was caught. The American African squadron had been more active that year as well, to judge from British reports. In September and October of 1860 alone, a British officer noted, the American navy had captured six slavers and freed over 4,200 slaves. Bowing to the necessity of war, the United States African squadron returned home on August 9, 1861, leaving one corvette on patrol. By the following April 7, the Lincoln government finally negotiated a treaty with Britain for the suppression of the African slave trade, at last granting the British the right to search American slavers. Although the Confederacy made fitful attempts to import African slaves, they met with little success. With the onset of the Civil War, the infamous trade soon died, and by 1867 the British disbanded their slave patrol.

The Slave's Dilemma

The end of the slave trade coincided with the beginning of the end of slavery itself in the United States. For the slave, no matter how often he was allowed a holiday, or how deeply religion moved him, his world remained the narrow world of the plantation. The big world beyond the plantation frightened him, for he knew and understood little about it. His own world was bereft not only of education and knowledge, but of freedom and dignity. He knew little of his African cultural heritage, and still less as one generation followed another and the memory receded into near obscurity. Nor was he able to develop a new culture, because of the circumscriptions of his daily life.

Like other immigrants, slaves adapted as best they could to the civilization in which they lived, showing in many ways a preference for copying the white civilization that was their only example. Many, like Vesey, refused to return to Africa when the opportunity presented itself. Slave or free, consciously or unconsciously, most of the slaves were no longer Africans, but Americans. They demonstrated this preference as those who were American-born looked down upon new African imports; as free black Americans held slaves of their own; and as others chose to compete, one way or another, in white society and white business.

Yet neither the free black American nor the black American slave could share the best of white culture. His African heritage lost to him, "he lived," wrote Stampp, "in a twilight zone between two ways of life," in a vacuum, as it were, between cultures. The result deeply affected white society as well. Slaveholders seldom questioned true democracy openly, for political reasons, but they saw potential danger both in it and in humanitarian reform. Both were only a short step from equal rights, civil and human, for both races. The rest of the world outside the South nagged the slaveholder, as did his conscience—as he demonstrated with his various pseudoethnological, pseudoscientific, pseudointellectual, and even pseudoeconomic defenses of slavery. He tried ceaselessly to convince himself that slavery was the positive good he said it was.

3
North of Slavery

New England writer and reformer Orestes A. Brownson, in an 1840 issue of the *Boston Quarterly Review*, noted the similarities of wage and slave labor: "Wages is a cunning device of the devil, for the benefit of tender consciences who would retain all the advantages of the slave system without the expense, trouble, and odium of being slaveholders." Brownson's concern for the laboring population illustrated the anxiety growing in various circles, especially in the Northeast, over one of the social effects of the Industrial Revolution. Factories dotted the valleys of New England, New York, Pennsylvania, wherever water provided cheap power or fuel for steam was convenient. Industrial enterprises of various sorts had, by the 1840s, located in parts of the South and Northwest as well, but the densest concentration by far remained in the Northeast.

In 1849 Alexander Mackay, an English lawyer travelling in the United States, pointed out that the industrial progress in the North had shattered the lively trade that had for so long linked the Northwest and the Southwest along the great natural north-south river basin of North America. Mackay singled out the railroad as the one achievement of American industry that had particularly altered the patterns of sectional alignment in the country. The iron rails of the railroad, he declared, had cemented the ties between the Northeast and the Northwest that the canals had fostered. By so doing, the "strong tie of material interests" now also bound the "political sentiment" of the Northeast to the Northwest; the two sections had become one "by making the Atlantic more necessary to the West than the Gulf," he wrote, "by removing the Alleghenies."

Although Brownson and Mackay recited a couple of facts about sectionalism, the idea of sectionalism itself was not new. Americans had lived with sectional divisions of one sort or another since colonial times. Journalists and historians, as they commented upon the American scene, had never failed to relate how East-West or North-South groupings had resulted from different economic or political aspirations.

The Sections

By the 1840s, when Mackay toured the United States, Americans spoke in terms of three sections comprising the nation. When they talked about the East, they meant, in fact, the Northeast— New England, New York, New Jersey, and Pennsylvania—with its merchants, bankers, and factories. When they mentioned the West, they generally meant the area once included in the Northwest Territory: Ohio, Indiana, Illinois, Michigan, Wisconsin Territory, and perhaps Missouri and Iowa Territory as well (the last two were still very much frontier areas and beyond the boundary of the Old Northwest). Their West, more accurately, their Northwest, was a land inhabited mostly by farmers, but with a growing industrial and urban population. When they considered the South, they meant the slave states, the entire area that permitted slavery and was primarily influenced by the economy based on the production of the plantation staples.

That sectional boundary lines were not always clear in the popular mind of the time is indicated by the fact that Missouri, a slave state, was sometimes considered West, that Kentucky and the western part of Virginia to some ranked with the Ohio Valley as part of the Northwest, that portions of Maryland, Delaware, and Virginia might well belong with the Northeast, and that one had to create yet a fourth section, the Far West, if one considered California, Oregon, and the seemingly remote territories acquired in the war with Mexico. And all of that failed to take into account the differences within the sections themselves, as for example, the Northwest's great subsections, the Ohio Valley and the Great Lakes. Yet over all, the major divisions had political and economic characteristics that made them distinct from one another.

The Northeast, with its factories, factory masters, merchants, and workers, claimed manufacturing as its key economic activity, even though many still farmed and lived a rural life. The merchants and factory masters who controlled the economy naturally also sought, with considerable success, to control the section's politics. The South, though it contained many elements of the other sections, depended upon a system of staple production markedly different from any other section. Just as the businessmen dominated the economic and political life of the Northeast, so did the planters dominate the economic and political life of the South. Overwhelmingly agrarian, like the South, the Northwest as a section was economically and politically directed by its major economic group, the farmers. Unlike their counterparts in the Northeast and South, the farmers of the Northwest represented a majority of the population.

By the 1850s politicians and other observers increasingly spoke of just two sections, the North and the South. Different though they may have been, the North included the Northeast and Northwest. The Far West was seldom considered in this division, except as either Northerners or Southerners viewed portions of it as vital to their own aspirations. Disagreement as to which section should exert control in the Far West did, however, play an integral role in the North-South conflict.

Even though the Northeast and Northwest came to be viewed as one, the political and economic leaders of both sections often opposed one another on a variety of issues. When business and agricultural interests clashed on questions of national policy, the Northeast often stood against the Northwest and the South. When Northwesterners clamored for expansion, they often fought the Northeast and the South. On questions of slavery, the South by itself challenged the Northeast and the Northwest.

With generally different economic systems at mid-century, the sections of the nation had enough national problems to quarrel about without the growing intrusion of the question of slavery, which complicated and often magnified other disputes. Yet slavery continued to intrude, so much so that by the 1850s virtually no question of national significance could come before Congress for debate without breaking down into a North-South quarrel, with the issue of slavery somewhere at its roots.

The Northeast

The Industrial Revolution had pushed the United States into second place, behind Great Britain, among the world's manufacturing nations. At the same time it had wrought substantial organizational and financial changes in American industry. A full-blown factory system had replaced the earlier household or domestic systems of production, as efficiency and growing technology required all manufacturing operations—from the acquisition of raw materials to the distribution of the finished product—to come under the control of one company. The intermediate steps were no longer contracted out to individual households. Economic power had shifted from the merchant-capitalist (primarily a trader) to the industrial-capitalist (primarily a manufacturer). The corporation form of business organization quickly supplanted earlier partnerships and joint-stock companies because it allowed for raising the much larger amounts of capital necessary to the larger undertakings.

The tremendous effect of the Industrial Revolution on the Northeast was reflected in the section's claim to over half of the nation's factories, over half the total industrial investment, and over two-thirds of industrial products by value. Two-thirds of the country's industrial laborers toiled in the Northeast. As an indication of growth, the value of manufactured goods in the United States in 1840 came to $483,000,000, rose to $1,015,900,000 in 1850, and hit $1,876,900,000 in 1860. The Northeast alone accounted for $1,213,900,000 of the total in 1860, with the Northwest ($346,-675,000) and the South ($245,090,000) distantly second and third.

The Northeast could not have achieved its industrial supremacy nor its awesome industrial growth without access to markets and raw materials. For effective transportation and intersectional trade the nation depended greatly on its expanding network of roads, canals, and railroads. Agriculture declined in New England, for example, in the face of western competition as the transportation network developed enough to make it economically feasible to haul farm products east. Transportation opened the way for raw materials to move east, and for industrial products to move west and south.

The completion of the Erie Canal in 1825, connecting New York City with Buffalo and the markets of the West, broke the Mississippi River's monopoly on the Northwest grain trade. Other canals soon gathered in a share in the transportation of bulk goods, so that by 1850 the state of Ohio alone had completed more than a thousand miles of canals. Total national canal mileage increased from just under 1,300 miles in 1820 to about 3,700 in 1850. New York, Pennsylvania, and Ohio ranked first, second, and third, with Virginia fourth by a few miles over Indiana, and with the rest of the Union far behind. Ohio's canals connected the Ohio River with Lake Erie, providing, with New York's Erie Canal, a water route from the Northeast and Upper South to the Atlantic.

The golden age of canal building was the decade of the 1830s. By then the steamboat had been introduced both on eastern and western waterways. Robert Fulton and John Livingston made a start in the Northeast by navigating the Hudson River from New York City to Albany in 1807, and four years later Nicholas J. Roosevelt built the *New Orleans* in Pittsburgh and sailed her to New Orleans. There followed a spectacular growth on the western rivers in particular, with 69 vessels operating there in 1820 and 727 only thirty-five years later. The number of steamers on the Great Lakes grew more slowly, since sailers could compete on the lakes better than they could on the rivers. Still, by 1860 nearly 400 steamers plied Great Lake waters.

The waterways of the country, especially those of the Northwest, bustled with all types of commerce in the antebellum period. The more leisurely downstream commerce to the Gulf felt the competition from the new waterways that drew trade to the Northeast. Nevertheless, the great challenger for business proved to be the railroad. Railroads developed almost simultaneously in England and the United States, and both nations counted experiments in the years between 1825 and 1830. In the United States, business leaders of Baltimore sought a way to compete for the commerce of the West —New Yorkers had their Erie Canal; Washington, D.C., and the Potomac area used the Chesapeake and Ohio Canal, but Baltimore was left out. Securing a railroad charter in 1827, Baltimore leaders launched service on the Baltimore and Ohio Railroad in limited fashion in 1830. From Charleston, South Carolina, the Charleston and Hamburg line was inaugurated in the same year.

These early beginnings quickly spawned other ventures. By 1840 the United States had 2,800 miles of railroad, over 9,000 miles by 1850, and, as a result of the antebellum heyday of rail construction, 30,600 miles by 1860. About a third of the railroad mileage was built in the South, but most lines were short and there were few through roads. The Northeast had somewhat less than a third, and the Northwest a bit more than a third of the nation's track, with, by 1860, many through lines and generally good connections from west of the Mississippi to the Atlantic coast. In commerce, railroads enjoyed some advantages over water transportation. Railroads did not freeze over in winter, and they generally were more direct and faster. Water was cheaper, but the United States seemed to be a nation in a hurry, and the railroad had the speed. As railroads linked the Northeast and Northwest, the volume of canal traffic declined. By 1860 when one thought of transportation, one automatically thought of the railroad. It became more than a means to move passengers and freight, it became an industry in itself which consumed great quantities of iron, labor, capital, and imagination. Mackay's observation that the railroad had subtracted the Alleghenies and married the Northeast and Northwest, virtually jilting the South, was indisputable by 1860.

Tied into a great and almost bottomless national market by smoking steam engines on railroads and rivers, the Northeast led all other sections in the production of cotton textiles, wool, silk, iron and coal, textile machinery, steam engines, machine tools, firearms, ships, clocks, furniture, shoes, and rubber goods. As rapidly as it grew, Northeastern industry never quite caught up with demand. Cotton manufacturers kept expanding their productive capacity, more than doubling the number of spindles in operation between 1840 and 1860. But they continued to concentrate on the production of coarse goods. England dominated the United States market for fine cottons and woolens.

The vitality of American industrial progress was illustrated in many ways. American machine tools were acknowledged as the finest in the world. American factories applied to production the idea of interchangeable parts, insuring great efficiency, thanks to Eli Whitney and his efforts to mass-produce guns. American inventors or promotors, or both, produced the telegraph and cylinder printing presses which together brought more news to Americans more quickly and cheaply than ever before, a factor in speeding up sectional quarrels. The combination of sewing machines and vulcanized (stabilized) rubber stimulated a ready-to-wear shoe industry; the textile manufacturers and sewing machines produced the ready-to-wear clothing industry—both of which had great implications for the support of mass armies.

Although the industrial-capitalist dominated the Northeast's economic and business structure, the merchant-capitalist continued to be active. His foreign and domestic trade ventures and accumulated profits provided financial assistance and investment dollars from time to time for the industrial-capitalists. Headquartered in Northeastern port cities, especially New York and Boston, the merchant-capitalists were leaders in shipping, both in the coastal trade from New Orleans to Boston and in the overseas trade to every part of the globe. During the golden age of the 1840s and 1850s, their beautiful and fast clipper ships logged 300 or more miles a day at sea, helping increase the dollar volume of American sea trade by over $210,000,000 in the two decades. They made the British ocean-going steamers seem like "seagoing teakettles" or slow washtubs in comparison. Yet by 1860 the ocean steamer had made considerable inroads into world shipping, with the United States registering over 97,000 tons steamship displacement in that year. Clippers sacrificed cargo space for speed, while the steamers sacrificed cargo space for fuel. Since the steamship could maintain a regular speed, it averaged better time in a trans-Atlantic crossing, even if it could not surpass a clipper in a fair wind.

Daniel Webster provided a nearly perfect example of the sort of man Northeastern businessmen wanted as their spokesman in Congress. Webster first followed the inclinations of the merchant-capitalists, who opposed tariffs as devices that only troubled and complicated their trade. By 1824, however, the industrial-capitalists had wrested away economic control in the Northeast, and Webster then became a champion of tariffs that protected from foreign competition the profits of industrial-capitalists. Webster accurately reflected the change in the Northeast without losing political stature for his position switch on the tariff question. He remained a defender of majority rule and maintained that the federal government had a duty to bolster the economy. If a protective tariff assisted the industrial-capitalist, it also thereby increased national wealth and indirectly the well-being of all citizens. Like Alexander Hamilton before him, Webster believed a sound system of government finance would preserve and strengthen the Union, by at once protecting business property and binding business interests to national interest.

Agriculture declined in the Northeast as industry grew, largely because of the expanding transportation network. Northeastern farmers with poorer soil than their Northwestern brothers could not successfully compete with them even in Northeastern markets, in spite of transportation costs. As a result, the focus of agricultural production shifted west. By 1860 Ohio, Illinois, Indiana, and Wisconsin, for example, replaced New York, Pennsylvania, and Virginia as the leading wheat producers. Similar changes occurred in corn and beef production, though Texas emerged as an important beef producer. Chicago and Cincinnati ousted New York as the major cattle and hog market. During the 1840s many Northeasterners left their farms; many who remained turned to truck farming of fruits and vegetables to supply eastern industrial cities, or to dairy farming. Of those who departed, a few went west to begin again while others became factory hands in the mill towns.

Nearly half the factory workers were women and children, except in the textile industry, where they were in even greater proportion. The drab mill towns offered no better life than the failing farms: Depending on the season of the year, the workday stretched from twelve to fifteen hours. Unskilled workers earned from $1.00 to $6.00 a week, with skilled hands making perhaps $4.00 a week more. Laborers were unable to change the situation, for their organizations were weak, poorly supported, and unrecognized in law. The Massachusetts Supreme Court decision in *Commonwealth* v. *Hunt* (1842) at least gave workers the legal right to organize and brought the weapon of the strike within the law, but it took the better part of a century for labor successfully to assert itself for its own protection.

Immigrants, too, swelled the labor supply. Between 1840 and 1850 better than 1,500,000 arrived in the United States, and between 1850 and 1860, 2,400,000 more made the journey, part of the greatest voluntary migration in history. This migration marked America throughout the entire nineteenth century but seldom touched the South. The immigrants came in waves that cast ashore millions who attempted to escape Europe's famines, poverty, politics, and wars. The Irish, so numerous in these middle years of the century, fled potato famine and English rule; a large contingent of

Germans escaped the consequences of the failure of the revolutions of 1848. In some centers the immigrants overwhelmed the native laboring population, as did the Irish in Boston.

The Irish newcomers, who wanted little to do with the farming that had impoverished them at home, avoided competition with slave labor in the South. Many Germans continued across the country and settled in the Northwest; they had not the money nor the agricultural training to set themselves up as growers of Southern staples. Because the immigrants provided employers with a cheap source of labor, they unconsciously delayed the development of labor organizations and helped to keep wages depressed. A few skilled workers, such as machinists and printers, maintained effective labor organizations bordering on guilds, but the great majority of laborers could not. Curiously, the philosophy of individual success in America and the constant dilution of the native working force with foreign labor kept class-consciousness from becoming a factor on the American labor scene in the nineteenth century.

The Northwest

Although far behind the Northeast, industry also made headway in the Northwest. By 1860 Northwestern manufacturing establishments were capitalized at $173,956,000 with 189,000 workers in 33,335 plants that produced goods valued at over $346,675,000. Booming Chicago along with Cincinnati and Cleveland became the major centers for the production of farm machinery, leather and wooden goods, distilled liquor, flour milling, and meat packing. Nevertheless, agriculture remained the most important activity in the Northwest.

The average size of the Northwestern farm was about 200 acres, and it was owned by and worked by individual families. Although some holdings were much larger, the Northwest had no installations similar in function to the plantation of the South. Northwesterners produced great amounts of corn and hogs, wheat, cattle, and sheep, with good reason. Just as the Industrial Revolution stimulated cotton production in the South, the same process created a Northeastern urban demand for foodstuffs. Simultaneously, Europe increased its importation of agricultural goods. The 1840s and 1850s were decades of constantly ascending demand for farm products and, consequently, of increasing prosperity for the farmer. The Northwestern farmer specialized more and gleaned the advantage of greater income, but as he did so, he became part of a larger economic pattern, more and more dependent upon the demands of his market in the industrial-urban Northeast. The economy of the two sections proved highly complementary, as the Northeast became the Northwest's best customer and the Northwest provided a growing market for the products of the Northeast.

In this way the economic ties between Northeast and Northwest were direct and vital. Railroads literally riveted the sections together, with their fast, all-weather connecting routes. By 1860, Northwestern farmers no longer depended upon the waters of canals or rivers to carry their freight east. As Mackay had observed, another link between the Northwest and the South vanished, as the Ohio and Mississippi waterways decreased in commercial importance.

Although primarily powered by the horse, the variety of farm machinery grew as the demand for farm products increased and as the frontier receded farther into the Indian country west of the Missouri River. At Moline, Illinois, John Deere produced plows with steel moldboards that more efficiently turned under the prairie sod. At Chicago, Cyrus McCormick sold 20,000 reapers a year by 1860, greatly reducing the time and manpower necessary for harvest. At Racine, Wisconsin, Jerome Case built threshers that could do in one hour what the older methods did in a day. When young Northwesterners marched off to the Civil War, they were partly replaced by machines. Mechanization of the farms increased and brought the vast agricultural potential of the section to the assistance of the Union.

By the 1860s the Northwestern farmers who controlled politics in their section tended to be conservative. They were middle income landowners, who reinvested their profits in their enterprises in the search for even greater profit. These agrarian capitalists claimed no great spokesman for their group on a par with John C. Calhoun or Daniel Webster, and Henry Clay of Kentucky was not really one of them. Although almost unknown outside of his own state until 1858, Abraham Lincoln, the Illinois Whig turned Republican, echoed many of their opinions. Lincoln believed America should make it possible for men to become property owners, even if some men would acquire more than others. Lincoln opposed obstacles to "getting rich," for he felt that in "free society" men knew they could "better" their "condition," knew that they faced "no fixed condition of labor" all their lives. Lincoln, when he spoke of "all men," meant all white men, for he confessed later that he did not know how to handle the problem of race. At the time, the society of which he spoke in the Northwest was overwhelmingly a white society which knew little of race problems. The question of slavery was another matter, one that Lincoln, like many of the people in his section, came to view in a moral and political, not a social and economic light.

Among the general factors that seasoned the conservative politics of the Northwest, westward expansion, free or nearly free land, and internal improvements ranked high. They objected to centralized banking control by the federal government, such as the old Bank of the United States had been. In that regard, Andrew Jackson remained their hero for his successful "war" against the Northeastern-controlled institution. Northwesterners wanted no federal restraints on their credit like that which the bank had imposed. At first, the tariff question interested Northwesterners only as a device they could use to logroll for their own projects; but by 1860, given the section's growing industry, they came to favor protectionism, which became another point of conflict with the South.

Northwesterners, Lincoln included, believed that the federal government could not interfere with slavery in the Southern states that permitted it without trampling the right of a state to control its own affairs. At the same time they frowned on black immigration into their section, whether slave or free. They emphatically insisted that the territories be kept white, for Northwesterners looked upon those areas as theirs for expansion. In this sense they were white supremacists, determined to keep both slavery and the black man in the South.

Northern Culture

Northerners still assumed, in the antebellum days, that America was capable of becoming an earthly paradise. Their confidence and optimism lent them an air of superiority over foreign cultures and systems in the realm of both material and spiritual progress. Northerners seemed to believe that progress itself, or at least the idea of progress, was their exclusive property. The optimism various writers noted following the War of 1812 continued as an American trait. During the expansionist, "manifest destiny" years of the 1840s prominent Americans widely proclaimed it America's mission, even her destiny, to bring the advantages of her free civilization to the rest of the world. As a result, some Northerners felt Southern slavery was awkward, but most had no notion of letting slavery impede the nation's progress.

American brashness, the very crudity and naïveté of Americans, drew foreign criticism, which Americans returned with swift and uncompromising rejoinders. Still, Americans unhesitatingly found fault with themselves, or with anything that appeared to stand in the way of whatever they thought progress to be. One author aptly labelled this "freedom's ferment," and much of the ferment stirred the South as well as the North unless it in any way threatened their own slave institutions. American writers played a more important role in the ferment than they were given credit for in their own day.

While Americans resented general foreign criticism, they accepted it in the realm of literature. An American writer seldom won critical acclaim at home unless he had first won it abroad. Even with that handicap American literature, which had budded as early as the 1820s, blossomed in the decades prior to the Civil War. New Yorkers Cooper, Irving, Melville, Walt Whitman, and New Englanders Emerson, Thoreau, and Hawthorne established reputations both abroad and at home—not only for their literary skills but also for their social commentary.

Behind the adventure and romance of James Fenimore Cooper's Leatherstocking sagas was an exposition of society's tensions, including that between civil law and natural rights. Cooper also lashed out at America's English critics in *Notions of Americans* (1828); he followed that, a few years later, with lectures on conservatism in *A Letter to His Countrymen* (1834), scorching Americans for their abuse of democracy. American critics were hard on this conservative who bordered on the aristocratic, and Cooper challenged them in libel suits that he usually won.

Unlike the sometimes cranky Cooper, Washington Irving was admired and imitated in the nineteenth century, although he, too, observed shortcomings in American society. Irving, though, presented his land-hungry, pleasure-loving, ignoble settlers in a comic masterpiece, *Diedrich Knickerbocker's History of New York* (1809). This Federalist critique of Jeffersonian democracy allowed "Diedrich Knickerbocker" to convey Irving's views in a popular way.

Melville, more abstruse and sophisticated than either Irving or Cooper, worked his philosophy into his stories with a symbolism that his contemporary readers often missed. His career passed virtually into limbo after *Moby Dick* (1851), in which he sermonized about the useless but heroic effort to eradicate evil in the universe. Expressed in masterful prose, clever social criticism, and a mature philosophy, Melville's genius went unrecognized until the twentieth century.

Walt Whitman, abolitionist, libertarian, equalitarian, and self-proclaimed poet of democracy, entered politics as a Democrat and later turned Republican. His sympathy with Free-soilers and abolitionists prompted the Brooklyn *Eagle* to discharge him as editor (1846–1848), while the views he expressed in his main work, *Leaves of Grass* (1855), scandalized most of his readers. Whitman championed both the brotherhood of man and the dignity of the individual, reconciling for himself the tension between the two.

By the 1840s the tiny New England village of Concord, Massachusetts, replaced New York as the center of American literary creativity. After Harvard-educated Ralph Waldo Emerson left his Unitarian ministry of the Second Church of Boston in 1832, he gathered together in a series of essays, *Nature* (1836), an explanation of his optimistic and individualistic philosophy called Transcendentalism. He repeatedly applied this philosophy to American cultural and national problems, especially in *The American Scholar* (1837) and in *Dial* (1840–1844), a quarterly review he and other Transcendentalists published. Emerson shocked the East by identifying himself with black emancipation when it was still an unpopular cause, but by 1850 he was widely sought as a lecturer everywhere but in the slaveholding South.

Among those gathered around Emerson at Concord was Henry David Thoreau, a fellow Harvard graduate. Although he wrote very little on political and economic issues before the Civil War, he was an activist whose personal conduct revealed his position. Thoreau was jailed for refusing to pay a poll tax in support of the Mexican War, which he viewed as a slaveholder's scheme to obtain land for the expansion of slavery. He spoke often and fervently against the institution, was accused of harboring fugitive slaves at Walden, and condemned both the indictment and conviction of John Brown in ringing public addresses. He expressed his concern with nature and the individual in his book *Walden* (1854).

Nathaniel Hawthorne joined the literary colony at Concord in July, 1842. A native of Salem, Massachusetts, and a student of New England Puritanism, he commented on the contemporary scene in *Blithedale Romance* (1852). A thinly disguised account of his six-month stay at the utopian Brook Farm community, it indicted certain reformers for their narrow pursuit of limited goals at the expense of a general reform of society. The fame of his colleague, Harvard professor Henry Wadsworth Longfellow, rested on gentle poems like *The Courtship of Miles Standish* (1858), though Longfellow's antislavery views were reflected in *Poems on Slavery* (1842). John Greenleaf Whittier, with little formal education and a Quaker background, spoke often and ardently at antislavery meetings while a Massachusetts legislator. His first poems were published in *The Liberator*; but later Whittier turned to editing, serving as editor of the *Pennsylvania Freeman* (1838–1840) and the *National Era* (1847–1860), which published the serialized version of Harriet Beecher Stowe's *Uncle Tom's Cabin*.

James Russell Lowell owed some of his vibrant abolitionist convictions to his wife, Maria White, a poet and Transcendentalist in her own right. Lowell contributed to and edited the *National Anti-Slavery Standard* from 1848 to 1852 and later wrote for the *Pennsylvania Freeman*. A staunch Republican and a critic of England's role in the Civil War, Lowell was devoted to the preservation of the Union. William Cullen Bryant, though New England born and raised, edited the *New York Review and Athenaeum Magazine*, successor to the *Atlantic Magazine*, for two years from 1825 to 1826. In 1829 he took over as editor-in-chief of the New York *Evening Post*, remaining at the helm for nearly fifty years. He vigorously advocated the abolition of slavery, championed the Free-soil platform, and supported John Brown. Oliver Wendell Holmes, M.D., the essayist and lecturer, included antislavery sentiment in his reformist thought.

By the 1840s American publishers had come into their own, and better than two-thirds of the books sold in the States had been printed there. Even so, English authors like Charles Dickens and Sir Walter Scott dominated the scene. The absence of an international copyright law made it easy for American publishers to pirate British works and capitalize on their popularity, to the detriment of American authors who had to be paid. On the other hand, American authors successfully invaded the booming magazine field. Though their life span was usually short, numerous magazines appeared in the United States, hundreds in the decade of the 1850s alone. They included Bryant's *New York Review and Athenaeum Magazine*, the *Atlantic Magazine* that preceded it, and the *United States Literary Gazette* with which it merged. But Americans also read American authors in *Putnam's Monthly Magazine* (begun in 1853), the scholarly *North American Review* (founded 1815), and the *Atlantic Monthly* (1857). *Harper's Monthly Magazine* (1850), with a strong dose of English-born prose, sold in the South as well as the North. Even *Godey's Lady's Book* (1830), the pace setter for women's styles, included Holmes, Hawthorne, Emerson, Poe, and William Gilmore Simms among its contributors.

The connection between the magazine and newspaper world was closer than many suspected, for some of America's best writers edited newspapers or magazines or both, frequently simultaneously and often anonymously. Newspapers furnished American authors with an outlet for their fiction as well as for their reporting, although the papers most often bore the distinctive stamp of editors-in-chief like James Gordon Bennett of the New York *Herald* or Horace Greeley of the New York *Tribune*. The New York *Sun* revolutionized journalism in 1833 with its penny an issue price, and other New York papers quickly followed suit. Many newspapers also published a weekly mail edition—the New York *Tribune's* rapidly became popular across the North. The *Tribune*, whose columns were open to abolitionists and other social reformers, contributed to an increase in sectionalism.

The theater sought respectability by involving itself with reform, through temperance melodramas such as *Ten Nights in a Barroom* or abolition plays like *Uncle Tom's Cabin* (adapted for the stage). The popularity of the theater increased as stock companies traveled between the larger cities of the North using the star system to fill theaters. Dark, graceful, patrician Fanny Kemble came to the United States from England with her father, a Shakespearian actor, in 1832 and was an immediate hit. Leading men included the Englishman William C. Macready and the Americans Edwin Forrest and Joseph Jefferson.

The theater faced stiff competition on the entertainment circuit, especially from circuses, minstrel shows, and exhibitions like those managed by Phineas Taylor Barnum. In 1842 amidst much advertising Barnum opened his American Museum in New York City, presenting for the amazement of his patrons "General Tom

Thumb," the midget; the "Fiji Mermaid," half-monkey, half-fish; and Siamese twins. He managed the 1850 American tour of "the Swedish nightingale," Jenny Lind, which netted both of them fortunes. Minstrel songs flowed from the pen of Pennsylvanian Stephen Collins Foster, whose secondhand knowledge of black Americans showed in popular hits such as "Oh! Susannah" (1848), "My Old Kentucky Home" (1853), "Jeannie With the Light Brown Hair" (1854), and "Old Black Joe" (1860). Foster wrote more than 200 other songs, but with no head for business and a taste for the bottle, he died in poverty in 1864. For lovers of classical music, Boston, New York, and Philadelphia boasted symphony orchestras by the 1840s.

Northern Reform

Outstripping the South in industry, population, and the arts, the North also led in humanitarian reform. Foreign visitors observed that Americans formed all sorts of organizations and were almost compulsive joiners. Americans fashioned organizations to fight moral enemies and vices as well as to promote everything from commerce and industry to religion. Gilbert Seldes remarked that "the air was full of voices," from the arguments of De Witt Clinton plugging the Erie Canal to the shouts of Boston mobs as they attacked lawmen who sought to return fugitive slaves. Most of the idealistic reformers believed they could right the wrongs of society in their own time. Their reform spirit was inspired by many different sources, from Christianity's emphasis on human worth, to America's belief in the equality of men, to a reaction against the social and economic dislocations of the Industrial Revolution, or a faith that material progress would create a life of abundance. Their confidence emanated from the optimistic view Americans had of their own destiny, of their mission to create a better way of life.

"Whoever has had an opportunity of acquaintance with society in New England during the last twenty-five years," Emerson lectured one Sunday early in 1844, "will have been struck with the great activity of thought and experimenting." Emerson observed how the churches had been in ferment, how churchmen had taken to temperance, abolitionism, and even socialism, and had divided among themselves. "What a fertility of projects for the salvation of the world!" he exclaimed. "One apostle thought all men should go to farming," another "that the use of money was the cardinal evil," others that "We eat and drink damnation." There also appeared "the adepts of homeopathy, of mesmerism, of phrenology. . . ." Some attacked particular vocations, "as that of the lawyer, . . . the merchant, . . . the manufacturer, . . . the clergyman, . . . the scholar. Others attacked the institution of marriage. . . ."

"With this din of opinion and debate," Emerson remarked, "there was a keener scrutiny of institutions and domestic life than any we had known; there was a sincere protesting against existing evils." It was "a restless, prying, conscientious criticism" that broke out, he noted. Later observers of the American scene remarked how the "restless" criticism continued far past 1844 and touched upon not only those subjects Emerson mentioned, but many others as well. There were those who sought to discard society as they knew it and entirely rebuild it. They advocated or founded idealistic enclaves often in the backwoods or on the edge of the frontier that would be free of crime, poverty, exploitation, and other evils, communities that would shine as examples to society. As society found the truth in this new communitarian spirit, the land would be covered with similar societies, they hoped, and evil would disappear from the nation. Unfortunately, society failed to copy them, and most of the efforts themselves ended in collapse.

Although some of the communitarians were of a religious bent —people like George Rapp, who sold his community to Robert Owen, or the Shaker, Amish, or Mormon communities—the largest number embraced rationalism, not religion. Robert Owen of New Lanark, Scotland, bought New Harmony, Indiana, in 1825, only to have it disband in 1828. Etienne Cabet, a Frenchman, twice tried unsuccessfully to establish similar communities, first on the Red River in Texas and then in Nauvoo, Illinois, after the Mormons fled.

Charles Fourier, another Frenchman, dreamt of an elaborate organization called Phalanastery, a division of society into groups or Phalanxes of about 1,500 people each, living together and working cooperatively. American followers of Fourier called themselves "Associationists," and between 1840 and 1850 they tried Fourier's ideas in perhaps fifty different short-lived communities. Some, like Brook Farm, attracted a great deal of attention. John Humphrey Noyes, a former preacher, established perhaps the most radical community at Oneida, New York, in 1848. Though this community lasted in corporate form for more than a decade after the Civil War, the participants themselves were unable to establish the perfect society they sought.

While the communitarians attempted to reform all society, others chose to work within it and correct specific evils. Dorothea Dix tried to improve the lot of the insane, to get them out of "snake pits" and jails and into hospitals and asylums. Horace Mann sought to upgrade education by establishing training schools for teachers. Samuel Gridley Howe successfully struggled to find a way to educate the blind. Others, recoiling from the horrors of war, founded the American Peace Society in New York, and still others advocated a world court of justice.

Hydropathy became fashionable as people took the "water cure" at spas like Hot Springs, Virginia, bathing in and drinking the allegedly beneficial waters. Orson Fowler, and later Samuel Gridley Howe, attempted to find a better life for mankind through phrenology, the understanding of man and his character by reading bumps on the head. Sylvester Graham advocated a vegetable diet for man and the use of coarsely ground wheat flour.

Reformers investigated mental illness, poverty, and crime and deduced that one cause, perhaps the major cause, of evil was alcohol. The movement against "demon rum" began in earnest in Boston in 1826 with the formation of the American Temperance Society. Horror stories, such as Timothy S. Arthur's *Ten Nights in a Barroom and What I Saw There* (1854), and spellbinding lectures of reformed drunkards put fear into men's hearts. Temperance societies multiplied, even in the South, as crusaders divided over total abstinence versus the prohibition of hard liquor only. In 1851 Maine enacted a law forbidding the manufacture or sale of liquor, and about a dozen other states followed with similar legislation before the Civil War.

Women actively involved themselves in the temperance crusade, and just as industriously worked to improve their own condition. Women were legally treated as children in the United States, subject to corporal punishment by their fathers or husbands, denied the right to own property, and denied the suffrage. Among those who sought to change the situation were the Quakeress Lucretia Mott, Mrs. Elizabeth Cady Stanton (who insisted the word "obey" be omitted from her marriage vows), Miss Susan B. Anthony, one of the great lecturers, and Mrs. Amelia Bloomer (inventor of "bloomers" for women to replace the long, ground-sweeping dresses). Meeting at Seneca Falls, New York, in 1848, women's rights crusaders adopted a "Declaration of Sentiments" to let America know how they felt. A parody on the Declaration of Independence, it began: "All men *and women* are created equal." Though society considered it in bad taste for "nice" ladies to speak before mixed audiences, the feminine activists ignored the taboos. Quickly the speaking barrier dropped as abolitionists and other reform groups allowed women to address their meetings.

Reform movements drew their strength from the middle class, from the clergymen, writers, editors, lawyers, small businessmen, and prosperous farmers. As many of these people were politically conservative, the Whig party was affected to a greater degree than the Democratic party. Most Democrats worried more about suffrage reform (though not the extension of the vote to women) and the breakdown of financial monopoly. Both parties represented a broad spectrum of the population, however, and both sought to remain aloof from social reform for fear of alienating segments of their support. The Whigs were the least successful, and the party shattered over sectional disagreements over slavery in the early 1850s. The Democrats came to grief in much the same way, but were able to sustain themselves nearly a decade longer. Labor leaders shunned reformers, except those connected with the movement for public education, largely because conservative reform leaders frowned on unions and strikes and were unfamiliar with other labor problems.

The Antislavery Movement

Antislavery dwarfed the other reform movements by the mid-nineteenth century. Though its roots reached back before the American Revolution and though it underwent periods of ferment, it had little impact prior to the 1830s. Founded in 1817, the American Colonization Society attempted to colonize freed blacks in Africa. In 1822 agents of the organization purchased land on the west coast of Africa. Primarily supported by private contributions, the Society did receive some state funds from Maryland and Virginia. After a time Northern members began to suspect that their Southern counterparts were using the organization to sustain slavery rather than to hasten its demise; they accused Southerners of de-

porting freed slaves in order to be rid of them and of caring little
about ending slavery. Philadelphia blacks, led by James Forten,
had condemned colonization from the first, arguing that slavery
would be more secure if free blacks emigrated and that colonization
would raise the price of slaves and thus make emancipation less
likely; they regarded colonization as a threat of exile. "We are *natives* of this country," said Peter Williams, a black preacher in New
York, ". . . our fathers suffered and bled to purchase its independence." Black opinion had its effect upon white antislavery groups,
leading men such as Lewis Tappan and William Lloyd Garrison to
oppose colonization as well. By the 1830s colonization had been
"dislodge[d] . . . from the abolitionist movement," wrote Benjamin
Quarles.* Over a period of ten years, the Society sent fewer blacks
to Liberia than were born in America each month.

Antislavery journals mushroomed after Benjamin Lundy
launched the *Genius of Universal Emancipation*, a weekly, at Mt. Pleasant, Ohio, in 1821. Lundy, who gave up a lucrative trade as a sad-
dler to devote his life to abolition, favored colonization, touching a
chord of responsiveness among white Northerners who saw it as a
means of ending the race problem. Garrison assisted him for a time
in 1822, but Lundy proved too mild for Garrison. The *Genius* ceased
publication in 1835, and Lundy soon established the Philadelphia
National Enquirer. John Greenleaf Whittier took over the editorial
duties in 1838, when the paper became the *Pennsylvania Freeman*.

The most famous abolitionist journal appeared in 1831 when
Garrison's own paper, *The Liberator*, made its debut. Garrison fearlessly published his outspoken sheet until after the passage of the
Thirteenth Amendment in 1865. Though the paper never topped a
circulation of 3,000, it became famous for its uncompromising demand for the immediate and complete abolition of slavery and for
its intemperate language. Garrison fixed his direction in the very
first issue:

> I am aware that many will object to the severity of my
> language; but is there not cause for severity? I *will* be
> harsh as truth, and as uncompromising as justice. On this
> subject I do not wish to think, or speak, or write with
> moderation. No! No! Tell a man whose house is on fire to

* Benjamin Quarles, *Black Abolitionists* (New York: Oxford University Press, 1969), pp. 4–7,
19; and Louis Filler, *The Crusade Against Slavery* (New York: Harper and Brothers, 1960), pp.
21–22, 61–62.

give a temperate alarm; tell him to moderately rescue his wife from the hands of the ravisher; tell the mother to gradually extricate her babe from the fire into which it has fallen;—but urge me not to use moderation in a cause like the present. I am in earnest—I will not equivocate—I will not excuse—I will not retreat a single inch—AND I WILL BE HEARD.

In spite of his language, Garrison believed in moral persuasion and rejected both the use of force and the ballot. In 1832 he helped organize the New England Anti-Slavery Society, and then in 1833 with Arthur and Lewis Tappan, the American Anti-Slavery Society. Garrison advocated Northern separation from the South because the Constitution permitted slavery. To him, the Constitution was a "covenant with death and an agreement with Hell." He opposed the churches as well, considering them supporters of slavery. When he insisted that women had the right to speak before the Society, he caused the membership to split.

An advocate of women's rights and temperance as well as abolition, Garrison was a difficult man whose qualifications as an organizer were questionable. His language antagonized others, and in 1835 a Boston mob attempted to throttle him. But he succeeded in attracting attention, for at least a few Southern newspapers occasionally printed quotes from *The Liberator* as examples of Northern abolitionist sentiment in its most extreme form. Many black Americans supported and subscribed to *The Liberator*, a very important fact considering its small circulation.

Black journalists contributed heavily to abolitionist literature, publishing some seventeen newspapers before the Civil War. Samuel Cornish and John B. Russwurm founded *Freedom's Journal* in New York in 1817. Like its successor, *The Rights of All*, the *Journal* emphasized the need to fight the institution of slavery. *The Colored American* sought and obtained a wide, if selective, audience from Boston, New York, and even Cleveland. David Ruggles published the *Mirror of Liberty* in the East, John E. Stewart produced *The African Sentinel and Journal of Liberty* in Albany, New York, and in the 1840s and 1850s Frederick Douglass edited *The North Star*, and later *Frederick Douglass' Weekly* in Rochester.

Newspapers propagandized for the abolitionist cause, but they were only a part of the picture. For all of his bluster, other abolitionists were more important in New England than Garrison—for example, Wendell Phillips, the Boston lawyer who joined the anti-slavery cause when Garrison was attacked by the mob in Boston. With an independent income, and a wife who prodded him, Phillips left the bar to crusade for abolition. He contributed to *The Liberator*, but was more effective as a lecturer. He opposed the Mexican War and the annexation of Texas, like Thoreau viewing the situation as a Southern plot to expand slavery. Like Garrison, he advocated dissolution of the Union if that was necessary to rid the North of its tie with slavery.

Churchmen joined literary figures to provide additional momentum to the abolitionist cause. Congregationalist Charles Grandison Finney, a professor of theology at Oberlin in 1837 and its president in 1851, influenced churchgoers in upstate New York and Ohio from the 1820s on, making Oberlin a center of abolitionist activity. Theodore Dwight Weld devoted most of his energy after 1830 to antislavery, working with the Tappan brothers, James G. Birney, and with the Grimke sisters, Sarah and Angelina (he married Angelina in 1838). At Lane Theological Seminary in 1834, Weld organized a series of antislavery debates that led to his dismissal, followed by a walkout of nearly the entire student body. From then on Weld was in the forefront of the abolitionist movement, editing the American Anti-Slavery Society's paper, *The Emancipator*, in New York for a time; assisting John Quincy Adams in the fight against the "gag rule" in Washington; and advising antislavery Northern Whigs like Benjamin Franklin Wade and Thaddeus Stevens. He retired in 1844 to found a school in New Jersey but then actively stumped for the Republican cause during the Civil War.

The work of Finney and Weld had a tremendous impact on Protestant churches, especially the Presbyterian and Congregational, which produced more reform leaders in the antebellum period than any other churches. Parishioners often denounced their churches as agents of the status quo if the clergy would not take a firm moral stand, and congregations splintered as the more reform-minded churchgoers founded their own new congregations. Churchmen demanded that their places of worship take moral stands not only on abolition, but also on temperance and other reform issues.

Those Americans who joined abolitionist societies—by 1840 about 200,000 belonged to local chapters—generally wanted to work gradually toward an inclusive, and perhaps sudden, end to slavery. They hoped to end the institution completely and without compensation to slaveowners, but they recognized they could not accomplish their task overnight. The abolitionist program differed from that put forth by other antislavery partisans. The antislavery camp could count in its ranks those who opposed Southern dominance in politics, and especially those who worried that the fugitive slave laws, the "gag rule," and the other manifestations of the institution threatened the entire structure of American civil liberties, including the highly prized freedom of speech. Still others were devout churchgoers, who saw slavery as a moral wrong, and condemned it as such, but who were not formally abolitionists; they would support colonization or any gradual scheme that would ultimately bring an end to the peculiar institution. Determined Free-Soilers opposed opening new territories to slavery, and though some belonged to the abolitionist camp, many others clung to the doctrine as a way to keep the territories white. Many antislavery workers and abolitionists were no less racist than Southern non-slaveholders who sought to maintain slavery as a means of protecting white social superiority. Black abolitionists realized this, as they alone championed not only freedom for slaves, but also an end to racial discrimination against the free black man in the North or South.

Originally abolitionists hoped to persuade slaveholders that slaveholding was a sin, a moral offense. Slaveholders reacted with rigid defenses of slavery, including those based on the Bible. Some abolitionists like James G. Birney undertook political action to bring pressure on free-state governments and the federal government for assistance. A Kentucky lawyer who served a brief term in Alabama's state legislature and was once an agent of the American Colonization Society, Birney freed his slaves in 1834. In 1835 he formed the Kentucky Anti-Slavery Society, became executive secretary of the American Anti-Slavery Society in 1837, and in 1840 served as vice president of the World Anti-Slavery Convention in London. An advocate of political action, Birney put his views on the line as the presidential candidate of the Liberty party in 1840 and again in 1844. In 1842 under the direction of Weld and with the co-operation of men like Joshua R. Giddings, a Whig congressman from Ohio's Western Reserve, Birney founded an antislavery lobby in Washington. Giddings was censured by Congress in 1842 for his militant antislavery speeches; he resigned, stood for reelection, and won despite his party's opposition in the campaign. Giddings became a Free-Soiler in 1848, and a Republican by 1856. The lobby, which included Birney, Weld, Giddings, Seth Gates of New York, and William Slade of Vermont, with the association of John Quincy Adams from time to time, proved effective in providing abolitionists with a national platform, keeping the issue of slavery very much alive in Congress, and helping to break the infamous "gag rule."

From Quaker meetings and abolitionist societies, petitions poured into Congress demanding the abolition of slavery and the slave trade in the District of Columbia. The District provided a convenient transfer point for slaves from both Maryland and Virginia into the South, and coffles of slaves were a common enough sight in the city to disturb some Northern politicians as well as visitors who thought the national capital should not be thus dishonored. Since Congress had jurisdiction in the District of Columbia, the petitions were a natural form of pressure. Congress, according to the Constitution, also had control of interstate commerce, and some of the petitions asked for the abolition of the interstate slave trade as well. Since nearly everyone agreed Congress could not take legal action against slavery in the states themselves, the petitioners urged Congress to attack slavery in these Constitutionally sanctioned ways.

Most Southern congressmen agreed with John C. Calhoun that Washington must be held as slave territory at all costs, lest the petitioners attempt to close slavery out of the Western territories as well. Besides, if Southerners could hold the line against these abolitionist attacks, they hoped the movement would die in frustration. Southern congressmen won the showdown in 1836 by pushing through the "gag rule," a resolution that required all petitions regarding slavery to be laid upon the table without being read or acted upon.

Former president John Quincy Adams had returned to Washington as a representative from Massachusetts in 1831, and though not an abolitionist, he recognized the danger to civil liberty inherent in the newly passed rule. Tireless, eloquent, master of parliamentary tactics, Adams, with the help of the antislavery lobby, fought tirelessly to secure repeal of the resolution. His opponents threatened him, attempted to censure him, but were unable to stop him. The persistent Adams finally succeeded in 1844, with increasing help from Northern congressmen. The eight-year struggle to repeal the "gag rule" brought a broad spectrum of civil libertarians into sympathy with the abolitionist cause, since the antislavery forces had stood as the bulwark in defense of free speech.

Abolitionists clandestinely abetted the escape of slaves who sought freedom in the North or in Canada, over what became known by the 1840s as the "underground railroad." In the railroad jargon, fugitives were "passengers," the hiding places along the way were "stations," and the guides were "conductors." Although a loose organization existed in localities such as Cincinnati, Wilmington, and Philadelphia, the underground railway was not the well-organized system the name implied. Usually the assistance was spontaneously offered by Quakers, Northern free blacks, and abolitionists. The underground railroad provided the abolitionists with propaganda about the evils of slavery and conversely supplied Southerners with news of fugitive slave law violations. Only the routes were secret and each escape was publicized as widely as possible. Frequently the real daring and bravery of the slaves who had successfully escaped bondage was obscured by the "railroad's" propaganda. The runaways' true courage is emphasized by the fact that less than a thousand slaves a year escaped in the two decades before 1860.

In 1838 slave Frederick Douglass, born near Easton, Maryland, escaped to New England. He found work in New Bedford, Massachusetts, and in 1841 so impressed the Massachusetts Anti-Slavery Society with an address at one of their meetings that they recruited him as an agent. Douglass' Maryland owner had taught him to read and write, and he proved an extremely apt pupil, publishing the *Narrative of the Life of Frederick Douglass* in 1845. But his book and his activities as a lecturer for the Society awakened Douglass' fear of recapture, so he spent the next two years safely out of reach in England and Ireland. English friends enabled the exile to return to the United States by purchasing his freedom. Upon his return he began his newspaper career, choosing to follow Birney's lead with political action rather than Garrison's nonpolitical agitation.

According to the fugitive slave law, an agent or his master could reclaim an alleged runaway merely by swearing to the black man's identity before any magistrate. The accused had no recourse in law. Professional slave-catchers, working for rewards or commissions, cared little if they found the right man or not. Kidnapping of free blacks became so common in Pennsylvania in 1825 that the state passed personal liberty laws which made it nearly impossible for any claimant to establish the identity of an alleged fugitive. Several other Northern states copied the law. In 1842 the Supreme Court, in *Prigg* v. *Pennsylvania* held that the states were not bound to assist in the enforcement of the federal fugitive slave law. The decision led to the passage of more personal liberty laws which specifically forbade state officers to participate in the return of fugitives.

With little difficulty, abolitionists turned resentment against kidnapping, against the lack of due process protection for the fugitive, and against Southern attempts to force Northerners to help protect slavery, into an issue that won the antislavery cause considerable popular support. Without local assistance, slave-catchers found their task nearly impossible, and when they did capture a fugitive they often had to face angry Northern mobs. Abolitionists gained much sympathy from nonabolitionists in the North because of the stories portraying Southerners not only as ogres who would smother freedom of speech but also as tyrants who would highhandedly kidnap or deny due process to free black men in the North.

Black Americans helped organize and staff the American Anti-Slavery Society and proved extremely effective as agents and speakers for local chapters. They brought to white audiences as nothing else could living proof that the black man was as human, as American, and as much in need of help as the white abolitionists had claimed. Not only Douglass, but William Jones, Theodore S. Wright, the colorful Sojourner Truth, and a host of others spoke to anyone who would listen. Sojourner Truth, a freed slave originally known as Isabella, felt she had a divine mission to bring the message of emancipation and women's rights to the nation. Though unschooled, this remarkably fluent woman traveled through the North making an effective case before antislavery and reform groups.

Not surprisingly, black abolitionists divided among Garrison-like militants, Birney-like political actionists, and gradualists. In 1829 David Walker denounced slavery in terms Garrison might well have envied. Free-born in North Carolina but living in Boston, his pamphlet, "Walker's Appeal in Four Articles," asked fellow blacks: "Are we MEN? Did our creator make us to be slaves to dust and ashes like ourselves? . . . America is more our country than it is the whites—we have enriched it with our *blood and tears.*" Walker called for militancy and action, as Garrison did in *The Liberator* two years later. Other militants in New York City established vigilance committees in the mid-1830s to prevent kidnapping and to assist fugitive slaves. In 1843 Henry Garnet told a Buffalo convention that black men had to "strike for your lives and liberties. Now is the day and the hour. . . . the days of slavery are numbered. . . . Awake! Awake!" Moses Dickson founded the Knights and Daughters of Tabor in Cincinnati in 1844 and the Knights of Liberty in St. Louis in 1846, both fraternal organizations dedicated to the overthrow of slavery.

Actually, American blacks had been involved in organizational work long before the formation of abolitionist societies by whites. The American Convention, a federation of early state antislavery societies that first met in Philadelphia in 1794, had continued as a viable black organization for several decades. It was before that group that James Forten had denounced colonization in 1818. The American Convention's full title spelled out its aims: "The American Convention for Promoting the Abolition of Slavery and Improving the Condition of the African Race." Essentially they concerned themselves not only with the lot of their brethren in Southern chains, but also with the condition of their Northern friends. Northern racial animosity occasionally flared into riots in the 1830s, which lent a dual meaning to the speeches of black Americans on the subject of emancipation.

Black leadership in the North before the Civil War came largely from the pulpit, for the simple reason that black Americans in other professional walks of life were scarce. Black Americans had formed their own churches around 1800, and though some remained within white churches, especially the Methodist Episcopal, most black Americans associated with either the Bethel Methodists (AME) or the Zion Methodists (AMEZ). The black church gave the black man, as Ohio attorney John M. Langston claimed, a chance to be and express himself. Black churches criticized white churches for supporting colonization and for failing to come to grips with the moral question of slavery. Black churches endorsed movements to boycott slave-produced goods; they opened their doors for abolitionist meetings; and they never hesitated to denounce slavery in the South or prejudice in the North.

Critics of Reform

White or black, abolitionist crusaders often faced violent opposition in the North. Even in New England, when Prudence Crandall decided to admit black children to her private school in Connecticut in 1833, the community solidly opposed her and had her school closed. Although she won her case on appeal, she was prevented from carrying out her plans. In addition to the hostile mob that attacked Garrison in Boston, another took the life of antislavery editor Elijah Lovejoy in Illinois in 1837. Antislavery agents and lecturers risked their lives pleading the cause across the North. They were beaten, pelted with rotten eggs, tomatoes, and stones, and sometimes tarred and feathered.

Southern reaction to abolitionist pressure was still greater. They blamed Turner's uprising on the abolitionist influence. They tightened up their slave codes. They destroyed mail sacks presumed to contain abolitionist literature, or at the very least, Southern postmasters refused to deliver such literature. Southern state legislatures resolved that their Northern counterparts be obliged to suppress abolitionist activity. Known antislavery partisans in the South found it necessary to go North, or face physical abuse—as did Birney, the Grimke sisters, and later Hinton R. Helper, author of *The Impending Crisis of the South*, an indictment of slavery. Like the fugitive slave law and the gag rule, the mistreatment of abolitionists North and South helped swing additional sympathy to the cause.

All the reformers of the time, abolitionists included, came in for criticism from segments of the Northern intellectual community. Emerson wrote, "many a reformer perishes in his removal of rubbish; and that makes the offensiveness of the class. They are partial. . . . They lose their way; in the assault on the kingdom of darkness they expend all their energy" on one object. In Emerson's opinion it did not matter "that one or two or twenty errors of our social system be corrected" but it mattered a great deal that "man be in his senses."

"It is handsomer," Emerson continued, "to remain in the establishment . . . and conduct that in the best manner, than to make a sally against evil by some single improvement, without supporting it by a total regeneration." Emerson advised, "Do not be so vain of your one objection. Do you think there is only one? Alas, my good friend, there is no part of society or of life better than any other part."

The one-sided view of society so often presented by reformers repelled Emerson. They lost their perspective when they believed the world could be bettered through the elimination of one vice out of many. Hawthorne's *Blithedale Romance* echoed Emerson's thought. While Hawthorne generally portrayed reformers sympathetically, he, too, attacked the blindness of the reformer committed to a single cause. In the book, Hollingsworth, a blacksmith, joined the utopian colony in order to convert its resources and members to a reform project of his own. For Hollingsworth, everything was black or white, one either was in favor of his project or against it, for he saw no middle ground. In the end his plans worked against him, leaving him a shattered man. Hawthorne moralized that while Hollingsworth's aims might have been useful, his shortsighed concentration upon them destroyed other, equally useful impulses in the process.

William Ellery Channing, called "the apostle of Unitarianism," denounced slavery and war and influenced Emerson, Holmes, and Bryant. He never became an abolitionist, and like Emerson, Hawthorne, and later, Webster, believed that the best solution for social problems in a democracy was rational discussion. Channing and the others pointed out that rational discussion was impossible when reformers became so excited that they refused to participate or when they deliberately inflamed public opinion through propaganda. They saw propaganda as both unfortunate and dangerous to society when its excesses made compromise impossible and destroyed the civil and political rights of moderate or conservative dissenters.

When he supported the Compromise of 1850 with his Seventh of March speech, Webster lashed out at the abolitionists for that very reason. "In their sphere of action, they do not see what else they can do than contribute to an abolition press, or an abolition society, or to pay an abolition lecturer." In times past, Webster continued, as in Virginia in 1832, members of that legislature were "not unwilling nor afraid to discuss this question [abolition]" but such was not the case by 1850. "And everything this agitating people have done, has been, not to enlarge, but to restrain, not to set free, but to bind faster, the slave population of the South." Just as extreme proslavery advocates had closed the South to abolitionists and their literature, so did extreme abolitionists close the North against moderates like Webster. Although Webster considered slavery to be a great evil, he thought disunion was an even greater evil. For his stand on the compromise, Webster was ostracized in New England.

The Political Scene

Antebellum Northern society manifested abundant energy with its industrialization, population growth, cultural activity, and humanitarian reform. Southern society in the same period focused upon the plantation economy and greatly expanded the production of cotton; increasingly defensive on matters of slavery, some Southerners participated in some of the reform activities. Yet the overwhelming thrust of the South's intellectual, cultural and political life was to defend slavery. While both segments of American society had much in common, they also manifested great differences as well by 1850. Nothing seemed to accentuate North-South differences better in 1850 than activities in the political arena.

With the election of President William Henry Harrison in 1840, Senator Henry Clay and the Whig party at last had an opportunity to put the Whig program in effect. At Clay's insistence, Harrison called a special session of Congress to repeal the Democrats' independent treasury system, to create a new national bank, to raise the tariff, and to pass new laws for the distribution of the public domain. Unfortunately for Clay and the Whigs, "Old Tippecanoe" Harrison died within a month of his inauguration and left the Whigs to deal with John Tyler.

A Virginian, Tyler had left the Democratic party in 1832 yet still had little in common with the Whigs. He blocked implementation of all their programs except the Tariff of 1842. Furious, Whig congressmen read the President out of the party. Every member of the cabinet resigned but Secretary of State Webster, who waited until the Maine-Canada boundary dispute was settled with the Webster-Ashburton Treaty of 1842. In a stunning political reversal, the Whig victory of 1840 had been turned into a shambles by the renegade Democrat whom the Whigs had made vice president and whom death had moved into the White House.

Hated by the Whigs and mistrusted by the Democrats, Tyler then sought an issue that might win him reelection either as an independent or as a pro-expansionist Democrat. He embraced the explosive political question of the annexation of Texas, which Democrats Jackson and Van Buren had both sidestepped for the sake of party unity. From the moment of Texan independence in 1836, antislavery men had denounced the possible annexation of Texas as nothing more than a Southern plot to extend slavery; leaders on both sides had sought to avoid a confrontation between the Northern and Southern wings of their party over the issue.

President Tyler brought Democrat John C. Calhoun into the cabinet to replace Webster and to undertake secret negotiations for an annexation treaty. Tyler sent the treaty to the Senate in the spring of 1844; but at the same time a Calhoun letter that justified annexation as an asset for slavery surfaced, infuriating the antislavery forces, dooming the treaty in the Senate, and unleashing violent sectional passions on the eve of the 1844 nominating conventions.

Both Whig party leader Clay and Democratic party leader Van Buren expected to be nominated by their parties, and both wanted to keep the question of Texas and the issue of slavery out of the campaign. Both published letters opposing the annexation of Texas. The Whigs nominated Clay, but after a deadlock between Van Buren and Lewis Cass of Michigan, the Democrats settled on James K. Polk of Tennessee, a slaveholding expansionist. Tyler was squeezed out of the race altogether.

To neutralize sectionalism, the Democrats adopted a platform that called for the annexation of both Texas and Oregon. By linking the two and playing down the sectional dispute, Polk won the election by a narrow margin. New York Whigs who deserted their party to vote for Birney, the Liberty party candidate, assured Polk of New York's conclusive electoral votes.

Viewing the results of the election of 1844 as a mandate, the lame duck Congress annexed Texas by joint resolution just before Polk's inauguration. Once in the White House, Polk and the Democrats reinstituted the independent treasury system, revised the tariff downward, and blocked Whig-sponsored internal improvement bills. The boundary of Oregon was settled, and Oregon Territory became a part of the United States. Polk, however, wanted more than just Oregon and Texas; he wanted California, New Mexico, and Utah as well, and he got them in the Mexican War.

Impatient over both major parties' unwillingness to deal with slavery questions, antislavery Northerners had supported the creation of a third party. Founded in 1840, the Liberty party espoused the avowed purpose of keeping slavery from the territories, although its "free-soil" stand was by no means abolitionist. Some party members were indeed abolitionists, but many were Negrophobes who sought only to keep the West a white man's country. The Liberty party provided a dramatic illustration of the disruptive power of a sectional, one-purpose party, for it had in effect thrown the 1844 election to Polk.

As national political parties, the Whigs and Democrats accommodated within their ranks very discordant elements; by avoiding disruptive sectional issues, they not only held themselves together, but the Union as well. The major parties were in fact loose organizations with weak central control, little more than federations of state organizations. To win nationally, they had to minimize their divisions and put up a united front in national elections.

The Liberty party, on the other hand, exploited sectional differences, as did its successors, the Free-Soil party and, later, the Republican party. As the moral question of slavery came to the fore, Northern Whigs tended to vote according to their consciences; this brought them to the Liberty party in small numbers, then to the Free-Soil party in larger numbers, and by the late 1850s to the Republican party en masse. As the Whig party thus broke up, a process hastened by the deaths of its leaders, Clay and Webster, Southern Whigs had no place to go except into the Democratic party. That party remained a national party until 1860, although it became more Southern-oriented than many of its Northern and Western members wished. In addition to the accession of Southern Whigs, the influence of Calhoun after 1843 was crucial to the shift. Calhoun desired to reform the Democratic party and win it over to the defense of "states' rights" in order to prevent an increasingly Northern-dominated federal government from damaging the South's system of slavery. Although Calhoun died in 1850, he had done his work well among Southern Democrats.

The seeds of disruption were thus planted within the major political parties in the 1840s. In 1848 the Whigs managed to elect Mexican War General Zachary Taylor to the presidency, but Taylor had neither the experience nor the skill to keep the divisive issue of the expansion of slavery from nearly wrecking the Union in 1850. With Clay and Webster dead by the end of 1852, the Whig party was doomed. The nation had to face the political implications of geographical changes brought by the Mexican War: the thorny question of expansion into the vast areas added to the Union. Handicapped by the demise of the Whigs, a conservative force in American affairs, by the growing Southern influence in the last national party, the Democrats, and by the appearance of a purely sectional Republican party, national politicians faced possibly the sternest test of statesmanship ever in the history of the United States.

Courtesy of The New-York Historical Society, New York City.

PART TWO

YEARS OF CRISIS ———

Spring, 1854: For several years friends from other states had to come over and help Kansas bury its dead.

Fall, 1860: Lincoln was elected, which reminded him of an anecdote.

Winter, 1861: Everything belonging to the United States not thoroughly fastened down was carried away by the Confederacy, while President Buchanan looked the other way.

Spring, 1861: A deaf and dumb asylum in Northern Michigan was about the only safe place for a peaceable man at that time.

Bill Nye's *Comic History of the United States*

4
The Disruptive
Years, 1848–1856

In the winter of 1848, discussion of the victories at Monterrey, Buena Vista, and Molino del Rey still spiced American conversation. The battlefields had been quiet since October, and Americans waited only for a formal peace treaty to conclude the war with Mexico. Americans contemplated the addition of vast southwestern areas that would round out the continental limits of the United States. California, along with recently acquired Oregon, completed the nation's Pacific coast frontage, while in the interior east of California, huge, rugged, New Mexico beckoned.

Up in California's Sacramento Valley, along the American River, John Augustus Sutter maintained a large estate called New Helvetia. Sutter's establishment often sheltered newcomers who trickled into California after the long overland trek. Besides raising cattle and fruit, Sutter operated a sawmill managed by James W. Marshall. On January 24, 1848, Sutter awakened from his afternoon siesta and began a letter to a Swiss relative. Suddenly Marshall burst into the room and flung "a handful of scales of pure virgin gold," found in the millrace, on Sutter's desk. Further investigation located evidence of gold in the stream-bed and in some of the tributaries. Though Marshall and Sutter had agreed to keep the discovery a secret, workmen at the sawmill had also noticed traces of the metal. "Oro!—Oro—Oro!!!" cried one of the Indian workers, holding gleaming specimens in his palm.

The California Question

The discovery of gold in California precipitated the great crisis in American politics that ominously opened the decade of the 1850s. Newly acquired California (the Treaty of Guadalupe Hidalgo ending the Mexican War was signed nine days after Marshall found the gold) was administered by the military, responsible to their commander-in-chief, the president. A civilian government had not yet been established. Normally, this temporary preterritorial arrangement would not have caused any serious problems, but with the discovery of gold and the inrush of gold seekers, the situation was not normal. The news of the find traveled east and even to Europe by midsummer, and then to the rest of the world. Afflicted with gold fever, people poured into California by every route and means possible. They came by wagon overland, by ship to the Isthmus of Panama and by another ship to San Francisco, or by ship clear around the horn of South America. Over 80,000 people arrived in California in 1849; by 1850 the population reached nearly 100,000, surpassing that of neighboring Oregon and New Mexico combined and that of Delaware, Florida, and the District of Columbia as well. Still they came, over 380,000 by 1860.

The newcomers completely overwhelmed the military government, for it was not equipped to handle the sudden influx of settlers in such great numbers. San Francisco, Sacramento, and Stockton grew from villages to cities in a few months. "In 1850," wrote Tom Clark in *Frontier America*, "San Francisco was a jungle of tents and flimsy wooden shacks. . . . Barrooms, brothels, and jerry-built stores sprang up" only to burn down the next year and rise again nearly overnight. As in any great migration, along with respectable persons came a lawless element of fugitives and criminals from the East and abroad who sought to get rich by any possible means. Crime of all sorts flourished, mining titles were insecure, and often the only protection individuals had was their own prowess with guns or fists. Unable to handle the situation, the military gave way before vigilante committees that organized to counter, in their own lawless way, organized bands of criminals.

In March 1849 Mexican War hero Zachary Taylor became president of the United States. Overcoming opposition from the "conscience" wing of his own party, led by antislavery spokesmen like William H. Seward of New York, Taylor secured the Whig nomination and then defeated the Democratic candidate, Lewis Cass of Michigan.* Taylor, the old soldier, believed statehood to be the answer to California's problems, as well as to the question of slavery in any of the territories won from Mexico.

The issue of slavery and the territories had already been brought into focus by Representative David Wilmot of Pennsylvania in his amendment to an appropriations bill prohibiting slavery in any territory acquired from Mexico. The bill had passed the House on August 8, 1846, but was rejected by the Senate. The Wilmot Proviso served notice on the South that Northerners intended to halt the spread of slavery; Southerners regarded it as an attack on slavery itself. In effect, Wilmot's Proviso announced an end to the old constitutional custom of allowing slavery in the Southern territories and prohibiting it in the Northern. The custom dated back to the Northwest Ordinance in 1787 and had been perpetuated in other territorial acts and in the Missouri Compromise. The Wilmot Proviso raised a storm of public protest and controversy, which was reflected in heated congressional debates, January through August 1848, over slavery in the Oregon Territory. Oregon remained free in a compromise that left the status of slavery in California and New Mexico unsettled.

President Taylor found the persistent argument over slavery in the territories irritating and needless. He believed that since both sides to the controversy agreed that a territory, as it became a state, could do what it chose with slavery, then statehood was the answer. As far as he was concerned, both California and New Mexico should draft state constitutions immediately and seek admission to the Union. Not only would California's current problem be solved, but so would the conflict over slavery in the two areas.

At Taylor's suggestion, California, New Mexico, and even

* Antislavery groups, meeting in Buffalo, New York, August 9, 1848, formed a third party called the Free-Soil party out of the New York "Barnburner" faction of the Democrats, the eight-year-old Liberty party, "conscience" Whigs, and others. They ran Martin Van Buren and polled over 291,000 votes (no electoral) to Taylor's 1,300,000 and Cass's 1,200,000.

Utah proceeded to draw up constitutions. Since few Californians or New Mexicans were from the South, it was quite likely both places would opt for free-state charters—a probability Taylor must have realized. Yet he made a major tactical error in trying to resolve debate; he failed to deal with the fact that Congress ultimately had to consent to statehood applications.

California moved swiftly. Driven by an urgent need for civil government and encouraged by Taylor's emissaries, Californians wrote and ratified a free-state constitution, and elected state and national officials by October 1849. By the following May, New Mexico, too, produced a free-state constitution. In Utah, Mormons composed an antislavery constitution, elected their leader, Brigham Young, governor of a state they called Deseret, and applied for admission to the Union. Meanwhile, the Thirty-first Congress convened in December 1849, and heard Taylor advocate California's admission to the Union under its antislavery constitution, and urge Congress to accept New Mexico slave or free as it might decide. Taylor made no reference to Utah, but advised Congress to "abstain from the introduction of those exciting topics of sectional character which have hitherto produced painful apprehensions in the public mind."

The House of Representatives had already endured a brief, but noisy, skirmish over "topics of a sectional character," as Joshua Giddings led Free-Soilers in an attack against the Whig candidate for Speaker on the grounds that he was not an antislavery man. Giddings and his group miscalculated, and the result was the election of Howell Cobb, a Georgian and a proslavery Democrat, to the chair. During the debates over the speakership, two Whigs from Georgia, Robert Toombs and Alexander Stephens, had served notice that the Wilmot Proviso would not be acceptable to the South. Toombs warned, "if you seek to drive us [slaveholders] from . . . California and New Mexico . . . *I am for disunion.*" So by the time Taylor's message was received by Congress, his admonition had considerable meaning.

Obviously Congress had no intention of taking Taylor's advice either on the question of avoiding sectional debate or on the admission of California and New Mexico. Not only had Taylor completely disregarded proslavery sentiment in his actions, he had ignored Congress. Even without sectional issues, congressmen viewed the executive branch with apprehension and were determined to deny the White House power at their expense.

Ever since the introduction of the Wilmot Proviso, emotions had run so high in Congress that many congressmen felt the Union was in serious danger. Congress included at the time many of the ablest men ever elected. Veterans Clay, Calhoun, and Webster had public careers in national service dating back nearly forty years; men such as William H. Seward, Salmon P. Chase, Jefferson Davis, Stephen A. Douglas, Thaddeus Stevens, and Alexander Stephens had all been in Congress less than a decade. Ironically, Calhoun, Clay, and Webster, who had been the young stars of Congress during the War of 1812, now faced a challenge from a new group of young leaders. Even in less emotional times, so distinguished a group could hardly have sat by and allowed a military man to handle so important a matter with such complete disregard for Congress.

Congressmen recognized Taylor's failure to confront subsidiary questions that seethed round the issue of slavery in the territories. Texas, for example, claimed that the Rio Grande formed its western boundary, thereby claiming all of New Mexico east of the river, including Santa Fé. This meant that Texas, a slave state, would have a considerably enlarged area at the expense of New Mexico, in all probability a free area. Southerners supported the Texas claim, Northerners, that of New Mexico. Neither could Southerners ignore the continuing demand of Northerners that the shameful slave trade be abolished in the District of Columbia. The personal liberty laws of the North galled the South, and in the light of *Prigg* v. *Pennsylvania*, Southerners demanded a new and effective federal fugitive slave code.

Taylor counted on the support of most Northern Whigs, including Seward, Free-Soilers like New Hampshire's John P. Hale and Ohio's Salmon P. Chase, and senior Democratic Senator Thomas Hart Benton of Missouri. He doubtless hoped for the support of the popular-sovereignty advocates, those who believed that the people of a territory should decide for themselves the question of slavery; most prominent among these were Northern Democrats Lewis Cass and Stephen A. Douglas. A few Southern Whigs believed the popular sovereignty position promised peace, but most of the Southern Democrats continued to insist on the extension of slavery into the territories. Southerners who supported Taylor either opposed efforts at compromise or disagreed with other members of Taylor's hoped-for coalition on specific questions involved in the dispute.

Of course, another important factor was the impact of admitting two more free states to the Union. Northerners were not adverse to that, but Southerners were aware it would destroy the Senate balance of fifteen free and fifteen slave states. To Southern leaders, this balance was their last bulwark in Congress, for their strength had already ebbed in the House. In 1789 the South had controlled 46 percent of the House seats, compared to only 38 percent in 1850. Electoral College percentages had declined in like proportion. The South's political means of protecting slavery from Northern encroachment was collapsing. Behind California and New Mexico, stood Utah, Oregon, and perhaps Minnesota in line for statehood. Since most Southerners conceded that any state could control its own position on slavery, they could not oppose the admission of a state merely because it was free. Instead, they vented their anger on Taylor, claiming he and his military men had strong-armed California and New Mexico into asking for statehood. If the territories had not freely chosen to apply, Congress could refuse their petitions. Southerners considered it both difficult and dangerous to reconcile themselves to an eventual minority status in the Union, and talk of secession blossomed among Southern congressmen.

Meanwhile, in June 1850, Southern representatives convened at Nashville, Tennessee, at the urging of Mississippi leaders, for the express purpose of discussing secession. Delegates came from Virginia, South Carolina, Georgia, Alabama, Mississippi, Arkansas, Florida, Tennessee, and Texas. Southern Whigs generally opposed the meeting; Southern Democrats mainly supported it. Public enthusiasm for the move, strongest in Mississippi and South Carolina, lagged, but clearly reflected Southern fears. Northerners reacted more strongly during those uneasy weeks, as state legislatures passed resolutions demanding the exclusion of slavery from the western territories, public meetings endorsed the Wilmot Proviso, and the press carried on a continual harangue against Southern efforts to extend slavery.

The Union was on the verge of a serious impasse. Northern public opinion supported the efforts to block the return of fugitive slaves, while Southerners considered legislation to prevent the retail sale of Northern products. Virginia's governor proposed taxing the products of all Northern states with stiff personal liberty laws. The crisis in Congress and sentiment across the nation demanded positive action lest the Union face disruption.

The Compromise of 1850

Congressmen who felt the preservation of the Union to be more important than sectional differences looked to Henry Clay to work out a compromise. Along with many other politicians, Clay felt that if the difficult question of slavery could be ended in the political arena, the nation could deal with other demanding national problems in a less emotional atmosphere, and the danger to the Union and the division of political parties would come to an end for the time being. Clay hoped to bring "peace, concord, and harmony" to the Union for at least as long as the Missouri Compromise had lasted.

On January 29, 1850, Clay introduced in the Senate a series of resolutions dealing with all the major questions at issue. They were:

1. Admit California as a free state.
2. Establish territorial governments in the remainder of the Mexican cession without any restrictions on slavery.
3. Establish a reasonable western boundary for Texas.
4. Assume the part of Texas' public debt contracted prior to annexation, provided Texas gives up her claim to part of New Mexico.
5. Abolish slavery in the District of Columbia only if the people of both Maryland and the District consent, and then only with compensation to slaveholders.
6. Prohibit the slave trade in the District of Columbia.
7. Enact a new and effective fugitive slave law.
8. Affirm that Congress has not the power to deal with the interstate slave trade.

Clay's resolutions touched off one of the greatest debates in American congressional history. For nearly nine months, not only in Congress, but across the nation, Americans wrestled with the effort to find a solution to the problems of the Union.

Clay, seventy-three years old, weak and in poor health, rose in the Senate to defend his resolutions on February 5. The galleries were so tightly packed that a correspondent for the New York *Tribune* could not get close enough to hear. Clay told the assemblage that his compromise measures would not involve the sacrifice of "any great principle" by either section. Yet concession, "not of principle, but of feeling" was necessary by both sides. The admission of California was standard procedure. But what of the application of the Wilmot Proviso in the rest of the territory?

> What do you want who reside in the free states? You want that there shall be no slavery introduced into the territories acquired from Mexico. Well, have you not got it in California already, if admitted as a state? Have you not got it in New Mexico, in all human probability, also? What more do you want? You have what is worth a thousand Wilmot Provisos. You have got nature on your side.

On the subject of a new fugitive slave law Clay remarked that not only was it necessary in order to win Southern support for the compromise, but also "it is our duty to make the law more effective." Clay explained to the South the folly of secession. "War and dissolution of the Union are identical," he warned, painting a word picture of a fierce and bloody struggle of "interminable duration." He appealed to the common sense of both sides to prevent such a disaster, to quiet the clamor of the nation.

John C. Calhoun continued the great oratorical contest with his speech on March 4. Very ill, unable to speak in person, Calhoun sat wrapped in flannels, his eyes half-closed while Virginia Senator James M. Mason read his speech. The "great and primary cause" of Southern discontent, Mason said, "is that the equilibrium between the two sections has been destroyed." He traced this destruction to Northern growth and expansion, citing how the Northwest Ordinance first, the tariff system second, and the assumption of power by the federal government third, had injured the South. Many cords binding the states together had begun to snap. Religious ties had already broken, and he warned, "if the agitation goes on, the same force . . . will finally snap every cord," political and social as well as religious, and "nothing will be left to hold the states together except force."

The Union could be saved, Calhoun continued, but neither by Clay's compromise nor Taylor's action. The North held the key. The North had to concede that the territories belonged to the South as well as the North, return the fugitive slaves, refrain from attacking slavery in the South, and consent to a constitutional amendment that would preserve equilibrium of the sections in Congress. California's admission to the Union would provide a test of Northern intentions, for if the North acted to admit California as a free state the North would be serving notice that it intended to "destroy irretrievably" the sectional balance. "If you who represent the stronger portion cannot agree to settle" the disputes between us "on the broad principle of justice and duty, say so; and let the states we both represent agree to separate and part in peace. . . ." Calhoun, who died within the month, had asked for complete capitulation by the North.

Three days later Webster delivered his famous "Seventh of March" speech, "the most important" of his life, he believed. Webster began: "I wish to speak today, not as a Massachusetts man, nor as a Northern man, but as an American. . . . I speak today for the preservation of the Union." He had no desire to disturb slavery where it exists, he said, and pledged "I will not violate the faith of the government." So far as California and New Mexico were concerned, Webster held "slavery to be excluded from those territories by a law even superior to that which admits and sanctions it" elsewhere. "I mean the law of nature." Webster admonished: "That law settled forever, with a strength beyond all terms of human enactment, that slavery cannot exist in California and New Mexico." For that reason, he would support "no Wilmot Proviso for the mere purpose of taunt or reproach. . . ."

On the burning question of fugitive slaves, knowing full well how his own section felt on the matter, Webster bravely asserted that he believed the complaints of the South had merit and that the North had failed to do its duty. Webster claimed Northern abolition societies were not "useful." For "the last twenty years [they] have produced nothing good or valuable," and have only added to division and perpetuated discord. Turning to the South, he warned as Clay had of the fallacy of peaceable secession. "Instead of speaking of the possibility or utility of secession, instead of dwelling in those caverns of darkness . . . let us come out into the light of day; let us enjoy the fresh air of liberty and union."

Northern reaction against Webster's speech was instantaneous. The Massachusetts legislature debated a resolution to instruct Webster to support the Wilmot Proviso, and though it failed to pass, Horace Mann lamented "Webster is a fallen star!" Theodore Parker, in a meeting at Boston's Faneuil Hall, said that he knew "no deed in American history done by a son of New England to which I can compare this but the act of Benedict Arnold." Webster had slapped the abolitionists hard and punched them with his support of a new fugitive slave law. His career in Massachusetts seemed ended, a fact the Senator must have considered as he wrote his words. Courageously, he had been willing to trade his career and reputation for the preservation of the Union. Yet near the end of March, eight hundred men of Boston sent him a testimonial for his "broad, national, and patriotic views." Webster won praise from the Washington, D.C., newspapers, and from the Charleston *Mercury*. Calhoun thought Webster showed a commendable "yielding on the part of the North."

Yet Webster changed few votes. Northern Whigs still remained faithful to Taylor; Southern Whigs divided between Clay and the Democrats; and the Democrats remained divided between Calhoun and those who followed Douglas, who supported Clay. Outside of Congress, Webster probably swung a segment of Northern opinion toward compromise.

Seward spoke on March 11. Although a novice in Congress, he was well known as a former governor of New York and as an able lawyer. Seward echoed the antislavery views of his friend John Quincy Adams, and his fellow Whigs knew he would lash out against the compromise. They were not disappointed. Supporting the admission of California, Seward stated, "I am opposed to any such compromise, in any and all the forms in which it has been proposed." He told the South they were "entitled to no more stringent [fugitive slave] laws; and that such laws would be useless," for no government has ever succeeded in "changing the moral convictions of its subjects by force." In regard to the territories, Seward remarked that although the Constitution regulated the nation's stewardship, "there is a higher law than the Constitution." On the question of secesssion he proved more prophetic than any of the other speakers. He asked his audience whether the Union should remain as it is and slavery be gradually removed by peaceful means, or whether the Union should be dissolved and civil war follow, "bringing on violent but complete and immediate emancipation." The South balked at Seward's assumption that slavery would perish one way or another, but that was Seward's view, and in that light the sectional quarrel was useless. "You cannot roll back the tide of social progress." Seward closed with an appeal for the Union.

A friend of the President and a leader of the "conscience" Whigs of the North, Seward had shocked no one by his support of Taylor's position on California nor by his defense of Northern efforts to protect fugitive slaves nor by his desire to keep slavery out of the territories. What stunned Southerners and disturbed even Taylor was Seward's reference to "a higher law." That also troubled New York political boss Thurlow Weed, an associate of Seward's. Seward had put into political terms the notion that manmade laws and God's laws must be compatible for law to be meaningful, a notion Transcendentalists like Emerson had propounded earlier.

Jefferson Davis spoke on March 13. He advocated nonintervention in Southern affairs and equal rights in the territories. He agreed to an extension of the Missouri Compromise line west through the territories acquired from Mexico. By mid-March all positions had been heard. Clay, the Southern Whig, spoke for his compromise; Calhoun, the Southern Democrat, had denounced it; Webster, the Northern Whig, had supported it; Seward, another Northern Whig had opposed it; and Davis, another Southern Democrat, had opposed it. Others spoke, echoing or expanding the speeches of these men. The debate became so heated that the venerable Senator Thomas Hart Benton of Missouri physically threatened Senator Henry S. Foote of Mississippi who had taunted him as a traitor to the South. Benton chased Foote from his seat. Foote fled to the foot of the rostrum, drew a loaded revolver, and aimed at Benton. Their colleagues intervened in the nick of time.

On April 18 Clay's resolutions were referred to a fairly moderate committee chosen on sectional lines. On May 8 they reported back to the Senate a somewhat altered set of resolutions, and the debate continued for another five months. Senators Clay, Webster, Cass, Douglas, and Foote argued in favor of the committee position; Senators Seward, Chase, Benton, and Davis joined President Taylor in opposition. Ironically, the opposition included the Northern Whig and Southern Democrat extremists, while the supporters included Whig and Democrat moderates from both sections. Hanging over a successful compromise bill, should one pass, was the cloud of Taylor's possible veto.

Outside of Congress, as the spring and summer of 1850 wore

on, public sentiment appeared to favor adoption of the compromise. The nation enjoyed the rising prosperity that followed the expansion of the railroads, the influx of gold from California's mines, the increase of foreign trade, and the growth of industry. Businessmen hesitated to support any measure but compromise for fear of blocking the road to increased profits with sectional disruption. Northern merchants and manufacturers hoped to conciliate the angry South and preserve their lucrative markets, and Southern cotton producers and brokers wanted nothing to interrupt their booming foreign trade. The moderates took over the Nashville convention and recessed to watch the outcome of events in Congress.

During the summer the various impediments to compromise began to dissolve. President Taylor died July 9, of an illness that began July 4, probably acute gastroenteritis. Millard Fillmore of New York, a Whig who had supported John Quincy Adams in the House fight over the gag rule, succeeded to the presidency. Fillmore appointed Webster to the top State Department post, and Clay became a White House spokesman. The compromise now received the backing of the administration. Clay, worn out by his futile attempts to get his omnibus measure passed and by the summer's heat in Washington, left the capital early in August for a month's rest in New England by the sea. Inadvertently, by keeping the compromise measures together in one bill, the "omnibus bill," had drawn "all the malcontents" into combination against it. Clay's absence gave Illinois Senator Stephen A. Douglas the opportunity to submit the compromise as a series of individual bills, which he believed would pass singly, with different majorities on each. Where it had been impossible to obtain a single majority for the omnibus bill, it was now possible to win the vote. In order of passage, the Compromise of 1850 included these separate laws as it left the Senate:

1. Texas relinquished her claim to New Mexico's territory for $10,000,000 (the vote was 30 to 20, with the opposition including 12 Southerners and 8 Northerners, mainly extremists from both sections).
2. California was admitted as a free state (the vote was 34 to 18, with 26 of the yea votes from Northern Democrats and Whigs, and all of the negative votes from Southerners, mostly Democrats).
3. New Mexico was created as a territory without reference to the Wilmot Proviso (27 to 10, all negatives from the North).

4. A new and tougher fugitive slave law was enacted (27 to 12, 8 Northern Whigs, 3 Northern Democrats, and Free-Soiler Chase opposed; 15 Northern senators did not vote).
5. Slave trade in the District of Columbia was abolished (33 to 19, 13 Southern Democrats and 6 Southern Whigs opposed).

Douglas had been correct. He had succeeded in getting the Senate to pass the measures individually, and in so doing, was able to pass the substance of Clay's compromise.

The House of Representatives made a few changes in the final compromise, but the whole secured easier approval than in the Senate. As signed by Fillmore in September, the final version looked like this:

1. New Mexico was created a territory without the Wilmot Proviso, and Texas's claim to part of New Mexico was vacated for an indemnity of $10,000,000.
2. California was admitted as a free state.
3. Utah was created a territory without the Wilmot Proviso.
4. A more stringent fugitive slave law was enacted.
5. The slave trade was abolished in the District of Columbia.

America remained on edge even after the compromise passed, for it meant nothing if the nation did not accept it. The political parties were badly scarred by the sectional issues, a bad omen indeed. The Nashville Convention reassembled in November, denounced the Compromise of 1850, and urged that a new convention meet to discuss ways of protecting slavery or to consider secession. Alabama, Georgia, Mississippi, and South Carolina convoked special state conventions to discuss secession, and hope for the compromise looked bleak. But the Nashville Convention's recommendations were not followed; in the last analysis none of the four state conventions favored secession, although South Carolina would have moved in that direction had she had support. Sentiment throughout the South echoed the Georgia convention's resolutions: Georgia accepted the compromise as a "permanent" solution to the problem of sectionalism but warned the North that preservation of the Union depended upon how well the North observed the new fugitive slave law.

That new fugitive slave law was bitter medicine for the North.

Under the new provisions, anyone accused of being a fugitive was not allowed to testify, had no right to a jury trial, and could be turned over to his master or his master's agent with only an affidavit or a sworn statement that the fugitive belonged to the master. The fugitive's fate was decided by either a federal judge or a court-appointed commissioner. The act contained *ex post facto* provisions, for it applied to any slave who had escaped at any time in the past. A commissioner earned $10 for a decision in favor of the master, $5 for one in favor of the fugitive. Federal marshals and their deputies were directed to enforce the act, and anyone convicted of aiding a fugitive faced a fine of up to $1,000 or six months in prison, plus liability in a civil suit of $1,000 damages to the slave owner. Obviously the law was aimed squarely at the abolitionists.

Fillmore might have vetoed the act had it appeared clearly unconstitutional to him, and he was not certain but that it would fail to stand up to Supreme Court scrutiny. Yet Attorney General John J. Crittenden advised Fillmore the law was constitutional, and so did Webster, whose opinion Fillmore also sought. Constitutionality aside, if Fillmore had vetoed the measure, he would probably have destroyed the compromise and reopened the entire slavery debate. He had little choice.

In Boston, within days of the passage of the fugitive slave act, 40 former slaves departed for Canada. Before the law was signed, an estimated 200 blacks left Pittsburgh for north of the border, and 600 more joined them shortly. Others followed. Black churches suddenly lost their members. Other blacks remained to fight. Throughout the North, antifugitive slave law meetings were held. A particularly large one took place in New York in October, where about 1,500 black New Yorkers listened to William P. Powell; asked if they would submit peacefully, if they would kiss their chains, they shouted in reply, "No, no!" They dispatched petitions denouncing the law to the state legislature and to Congress. Robert Purvis told a meeting of the Pennsylvania Anti-Slavery Society that if "any pale-faced spectre" entered his house to execute the fugitive slave law, "I'll seek his life, I'll shed his blood." All across the North, the reaction of the black community was similar.

Northern white reaction was divided. At Faneuil Hall in Boston on October 14, Charles Francis Adams presided over a meeting where Theodore Parker and Wendell Phillips urged the audience to action, denouncing the fugitive slave law as contrary to God's law, the Declaration of Independence, and the Constitution. In Chicago, almost half a continent away, the city council agreed and likened those who voted for the law to the "traitors Benedict Arnold and Judas Iscariot." Yet in November, Charles Sumner told another meeting at Faneuil Hall that he advised "no violence" on the question. Let the power of public opinion make the bill "a dead letter," he said. Sumner's moderation was taken a step farther by Douglas at a large meeting in Chicago, where he pushed through a resolution that all of Congress's laws ought to be obeyed.

In fact, most Northern agitations seemed to be in support of the compromise. Bostonians saluted the measure with a hundred-gun salute fired on the Commons. Called by a petition said to be signed by 10,000 people, a Union meeting in New York City enthusiastically approved the compromise, including the fugitive slave law. Other large meetings in New York, Pennsylvania, and Ohio thundered their approval as well. In January 1851, 44 congressmen from both major parties and sections signed a pledge to oppose any candidate for office who did not accept the compromise as final.

The Election of 1852

For nearly two years sectional strife waned and the compromise seemed to work. In preparation for the presidential campaign of 1852, the Democratic party platform endorsed the compromise and made it plain that the party would resist any effort to renew the question of slavery. The platform caused the Democratic delegates little difficulty, but they had a more difficult time selecting a candidate. The leading contenders were Douglas, at age thirty-nine called the Representative of Young America; Cass, almost seventy but vigorous; James Buchanan, age sixty-one; and William L. Marcy, age sixty-six, the New York politician who had been Polk's secretary of war. After forty-nine ballots, dark horse Franklin Pierce, age forty-eight, stampeded past the others to claim the prize. Although his nomination came as a surprise to the nation, it had in fact been carefully engineered by New England Democrats who felt that neither Cass, Douglas, Buchanan, nor Marcy could win the nomination. Accepting the nomination, Pierce wrote that he would abide by the platform not because it was expected of him, but because it squared with his own opinion. The Democrats faced the electorate in 1852 standing firmly in support of the compromise.

The Whigs held their convention two weeks after the Democrats, and were initially as divided over the platform as over nominees. Nevertheless, the Whigs also endorsed the compromise, adopting that plank of the platform with a 227 to 66 vote, the 66 negatives all from Northern delegates who refused to accept the fugitive slave law. The leading candidates were Webster, Fillmore, and General Winfield Scott of Mexican War fame. Rather than nominate Fillmore or Webster, who had both been important figures in the passage of the compromise and who therefore had little support from the Seward antislavery wing, the Whigs turned to Scott on the fifty-third ballot. Whigs across the country received the outcome of the convention without enthusiasm. Those who favored the platform frowned upon Scott, and those who favored Scott frowned upon the platform. Some Southern Whigs, like Georgians Alexander Stephens and Robert Toombs, announced they would not support Scott because he would be controlled by Seward and the "conscience" Whigs of the North. They and quite a few of the anti-Seward Northern Whigs would have been happier with Webster.

The Free-Soilers, hurt by the return of the Van Buren Democrats to their own party, nominated John P. Hale of New Hampshire and openly opposed the compromise. Hale had the support of Charles Francis Adams of Massachusetts and Joshua Giddings of Ohio, both former Whigs. They stood for, they said, "Free soil, free speech, free labor, and free men."

The two great Whigs, Clay and Webster, died on June 29 and October 24, before the election in November. Their deaths foreshadowed the demise of their party, for 1852 marked the Whig party's last, and far-from-exciting campaign. No one but the Free-Soilers addressed the real issues that year, and everyone knew they stood no real chance to win. For lack of anything to say, the campaigners attacked Scott and Pierce. The Whigs accused Pierce of cowardice on the field of battle and of being a drunkard; the Democrats assailed Scott's vanity and ridiculed his army nickname of "Fuss and Feathers." Scott campaigned actively across the nation, while Pierce remained home in New Hampshire, making a few speeches, writing letters, and letting his party carry the burden of the campaign.

The election results surprised few Americans, as Pierce, the Democrats, and the Compromise of 1850 swept the election. The

Pierce landslide carried 27 states to Scott's 4; 254 electoral votes to 42. Yet the popular edge for Pierce was not so great: 1,601,274 to 1,385,580. Hale, who won no electoral votes, ran a distant third with 155,825, as the Free-Soil vote fell to about half its 1848 total. If the third party vote is construed as opposition to the Democrats, Pierce's popular victory was quite narrow.

Slender, handsome Franklin Pierce was the son of a New Hampshire governor, a graduate of Bowdoin (1824), and a Jacksonian Democrat. He had served without particular distinction in the New Hampshire legislature, the House of Representatives, and the United States Senate. He resigned his Senate seat in 1842 because of his wife's illness and conducted a profitable law practice in Concord, New Hampshire. He had served as a brigadier general of volunteers in the Mexican War, a war he had enthusiastically supported. Because he had made few enemies in his brief political career, except for his support of the war, he proved attractive as a political candidate in 1852. Aged forty-nine at inauguration, he was the youngest president of the United States up to his time.

As president, Pierce lacked firmness and direction. Always kind and polite, he directly or indirectly promised office and favor seekers everything they asked for, thus disappointing those who ultimately found that they had won neither the office nor the favor they thought they had secured. Some said Pierce was influenced by Secretary of State Marcy, or Attorney General Caleb Cushing, or Secretary of War Jefferson Davis. In fact, Pierce was a middle-of-the-road administrator who tried to hold together the various party factions without alienating any strong segment.

In his mild inaugural address, delivered without notes, Pierce reaffirmed his support of the Compromise of 1850, denounced sectional discord, extolled expansion, and proved himself a fine speaker. If Pierce seemed lacking in leadership to some of his intimates, his inaugural reflected the hopes of many Americans. Tired of the sectional dispute, people wanted reassurance that the Compromise of 1850 had taken slavery out of politics. Business supported peace and tranquility and therefore the Democrats. Trade blossomed, the nation prospered and was likely to continue so long as political conditions remained stable. The business community felt the Democrats promised that stability better than the openly divided Whigs, the nation felt that Democratic commitment to the compromise was stronger than that of the Whigs, so the Democrats had a clear mandate in Congress as well as the White House.

Pierce, influenced by the expansionist-minded Young America* movement, thought not only in terms of westward expansion but also in terms of expansion into the Caribbean. Manifest Destiny appealed to Pierce, as it did to many Americans, so in that sense he followed in the footsteps of Polk. If Pierce saw expansion as a healthy replacement for sectionalism, he should have remembered that the acquisition of California and New Mexico had led to increased sectional dispute and the Compromise of 1850. In any event, the Pierce administration cast covetous eyes on Cuba.

Intrigue concerning the island harked back to before the days of the Monroe Doctrine, and involved Spain, England, and the United States. England found the slaveholding island an obstacle in her efforts to suppress international slavetrading and had hoped either to acquire or to neutralize the island in some way, perhaps by creating a militant black republic there. Southerners worried about such a prospect, particularly since some of them considered Cuba a natural area for Southern expansion; they hoped that the extension of the plantation system outside continental boundaries might be better received by Northerners than slave expansion westward.

The Cuban issue had been much discussed by 1853, when Pierre Soulé of Louisiana was named minister to Spain. Soulé, an open advocate of Cuban acquisition, met in October 1854 at Ostend, Belgium, with James Buchanan, minister to Great Britain, and John Y. Mason, minister to France. They advised Pierce to offer to buy Cuba from Spain and, if Spain refused, to take the island. This "manifesto" was condemned by Northerners who suspected that the South, through Pierce, sought only to increase slave territory. Secretary of State Marcy repudiated the document; Soulé resigned his post. The "Ostend Manifesto" abruptly ended expansion in the Caribbean.

Pierce's aggressive foreign policy was more successful in opening trade with Japan (1854) and extending American influence in the Pacific with China and Hawaii. The administration also concluded a reciprocal trade treaty with Canada (British North America) in 1854 that broadened U.S. fishing rights on the Great Banks and established tariff-free agricultural exchanges. On the other

* The term was used in reference to a strong nationalist movement with overtones of Manifest Destiny. They often wished to aid revolutionaries abroad who sought democratic overthrow of autocratic regimes as well as to promote acquisition of new territories by the U.S.

hand, relations with England were strained over Pierce's implicit approval of William Walker's filibustering in Nicaragua.

Breakdown of the Compromise

Pierce and the Democrats had won America's public trust because they opposed the agitation over slavery and accepted the Compromise of 1850. A strong president presiding over a united party might have been able to carry out that mandate, but Pierce was not a strong man, and he in fact presided over a deeply divided party. In fairness to Pierce, the Compromise of 1850 was in trouble from the start. The abolitionists refused to be intimidated by it. Even while the campaign of 1852 was underway, Charles Sumner ignored the political question and agitated for repeal of the new fugitive slave law. No matter if the law was constitutional, which he doubted, he told fellow senators: ". . . it lacks that essential support in the public conscience of the States where it is to be enforced, which is the life of all law, and without which any law must become a dead letter."

Nor was Sumner alone, for other Free-Soilers joined in denouncing the law in Congress, in particular the Ohioans, Chase, Wade, and Giddings. Abolition societies attacked the measure with renewed fury and joined in the rescue of fugitives. A predominantly black mob rescued Fred Wilkins, or Shadrach as most knew him, from a Boston courtroom in February 1851. Thomas Sims, another fugitive, was successfully returned to Georgia in April 1851, but only because the police escort to the Boston docks outnumbered his would-be rescuers.

Horace Greeley offered the columns of the New York *Tribune* as an abolitionist forum. From abolition centers all across the North, from the pages of the *Tribune*, whose weekly editions circulated widely across rural America, and from the halls of Congress echoed persistent, loud protest over the fugitive slave law. And from the pen of Harriet Beecher Stowe came one of the most powerful pieces of all abolitionist propaganda, *Uncle Tom's Cabin*.

Daughter of the famous minister Lyman Beecher, sister of the sensational preacher Henry Ward Beecher, and wife of Reverend Calvin Stowe, Mrs. Stowe dwelt in a Calvinistic atmosphere. Many of her formative years were spent in Cincinnati, Ohio, just across the Ohio River from the slave state of Kentucky. Her father, president of the Lane Theological Seminary, sheltered fugitives in their home, and young Harriet heard the runaways' stories first hand. Only once did she visit slave country, on a brief trip with friends to Maysville, Kentucky, in 1833.

Harriet returned to New England with her husband in 1850, when he took a professorship at Bowdoin. New England had erupted in a furor over the new fugitive slave law, and stories of blacks long free being remanded to slavery helped arouse the people. Brother Edward denounced slavery from his Boston pulpit, and brother Henry auctioned slaves, often females, in his Brooklyn church to raise money to redeem them. Urged by her sister-in-law to write something that would make the nation "feel what an accursed thing" slavery was, Harriet, who occasionally sold stories to genteel women's magazines, gave the idea thought. Later she recalled that the climax to *Uncle Tom's Cabin* had come to her during a church service, and she had written it down that same afternoon while it was fresh in her mind. Having composed the climax, she set to work to write the remainder of the novel.

Gamaliel Bailey, an editor of the *National Era* and a friend of the Beechers from Cincinnati, bought the story for $300 and began serialization in June 1851. Although the magazine's circulation was small, the story won immediate acclaim. Even before the last chapter appeared, John P. Jewett of Boston had published the whole in book form. Jewett had misgivings about his publishing venture for several reasons: the author was a woman, the subject was controversial, and the manuscript was so long it had to be published in two volumes. He printed 5,000 copies, which to his astonishment sold out in two days. Within one week 10,000 copies vanished from bookstore shelves, with orders for more arriving faster than Jewett could honor them. Within one year the book sold over 300,000 copies in the United States alone. The publisher ran eight steam presses around the clock, bought out the produce of three mills to supply the necessary paper; still he failed to keep pace with demand. Unhampered by international copyrights, 18 English presses turned out over 40 different editions. On the continent yet other publishers translated and produced the book. *Uncle Tom's Cabin* outsold any other volume in the history of printing except for the Bible, a record that remained intact until recent times. In addition, the story was soon transformed into a highly successful stage play, seen by thousands.

Uncle Tom's Cabin was important because of its impact on contemporary opinion, not because of its literary quality. It aroused sentiment and compassion in thousands of individuals as no abstract attack on the institution ever could. The strong religious overtones of the volume emphasized that slavery dealt in human souls. Although Mrs. Stowe had not intended to inflame passions, her book contributed directly to Northern determination to evade the fugitive slave law. It spawned a literature of imitation in the North, and if the *Spectator* in London could label the attention *Uncle Tom* attracted "Tom-mania," that description was even more apt for the United States. From the number of volumes sold and the countless thousands who viewed the stage play, it would seem that every literate Northerner knew the story. Southern critics soon denounced Mrs. Stowe and her book, for they were stung by its powerful effect on the North.

As repulsion for slavery grew, the abolitionist attack came to include everything connected with the system, including all of Southern life and culture. While Southern politicians probably understood that the most avid of the abolitionists represented a Northern minority, they found it good politics to keep their constituents believing all Northerners were extremists. Southerners worried about the future of Southern life in an obviously unfriendly Union.

Southern fears coalesced in a retaliatory attack on Northern culture. George Fitzhugh in *Sociology for the South* exhorted Southerners to "indignantly hurl back upon our assailants the charge, that there is something wrong and rotten in our system." Why, Fitzhugh exclaimed, "From their own mouths we can show free society to be a monstrous abortion, and slavery to be healthy, beautiful and natural," a system "they are trying, unconsciously, to adopt." Fitzhugh and other authors of Southern "Anti-Tom" literature attracted little attention in their own section, but they helped convince Northerners that slaveholders meant to enslave them as well.

Kansas-Nebraska

Out west, settlers began drifting into the Indian reserve beyond the Missouri River in order to farm the plains. The continuing course of normal frontier expansion, the influx began as Northwesterners in particular discovered that the area long known as the Great American Desert was in fact fertile. Once more, Northwesterners clamored for the federal government to clear out the Indians, establish territorial government, and ready the area for development. All along, Senator Benton of Missouri had urged building a national transportation link with the Pacific coast, on the grounds that it would help to promote trade with the Orient. With the obvious movement of the frontier west, Benton and others now observed that a transcontinental railroad would hasten settlement of the area, open new markets for industry, provide industry with easy access to raw materials, foster national prosperity, and also furnish much-needed communication links between the Pacific settlements and the east.

It was the consensus of most Americans that a transcontinental railroad should be constructed with federal aid, that it must connect with the eastern rail network, and that it should take a logical course to the coast. Consensus ended there. Chicago, St. Louis, Memphis, New Orleans, and other cities clamored to be the gateway to the far west. The healthy rivalry for municipal trade advantages rapidly took on different overtones as it became clear how deeply the location of the terminus would affect the western expansion of either slave or free society. The controversy over the construction of a transcontinental railroad became another phase in the sectional contest.

Army topographical engineers had studied the construction of a transcontinental rail line in 1853, concluding that routes with eastern terminals at Memphis and New Orleans, both "Southern" routes, and at St. Louis and Chicago, central and "Northern" routes, could be built. The engineers observed that the southern routes were less difficult from a construction viewpoint and would pass through settled country. The central or northern roads presented greater engineering problems and would have to traverse unsettled territory and large Indian reserves. Yet the central or northern route would follow the most-used overland western trail, the well-beaten path of the Oregon, Mormon, and California trails.

To make a southern road more attractive, War Secretary Jefferson Davis acquired from Mexico that arid piece of Southwestern real estate called the Gadsden Purchase. The army claimed that the best southern route was via the Gila River Valley, the southern part of which was then in Mexico. President Pierce, urged by Davis, sent James Gadsden to buy the necessary land from Mexico, which he did for $10,000,000. Meanwhile, Senator Stephen

Douglas, whose home was in Chicago, attempted to dissolve the main objections to a central or northern route by organizing unsettled Indian country into a territory. In so doing, Douglas shoveled the final clods on the grave of the Compromise of 1850.

Chairman of the Committee on Territories, darling of the Northwestern Democrats, and representative of the expansionists, Douglas authored a bill early in 1854 to create the vast territory of Nebraska west of Iowa and Missouri. North of the Missouri Compromise line in the old Louisiana Purchase, Nebraska would be free territory. To overcome Southern objections to such a large new free area and in line with his own views on popular sovereignty, Douglas determined that the territorial legislature would decide the question of slavery for Nebraska. But Southerners balked, especially Missouri Democrats who feared that the slave state of Missouri would be virtually encircled by free territory. Douglas then modified his bill with a specific repeal of the Missouri Compromise and a proposal to divide the territory in two, Kansas, the southern portion, and Nebraska, the northern. Kansas lined up immediately west of Missouri, and by implication would become slave territory. The Douglas bill, called the Kansas-Nebraska Act, proved to be the fuse that blew the slavery controversy wide open.

While bending to Southern sentiment to get votes for his bill, Douglas clung to his principle of popular sovereignty and to his sincere belief that climate and geography would make slavery all but impossible in the area anyway. By making a gesture to the South, he also hoped to win support from the Southern Democrats for his drive to become a Democratic president. Douglas knew only too well, as one of the nation's leading politicians, that the Compromise of 1850 was exhausted. He knew, too, that another solution to the problem of the expansion of slavery was necessary, and in his mind popular sovereignty provided the answer. The morality of the slave problem failed to excite him. Douglas apparently felt his modification of the bill represented no real concession to the South.

As a Northwesterner and a Chicagoan, Douglas wanted the advantages of the railroad to accrue to his section, to his city. So he believed he had accomplished a great deal with the Kansas-Nebraska Act, for himself, for his area, for the nation—if the country accepted popular sovereignty. But Douglas had accomplished a number of other things as well. Repeal of the Missouri Compromise technically opened the whole Louisiana Purchase territory to slavery, which, while it pleased Southerners, appalled many Northerners. Southerners found themselves on the horns of a dilemma, for by accepting the act, they conceded that a territory could ban slavery, a point they had previously been unwilling to grant. Southerners further supposed that Missourians could settle Kansas and make it a slave area, overlooking the fact that Missouri had too few slaveholders to accomplish the task. Politically, they opened themselves to the charge of renewing the sectional controversy. If the North had buried the Compromise of 1850 under a stack of personal liberty law legislation and open defiance of the Fugitive Slave Act, then the South, if it accepted Kansas-Nebraska, could no longer react as the injured party since it too would have played a part in destroying the same compromise.

The Kansas-Nebraska bill became an administrative measure when Pierce, who advocated expansion, gave it his support. The measure met considerable resistance in Congress that delayed its passage for four months. Almost all Southern Whigs and Democrats favored the measure, practically all Northern Whigs stood against it, and the Northern Democrats divided. Outside of Congress, the North reacted angrily and indignantly. Chase, Giddings, Sumner, and Gerrit Smith published a flaming "Appeal of the Independent Democrats in Congress to the People of the United States." Signed by others as well, including many Free-Soilers, it arraigned the Kansas-Nebraska Act as "a gross violation of a sacred pledge; as a criminal betrayal," and as part of "an atrocious plot" to convert Kansas-Nebraska into a "dreary region of despotism inhabited by masters and slaves." Although written by highly literate men, they still felt that "language fails to express the sentiments of indignation and abhorrence" of this "bold scheme against American liberty worthy of an accomplished architect of ruin." Their words were reprinted by most free-state newspapers, which took up the argument with gusto. Douglas and the act were denounced with equal vigor. Amazed at the Northern reaction, the Richmond, Virginia, *Whig* announced that it had never before known "such unanimity of sentiment at the North upon any question affecting the rights of the South as now prevails. . . ."

Meetings in major cities and state legislatures condemned the act and its implications. Reluctantly, the Illinois legislature supported favorite son Douglas, but petitions, resolutions, and memorials against the act flooded Congress. The South reacted less warmly in favor of the bill than the North did against it, yet by the time it became law Southern legislatures and newspapers had come to its support. Greeley put the matter quite accurately when he summed up the Kansas-Nebraska quarrel by remarking that Pierce and Douglas made more abolitionists in three months than Garrison and Phillips could have in fifty years. As Douglas later observed, he could have journeyed "from Boston to Chicago by the light of his own [burning] effigies."

The Kansas-Nebraska Act so blurred party lines in the nation that men became known as "Anti-Nebraska Whigs" or "Anti-Nebraska Democrats." Finally divided, the Whig party disappeared in most of the North and South. Some Southern Whigs reluctantly joined the Democratic party, increasing the Democrats' Southern orientation; others voted with the American party in 1856 and with the Constitutional Unionists in 1860. United in their opposition of the spread of slavery into the territories, anti-Nebraska Whigs and Democrats in the North joined together in a new party. The Republican party grew out of independent political meetings in the North and by the spring of 1854 had evolved an organization based on the single purpose of opposing slavery in the territories. A clearly sectional party, it flexed a surprisingly mature muscle in the congressional elections of 1854 by winning a majority in the House of Representatives and several Northern state legislatures.

Trouble in Kansas

Most of the settlers moved to Kansas, after the Kansas-Nebraska Act was passed in 1854, rather than to Nebraska, for several reasons. It was better known, for the Santa Fé and the Oregon Trails both passed through; nearby Independence, Missouri, was a jumping-off place for both routes west. Further, since Americans assumed Nebraska would become a free-state area, and Kansas a slave-state area, the point of contest focused on Kansas. In each section, North and South, publicity given to Kansas attracted settlers. Many different sorts of people came, as they did to every new frontier: settlers whose motives were simply to farm and raise families; real estate dealers and land speculators determined to make fortunes; and fugitives from justice and the lawless who sought their own particular opportunity. But the makeup of Kansas was unique because of its position in the quarrel between the sections: some came specifically to make Kansas slave or free; the speculators were quite willing to be partisans of slavery or freedom as necessary; and the lawless championed either side as it suited their purposes.

Abolitionist press, pulpit, and publications in the North urged free-staters to migrate to Kansas to save the place for freedom. In July 1854 Eli Thayer led the vanguard of those sent by the New England Emigrant Aid Company, which had been created to help make Kansas free. They received much publicity in the columns of Greeley's weekly *Tribune* and the other Northern papers that reported their progress and requested support. Nevertheless, most of the free-state immigrants came from Iowa, Illinois, and Indiana, and were those who would normally have peopled the neighboring frontier. For the most part, they located along the Kansas (Kaw) River, and created towns like Franklin, Lawrence, Tecumseh, and Topeka.

An example of the sort of Northern propaganda that encouraged people to go to Kansas to make it a free state is this 1854 poem by John Greenleaf Whittier.

The Kansas Emigrants

We cross the prairie as of old
    The pilgrims crossed the sea,
To make the West, as they the East,
    The homestead of the free!

We go to rear a wall of men
    On Freedom's southern line,
And plant beside the cotton-tree
    The rugged Northern pine!

We're flowing from our native hills
    As our free rivers flow;
The blessing of our Mother-land
    Is on us as we go.

      •   •   •

No pause, nor rest, save where the streams
    That feed the Kansas run,
Save where our Pilgrim gonfalon
    Shall flout the setting sun!

We'll tread the prairie as of old
    Our fathers sailed the sea,

And make the West, as they the East,
The homestead of the free!

Southerners who migrated to Kansas to participate in the sectional struggle were encouraged to do so under much the same sort of influence as moved free-staters. Yet few came from the deep South; most of the proslavery settlers in Kansas were from neighboring Missouri, and they remained close to the Missouri River and built Leavenworth, Atchison, Doniphan, Troy, and nearby towns. Reacting against the New England Emigrant Aid Company, Missourians formed organizations for the purpose of saving Kansas for slavery either by moving to Kansas or by voting in Kansas territorial elections.

Pierce sent Andrew Reeder of Pennsylvania, a Douglas Democrat, to Kansas as territorial governor. Reeder specified November 29, 1854, as the date for the first territorial congressional election. To insure the choice of a proslavery partisan, Missourians swarmed into the territory and swelled the count for their candidate. The free-staters paid little attention to the election, for they believed that the question of freedom or slavery was not involved. Instead, the free-staters looked ahead to March 30, 1855, the date set for the election of a territorial legislature. For the second time, Missourians staged their election-day performance, and armed with rifles, revolvers, and whiskey, they followed Missouri Senator David R. Atchison into Kansas. Their might overawed election officials, and, of perhaps 1,500 legal voters in Kansas, 6,307 votes were cast. Governor Reeder, though not opposed to the election of a proslavery legislature, could not but declare the election a farce. Angry, proslavery partisans threatened to shoot the governor if he voided the election.

Reeder met with the thirty-nine legislators-elect in his office. They arrived armed and faced the governor and fourteen armed bodyguards. With cocked pistols on the table near his hand, the governor voided the election of seven members from whose districts protests of fraud had been raised, and issued certificates of election to all the others. The victory clearly went to the proslavery partisans.

News of the fraud in Kansas traveled rapidly throughout the free states, in newspaper accounts and in letters from the Kansas free-staters. Governor Reeder, back home in Easton, Pennsylvania, added to the furor by telling of the invasion of armed Missourians and how they had intimidated the polls. Across the North, a wave of indignant anger swept over concerned citizens.

Southerners justified the Missouri intervention as necessary to counter the purpose of the Emigrant Aid group and attacked the abolitionists for emigrant activities, including Garrison and his paper even though *The Liberator* had actually discouraged such tactics. Nonetheless, Southerners believed the unruly Missourians had only met force with force.

Under great pressure from Secretary of War Davis and Senator Atchison, Pierce asked Reeder to resign. Refusing, Reeder bravely returned to Kansas where he had virtually no control. The territorial legislature met in July and ousted the seven free-staters who had been returned in the seven contested districts. Reeder was saved from further action as Pierce soon replaced him with Wilson Shannon as governor. Shannon, a Democrat who had served as governor of Ohio (1838–1840), had voted for the Kansas-Nebraska Act as a congressman.

The proslavery legislature enacted a legal code for the territory that in effect legalized slavery, imposing stiff penalties, including death, for advising slaves to rebel. Leadership of the free-staters fell to Dr. Charles Robinson, Massachusetts-born agent of the New England Emigrant Aid Company who had lived in California (1849–1851) and participated in the California legislature. James H. Lane, a Hoosier, Mexican War veteran, and congressman who had voted for the Kansas-Nebraska Act paired with Robinson. Along with ex-governor Reeder, they hatched a plan to recapture Kansas for the free-staters. They proposed a constitutional convention which would draw up a free-state constitution and apply for admission to the Union. They repudiated the territorial legislature as illegal.

Under the guidance of the proslavery legislature, Kansans on October 1 elected a proslavery partisan as territorial delegate to Congress, while on October 9 the free-staters held their own election and returned Reeder as territorial delegate. In the constitutional convention held at Topeka on October 23, the free-staters framed a constitution prohibiting slavery; they submitted the document to the people on December 15, along with a proposal to exclude free blacks from the state. Both the constitution and black exclusion were approved, 1,731 to 46, and 1,287 to 453 respectively.

Kansans with New England backgrounds generally opposed the black exclusion, while those formerly from the Midwest supported it. With the vote, Kansas had two hostile governments.

Meanwhile on October 25 the proslavery people had held an organizational meeting at Leavenworth, taking the name of the "Law and Order" party and choosing Governor Shannon as convention president. Shannon reaffirmed the legitimacy of the proslavery legislature and pictured the free-state movement as revolutionary. He warned the free-staters that disobedience of the territorial legislature amounted to treason, and announced that he intended to enforce the law.

Both sides in Kansas were highly charged emotionally, and the situation was ripe for violence. The clash came over a land claim as a proslavery squatter shot a free-stater and fled. Free-staters, demanding justice, retaliated by burning the murderer's cabin and the homes of his friends. The sheriff of Douglas County, a proslavery man, in turn served a peace warrant against a friend of the slain man for threatening violence. A posse of free-staters rescued the prisoner without firing a shot and fled to Lawrence to confer with Dr. Robinson. The citizens of Lawrence took no action against the rescuers but feared possible retaliation by the proslavery people. They formed a committtee of safety to organize the town defense.

The Douglas County sheriff appealed to Governor Shannon for three thousand militia to enforce the law, and as a former Missourian he also appealed to Missouri for help. Shannon ordered out the Kansas militia, still in an embryonic stage of organization, and managed to raise about fifty men, who were swiftly reinforced by about twelve hundred armed Missourians spoiling for a fight. By December 1 this makeshift army assembled south of Lawrence on the banks of the Wakarusa River. They awaited the opportunity to destroy the town for its association with the hated Emigrant Aid Company.

In the interim, the defenders of Lawrence had constructed earthworks and manned them with perhaps six hundred men, a number of whom were equipped with the famous Sharps carbines. They had also readied a howitzer contributed by free-state sympathizers from the North. Confident of victory, Dr. Robinson believed his Sharps carbines would make the difference. Aware that the defenders were equipped with efficient breech-loaders, the army of militia and Missourians paused, but it was Governor Shannon's intervention that kept the "Wakarusa War" from exploding into violence.

The sheriff feared that the situation would get out of hand since the Missourians clamored to level the town rather than just help recapture his prisoner. He unsuccessfully appealed for federal troops from Fort Leavenworth, but the governor refused, fearing that a proslavery attack on Lawrence would arouse the whole North and provide antislavery groups with additional political ammunition. Senator Atchison, who had gone to the Wakarusa with the Missourians, worried about the same thing and supported Governor Shannon. Shannon went into Lawrence and negotiated a peace treaty, signed by himself, Robinson, and Lane. In this remarkable document, Shannon repudiated the support of the Missourians and in return the free-staters denied that any organization existed to resist the laws of the territory. Atchison, meanwhile, told the Missourians, "If you attack Lawrence now, you attack it as a mob; . . . You would cause the election of an abolition President and the ruin of the Democratic party." The Missourians returned home albeit unhappy with the outcome.

On January 15, 1856, the Kansas free-staters chose Dr. Robinson governor and elected a new legislature. The proslavery people generally did not interfere, considering the election a useless free-stater gesture. Seven weeks later the free-state legislature met in Topeka and petitioned Congress for admission to the Union as a free state under the Topeka Constitution. President Pierce branded the action treasonous and unlawful and threw the weight of the United States behind the proslavery territorial legislature.

The Thirty-fourth Congress assembled in Washington on December 3, 1855, with a Republican majority of 108 over 83 Democrats and 43 others, mostly Whigs.* Political observers in the nation's capital counted an anti-Nebraska plurality of 117. Congressmen identified themselves with a variety of party tags, including administration and anti-administration Democrats, slavery and antislavery Know-Nothings (or Americans), Whigs, Free-Soilers, or Republicans—which made organization of the new House very difficult. Moreover, the Republican majority represented a turnabout of the previous Democratic majority of 159. William A. Rich-

---

* Of the Democrats, 79 were Pierce Democrats, only 20 of whom were Northerners. There were 37 Whigs, but only 3 from the North. Approximately 75 Republicans and others had been elected under the Know-Nothing label.

ardson of Illinois, the jolly fat man who worked with Douglas on both the Compromise of 1850 and the Kansas-Nebraska Act, was Pierce's choice for Speaker. The Anti-Nebraska forces entered a large number of candidates, among whom was Nathaniel Banks of Massachusetts, a Democratic congressman in the previous Congress who had won reelection as a Know-Nothing and who turned Republican shortly before Congress convened. But congressmen could not make up their minds on the speakership, and as the clerk called the roll for vote after vote, December and January slipped by. On February 2 the House changed its rules to provide for the candidate with the most votes to win the chair, majority or not. When the roll was called the 133rd time, Banks won the Speakership by three votes over a South Carolinian.

In his annual message Pierce appeared unconcerned about the electoral process in Kansas, reaffirmed the legality of the proslavery legislature, placed the army stationed at forts Leavenworth and Riley at the call of Governor Shannon to enforce the law, and failed to propose any constructive measures for the situation. In effect Pierce left the initiative with Congress to find a solution for Kansas and thus managed to incense the antislavery group. An attempt to restore the Missouri Compromise passed the House by one vote but failed in the Senate.*

Unable to decide which Kansan represented legitimate government, the proslavery John Whitfield or the antislavery Reeder, the House appointed a committee to investigate Kansas. In the Senate that March, legislators debated a Douglas report backing Pierce and a Seward proposal to admit Kansas as a state under the Topeka Constitution. But 1856 was an election year, and the debates lacked crispness at the very least and statesmanship at the most. Two rival governments persisted in Kansas.

Senator Sumner, though, had no intention of letting the debate over Kansas languish in mediocrity. He told Theodore Parker that he intended to "pronounce the most thorough philippic" that anyone had ever made in a legislative hall. Subsequently published as "The Crime Against Kansas," Sumner's speech vibrantly announced that the only Kansas remedy he could accept was the immediate admission of that place as a free state. Speaking on May 19 and 20, he thundered, "against this territory a crime has been com-

---

* Composition of the Senate was 40 Democrats, 15 Republicans, and 5 others.

mitted which is without example in the records of the Past." Democracy in Kansas has been raped, Sumner charged, by those who have "a depraved longing for a new slave State . . . in the hope of adding to the power of slavery in the national government. . . . [H]ere in our republic *force* . . . has been openly employed in compelling Kansas to this pollution, and all for the sake of political power. . . . Such is the crime," Sumner shouted.

Sumner attacked personalities directly. Former Senator Atchison "stalked into this chamber, reeking with conspiracy . . . and then . . . he skulked away to join and provoke the conspirators" in Kansas. Atchison led "murderous robbers from Missouri," who were "hirelings picked from the drunken spew and vomit of an uneasy civilization." He attacked Senator Andrew P. Butler of South Carolina as slavery's Don Quixote, one who made his vows to a mistress "who, though ugly to others, is always lovely to him; though polluted in the sight of the world, is chaste in his sight—I mean the harlot slavery." He pictured Douglas as slavery's squire, "its very Sancho Panza, ready to do all its humiliating offices." Returning to Butler, Sumner raged at his colleague's support for the proslavery forces, and denounced him as one who, "with incoherent phrases, discharged the loose expectoration of his speech, now upon" the representatives of Kansas, "and then upon her people." There was no "possible deviation from the truth which he did not make." Butler touched nothing "which he did not disfigure. . . . He cannot open his mouth but out there flies a blunder." Sumner ended with an attack on Senator James M. Mason of Virginia, a state "from which Washington and Jefferson now avert their faces, where human beings are bred as cattle for the shambles."

Sumner shocked many who heard him, but thick-skinned Douglas worried only that "that damn fool will get himself killed by some other damn fool," and he dismissed Sumner's speech as obscene libel and insult that added nothing new to the debate. Other senators denounced Sumner, especially Lewis Cass and Mason. Seward, Wade, Henry Wilson, and Edward Everett thought Sumner too intemperate and personal. Preston Brooks, congressman from South Carolina, a cousin of Butler, and a moderate in the House debate on Kansas, heard the speech from the gallery and vowed to avenge the insult to his kinsman and to his state. By the Southern chivalric code Brooks could call Sumner out for a duel, but he considered Sumner not his equal, and one only dueled with equals. To be chastised by the code Sumner had to be beaten with a whip or a cane.

When the Senate adjourned shortly after noon on May 22, Sumner remained bent over his desk writing letters. Brooks then strolled down the aisle and said, "Mr. Sumner, I have read your speech twice over carefully. It is a libel on South Carolina and Mr. Butler, who is a relative of mine." Nearsighted Sumner looked up without recognition, as Brooks brought his gold-headed cane down hard upon his head, striking him again and again. Dazed, his head covered with blood, Sumner rose, ripping his desk from the bolts that secured it to the floor. Brooks continued the beating even though his cane broke, grabbing Sumner by the lapels to keep the insensible man from falling as he continued. The whole episode took about a minute, and before it was over Brooks and Sumner were surrounded by excited senators, some imploring Brooks to stop, others demanding no interference.

Brooks instantly became the hero of the Southern fire-eaters, who threatened other Northern leaders with the same fate. Arrested on a charge of assault, Brooks remained free on $500 bail. The Senate took no action; the House investigated. Tempers flared across the North and protest meetings occurred in virtually every Northern city. The House failed to muster the two-thirds vote necessary for the expulsion of Brooks, who resigned, stood for reelection, and was returned to his seat by a nearly unanimous vote in his district. Almost simultaneously with Sumner's beating, trouble flared anew in Kansas.

With the coming of spring, more settlers from the free states arrived in Kansas, threatening to tip the population balance permanently in favor of the free-staters. In April, the sheriff who had ignited the Wakarusa War was wounded while in Lawrence attempting to arrest some free-staters. With the lawman erroneously reported dead, an excited proslavery grand jury responded by indicting Lane, Reeder, and Robinson, among others, for treason. The jury also recommended that Lawrence's stone hotel, a possible military bastion, be leveled and further, that two free-state newspapers be suspended.

Robinson, traveling east, was arrested in Missouri and returned to spend four months in a Lecompton jail. A United States marshal called upon fellow citizens to assist him in serving his warrants in Lawrence, and a mob of armed proslavery men responded, including a rifle company from Missouri commanded by Atchison. On May 21 the marshal's posse encountered no resistance in arresting those named in the warrants. The sheriff, meanwhile, destroyed the two newspaper offices and turned a cannon on the stone hotel. The edifice was so strongly constructed that it withstood the blasts; in their fury the proslavery mob burned it after liberating its store of wine and liquor. Then they burned Robinson's house and sacked others. In all the melee one man was killed, a proslavery partisan struck by a brick falling from the stone hotel. The free-staters had not resisted; the president, who had an opportunity to intervene, chose not to.

"Bleeding Kansas" and "bleeding Sumner" aroused the North and provided the Republicans with fine material for the coming presidential campaign. Secretary of State Marcy observed that exploitation of the events in the antislavery press would cost the Democrats hundreds of thousands of votes in November. Some free-staters in Kansas, like John Brown, thought in terms of revenge. Brown, a Puritan by temperament, emotionally unstable, a failure in business and deeply in debt, hated slavery with a peculiar burning passion all his own. He had to avenge the proslavery attack on Lawrence. "I have no choice," he told a neighbor, "it has been decreed by Almighty God, ordained from eternity. . . ."

Brown struck along Pottawatomie Creek May 24. Because he reckoned that five free-staters had been killed, he now slew five proslavery men in cold blood. Brown and his band of seven wreaked a terrible vengeance, mutilating the bodies of their victims. When the horrible deed became known, Kansas, free-staters and proslavery alike, denounced the murders; free-staters fervently vowed they had had nothing to do with the attacks. Although he provoked guerrilla warfare in Kansas, Brown escaped punishment for his deed, and some even lauded him as the liberator of Kansas.

The week of May 19–24, 1856, had been a violent one. Sumner had spoken on May 19–20; the sack of Lawrence followed on May 21; Sumner suffered his beating on May 22; and the Brown murders took place on May 24. An ominous sign, this bloody week came on the eve of the presidential nominating conventions. It seemed as if debate and ballot, the normal method of settling political differences, would fail.

The Presidential Campaign of 1856

The Democratic platform, adopted at Cincinnati on June 2, praised the Kansas-Nebraska Act as "the only sound and safe solution of the slavery question" and declared that the party would "resist" all attempts to reopen the slavery controversy. When it came to selecting a candidate, party leaders understood the necessity of nominating a man who could win votes not only in the South but also in the North. Most of the slave states would vote for a Democrat, but it would take Northern electoral votes to put a nominee in the White House. Pierce and Douglas, advocates of popular sovereignty, were logical candidates to share a popular sovereignty platform. But the Kansas-Nebraska Act with its repeal of the Missouri Compromise had been patently unpopular in the North and had led to the trouble in Kansas and indirectly to the beating of Sumner. Doubting that either Pierce or Douglas could get the Northern votes needed for victory, practical Democrats closed behind James Buchanan of Pennsylvania.

Buchanan had been a reliable Democrat for forty years, a lawyer who had served in the Pennsylvania legislature, the House of Representatives (1821–1831), minister to Russia (1832–1833), the United States Senate (1834–1845), as secretary of state under Polk (1845–1849), and most recently as minister to England under Pierce (1853–1856). Because of his duties in England, he had been out of the country during the recent uproar, had not been involved, and had not taken a public position on the latest issues. He had therefore not made the enemies Pierce and Douglas had and was eminently available for the nomination. His state, Pennsylvania, was also a key Northern state that could provide important electoral votes. His views had not been advertised, but Buchanan had assured Southern Democratic leaders before the convention that the Kansas-Nebraska settlement should be maintained. Although he led on the first ballot, it took fifteen ballots to secure the nomination. John C. Breckinridge of Kentucky won the vice-presidential nomination.

The new Republican party entered its first presidential race with a zest born of its 1854 achievements. They met in Philadelphia on June 17, more concerned with the choice of a candidate than with the platform. As expected, the platform denounced the Kansas-Nebraska Act, advocated the immediate admission of Kansas as a free state with its free-state constitution, and resolutely demanded the prohibition of slavery in the territories. The platform also included approval of certain internal improvements, a gesture to Northern economic interests.

Frémont's nomination had been virtually settled before the convention. Logic might have suggested Seward, in spite of his tardy conversion to Republicanism, but Seward did not have the unqualified support of party leaders. Neither did Seward attempt to secure the nomination, heeding advice from Thurlow Weed, his political advisor in New York. Chase emerged as a candidate, but party members objected that like Seward, Chase had such strong antislavery views as to prejudice his chances nationally. In April, Frémont expressed sympathy with his old friend from California, Dr. Robinson, serving notice of his availability for the nomination. Frémont's assets included his fame as an explorer and the fact that he had been a Democrat as well as his silence on both slavery and Kansas-Nebraska. Thaddeus Stevens of Pennsylvania campaigned hard for John McLean, an Ohioan who sat on the Supreme Court and who, Stevens believed, could carry Pennsylvania. But Frémont captured the nomination easily on the first ballot, receiving all but a handful of votes. William L. Dayton of New Jersey shared the ticket.

The American party, popularly called the Know-Nothings, nominated Fillmore in their regular convention, while some who were unhappy with Fillmore and who cared little for nativism seceded from that gathering and nominated Banks. Banks refused the nomination, and the dissidents, calling themselves the North Americans, endorsed Frémont. A Whig convention met at Baltimore on September 17, the anniversary of Washington's Farewell Address. Much reduced in numbers, the unhappy Whigs condemned both major parties and nominated Fillmore.

The campaign of 1856 was conducted amidst national excitement over events in Kansas plus all the ballyhoo the Republicans could bring to a campaign. Toombs of Georgia introduced a bill in Congress to provide for a census and carefully supervised elections in Kansas, which the Senate passed but which the House never considered. Republicans rejected the obvious attempt at compromise, for while the Toombs bill would probably make Kansas a free state, the outcome was not certain. Engaged in a campaign on a platform of free territories, the Republicans would not take the gamble. They made their position clear by introducing a bill in the House that would admit Kansas as a free state under the Topeka Constitution. The Democrats condemned the Republicans for their refusal to compromise. The House investigating committee had in fact advocated the sort of procedure contained in the Toombs bill, but had concluded its report by stating that under the circumstances the Topeka document represented "the will of the people."

Republican newspapers used the conclusion of the committee report to support their stand on Kansas. The House Elections Committee endorsed Reeder as the Kansas territorial delegate, but the House refused by large margins to seat either Whitfield or Reeder. John Sherman of Ohio introduced a rider to an appropriations bill for the army, prohibiting the president from using the army to enforce the will of the proslavery legislature in Kansas; but the Senate refused to comply, and the session ended without any army appropriations. Pierce called a special session, and after a hot fight the measure passed without the rider.

The campaign moved out of the halls of Congress when it adjourned for the second time August 30. Republicans, shouting "Free Soil, Free Speech, and Frémont," held rallies all around the North and produced massive amounts of campaign literature. They claimed the Democratic party had been captured by the slaveholders, whose Northern puppets like Buchanan masked an effort to break down all restraints against slavery. Those who condemned the repeal of the Missouri Compromise supported Frémont, as did those who demanded the admission of Kansas as a free state and the prohibition of slavery in the territories. The uncompromising nature of the Republican campaign and the obviously sectional nature of the party worried moderates, who feared that Republican success could bring disunion.

Although Buchanan accepted the Democratic platform without reservation, he appealed to moderates and conservatives in the North by reminding them that the Democratic party was a national, not a sectional party, and that the Democrats pledged themselves to the Constitution and the Union. Buchanan's appeal was effective, judged in the light of voter response. Moderates and conservatives certainly did not want the Kansas strife to spread, and very likely many voters had tired of the Kansas issue.

While the campaign thundered on in the East, guerrilla warfare took its bloody toll of the settlers in Kansas. Anarchy prevailed as Missouri and Kansas border goons robbed and plundered and murdered, and free-state marauders retaliated. Men slept with weapons at hand and feared for the lives of their families. Lane directed the free-staters as Reeder remained in the East pleading free Kansas' cause and Robinson languished in jail. John Brown joined Lane as a guerilla leader, but most free-staters deplored the violence and in the end prevailed. The Republican press ran one atrocity story after another, real and imagined; Democratic journals cried out "exaggeration" and tried to ignore the situation. Meetings for the relief of Kansas mixed with Republican campaign rallies across the North. Pierce assisted the Democratic campaign by replacing the controversial Kansas territorial governor, Shannon, with John W. Geary, a respected Pennsylvanian, whose mission was to bring order to Kansas. Geary reported on September 30 that "peace now reigns."

In November, voters across the nation put Democratic majorities in both houses of Congress and Buchanan in the White House. Buchanan garnered 1,839,237 popular votes to Frémont's 1,341,028 and Fillmore's 849,872. In the Electoral College, it was Buchanan with 174, Frémont 114, and Fillmore 8. Buchanan carried all the slave states but Maryland and the Northern states of Pennsylvania, New Jersey, Illinois, Indiana, and California. Frémont took the votes of the remainder of the Northern states and trailed Buchanan closely in those he lost. Fillmore's eight electoral votes came from Maryland; Frémont won virtually no popular votes south of the Ohio River.

Moderation prevailed, and the Democratic party, nominally a national party, won again. Clearly, as demonstrated by the returns, the Republican party was still a sectional party. The Democrats, however, had become captives of the South, for without that section they could not have won the election. And, ominously, had a few votes in Pennsylvania and Illinois gone the other way, Frémont would have had the victory. Thus in reality both parties owed their strength to sections, and the election was much closer than it appeared; the Republicans were much encouraged by their effort while the victorious Democrats faced the future with misgiving.

The election over, even Republican newspapers took note of the fact that Kansas had indeed quieted down. Encouraged, Northerners felt that a large emigration of free-staters would occur again in the spring, and they looked to Kansas to enter the Union soon as a free state. Although they mistrusted Governor Geary at first, the free-staters came to lend him their support, particularly after Robinson was released from prison and Lane and Brown left the territory. Yet the free-staters had boycotted the October 1856 territorial elections, unwilling to admit the legality of the proslavery legislature. That legislature, with its determination to keep Kansas for slavery, soon came into conflict with Geary, who spoke of "equal and exact justice to all men." The proslavery partisans saw Geary as a threat, denounced and threatened him, and agitated for his removal. The lame-duck administration of Pierce listened to them and never tendered Geary the support he had a right to expect from those who had appointed him. Looking ahead, the Republicans generally expected nothing better from the incoming administration; some Northern Democrats still hoped for an improvement in the fortunes of Kansas free-staters under Buchanan.

5
The Crisis Years, 1856–1861

Republicans who feared the Democratic Buchanan administration would be no more enlightened on the question of slavery in the territories than the Democratic administration of Pierce were not proved wrong. Forewarned that the Supreme Court was about to consider the issue, Buchanan observed in his inaugural "what a happy conception" it was that Congress in its wisdom had applied popular sovereignty to the territories in the Kansas-Nebraska Act. "The will of the majority," he proclaimed, "shall govern . . . the question of domestic Slavery in the territories!" In reference to the pending court decision, he noted "a difference of opinion has arisen in regard to the point of time when the people of a territory shall decide this question." But that no longer had importance, the new president remarked, for it was a "judicial question" that belonged "to the Supreme Court," where it would "be speedily and finally settled." With that decision, and with the acceptance of popular sovereignty, "no other question [regarding slavery] remains for adjustment," and, Buchanan hoped, "the long agitation on this subject" was at an end. With the conclusion of the slavery controversy, "the geographical parties" spawned by it would also "speedily become extinct." Unhappily for the president, neither the "long agitation" nor the Republican party met the fate Buchanan predicted for them.

Two days after Buchanan's inauguration, the Supreme Court handed down its decision in the case of *Dred Scott* v. *Sanford*, fanning the flames of sectionalism anew. Scott, a slave originally owned by an army doctor from Missouri, had traveled with his master into the free state of Illinois and the free territory of Minnesota. While stationed at Fort Snelling, Minnesota Territory, Scott in 1836 had married another of the doctor's slaves. They had two children, Eliza born in free territory, and Lizzie, born after their return to Missouri. Subsequently the doctor died, and his widow wed a New York abolitionist, John F. A. Sanford. Scott sued for his freedom contending that his residence in free territory had made him a free man. A St. Louis state court decided in his favor, but the Missouri Supreme Court reversed the decision. With abolitionist support, the case was appealed to federal courts, and eventually argued before the United States Supreme Court in February 1856.

At first the justices were inclined to dismiss the case on jurisdictional grounds. But when Justice John McLean, an Ohio Republican originally appointed to the court by Andrew Jackson, and Justice Benjamin Curtis, a Massachusetts Whig appointed by Millard Fillmore, announced their intention to voice dissenting opinions that would include discussion of slavery in the territories, the majority decided to prepare an opinion on that phase of the suit. Of the nine justices, seven were Democrats, five of them from the South. Roger B. Taney of Maryland, whose tenure on the high bench also dated back to Jackson, served as chief justice. Although each of the justices wrote separate opinions, Taney's was taken as representative of the majority.

As Taney saw it, Scott could not sue in federal courts because he was not a citizen of the United States. He contended that no black, not even a freedman, could become a citizen of the United States. Taney created the doctrine of dual citizenship, avoiding the fact that blacks had been citizens of certain Northern states since the Revolution. He held that states could make whomever they chose into state citizens, but only Congress could confer federal citizenship. The question of citizenship in Scott's case, however, did not even depend upon such a distinction, according to Taney, since

Scott was a slave. Taney could have referred to the decision in the Missouri courts and the precedent of *Strader* v. *Graham*, and gone no further. Instead he enlarged upon the point.

With regard to Scott's residence on free soil and his claim of freedom as a result, Taney decided that the federal government had no general authority over the territories at all. Congress, Taney claimed, could acquire territory and make rules for statehood, but it could not exercise internal control of the territories or rule the people in them as colonists. Congress could also establish territorial government, but that government could not touch "local rights of person or rights of property." As a result, Congress could not prohibit slavery in the territories, since slaveholding was a local property right. Douglas, Cass, and popular sovereignty advocates had made this argument in Congress for years. On the other hand, Congress had historically exercised a general police power in the territories of precisely the sort that Taney now denied.

Taney went further still. He held that federal authority in the territories was limited by various provisions in the Bill of Rights, specifically that section of the Fifth Amendment that guaranteed due process of law. A law of Congress that deprived a citizen of his property just because he took that property into a particular territory violated the principle of due process of law, he argued. As a result, the chief justice concluded that the Missouri Compromise, which prohibited slavery in the northern two-thirds of the Louisiana Purchase territory, was void. In other words, since the federal government could not exclude slavery from any territory, Scott's sojourn in so-called free territory had not freed him.

Curtis and McLean disagreed with the majority on both the question of Scott's status and on the validity of the Missouri Compromise. Curtis pointed out that blacks had been citizens of Northern states prior to 1787; that the Constitution did not provide for federal control of citizenship except for naturalization of foreigners, and therefore state law took precedence; and that Scott had indeed become a freedman by virtue of his residence in free territory. Curtis contended that the Fifth Amendment applied to procedural guarantees, not to legislative rights to restrict property in the public welfare. He pointed to English law that made slaves free when they entered Britain and to similar laws in Northern states, such as Illinois. He held that according to the Constitution each state had to recognize the laws of the others; Missouri had therefore ruled improperly by not recognizing the effect of Illinois law on Scott. Curtis attacked the contention that the Missouri Compromise was invalid with an impressive array of examples of the exercise of federal power in the territories. Curtis clearly intimated that the judgment of the majority was contrary both to law and fact, and that Taney and the majority knew that.

No Supreme Court opinion had excited Americans as much as *Dred Scott* v. *Sanford*. Southerners gloated because the court had sanctioned their arguments. "The blackamoors . . . are not citizens," exclaimed a Virginia newspaper, they cannot hold any position in society other "than an inferior and subordinate one—the only one for which they are fitted." Not only could slavery enter the territories, but Congress was obliged to defend it! Southerners laughed at the Republicans, for the decision rendered their political platform void. Even they would have to honor the decision!

A Republican writing in the New York *Tribune* charged that the court had "descended into the political arena . . . [and] polluted its garments in the filth of pro-slavery politics." *The Liberator* advised Northerners to disregard the court's opinion, for the judges had conspired with Southern politicians "who have been for the space of a generation plotting against the Union" and who now have "dared" to include the Constitution. "It is a sacrilege. . . . No man . . . can actively submit to their decree." Abraham Lincoln announced that "the Dred Scott decision . . . [was] erroneous. We know that the court that made it has often overruled its own decisions, and we shall do what we can to have it overrule this." Republicans pointed out that the portion of the decision concerning slave expansion in the territories was just *obiter dictum*, without legal justification.* They even threatened to pack the court, if necessary, to secure a reversal. Outwardly, Northern Democrats abstained from criticizing the court, but the decision worried them. Territorial legislatures were creations of Congress, so if Congress could not exclude slavery from a territory, it followed that a territorial legislature similarly lacked the power. The decision meant that popular sovereignty had been destroyed just as had the Republican platform.

* On the question of *obiter dictum*, it has been pointed out that the case came before the court on a writ of error and that current practice permitted the court to examine all parts of an opinion brought before it on such a writ. Also, if the court found Scott a slave, the case would be stronger were he not a citizen. So Taney's inquiry into Scott's residence in free territory was not immaterial. (See Alfred H. Kelly and Winifred A. Harbison, *The American Constitution* [New York: W. W. Norton, 1963, 387–8].)

For the black man, the decision was discouraging. Some blacks, lamenting that the "ship is rotten and sinking" moved to Canada, but most reacted with protest meetings that recurred for at least two years, beginning with Crispus Attucks Day celebrations in Boston. The decision appeared to increase black militancy in the North. Charles L. Remond told a New Bedford, Massachusetts, audience that he would spit on Taney's decision and urged that it be defied and further that the slaves be encouraged to rebel.

The Lecompton Constitution

Just as Buchanan believed the Dred Scott decision would end the slavery in the territories controversy, he also thought that Kansas' problems would end if it were accepted into the Union as a slave state. The proslavery legislature had taken steps toward that end by scheduling an election of delegates to a constitutional convention for June 1857. Buchanan, eager to smooth the way for statehood, removed Geary as governor and appointed Robert J. Walker in his stead. A native of Pennsylvania, Walker lived in Mississippi. He had authored the Tariff of 1846, had served both in the United States Senate and as treasury secretary under Polk; he promised to be a superior appointee. Walker hesitated to accept the post, but gave in to Buchanan's insistence.

After arriving in Kansas, Walker urged all residents to participate in the June elections, but the free-staters again declined. Only 2,200 of the 9,251 eligible voters balloted. Walker soon discovered that the change in occupants of the governorship had not changed the situation in Kansas. His efforts to unite the free-state Democrats and slave-state Democrats and his attempt to convince moderate Republicans that they could expect justice from him only brought the wrath of the extreme proslavery groups upon him. Outside of Kansas, Southern politicians, including Jefferson Davis, denounced Walker; Southern newspapers asked for his removal. At this stage, Buchanan stood behind Walker, writing him on July 12 that "on the question of submitting the Constitution [of Kansas] to the *bona fide* resident settlers of Kansas, I am willing to stand or fall." Also, at least through July, most of the delegates to the Kansas constitutional convention understood, as Buchanan appeared to understand, that Walker was determined to submit their product to the voters.

The constitutional convention met briefly at Lecompton in September, then adjourned to await the outcome of the territorial legislative elections in October. By then Walker had convinced the free-staters to participate. In the election they won 24 of 39 representatives and 9 of 13 in the council. The free-state victory in the territorial legislature was assured when Walker and Territorial Secretary Frederick P. Stanton of Tennessee threw out over 2,800 fraudulent proslavery votes. The free-state victory put the Lecompton convention in a dilemma, for the proslavery delegates were charged with drafting a constitution for an obviously free-state electorate.

The constitution-makers in Kansas produced a document that protected slavery. Aware that the electorate would refuse to accept it, the convention decided to let the electorate express itself only on the constitution with slavery or the constitution without slavery. Either way, the Lecompton Constitution would pass; and either way, slavery would exist in Kansas. The convention cleverly had arranged the document so that if the voters selected the constitution without slavery, the institution would not exist officially, yet slave property would be protected by other clauses. The constitutional delegates had thus given the electorate a two-headed coin to flip, and had circumvented the governor's determination to submit the entire document to the electorate.

Distressed, Walker considered "submission of the question a vile fraud" and refused to support the convention's decision. On this matter he lost Buchanan's support, for the president staunchly upheld the convention. Southern Democrats had made it clear that the administration must back the Lecompton Constitution or face a party split. The split appeared anyhow, for the Lecompton convention shocked Northern Democrats. Douglas, seeing a mockery of popular sovereignty, confronted Buchanan, who in turn threatened Douglas with party ostracism should he oppose the convention's chicanery; Douglas refused to be intimidated. In December 1857, Douglas rose in Congress to condemn the deceptive ratification the Lecompton constitution-makers intended to perpetrate in Kansas.

Earlier, in November, when Walker arrived in Washington, he had quickly discovered he had lost the administration's confidence. Opposed to the Lecomptonite policy and without Buchanan's support, he had little choice but to resign. Back in Kansas, outraged free-staters demanded that the newly elected territorial legislature be called into special session, and Territorial Secretary Stanton complied. Meanwhile, the Lecompton convention scheduled a ratification vote on their terms for December 21. In special session, the territorial legislature denounced the Lecompton convention's ratification plan as fraud and established January 4 as the date when Kansans would consider the Lecompton Constitution as a whole. When that news reached Buchanan, he fired Stanton at once for having called the legislature into special session.

On December 21 free-staters boycotted the Lecompton-mandated election. Without them, the constitution with slavery received 6,226 votes; the constitution without slavery, only 569. An investigating committee later discovered 2,720 fraudulent votes. James W. Denver, Buchanan's new appointee as territorial secretary, arrived in time to oversee the January 4 election that the president reluctantly allowed to proceed. The January vote was 10,226 against the constitution as a whole, 138 for the document with slavery, and 24 for it without slavery. Denver, as acting governor, certified the election to Buchanan and in so doing joined all his predecessors in backing the free-state cause.

Ignoring the January vote, Buchanan sent the Lecompton Constitution to Congress on February 2, 1858, and asked Congress to admit Kansas to the Union under that document. He told Congress that the Lecompton Constitutional Convention had been a lawful body with the power to write a constitution. The convention, Buchanan said, "did not think it proper to submit" the entire constitution to the people, but asked them to vote on it with or without slavery. According to the Supreme Court, Buchanan continued, slavery properly existed in Kansas, and therefore Kansas was as much of a slave state as any in the Deep South.

Southerners in Congress firmly backed the admission of Kansas under the Lecompton Constitution, and just as solidly, Northerners opposed it. In the midst of heated arguments, a fist fight involving nearly thirty congressmen broke out in the House. A bill to admit Kansas passed the Senate, 33 to 25, with Douglas energetically but vainly leading the opposition. Since it was obvious that the bill would not pass the House unless amended, a joint House-Senate conference worked out a compromise called the English bill. Essentially the English bill provided yet another opportunity for Kansans to consider the Lecompton Constitution, under the guise of accepting or rejecting a federal land grant. If accepted, Kansas would become a state with the Lecompton Constitution and a 4,000,000-acre federal grant. If rejected, Kansas would have to wait for statehood until it had a population equal to that necessary for one representative in Congress, then about 93,000. After initially hesitating over the English bill, Douglas followed the lead of his Illinois partisans who opposed it. Administration supporters, however, successfully maneuvered the bill through both houses of Congress by the end of April. So Kansans returned to the polls for final consideration of their constitution on August 2, 1858. Refusing to be bribed, they rejected it and the land grant by 11,300 to 1,788 and remained a territory.

The Panic of 1857

On August 24, 1857, six months following the Dred Scott decision and one month after Walker first arrived in Kansas, the Ohio Life Insurance and Trust Company failed, causing a widespread financial crunch. Rapid growth in all segments of the economy had marked the 1850s, much of it credit financed, often by European capital. The expansion had been accompanied by widespread speculation both in land and in the market. Inflation accompanied growth and speculation, and raged unchecked by any federal control such as the former Bank of the United States had once provided.

Industrial production outran demand, and overextended companies found they could not pay their debts out of their revenues. Virtually unregulated, most state-chartered banks had issued currency far past their reserves; when the panic struck they were unable to meet their obligations. The demands of the Crimean War had put a premium on the products of American agriculture, but when the war ended in 1856 so did European requirements, and the value of American agricultural commodities plummeted.

Though the recession touched all sections of the country, it affected them in different degrees. The South, with much less industry than the North, felt the pinch less. World cotton prices had dipped but recovered rapidly, enabling the South to shake off the effects of the recession before the North could. The situation convinced Southern leaders of the excellence of their economic system as compared to the North; the slaves at least were spared the desperate circumstances of Northern free laborers, thousands of whom were plunged into desperate poverty. Southern extremists argued that the South would fare better outside of a nation that was at the mercy of such financial catastrophe.

As usual in American politics, the administration had to bear the cross. Manufacturers in the East and farmers in the West blamed the financial policies of the Pierce and Buchanan administrations for their plight. As the South pulled out of the recession, Northerners and Westerners claimed that Democratic controlled administrations had neglected their interests, a viewpoint that strengthened the Republican party. Manufacturers favored a tariff; Westerners favored a homestead act; and former Whigs North and South favored internal improvements. All of these groups believed their proposals would not only benefit the nation in normal times, but were crucial to bringing an end to the recession. Southerners disagreed both with the proposals in themselves and as solutions for recession, since the South did not need a cure for an illness it did not have. Southern votes killed a Western-sponsored homestead act early in Buchanan's term, and when another passed Congress later, the president vetoed it. Since Southern Democrats blocked economic measures that powerful Northern groups desired, Northern businessmen and expansionists looked to the Republican party to implement their goals. In the end, the Panic of 1857 and the recession of the following years helped the new Republican party. Americans, especially those in the North who mistrusted Southern ambition, Southern-controlled economics, and the Southern-oriented Democrats whose policies had brought on the recession, put the Republican party again in control of the House of Representatives in 1858.

Lincoln versus Douglas

The Dred Scott decision, the Panic of 1857, and the controversy over the Lecompton Constitution in Kansas muddied the waters of national politics as the congressional elections of 1858 approached. Douglas, spokesman of the Northern Democrats, had to clear the hurdle of reelection in 1858 before sprinting toward the goal of the White House in 1860. His opposition to Buchanan over the Kansas question had won him the admiration of Eastern Republicans, such as Seward and Greeley, who found him so attractive that they advised their party not to run a candidate against him.

The New York *Times*, a Republican paper, speculated on the possibility that a new political party composed of Douglas Democrats and Republicans might emerge.

From his vantage point as governor of Ohio, Salmon P. Chase opposed the Republicans' wooing of Douglas. Chase admired Douglas' stand on the Lecompton Constitution and the English bill, but he warned fellow Republicans that Douglas "has steadily avowed his equal readiness to vote for the admission of Kansas as a slave or free state" and that Douglas "constantly declared his acquiescence in the Dred Scott decision." But Chase need not have worried, for Illinois Republicans had no intention of supporting Douglas. On June 16 the Republican State Convention unanimously nominated Abraham Lincoln to oppose Douglas for the Senate seat.

Douglas, of course, was well-known across the country as a prominent Democrat, whereas Lincoln was a political unknown outside his native Illinois. Born in Kentucky, raised in frontier Indiana and Illinois, and self-taught, Lincoln had devoted himself early to law and politics. He had become a leader in the Whig party in Illinois and had served in the Illinois legislature, but his national experience was limited to one term, 1847–1849, in the House of Representatives. Although he had defeated the popular preacher Peter Cartwright to win his House seat, his opposition to the Mexican War, a popular war in Illinois, cost him reelection. After 1849 he returned to his law practice in Illinois. While he was no more than an average lawyer on the circuit, where cases had to be hurriedly prepared, he had an outstanding record in the higher courts. During this period, Lincoln's wit and reputation as a story-teller created a demand for his services as a speaker.

In contrast to the rotund Douglas, Lincoln stood a lean six feet four inches. A large nose and hollow cheeks dominated his rugged, lined face. Carl Schurz, a well-educated, German-born liberal, was taken aback by the "uncouth" appearance of Lincoln at their first meeting in 1858. Unlike the more dapper public figures of the time, including Douglas, Lincoln projected a casual, homespun frontier image. Schurz described in disbelief Lincoln's battered stovepipe hat (often stuffed with papers), his "rusty black dress coat" with sleeves too short for the tall man, and black trousers that ended abruptly above the ankles. Lincoln wore "a gray woolen shawl" or cape and in his left hand carried a well-worn satchel and a bulging umbrella, which William H. Herndon, Lincoln's law partner, said was usually tied with cord to keep it from falling open. His right hand Lincoln kept "free for handshaking," according to Schurz. "I had seen, in Washington, several public men of rough appearance, but none whose looks seemed quite so uncouth, not to say grotesque, as Lincoln's," wrote Schurz, in mild astonishment.

Yet Lincoln cultivated his homespun appearance as he did his southern Illinois drawl, for he knew how effective a contrast he was to most other lawyers and politicians. People who saw or heard him could not easily forget the ungainly man from Illinois. Lincoln also had a way with words, of expressing himself clearly and succinctly when he chose. On June 16, accepting the nomination to oppose Douglas in the race for senator, he told the Republican State Convention that "a house divided against itself cannot stand. I believe this government cannot endure permanently, half slave and half free." Yet he also believed that the Union would not dissolve, but would "cease to be divided. It will become all one thing, or all the other." Lincoln denounced the Dred Scott decision as part of the proslavery conspiracy.

Ordinarily, congressional elections outside of presidential years attracted less attention and provoked less excitement than when the nation had to choose a chief executive. But those of 1858 proved an exception because of the sectional excitement; and of all the contests that year, the senatorial election in Illinois drew the widest public attention. The election was critical for Douglas, a must if his presidential ambitions were to be satisfied, and difficult not only because of Lincoln's candidacy, but also because Buchanan Democrats opposed him in many Illinois districts. The state legislature to be chosen by Illinois voters would decide whom to send to the Senate, so Douglas had to see his supporters elected over both Republicans and administration Democrats.

Douglas took the lead in campaigning, leaving Lincoln to speak in his wake. In order to confront Douglas more directly, Lincoln, on July 24, 1858, challenged the senator to a public debate, and Douglas agreed. News coverage of the seven debates with the illustrious senator brought Lincoln to the country's attention. From Ottawa, Illinois, on August 21, to Alton, Illinois, on October 15, the contenders squared off before emotional and partisan crowds. Douglas traveled in his private railroad car, while Lincoln rode ordinary coach, an added contrast between the two.

The debates were not cooly reasoned, calm considerations of

the issues, but political attacks characteristic of western stump campaigning. Yet they never degenerated into name-calling or mudslinging personal assaults, for behind the banter and wit there was a seriousness of purpose on the part of each contestant. Lincoln tried to exploit the split in the Democratic ranks by pointing out the inconsistency between popular sovereignty and the Dred Scott decision, both of which Douglas supported. Lincoln denounced Douglas for not taking a moral stand on slavery. Lincoln's conservatism appeared as he disavowed abolitionist ideals such as unconditional repeal of the Fugitive Slave Act and political or social equality of the races. Douglas countered by branding Lincoln and the Republicans as promoters of sectional strife, racial equality, and the end of slavery even within the Southern states.

During the course of the debates it became clear that both men were in accord on some of the issues. Both opposed any sort of black equality. Both opposed the spread of slavery into the territories, but through different means. In the August 27 debate at Freeport, Lincoln asked Douglas, "Can the people of a United States Territory, in any lawful way, against the wish of any citizen of the United States, exclude slavery from its limits prior to the formation of a State Constitution?" Rephrased, Lincoln in fact asked if popular sovereignty was still viable considering the Dred Scott decision. The question was designed to snare Douglas, for any position he took would cost him something. If he shrugged off popular sovereignty and supported the Dred Scott decision, he would lose the Illinois election and his career would be over. If he continued to support popular sovereignty, he would lose the support of the Southern wing of his party and with it, any hope of becoming the Democratic presidential candidate in 1860. The question was not as clever as it seemed, for Lincoln had already perceived Douglas' answer from the senator's earlier statements. Lincoln wanted only to force Douglas into a public position that the press would report and that Douglas' party could not ignore.

Douglas replied fearlessly, "I answer emphatically, as Mr. Lincoln has heard me answer a hundred times from every stump in Illinois, that in my opinion the people of a territory can, by lawful means, exclude slavery from their limits prior to the formation of a State Constitution." After the applause died down, Douglas continued, "It matters not what way the Supreme Court may hereafter decide as to the abstract question whether slavery may or may not go into a territory under the constitution, the people have the lawful means to introduce it or exclude it as they please, for the reason that slavery cannot exist a day or an hour anywhere, unless it is supported by local police regulations." Douglas concluded: "The right of the people to make a slave territory or a free territory is perfect and complete under the Nebraska bill." So, Supreme Court opinion or not, local territorial laws were capable of excluding or accepting slavery. Northerners called Douglas' answer the Freeport Doctrine, while Southern Democrats labeled it the Freeport Heresy. The senator's answer was popular enough with Illinois voters to secure him the Senate seat,* but his stand on the issue widened the split in his party on the national level.

Though Douglas won, his party suffered across the North. Pennsylvanians reacted against the Democratic low-tariff policy and blamed the recession on Buchanan as well. Elsewhere, voters manifested their displeasure over the way in which the administration had handled the Kansas situation. Republicans took control of the House of Representatives, although the Democrats retained the Senate.

Democratic Division and
Northern Frustration

In his December 1858 message to Congress Buchanan took credit for peace in Kansas and discussed the acquisition of Cuba, a subject dear to the hearts of slaveholders. With Cuba in hand, a new slave area would be available to the South that would offset the free states that were coming into the Union. Buchanan asked for a congressional appropriation as an immediate down payment should negotiations proceed favorably. The Spanish, of course, were insulted, and that should have ended the matter, but it did not. Some Americans believed Spanish officials could be bribed to sell the Island, while others still advocated taking it if the Spanish refused to sell.

The Cuban matter became entangled with an effort to pass a homestead bill. Republicans wanted the measure, which had passed the House, to come before the Senate in the 1858 session. February

---

* Although Douglas won in Illinois, the Lincoln campaign had been effective. Republicans carried districts with a larger population than the Democrats did, but unequal apportionment gave the Democrats a majority in the legislature, thus assuring Douglas his Senate seat.

was drawing to a close, and the short session of the lame-duck congress neared adjournment. In the order of precedence, the Cuban bill came first. Seward argued to set the Cuban bill aside in favor of the homestead act, for as he said, the one was "a question of homes, of lands for the landless freemen," while the other was a "question of slaves for the slaveholders." A short but heated debate followed, and a motion to put the Cuban bill on the table failed by a 30 to 18 vote. Having defeated Republican aspirations, the Democrats then withdrew the Cuban bill.

The schism in the Democratic party widened as Senators Jefferson Davis and Stephen Douglas argued over the question of popular sovereignty. Douglas declared that he believed no Democrat could carry any Northern state "on the platform that it is the duty of the federal government to force the people of a territory to have slavery when they do not want it." Davis replied that "when men are to lose the great States of the North by announcing" that protection for slavery, conceded by the Constitution-makers, is an unpopular doctrine, then "I wish it to be understood that my vote can be got for no candidate who will not be so defeated." Douglas announced that Davis appeared to want him to leave the party, but rather he would "stand on the platform" and others would have to jump off and "go out of the party," not he. Senators from the free states for the most part sided with Douglas, while Southern senators seconded Davis. The division in the party was in the open, a clear and ominous omen for 1860; Douglas outspokenly lectured his party, in part because he still smarted from having been removed from the chairmanship of the Senate Committee on Territories, the administration's revenge for his stand during the Lecompton debates. The Buchanan wing of the party had failed to prevent his re-election, but they had used their power to strip him of his chairmanship.

The debate with Davis raised questions among Democrats regarding Douglas' position on popular sovereignty, particularly since they knew he would be a contender for the nomination. Douglas had tried to make his opinion very clear in speech after speech, yet apparently he still felt the need for a public restatement that no one could mistake. His definitive exposition came in *Harper's Magazine* in September 1859. Entitled "The Dividing Line between Federal and Local Authority: Popular Sovereignty in the Territories," Douglas sought to establish historical precedent for his doctrine and to support popular sovereignty with constitutional arguments. He concluded that "every distinct political community . . . is entitled to all the rights, privileges, and immunities of self-government in respect to their local concerns . . . subject only to the Constitution of the United States."

The appearance of the *Harper's* article stirred widespread debate across the nation. Some saw popular sovereignty as a compromise between the Southern position and the Republican position, others argued for the extremes. Most felt it was the opening gun in Douglas' campaign for the Democratic nomination. Few asked for further clarification. Lincoln responded in Columbus, Ohio, in mid-September. Douglas meant, Lincoln proclaimed, by popular sovereignty, once all the "chaff was fanned out of it, . . . [that] *a thing may be lawfully driven away from where it has a lawful right to be.*" Lincoln called the *Harper's* essay "explanations explanatory of explanations explained," and noted that "he has a good deal of trouble with his popular sovereignty." The Louisville *Courier* wrote that some Southern supporters of Douglas had found Douglas' Lecompton stand poor, his Freeport Heresy even poorer, and his *Harper's* "Squatter Sovereignty" article the "worst of all." Other Southerners saw popular sovereignty as yet another antislavery gimmick.

Meanwhile, in Congress Republicans failed to get past Democratic opposition a Pacific railroad bill, an increase in the tariff, and federal land grants for agricultural colleges. Northern economic interests were frustrated as were Western aspirations. These matters assumed greater importance in the face of the division in Democratic ranks over popular sovereignty, for it appeared as if a united Republican party might well be able to overcome Southern Democratic opposition to Northwestern needs if they won the next election.

Fugitive Slaves and Public Excitement

The popular sovereignty debate and Northwestern disappointments in Congress mingled with popular commotion over the fugitive slave problem. In September 1858 a slave catcher apprehended a fugitive near Oberlin, Ohio, and took the unfortunate to nearby Wellington to appear before a federal commissioner as provided by the Fugitive Slave Act of 1850. A crowd from Oberlin rescued the slave and hastened him on his way to safety. A federal grand jury indicted thirty-seven for their act, including a professor and several students from Oberlin College. They were defended by prominent Cleveland attorneys, among them Albert Gallatin Riddle. At their trial, the courtroom exploded in applause when Riddle invoked a "higher law" than that which man made and declared that if a fugitive came to him needing rest, comfort, protection, and means of "further flight, so help me the great God in my extremest need, he shall have them all." When the district attorney condemned the Republican press in Cleveland and the audience in the courtroom, the audience hissed him. Still, one by one, the defendants were found guilty. Clevelanders organized mass meetings in support of the defendants, and Governor Chase suggested that Ohioans use the ballot box to remedy the situation.

Meanwhile, under an 1857 Ohio law that frowned on kidnapping fugitives, a Lorain County grand jury indicted the slave catcher and those who had cooperated with him; county officials arrested the accused. A hurried compromise narrowly averted a confrontation that might have found the federal court imprisoning the rescuers and the county court imprisoning the slave catcher and the federal prosecutors. Lorain County authorities dismissed their suits as the United States quashed prosecution of the remaining cases and freed the Oberlin prisoners. Citizens in both Oberlin and Cleveland celebrated. The proceedings led to an appeal from Ohio and the New England states for the repeal of the fugitive slave law.

In August 1858 the slave ship *Echo*, captured by a United States Navy cruiser while bound for Cuba, was brought to Charleston, South Carolina. Three hundred blacks were returned to Africa by the Colonization Society. The crew was tried for piracy under a federal law of 1820, but a Charleston jury found them not guilty. When the yacht *Wanderer* deposited a cargo of slaves in Georgia late in 1858, no jury could be found to convict that crew either. In the South as well as the North, federal law went unenforced if citizens found it intolerable. The sectional controversy threatened to undermine law enforcement as seriously as it did the stability of politics.

News from California concerning the death of Senator David C. Broderick further excited Americans. Broderick, a transplanted New Yorker, had led the anti-Lecompton wing of the Democratic party in California, against Senator William S. Gwin and the Buchanan wing. The September 1859 election in that far western state climaxed a hard fought, bitter campaign between the two factions.

The Broderick faction lost, whereupon California Chief Justice David S. Terry, a former Texan and Gwin supporter, challenged Broderick to a duel. Terry killed Broderick, making Broderick a martyr in the eyes of antislavery Californians. So great was the change in public opinion in California that the Gwin faction lost power in the next election. Just as important, Easterners mourned Broderick as a victim of the slave powers.

John Brown

Fugitive slaves, slave ships, Congressional debates, the Broderick-Terry duel, all paled before John Brown's attack on the United States arsenal at Harpers Ferry, Virginia. The Kansas avenger of Pottawatomie Creek fame appeared in the neighborhood of Harpers Ferry early in the summer of 1859, rented a place across the river in Maryland, and began accumulating arms for his new project. He aimed to seize the arsenal at Harpers Ferry and the arms stored there, make raids into the slave countryside, arm the slaves, organize them, perhaps erect a black state, and use his military leverage to force emancipation on the South.

Impatient with the progress of the abolition movement, Brown chose instead determined action. At a New England antislavery society meeting in Boston in May 1858, Brown allegedly snorted: "These men are all talk; what is needed is action—action!" He enlisted the support of several antislavery luminaries from New England, for he needed money and weapons. Shocked at the daring of his plan, his backers wavered, and asked how he could hope successfully to defy the slavocracy with only a handful of men. He replied with evangelistic zeal: "If God be for us, who can be against us?" His confidants in New England, Theodore Parker, Samuel Gridley Howe, Gerrit Smith, and others, withheld full approval of his plans, but nevertheless supported him financially.

Brown took care to attract as little attention as possible while he readied his band for their adventure. His task force totaled twenty-two, including himself and five blacks; his arsenal contained pikes, revolvers, and Sharp's carbines. On October 16, 1859, a chilly Sunday night, Brown led eighteen men to Harpers Ferry and "proceeded immediately to take possession of the buildings of the armory and arsenal of the United States." Brown and his raiders overpowered the watchman and turned the brick engine house into a stronghold. When dawn broke, Brown's men made prisoners of the inhabitants of Harpers Ferry. News of the raid spread rapidly, and armed citizens soon liberated most of the prisoners and besieged Brown's party. A detachment of marines, under the command of Army Colonel Robert E. Lee, hastened up from Washington, stormed the engine house, and captured Brown.

According to a United States Senate *Report*, Brown's raiders had killed three Virginians, one marine, and had wounded another. Of the original group, which included three of Brown's sons, seven actually came to trial. The remainder either escaped or were killed. Two of the blacks were slain, two were subsequently hanged with Brown, and one escaped. But the casualties were scarcely as important as the psychological effect of the raid on the nation. The shock of the news of the raid equalled that of the Japanese attack on Pearl Harbor eighty-two years later.

An Associated Press wire reported on October 17, "a dispatch just received . . . states that an insurrection has broken out at Harpers Ferry, where an armed band of Abolitionists have full possession of the Government Arsenal. . . . The insurrectionists number about 250 whites, and are aided by a gang of negroes. . . ." A shudder of fear trembled through the South, for it seemed as if the abolitionists had come sword in hand to liberate the slaves, to encourage them to rise up and slay their masters. Tension and anger raged in the South, even when subsequent dispatches revealed that the raid had failed and most of the insurrectionists had been killed or captured.

A week after the raid a Richmond newspaper announced that the "invasion has advanced the cause of Disunion more than any other event" in the history of the nation. Southerners are saying, the paper continued, " 'let disunion come.' " Southern propagandists identified John Brown as a man who enacted the North's true purpose, playing on the South's constant dread of servile insurrection, now compounded with the evil of white abolitionist leadership. Documents captured with Brown seemed to indicate a wider conspiracy, with Harpers Ferry only one of a number of uprisings planned in other Southern states. It seemed as if Brown had agents all through the South, and reports persisted that Brown's agents had been seized and punished in all parts of the section. Southerners saw an abolitionist or an insurrectionist in every stranger, and mob reaction was swift and unquestioning. A Texas minister, an old

man, screamed as seventy lashes tore into his back for remonstrat-
ing about poor treatment of slaves. A New Yorker, newly installed
as president of an Alabama college, fled for his life. The crew of a
Yankee ship was brutally beaten by irate Georgians. Others suspected of Northern sympathy were tarred and feathered, arrested as
agents of Brown, or driven out of town or out of state. Northern
businessmen in the South, unable to continue their pursuits, returned North.

In an effort to make political capital of the Brown raid, Northern Democrats charged that Seward and other prominent Republicans were associated with Brown. Alongside news of the incident at
Harpers Ferry, the New York *Herald* printed Seward's "irrepressible
conflict" speech, called Seward the "arch agitator who is responsible," and suggested that he be prosecuted. To head off his possible
candidacy in 1860 and to discredit the leader of the Republican
party, Southern Democrats accused him of being the evil genius behind Brown, or at the very least, the type of abolitionist who sought
the destruction of slavery by any means. Seward made no reply, not
out of prudence, but because he was in Europe at the time.

Veteran newsman Horace Greeley published a Republican
refutation in the New York *Tribune*. Brown and his raiders were
"mistaken men," wrote the editor, maintaining that Republicans
stood for "peace, discussion, and the quiet diffusion of sentiments of
humanity and justice. We deeply regret this outbreak." In Kansas,
Lincoln denounced the Brown raid as both a violation of the law
and as a futile effort to eradicate the evils of slavery. At Cooper
Union in New York City, Lincoln described "John Brown's effort
. . . [as] so absurd that the slaves, with all their ignorance, saw
plainly enough it could not succeed."

On Monday, October 31, the fifth day of Brown's trial, a circuit court in Jefferson County, Virginia, found him guilty of treason
and first degree murder. The court selected Friday, December 2, as
the date for Brown's hanging. To the end Brown remained convinced that he had been an instrument of God and therefore had
acted properly. He saw his movement as a religious undertaking,
the purpose of which was to right "a great wrong against God and
humanity." He warned congressional investigators that "you may
dispose of me very easily. . . . but this question [slavery] is still to be
settled . . . the end of that is not yet."

Amid fears that an attempt would be made to rescue him, perhaps as a signal for an extended slave uprising, Brown and six of his followers went bravely to the scaffold. Had Brown been confined as insane his martyrdom might have been prevented. Louisa May Alcott wrote about "Saint John the Just," Longfellow saw the coming of a new revolution, and *The Liberator* eulogized him. Thoreau remarked at Concord that "Christ was crucified" eighteen hundred years ago, and "this morning . . . Captain Brown was hung." Thoreau feared that "I may yet hear of his deliverance, doubting if a prolonged life, if any life, can do as much good as his death." Brown's martyrdom became real for many Northerners.

Hinton Helper and the House

Congress assembled three days after Brown went to his death. The Democrats had clung to their majority in the Senate, but no party had a majority in the House. There were 109 Republicans, 101 Democrats (13 of whom were anti-administration by virtue of their stand against the Lecompton Constitution), and 27 from the American or Know-Nothing party (23 of whom were Southerners). Under the circumstances, a spirited contest over the speakership loomed.

As the House attempted to organize, a Missourian presented a resolution barring from election as speaker anyone who had endorsed Hinton R. Helper's book, *The Impending Crisis of the South* (1857). Southerners had come to regard the book, a different sort of attack on slavery by a North Carolinian, as especially dangerous. A number of Republicans had endorsed the volume, including some of the possible candidates for speaker.

During the debate over the resolution, the clerk found it impossible to keep order as Republicans and Democrats shouted and threatened each other. Emotionally keyed up since the Brown affair, Southern orators condemned Helper and his sympathizers. Thaddeus Stevens warned the Southern members that they could not intimidate Northerners. A New York Democrat accidentally dropped a revolver, causing near pandemonium, but bringing to light the fact that both Northern and Southern congressmen carried weapons on the floor of the House. Forty-four ballots and two months later, February 1, 1860, William Pennington of New Jersey, a conservative Republican, received 117 votes, the exact number necessary for election. Pennington beat out John Sherman, who though he had been the front runner most of the time had endorsed Helper's book and was not acceptable to the South.

The crisis in the House over Helper's book served only to prolong and intensify, not just in Congress but throughout the nation, the moral and emotional differences that had been building for over a decade. In itself the book remained relatively unimportant except as another symptom of sectional division. The passionate reactions stemmed from the psychological impact of the Helper book on the South. Helper used statistics to compare and contrast the material growth of the sections, seeking to prove that slavery enriched only a few planters to the detriment of the mass of nonslaveholding farmers. Helper believed that the lot of the Southern farmers was eventual poverty unless they destroyed the economic and political power of the slaveholders and the institution of slavery itself. "In our opinion . . . the causes which have impeded the progress and prosperity of the South, . . . sunk a large majority of our people in galling poverty and ignorance, rendered a small minority conceited and tyrannical, . . . and brought us under reproach in the eyes of all civilized . . . nations—may all be traced to one common source, . . . the most hateful and horrible word, that was ever incorporated into the vocabulary of human economy—*Slavery!*"

That one marathon sentence summed up Helper's viewpoint. Coming from a Southerner, not from an abolitionist or a Northerner, and appealing to the economic interests of the Southern white majority, this appeared to slaveholders as an extremely dangerous attack, one to be suppressed. Southern postmasters could refuse to deliver Helper's book, as they did abolitionist materials, until the Republicans controlled the government, appointed Republican postmasters, and flooded the South with antislavery literature and the Helper book. Southerners rose to the defense of slavery at every level, on every conceivable occasion that winter in the House of Representatives.

The Presidential Campaign of 1860

As the speakership battle took place in the House of Representatives, delegates to the 1860 national political conventions were being selected. Leading candidates for the Democratic nomination were Jefferson Davis and Stephen Douglas. Head of the Western and Northern wings of his party, Douglas' opposition to Republican aggressiveness had cost him the sympathy of many Northern anti-slaveryites, but Democratic leaders believed that that very fact would win both moderate and former Whig support. Southern Democrats had become increasingly disenchanted with Douglas and were unwilling to lend him their support.

Southerners now looked to Davis as their spokesman. He delighted them when, on the day the House settled the speakership question, he introduced four resolutions in the Senate that expressed their point of view. Davis restated the Dred Scott decision by declaring that neither Congress nor a territorial legislature could prevent citizens from taking slave property into the territories of the United States and that the federal government was obliged to protect slave property in the territories just as it had to protect any other sort of property. The Davis resolutions were modified slightly by a Senate Democratic caucus, the aim of both Davis and the caucus being to find a compromise between Douglas' popular sovereignty and the position of Southern extremists who demanded unconditional protection of slavery in the territories. Clearly the Davis resolutions represented the highest degree of moderation possible for Southern Democrats and was a bid to have the 1860 platform drafted on those lines.

Douglas could not agree to the Davis resolutions without discarding his Northern friends and his chances for the nomination, a fact recognized by Davis and the Southern Democrats. The Douglas people still hoped to work out some sort of compromise in the convention, though they deplored the overt Southern effort to take over their party. Eastern Democrats bided their time and apparently were willing to side with whichever faction promised to win in November.

Most Republicans looked to Seward as the party leader. In 1859 he made an effort to consolidate behind him the few remaining reluctant party leaders. It appeared that Greeley had joined the Seward camp after lunching with him in the spring and that Seward had placated Simon Cameron after visiting with him in Philadelphia. His fences thus mended, Seward departed on a Mediterranean cruise. Seward was abroad during the Brown raid and the speakership battle, as well as during the Democratic assault on his antislavery views. Democrats pointed out how Seward, in his opposition to the Compromise of 1850, had invoked a higher law than the Constitution for a mandate to end slavery; they recalled his "irrepressible conflict" speech of 1858; and they accused him of complicity in the Brown affair at Harpers Ferry. This man of "evil passion," they observed, was a prime contender for his party's nomination.

On his return, Seward attempted to cool down Southern accusations. In a Senate address early in March 1860, Seward remarked that if thirty million people "cannot so combine prudence with humanity" in dealing with slavery, "as not only to preserve our unequalled institutions of freedom, but also to enjoy their benefits with contentment and harmony," then those people would be covered with "shame and sorrow." He deplored hasty threats of disunion as "unnatural" and proclaimed that the motto of the Republican party would be "Union and Liberty." He warned Southern Democrats that if they chose to "rule by terror, instead of ruling through . . . public confidence," then it was time for a change. Seward's effort to rebuild his image into one of moderation inflamed the abolitionists, who, like Wendell Phillips, accused him of moderating his position in the face of slave-power pressure "so as to suit Wall Street."

Two days before Seward spoke to the Senate, a much less well-known Republican appeared at a youth rally at Cooper Union in New York City. There Abraham Lincoln of Illinois told his audience that it made little sense for the South to claim it would secede from the Union rather than tolerate the election of a Republican president in November and then blame the North for the disruption. "That is cool! A highwayman holds a pistol to my ear, and mutters through his teeth, 'Stand and deliver, or I shall kill you, and then you will be a murderer!' " Republicans should not be so easily intimidated, Lincoln said. "Wrong as we think slavery is, we can yet afford to let it alone where it is, because that much is due to the necessity arising from its actual presence in the nation; but," Lincoln asked, "can we . . . allow it to spread" into the territories and even "overrun us here in these Free States?" Republicans should not be diverted from their principles by threats of disunion or "false accusations." Lincoln's moderate and even conservative speech belied the Southern charge that Republicans were all abolitionists and aimed to allay Southern fears that slavery would perish in the hands of a Republican president. Lincoln would not touch it in the states, but he would prohibit it in the territories. Even if the South was not reassured, the speech appealed to Lincoln's auditors, including Greeley, who called it "the very best political address" he had ever heard, including "some of Webster's grandest."

In the Republican party, Lincoln emerged as a moderate who stood between the conservatives and the radicals. He clearly desired party unity, and opposed radical Republican platforms in some states that included demands for fugitive slave law repeal. He was equally against the efforts of other Republicans to modify the Republican stand to attract Douglas Democrats. He wanted to toe the mark carefully, to prevent the extension of slavery to the territories, according to the single plank that held the party together. In his Cooper Union speech and others that followed, Republicans came to know him as very much a moderate—an important impetus to his role in the forthcoming convention.

Yet Lincoln was not the most prominent of contenders for the nomination as 1860 opened. Seward of New York was the favorite still, with Benjamin F. Wade, Salmon P. Chase, and John McLean of Ohio, Edward Bates of Missouri, Simon Cameron of Pennsylvania, Nathaniel P. Banks of Massachusetts, and far down the list, Lincoln of Illinois, among the challengers. As the candidates and their supporters vied for position, the House of Representatives erupted in near physical violence in response to a stinging antislavery speech by Owen Lovejoy of Illinois.* The House roared to its feet, and a riot was narrowly averted. Representatives from Wisconsin and Virginia respectively agreed to a duel as a result of the fray, though in the end that, too, was averted.

On April 23, 1860, the Democratic Convention met in Charleston, South Carolina. The Democrats immediately quarreled over the platform, as Southerners endorsed the Davis Resolutions and Westerners supported popular sovereignty with the additional stipulation that questions of slavery in the territories be left to the Supreme Court. Westerners hoped that their statement could be accepted as a compromise, but Southerners disappointed them. William L. Yancey, as extreme a Southern "fire-eater" as Garrison was an abolitionist, denounced the compromise efforts and Northwestern Democrats as well. Yancey claimed that if Northern Democrats had met the issue squarely and declared slavery a positive good, then the abolitionists would have long since been silenced and har-

* Brother of Elijah P. Lovejoy, killed in 1837 while defending his abolitionist press against an unsympathetic mob at Alton, Illinois.

mony would reign in the party. But they had not, Yancey held, and now Southern Democrats could accept nothing less than the Davis Resolutions. Northern Democrats replied that they were unable to accept the Davis ultimatum. When the platform came to the floor, the Western plank was adopted by a 165 to 138 vote.

As a result, the Alabama delegation announced that according to their instructions, Alabama would withdraw from the convention. Yancey led the Alabamans out, and they were followed by the delegations from Arkansas, Florida, Georgia, Louisiana, Mississippi, South Carolina, and Texas. The seceders hoped that they would force the convention to adopt the Southern platform and a compromise candidate instead of Douglas. But the convention labored on without them. By May 3, after nearly sixty ballots, Douglas commanded a majority though he was unable to get the two-thirds necessary for nomination. Rather than give in to the seceders, who met in a convention of their own, the Douglas men decided to recess the convention for six weeks in order to capitalize on fears of party disunion. They hoped enough pressure would build up so that the walk-out delegations would be replaced by others who might join in nominating Douglas. The seceders were caught by surprise and recessed the rump convention. For many Democrats it was a solemn moment; they feared the great party of Andrew Jackson had committed suicide.

On May 9 a new party composed of old conservatives met in convention at Baltimore. Primarily former Whigs and Americans, they took the name of the Constitutional Union party. They proclaimed a platform of "the Constitution and the country, the union of the States, and the enforcement of the laws," designed to appeal to men of patriotism and supporters of union and order. Their place in the political spectrum of 1860 was akin to that of Fillmore's coalition of Whigs and Americans in 1856. They knew they could not elect a president but hoped they could prevent anyone else from electing one; and should the election be thrown into the House of Representatives, they hoped to use their influence to pick a conservative. For president and vice president they named John Bell of Tennessee, a former Democrat who had broken with Jackson and become a leading Southern Whig, and Edward Everett of Massachusetts, former president of Harvard and an old-line Whig himself.

On May 17, Davis and Douglas debated in Congress. Davis scolded: "I would sooner have an honest man on any sort of a rick-

ety platform . . . than . . . a man I did not trust on the best platform which could be made." Douglas asked in reply, if the platform
was of so little consequence, "why [did you] press that question to
the disruption of the party?" Meanwhile the Republican convention had opened in Chicago on May 16.

Overjoyed at the Democratic split, the Republicans felt assured of the presidency if they chose their candidate and wrote their
platform with care. Many Republicans felt the candidate should
project a conservative image rather than the image of a radical who
sought fundamental changes in the system, such as the abolition of
slavery. Conservatives looked to Bates or McLean. Cameron remained a favorite son of Pennsylvania. Wade hoped to be a dark
horse in the event of a deadlock, while Chase, unable to get the
united backing of the Ohio delegation, leaned toward Seward. In
fact, Seward appeared to have a considerable edge over all the others. Scarcely noticed before the convention, Lincoln had the support of the Westerners in Indiana, Illinois, and Iowa.

The Republican platform rejected secession as treasonous,
called the Dred Scott decision "dangerous," denounced the Brown
raid as a "grave crime," and stood firmly opposed to the extension
of slavery into the territories. Searching for the support of Northern
economic groups, Republicans endorsed a high tariff (a plank
aimed to win Pennsylvania and other industrial areas), internal improvements (dear to former Whigs), a Pacific railroad to be built
with federal assistance, and a homestead bill (popular Western demands). The platform, bearing some resemblance to Henry Clay's
Whig program of decades before, remained discreetly silent on the
fugitive slave law, abolition of slavery in the District of Columbia
(radicals sought to have those slaves incorporated), and personal
liberty laws (conservatives and moderates would have preferred a
mild statement against them).

Abolitionists thought the platform too conservative. Joshua
Giddings, for one, accused the Republicans of moral bankruptcy.
They should have boldly condemned slavery as it existed even
within the Southern states, he felt, and at the very least they should
have reaffirmed their adherence to principles of the Declaration of
Independence. Giddings sought to address the convention, and in
spite of efforts by David Cartter of Ohio to prevent him, successfully
offered an amendment to the platform based on the language of the
Declaration of Independence, reasserting mankind's right to life,

liberty, and the pursuit of happiness. He reminded the party that it had been formed on that basis, "and when you leave out the truth, you leave out the party." Giddings' amendment was defeated. As the old abolitionist rose to leave, he remarked to nearby delegates: "I see that I am out of place here." George W. Curtis of New York promptly asked the convention to reconsider its vote on Giddings' amendment. Were not the words "of the men of Philadelphia in 1776" good enough for Republicans of 1860? On a second vote, the amendment passed, and Giddings strode back into the hall "amidst thunderous applause." To Giddings and other abolitionists, the amendment, while not a significant part of the platform, committed the party to oppose white supremacy and hence the institution of slavery.

Except for the Giddings amendment, the platform sailed through without difficulty. Republicans now bent to the choice of a candidate. Newsmen like Murat Halstead of the Cincinnati *Commercial* and Greeley of the New York *Tribune* fully expected Seward's nomination, although Greeley backed Bates or anyone except Seward. Led by Thurlow Weed and William M. Evarts of New York, Carl Schurz of Wisconsin, and Austin Blair of Michigan, the Seward machine appeared ready to roll over all opposition. Yet Indiana and Pennsylvania delegates warned the party that they could not carry their states for Seward, and Ohio's delegation was hopelessly divided. Pennsylvania and Indiana, along with Ohio, were important, for they held their state elections in October, and might well affect the outcome in the November presidential election if they failed to make strong Republican showings.

David Davis of Illinois, Lincoln's campaign manager, wooed Indiana for Lincoln by promising a cabinet post to Caleb Smith, an important man in the Hoosier delegation. Pennsylvania was pledged to Cameron at least for the first ballot, but Davis enticed Cameron with another cabinet post provided he would throw his support to Lincoln and not to Seward on later ballots. Davis struggled hard to gather the anti-Seward votes, yet it remained uncertain that conservative anti-Sewardites could concentrate enough support for any one candidate to defeat the favorite.

On Friday morning, May 18, Seward's band, wearing white and scarlet feathers in their caps, led a long column of Seward supporters to the Wigwam, the specially built convention hall. Delegates and visitors crammed into the hall, while thousands milled around outside, unable to enter. Both Seward's and Lincoln's managers had hired men of prodigious lung power to shout and scream every time the name of their benefactor was mentioned, a tactic commonly used and intended to magnify the support of the rank and file.

Nominations and seconds began promptly. The Seward and Lincoln men vied with one another to produce the most noise, and according to Halstead, it was a magnificent shouting match. When Blair seconded the nomination of Seward, Sewardites were compelled to outdo a previous Lincoln shriek that had been tremendous. Their response, wrote Halstead, "was startling. Hundreds of persons stopped their ears in pain. . . . No Comanches, no panthers, ever struck a higher note, or gave screams with more infernal intensity." As he looked down from the stage, "nothing was to be seen below but thousands of hats—a black, mighty swarm of hats—flying with the velocity of hornets over a mass of human heads, most of the mouths of which were open."

When an Ohioan seconded Lincoln's nomination, "the uproar was beyond description," wrote Halstead, who proceeded to describe it. "Imagine all the hogs ever slaughtered in Cincinnati giving their death squeals together, a score of big steam whistles going . . . and you conceive something of the same nature." Then the Lincoln boys "took deep breaths all around, and gave a concentrated shriek that was positively awful," at the same time stamping their feet so that "every plank and pillar in the building" quivered. "The Lincoln *yawp*," Halstead noted, "swelled into a wild hozanna of victory."

The balloting began, with 233 votes necessary to win. On the first Seward led with 173½ to Lincoln's 102 *; on the second, Lincoln closed the gap with Seward at 184½ to his 181. On the third ballot, Lincoln took the lead, 231½ to Seward's 180, but before the result was announced, Cartter of Ohio leaped up on a chair and got the floor, bringing a smile to Halstead, who later remarked, "I had imagined Ohio would be slippery enough for the crisis." Cartter shouted, "I rise, Mr. Chairman, to announce the change of four votes of Ohio from Mr. Chase to Mr. Lincoln."

* In addition to Lincoln and Seward, the nominees and their votes on the first ballot were: Bates (of Missouri) 48; Cameron (Pennsylvania) 50½; McLean (Ohio) 12; Chase (Ohio) 49; Wade (Ohio) 3; William L. Dayton (New Jersey) 14; John M. Reed (Pennsylvania) 1; Jacob Collamer (Vermont) 10; Sumner (Massachusetts) 1; and Frémont (California) 1.

It was over. Lincoln had won the nomination! There was a moment of quiet, Halstead observed, as everyone took deep breaths "like the rush of a great wind, in the van of a storm" and then the storm broke. "Thousands cheered with the energy of insanity." To Halstead it sounded like "the breaking up of the fountains of the great deep," occasionally drowning out the blasts of the cannon salute fired outside.

In contrast to the acrimonious adjournment of the Democratic convention, Chicago hosted a joyous celebration. "The town," Halstead wrote, "could hardly contain itself. There were bands of music playing, and processions marching, and joyous cries heard on every hand." Amidst the festivities, the convention reassembled that evening to choose the second spot on the ticket. With shouts of "Clay! Clay!" boosters of Cassius M. Clay of Kentucky touted their candidate. Hannibal Hamlin of Maine, a friend of Seward (the New York delegation would not enter Seward's name), a former Democrat, and a better geographical balance for the ticket than Clay, turned out to be the convention's choice. Republicans, explained Halstead, "deemed [it] judicious to pretend to patronize the Democratic element" with Hamlin's nomination and by so doing answer charges that the convention smacked far too much of conservatism, "an old Whig affair." After wrap-up speeches the convention adjourned, its work completed. Back out into the Chicago night the celebration continued with obvious relish. "The 'Old Abe' men formed processions and bore rails through the streets," Halstead reported, presumably some of those "three thousand" split by Lincoln thirty years before down Sangamon River country way. "Torrents of liquor were poured down the hoarse throats of the multitude. A hundred guns were fired from the top of the Tremont House."

Lincoln had been eminently available for the nomination in the classic sense. Although not a complete unknown politically, neither was he widely known outside of Illinois, and as a result he had not made the enemies on a national scale that Seward had. Southerners had focused their hatred on Seward, who, under the circumstances, could have been considered nothing more than a sectional candidate. It was ironic that Lincoln's "house-divided" speech had failed to attract the same sort of attention as Seward's "irrepressible conflict," but it had not. Lincoln was a Westerner of Kentucky (at least border, if not Southern) background and not an abolitionist. As it turned out, Lincoln appealed little to Southerners either, but the party felt he projected a more conservative image than Seward.

When the Democrats reassembled in Baltimore on June 18, they had to face the fact that the Republicans were united and enthusiastic and intended to wage a very hard campaign. Clearly party unity was necessary for a Democratic victory in November. However, the adjournment at Charleston had not healed the split in the party, as was apparent from the beginning. The Douglas men controlled the Baltimore meeting. They refused to seat anti-Douglas delegates from those Southern states that attended, and questioned the credentials of others. Virginia led a new walkout, followed by delegations from North Carolina, Maryland, Kentucky, and Tennessee. Those Southerners who remained refused to budge from their previous anti-Douglas stand just as the Douglasites remained firm, comforted by the knowledge that they controlled the meeting.

Douglas realized that in the interests of party harmony it might be wise for him to withdraw in favor of another candidate, provided the candidate was a pro-Union man and provided the convention could find a suitable substitute. His supporters, however, suppressed his offers to withdraw, and when he received all but a handful of the votes cast on the second ballot, the convention declared him nominated on the grounds that he had received more than the necessary two-thirds vote of those delegates present. The convention nominated as his running mate Herschel V. Johnson, a former governor of Georgia who opposed secession.

Dissident Southern Democrats, the seceders from Charleston and the Baltimore bolters, held a meeting of their own in Baltimore on June 28. They quietly adopted the Southern platform that had been turned down at Charleston and nominated Buchanan's vice president, John C. Breckinridge of Kentucky, as their presidential candidate. Second spot on this "National Democratic" ticket went to Senator Joseph Lane of Oregon.

Four Americans now vied for the office of president. Douglas needed either a solid North or some combination of Northern and Southern electoral votes to win, while Lincoln needed all the states Frémont had carried in 1856 plus Pennsylvania and Indiana. Breckinridge and Bell needed a miracle, but together they might have taken enough votes from the front runners to throw the election into the House of Representatives. Pennsylvania appeared to be the keystone to victory for either Lincoln or Douglas. Since the state held its elections for state offices in October, a Republican or Democratic victory there could easily influence the national outcome in November.

The recession of 1857 had hurt Pennsylvania's industry, especially the iron industry. Pennsylvania industrialists looked to a tariff to cure their ills, but the Democrats in Congress had only recently blocked a protective tariff proposed by Justin Morrill. The Republicans pointed gleefully at their tariff plank, while both Douglas and Breckinridge stood on platforms that emphasized free trade. The tariff issue was important in Pennsylvania, but outside of that state it was seldom mentioned. The campaign in New England proved dull, for while Bell had some support in Massachusetts, neither he nor Breckinridge emerged as contenders there. The divided Democratic vote in New England hurt Douglas, while Lincoln had a clear edge. In the slave states other than Missouri, the election was between Bell and Breckinridge primarily, with Douglas a poor third and Lincoln unacceptable.

During the race Lincoln made no speeches, as was the practice then, leaving the campaigning to his party. Lincoln also declined to issue written statements of his position, wisely believing that anything he wrote would be seized upon and misrepresented by Southerners. Douglas, on the other hand, campaigned hard, even making an unprecedented speaking tour of the South denouncing Breckinridge backers as disunionists. Not every Breckinridge man was a disunionist, Douglas quipped, but every disunionist in America was a Breckinridge man. Douglas warned the South that the Union could not be broken. In August, he told an audience at Norfolk, Virginia, that seceders ought to be treated as "Old Hickory treated the Nullifiers in 1832." His references to Jackson were frequent. In Northern speeches he advocated burying Southern disunionism and Northern abolitionism together, for Jackson would have hanged "Northern and Southern traitors on the same gallows."

John L. Scripps, a Chicago *Tribune* editor, obtained a twenty-five-hundred-word autobiography from Lincoln and from it wrote a campaign biography that the Chicago and New York *Tribunes* sold by the hundreds of thousands at a nickel each. Americans now read about the rail-splitting, honest, charitable, and perhaps heroic Illinois lawyer about whom they knew so little. "Abe," "Honest Abe," "the Rail-splitter," was praised and bally-hooed by hundreds of party orators across the North. The Republicans held parades and mass meetings and distributed literature in a manner old-timers thought reminiscent of the 1840 election.

Douglas was in Cedar Rapids, Iowa, when he learned that the Republicans had swept Pennsylvania in their October elections. He told his secretary, "Mr. Lincoln is the next president." Douglas felt then that he had to try to help save the Union, and toward that end he toured Tennessee, Georgia, and Alabama, hammering away against disunion in spite of the jeers and ripe fruit that voters often greeted him with. Southern threats of secession seemed to grow louder as a Republican victory became a possibility. The Northern public received secession threats with mixed emotions, uncertain about their sincerity. In Cleveland, for example, Edwin Cowles, antislavery editor of the Cleveland *Leader*, told his readers that Lincoln's election would expose the South's "empty" threats of secession and result in a final settlement of the sectional agitation. The Douglas-oriented *Plain Dealer* in Cleveland stressed the sincerity of the disunion threats and urged its readers to support Douglas as the "only" nonsectional candidate. Both papers insisted that the Union must be preserved.

James Russell Lowell had no doubts about the importance of the election, the question at issue, or fears of secession. In the October issue of the *Atlantic Monthly* he wrote: "The slaveholding interest has gone on step by step, forcing concession after concession, till it needs but little to secure it forever in the political supremacy of the country. . . . let it mould the evil destiny of the Territories,—and the thing is done past recall. The next Presidential election," Lowell warned, "is to say *Yes* or *No*." The importance of the election was clear, it "is a turning-point in our history; for, although there are four candidates, there are really . . . but two parties, and a single question that divides them." That question was slavery. "What unites the Republicans is . . . a common resolve to resist its encroachments everywhen and everywhere. . . . It is in a moral aversion to slavery as a great wrong that the chief strength of the Republican party lies."

Lowell continued: "It is idle to talk of sectionalism, abolitionism, and hostility to laws. The principles of liberty and humanity cannot, by virtue of their very nature, be sectional. . . . Prevention is not abolition." It was not treason to question "the infallibility of a court; for courts are never wiser or more venerable than the men composing them," Lowell lectured, alluding to the Dred Scott decision. "Truth is the only unrepealable thing." Lowell asked: "Will the election of Mr. Lincoln endanger the Union? . . . Mr. W. L. Yancey, to be sure, threatens to secede; but the country can get along without him, and we wish him a prosperous career in foreign parts." Secession was "the old Mumbo-Jumbo" that had been "occasionally paraded at the North, but, however many old women may be frightened, the pulse of the stock-market remains provokingly calm." To Lowell "the old cry of Disunion has lost its terrors, if it ever had any." It was "a manifest absurdity" to think that Republicans would disturb slavery in the Southern states themselves, and Lowell thought the South knew that by October. "We are persuaded that the election of Mr. Lincoln will do more than anything else to appease the excitement of the country," Lowell concluded. In one way or another, other literary figures, including Holmes, Whittier, and Bryant, echoed Lowell.

Yet Lowell and the others were mistaken. Southerners were convinced that the Republicans would attack slavery, perhaps first in the territories, but sooner or later in the South itself. The hysteria over John Brown's raid had not yet abated, and nothing the Republicans could do or say would convince or reassure Southerners that Brown was not representative of the new party. They believed Lincoln to be a simple Western hick whom the Republicans had put up as a screen for Seward and the radical wing of the party. The rumor that Hamlin was a mulatto circulated widely in the South. Southern politicians successfully convinced Southern poor whites that Lincoln's election meant black equality and black citizenship. Douglas, having toured the South, was more acutely aware of Southern attitudes than most Northerners. Early in October he told a Chicago audience that he believed "this country is more in danger now than at any other moment" since he had been in public life. Republicans like Lowell refused to listen to Douglas or Bell, who also saw the danger; they preferred to consider the threat of secession as a scare tactic designed to frighten people away from the Republican ballot. Early in November, Seward reminded New Yorkers that Southerners had made the same threats for twenty years, conveniently before each election. He did not doubt, he said, that Southerners thought they would "dissolve the Union, but I think they are going to do no such thing."

Election day November 6, 1860, passed in an orderly and quiet manner. The October voters in Pennsylvania, Indiana, and Ohio proved to be accurate forecasters in electing Republican governors. In November the Republicans captured the White House for Lincoln with 40 percent of the popular vote; Douglas ran close behind with 29 percent, second in the popular total, but last in the electoral column. Breckinridge and Bell followed in the popular count in that order.* Lincoln carried every free state except New Jersey, which he split with Douglas four electoral votes to three. Breckinridge took every state of the Lower South, and North Carolina, Maryland, and Delaware as well. Bell won Virginia, Kentucky, and Tennessee; Douglas only Missouri.

Out of the mass of statistics and the many interpretations of the election, an overwhelming 69 percent of Americans had endorsed Lincoln and Douglas. By one method or another both men were committed to keeping slavery from the territories. The heavy vote against the expansion of slavery was a stunning fact for the South to accept. Their choice seemed clear enough, they could accept the will of the majority or they could attempt to preserve their institution through secession.

The Republicans may have put the Illinois lawyer in the White House, but the composition of Congress was not yet fully settled, for all members of the Thirty-seventh Congress had not yet been elected. The Republicans eventually fell short of majorities in both houses. An early report in the *National Intelligencer* showed that the Republicans lacked eight seats for a majority in the Senate, and twenty-one fewer than a majority in the House. Other newspapers concurred with slightly different figures. Not subject to election, the Supreme Court also remained unchanged. Only the executive branch of the government had succumbed to the Republican assault.

Black Americans had no real champion in the contest of 1860. Frederick Douglass saw nothing to cheer him in Lincoln's stand, or that of the Republican party, except that Lincoln opposed the extension of slavery. No candidate proposed to end the institution, and none even considered the plight of the free Northern blacks. Black Americans would have preferred Chase or Seward to Lin-

* Election results:

CANDIDATE	PARTY	ELECTORAL VOTE	POPULAR VOTE	%
Abraham Lincoln	Republican	180	1,867,198	39.8
Stephen A. Douglas	Democrat	12	1,379,434	29.4
John C. Breckinridge	National Democrat	72	854,248	18.2
John Bell	Constitutional Union	34	591,658	12.6

coln, but Lincoln was the lesser of the other evils: Douglas, Bell, or Breckinridge. As a group, black Americans had very little political influence in 1860. Yet, ironically, for many white Americans that part of the black population in chains played a very real role in the election.

6

Secession, Constitutional Controversy, and Sumter

During the four-month interim between Abraham Lincoln's election on November 6, 1860, and his inauguration on March 4, 1861, seven states of the Lower South seceded from the Union. Governor William Henry Gist of South Carolina, planter turned politician and ardent secessionist, paved the way. Prior to the election Gist had informed the governors of all the other cotton states but Texas that in the event of Lincoln's election South Carolina would call a special state convention to consider secession. He asked his fellow cotton state governors to cooperate. When Pennsylvania and Indiana went Republican in October, Gist alerted his legislature for action; on the eve of the election, he recommended that they prepare to call a special state convention, for it appeared Lincoln would win.

The people of South Carolina were also prepared for action. "The tea has been thrown overboard—the revolution of 1860 has been initiated," announced the Charleston *Mercury* after the election. South Carolina officials who held federal posts promptly resigned. On Saturday, November 10, the legislature unanimously passed a bill to call a state convention to meet on December 17 for the express purpose of considering secession. Throughout the state, public meetings endorsed the action; everywhere palmetto flags flew and South Carolinians celebrated. Sympathy ran so high in the other cotton states that, unlike the situation during the nullification controversy of 1832, it seemed certain that South Carolina could count on support from her neighbors.

Aware that he faced a great crisis, President Buchanan adopted a wait-and-see policy, hoping he would not be the cause of violence or secession either in South Carolina or in any other cotton state. He chose not to make a show of force by reinforcing the federal garrisons in the state as Jackson had done in 1832. Though Attorney General Jeremiah S. Black advised the president that he had the right to take steps to protect federal property, Buchanan took none, feeling that such an act would solidify the South behind South Carolina more firmly than ever.

In his annual message to Congress on December 4 Buchanan pointed out how Northern antislavery agitation deeply disturbed the South and asked the Northern states to repeal their personal liberty laws. He reminded the South that the founding fathers had made no provision for the dissolution of the Union. "Secession," Buchanan warned, "is neither more nor less than revolution." The rights of Southern states had not been trampled by Congress, Buchanan argued, so threats of disunion stemmed from apprehension of future danger, which in his opinion failed to provide cause for revolution. He told the South that it was his duty to protect the property of the United States in the South; that federal officers had been so instructed; that Southern attempts to take over federal property would put the responsibility for the consequences with them. At the same time Buchanan denied that Congress could coerce a state, probably in an effort to reassure Southern states of their safety in the Union; whatever his intent, the statement caused considerable confusion and weakened his policy. The message failed to satisfy anyone in the South except the Unionists within the cotton states.

On December 6 South Carolinians elected delegates to their secession convention scheduled to meet in Columbia. A Charleston newspaper reported that of the twenty-two delegates, seventeen stood for immediate secession, three for secession when the time was right, and two failed to respond. On December 20 the convention solemnly and unanimously declared "that the union now subsisting between South Carolina and other States, under the name of the 'United States of America,' is hereby dissolved."

Republicans and Compromise

Republican satisfaction at having won the White House gave way to concern over the events in South Carolina. Horace Greeley represented one segment of Republican opinion, suggesting in his newspaper that if the cotton states wanted to leave the Union, "we insist on letting them go in peace." Greeley felt separation was preferable to pinning one section to the other "by bayonets." The great preacher Henry Ward Beecher agreed, and so did the Garrisonians, who were delighted to be rid of slavery by any means. Others advocated compromise. In his Albany newspaper, Thurlow Weed, a Whig political boss in New York, called for a revised fugitive slave law that would allow the purchase of a runaway's freedom and also for the extension of the Missouri Compromise line westward to the Pacific. Many Republicans, however, believed that the election had been lawfully carried out and that the South had a duty to abide by it, distasteful as it might be.

Early in December the House appointed a Committee of Thirty-three to work out a solution to the crisis. Obviously the Republicans were the key, for no measure they opposed could become a viable compromise. Aware of this, cotton-state Democrats would accept no proposal that had not the full support of the Republicans. And the Republican position was clear. Lincoln, in a series of communications to party members, to Lyman Trumbull on December 10, to William Kellogg of the House committee on December 11, and to Weed on December 17, firmly opposed any compromise on the extension of slavery, including the extension of the Missouri Compromise line or the legalization of popular sovereignty. Only a steadfast course could preserve the Republican party and Lincoln knew it. To compromise on the extension of slavery would have been to deny the very foundation on which the party had been founded and to repudiate the platform on which he had been elected. By the end of December even Greeley swung around to Lincoln's view.

As the South Carolina convention gathered, the House of Representatives with Republicans and Douglas Democrats in the majority voted 153 to 14 to recommend repeal of the personal liberty laws; but that was not enough for Southern Democrats. Jefferson Davis doubted if the repeal of the laws would secure Southern rights. Senator John J. Crittenden, a seventy-three-year-old former Kentucky Whig, introduced a compromise plan into the upper house on December 18. Crittenden's plan included constitutional amendments that would have extended the Missouri Compromise line; guaranteed the preservation of slavery where it then existed; and prohibited the abolition of slavery in the District of Columbia unless District citizens, along with those of Maryland and Virginia, consented, and only with compensation to slaveholders. The Crittenden proposals were debated by the Senate Committee of Thirteen two days after South Carolina seceded, but Republicans and Southern Democrats combined to reject it. The main contention was over the extension of the Missouri Compromise line, which Robert Toombs and Davis apparently would have accepted if a majority of Republicans had also agreed. In the end, only Douglas Democrats and a few border-state Democrats gave it the nod.

On December 24 Seward offered the Senate Committee of Thirteen three propositions, composing a Republican compromise. The first of these, a suggested constitutional amendment, would have restrained Congress from ever abolishing or otherwise interfering with slavery in the states. The second called for amendments to the fugitive slave law in order to grant the runaway a jury trial, and the third recommended that Congress ask the Northern states to repeal their personal liberty laws. Seward claimed the resolutions were in accord with Lincoln's views. The committee accepted only the first proposal; they opposed the second after Democrats amended it to provide for selection of the jury from the state whence the fugitive had fled; and they rejected the third proposition out of hand. By December 28 the Committee of Thirteen reported to the Senate that they had been unable to agree on a plan of settlement. The same fate had befallen the House Committee of Thirty-three. Both houses of Congress, however, later voted by two-thirds majorities to amend the Constitution in order to deny to Congress forever the right to abolish or to interfere with slavery in any of the states. That vote came on March 3, 1861, but only Ohio, Illinois, and Maryland had ratified it before the press of events crowded it out. Ironically, the Thirteenth Amendment that was later adopted abolished slavery.

South Carolina's initiative, the election of Lincoln, Buchanan's caution, and the inability of Congress to reach a compromise spurred secessionist activity in other states. Led by men like Robert Toombs and William L. Yancey, secessionists claimed that the interests of the South were in serious danger so long as the South remained in the Union, and they demanded immediate secession before Lincoln took office. The Unionists in the Southern states strongly opposed hasty action.

Alexander Stephens told his fellow Georgians on November 14 that the election of Lincoln in itself was not a cause for secession. While the House and Senate were not in Lincoln's hands, Stephens reasoned, the president would be "powerless" to do the South "any great mischief." Stephens reminded Georgians that the tariff was not a valid complaint either since Southerners had supported the current tariff. The personal liberty laws *were* a bona fide grievance, he admitted, but redress should be demanded within the Union. Stephens urged delay and consultation before secession, and begged his colleagues to exhaust every possible remedy within the Union. Yet by the time November 1860 had passed, Stephens had come to believe that his own Georgia, plus Alabama, Mississippi, and Florida would follow South Carolina. "The odds are against us," he said of the Southern Unionists, it was too late to reason. "The people are run mad. They are wild with passion and frenzy, doing they know not what." The well-organized advocates of secession had drawn a rosy picture of life outside of the Union: direct trade with Europe without bothersome tariffs; lower taxes; an end to abolition agitation; an end to dependence upon the North for the necessities of life; an end to Northern debts; the reopening of the slave trade; expansion into the Caribbean or Central America; and the creation of a great Southern Union backed by Britain and France and financed by cotton.

Southerners had felt for years that they lived under a cloud of impending disaster so long as they remained in the Union. The tension created by the Brown raid, followed by the election of a Republican president, added significantly to the fear that the Southern way of life would be extinguished in the near future. They wondered what they stood to gain by delaying secession when that simple act would save Southern society, maintain white supremacy, protect slave property, soothe their tension, and end Northern meddling in Southern affairs. Between November 18 and December 11 conventions to study the crisis were called in each of the cotton states except Texas, where Unionist Governor Samuel Houston blocked secessionist moves. Sentiment in support of South Carolina snowballed.

State after Southern state joined South Carolina throughout January 1861: Mississippi on January 9 by a convention vote of 84 to 15; Florida on January 10 by 62 to 7; Alabama on January 11, 61 to 39; Georgia on January 19, 208 to 89; Louisiana on January 26, 113 to 17; and finally, on February 1, Texas by a vote of 166 to 8, Sam Houston notwithstanding. The final votes in the conventions failed to show the extent of Unionist sentiment; in Alabama and Georgia, for example, the Unionists failed by narrow margins to delay a decision but when it appeared the secessionists would carry the day, many voted along with the majority to present as united a front as possible.

Representatives of the seceded states met February 4, 1861, at Montgomery, Alabama, to form a new nation called the Confederate States of America. On the same day, in Washington, D. C., representatives from twenty-two states met at the invitation of the Virginia legislature to find a last compromise. Presided over by former President John Tyler, the Peace Conference debated behind closed doors and came up with a proposed constitutional amendment similar to Crittenden's. The main difference between the two was the stipulation that new territory could be added to the Union only with the consent of a majority of both free- and slave-state senators. Opposed by Virginia and other Southern states, the proposal stirred little support when submitted to the Senate.

The long and bitter sectional agitation had taken its toll. All attempts at compromise failed in part because men in political life, both North and South, felt that they had yielded enough and that, regardless of the consequences, their consciences and their constituents would allow them to bend no further. And compromise failed in part because Southerners realized that no compromise plan safeguarded their diminishing power inside the Union to protect their peculiar institution and white supremacy. Compromise also failed because Northerners would no longer tolerate the dictates of a Southern minority on questions of national policy. Just as Southerners refused to commit institutional suicide neither would Republicans commit political suicide.

The Constitutional Controversy*

In the decade and a half prior to secession, the public debated the extension of slavery, the fugitive slave acts, the personal liberty laws, and the role of the federal government on an emotional and intellectual level. Both sides formulated constitutional arguments to support their positions before the lower courts and especially before the Supreme Court.

Northern lawyers cited personal liberty laws to protect black citizens from the fugitive slave laws and relied upon the use of the "police powers" ** in the territories to exclude slavery. Northerners in general depended upon time, the growth of the population, and the expansion of free state rule to bring the institution of slavery to a legal end through parliamentary majorities.

Southern lawyers sought to preserve slavery by building into the federal system legal means of protecting slavery in the territories and of upholding the fugitive slave laws. They worked out an elaborate program whereby the laws of the slaveholding states would be the controlling laws so far as slavery in the territories and the fugitive slave laws were concerned; they depended on the federal government, especially the Supreme Court, to effect their program. Their ally, Chief Justice Roger B. Taney, brought their program to fruition in the Dred Scott case (1857) and Booth or Fugitive Slave case (1859). Jefferson Davis formulated the completed proslavery program in his Senate Resolutions of 1860.

States' Rights and Slave Sovereignty

Astute lawyers representing the North and the South in Congress understood one another's legal arguments and terminology very well, even though in political rhetoric terms like "states' rights" or "state sovereignty" projected emotional overtones that lent them a certain ambiguity and made them useful in political debate. These terms held meaning for the constitutional and legal ar-

---

* For a thorough examination of this subject, see Arthur Bestor, "State Sovereignty and Slavery: A Reinterpretation of Proslavery Constitutional Doctrine, 1846–1860," *Journal of the Illinois State Historical Society* (Summer 1961), pp. 1–64.

** A government's "police power" is its ability to legislate for the health, morals, and general welfare of the community.

guments as well, and both parties used them occasionally, though not always in the same manner.

"States' rights" was defined consistently. It meant that a state could use its powers, within its jurisdiction, to prevent the federal government from tampering with the rights of its citizens. It provided a means of defense against the national government, a way to weaken federal authority within a state, but it was not applicable outside of the state. For example, as it broke its ties with the Union in 1860, South Carolina applied states' rights in the most positive way it could. South Carolina claimed that by remaining within the Union it would be unable to protect the rights of its citizens to slave property, so it imposed its power through secession to protect its citizens from interference by the federal government. As used in the secessionist movement during the winter of 1860–1861, states' rights was clearly a defensive concept.

But a defensive weapon could not be used to build protection for slavery into the federal system. Between 1846 and 1860, Southern leaders hoped to find a way to protect slavery within the Union; secession, though it was always an option of last resort, was not the answer they sought. It made better sense to proslavery leaders to use the historic constitutional system if they could, and the program they evolved was based on a clever combination of state sovereignty and constitutional interpretation.

Between 1846 and 1860 Southern leaders backed away from local autonomy, a concept basic to the theory of states' rights. Their attitude toward slavery in the territories provides an illustration. Stephen A. Douglas and his doctrine of popular sovereignty exemplified local autonomy applied to slavery in the territories. Southern leaders supported him at first when his position seemed a way to open Kansas and Nebraska to slavery; but when it appeared popular sovereignty would be disadvantageous in Kansas they rejected the idea so violently that they chose to destroy the Democratic party in 1860 rather than allow their opponents to incorporate popular sovereignty into the platform.

Southern leaders also vigorously opposed the doctrine of states' rights as it was used by Northerners. South Carolina, author of the only nullification ordinances in American history (1832–1833), announced in 1860 that the Northern states shirked their constitutional duty through the passage of personal liberty laws that nullified the fugitive slave laws. Proslavery leaders insisted from the first that the federal government had to enforce the federal fugitive slave ordinances.

The terms states' rights and state sovereignty were not used by the Constitution-makers in 1787. They accorded only powers, not rights, to federal and state governments. They carefully assigned rights, privileges, and immunities to individuals, not governments. They took care to protect the rights of individuals by listing them specifically or by prohibiting a government from exercising a power that would infringe upon them. So governments either exercised or were denied powers, and citizens possessed rights, a usage that was consistent in the Constitution.*

The term states' rights was therefore meaningless in the phraseology of the Constitution. Historically, the term first appeared in 1798 and then as a convenient label rather than a doctrine. According to the Kentucky and Virginia Resolutions, presented to defend the constitutional right of freedom of the press, the power of a state could be used to protect the rights of a citizen. The condensation of terminology from "state interposition of power to protect the rights of its citizens" to "states' rights" described what a state could do against a law of the United States that state authorities believed transgressed a given constitutional right. The same label just as appropriately described state interposition against the fugitive slave law of the 1850s. But the institution of slavery needed protection beyond the borders of the slave states in order to recover runaways and insure the safety of the institution in the territories. States' rights was not sufficient for the task.

The defenders of slavery therefore settled upon a more viable premise, state sovereignty. They held that each state of the Union was a sovereign state and had been so even before the compact of Union was made. They considered sovereignty an indivisible power wielded by the state, with the state as the only judge of its authority. American revolutionaries, in both the Articles of Confederation (1781) and the Constitution, had associated indivisible sovereignty of that sort with the British system, where the King in Parliament made law that bound the whole empire, and rejected it. Instead, Americans had adopted a contrary system of sovereignty that was divided between the states and the federal government. States' rights as a protective device worked only within the framework of

---

* This consistency of language extended to the Declaration of Independence.

divided sovereignty. But state sovereignty as developed by the pro-slavery group represented a return to the older British view that sovereignty was indivisible.

Such a doctrine was much better fitted to intrude aggressively into the workings of the federal government, and its effects might even be felt beyond the boundaries of the slaveholding states for the protection of slavery in the territories and the return of fugitive slaves. State sovereignty, then, had little to do with rights and a lot to do with power.

State Sovereignty and Slavery in the Territories

Neither the right to carry slaves into a territory nor the right to prohibit slavery there was mentioned in the Constitution. Any legal theory about the status of slavery in the territories had to be based on legal precedent or interpretation of the Constitution. In practice, slavery in the territories either existed or was prohibited according to territorial regulations on the subject—the exercise of the police powers of the territorial legislature. Although the territories were created by Congress, control of those police powers remained with the government of the territory. This practical state of affairs normally mattered little, for the expedient legislation of the territorial period could be regularized with the coming of statehood. The issue of slavery in the territories altered the normal situation, however, for the early use of the police power determined the subsequent existence or prohibition of slavery.

Both parties to the dispute understood that implication perfectly. In 1854 Lincoln had questioned the wisdom of letting the first settlers in a territory fix policy, lest they deprive latecomers of a choice. Proslavery leaders agreed, because if slavery was not protected from the beginning in a territory, slaveholders would not migrate there. Since original decisions in a territory could fix its future domestic social policy, both sides knew how important those original decisions were.

That was exactly why the Wilmot Proviso of 1846 catapulted into the arena of national politics the issue of slavery in the territories. "Neither slavery nor involuntary servitude shall ever exist in any part of the said territory" acquired as a result of the Mexican War, the proviso read in part. Though the House had passed the measure, proslavery partisans successfully quashed it in the Senate. Still the Wilmot Proviso served notice on the South that the North intended to do away with the custom of allowing slavery in the southerly territories and banning it in the northerly ones. From then on, sectional battle lines were drawn on the issue.

The language used in the Wilmot Proviso had appeared in the Northwest Ordinance of 1787, reenacted by Congress in 1789. Congress used those words in the territorial acts of Indiana, Illinois, Michigan, Iowa, and Wisconsin, as well as in the Missouri Compromise of 1820. Congress' power on the matter had not been challenged, but a time-honored custom had been. As a result, both sides re-examined the constitutional precedents of slavery in the territories during the decade and a half following the Wilmot Proviso.

The proslavery group knew they had to construct a definition of slavery in the territories that denied the legality of every measure that had ever been used to prohibit slavery from any territory from the time the Union was established. While Article IV, section 3, clause 2 of the Constitution gave Congress the power "to dispose of and make all needful rules and regulations respecting the territory or other property belonging to the United States," the language was not as explicit as that in Article I, section 8, clause 17, which granted Congress the power "to exercise exclusive legislation in all cases whatsoever" over the District of Columbia and "forts, magazines, arsenals, dock yards" and the like.

Southern leaders concluded that Congress therefore had not been granted full legislative powers over the territories. Thus the power of legislation for the territories must belong to the inhabitants of the territories, as Jefferson suggested in the Ordinance of 1784 and as Douglas had concluded in the doctrine of popular sovereignty. So for a time popular sovereignty appeared to be an effective defense against the Wilmot Proviso, at least until the late 1850s when the struggle in Kansas opened previously undetected loopholes.

Discarding popular sovereignty, proslavery partisans returned to an adaptation of state sovereignty. They claimed that only a sovereign could exercise police power, and that the people of a territory had not attained sovereignty. Neither did the Constitution grant the federal government a sovereign's power in the territories. Therefore that power was reserved to the states by the Tenth Amendment.

To prevent all of the states of the Union from enforcing their powers in the territories, which would be chaotic, proslavery groups asserted that the federal government could act as the agent of the sovereign states in the territories. Acting only as an agent meant the federal government would have no policy-making power of its own, but could enforce the rights of United States citizens in the territories. The proslavery argument also provided whose law on slavery in the territories should be enforced: not the law of Congress, since it held Congress had no power delegated to it that would allow it to legislate on slave matters; not any policy set by the executive branch, since the federal government could intervene only as an agent of the states; but the only laws on slavery made anywhere in the United States, the slave laws of the slaveholding states. Southern leaders argued that since the Constitution recognized slavery, the institution had to be protected, defined, and provided for in law, and the only place that protective law was found was in the sovereign slaveholding states themselves.

This proslavery position was given legal sanction by Chief Justice Taney in the Dred Scott case. The federal government, Taney found, could interfere in the territories for no "other purpose but that of protecting the rights of the [slave] owner." He implied that it was unconstitutional for the federal government to use its power in the territories so far as slavery was concerned in any other way than for the protection of the institution. As Southern leaders worked the program out, and as Taney implemented it, the laws of the sovereign slaveholding states would extend beyond their boundaries and be enforced by the federal government in the territories on the question of slavery. Essentially then, the slaveholding states made policy not just for themselves, but for the territories as well.

The proslavery argument then became a nationalistic, not a localistic one, for the Constitution, as Southern leaders interpreted it, and the federal government, according to the limitations placed on it by the Supreme Court, were vital to the success of the state sovereignty program. Only through the federal government could the proslavery state sovereignty scheme operate beyond the boundaries of the slave states to protect the institution of slavery in the territories. The beauty of the state sovereignty theory as expounded by Southern leaders was that it also invoked a sovereign's immunity from federal interference in state affairs.

State Sovereignty and the Fugitive Slave Law

Along with protecting slavery in the territories went the question of reclaiming fugitive slaves. State sovereignty arguments to that end were even clearer than those used to protect slavery in the territories, for the Constitution, in Article III, section 2, recognized the right of a slaveholder to his runaway slave. As the supreme law of the land, the Constitution rendered void any free-state law that hindered the recovery of an escapee and in so doing recognized the property right of a slaveholder to his slave. This was a vital provision for slaveholders who were determined to resist any attempt to erode it by the Northerners.

Yet to Northerners, whose personal liberty laws were used to nullify the fugitive slave laws, such statutes were unconstitutional. The law of 1850 especially offended antislavery men because it denied a fugitive the normal legal safeguards of due process of law, a jury trial, or a writ of habeas corpus—a violation of the civil liberties of their citizens that was far more important to Northerners than the protection of property.

The Northern personal liberty laws, designed to protect black citizens from the terrible practice of kidnapping by professional slave catchers, erected legal barriers to block the recovery of alleged escapees by supposed masters or by professional slave hunters. These laws bore a direct relationship to the Kentucky and Virginia Resolutions of 1798, for both the Alien and Sedition Acts (1798) and the Fugitive Slave Act (1850) deprived individuals of freedom and thus violated the letter and spirit of constitutional guarantees of individual rights. On both occasions opponents of the federal statute argued that a state could interpose itself between the federal government and the state's citizens to protect those citizens in the exercise of their civil liberties.

The conflict over the enforcement of the fugitive slave law climaxed in the Booth cases. These cases, argued in both Wisconsin state courts and federal courts, concerned the rescue of a fugitive slave in 1854. Sherman M. Booth, a Wisconsin abolitionist editor, led a mob that rescued a fugitive from his captors and sent him off to Canada. Federal authorities prosecuted Booth as a violator of the

Fugitive Slave Act, but twice the Wisconsin Supreme Court freed him on writs of habeas corpus. The Wisconsin Supreme Court argued that a state had the power to free its citizens from imprisonment under an unconstitutional law in order to protect the civil liberties of its citizens.

In March 1859 Taney, speaking again for the Supreme Court, overruled the Wisconsin court on every point. He held that the federal government had to be supreme in the sphere of action assigned to it by the Constitution, and that Wisconsin courts did not possess the jurisdiction they claimed. The federal government, Taney proclaimed, "should be supreme, strong enough to execute its own laws, by its own tribunals, without interruption from a State or State authorities."

Proslavery partisans cheered the decision, for although it seemed to exalt national supremacy, it in fact exalted federal judicial supremacy only. Taney confined himself to that single aspect and reminded his auditors that the court had a duty to strike down unconstitutional laws, for by so doing, the court would "guard the States from any encroachment" on the rights reserved to them by the Constitution. By enhancing federal judicial supremacy only and thus strengthening enforcement of the fugitive slave law through the Booth case, and by denying Congress any policy-making function regarding slavery in the territories as a result of the Dred Scott case, Taney provided legal sanction for the state sovereignty contention that slave state laws operated outside of state limits and that Congress and the courts were bound to sustain them.

The Davis Resolutions

With the Supreme Court setting the major outline of the state sovereignty position, Southern leaders continued to work out the details. These were enumerated in a set of four resolutions that Jefferson Davis introduced into the Senate in February 1860, adopted the following May. The resolutions maintained that the states had acted as "free and independent sovereignties" when they had approved the federal Constitution; the fourth resolution propounded the new state sovereignty thesis with the declaration that neither Congress nor a territorial legislature possessed the power to impair the constitutional right of any citizen "to take his slave property into the common territories." Rather, it was the "duty of the federal government" to protect slave property like any "other species of property." Should the court not have the power to protect slavery adequately in the territories, then it would become "the duty of Congress to supply such deficiency."

Defenders of slavery insisted that the Davis resolutions be incorporated into the Democratic party platform, forcing a party split and paving the way for the victory of Abraham Lincoln and the Republican party in November 1860. Implacable in their opposition to the Dred Scott decision, the Republicans clearly threatened the entire proslavery state sovereignty position as outlined by Taney and Davis. Lincoln could not be counted on to enforce the law, especially since he sought a reversal of the Dred Scott decision. Moreover, though Lincoln did not have congressional majorities behind him, he could still veto any federal slave code Congress might enact. Lincoln could also appoint the territorial governors, who had veto powers of their own over acts of territorial legislatures. Proslavery partisans admitted Lincoln's election was not a menace to slavery within the slave states, but they recognized the direct threat to slavery in the territories and to their carefully constructed scheme to protect slavery through the state sovereignty approach. According to both the defenders and the opponents of slavery, extinction of slavery in the territories meant the eventual extinction of slavery in the states.

Proslavery leaders finally turned to the option of secession. Not an end in itself, secession was viewed as a means to the end of creating a new constitutional system that would protect slavery. Slavery's defenders quickly built that protection into the Constitution of the Confederate States of America, adopted at Montgomery, Alabama, March 11, 1861.

The Confederate Constitution

The new Constitution, parallel to the old one in most respects, remained silent on the "right" of secession just as the old one had. The balance of powers between the states and the federal government remained about the same. The striking difference was the protection afforded slavery. In that respect the Confederate Constitution created a much more consolidated union than had the old and thus enabled the Confederacy to discard the state sovereignty theory.

Southern leaders had claimed that the old Constitution gave Congress no power to legislate on the question of slavery in the territories; now, rather than specifically reserve that power to the Confederate states, Confederate constitution-makers granted that power to their Congress. That was exactly what the opponents of slavery had insisted the old Congress had a right to do. The Confederacy thus abandoned the idea that Congress must act as a trustee for the states in matters of slavery and the territories; it eliminated the premise on which the Dred Scott decision had rested. The Confederate constitution-makers were able to do so because they wrote into their document a mandate for the protection of slavery in the territories, something they had had to infer and deduce from the old Constitution.

With slavery under firm national protection in the territories, they had no use for any theories of state sovereignty on the subject, for it could only prove embarrassing. There was no reason for the laws of the several states to reach through the national government and operate in the territories of the Confederacy the way the Dred Scott decision and the Davis resolutions had permitted.

Other sections of the Confederate Constitution prohibited the Congress from passing any law "impairing the right of property in negro slaves" or the right to move slave property from state to state or territory; the fugitive slave clause was enlarged; and states were forbidden from emancipating the slaves of the citizen of another state no matter how the slave arrived in the second state. The Confederate Constitution denied its states any local autonomy whatever on the matter of slavery, so in respect to the peculiar institution the Confederacy was a national, not a federal, state.

At Savannah, Georgia, a little over a month after the adoption of the Confederate Constitution, Stephens observed "the new constitution has put at rest, forever, all the agitating questions relating to our peculiar institution, African slavery, . . . the proper status of the Negro in our form of civilization. This was," the new vice president of the Confederacy emphasized, "the immediate cause of the late rupture and the present revolution." Although Stephens changed his mind after the war,* in this speech he stripped away all other reasons for secession and bared the fundamental one: the

---

* In 1868, Stephens published his *A Constitutional View of the Late War Between the States*, in which he held that the reason for secession was opposition to the encroaching of the federal government on the sovereignty of the states, not slavery.

preservation of slavery. The founding fathers, Stephens said, really never understood how to deal with the institution. They thought that "somehow or other, . . . the institution would be evanescent and pass away. This idea, though not incorporated in the Constitution, was the prevailing idea at the time." Stephens implied that sophisticated Southern interpretations of the Constitution that led to their aggressive state sovereignty view conflicted with the intent of the framers.

"Our new government," Stephens continued, "is founded upon exactly the opposite idea; . . . its cornerstone rests, upon the great truth that the Negro is not equal to the white man; that slavery—subordination to the superior race—is his natural and normal condition." This affirmation of white supremacy drew a hearty round of applause. "This, our new government," he concluded, "is the first, in the history of the world, based upon this great physical, philosophical, and moral truth." Stephens and other Southern leaders had met in Montgomery to draw up a form of government with protection for slavery built into it, which was exactly what they had attempted to do with their old theory of state sovereignty prior to 1860.

The defenders of slavery used the theory of state sovereignty to suit themselves, as a doctrine of power, not of right. They attempted to protect the power of the slaveowners, a regional elite, rather than to protect the rights of any minority. Slaveholders attempted to grasp the power to enable them to dominate all minorities within their reach. A minority themselves in the nation as a whole, the use of sovereignty and its language was designed not to protect themselves but to assure themselves of absolute power. That power would have enabled them to keep human beings in bondage and to deny them the elementary right of freedom, even beyond the borders of their states.

The Road to Sumter

As the cotton states followed South Carolina out of the Union, Northern conservative and business interests became alarmed. Republicans, who had belittled the threat of secession in the fall, were confused and angry. Generally they looked to Seward for leadership rather than to the less experienced and less well-known president, for Seward appeared to them as the real leader of the Republican party. Lincoln had tendered Seward the position of secretary of state in December 1860, and by early January Seward's selection had become public knowledge.

Yet Seward exercised no really effective leadership. He failed in an effort to influence the Senate Committee of Thirteen, largely because Lincoln would not bend on excluding slavery from the territories. Rumor had it that Seward supported the Crittenden compromise, yet he never publicly announced in its favor. Late in January 1861, a New York newspaper interpreted a speech of his as an effort to create a Union party in place of the Republican party, and critics accused him of attempting to seduce the South into returning to the Union. Yet Seward had not in fact advocated such a change. His mind wandered over the range of other possibilities of reuniting the sections, including the use of a foreign war for that purpose. He even suggested that violent alternative to Lincoln as late as April 1, 1861, nearly a month after the inauguration.

Like Seward, the nation seemed to drift throughout the winter of 1860–1861, with no real national policy. Buchanan had denied the right of secession but he had taken no positive steps to prevent it in hopes of avoiding war. Having announced his intention of maintaining the authority of the national government by holding federal property in the South, the lame-duck president stood silently by as the various seceding states took possession of some of the federal property within their boundaries. Yet they had not the strength to seize certain garrisoned forts, such as Fort Sumter in Charleston harbor, South Carolina, or Fort Pickens in Pensacola harbor, Florida, and Buchanan refused to surrender these posts even when asked to do so by Southern commissioners. He directed an unarmed merchant ship, the *Star of the West*, to take supplies to Sumter in January, but Confederate shore batteries drove the vessel away. This open and defiant act on South Carolina's part failed to provoke the North into an indignant outburst, evidence that the North had not yet settled upon any collective policy to resolve the situation.

Many in the Confederacy had come to believe that the North would ultimately let them go in peace, and they had some evidence in early Northern reactions to support that view. Southerners even assured anxious Northwesterners that the historic Mississippi River would always remain open for commerce. Both Stephens and Davis nevertheless warned the Confederacy to prepare for a long and bloody war, a message that fell on deaf Southern ears, unwilling to believe that the North could or would fight.

Nothing had been resolved when Lincoln was inaugurated on March 4, 1861, except the Republicans' steadfast refusal to sanction an extension of slavery into the territories. Lincoln stated his position as frankly as he could in his first inaugural address: "The Union is perpetual, . . . [it] is much older than the Constitution." No state, he warned, "upon its own mere notion, can lawfully get out of the Union," and ordinances of secession are illegal. "Acts of violence against the authority of the United States, are insurrectionary or revolutionary, according to circumstances." The new president said he considered it his constitutional duty to see that "the laws of the Union be faithfully executed in all the States." Since he affirmed he would do this "to the extent of my ability," he implied that he would use force to save the Union if necessary. Lincoln left the door of conciliation open: "There needs to be no bloodshed or violence; and there shall be none, unless it be forced upon the national authority." Yet Lincoln made it clear the federal government could make no compromise other than through a constitutional amendment should the seceders choose to return.

In his opening words, Lincoln tried to allay Southern fears of a Republican administration. "There never has been any reasonable cause for such apprehension," Lincoln smiled, and went on to quote himself: " 'I have no purpose, directly or indirectly, to interfere with the institution of slavery in the states where it exists. I believe I have no lawful right to do so, and I have no inclination to do so.' " Slavery in the South was safe with him, as both he and the Republican platform had maintained. Lincoln plainly said he would carry out the law regarding fugitive slaves, but he believed that "all the safeguards of liberty" ought to be introduced into the law, "so that a free man be not, in any case, surrendered as a slave." He did not mention the territories.

In spite of his firm views on secession, he argued against the wisdom of it as calmly and rationally as possible. Nonetheless, he left little doubt that if the South persisted in its course it meant war. "In *your* hands, my dissatisfied fellow countrymen, and not in *mine*, is the momentous issue of civil war. The government will not assail *you*. You can have no conflict, without being yourselves the aggressors. *You*," Lincoln emphasized, "have no oath registered in Heaven to destroy the government, while *I* shall have the most solemn one to 'preserve, protect, and defend' it."

Unfortunately the South took Lincoln's composure for weakness and misread the gesture of friendship. Douglas supported Lincoln's determination to maintain the Union by sharing the platform with him. Northerners, except for ardent abolitionists, accepted Lincoln's address as moderate, perhaps conservative, and thus necessary in such uncertain times. Few Southerners either read it or heard it. Those that heard about it, or read Southern papers that discoursed upon it, took it to be the speech of an abolitionist who headed the party of Sumner and Brown, the party that still refused to accept the Dred Scott decision. To the South, Lincoln remained the same threat he had been in November.

Lincoln soon learned that Fort Sumter's commander, Major Robert J. Anderson, needed provisions and at least 20,000 reinforcements in order to hold his position. Anderson favored evacuation of the fort, echoing the opinion of old General Winfield Scott, ranking officer in the army and therefore its top commander. Seward also pressed Lincoln for evacuation, in hopes of avoiding war and providing time for the Confederate states to see the error of their ways and repent. The cabinet overwhelmingly favored Sumter's evacuation, with only two members, Salmon P. Chase and Montgomery Blair, in favor of a relief expedition. Even they were uncertain about attempting to relieve the fort if the act would provoke war.

Thus the rumor spread in Washington that the government meant to evacuate Sumter. Seward gave the rumor further credence by dealing with Confederate commissioners who had come to Washington to negotiate for the surrender of federal property in the South. To avoid recognizing the existence of the Confederate government, Seward dealt with the commissioners unofficially, through the intercession of two Supreme Court justices. He gave the commissioners his personal assurances that if the Confederacy was patient, evacuation would ultimately take place. The Confederate Commissioners became uneasy when counterrumors began to circulate to the effect that the fort would be reinforced, but Seward continued to placate them. In his last message to them on April 7, he said: " . . . faith to Sumter kept; wait and see." On April 8 the relief expedition left New York.

Meanwhile Lincoln had decided, independently of the cabinet

and as early as April 1, that the forts must be maintained and that two relief expeditions must be sent, one for Sumter and the other for Pickens. Seeking advice all around, Lincoln had first spoken with Unionist members of the Virginia secession convention, suggesting an evacuation of Sumter if Virginia would remain in the Union. He also had sent Ward H. Lamon, a friend from Illinois, to Charleston to see if any Union sentiment existed there. Lamon could find none; on his own authority he apparently suggested to both South Carolina's governor and to Anderson that the government intended to abandon Sumter. Lincoln decided that evacuation would solve nothing, for it would make it difficult to convince the North as well as the South that he meant to keep his word to sustain the Union. The president had to act before supplies at the fort were exhausted.

On April 1 Lincoln issued orders to the Navy Department to ready ships for the two expeditions. On April 6 he sent a state department clerk and an army captain to Charleston, to deliver to Governor Francis W. Pickens of South Carolina a message that "an attempt will be made to supply Fort-Sumpter [*sic*] with provisions only; and that, if such attempt not be resisted" there would be no effort to reinforce the garrison. This notice put the Confederate government in a quandary, for if they allowed the Sumter expedition to reach the fort, they would have bowed to federal authority and might have destroyed the illusion that an effective Confederate government existed. The only Confederate option was to reduce the fort before the expedition arrived or to fire on the expedition itself, which certainly meant war. Lincoln had hoped to make his intentions perfectly clear by informing Governor Pickens of the action and by emphasizing the nature of the expedition, "provisions only" unless the expedition met with a hostile reaction. Confederate officials apparently misunderstood this caution and felt themselves in the position of being forced to fire the first shot.

The Confederate cabinet met at Montgomery, Alabama, and instructed Secretary of War Leroy P. Walker to order General Pierre G. T. Beauregard, who commanded at Charleston, to demand evacuation of the fort and, if refused, to reduce it. Even had that order not come, anti-Union feeling ran so high in South Carolina that the state might have taken the initiative alone, a factor the Confederate cabinet considered.

Following orders, Beauregard sent two officers under a white flag to visit Anderson on April 11, with the surrender demand. Anderson refused, but he told the Confederate officers that his garrison would run out of provisions in a few days. Walker sent another message to Beauregard the same day, cautioning the officer: "Do not desire needlessly to bombard Fort Sumter." Another delegation visited Anderson that night with additional instructions from Walker: if Anderson would say when he would evacuate, Beauregard was ordered to agree; if he would not so state, then Beauregard was to reduce the fort. Anderson replied that he would "evacuate Fort Sumter by noon on the 15th" if not sooner fired upon and if he received no instructions to the contrary from his government "or additional supplies."

Meanwhile, word had come to the Confederate authorities of the impending arrival of Lincoln's expedition. Beauregard's officers did not wait to transmit Anderson's reply to the general; instead they served notice on Sumter that the shore batteries would open fire within the hour. At 4:30 A.M., April 12, 1861, a mortar shell arched high above Charleston harbor and exploded in a flash of light above Fort Sumter. The signal had been given, and from around the harbor other batteries responded. Within minutes the flashing and booming of the cannon and bursting of the shells around the fort signalled the beginning of the Civil War.

Anderson knew that his best chance was to hold out until the relief expedition arrived. But through a bureaucratic mishap, the expedition was weakened by the assignment of the warship *Powhatan* to the Fort Pickens fleet rather than to the Sumter expedition as originally planned. Without the *Powhatan*'s firepower and with the expedition's tugs detained by a gale, the relief force was unable to help. They discovered by noon of April 12 that the firing had already begun and they could only stand off and watch. The Confederate bombardment lasted all day April 12 and most of April 13 before Anderson agreed to terms of surrender. About noon on Sunday, April 14, his band playing "Yankee Doodle," Anderson and the garrison boarded a steamer from the relief expedition, and evacuated the fort according to the final surrender terms. As the Yankees departed, the Confederates celebrated their first victory. They raised a Confederate flag over the battered fort; sightseeing boats carried the curious out to see the ruins. Over 4,000 shells had been fired during the bombardment, yet no one, on either side, had been killed.

When the bombardment of Sumter began, the news hummed

across the nation by telegraph. "The ball has opened," the New York *Times* announced, "war is inaugurated." Northerners hesitated no longer, their indecision over. Thousands immediately volunteered to fight even while bombs continued to burst over Sumter. In Ohio alone twenty companies were raised before the shelling stopped. States and cities hurried to raise men and money for the war.

Excitement swept the South as well. A correspondent for a foreign newspaper on his way to Charleston found bands loudly trumpeting "Dixie" and crowds hailing President Davis and the Confederacy. In Richmond a mob with a Confederate flag hauled a cannon from the ironworks to the state capitol and fired salutes. The states of the Upper South—Virginia, Tennessee, Arkansas, and North Carolina—now seceded from the Union and joined the Confederacy. Emotion tore at the loyalties of citizens in the slave states of Maryland, Kentucky, and Missouri, though those states ultimately remained in the Union.

On April 13, Lincoln addressed delegates from the Virginia secession convention, reaffirming the position he had taken in his inaugural, and added that he would "hold myself at liberty" to repossess any places seized, but beyond that "there will be no invasion," no use of force "against, or among the people anywhere." Two days later, Lincoln called for 75,000 militia to suppress the "combinations too powerful to be suppressed" by the ordinary means of law enforcement, and commanded "the persons composing the combinations . . . to disperse . . . within twenty days from this date." At the same time he summoned Congress to meet in special session on the Fourth of July to consider "such measures" as "the public safety, and interest may seem to demand." Lincoln continued to move calmly, perhaps in the hope that the violence at Sumter would bring citizens, North and South, to their senses.

PART THREE

THE FIELDS
OF BATTLE

Beside a stricken field I stood;
On the torn turf, on grass and wood,
Hung heavily the dew of blood.

Still in their fresh mounds lay the slain,
But all the air was quick with pain
And gusty sighs and tearful rain.

Two angels each with drooping head
And folded wings and noiseless tread,
Watched by that valley of the dead.

"How long!"—I knew the voice of Peace,—
"Is there no respite? no release?
When shall the hopeless quarrel cease?"

Then Freedom sternly said: "I shun
No strife nor pang beneath the sun,
When human rights are staked and won."

JOHN GREENLEAF WHITTIER, *"The Watchers,"* 1862

7

The Union and the War

Lincoln enjoyed little prestige when he moved into the White House. "The unpopular Mr. Lincoln," as James G. Randall called him,* did not enjoy a good press. Charles Francis Adams, son and grandson of former presidents and later Lincoln's minister to Britain, cried out that in the great crisis then facing the nation this "absolutely unknown" Lincoln was "perambulating about the country, kissing little girls and growing whiskers!" Even William H. "Billy" Herndon, Lincoln's former law partner, wondered if Lincoln supposed he could suppress this "huge rebellion by pop guns filled with rose water." Reporters gleefully bent to the task of ridiculing the gangly Westerner, calling his speeches "crude, ignorant twaddle," and caricaturing him as a baboon. Through it all, Lincoln, who had grown up in the rough and tumble atmosphere of frontier politics in Illinois, kept his poise.

Lincoln demonstrated confidence in his own ability to govern

* James G. Randall, "The Unpopular Mr. Lincoln," *The Abraham Lincoln Quarterly*, Vol. II, No. 6 (June 1943), pp. 255–280.

the nation by appointing a cabinet filled with prima donnas, all of whom felt they could do a better job than he at the helm of the ship of state. Seward won the job of secretary of state largely because of his influence within the party. Thinking he would be paramount in the administration, he had sent Lincoln a list of "considerations" on April 1, aimed at changing the focus of politics from the question of slavery to the issue of union or disunion, or perhaps even provoking a foreign war. Lincoln replied that if a policy must be adopted, "*I must do it.*" After Lincoln's unilateral decision on Sumter, Seward learned the president was in earnest.

Salmon P. Chase of Ohio, an antislavery leader and a rival candidate for the nomination, accepted the post of secretary of the treasury. Chase never ceased to feel that he was a better man for the presidency than Lincoln, and he often criticized Lincoln's "blunders." Yet Chase, like Seward, proved to be an able administrator, and Lincoln kept him in the cabinet until political events forced a parting of the ways in 1864. Simon Cameron, a Republican political boss from Pennsylvania, took over the important post of secretary of war. Cameron's appointment resulted from a convention bargain that Lincoln honored although he would have preferred someone else. The War Department quickly proved to be beyond Cameron's slender abilities, and Cameron knew it. In less than a year Lincoln bowed to his request for a diplomatic post, and appointed Edwin M. Stanton to replace Cameron. Stanton had served in Buchanan's cabinet as attorney general, and, under Lincoln, became an outstanding secretary of war. A man of forceful personality, Stanton, too, believed his talent superior to Lincoln's.

Lincoln chose a former Democrat and New Englander, Gideon Welles, for his navy secretary. Edward Bates of Missouri, another contestant for the presidential nomination, was named attorney general. Caleb B. Smith of Indiana became secretary of the interior, again in payment for convention support. Maryland's Montgomery Blair, as postmaster general, rounded out the cabinet. Lincoln's ability to work with and manage an assortment of personalities such as those who made up his cabinet was a tribute to his talent and an illustration of his own self-confidence and poise. He had begun his administration with a firm, yet calm inaugural, paid attention to the hundreds of office-seekers and the details of myriad appointments, remained cool at the time of Sumter, and issued a reasoned, unruffled proclamation in response to it. His patience and almost casual competence augured well for an administration baptized in secession and war.

Raising an Army

In raising and equipping an army, Lincoln's administration ran headlong into the inclination of the Northern states to raise and control their own troops. There was no unity in the North powerful enough to hold the various subsections together the way the desire to protect and preserve slavery and white supremacy, plus the threat of invasion, cemented the South. New Englanders, who had nearly seceded in 1814 when they found themselves a minority in the Union, had embraced national concerns only when they found that their manufacturing interests could control the nation's markets with federal aid. After that, New England had favored national supremacy and denounced nullification; opposed the annexation of Texas and the Mexican War as devices to strengthen the other sections; condemned Webster in 1850 and Douglas in 1854 for bowing to popular sovereignty; welcomed the antislavery constitution of California and openly aided the free-staters in Kansas. In 1860 some New Englanders had been ready to secede if Breckinridge won the election, for New England manufacturers and commercial interests were as determined to protect their mercantile supremacy as the cotton barons of the South were resolved to protect slavery. As a result, New Englanders refused to be bound to any strong, national position when the shooting started.

Politically flexible, the Northwest had been quite willing to bargain with either the East or the South as it gained sectional advantage. The Northwest had joined with the South in the effort to acquire both Texas and Oregon; it had favored the Mexican War as an excuse for acquiring new lands, providing Westerners with a strong argument for expanding into and organizing the territory between the Missouri River and Oregon. The West's motive was expansion, popular sovereignty its doctrine. So Westerners would have sacrificed Kansas in order to develop the remainder of the West, but the Dred Scott decision robbed it of that opportunity. Westerners then turned Republican, determined to keep the western territories both open and white. In the older sections of the Northwest, such as Illinois, Indiana, and Ohio, tradition and regard for the Union were stronger motives than expansion.

But in some ways the old Northwest was the weakest link in the Union, as its people were, and remained, more divided in their sympathies on the issue of slavery. In areas like Ohio's Western Reserve, antislavery sentiments were as strong as anywhere, but in southern Ohio, Indiana, and Illinois the peace Democrats and copperheads commanded a substantial number of followers during the war.

The Union slave states faced the most complex problems. Delaware, Maryland, Kentucky, and Missouri, along with the western portions of Virginia, were not cotton states and had strong economic links with the Union. They faced the dilemma of simultaneously trying to preserve slavery and to preserve the Union, and as a result were almost ruinously divided when war came. It took both diplomacy and military force to keep them in the Union, and the dilemma caused the permanent division of Virginia.

The mid-Atlantic states, especially urban New York and Pennsylvania, had large numbers of immigrants who had little direct interest in the quarrels of the North and South but who strongly opposed emancipation of blacks in fear of their competition on the labor market. The Irish, who hated the British, would fight with whomever Britain aided. The Pietists and Quakers of upstate New York and back-country Pennsylvania remained morally opposed to slavery and consequently backed the North.

The subsections of the North included a wide array of social elements motivated by diverse beliefs who could be represented only with great difficulty in any united movement. Therefore, the diversity was imperfectly represented by the states. In armies raised by the federal government on a national scale, one subsection or another might predominate; but that would be less likely if the forces were raised by the states. State interest thus dictated that troops should be raised and managed and war politics controlled as far as possible on the state level. With their stable governments and sound financial bases, the Northern states had certain advantages over the federal administration. Nearly every one had a complete military organization, if often more elaborate than efficient. Their legislatures were willing and able to pass military legislation and appropriate money. Their financial institutions and private organizations and individuals were eager to loan or even donate money to arm and equip volunteers.

State governments vigorously responded to the Union's cause, often without awaiting a call for troops from the federal government. Volunteers filled the streets of Ohio's capital before the shelling of Sumter ended, while Wisconsin's legislature, in session at the time, passed a war act on April 13 giving the governor broad authority to raise troops and $100,000 to use for that purpose. On April 15, the very day Lincoln called for 75,000 militia, New York appropriated $3,000,000 to raise 30,000 militia for two years' service. Two days later Rhode Island voted $500,000. Other legislatures were called into session as hastily as possible. By the end of April New Jersey and Pennsylvania enacted emergency measures, and before the end of May Massachusetts provided a $10,000,000 war fund. Individuals and financial institutions hurried to make credit or cash available to the various states; the Cincinnati City Council, for example, offered Ohio $225,000.

In sharp contrast to the states, the federal government moved cautiously, even though the firing on Sumter and a Baltimore mob's attack on a Massachusetts regiment marching to Washington dramatized the volatile situation. After Sumter Lincoln requested 75,000 militia for ninety days service; four days later, on April 19, he proclaimed a blockade of Southern ports; on May 3 another presidential proclamation called for 42,034 volunteers to serve for three years, for an increase of 22,714 in the regular army and 18,000 sailors in the navy. Not until Congress met in July did it ratify Lincoln's calls, and in addition provide for 500,000 volunteers to serve for three years. Lincoln's first militia call appears absurdly small when compared with New York's call for 30,000, a similar number by Indiana, and Pennsylvania's determination to raise 75,000 by herself. Those states alone volunteered nearly twice as many men as Lincoln asked for.

Rather than accept the early volunteers into federal service, the Lincoln government accepted only some of them by apportioning the 75,000 militia to the states according to their population. New York's quota was seventeen regiments (about 17,000 men), Pennsylvania's was fourteen, Ohio's thirteen, with the other states responsible for from one to six regiments each. All of the officers, including generals, were to be supplied by the states. The quotas were filled within a week, and the governors badgered the War Department and the president to accept the surplus. The president's May 3 proclamation came in response to this demand but fell far short of the number of volunteers available.

The War Department and Simon Cameron could not keep up with the emergency. Whatever order was maintained in the department came through the influence of Chase. Cameron accepted, and Lincoln encouraged Chase's efforts. Chase had drafted the May 3 proclamation; he advocated keeping the peace forcibly in Maryland; he directed the organization of Western troops; and at least shared the responsibility, later, for putting George S. McClellan in command. Yet for all of his energy, Chase could not manage two government departments. As a result, no cabinet officer devoted his entire attention to mobilization.

As of January 1, 1861, the regular United States Army numbered about 16,000. They were a well-trained, disciplined group, but were scattered, usually in company strength, on the frontier. Robert E. Lee was proposed for command of the armies, both regulars and volunteers, but Lee declined, resigned, and went to the Confederacy with his state, Virginia. A number of other able officers with cotton-state backgrounds followed suit. Yet the percentage of enlisted men who resigned to serve with the South remained very small, less than 1 percent, so that the strength of the regular army was not much diminished.

By April 15 thirty-four regular army companies of infantry, cavalry, and artillery were within easy reach of Washington, D. C., had the War Department seen fit to concentrate them. Another thirteen companies had been captured in Texas right after Sumter, and the remainder of the army was either in transit or still stationed on the frontier. Had the regular army been mobilized and used immediately the war might have been shortened. Or had this regular army later been made the cadre of a national army, it might have provided superior discipline and effectiveness and shortened the war in that manner. The first Battle of Bull Run, for example, might well have had a different outcome.

Even though the states acted vigorously to raise troops, they had disabilities of their own. One might have expected the Western states, which had to deal with the Indians from time to time, to be well organized but the opposite was the case. Iowa, where the Spirit Lake Massacre (1857) had recently taken place, owned few arms. The governor estimated that at the time of Sumter the state owned about 1,500 muskets, 200 rifles, and four 6-pound guns. A Wisconsin militia company had arms for about 40 men (borrowed from the state) and uniforms for about 20. Ohio faced many of the same

problems, issuing its volunteers nothing better than flintlock muskets altered by the addition of percussion caps. Volunteers frequently refused to have anything to do with such antiques and had
to be persuaded to learn to use them. Uniform issue often followed
mustering in by weeks, or even months, while volunteers learned
about drill and camp life in their civilian clothes.

When Congress met on July 4 and provided for 500,000 three-
year men, all the Union had to rely on at the time was a widely
scattered regular army, 75,000 largely untrained and inadequately
equipped militia whose time by then was nearly up, and an additional 42,000 three-year volunteers who were also poorly equipped
and had received only the most elementary training. It was just
such an untrained mob that General Irvin McDowell reluctantly
led against a similarly green Confederate army at the first Battle of
Bull Run on July 21. The bulk of the national army, the 500,000
authorized by Congress, did not materialize or become useful much
before the end of 1861.

The military ineptness of the Union government contrasted
not only with the frenzy of activity in the Union states, but also
with the Confederate government. On May 8 the Confederate legislature voted to enlist an army of 400,000 volunteers, adding to earlier legislation providing for a total of 100,000, or 500,000 all together. Confederate legislation at least provided for a more realistic
approach in terms of numbers, even if their equipment and training
proved no better than that of the Union.

The Union made only the feeblest effort to increase the size of
the regular army. By December 1861 when the volunteer army exceeded 640,000, the regular army had grown to only about 20,000.
Throughout the war it never reached its authorized strength of
42,000. This was partly explained by the attractiveness of state service, with its popular election of officers, bounties, and fraternal aspects, and partly because of states' rights. Congressmen conceived of
no other way to create a huge national army than by asking the
states to do the job, and the administration in Washington, if it considered the question at all, agreed. Not only did the United States
lack a military tradition that might have decreed otherwise, but
also the ideal of local autonomy had a tight hold on the popular
mind. Many Americans felt that a huge regular army would im-
peril the integrity of the federal system.

Feeding and Clothing the Volunteers

It was the duty of the states to care for the volunteers only until they were sworn into federal service, but the War Department lacked the resources to take over. All the War Department could do was to advise the states to continue to furnish the necessary supplies and present the bills to the federal government. Congress set aside money for that purpose, and the states proceeded to do what they could. The resultant confusion, graft, and hardship were not wholly the fault of the states. They purchased supplies on the open market by contract, in the United States and abroad. The generosity of state legislatures, the zealousness of governors and their agents, and the great need made the army contract business very profitable. There would have been difficulties enough had only the federal government been in the marketplace, but the problems were compounded by a score of states bidding against each other and against the federal government. The chaos produced a series of scandals that echoed across the Union.

With an army of lobbyists, contractors, and speculators descending upon the state capitals and Washington, state and federal officers hastily and carelessly accepted almost every offer and paid almost any price. As a result, *Harper's Weekly* observed, soldiers often got sand for sugar and rye for coffee; brown paper for leather; and "spavined beasts and dying donkeys" for horses and mules. Rather than serviceable weapons they received "the refuse of shops and foreign armories."

Early in 1861 the New York *Tribune* exposed a scandal in the supply of uniforms. A supplier contracted for 12,000 uniforms at $9.50 each, but they turned out to be entirely unsatisfactory, made of inferior material, of odd and unusual cut, and often without pockets, buttons, or other necessities. This led to a congressional investigation of the contract business and the exposure of extensive fraud and illegal practices, implicating numerous high government or military officials. The investigating committee found General John C. Frémont, commander of the military Department of the West, particularly irregular. In June 1861, the War Department sold 5,000 Hall carbines to Arthur M. Eastman of New Hampshire for $3.50 each. At a cost of $.75 to $1.25, Eastman altered those guns and sold them to Simon Stevens of Pennsylvania for $12.50 each. Stevens then sold them to Frémont for $22 apiece. The transaction raised several questions for the investigators. Why did the War Department sell the arms when it needed them and was simultaneously buying worthless Austrian muskets at $6.50 each? They found it a curious kind of honesty that allowed the same guns to be repurchased at six times the sale price within a few weeks' time. Even more disturbing was the fact that 790 of the weapons had been condemned by the War Department before the war and disposed of at a token price. After Sumter they were resold to the government for $15 each, then included in the lot sold to Eastman for $3.50, and then repurchased with the others by Frémont for $22. "The liberality of the government is . . . striking!" the committee report announced with considerable understatement.

The shady deal was repeated over and over. One firm contracted for beef at $.08 a pound, then subcontracted the entire amount to a second company for $.06½ a pound, making over $32,000 without risking a dime. Horse traders made fortunes. They hiked their prices by rebranding cavalry horses that sold at $119 each as artillery horses that commanded $150 apiece. In October 1861 a board of survey discovered that only 76 of 411 cavalry horses sent out from St. Louis were fit for service. Of the remainder, 5 were dead, and 330 were either undersized, overaged or underaged, blind, disabled, or otherwise unfit. The government took a loss of $40,000 on that one lot. A St. Louis firm supplied Frémont with all sorts of equipment and clothing, on contracts of over $800,000, "without the price of a single article being previously determined." Secretary of War Cameron delegated the purchase of supplies in New York City to friends and put $2,000,000 at their disposal without making them accountable to anyone.

After Stanton took over the War Department, he set up a special committee to investigate arms contracts. Investigation revealed, among other things, that Remington sold the War Department Colt revolvers for $25 each, the same Colt that could be purchased in stores across the country for $14.50. The company made in the course of one year, the committee estimated, $325,000 in excess profits. Further efforts of the committee, headed by Colonel Joseph Holt, saved the War Department thousands of dollars on current and future contracts.

By the end of the first year, the federal government had paid nearly $50,000,000 for subsistence and a similar sum for quartermaster supplies. By the war's end, the Commissary General's Department within the War Department had spent $369,000,000, and the Quartermaster's Department over $678,000,000. Adding other expenses of contract business plus the contract business of other branches (the Ordnance Bureau spent $163,000,000), plus contract transportation, army contractors handled at least $1,000,000,000 during the war, and according to Professor Shannon's estimate, "retained a half of it." *

A tremendous outcry erupted against profiteering and corruption, and as the war progressed, more preventive measures were instituted. After Stanton came into the War Department in 1862, the department's purchasing practices were more carefully scrutinized. A newspaper campaign against flagrant evils caused the states to tighten up their practices as well. *Harper's Weekly* ominously printed an extract from Admiral Charles Napier's Crimean War dispatches. Napier wrote: "After we hanged a few contractors, . . . the quality of beef . . . improved amazingly."

By and large the Union soldier was adequately supplied with food. Only occasionally did he have to live on government rations of salt or fresh beef, flour or bread, tea, coffee, and sugar. Soldier's Aid Societies supplied state regiments with vegetables, dried fruit, eggs, butter, cheese, beer, ale, fish, and the like. Foraging and the army sutler (the post exchange of the era) supplied the soldiers well. Enterprising citizens within the areas where troops were stationed also supplied a variety of produce.

The army encountered greater problems in the matter of uniforms, in particular because of the great variation. Three Iowa regiments, for example, had no less than five distinctive colors of uniforms: blue, gray, black and white, dark blue and green, and light blue. Some Wisconsin regiments wore light gray trousers, gray blouses, and light hats. Most popular was the Zouave uniform with its baggy breeches, turbans or fezes, and a predominance of bright red that made the Algerian soldier seem dowdy in comparison. Unfortunately, the Confederates dressed in a similar array of uniforms, which caused bewilderment on the battlefield early in the war. The Union army was not completely uniformed in regulation blue before January 1863.

Uniform shortages appeared from time to time as the quarter-

---

* For a full account of the scandals and the contract business, see Fred A. Shannon, *The Organization and Administration of the Union Army, 1861–1865* (Gloucester, Mass.: Peter Smith, 1965).

master struggled to supply the volunteers with clothing in the face of defective manufactures, shoddy materials, and distribution difficulties. Uniform "cloth" occasionally dissolved in the rain, and one Wisconsin regiment "in order that they might with decency be seen upon the streets" were given blue overalls to replace uniforms issued ten days earlier. An Iowa soldier remarked that his "regiment would not run from a lady or the enemy. For very shame's sake they would not dare turn ought but their faces to either."

Blankets were in short supply from the beginning of the war, and soldiers had to supply their own as late as 1863. Those that were furnished were few and of poor quality. An observer noted that one such blanket measured about a third regulation size and was "so rotten a finger could be poked through it." Another found a blanket to be "of such light and open weave as to protect neither against cold or rain, and addicted to falling apart without previous warning." A reporter for the New York *Tribune* concluded a blanket he inspected was made of horsehair and broom corn. Shoes were also of inferior material, often with wooden soles and brown paper uppers.

A soldier could outfit himself for about $28, and since the government allotted him $42 a year he had to take good care of what he had. By the end of the war, however, the Quartermaster General's Department had become quite efficient at supply, and shortages were much less frequent. Both the quartermaster and other government departments had become more quality conscious and successfully applied basic rigid standards.

Munitions Supply

Although the Union, because of its ability to purchase abroad and to manufacture arms more easily than the South, could theoretically exercise more discretion in the choice of arms than the Confederacy, in practice, it generally did not. The standard infantryman's weapon was the traditional muzzle-loading musket of the American Revolution, altered only by the addition of a percussion cap and rifling. These were the same as weapons available to the South.

It would have been possible to supply all but the first hundred thousand volunteers, and perhaps some of them as well, with a high-grade, breech-loading rifle, complete with copper cartridges with built-in percussion caps, that could be quickly and simply loaded, and against which only a similarly equipped army could have competed. The Spencer carbine could be fired fourteen times a minute, yet by 1865 the Union had only about 100,000 in use. Such weapons had not become standard arms because early models had been unsafe and because the War Department had only the most rudimentary testing and evaluation procedures. But their fire power was indisputably superior to the modified antiques that were standard issue.

The War Department obtained the muzzle-loading muskets from stockpiles in government armories, from contracts with manufacturers and jobbers, or through purchase abroad. Even though the prewar army numbered less than 20,000, the government kept about 700,000 muskets on hand. Of those, only about eight in a hundred had been rifled, and over 24,000 remained unaltered from the flintlock type. Many that were altered were nearly worthless. It would have been a stroke of military genius, commented an observer, to let the enemy steal them all, for they were much more dangerous to friend than foe, "and would kick further than they would shoot."

The immediate demand for weapons sent purchasing agents flocking to Europe, authorized by the states, the War Department, various departments of the army, and on private speculation. In August 1861, a War Department agent discovered that all the arms manufacturers of Birmingham and London, England, were working to fill contracts for Ohio, Massachusetts, and Connecticut. In desperation buyers sought arms everywhere, purchasing anything that even looked as if it might shoot. Prices soared. At the time European armies were modernizing their equipment and shifting to breech loaders and thus had thousands of obsolete weapons to dispose of. By June of 1862 the War Department had secured 170,000 Austrian muskets, 112,000 Prussian muskets, 58,000 Belgian muskets, and 203,000 "miscellaneous" muskets. The best of the lot included 117,000 British Enfields and 48,000 French rifled muskets, all quite serviceable, for muskets.

At the same time, the government stepped up its own production of muskets. With the arsenal at Harpers Ferry already destroyed, only the Springfield armory remained. With new equipment the armory turned out over 6,900 in October 1861, working toward a production goal of 10,000 a month for December. The private manufacture of small arms boomed similarly, so that by January 1862 the total Union capacity for producing small arms reached about 700,000 a year. The Union soldier perhaps had not the best weapon available, but after January 1862 he always had enough.

Quite a variety of weapons appeared in a single regiment. An Iowa regiment catalogued in 1861 Austrian and Prussian muskets, Belgian rifles, Colt rifles, Minie rifles, Colt revolvers, navy revolvers, and still other types. A Minnesota regiment refused to use an obsolete lot of Belgian muskets and instead armed themselves with squirrel guns, shotguns, and long Kentucky rifles. Another Minnesota regiment in the winter of 1862–1863 had their Belgian muskets replaced with Austrian muskets, and finally with Springfields. The variety of weaponry raised tremendous problems of supply. Portions of a Minnesota regiment, sent out to protect the frontier from rampaging Sioux, discovered after being pinned down by the Indians that their .62 caliber ammunition supply was unsuitable for their .58 caliber guns.

Between 1861 and 1864 over 4,000,000 small arms and 7,892 cannon were issued to Union soldiers, demonstrating that it was an infantryman's war. Breech-loading and rifling were only then being applied to cannon, as cannon of all types were pressed into service. Another new weapon, a prototype of the machine gun, went unappreciated until it was too late. Richard Jordan Gatling made the first model of his Gatling gun in Indianapolis in 1862. Mounted on a light gun carriage, it could fire 250–300 shots a minute. The War Department bought a dozen, but ordnance officers were not sufficiently impressed to order more until after the war, when an improved type went into service.

Organization and Discipline

The lack of a military tradition in American society and the application of the jealously guarded democratic tradition normally served Americans very well, but not in war, and especially not in the army. The insistence of the states that they run their own regiments and the early application of democratic methods in the choice of officers led to a waste of life on the battlefield. The federal government left the training and staffing of regiments to state officials, giving them little more than guidelines on how to set up camps. Aside from learning marching formations, the barest elements of military courtesy, and how to load and shoot their weapons, recruits received most of their actual training under fire on the battlefield in the ranks alongside veterans. This painful training meant that raw recruits had to become veterans themselves before they were of real use to a fighting army.

The same applied to officers. An officer with courage and ability and professional training could make soldiers out of almost any volunteers when given the opportunity. Untrained officers with all the personal bravery in the world made errors in judgment that cost thousands of lives. Yet the problem of selecting officers remained in the hands of the state governors. When they could, they engaged trained soldiers like Grant and McClellan, and old soldiers with any experience often received commissions or at least served as sergeants. But so did political favorites. Since there were not enough experienced men to go around, there often was a simple election of officers by the volunteers themselves—a system Congress sanctioned in July 1861. The majority of officers so elected ranged in ability from totally ignorant to incompetent to incapable of learning. Fortunately for the Union there were enough exceptions to the rule to provide a modicum of discipline for the army.

As a group, the volunteers were nearly totally untrained and had little comprehension of the job they faced. Their enthusiasm, plus time and experience, generally overcame their lack of military education, and discipline might have made them matchless soldiers. The weakness of the volunteer system was that the citizen-soldier hated taking orders and the volunteer officer hesitated to command. Most volunteers would comply with a reasonable order, but did so because the order was reasonable, not because it was an order. Officers who issued unfair orders, or orders that seemed needless, found that they were dealing not with soldiers but with free and independent citizens who had an almost traditional distaste for army discipline.

Lack of discipline manifested itself on the drill field, in sanitation, and in morale. Desertion was frequent. Mutiny was incipient, though usually squelched. McClellan, who turned 100,000 loosely organized troops in and around Washington, D. C., into a well-disciplined army, and Grant, who made soldiers out of the uniformed mob gathered at Cairo, Illinois, contributed most to army discipline. As officers gained knowledge, and courts-martial and examining boards clamped down, and death under fire increased, the army gradually improved. Soldiers learned to vote for, and officials learned to appoint, efficient and courageous men. By 1863 veteran Union armies could meet any opposition.

Enrollment and Draft

For a while after Sumter enough men volunteered to fill the armies. After the first blush of enthusiasm wore off, however, enlistments diminished, and states, cities, and even the federal government came to rely more heavily on cash bounties. The practice of paying a bounty for army enlistment had been used since Revolutionary days, when free land had been the common bait. Thus it was not unusual that with the call for volunteers men were offered compensation above the regular $11 a month.*

On April 17 Rhode Island voted each of her volunteers $12 a month in addition to their federal pay, and almost immediately other localities in the East followed suit, with the city of Boston providing $20 additional. Before the summer of 1861 ended, Ohio, Michigan, and Wisconsin enacted legislation to provide relief for the families of volunteers, which was a basic reason for the bounty to begin with. After the Union defeat at First Bull Run, men were much less eager to enlist, and the use of bounties as an inducement became much more important.

In August of 1861 Governor Edwin Morgan of New York offered $2 for each person recruited by individuals who raised at least thirty-two volunteers, an indication that competition between the states and localities to fill their quotas had become keen. Governor Samuel J. Kirkwood of Iowa even issued an order forbidding Iowans to enlist outside of their state. The federal government, according to a War Department order of May 4, 1861 (legalized by Congress the following July), tendered a bounty of $100, payable upon discharge, to all volunteers enlisting for three years and to all those who enlisted in the regular army. In 1862 the regulation was altered to allow a payment of $40 cash at enlistment, which with an advance of one month's pay could come to $53. In June 1862, Congress resolved to apply the New York governor's premium system, without restriction on the number of volunteers required. Curiously, no one advocated merely raising the soldier's pay.

* The pay of a private, $11 a month at the beginning of the war, was raised to $13 a month August 6, 1861, and then to $16 a month on June 20, 1864. Foreign observers considered the pay quite high compared with European soldier pay schedules, but American volunteers considered it a pittance. Once they were paid in depreciating greenback dollars, the volunteers themselves estimated they made at most $8 a month in actual wages.

The passage and implementation of the Militia Draft Act of July 17, 1862, again altered the bounty situation. The act provided for payments of $25 and $50 for nine-month and twelve-month volunteers, but since no one-year men were accepted the $50 bounty never was paid. Almost 19,000 nine-month Pennsylvania volunteers received the $25 bounty, as did nearly 4,000 Vermont militia. Citizens across the country opposed draft legislation and ostracized draftees in peculiar ways that did not apply to the soldier who volunteered to escape the draft. Officials, from governors down to and including recruiting officers, described the horrors of the draft and advertised the bounties available to volunteers.

Across the nation officials agitated for larger bounties. Some counties in Iowa offered $75 cash; Rhode Island localities advertised as much as $350. In 1863, Congress passed the Enrollment Act, allowing a stand-in $300 plus $100 bonus for replacing a draftee. Subsequently most localities boosted their bounties to the same level. In June 1863, the federal government further offered a $400 bounty to all men enlisting in the regular army for five years or to volunteers who reenlisted for three years. The army still paid only $40 in advance (raised to $75 in 1864), with the remainder distributed in $50 portions throughout the enlistment term. This amounted to raising the pay of the soldier by that amount and to some extent frustrated the efforts of bounty deserters and bounty brokers. For a short time toward the end of 1863, the government extended a $300 bounty for all three-year volunteers, a practice ended by Congress on January 5, 1864, largely because Senator John Sherman pointed out that the Treasury simply did not have the money to continue payments. In response to popular clamor, Congress extended the practice to April 1, 1864.

The bounty, of course, gave tremendous advantage to the locality able to pay the most. Recruits traveled long distances, often out of state, to collect. Many men went into the bounty business for all they could get, collecting, deserting, and collecting again, never intending to become soldiers. A large number of those listed on the rolls as deserters were bounty jumpers. The bounty business was also profitable for gangs who used all manner of disguises and tricks to collect.

When the first round of relatively reasonable bounties failed to draw enough men, the militia draft was instituted in July 1862. The militia included all able-bodied men between the ages of eighteen and forty-five, and the states were authorized to draft militia if they were unable to fill their quota of volunteers. The states, hesitant to do so, continued to rely on bounties, beginning the second round. When some states still had difficulty meeting volunteer quotas, Congress reluctantly passed the Enrollment Act of March 3, 1863.* Enlistments had been much discouraged by setbacks at Bull Run, Antietam, Perryville, Fredericksburg, and other engagements, while the fighting had cost the Union armies about 75,000 in dead, wounded, and deserters.

The measure provided that all able-bodied males between twenty and forty-five if unmarried, or twenty and thirty-five if married, were liable to military service for three years. Few exceptions were permitted: those who were physically or mentally unfit or who had been convicted of a felony, high national and state officials, and those who were the sole support of a dependent family. However, under section 13 of the law it was possible to purchase exemption. Anyone who could afford to hire a substitute to go in his place or pay the government a $300 commutation fee could remain safely and legally at home.

Section 13 thus opened the door for an evil as great or greater than bounty jumping. Since a substitute could claim a bounty in addition to his fee, which usually equalled the commutation fee of $300, he could make $400 and perhaps more. Then if he could desert and repeat the process, he could garner his own small fortune. Many tried. The law also gave rise to the substitute broker who, for a fee in addition to the $300, would provide substitutes. One newspaper correspondent discovered that "cripples from birth, men partially blind, idiots from town poor farms, . . . puny boys of 14 or 15, escaped prisoners, paralytics, [and] men who cannot speak English" were sent to the army as recruits. In the Northwest substitute brokers added kidnapped Indians to the list. This portion of the legislation was denounced as class-favoritism and was eventually repealed, but not until the summer of 1864.

Rather than imposing a direct draft, the law spurred enlistments by threatening to invoke conscription. Each state was divided into enrollment districts, and at stated intervals was assigned a quota to raise. If a state could fill its quota through the use of

* The first national conscription act in United States history. However, it followed a similar law enacted by the Confederacy in 1862.

bounties or by any other means, the draft remained inoperative in that state. When districts failed to meet their quota, a sufficient number of men were drafted to make up the difference. Thus some states and many districts never resorted to conscription. The draft acts altogether produced about 170,000 men, of whom nearly 120,000 were substitutes. During the same period, well over 1,000,000 volunteers joined. There was no way to determine how many volunteers had signed up simply to avoid being drafted.

The Enrollment Act meant essentially that every male of proper age would be subjected to a military census. An enrolling officer of the provost-marshal's office canvassed his district house-to-house. Obviously the easy way to escape service was to be absent during the enrollment period. A district commander in Iowa lamented that in enrolling season Iowa was full of Minnesota boys who had come to visit and empty of Iowa lads. Some citizens even preferred the uneasy and hostile Indians of the plains to the enrolling officer, and migration west continued unabated during the war. In 1864 alone, an estimated 150,000 persons, mostly men, crossed the Missouri River heading westward.

Persistent and violent opposition to the draft erupted in almost every state in the Union where the draft was tried. Enrolling officers were murdered, tarred and feathered, and greeted by hostile opposition. Resistance was sometimes organized by groups such as the Knights of the Golden Circle, the Sons of Liberty, the Circle of Honor, or, as all were called in common language, the butternuts.

The Knights of the Golden Circle did not stand officially for violent draft opposition. They included all shades of opinion in their ranks, from individuals mildly opposed to the war to outspoken Confederate sympathizers, yet they were blamed for the shooting of enrolling officers in Iowa, Indiana, and Illinois in 1862 and Maryland, Pennsylvania, and Wisconsin in 1863. The butternuts were accused of delaying recruiting in Ohio, Indiana, and Illinois, and of instigating draft riots in New York.

Whether the Knights deserved all the charges hurled at them is questionable. In Pennsylvania draft resistance centered in the coal mining districts, where it had its roots in a much deeper struggle involving capital versus labor and the famous "Molly Maguires." In Wisconsin German-American pacifists of Ozaukee (Milwaukee) and neighboring counties forced enrolling officers out of the area. It took 600 troops to enforce the law, and 150 resisters were arrested.

The most infamous incident took place in New York City, July 13–16, 1863, where Irish immigrants opposed being compelled to fight to free blacks. A mob of seventy-five to a hundred persons broke up enrollment proceedings in one New York district by showering officers with brickbats and setting fire to their headquarters. The crowd swelled rapidly out of control, and as the disturbance grew into a riot the original protest was forgotten. The mob pillaged saloons, stores, and hardware stores where guns might be obtained, venting its anger in passing on blacks and suspected abolitionists. At least eighteen persons were murdered without provocation, most of them black. Finally troops moved in to restore order, suffering perhaps a score dead and twice that number wounded; but they in turn took a frightful toll of the mob, killing or fatally wounding between four and five hundred. Property losses ran to over $1,500,000.

Other riots, minor in comparison, occurred in Troy and Boston. As a crowd attempted to batter its way into Boston's Cooper Street armory, soldiers fired a cannon-load of canister and followed with a bayonet charge. Six or eight persons were killed, including a woman, and several more were wounded. There were incidents in almost every Northern state, and the federal peacekeeping troops that would have been labeled interference in 1861, were eagerly sought in 1863. In this small way the draft and its enforcement contributed to the creation of a stronger national government and weakened the states' rights concept in the North.

Northern recruiters also sought to enlist men from the Southern states. In September 1863 General Nathaniel P. Banks, commanding in New Orleans, announced a draft "in accordance with the provisions of the law of conscription" so far as it could be applied in his department. In November 1863 General Stephen A. Hurlbut issued an order for impressment of able-bodied men into the army at Memphis, Tennessee, and mustered twenty-seven companies for home guard service. The military Department of the South issued similar orders in January and June 1864, including all refugees between eighteen and fifty years of age. General Edward R. S. Canby ordered a draft in the Department of Western Mississippi in July 1864 and expanded it in January 1865 to include the Department of Arkansas, Mississippi, and the Gulf. Confederate deserters were excepted, but they were allowed to volunteer to fight Indians in the Northwest.

Though these efforts were limited and not very effective, they did turn up over 100,000 blacks and 54,000 white volunteers for the Union from Confederate states. The number is even more impressive when added to the numbers furnished by the loyal slave states for a total of 445,000. Thus the slave states combined to send into Union forces between 40 and 50 percent as many men as the slave states furnished to the Confederacy. Recruiting among Confederate deserters, a dangerous business, was tolerated for a while, then ended in December–January 1863–1864, when first Grant and then the provost marshal's office declared such persons not subject to draft or acceptable as recruits. Lincoln later ordered the provost marshal to accept nearly two battalions of Confederate prisoners of war in October 1864 for frontier duty in regiments called United States Volunteers. A few found their way into state regiments as well.

For more than a year, federal officials refused to permit the recruiting of even free blacks. While many in the North hoped to end slavery, many also intended to keep the North white. Westerners fought to make the territories white-man's country, and many elsewhere protested the danger of black competition. In Florida, Maryland, West Virginia, and the Department of the West, fugitives making their way into Union lines were returned to their masters or otherwise discouraged from their attempts to gain freedom. Yet from the beginning of the war, ardent abolitionists demanded that blacks be recruited despite firm opposition from Lincoln and the Secretary of War. On July 9, 1861, the House passed a weak resolution declaring that the army had no duty to return fugitives; but the resolution failed to settle the matter. General Butler at Fortress Monroe, Virginia, refused to return fugitives and considered them as contraband of war, a policy apparently honored by the War Department so long as the fugitives came from rebellious states and not Union slave states.

In October 1861 Butler's successor, General Thomas W. Sherman, was given authority to create military units composed of fugitives. Sherman failed to take advantage of the order except for hired laborers, but his successor, David Hunter, did. On May 9, 1862, Hunter issued a proclamation for the emancipation of slaves in Georgia, Florida, and South Carolina, which Lincoln repudiated a couple of days later. Hunter had already taken advantage of the previous order and organized at least one regiment of blacks, the First South Carolina Regiment of Volunteers, but failing to secure political support for his efforts, he had to disband his regiment and send them away on August 10, 1862.

No sooner had Hunter disbanded his troops, than the War Department changed its mind and renewed efforts to recruit blacks, citing a couple of laws passed in July 1862 that gave the president discretion in the disposition of blacks. Though little was accomplished in 1862, General Rufus Saxon in the Carolinas, General Butler in New Orleans, General Augustus L. Chatlain in Tennessee, and others recruiting free blacks in the North had done enough by the end of the year to promise a much brighter future. In the spring of 1863 black recruiting was systematized. In the end a recorded 186,017 blacks fought in the Union army, and of those, 104,387 were recruited in Confederate territory. At first, under the language of the Militia Act of July 17, 1862, black soldiers were discriminated against in pay rates—$7 a month as compared to $13 a month for white soldiers. It took from June 1864 to March 1865 to end pay discrimination. Similar discrepancies in bounties plagued black soldiers.

The total enrollment in the Union army reached 918,191 on January 1, 1863, and 1,000,516 on May 1, 1865. The fact that the increase in the last two years was only about 82,000 is explained by the early acceptance of thousands of militia and the varying terms of service of men recruited in the territories and Confederate states. The latter made up a transient contingent of over 350,000 men, most of whom had completed their service by mid-1863. Add another 658,000 three-year men whose terms expired in 1864, and 360,000 deaths from all causes, plus 275,000 wounded, and it is clear that the army was fairly stable in size during the last two years. The total number of enlistments ran to about 2,900,000 for the war; and a reasonable estimate was that about 1,500,000 served for three years.

Financing the War

Energetic and honest, Treasury Secretary Chase and his successor in June 1864, William P. Fessenden, both had a good deal of innate ability but little financial training. Chase failed to propose

tax measures at a time, early in the war, when the public was enthusiastic about restoring the Union and would have supported
heavier tax burdens. Instead the government relied largely upon
borrowing and secured twelve major loans with interest rates ranging from 5 to 7⅓ percent. Because Chase refused to sell the bonds
below par value, speculators would not buy them in volume; as a
result, the government experienced some difficulty in marketing
bonds for the first two years. After January 1863 the situation improved. Congress passed legislation to permit the sale of bonds for
whatever the market would bring, and by that time, greenbacks
had so declined in value that their conversion into bonds was financially attractive.

The government hired as its broker Jay Cooke, who imagina-
tively disposed of the bonds to businessmen, financiers, and institutions, as had been the usual custom, and to the general public as
well. His commission of ⅜ percent brought him close to half a million dollars by the close of 1865. Wisely, Chase set the redemption
period of the bonds at an undetermined number of years, such as
five to twenty or ten to forty. The object was to make it possible for
the government to redeem the bonds at a lower rate of interest after
the war, thereby saving considerable sums of money. That, too,
frightened prospective purchasers and was another reason why the
bonds sold slowly at first.

The issue of legal-tender paper money offered another method
of financing the war. The bills provided less income than bond
sales but had consequences far beyond the war period. Under legislation of July and August 1861 and especially of February 25, 1862,
the government issued notes that were "legal tender . . . for all
debts public and private except duties on imports and interest on
the public debt." The public generally approved of the issue, but
the bankers firmly opposed it. The growing cost of the war and the
desire to stimulate bond sales encouraged further issues, and the
United States Notes, or greenbacks, totaled $450,000,000 by March
3, 1863.

The United States Notes, unsecured by any redemption fund
of gold, silver, or bonds, were fiat money secured only by the credit
of the United States. The exemption that prohibited their use for
import duties clearly recognized the possibility that they might de-
preciate in value vis-à-vis gold. Imports were assessed on a gold
value, hence duty payment in shrunken dollars would shrivel both

revenue and tariff protection for manufacturers. Prohibiting United States Notes from being used for interest payments on the public debt was an inducement for purchasing bonds. An investor in 1864 could change $400 in gold for $1000 worth of greenbacks, purchase a $1000 bond, and net $60 a year interest in gold for a 15 percent return on his original $400. Based as they were on the credit of the United States, the greenbacks fluctuated in direct proportion to the Union's military successes. Thus they shrank in value rather steadily until July 1864, when they reached a low of about $.35 compared to the gold dollar. This depreciation added greatly to the cost of the war, though the consequent inflation bolstered the illusion of general prosperity.

The greenback issues drove other currency, including coins, out of circulation before mid-1862. Making change became a real problem. Bus tickets, street-car tokens, personal notes, even beer checks were used as makeshift. In July 1862 Congress authorized the use of postage stamps as currency, even issuing stamps without gum on the reverse side. On March 3, 1863, Congress provided for greenbacks in fractional amounts, and notes of three to fifty cents were printed. The public called all the substitutes for change "shinplasters."

Taxation provided only about 20 percent of the revenue for 1861–1863. Few in or out of government recognized the magnitude of the war and the large sums necessary for its prosecution, a fact attributable partly to the lack of a military tradition in the United States and partly to inexperience with public funds on so vast a scale. By the middle of 1862 a direct tax of $.22 a head and a 3 percent levy on incomes of over $800 a year had been decreed. The income tax rates changed in 1863 and again in 1865, with the exemption lowered to $600 and the tax graduated from 5 to 10 percent, with the higher figure applicable to incomes over $5,000. The tax bothered relatively few, with just over 460,000 paying in 1866. Most of the income tax revenue found its way to the Treasury only after the end of hostilities.

On July 1, 1862, the government revived long dormant internal revenue duties. The Treasury proposed to tax as many articles as possible rather than place a high tax on just a few items. Manufactured products were taxed at various stages of production as well as in the finished state. Cigars, taxed at 4 cents each, and hard liquor, at $2.00 a gallon, were tagged with the highest rates. In 1864 the national income from internal revenue duties, including the income tax, surpassed customs receipts in volume for the first time in the nation's history. In order to provide relief for manufacturers and protection from foreign competition during the emergency, the tariff rates were raised in 1862 and again in 1864.* The average rate under the 1864 measure was 47 percent, which remained the fundamental basis for the tariff for about twenty years.

Business conditions fluctuated with the successes and failures of the war. The financial crisis of 1861, precipitated largely by the repudiation of Southern debts (as much as $300,000,000 worth), was only slightly less profound than the Panic of 1857. The recession continued until the winter of 1861–1862, when both war profits and greenbacks stimulated business. Banking in 1861 found itself in as precarious a situation as ever. Some institutions issued notes two or three times in excess of their capital, and all bank notes varied considerably in value as a result. The public summarily dismissed bank notes as "stumptail, wildcat, yellow dog, and red dog," depending upon their worth. Most of the banks suspended specie payments late in 1860, and the Treasury followed suit a year later (except for interest on bonds). Many banks failed, especially in the mid-West. After the suspension of specie payments it was nearly impossible to calculate the value of bank notes, and notes from hundreds of extinct and discredited banks continued in circulation alongside those from nearly 1,600 institutions that remained solvent. With the several denominations of bills and the many different designs, businessmen and bankers had to be knowledgeable about nearly 12,000 kinds of notes. Cautious transactions slowed business to a crawl, as creditors agonizingly examined each bill.

The situation was intolerable in the emergency, and it took federal action to solve the problem. To regularize business transactions Chase advocated a uniform national system of banking in December 1862, and Congress set up the system in February 1863.** The National Bank Act stipulated that any bank complying with federal regulations could deposit government bonds with the Treasury and issue national bank notes up to 90 percent of their value.

* The Morrill Tariff of February 1861 afforded moderate protection, a return to the low rate schedules of the Walker Tariff of 1846. An act of August 1861 was primarily revenue producing. The acts of July 1862 and June 1864 were frankly protectionist, and the rates rose considerably for items produced abroad.

** Congress redrew the law in June 1864.

Western cities led in supporting and nurturing the national bank plan. Chicago merchants and bankers discounted all paper money except greenbacks and national bank notes and presented all state bank notes for redemption. The nonurban West fell into line, for it became very difficult for banks outside the system to stay in business. On March 3, 1865, Congress levied a 10 percent tax on state bank notes, virtually bringing those issues to an end. By 1866 the nation counted 1,634 national banks and only 297 state banks.

Wartime Politics

Lincoln's theories concerning the exercise of emergency war powers and the relationship of the executive to Congress and the Constitution emerged almost immediately after Sumter. Where the Constitution failed to indicate clearly who should wield certain powers, Lincoln preferred that the chief executive exercise them. Unswerving in his determination to preserve the Union, Lincoln observed that he would rather violate the Constitution than have it rendered useless.

On April 15, 1861, he published a proclamation designed to suppress by force if necessary any "said combinations" that thwarted law enforcement. Although fighting began with the firing on Sumter, Lincoln's carefully structured proclamation was tantamount to a declaration of war, an act that constitutionally belonged to Congress. The same spirit marked his blockade proclamation of April 19, for in it he recognized the belligerency of the Confederacy and tacitly admitted, so far as international law was concerned, that a rebellion existed. The May 1 proclamation that called for additional volunteers to serve for three years had no basis in the militia law of the time, while the section enlarging the regular army and navy transgressed the power of Congress.

In his April 15 proclamation Lincoln called for Congress to meet in special session July 4, not sooner, which allowed him two and a half months to bring the South to its senses. His proclamations of April 15, 19, and May 1 were designed to let the South know he meant business, but to allow time for a possible reconciliation should Southerners realize the seriousness of the situation and to avoid the complications Congress might cause by immediate all-out prosecution of the war. They also gave Lincoln time to implement war measures, so that when Congress met it would be faced with a fait accompli. Congress, in fact, quickly rubber-stamped Lincoln's extra-legal activities after it convened.

Lincoln used any measures he thought necessary to prosecute the war without undue interference from Southern sympathizers, those who condoned separation and the splintering of the Union, or those who opposed the war effort or any part of it for the sake of political advantage. Lincoln several times repeated his warning that he intended to preserve, protect, and defend the Union after first warning the South in his inaugural. He told a New York delegation that his sentiment was "for the good of those" who lived in the North as well as the South. He told a delegation from Massachusetts and a committee from Baltimore the same thing, and subsequently, through word and deed, reiterated this belief. As early as April 27 he advised General Winfield Scott that he could suspend the writ of habeas corpus "at any point on or in the vicinity of " resistance to the movement of military forces.

Lincoln and Civil Liberty

Lincoln aroused considerable popular criticism for his actions affecting civil rights. Much of the censure directed at the president originated with pro-Southern citizens in Union states and from a faction of the Democratic party. Splintered by the election of 1860, the Democrats remained fractured into at least three parts throughout the war. Those who assailed Lincoln often represented the peace Democrats, or copperheads, who desired to end the war with a truce. Other Democrats backed the war effort and assisted the Republicans in its prosecution. When the Republicans took the name of the Union party after their reverses in the congressional elections of 1862, many of the war Democrats joined them as Unionists. Most of the Northern Democrats fell into neither peace nor war categories, remained in their party and condoned the war, but criticized its management as well as specific acts of Congress.

The Lincoln administration found the copperheads the most troublesome. Centered in southern Ohio, Indiana, and Illinois, they feared that their agrarianism suffered at the hands of the industrialists who controlled the Republican party. They also feared that a new nationalism might curtail much of the local autonomy the states had enjoyed in antebellum days, when the agrarian South and West had ruled the nation. They wanted to bring about a truce, call a national meeting with the Confederate Southern states in attendance, and work out a constitutional compromise that would restore the Union and the autonomy of the states and put the old agrarian coalition back in control of the government. They appeared blind to the fact that the seceded states had had several opportunities in the winter of 1860–1861 to agree to compromise proposals that would have accomplished much the same thing, as well as to the fact that the South now found such a prescription repugnant. For all of their so-called copperheadism, the peace Democrats were Unionists in that they favored a restoration of the Union.

Congress strengthened Lincoln's hand in fighting antiwar activities with a conspiracies act (July 1861) and a treason act (the second Confiscation Act, July 1862).* Some grand jury indictments did result, but most court cases were postponed time and again as the suspects went free under their own responsibility to appear if called. Usually the courts dropped the indictments after a time. The administration knew that a conviction for treason was most difficult to obtain and once convicted, a man might become a martyr.

Rather than wait for treasonable activities to materialize, Lincoln arbitrarily arrested potentially dangerous war opponents. He suspended the writ of habeas corpus to enable an alleged offender to be detained and held without trial, though usually for only a brief period. In the few instances that suspects did come to trial, they appeared before military tribunals, not civilian courts. Originally Lincoln suspended the writ only in certain areas, then on September 24, 1862, he extended the suspension to "all Rebels and Insurgents, their aiders and abettors within the United States, and all persons discouraging volunteer enlistments, resisting militia drafts, or guilty of any disloyal practice" as well as all persons arrested or imprisoned by "any military authority" or by the sentence of a military court. This sweeping authority for arbitrary arrest netted over 13,000 suspected individuals, who were kept in federal custody for varying short periods of time. Lincoln found arbitrary arrest more convenient and more expedient than action under the treason act. At first, throughout 1861, Seward and the State Department handled these arrests; but beginning in 1862 the War Department took over. A War Department commission examined each case and ordered many releases.

---

* The first Confiscation Act passed Congress August 6, 1861. It provided for the seizure of property used for "insurrectionary purposes."

A few of those arrested managed to bring their plight to the attention of civil courts through their attorneys. John Merryman, a Maryland secessionist leader, had been arrested and confined in Fort McHenry. Chief Justice Taney directed that the writ of habeas corpus be served to produce Merryman in court and examine the reason for his arrest. Following orders, the officer in charge refused to surrender Merryman. Taney then issued a writ of attachment for contempt against the officer, but the marshal was unable to serve it. Taney then prepared an opinion that denied the president's authority to suspend the writ since only Congress had the power. Taney had gone on record in the circuit court, for the Chief Justice had acted in his capacity as circuit judge;* the case never came before the Supreme Court.

The case of Clement L. Vallandigham, an Ohio Democrat, eventually reached the high bench. In the spring of 1863 Vallandigham spoke at Mount Vernon, Ohio, and denounced the government for unnecessarily continuing the war, which he claimed was fought to free blacks and enslave whites, not to maintain the Union. General Ambrose E. Burnside, commander of the military Department of Ohio, had earlier issued an order that his department would "no longer" tolerate expressions of public sympathy for the Confederacy and would punish offenders. Vallandigham was duly arrested, denied habeas corpus, and tried by a military commission. Found guilty, he was sentenced to prison for the duration of the war. From his cell in Cincinnati, he proclaimed his only "crime" to be that he was a Democrat who stood for the Union, Constitution, law, and liberty. He received wide publicity and embarrassed the Lincoln administration.

Since there were many war critics, the administration feared that Vallandigham's arrest and imprisonment would only make a martyr of him. Yet the administration could not afford to release him lest the whole episode be no more than a mockery of the government. Lincoln commuted the original sentence and banished him to the Confederacy, but Vallandigham made his way to Windsor, Canada, and continued to score the administration publicly. In disguise he returned to the United States; then discarding this disguise, he took part openly in the campaign of 1864. Lincoln chose

---

* Ever since 1789 Supreme Court justices had been required to do circuit court duty as well as to sit on the bench to which they were appointed.

to ignore him rather than return him to prison. Meanwhile, the Supreme Court heard the case, only to declare that its jurisdiction did not include the review of a military commission's findings. The court, in *Ex Parte Vallandigham,* thus refused in 1864 to rule against the administration.*

Lincoln publicly defended his arbitrary stance in his July 4, 1861, address to Congress. He acknowledged that the "propriety" of some of his actions had been questioned, and that many were concerned that "one who is sworn to 'take care that the laws be faithfully executed,' should not himself violate them." Referring to the suspension of habeas corpus, he told Congress, "are all the laws, *but one,* to go unexecuted, and the government itself go to pieces, lest that one be violated?" All the laws were going unexecuted in the states in rebellion. "In such a case," Lincoln continued, "would not the official oath be broken, if the government should be overthrown, when . . . disregarding the single law, would tend to preserve it?" And yet, he asked, was any law really being disregarded. The "Constitution itself, is silent as to which, or who, is to exercise the power" of suspending the writ; and clearly the writ's suspension "was plainly made for a dangerous emergency." He could not believe, he said, that the framers of the Constitution intended "that in every case" the "danger should run its course" until Congress could be called into session. That danger might very well prohibit Congress from assembling.

In 1863, in response to resolutions from the Ohio State Democratic convention concerning the Vallandigham affair, Lincoln added, "the military arrests and detentions, which have been made, . . . have been for *prevention,* and not for *punishment—* . . . as proceedings to keep the peace—and hence, like proceedings in such cases" have not been involved with indictments, or jury trial, "nor, in a single case by any punishment whatever" beyond that necessary for prevention. The attorney general concurred with Lincoln's right to suspend the writ, and Congress tardily responded with the Habeas Corpus Act of March 1863 that left suspension of the writ to the president's judgment.

Lincoln did not, as some accused, behave as a dictator. He made no effort to silence the opposition in Congress or to do away

---

* The court reversed itself in the case of *Ex Parte Milligan* (April 1866) when it held that martial law cannot exist where the courts are open, but only in "the locality of actual war."

with that body. He failed to use the emergency to extend arbitrary rule into other areas or to make himself a supreme ruler. He suspended no elections and fully expected to be defeated in 1864. If he interpreted the Constitution in a manner that permitted him to prevent dangerous situations from developing, he in no way attempted to replace or subvert the Constitution. In interpreting the Constitution he did only what other presidents had done, including the Democratic party's patron saint, Andrew Jackson.

Freedom of speech and the press flourished and only rarely were newspapers suspended. When General Burnside suspended the publication of the Chicago *Times* in the summer of 1863, Lincoln quickly reversed the order. A couple of New York papers were temporarily suspended after they published a fraudulent presidential proclamation, but resumed publication within three days. Two Baltimore papers, a Louisville paper, one in New Orleans and one from Philadelphia, among others, were also suspended for various periods. The Lincoln administration made no other effort to control or censor the news. Newspapers continued to attack the administration or to criticize its policies without interruption. They openly criticized military policy, a practice harmful to civilian and military morale. They maintained correspondents with both the army and navy, and frequently printed news of military preparations and operations, including the composition and whereabouts of units, their destinations and casualties—information that was of real use to Lee and other Confederate officers, who read Northern papers as regularly as possible. Indeed, much greater control was exercised in subsequent decades.

Radical Republicans

Many differences of opinion existed within the Republican party as they did within the opposition. A one-idea party before the war, cemented by opposition to the expansion of slavery into the territories, the Republican party encompassed men of all shades of opinion, who had not altered their often conflicting views on matters such as economic policy. The great division remained that of abolition versus antislavery. Abolitionists, like Senators Sumner of Massachusetts and Wade of Ohio and the great House leader, Thaddeus Stevens of Pennsylvania, squared off against the more conservative antislavery faction headed by Lincoln. Called Radical Republicans, the abolitionists viewed war emergency as a great opportunity to bring an end to slavery by proclaiming abolition a war aim. The party conservatives opposed so radical a social change. Lincoln, for one, feared the effect of a pro-abolition stand on the Union slave states and upon public opinion in other Northern states.

To bolster the conservative position, Congress passed the Crittenden Resolution in July 1861, specifically providing that slavery was safe within any state. By implication that made preservation of the Union the major war aim, as Lincoln's administration so often stated. The Radicals bided their time, aware that Northerners generally blamed the secession and war on slavery, and Northerners had no desire to let their young men die in a war that would preserve slavery. In the spring of 1862 the Radicals made their move, pushing through Congress the old abolitionist goals of excluding slavery from the District of Columbia and the territories. That accomplished, they launched an offensive against slavery in the states.

Although many Republicans and most Democrats believed Congress had no power to legislate an end to slavery in the states, the Radicals successfully hustled the second Confiscation Act* through Congress. The confiscation section provided for fines, imprisonment, and setting free the slaves of anyone engaged in rebellion against the United States, including the immediate confiscation of all the property of the officers of the Confederate government without notice and of other rebels within sixty days. It allowed the president to use blacks, even freed slaves, in the armed forces. A section on treason broadened penalties to include fines and imprisonment as well as death.

Essentially the act covered all persons living in the eleven Confederate states, including foreigners and those who remained loyal to the Union. Conservatives in the Republican party objected that thousands of innocent persons would suffer, yet the Radicals garnered decisive votes in both houses of Congress. Lincoln threatened to veto the bill on the grounds that confiscation without criminal conviction or a court hearing was unjust and that forfeiture of property beyond an individual's lifetime was unconstitutional. In a joint resolution designed to answer Lincoln, Congress declared that confiscation under the act would not apply beyond the lifetime of the

---

* The first Confiscation Act passed Congress in August 1861 and provided only for the seizure of property used in aid of rebellion.

accused. The resolution failed to meet all of Lincoln's objections, but he acquiesced to the Radicals and signed the bill.

The Confiscation Act actually freed no slaves and confiscated no property, for obviously the objects of confiscation were beyond the reach of the United States. Yet the act was important, for with it emancipation became a war aim and the abolitionists could feel they had accomplished their major goal at least in part. It also meant that the Radicals ruled the Republican party, and that Lincoln, aware of their power,,chose to yield on the question in order to maintain his chief purpose of preserving the Union. Not only would fighting the Radicals further divide the party, it would also alienate the staunchest and most enthusiastic war supporters who were essential to Lincoln's policy.

The Emancipation Proclamation

To garner abolitionist opinion both in the nation and in Congress, Lincoln considered using his executive power as commander-in-chief to issue a proclamation to liberate the slaves in the Confederacy. By July 1862 he no longer feared the effects of such a policy on the Union slave states, which would in any case be exempted. A proclamation would doubtless bring favorable comment from abroad, reversing criticism of the Union for waging an inhumane war merely to keep the Union together. If he published an emancipation order, it would be more effective following a military decision in the field, since a victory would undercut charges that the edict was designed to incite a slave rebellion.

Although Lincoln had reached his decision by July, he waited until after the Battle of Antietam to make his announcement. On September 22, 1862, he stated that as of January 1, 1863, he would free all the slaves in those states then actively engaged in rebellion. The preliminary Emancipation Proclamation gave the seceded states about a hundred days to reconsider their position and rejoin the Union. As with his proclamations following Sumter, Lincoln allowed the Confederacy time to save slavery and end the war. The Confederacy, of course, failed to respond, and on January 1, 1863, the final Emancipation Proclamation was published. Except for slaves in the Union slave states, and occupied areas of Tennessee, western Virginia, and southern Louisiana, slaves in the Confederacy were declared free.

The exceptions were made doubtless because Lincoln considered his war powers inoperative in any but enemy territory. Moreover, virtually no slaves were actually set free at the time of the proclamation, for the Union had no actual control over Confederate territory. Yet the proclamation would apply as Union armies recovered the specified areas. Neither was the institution of slavery itself destroyed—that final blow awaited legislation by the slave states or a Constitutional change. On the positive side, the Emancipation Proclamation encouraged those slaves who were able to learn that Lincoln wanted them free; and in the slave areas not covered by the proclamation, owners were in effect served notice that the end was just ahead. For them, the future was grim, but they understood perfectly what the future held. Maryland and Missouri abandoned slavery before Appomattox, as did occupied Tennessee, Louisiana, and Arkansas.

True to form, Southerners denounced the proclamation. They portrayed Lincoln as a "fiend" who would confiscate untold millions of dollars of property and incite the slaves to rebellion. Confederate President Jefferson Davis warned that, with emancipation, restoration of the Union became impossible. Other Southerners agreed and believed slave insurrection to be the only aim of the document. They also concluded that the Emancipation Proclamation illustrated the desperate condition of the Northern war effort, and would thus solidify the South in its determination to win independence.

The document received a mixed reception in the North. Thurlow Weed denounced it as a mistake that heartened the South and disappointed the North. Well aware of the limitations, Sumner and other abolitionists nevertheless gleefully supported the proclamation. The New York *Times* hailed the proclamation as one of the most important government documents ever issued. The black community agreed and celebrated across the North, with especially large gatherings taking place in Washington, D.C., New York, and Boston. Henry Ward Beecher declared from the pulpit of his Brooklyn church: "The Proclamation may not free a single slave, but it gives liberty a moral recognition." At New York's Cooper Union, veteran abolitionist Lewis Tappan foresaw a future in which the black man would play a normal role in society. In Boston's Music Hall Emerson read his "Boston Hymn" to the audience—"I break your bonds and masterships,/And I unchain the slave:/Free be his heart and hand henceforth/As wind and wandering wave." Hundreds of guns fired salutes, and blacks spoke of the "Year of Jubilee."

English abolitionists likewise hailed the proclamation but thought its debut as a war measure unfortunate; some British papers criticized its shortcomings. Yet general support for the measure was great enough to trouble Confederate agents and to cause Confederate Secretary of State Benjamin to despair. It led the South to agree to emancipate their own slaves in return for European recognition. As a diplomatic device to prevent recognition of the Confederacy and to swing public opinion back toward the North, the proclamation was an unqualified success.

Lincoln, of course, justified the proclamation as a war measure because in peacetime it would have been clearly unconstitutional. But the president believed that the Constitution invested him, as commander-in-chief, "with the law of war, in time of war." Wartime destruction of enemy property was normal, as was hurting the enemy in every possible way. Therefore, Lincoln held, "otherwise unconstitutional" measures become lawful if necessary for the preservation of the Constitution. Once more Lincoln illustrated his readiness to stretch the Constitution in order to accomplish his goals. By basing the proclamation on his war powers, he tacitly admitted that it probably had no standing in civil law. Lincoln recognized it as a temporary military expedient, not a permanent solution. In his message to Congress on December 1, 1862, he urged adoption of a constitutional amendment that would guarantee emancipation and gradual compensation to be accomplished by the year 1900. Congress recognized the need for an emancipation amendment all right, but the Thirteenth Amendment it approved early in 1864 lacked most of Lincoln's conditions. Ratified by the states on December 18, 1865, the amendment simply banished the institution of slavery, completing the abolitionists' program.

The Election of 1864

In a move designed to consolidate its hold on the government, especially after the reaction of critics to the second Confiscation Act, the setbacks in the congressional elections of 1862, and Democratic criticism of the Emancipation Proclamation, the Republican party formed the Union party, hoping to hold all war supporters together. They aimed, largely with success, to include the war Democrats. The new Union party's first challenge came in the general elections of 1864.

Everyone knew that Lincoln would be available as the Union party candidate, but the events of 1863 portended ill. Both the Enrollment Act and the Habeas Corpus Act passed Congress in March 1863, and neither was popular among large segments of Northern opinion. States' righters were disturbed by the increasing tendency to centralization seen in arbitrary arrests, conscription, national control of banking,* federal taxation, and other federal financial manipulations. Nor was the war progressing well. Chancellorsville occurred in May. July brought twin victories at Gettysburg and Vicksburg, but the celebration was tempered by the serious draft riots in Northern cities and the hard fact that Lee's army had not been destroyed. Toward the close of the year, Lincoln issued his Amnesty Proclamation, moving the Radicals to voice serious doubts about the president.

The Amnesty Proclamation of December 8, 1863, was Lincoln's first attempt to build a program of reconstruction. In it, Lincoln tendered a pardon to those Confederates who would take an oath to support the Union. He made clear his position on restoration by proposing to allow state governments to be reformed in recovered areas when 10 percent of those who could vote in 1860 took the oath, provided only that such governments outlaw slavery. The Radicals immediately rose in opposition, citing the proclamation as proof of his leniency toward the South. Immediately they met to find a more acceptable candidate, and settled on Chase. Radicals circulated the Pomeroy Circular, composed by Senator Samuel C. Pomeroy of Kansas, foreseeing the reelection of Lincoln as difficult and warning that Lincoln's arbitrary tendencies would only become more pronounced; Chase, they concluded, had the qualities necessary to run the nation.

The gulf between the Radicals and Lincoln widened when in February 1864 Francis P. Blair, Jr., a Lincoln spokesman in the House, viciously attacked Chase. Chase considered Blair's assault "malignant," and the Radicals interpreted it as a slap at them by Lincoln. Chase tendered his resignation which Lincoln shrewdly refused to accept. In so doing Lincoln kept Chase in the cabinet, and the Chase boom collapsed.

* The National Bank Acts of February 25, 1863, and June 3, 1864.

At the end of May Wendell Phillips and other radicals met in Cleveland to denounce the Lincoln administration and choose an alternate candidate. They settled upon Frémont for president and John Cochrane of New York for the second spot. But Lincoln partisans controlled the regular Republican organization, and when the Union party convened at Baltimore on June 7, it renominated Lincoln unanimously. Andrew Johnson of Tennessee, a war Democrat, won unanimous acceptance as the vice presidential candidate. The regular organization successfully outmaneuvered the Radicals.

The Radicals persisted in their opposition to Lincoln, and on July 2, 1864, passed the Wade-Davis Bill. Henry Winter Davis of Maryland and Benjamin Wade of Ohio, with support from Stevens and Sumner, produced a reconstruction measure designed to supplant Lincoln's Amnesty Proclamation. According to the provisions of the bill, a majority of the voting population of a state applying for re-admission to the Union would have to take the oath, no one connected with secession state governments or the Confederate government could participate, and slavery as well as the "rebel" debt would have to be repudiated. Lincoln applied a pocket veto to the bill, giving Congress no chance to override him. Both Davis and Wade waged a vindictive attack on Lincoln, the very man their party had launched toward a second term. Chase once more tendered his resignation, and to his chagrin, Lincoln accepted it this time. "You and I," Lincoln said, "have reached a point of mutual embarrassment" that cannot be overcome and is no longer in the interest of "the public service."

The obvious split in the Republican party, public dissatisfaction with the Lincoln administration's direction on states' rights, and the apparently futile military situation contributed to the gloom that Lincoln and others felt over the elections. The Democrats postponed their convention until August, quietly waiting to take full advantage of the situation. In Ohio Vallandigham spoke out for peace. In Lincoln's home state peace conventions met at Peoria and Springfield, and although they were denounced as copperhead meetings, the peace movement spread. Greeley advocated peace in his newspaper and wrote Lincoln, "our . . . dying country . . . longs for peace."

Lincoln replied that he would meet "any person, anywhere" who had Davis' authority to negotiate for peace under conditions of a reconstructed Union and the abolition of slavery. Lincoln nominated Greeley to meet with any such persons. Greeley went to Niagara to see two Confederate agents who, it turned out, had no authority to negotiate. Lincoln then published a memorandum in which he repeated his invitation to Greeley. In this spirit, he also encouraged the unofficial mission of two Northern peace agents who conferred unsuccessfully with President Davis, but Davis refused to consider peace on any terms other than Southern independence. Still another unofficial meeting came to a similar end in Toronto.

Under these circumstances, the Democrats met in Chicago on August 29. To reunite the war and peace Democrats, the party nominated General George McClellan of New Jersey and Ohio, and another Ohioan, George Pendleton, for vice president. A committee headed by Vallandigham drew up the platform. They produced a peace document, but not one that advocated peace at any price. Reunion remained a primary condition for peace. Still, the platform denounced the failure of the war and called for a truce to be followed by a national convention that presumably would try to piece the Union back together.

McClellan, in his acceptance letter, repudiated the platform. He intended to campaign on the grounds of continued prosecution of the war, and he had in fact been chosen in the first place because of his war record. Like other Democratic campaigners, he sidestepped the so-called "peace plank." In the ensuing campaign Democrats denounced Lincoln, his politics, his alleged dictatorship, and the Republican failure to save the Union.

Meanwhile Radical Republicans issued a call for another convention to meet in Cincinnati the end of September, to reconsider the state of affairs in the nation and to nominate a replacement for Lincoln "if necessary." Greeley and other editors, believing their cause lost, asked Northern governors to join in the effort to replace Lincoln. But the Democratic convention had upset their plans with McClellan and the peace platform. Lincoln remained unsatisfactory to the Radicals, but McClellan and a peace program were worse. Republicans closed ranks behind Lincoln; the Cincinnati convention never took place; Frémont withdrew from the race September 22; and the Republicans turned their wrath on the "copperhead platform" of the Democrats. Republican hopes revived as Atlanta fell early in September, and as Republicans scored victories in the October Maine and Vermont elections.

Lincoln won a landslide victory in November with 212 electoral votes to McClellan's 21. Only New Jersey, Delaware, and Kentucky went for McClellan. Lincoln's popular victory, 2,219,362 to McClellan's 1,805,063, gave the president a 414,000 vote edge. In retrospect, with the war moving swiftly to a conclusion, even a McClellan victory would have had little effect on the war. The new president was not inaugurated until March 4, 1865, and by that time a military decision had all but come.

The Northern Homefront

The people of the North were by and large spared the pain of hostile armies tramping across their countryside. Their houses, crops, cattle, mills, factories, and railroads remained intact. No blockaders closed Northern ports and foreign trade flourished. The financial recession of 1861 quickly faded away, people adjusted to war conditions and continued their regular occupations, as prosperous as ever and even wealthier in paper values. There was virtually no unemployment, for the demands of the military drew vast numbers of young men into the army. The largest percentage of Union soldiers were under twenty-two, and their absence was nearly unnoticed in the cities. In the smaller towns and on the farms women and children had to carry on, aided by the older men. Women replaced men as teachers in the schools.

Business flourished, manufacturing increased, and apparent wealth grew faster than at any time since before the Panic of 1857. Observers commented upon this fact and pointed out how New Yorkers, for example, put on an unprecedented display of luxury and used more foreign goods than ever before. Foreign luxury imports expanded in spite of inflation, heavy taxes, and the war. Women, promenading in public at the opera, the theater, and the parks, paraded an impressive array of silks, satins, and laces. Other women, daughters and wives of cabinet officers and congressmen, revolted against extravagance, pledging themselves through a "Ladies National Covenant" to buy American, to discourage luxury, and to adopt simple clothing as a symbol of support for the war. At Cooper Institute in New York City, 2,500 women met to implement the "covenant" and to form an organization to carry out their beliefs.

Yet if the press of that city served as a barometer, their deter-

mination went virtually unheeded. Female extravagance continued
unabated, perhaps fed by the inflation itself. The ladies paid sometimes a hundred dollars a bonnet in fashionable stores. Paper became very costly, yet more handbills and posters were visible than
ever before. Society folk had been content in prewar days with two
horses to draw their carriages, but during the war the four-in-hand
became a new status symbol. The theaters and other places of
amusement raised their prices as much as 50 percent and remained
as crowded as ever. The price of milk rose by 40 percent to an unprecedented ten cents a quart in New York, and went even higher
elsewhere. The price of bread doubled to ten cents a loaf; coffee sold
at seventy cents and sugar at thirty-five cents a pound. City restau-
rants charged as much for breakfast as they had previously charged
for dinner, but the hotels and dining rooms were packed. The famous penny newspapers doubled in price, magazines went up to ten
cents, yet total circulation increased. Rents in New York City rose
by 30 percent.

The newspapers pointed out the large role credit played in the
economy and warned people about mortgaging their children to the
third and fourth generation. The press observed that workmen who
made ten to twelve dollars a week before the war earned fifteen to
eighteen dollars during the war, but were paid in paper rather than
gold or silver. The paper dollar, editors lamented, was worth only
forty cents compared to gold, so workmen's real wages had shrunk.

In spite of inflation and constantly rising tax levels, railroads
continued building, horse-car lines in the cities were extended, and
court houses, city halls, churches, schools, waterworks, parks, and
private homes multiplied. Charitable works surpassed all known
records, as the Sanitary Commission, a sort of Civil War Red Cross
organization, raised millions of dollars to carry out relief work on
the battlefields and in the hospitals and camps. They raised additional millions in supplies, bedding, clothing, and food for the same
general purpose. Still further millions were contributed for nonwar
purposes, such as the building of colleges like Vassar, Cornell,
Swarthmore, the Massachusetts Institute of Technology, and scores
of others.

In the field of education Congress passed the famous Land
Grant College Act (Morrill Act) in 1862, ultimately turning over
10,000,000 acres of land to the states, the sale of which was to support at least one college in each state for "agriculture and the me-

chanic arts." The act culminated a movement for agricultural education that had begun at least a decade earlier.

Lured by the continued discovery of precious metals, by the enactment of the homestead law in 1862, and by a desire to escape enrollment for the draft, thousands of Americans headed west. By 1863 caravans of 900 to 1,200 wagons were not uncommon on the major trails. Over 14,000 homestead entries were made in Kansas, Nebraska, Iowa, Minnesota, and Wisconsin. A new gold and silver strike boosted the town of Virginia City, Nevada, from scratch to a population of 18,000 almost overnight. In Dakota Territory another Virginia City (now Montana) and Bannock City likewise mushroomed during the war because of the discovery of new lodes. Plains Indians took advantage of the war and the weakened frontier garrisons to wage wars of their own against settlers; in both the Southwest and Northwest they proved unwitting allies of the Confederacy.*

In the farm belt, wartime production of corn and tobacco declined, while the wheat harvest increased. Cotton production plummeted, and a government subsidy to encourage its cultivation had virtually no effect. Wool growers responded to wartime demands and nearly quadrupled the yield. Textile prices stayed up. The inaccessibility of Southern sugar mills caused a scarcity of that commodity, so Northerners used maple sugar and syrups as a substitute. Cattle and hog production remained stable, since the loss of Southern markets was offset by the demands of the army and increased exports. Unlike urban labor, farm labor was in short supply, due to the war's manpower demands and the increase in the number of farms. The scarcity of farm labor was not only alleviated by women, children, and the elderly, but also by an increase in the use of machinery, the sales of which more than tripled during the war years. Inflation gave farmers an opportunity to pay off their debts in money cheaper than that in which the debt had been contracted; but rising prices induced farmers to expand further, and many went still deeper into debt. Speculative farm expansion failed to pay off, and often after the war farmers faced the prospect of paying for their land and machines in much dearer currency.

Before 1861 expired, government contracts began to revive business; greenbacks, the tariff, and inflation acted as a further

---

* See Chapter 11, The War in the Trans-Mississippi West.

tonic. The textile industry, boosted by the great increase in the wool crop, flourished; woolen manufacturers declared dividends up to 40 percent, and formed the National Association of Wool Manufacturers in 1865 to protect their wartime gains. Although the cotton sector of the textile industry suffered from a lack of raw material, limited legal and illegal trading, the confiscation of Confederate supplies, and some importation prevented a complete shutdown. Wood pulp, straw, and other materials substituted for cotton in papermaking; and paper itself often substituted for leather. The ready-made clothing industry, established prior to the war, expanded with the growing use of sewing machines and often sweated labor to garner huge profits from war contracts.

Other industries that both expanded and fattened on war contracts included the iron industry, the lumber industry, meat packing, and distilling. Consolidation within industry took place partly as a result of the tax structure. A manufacturer who could purchase raw material and control all stages of manufacture to the finished product could save intermediate taxes and undersell his competitors. Expansion, consolidation, contracts, and war profits contributed to an increase in the number of millionaires and stimulated the growth of manufacturers associations for lobbying purposes and for setting industrywide price levels.

Railroad construction continued, but at a slower pace. Some Western railroads operated at capacity for the first time in their experience, partly because of the closing of the Mississippi River. Some Western as well as Eastern lines paid their first cash dividends and learned to use stock dividends to disguise profits. Railroad companies improved their roadbeds and increased their efficiency with double-tracking and the extension of the standard gauge. They tended, however, to neglect rolling stock and accidents mounted to scandalous proportions.

The United States merchant marine suffered a crippling blow from the war. Confederate cruisers like the *Alabama* accounted for a loss of $25,000,000 and 284 vessels, in all a minor loss compared to indirect consequences of the conflict. Marine insurance rates for American-owned vessels soared, giving a cost edge to competitors like the British, whose insurance houses wrote most of the marine insurance sold in the United States to begin with. Rising expenses, along with the war risk, led American shippers to seek shelter under foreign flags. Some 5,000 American vessels transferred their registry to British or other foreign protection in five years' time, virtually wiping out American oceanic commerce. Industry offered investors a more lucrative return for their money than shipping, and even the end of the war brought no relief since discrimination in insurance persisted and capital continued to flow to industry. The Civil War ended a golden age of American foreign shipping. Only a few clippers fought vainly to retain supremacy over European steamers after 1865; shipping in the coastal trade and that on the inland waterways made up the bulk of the once-thriving American merchant fleet after the war.

The laboring man and the salaried worker suffered from the war in spite of apparently higher pay and business prosperity. Wages rose by just over 43 percent, but purchasing power actually declined by a third. Wages for working women were particularly depressed, especially for seamstresses who made up about a fourth of all industrial laborers and averaged about $1.50 a week in greenbacks in 1865. All told, soldiers received about $1,500,000 in wages and bounties. But after deducting fees to bounty brokers, sutlers, gamblers, camp followers, and the like, they probably took home less than a third of that amount. Bank deposits grew from $149,278,000 to $242,619,000, but calculated in 1860 values, the gain largely disappeared. Skilled workers scored hard-won increases through collective bargaining, but employers vigorously opposed unionization and often used low-cost prison labor.

In spite of sweat shops, profiteering, the vagaries of business and finance, the North's attention remained focused on the war. At times the harsh reality, the defeats on the battlefield, the never-ending casualty lists, and the politicians' quarrels made dreary and unhappy reading in the press. But Northerners lacked no food or other critical supplies, they worked harder than ever, and they generally equated inflation with prosperity. Their morale, though challenged, remained high.

8

The Confederacy
and the War

On February 4, 1861, thirty-seven of the thirty-eight delegates chosen by the seceded states of Alabama, Florida, Georgia, Louisiana, Mississippi, and South Carolina met in Montgomery, Alabama, to form a new nation, for the individual states had never intended to set themselves up as small independent countries adjacent to the United States. A pleasant small town, the Alabama capital was chosen for its convenient location; though it lacked the office space and accommodations necessary to a national capital, Montgomery served the handful of delegates very well. The assembly named as its chairman Howell Cobb of Georgia, a slave owner experienced in both state and federal government and the most popular individual in Montgomery.

Joined shortly by colleagues from Texas, the delegates wasted no time completing a provisional Constitution for the Confederate States of America. Under the direction of South Carolina's Christopher G. Memminger, the drafting committee submitted a document almost overnight, and the convention adopted it unanimously on February 8. By its terms, the convention became the Congress of the

Confederate States and the document became law until a permanent constitution could be written or at least until one year from the
inauguration of a provisional president.

On February 9 in an effort to demonstrate their conservatism
to the world, the Congress chose Jefferson Davis president of the
Confederacy and Alexander Stephens vice president. In so doing
they bypassed many able men, including Robert Barnwell Rhett of
South Carolina, William L. Yancey of Alabama, Robert Toombs of
Georgia, and Cobb himself, in large measure because of their militant secessionist stand. The delegates regarded Davis as a moderate
and knew Stephens as a Unionist. For all his moderate views, Davis,
like many other members of the Confederate government, was a
first-generation cotton baron. In general, the old Southern seaboard
leaders had very little connection with the new government since it
was dominated by the cotton aristocracy. The Confederate statesmen at Montgomery moved rapidly in order to put a government
into operation before the Union could inaugurate Lincoln, and before any of the seceded states could precipitate an incident serious
enough to bring war while they were without a common organization. They knew that they must present a conservative as well as a
united front if they were to attract those slave states that had not yet
left the Union and if they were to convince the world that they were
not wild-eyed revolutionaries but serious men who were merely exercising their legal prerogatives.

Jefferson Davis had resigned from the United States Senate
only a few weeks earlier and had returned to Mississippi delighted
to discover that he had been appointed major general in command
of the state's troops. He had scarcely expressed his displeasure at
Mississippi's lack of arms, when news of his election to the presidency of the Confederacy reached him. He "was surprised, and, still
more, disappointed," he recalled later, since he thought himself
"better adapted to command in the field." Expecting his tenure as
chief executive to be temporary, he swallowed his preference and
departed for Montgomery.

After the inauguration, Davis formed his cabinet primarily on
a geographical basis. He found the task "more agreeable" than he
had expected, for no party structure existed to be "consulted and
accommodated." He named Toombs of Georgia secretary of state,
Memminger of South Carolina to the treasury post, Alabama attorney Leroy P. Walker to the war department (ironically, Walker felt

there was no danger of war), Stephen R. Mallory of Florida to the navy department, Judah P. Benjamin of Louisiana as attorney general, and John H. Reagan of Texas as postmaster general.*

The Confederate Congress at once set to work to write a permanent constitution. Rhett chaired a committee of two delegates from each state who, working smoothly and swiftly, closely followed the Constitution of the United States. Their labors ended when the Confederate Congress accepted their document unanimously on March 11. Aside from those sections that concerned slavery,** the Confederate Constitution differed from its model by setting six-year terms for the presidency and vice presidency and by making the president ineligible for reelection. In addition, the president was authorized to veto individual items in appropriations measures, all protective tariffs were prohibited, and internal improvements were virtually banned. The Confederate government was granted less power than the Union's federal government, while the states retained a bit more than they had in the Union. The new government was generally, however, a close copy of that of the United States.

The very traits that made it advantageous to name Davis head of the Confederate government played a significant role in the president's ultimate failure to create a nation. His conservatism and that of Vice President Stephens led them to act as if they headed a stable and established government, which in fact they did not. Both of them chose to observe carefully the provisions of the Confederate Constitution and to eschew pseudo-revolutionary action. In contrast, Lincoln as head of an established government behaved much more like a revolutionary, manipulating the U.S. Constitution whenever he thought necessary.

Davis' greatest disability was perhaps the trait he believed to be his greatest asset: trained at West Point, a veteran officer, and a former secretary of war as well, Davis fancied himself an authority on military affairs. He spent precious hours on military details as if he were the commanding general he would have preferred to be, refusing to delegate military tasks to his secretary of war or to his field commanders. His lack of confidence in the military ability of his officers and his refusal to accept their estimates of certain situations led him into needless conflict.

* Only Mallory and Reagan held their posts throughout the war. Toombs, R. M. T. Hunter of Virginia, and Benjamin took turns as secretary of state, and there were five different war secretaries, four attorney generals, and two treasury secretaries.

** See Chapter 6, pp. 169–170.

Intelligent, sensitive, and proud, Davis clung to his opinions even in the face of massive disagreement. Not only did he quarrel with his officers, he also antagonized others in his government who opposed him. His tendency to regard criticism at best as a personal affront and at worst as unpatriotic earned him many an enemy. Yet even his prickly personality might have been overcome had he had the charisma of a Jackson; instead he seemed cold and impersonal and never really stirred public enthusiasm.

In the political and constitutional struggle during the decade and a half prior to separation, Davis had supported Calhoun's states' rights ideas and incorporated them in modified form into his own thinking. As president of the Confederacy he correctly assumed that the success of the new nation depended upon unity, upon building a strong national feeling of pride and patriotism in the central government of the South. He was astute enough to shift from an emphasis on states' rights and to realize that the war could be used to turn sectional cohesiveness into national strength. Davis had an immediate advantage, for at the outset Southern morale was strong and his own popularity was at a peak. During the frantic first months of the Confederacy, Davis seemed successful, but by election time in November, signs of discontent had begun to show.

On the surface, it appeared as if Davis remained very much in command. Running unopposed for president and vice president, he and Stephens received a unanimous electoral vote. The unanimity was misleading, however, since it was the result partly of an absence of opposition candidates and partly of public preoccupation with the war. Southern leaders had called for a show of strength and support at the polls, but the election had been a humdrum affair. That, plus an undercurrent of criticism of the administration by Rhett and other officials, clearly demonstrated that popular support was hardly unanimous.

On July 20, 1861, the Confederate Congress had moved the Confederate capital to Richmond, Virginia. Confederate leaders had considered Montgomery a temporary site, and the small town had already proved inadequate. The importance and prestige of Virginia and the availability of ample accommodations led to the choice of Richmond, though Davis objected to its exposed location from a military point of view. Overruled, Davis took his oath of office as the first duly elected president of the Confederacy in Richmond on February 22, 1862, in the shadow of a statue of George Washington.

Raising the Armed Forces

Like the Union, the Confederacy first tried to build an army of volunteers. On February 18, 1861, a month and a half before Sumter and three weeks after the organization of the Confederacy, the provisional Congress at Montgomery passed an act to provide for the public defense. The law authorized Davis to receive into Confederate service "such forces" as might be in the service of the states "as may be tendered," or volunteers "by consent of their State," in whatever numbers the president might require for any time "not less than twelve months unless sooner discharged."

Davis believed that the Confederate Congress intended that a Confederate army "could only be drawn from the several States by their consent," that it would be organized by the states, that the officers would be appointed by the states except for general officers, and that arms and munitions already in the states belonged to them. His concept of an army controlled by the states paralleled the same notion in the North. The first attempts to create an army indicated that the Confederates anticipated either no war or, at best, one of short duration.

In response to Lincoln's inaugural address, the Confederate Congress reconsidered their military outlook. On March 6, "in order to provide speedily forces to repel invasion," Congress granted Davis the power to use the militia and to accept up to 100,000 volunteers. A second act of the same date created the Army of the Confederate States of America, a regular army as opposed to the provisional state-controlled army formed only a week earlier. The law specified that officers who had resigned from the United States Army would be employed with at least the same rank they had previously held.

The first three general officers to tender their services to the Confederacy were Samuel Cooper, whom Davis appointed adjutant general, Albert Sidney Johnston, whom Davis assigned to command the Confederate Army in the West, and Robert E. Lee, who took command of Virginia's forces.* Others who left United States serv-

---

* Cooper, a New Yorker, had resigned as adjutant general of the United States Army on March 7, 1861; Lee, called from Texas to Washington by General Scott, turned down a

ice to head various bureaus included Colonel Abraham C. Meyers as quartermaster general, Colonel Lucius B. Northrop as commissary general, and General Josiah Gorgas as chief of ordnance.

In order to enlarge the army and speed up its mobilization after Sumter, the Confederate Congress on May 8 and May 13 passed laws allowing Davis to accept up to 400,000 additional men as volunteers for three years or the duration of the war without waiting for the states to assent to the process. Under the Confederacy's earlier laws and state laws as well, some volunteers had enlisted for six months' time, others for twelve months. As in the Union, a confusing array of militia, state volunteers, and national volunteers appeared in the camps. Secretary of War Walker bore much of the responsibility for the ensuing confusion and proved as poor a leader as Cameron in the North. Davis and Stephens both predicted a long war and saw the need for more efficient army organization, but both were attacked and berated on the one hand by enthusiastic secessionists who feared a victory before they could participate, and on the other by jealous guardians of states' rights who dreaded the creation of a strong national government implied in a strong national army.

Volunteers flocked to Richmond as their counterparts converged on Washington. They were young, poorly armed, poorly equipped, and undisciplined; yet they arrived at the rate of about 4,000 a week. At Camp Lee outside the city well-drilled urban militia companies, rowdy westerners from Texas and Louisiana, Alabamans with scores of servants and baggage, mountaineers from Tennessee and Arkansas, and adventurers from the streets of St. Louis, New Orleans, and Nashville waited to be turned into an army. As in the Union, War Secretary Walker initially turned away nearly 200,000 eager volunteers. Then, as the first wave of enthusiasm subsided, volunteering fell off sharply. Following the victory at First Bull Run some felt that the war was over. To others, that bath of blood proved discouraging, for even victory came with pain and death, dimming the glow of the sport. Still others learned to their dismay that an army seldom fights, but often drills, marches, and most of all, waits in terrible boredom. A few young Southerners found army life worse than the lot of a slave.

Union command and resigned April 20, 1861, and took command of Virginia's troops April 23; Johnston, a native of Kentucky, resigned his command of the Department of the Pacific May 3, 1861.

Conscription

As 1861 turned into 1862, few new volunteers arrived to replace those veterans whose one-year enlistments expired in the spring. Confederate leaders faced the prospect of a Union offensive at the very moment their army melted away. The Confederate Congress vainly attempted to encourage reenlistment through promises of leaves and bounties, but Davis' call for "better measures" was finally honored on April 16, 1862, when the Confederate Congress enacted the conscription law. It put every white male in the Confederacy between the ages of eighteen and thirty-five under the jurisdiction of the president for military duty (removing state claims to their service) and extended the veteran's term to two additional years or the duration of the war, whichever might come sooner.* The law established a camp in every state to receive, organize, and train the new levies, under a commander responsible to Richmond. States' righters howled; Georgia Governor Joseph E. Brown told Davis that it was a usurpation of his sovereignty and that his state would resist the law.

Part of the law had been drafted by a member of Lee's staff at Lee's suggestion, but Congress had weakened the effect by allowing exceptions. As with the Union law a year later, a man could hire a substitute in order to avoid service. Moreover, if a person happened to be a school teacher, professor, minister, druggist, postal worker, telegraph operator, railroad worker, or a worker in various mills, mines, and foundries, a craftsman of certain types, an editor, or an officer of a state or the Confederate government, he was exempt. In addition to the long list of exempted groups, the law differed from the Union act in a unique feature: one overseer or owner for every twenty slaves could also claim immunity. Perhaps no more than two hundred persons qualified under the twenty-slave rule, but those less fortunate immediately denounced the provision, claiming it made the battle a rich man's war and a poor man's fight.

In September 1862 the upper age limit was raised to forty-five; and in February 1864 the limits were reset at seventeen to fifty, or

---

* Allan Nevins observed that this act was "a more Spartan measure than any other English-speaking land had ever enacted" and reflected that the Union passed no similar law for nearly a year, and that Britain put no such law on her books "until deep in the First World War." Allan Nevins, *The War for the Union: War Becomes Revolution, 1862–1863* (New York: Charles Scribner's Sons, 1960), p. 89.

the cradle to the grave as some opined. In December 1863 Congress closed the substitution loophole, and in February 1864 Congress removed the industrial exemptions and reduced the other categories. At the same time the twenty-slave rule became a fifteen-slave rule. As in the North, the main purpose of conscription was to encourage enlistment rather than augment the draft.

No set price existed for substitutes as in the Union. Each man had to make his own bargain or deal through substitute brokers. The price ranged up to $10,000 in Confederate currency. Governors were able to exempt militia officers, and in Georgia and North Carolina they used that device to thwart conscription. Governor Zebulon Vance of North Carolina supported the aims of the Confederacy but opposed conscription as illegal, and certified 16,000 militia as exempt. Georgia's Governor Brown favored both independence for the Confederacy and states' rights, though not in that order. He seemed determined to fight not only the Union, but also the Confederacy whenever it transgressed on Georgian sovereignty. Brown exempted over 15,000 persons from the draft, largely militiamen.

By the end of 1862 one estimate placed 500,000 men in Confederate service; but the conscription law clanked along inefficiently, providing fewer and fewer men while the armed forces dwindled steadily in size. As federal troops seized larger and larger areas of the South after 1862, they deprived the Confederacy of the manpower in those sections. The military reverses of 1863 convinced many others that the war was futile, thus increasing resistance to the draft. Desertions rose as well. By the end of 1863 about 465,000 men were listed on the muster rolls, but very likely fewer than 250,000 were actually present for duty.

Inflation and the Conscription Act operated to turn many Southerners against the government. No state had unanimously supported secession to begin with, and a few sections of the Confederacy contained active opponents. While most pro-Union Southerners had initially supported the secession of their states, the reality of war inspired mistrust of Richmond. Along with Unionists in the Appalachian regions, the Ozarks, the hill country of Alabama, and in Texas, they proved to be a disturbing influence on Confederate operations. In addition, deserters roamed virtually undisturbed through the backwoods. Secret societies advocating peace sprang up from Arkansas to Virginia. In North Carolina an opposition group called itself the Order of Heroes of America. The opponents of the

Confederacy, including Unionists, deserters, and peacemakers, encouraged desertion. That, plus the obvious Union gains by 1864–1865, caused morale to sag and over 100,000 to desert by early 1865. In a desperate effort to fill the ranks, the Confederate Congress authorized the conscription of 300,000 slaves in the last year of the war, but the fighting sputtered out before the act could be made effective.

Despite dissension and obstacles, in its four years of war the Confederacy drew an estimated 900,000 men into service, volunteers and conscripts together. The total represented a very high percentage of the South's white military-age population.

Military Supply

Jefferson Davis claimed there were about 15,000 rifles and 120,000 muskets "within the limits of the Confederacy" at the time the war broke out. He also found 60,000 flintlocks at Richmond, 10,000 Hall's rifles and carbines at Baton Rouge, "a few thousand stands" of small arms at Little Rock and some at the Texas Arsenal, for about 143,000 "serviceable arms" in all. In addition, the military organizations of the several states contributed a few thousand more, bringing the total to 150,000. Very little powder or ammunition had been stored in the Southern states, Davis noted, and he doubted if a million rounds of small arms cartridges were available.

Most of the accessible powder was captured at Norfolk early in the war, with small additional quantities at Southern arsenals, perhaps 60,000 pounds total, and most of that was "old cannon powder." At most the Confederacy had 250,000 percussion caps and no lead. There was very little artillery and no artillery or cavalry equipment. Before the fighting commenced, both the states and the central government had ordered supplies of gunpowder from the North, but shipments ceased with Sumter. Davis estimated that by June 1, 1861, the Confederacy would need 850,000 pounds of powder, a great deal more than the 250,000 pounds it had then amassed. At first the Confederacy had no machinery for the production of weapons, since, Davis lamented, "not an arm, not a gun, not a gun carriage, and . . . scarcely a round of ammunition, had for fifty years been prepared in the Confederate states." Nor, he added, were there any workmen skilled in armaments manufacture.

The Confederacy let contracts in Europe for $500,000 worth of small arms, and before Sumter they had obtained a few additional guns from the North. They removed the machinery from the Harpers Ferry arsenal and set up the rifled-musket equipment at Richmond and the rifles-with-sword-bayonets machines at Fayetteville, North Carolina. Small arms manufacture was instituted at New Orleans, but all the efforts suffered from lack of experienced workmen. The Tredegar Iron Works at Richmond cast most of the Confederate field artillery, although other small works at New Orleans, Nashville, and Rome, Georgia, made a few pieces.

The Confederacy established a powder mill at Augusta, Georgia, under the supervision of General George W. Rains, who had had practical experience in the business. By the end of 1861, Chief of Ordnance Josiah Gorgas had established eight arsenals* and four "depots" for the production of munitions and equipment. Even so, Davis observed, "the troops were . . . still very poorly armed." As with the Union, the musket was the standard weapon of the infantry, the artillery had few cannon, and the cavalry had makeshift equipment. Cavalry arms, according to Davis, included "sabers, horse-pistols, revolvers, Sharp's carbines, musketoons, short Enfield rifles, Holt's carbines, muskets cut off," and other non-regulation equipment.

By December 1861 arms began to trickle in from abroad. All told, about 600,000 stands of arms came through the blockade for both the Confederacy and the Southern states. "A good many Enfield rifles," Davis wrote, "were in the hands of the troops at the battle of Shiloh." The Confederacy further relied upon captured Northern weapons, and perhaps another 100,000 fell to them in that manner. Virginia mines supplied most of the lead, but agents collected it "throughout the country" and recovered it from battlefields as well. Davis noted that much lead was gleaned from the battlefield at Manassas. Almost every other item of supply was either nonexistent or scarce, and a priorities system was established, with shoes first on the list. Knapsacks, bridle reins, cartridge box covers, and saddle skirts were made of reinforced cotton.

The quartermaster of the Confederate Army, Abraham C. Meyers, had to secure millions of uniforms and shoes. With no existing factories that could handle the problem, the Confederate government set up its own. Diversity in uniforms plagued the Confed-

---

* The arsenals were located at Atlanta, Augusta, Charleston, Columbia, Fayetteville, Macon, Richmond, and Selma. The main depots were Richmond, Fayetteville, Charleston, and Selma.

eracy as it did the Union. At Richmond, early in 1861, Louisiana Zouaves wore red trousers, blue skirts, and embroidered vests; the Maryland Guard turned out in orange and blue Zouave attire; Georgia troops donned green, Alabama militia gray; and Tennesseeans wore fringed leggings. The task of uniforming the entire Confederate army was never completed, though the government-owned factories made progress in spite of inexperience, transportation problems, and material shortages. It was not unusual to find Confederate units wearing captured Union blue, riding saddles that were stamped "U.S.," and brandishing other items of Union equipment.

Once Kentucky and Tennessee were captured, the shortage of horses for the cavalry and artillery became acute; by 1864 one-quarter to one-third of the cavalry was dismounted for lack of animals. The troops grumbled both about those supplies the quartermaster did furnish and about those he was unable to supply. Wooden-soled shoes disgusted infantrymen, for example, and complaints rose to such a pitch that General A. R. Lawton, a Georgian, replaced Meyers in August 1863. In the end Lawton could do no better.

Northrop, the commissary general, faced the difficult task of feeding the army. In an agricultural region capable of raising enough foodstuffs to feed both the civilian population and the army, it seemed incredible to soldiers that the army experienced shortages. Davis exonerated Northrop, giving him "much credit . . . for his well-directed efforts to provide both for immediate and prospective wants"—widening the credibility gap that already existed between the president and the army. Davis explained that supply problems persisted because "the large supply of provisions which had been annually sent from the Northwest to the South could [no longer] . . . be relied on"; Southerners had not turned to food production early on because they were convinced that war would not follow secession; the railroads were "insufficient in number" and "poorly furnished with rolling stock," were dependent upon the North for rails and equipment, and were run by "Northern men" who deserted with every Confederate setback.

Northrop's inability to supply the army properly was in fact primarily due to the transportation bottleneck, and not to the reasons Davis enumerated. Although the Confederate rail network as a whole was insufficient, much of the difficulty could have been overcome had it been efficiently used. The crux of the problem lay in the Confederate conception of the strategic use of the rail network. While they understood the advantages in moving troops by rail, they never really understood the need to coordinate railroads for transporting supplies as well. Davis and his army chose to rely on the voluntary cooperation of railroad managers, rather than nationalize or militarize the roads. The operators consistently put their own welfare above that of the army, and consequently blocked any rational equipment pool or efficient schedule and effective rate control. In the spring of 1863 the Confederate Congress gave Davis the power to operate the railroads, but he never exercised the option. In February 1865 the Confederate Congress gave the secretary of war full power to bring all transportation facilities under his control, but by then it was too late. The rail network had simply disintegrated and was of no real use.

Confederate Economics

The wartime South endured deprivation, discomfort, and pain unknown in the North. In spite of a partially successful expansion of industry, it was impossible to provide either the military or the civilian population with the barest essentials. The Confederacy was forced to requisition shoes from civilians for the army, turn rugs into blankets, create cannon from plantation and church bells, and print state documents on wallpaper. The requirements of war in an industrial age put the agrarian South at a tremendous disadvantage. The need to impose a system of taxation and finance upon rural folk, who had protested the moderate demands of their former government in peacetime and who had expected relief from that burden through secession, startled Southerners like a bad dream.

The Union blockade, failure to obtain sufficient foreign financial and material assistance, and violent disagreements between the states and the central government, all contributed to the Confederacy's financial problems. The situation was exacerbated by the government's decision to finance the war by the traditional American method of taxation last. Neither Memminger nor George A. Trenholm proved capable of handling the problems as secretary of the treasury, although an expert probably could have done little better. The Confederacy appropriated the southern mint, customhouses, and subtreasuries, garnering a little over $1,000,000 in specie. State loans and private gifts provided a fraction more. A revenue tariff, of the sort Calhoun once tried to nullify, produced roughly $1,000,000 in gold value, and a tax of eight cents a hundred pounds on cotton exports brought in another $6,000 in gold value over a span of four years.

A direct tax of 0.5 percent on nearly all property yielded about $18,000,000 in paper by 1863. In that year, another act taxed various manufactures 8 percent, licensed some occupations, and levied a graduated income tax of 2 to 15 percent on incomes over $1,000. It also taxed wholesalers' profits at 10 percent, and included a levy in kind of 0.1 percent on all agricultural products. Those rates soared in subsequent measures and produced about $100,000,000 in paper, or about $5,000,000 in gold value. From all sources the Confederacy raised less than $20,000,000 in gold value, or about enough to finance the war on the Northern side for two weeks.

Loans in the form of both bonds and treasury notes were floated at frequent intervals. In February 1861, before the fighting began, the Confederacy sold $15,000,000 worth of five- to ten-year bonds at 8 percent interest. That loan produced a fair amount of specie, almost all of which was spent abroad for military materials. In the fall of 1861 the Confederacy issued produce bonds, twenty-year 8 percent loans, a more practical method of financing the war in an agricultural country. Similar loans followed, featuring the substitution of treasury notes for a specified portion of the bonds, enabling planters to sell their crops to the government, trade the bonds for notes, and spend the notes as money.

In 1863 the French firm of Erlanger and Company marketed $15,000,000 worth of cotton bonds for the Confederacy. The Confederacy netted $2,600,000; Erlanger netted considerably more in profits, selling the bonds at a 23 percent markup plus a 5 percent commission; and European investors, mostly British, lost nearly $10,000,000 with the fall of the Confederacy. The money that came to the Confederacy from the loan was invested in European-built cruisers and rams, which, due to the circumstances of the war, were for the most part never delivered. In short, the Erlanger affair aided Confederate finance very little.

A month before Sumter, the Confederate Congress authorized the distribution of treasury notes in the amount of $1,000,000 at 3.65 percent interest. Similar issues followed, some with interest, some without. By the end of 1861 over $100,000,000 worth of treasury notes circulated. In addition, states, cities, corporations, and railroad companies emitted notes in uncalculable quantities. In 1863 the Confederacy printed fractional notes to end the proliferation of private shinplasters, for as in the North, coins had been driven from circulation and change-making was difficult. Counterfeit notes circulated easily, some emanating from the Confederate military prison at Richmond. Northern presses ground out bundles of counterfeit as well, selling them at a discount to soldiers who passed them in the South. Northern greenbacks sold at premium prices. By 1863 the Confederate currency was so uncertain that many Southerners resorted to barter.

By mid-1864, $26 in Confederate notes would purchase a dollar of gold; by March 1865, it took $61, if one could find a buyer at all. In 1864 the Confederate private made $18 a month, the real value of which was $.90. As the war came to a close, the Southern soldier fought for a penny a day and failed to collect even that. From time to time, beginning in 1862, the Confederate government repudiated its currency and ordered a new issue. It began by reducing the interest rates and shortening the redemption period of bonds, then forcing the citizens to redeem their old currency in bonds or a new note issue. State governments tried the same sort of systematic repudiation, but efforts to overcome inflation in that way failed.

In spite of all note issues and attempts to manage the currency, inflation led to public complaints of a scarcity of money. The price of goods and produce remained high enough for merchants to cover any shrinkage of monetary value before the goods sold. Thus no matter how great the volume of money in circulation, it never proved sufficient for daily needs.

Southern bankers were generally more successful than the Confederate government in managing their affairs. Bankers suspended specie payment to protect their 1861 reserves of about $26,000,000, and they were cautious with their issues of bank notes, making the latter usually worth a good deal more than Confederate government notes. As an example, in 1864 they were quoted at about one to four with gold. Yet even these efforts were in vain, due to military confiscation, the collapse of the Confederacy in 1865, and military occupation of the South after the war.

On May 21, 1861, a month and a half after Sumter, the Confederate Congress passed a law sequestering all debts Southerners owed to the North, and ordering them paid instead to the Confederate government. The Union reacted by confiscating Confederate property in the North that might be used in aid of the South. The Confederacy imposed greater seizures, but none of them, including the sequestration act itself, proved beneficial. New Orleans merchants, for one example, promptly settled their accounts with New York bankers. Few planters made any effort to pay their Northern debts to the Confederacy.

The shift from cotton to food production provided the major economic change within the Confederacy. The blockade made cotton exports impossible, and the Confederacy urged planting of foodstuffs. The subsequent increased propagation of food, had there been a systematic distribution system, would have ultimately enabled all Southerners to avoid hunger. Farmers, however, hoarded their harvests to prevent seizure by the Confederate government. In its march to the sea Sherman's army found Georgia's smokehouses overflowing at a time when Lee's army was on half-rations.

The South also had a surplus of cotton on hand, despite greatly reduced cotton crops during the war years. Much was ruined by poor storage; more was destroyed to prevent Union troops from capturing it; many bales were used in fortifications; and, in the end, much cotton was captured. After 1866 cotton prices soared, but production remained below prewar levels for several years; growers' income was not sufficient to offset the great financial losses of four years of war nor the difficulties of reconstruction.

The Confederacy stimulated manufacturing, particularly of war materials. Production of textiles, leather, and the like also increased. Yet real advances in manufacturing were hampered by the Confederacy's inability to set up enough machine shops; and many new mills that survived the war despite the lack of machinery, skilled labor, and experienced management failed after the war. Southerners had no way to replace railroad rails or rolling stock that wore out or were destroyed by the Union armies, and wear and war reduced the rail system to junk.

Politics during the War

Unlike Union politics, Confederate wartime politics were nonpartisan. On the eve of the Civil War, the Democratic party in the South harbored many diverse elements ranging from former Whigs to Douglas and Breckinridge Democrats. Those divisions continued to fester, with new factions developing around issues of states' rights, war finance, and the prosecution of the war, but no political parties developed to provide a focus for disagreement or a platform for even a loyal opposition. Rather, Confederate political life suffered from personality clashes, and from factionalism that changed alignments as rapidly as the issues changed.

Planter-class Southerners and their allies, the traditional political leaders in the South, were the same individuals whose inflexibility on the national political scene had caused the breakup of the Democratic party. Unable to accept compromise or restraint before the war, they carried these same attitudes into Confederate politics. South Carolina's Rhett became one of the administration's earliest and loudest critics. Rhett, who would have liked the presidency for himself, was not even accorded a spot in Davis' cabinet. While he certainly supported Southern independence, his egotism and his concern for the Confederacy cast him in the role of a political Brutus.

Rhett had mistrusted Davis from the beginning since Davis's moderation had won him the presidency. Rhett always felt the new nation's leader should have been a revolutionary. Davis followed a defensive military policy, fighting only if attacked and then only to repel invasion. Rhett, along with Toombs and others, advocated an immediate invasion of the North. They reasoned that it would discourage the North, reduce it to impotence before it could mobilize its resources, and perhaps bring the Confederacy the foreign recognition it sought.

In the summer of 1861 Rhett assailed the administration for its military policy and criticized it for its lack of patriotism. By fall, Rhett was warning Southerners that Davis might become a despot under the guise of military necessity. Rhett's ranting inspired few supporters at first, and even Davis interpreted his own unopposed and unanimous election in November as a vote of confidence. But as the winter of 1861–1862 turned to spring, others besides Rhett came to blame Davis for the South's military disasters. Even before Davis' inauguration in February 1862 the line of defense in the west along the Ohio River had been shattered. Fort Henry on the Tennessee River and Fort Donelson on the Cumberland had been lost; many prisoners had been taken; and Albert Sidney Johnston's Confederate western army had been put in jeopardy. In the east, Roanoke Island fell, and the entrance to Albemarle and Pamlico sounds in North Carolina had been partly neutralized as a result. West of the Mississippi General Earl Van Dorn's loss at Pea Ridge sealed Missouri in the Union, and a few weeks later expansionist plans for the southwest territories exploded when General Henry H. Sibley's little army fled New Mexico after a skirmish at Glorietta Pass. In early April the defenses of the upper Mississippi River were broached as Island No. 10 fell, and on the heels of that came the catastrophe at Shiloh where A. S. Johnston died.

The stunning string of defeats provoked a chorus of protest against the Davis administration, including accusations of incompetency, inefficiency, and stupidity. In the face of this tide of criticism and sharply ebbing morale, passage of the new conscription law triggered what one historian called "the deadliest conflict within the Confederacy," * that of states' rights versus nationalism.

Governor Joseph E. Brown of Georgia denounced the conscription law as a wanton intrusion on the rights of the states, and Stephens, Toombs, and others joined Brown in questioning the constitutionality of the act. A furious attack upon the administration broke out in the Confederate Congress, led by Henry S. Foote of Tennessee in the House and Louis T. Wigfall of Texas in the Senate. Although Davis supporters in Congress defeated attempts to censure and otherwise disrupt the administration, the die was cast; the feud continued, and in the end the war-effort suffered.

Contentiousness slackened in the summer of 1862, as Lee repulsed Union efforts in the east, stopping McClellan at the gates of Richmond and sweeping to victory at Second Bull Run. George W. Randolph of Virginia, Jefferson's grandson and a leading secessionist, took over as secretary of war, contrasting favorably to the more tempestuous Benjamin, who moved to the State Department. Benjamin had come under violent attack from Davis' enemies for presiding over the winter and spring defeats. Randolph took over in time for the summer victories, and more importantly he interpreted the Conscription Act rigorously. As a result volunteering was stimulated and the armies of the Confederacy were in shape to meet the challenges of the summer.

While attacks on the Davis administration moderated during

* Charles P. Roland, *The Confederacy* (Chicago: The University of Chicago Press, 1960), p. 59.

that summer, they by no means ended or remained moderate. A credibility gap existed between the president and much of his Congress, and between Congress and many of the people. Davis often took action without informing either Congress or the people. Congress acted in secrecy, debating and legislating behind closed doors. Foote in the House and Yancey in the Senate wisely scorned congressional secrecy, but to no avail. The situation magnified public mistrust of both the administration and the Congress.

States' righters wrathfully zeroed in on the first limited efforts to suspend the writ of habeas corpus. Louisiana citizens loudly protested the suspension in New Orleans immediately prior to the Union occupation; and when General John H. Winder put Richmond under martial law to ferret out spies and other undesirables, his undiplomatic methods caused further repercussions. Alarmed, Congress curtailed Davis' authority to suspend the writ. Confederate commanders, especially in the west, also invoked martial law, sometimes over large areas. To Brown, Stephens, and Toombs, martial law and the suspension of the writ marked another step toward despotism. Foote led congressional enemies of the administration in another series of bitter attacks upon the president and the military.

In early 1863 a Mississippi representative introduced a bill to permit Davis to suspend the writ anywhere in the Confederacy as he thought necessary. Behind the bill, of course, was an effort to enforce the unpopular Conscription Act as well as to stop Unionist agitation. Nevertheless, states' righters denounced it as a menace to liberty and the constitution. Even supporters of conscription opposed the bill on those grounds, ignoring the fact that it would have provided an effective means of enforcement. With tales of ruthless generals oppressing innocent citizens ringing in their ears, Congress defeated the bill. Renewed opposition to conscription had already flared up with the passage of the Second Conscription Act in late 1862. That bill had raised powerful support, with even Yancey speaking in favor; but it also provoked determined opposition from Stephens, Brown, and Zebulon Vance, the governor of North Carolina.

Along with opposition to conscription, martial law, and anything that smacked of a threat to states' rights, the Davis administration faced still other threats to its popularity. The ruinous inflation in the South, coupled with the twin defeats in the summer of

1863 at Vicksburg and Gettysburg, turned Davis believers into disbelievers. The Confederate elections in November 1863 resulted in a tremendous growth of Davis opposition in Cóngress. Davis had no time to campaign for his supporters, but his popularity had dwindled so much that it would have been pointless even if he had. Many who still backed the administration went down to defeat, while former friends became enemies. The gulf between the president and his Congress grew so broad that no compromise could bridge it.

Yet when that new Congress met in December 1863, hostile as they were, desperate as they felt the situation was, they had virtually no alternative except to approve most of Davis' programs. Since they had no cure-all to administer, about all they could do was accept Davis' advice and grumble bitterly at the same time. They gave him a new draft law, a sharply limited Habeas Corpus Act, and a Currency Repudiation Act. At the same time they attempted to reduce his power by stripping him of the role of commander-in-chief and of various military assistants, especially the commissary general and the quartermaster general. Obstructionists Stephens, Brown, and Toombs continued their tirades, and on issues such as states' rights, Vance and other governors joined in. The states hoarded both men and supplies.

Governors Brown and Vance maintained their opposition to conscription, labeling it unconstitutional. They exempted so many militia in their effort to hobble the draft that according to one estimate about 100,000 Southerners remained in state service in early 1862. In 1864 Georgia had more men of military age at home than had been mustered into the Confederate army since the war began. Brown recalled state troops from Confederate duty when Atlanta fell, and turned a deaf ear to War Department pleas for their continued service. Unable to halt the passage of conscription laws in Congress, Governors Brown and Vance attempted to nullify their operation.

Ironically, revolutionary zeal neither overcame nor tempered the states' righters distaste for central control, however necessary, however temporary. Many preferred defeat to a victory that impaired local autonomy. Stephens told the Georgia legislature that he would not stand for independence now and liberty later. "Without liberty," he told them, "I would not turn upon my heel for independence." State sovereignty with its corollaries of local autonomy provided very little foundation for a nation. He believed that a strong Southern government was no better than a strong Northern one. "I was not born," Stephens exclaimed, "to acknowledge a master from either the North or the South."

The states' righters in the Confederacy were attracted by the idea of peace negotiations. Some clamored for a settlement on the terms of state sovereignty, especially the right of a state to run her own domestic institutions, which may have implied a restoration of the Union. Others clearly advocated peace with Southern independence as the primary condition. Vice President Stephens more than once led efforts to persuade the Georgia legislature to take the initiative in forcing the Confederacy to make a peace offer. Even in February 1865 Georgia's governor attempted to convoke a national constitutional convention in order to amend the document by replacing the president with a commander-in-chief. That complicated move would have deposed Davis and apparently would have been followed by peace overtures to the Union.

It may well be that the states' righters were prepared to effect a reunion of the nation if they could obtain a guarantee of state sovereignty and the preservation of slavery within their states. In that way the efforts of the peace advocates may have been partially to prepare Southern minds for a settlement without independence. The irony of the situation was that the Lincoln government had guaranteed as much to the South before Sumter. After emancipation, and control of the United States House of Representatives by the Radical Republicans, there was no longer any chance for a settlement of that sort.

At the Hampton Roads Conference of February 3, 1865, Davis was realistic enough to know that peace would come either by victory and Southern independence or by losing the war and capitulating to the North. Davis could not accept Lincoln's terms at the conference that the South return to the Union; but given the military and economic situation of the South and to prevent further useless bloodshed, it might have been the humane thing for him to have done.

Like Lincoln, Davis had great difficulty with his critics; but unlike Lincoln, Davis had not the power nor the ability to quiet them. Like Lincoln, Davis had a serious problem with martial law; but unlike Lincoln, Davis acted only as his Congress would permit. Davis lacked the ability to conciliate and manage people, one of the traits in which Lincoln excelled. Both men had trouble with their Congresses, but Davis vetoed over thirty bills, all but one of which was repassed over his veto; Lincoln seldom used that power. Nevertheless the situations in which each man operated were different, and comparisons are not quite fair. Had Davis operated like Lincoln, he probably would have fared little better.

Faltering Diplomacy

Remembering how important the alliance with France had been to the American revolutionaries less than a century before, Confederate leaders looked for a foreign alliance. They believed that the European appetite for cotton would provide France and especially England with an economic motive for extending national recognition. They predicted that without Southern fibers English and French mills would close and their national prosperity would be seriously threatened. Consequently, the nations of Europe in their desperation would then have to recognize the Confederacy, assist with money and possibly arms, and prevent the establishment of an effective Northern blockade.*

To bring about this result, Southerners imposed an embargo on cotton exports in the summer of 1861. The embargo was voluntary, not official, but it could not have been more complete. The 1861 crop, one of a string of heavy harvests, never left the country. Ironically, when Confederate agents protested the effectiveness of the Northern naval blockade, Europeans responded with the question: if the blockade was not effective then why was no cotton received in Europe?

In the spring of 1861 Davis sent three agents to Europe, and shortsightedly chose three men poorly fitted for the job: William L. Yancey, Louisiana's Judge Pierre Rost, and Georgia's A. Dudley Mann. Yancey was the best-known of the three, but he was not a diplomat. Cultured English leaders found it difficult to accept such an avid supporter of slavery, an institution they looked upon with obvious distaste. Yancey was also known as a ruffian who had slain his father-in-law in a brawl. The others were virtually unknown.

Toombs instructed the first mission to picture the Confederacy as a peaceful nation that had chosen to secede from the Union as a

---

* For the major outlines of the diplomatic struggle, see Chapter 13.

matter of constitutional right rather than continue to suffer oppression from the North through such devices as the protective tariff. Both the nonrevolutionary character of the South and the desire for free trade, Toombs believed, would strike responsive chords among the English. But the Confederate representatives received a chilly welcome from the British Foreign Office.

Any gains the South secured came not as a result of their mission, but as a consequence of British policy. In May, the unilateral proclamation of neutrality issued by the British government in effect recognized the belligerency of the Confederacy. If it raised Confederate hopes that recognition would follow, it failed to accomplish that end. Yancey quickly returned to the South and took up a more comfortable position as a senator; Rost and Mann fanned out to Spain and Belgium.

In the early fall of 1861 Davis sent off a new diplomatic mission, partially rectifying his earlier mistakes by now appointing men of ability. James M. Mason, former United States senator, planter, scion of a famous Virginia family, was dispatched to England, while former United States senator John Slidell of Louisiana, a New Yorker transplanted to New Orleans, headed for France. Slidell had married into the Creole aristocracy of Louisiana and spoke French fluently. The biggest drawback was Mason's avowed proslavery stand, especially undisguised because of his authorship of the controversial Fugitive Slave Act of the Compromise of 1850. British leaders may also have found his Virginia brand of English as curious as his habit of expectorating tobacco juice.

On their way across the ocean the U.S.S. *Trent* waylaid the pair, and the furor caused by their incarceration doubtless brought the British closer to the Confederacy than anything either of them was able to do after being released. According to their instructions, they, too, were to emphasize the importance of economics. Slidell had some success in France, if a sympathetic hearing could be judged success. Yet France refused to act without the support of Britain, which Mason found impossible to arrange. With Antietam and the publication of the preliminary Emancipation Proclamation all possibility of British intervention evaporated. Yet Mason and Slidell persisted. Only after Britain stopped the transfer of commerce destroyers to the Confederacy and after the Roebuck motion failed in Parliament, did it become clear even to Benjamin, by then secretary of state, how hopeless was the Confederate cause in London. Benjamin ordered Mason to Paris with Slidell, and expelled all British consuls from the Confederacy.

In addition, Davis sent Charles Helm, a Kentuckian, to Havana. Helm successfully allayed the fears Cuban leaders displayed over Southern motives since Southerners had cast covetous eyes on Cuba in the past; he set to work running the blockade from Havana. In contrast, the Davis government committed a terrible error in sending another Kentuckian, John T. Pickett, to negotiate with Juarez in Mexico. A filibusterer, Pickett had plotted Mexican annexation to the United States for years and was openly contemptuous of Mexican culture. He offered Mexicans no reason to look with favor on the motives of the Confederacy. Davis sent a more clever man, Juan A. Quintero, to northern Mexico, and Quintero successfully persuaded authorities at Matamoros to keep that port open so supplies could trickle into Texas.

Two more successful agents were James Spence and Henry Hotze in England. In his book, *The American Union*, Spence argued the constitutional legality of secession and the superiority of Southern life to Northern. Hotze established the *Index*, a pro-Southern journal that tastefully presented the Confederate case. Hotze emerged as the most influential Confederate in England.

However, the overall diplomatic efforts of Richmond suffered from the false illusion of the power of cotton, from second- and third-rate diplomatic personnel, from the English revulsion to slavery, and from English attitudes and foreign policies. Neither Davis nor his emissaries could convince the English that they should violate their carefully structured policy of neutrality. Southern handling of foreign affairs proved as disastrously inept as their handling of domestic affairs.

The Southern Homefront

The South—unrecognized abroad, largely cut off from foreign trade by the blockade, a fledgling in manufacturing, and deficient in transportation—provided a clear contrast to the North during the war. Southerners suffered from a lack of everyday necessities and from ruinous inflation. Southerners might have wondered where was the prosperity they had imagined and were promised would come with secession; they might have wondered how it was that the North went to war at all, or fought for so long, when they had assumed Yankees would do neither; they might have wondered why Great Britain had not come quickly to their aid, as everyone had supposed Britain would. It became clear that secession had created worse problems than those it had solved. In fact, Southerners were too busy grappling with their headaches and their war to spend more than idle moments complaining against those who had assured them a better place in a better world.

Not only did inflation hurt the ordinary people, but the various note issues confused them as well. The states issued treasury notes and treasury warrants, which were sometimes redeemable in Confederate treasury notes or in cotton bonds and most times were not redeemable until after the war; some were not exchangeable in any other form at all. As paper money flooded the South, prices floated atop the wave. Southerners saw little reason for the price rise, blaming it on speculators and profiteers. They protested. The citizens of Nashville, of Macon, and of Savannah held public meetings. Governors of Alabama, Georgia, Louisiana, Mississippi, and Tennessee urged their legislatures to curb speculation. The provost marshal issued an order fixing the price of produce and curbing speculators, but his order backfired. Farmers refused to market their goods, and within a month the order was rescinded.

Shortages became worse as the months passed. Tea and coffee cost too much even for people of means. Dried, ground cottonseed was added to coffee to extend it, or sweet potatoes were dried and ground to make a substitute. Acorns, washed, dried, parched, and roasted with bacon fat supposedly made "a splended cup of coffee." In 1862 in Charleston soap cost $.50 a bar, letter paper $18.00 a ream—and prices were still climbing. The scarcity of shoes brought wooden models to the general market. Citizens in the Confederate capital watched in amazement as a number of Confederate regiments marched past the War Department on Ninth Street in 1862, many of the troops walking barefoot in the melting snow, others with no blankets and no hats. In Alabama the legislature ordered the governor to seize all shoes in the state fit for soldiers. Southerners used the carpets from their floors as blankets for the army.

In December 1861 the secretary of the navy sent to Bermuda for office supplies such as letter paper, envelopes, ink, pens, erasers, and ledger books. Metal was so scarce that government agents in their search for lead took even window weights. Ordinance officials requisitioned every church and plantation bell in the South, promising replacement after the war.

Scurvy, a disease usually found only among men long at sea without fresh food, threatened the army. Every day, in place of vegetables, medical officers in the field gathered edible native plants and herbs growing near camps, from wild mustard, watercress, garlic, and sassafras to sorrel, pokeweed shoots, peppergrass, and wild yams.

For civilians, substitute medications were at hand. Dogwood berries replaced quinine. Blackberry roots and persimmons were cooked into a cordial for dysentery. Extract of wild cherry bark, dogwood, and poplar cured chills and fever. A syrup from mullein leaves and cherry bark was served for coughs and lung troubles. Finely ground charcoal was used "to keep teeth white and the breath sweet." One teaspoon of pulverized charcoal and one-third teaspoon of soda in hot water cured headaches.

Southerners made dyes as the Indians had, from berries, leaves, roots, and bark. Wood, seeds, and gourds were made into buttons; hats were fabricated from corn husks and straw. Recipes were ingenious. A wartime cookbook published in Richmond told how to make an apple pie without apples, a pie crust of boiled potatoes, salt, butter, and water, fried oysters without oysters, pumpkin bread, and a "Republican pudding" of boiled rice, milk, sugar, and butter. It included a recipe for "table beer" of treacle, ginger, and bay leaves, fermented with yeast. It advised those fortunate enough to have coffee grounds to chew them to stave off hunger and thirst.

In 1863 a Southern planter wrote that he had long since given up tea, coffee, and sugar. He observed that his coastal rice lands were so well guarded by Union gunboats that he could not market his crop. He had no more bacon for his slaves. Candles were so expensive that he burned lard with a paper taper. His family made homespun cloth.

Although in 1862 more acres had been planted in foodstuffs than in any year Southerners could remember, the crops had neither been abundant nor of good quality, especially in the southeast around Virginia. Transportation lags were felt even in the winter of 1862–1863, as the collection and distribution of crops proved difficult. In the parts of the Confederacy where people went hungry, they showed their displeasure. In Atlanta and in Salisbury, North

Carolina, mobs sacked provision shops. "Bread or Peace" placards popped up in Mobile.

Richmond witnessed a bread riot in April 1863, as militant Mary Jackson gathered women in Capitol Square to protest. The growing crowd paraded to Cary Street, looting shops of flour, meal, bacon, and any other sort of food; as they passed onto Main Street they took jewelry, millinery, clothing and similar items from the stores. Troops appeared; the Mayor of Richmond read the Riot Act; and the Governor of Virginia gave the women five minutes to disperse before he would order the soldiers to fire; bloodshed was narrowly averted as President Davis personally appealed to the ladies to go home. The next day a second crowd, of men as well as women, materialized, demanding bread, and a battalion of troops was ordered to scatter the mob. Such was spring 1863 in the Confederate capital.

Food, already scarce, became even scarcer after the passage of the Impressment Act in March. In Petersburg, near Richmond, the City Council complained that farmers withheld produce. In Savannah, a newspaper editor asked, "How are we to live?" He lamented the cost of flour at $120 a barrel and the scarcity of even a bushel of corn, meal, or grits in the city. Both grain dealers and planters fear the impressment officer, he complained; bread and meat will soon be as expensive as tea and coffee. It was November 1863.

In January 1864 the commissary general reported from Richmond that the city's supply of breadstuffs was exhausted and that Lee's army could not be supplied. Before the end of January Lee reduced army rations, telling his men he hoped the cut was temporary. Johnston's army had no meat, so the resourceful Johnston issued whisky instead. Georgia's governor refused to furnish grain for whisky because, he reminded Johnston, it was against state law. Even if it were not, the governor continued, there was not enough grain for both bread and liquor. Southern Georgia had a great deal of corn, but there was no way to transport it to Johnston or Lee.

By spring 1864 the situation had deteriorated still further. Barter was the only method of exchange in many localities. A Charleston salt maker offered a bushel of salt for five pounds of lard or bacon sides, two bushels of salt for a pair of shoes, four bushels of salt for five of peas or corn, and ten for a barrel of flour. Under the new currency repudiation acts, two dollars in new currency were paid for three of the old, so the new currency was immediately discounted by a third or prices were increased by two-thirds. Public confidence in paper money ebbed.

In 1864 the food supply in the cities was so low that thousands sought relief. Citizen protests were joined by the governors and the military, who complained about the difficulty of procuring food and who vainly appealed for a remedy. Three thousand barefoot men marched in Longstreet's army. Johnston's men had no blankets or clothing issues. Lee's army needed blankets and shoes. Bacon was nearly gone, old cattle had disappeared, and young animals were all being slaughtered. Many feared milk cows would soon be butchered for their meat and leather. The secretary of war complained that shortages of iron for the repair of farm implements held up planting food, but iron makers were busy with army contracts. The president of a Southern railroad lamented that his company had no tools for repairs and that he needed axes, shovels, and files; he proposed that the Confederacy trade cotton stores to the North for goods.

Blockade runners could have provided a great deal more assistance to the war effort than they did, but cargoes concentrated on civilian goods that would bring a large profit. They carried in cloth of all sorts (broadcloth, wool, flannel, alpaca) which retailed from $7 to $85 a yard, as well as linen shirt collars, handkerchiefs, hoop skirts, kid gloves, umbrellas, pins, needles, scissors, silver, and silver plate, all at great profit. In eight trips before she was captured, the *Banshee* made over 700 percent profit for her owners. The Confederate government attempted without success to regulate this trade. It was not difficult for vessels to transfer to foreign registry and evade all regulation, and the state governors resisted attempts to manage state commerce.

The desertions grew as the war dragged on. In mid-1864 Lee tried to bring deserters back into military service with a General Order promising leniency. Governors beseeched deserters to return to their units. Citizens asked the War Department for permission to raise regiments from among deserters provided the Confederacy would not prosecute them. A military commander in Alabama requested troops for enforcement of the Conscription Act, citing cases of unwilling conscriptees, tardiness in reporting for duty both originally and after furloughs, and obstruction of conscription by a large number of deserters. He claimed the "deserters book" in his office listed 8,000 men who had deserted between April and November

1864 from the armies of Tennessee and northern Virginia alone. Enrolling officers in Florida, Georgia, and Davis' own Mississippi reported that armed bands of deserters and "Tories" kept them from completing their work. Yet the Confederate soldier had good excuse for desertion: an army moves on its stomach, and theirs had little food; an army often marches, and theirs had few shoes; soldiers must sleep, and the army had few blankets; the wounded must be cared for, but medical supplies were at a premium; army morale depends partly on news from home, but Confederate news was not often good news.

For all the adversity that befell the Confederacy during the war, it still managed to wage a fearful defense of its desire for independence. In the eastern theater of operations the ragtag armies fought with a special discipline, effectiveness, and valor, under excellent commanders. In spite of the inflation, shortages, and other problems, the people of the Confederacy bore up for at least three years of the struggle, and some kept faith with the Confederacy until the end. And though events on the homefront and behind the battlelines contributed to the ultimate collapse of the Confederate cause, the war was still determined on the field of mortal combat.

9

The Eastern Theater
of Operations

Union armies undertook the complex assignment of invading the Confederacy, ending rebel resistance, and reestablishing the authority of the federal government, a task far more difficult than the Confederate army's single aim of defense. Union military leaders planned to send two armies south, one sweeping down east and the other west of the Appalachian Mountains. United, the two Union armies would deliver the fatal stroke to the Confederacy in the Deep South.

This strategy failed because the Confederates checked the Union advances in the East. But in the West, the Union army moved on steadily, wheeled eastward, and helped the Union forces in the East conclude the war. The heaviest fighting occurred then, in two main theaters of operation, the Eastern Theater and the Western Theater. But the war had ramifications for the entire United States, and some skirmishes took place west of the Mississippi, where a third military factor, hostile Indians, complicated the outcome. In addition, the war took on global implications as the Union navy, in addition to conducting a blockade of Southern ports, hunted Confederate raiders in both the Atlantic and Pacific oceans.

Prelude to War

Before Sumter, the United States Army served largely on frontier duty, scattered in scores of tiny garrisons from the Rio Grande to Vancouver Island, from Puget Sound to Minnesota. A few companies were located east of the Mississippi River, some in the vicinity of Washington, D.C., others at forts Sumter in Charleston Harbor, Monroe in Virginia, Taylor at Key West, Pickens at Pensacola, and a few more in the South, at Fayetteville, North Carolina, Augusta, Georgia, and Baton Rouge, Louisiana. The largest concentrations were in Texas and New Mexico, and it was in Texas that war seemed likely to explode.

The commander of the United States Army in Texas was General David E. Twiggs,* the seventy-year-old veteran of the War of 1812, the Seminole War, and the Black Hawk War, who earned his promotion to general officer for his distinguished service in the Mexican War. Located at frontier posts throughout the military Department of Texas, thirty-four companies of the regular army dutifully protected the frontier. They included part of the First Infantry, the Third Infantry, most of the Eighth Infantry, and the Second Cavalry, a total of 2,684 officers and men. On February 1, 1861, the Texas state convention voted to join other slave states in secession, if the people of Texas ratified their act in an election to be held three weeks later.

On February 5 the Texas state convention, anticipating a favorable result at the polls, appointed four commissioners to meet with Twiggs and secure the arms, supplies, and military installations in his department for the state of Texas. Three of them,

---

* Throughout the chapters on military history, each general officer will be referred to simply as "general," rather than "brigadier" or "major" general. Theoretically, brigades in the Union army would be commanded by brigadier generals, but they were usually commanded by colonels. A division theoretically would be commanded by a major general, and usually was, in Confederate service; in Union forces brigadiers usually commanded divisions. A Confederate lieutenant general commanded an army corps, but in the Union army they were commanded by major generals. The Union army's highest rank was lieutenant general, and the only one at that rank in the beginning was Scott. Subsequently Grant became the second. In other ways, rank was confusing. An officer might be a colonel in the regular army (his permanent rank) but become a brevet (acting) brigadier general, or perhaps have a volunteer rank conferred by a state of brigadier or major general.

Thomas J. Devine, Samuel A. Maverick, and Philip N. Luckett, met with Twiggs at San Antonio on February 8. A native of Georgia, Twiggs "expressed himself strongly in favor of Southern rights," the commissioners reported. Twiggs read the committee copies of his correspondence to the War Department, asserting that he would "not be instrumental in bringing on civil war." Cautiously, the commissioners concluded that that might have meant "something or nothing."

That Twiggs found himself in a dilemma is an understatement. Since December he had queried the War Department for instructions and had received none. The commissioners acted as if secession were a fact, although the people of Texas would not vote their seal of approval for another two weeks. Twiggs had asked to be relieved from duty back in mid-January, and he had not yet learned that his request had been granted on January 28, or that Colonel Carlos A. Waite, First Infantry, would succeed him. Mail moved slowly; the orders addressed to Waite arrived at San Antonio on February 15, and Waite was still sixty miles away at Camp Verde.

So Twiggs, confronting a difficult situation, told the commissioners of his willingness to maintain the status quo until at least March 2. Maverick, Luckett, and Devine believed a show of force on the part of Texas would be necessary to "compel a compliance." The Texas commissioners immediately asked Colonel Ben McCulloch (friend of Davy Crockett, Texas revolutionary, Indian fighter, Mexican War veteran, and former United States marshal) to raise a force of volunteers and report to San Antonio without delay; McCulloch promised to comply as rapidly as possible. On February 9 Twiggs appointed a military commission to meet with the Texans.

McCulloch arrived in San Antonio February 16 with about 250 men, holding another 250 in reserve about five miles outside the city. McCulloch's forces joined about 300 other armed Texans who waited in the city. With the Texans taking up commanding positions around the arsenal and the other buildings occupied by federal troops before five o'clock in the morning, the commissioners demanded that Twiggs give up all United States property in Texas. Twiggs complied and drafted General Order No. 5, which read in part, "the commanding general desiring to avoid even the possibility of a collision between the Federal and State troops," all military "posts will be evacuated by their garrisons, and these will take up as soon" as possible a "line of march out of Texas by way of the coast" with their arms, equipment, stores, and transportation, and will be ready "for attack or defense against aggressions from any source."

Twiggs surrendered the property of the United States to Texas, in return for which the Texans allowed the troops to march for the coast with their arms and equipment. The commissioners were elated, for they had carried out their instructions to the letter. They had avoided collision with the federal troops as instructed, secured the property, and peacefully removed the United States army. They would have preferred to have kept the weapons and equipment of the federal soldiers but feared they could not without a fight. "General Twiggs," the commissioners reported, "repeatedly asserted . . . that he would die before he would permit his men to be disgraced by a surrender of their arms."

While that drama played itself through, another took place. Lieutenant Colonel Robert E. Lee of the Second Cavalry, stationed at Fort Mason, Texas, had received orders from Twiggs in January to report to General Scott in Washington. Lee left Fort Mason on February 13, knowing that Scott had a special assignment for him, but hoping that it had nothing to do with any action against the Confederacy. He told friends he would resign his commission before he would fight against Virginia. By the time Lee reached San Antonio, Twiggs had completed the surrender. McCulloch's troops filled the city, and Lee feared for a moment that he might be held a prisoner. At his hotel, he changed his uniform for civilian clothes and soon discovered that Texans were in control. They intimated that unless he immediately joined the Confederacy, he might not be permitted to leave Texas. Lee rejected the overtures and replied that he would obey his orders to report to Washington. In the end the Texans let him go.

The situation proved ironic. A few months before, Lee had been acting commander of the Department of Texas during Twiggs' absence. Had the surrender demand been made at that time, Lee would certainly have refused; the first shot of the war would probably have come in Texas; and Lee would have occupied the place in history now accorded Major Anderson at Fort Sumter. On February 22 Lee reached the coast and took passage to New Orleans, arriving in Virginia on March 1.

Waite reached San Antonio on February 19, took over command, and made arrangements for the regulars to complete their

evacuation. Amid confusion and despite determination not to surrender to Texas authorities, the regular army units obeyed their orders and took up their march to the coast. On March 1 the War
Department in Washington issued a General Order No. 5 of its
own. "By the direction of the President of the United States," it
began, "it is ordered that Brig. Gen. David E. Twiggs . . . be, and
is hereby, dismissed from the Army of the United States for his
treachery to the flag of his country in having surrendered, . . . on
the demand of the authorities of Texas, the military posts and other
property . . . in his department and under his charge." Twiggs, infuriated, later threatened Buchanan with a duel over the "personal" insult to his honor. But the two old men never met. Twiggs
in May accepted an appointment as major general in the Confederate army.

On March 16 the Confederate secretary of war appointed as
colonel Earl Van Doren, a native of Mississippi, a West Pointer,
and until January an officer of the United States Army. Van Doren
was directed to go to Texas and secure "the U.S. troops for our
Army." Ten days later he reported from Texas that he anticipated
considerable success, but his efforts proved discouraging. Despite
the defection of a couple of officers, the enlisted men remained loyal
to the Union. Within another two weeks the bombardment of Sumter took place.

Meanwhile, the units of the First, Third, and Eighth Infantry,
and the Second Cavalry straggled to the coast, as vessels were being
made ready to embark them. On April 11, the day before Sumter,
Van Dorn received orders to "intercept and prevent the movement
of the U.S. troops" from Texas. "The whole of the U.S. force," read
the directive, "must be regarded as prisoners of war," and except for
those who chose to join the Confederacy, "must be held." The authorities in Texas, including Van Doren, carried out the order by
the end of April. Of the thirty-four companies originally in Texas,
the Confederates captured thirteen, including Colonel Waite. Portions of the First, Third, and Eighth Infantry surrendered at Saluria
and San Lucas Spring, Texas, and were ultimately paroled. Across
the North newspapers denounced "the traitor Twiggs" and the
Texas fiasco. A New York paper exhorted the Lincoln administration to exchange, "from among our first [Confederate] prisoners"
the exact number of those from Texas on parole, "giving the rebel

authorities notice that we do so in order to redeem the honor of our people, while we condemn . . . the acts of infamy which made them quasi prisoners of war."

The spark that would set off the war failed to ignite in Texas, the only place where substantial numbers of United States soldiers became prisoners. Neither did it ignite in Baton Rouge or Augusta, as the army evacuated those posts prior to April 15, 1861. The company at Fayetteville left after Sumter, while Forts Pickens and Taylor were reinforced before mid-April. The explosion came instead at Fort Sumter, where Companies E and H of the First Artillery, commanded by Major Anderson, took the first blow. After Texas and Sumter, several important but preliminary actions took place in 1861, one in the western counties of Virginia, one in Missouri, one in Kentucky, and one in Maryland, before the war settled down to two major theaters of operations.

Western Virginia

As Virginia seceded from the Union, so the western counties of Virginia seceded from the state in a move that climaxed with the creation of a new state, West Virginia. The military action that made West Virginia possible occurred as a Union force commanded by General George B. McClellan cleared the Confederate forces from the mountains. With one wing of McClellan's army rode Whitelaw Reid, twenty-three years old, a staff aide to General Thomas A. Morris and a war correspondent for the Cincinnati *Daily Gazette*.* Young and impatient, Reid learned, as soldiers have for centuries, of the interminably long and dull periods of waiting between the brief and exciting encounters with the enemy. As filler for his columns, published under the by-line "Agate," he commented on the fine morale, the poor uniform quality, and the character of the enemy (who exhibited an "extraordinary capacity for running").

"We are in the lull which, 'wise men' say, comes before the

---

* Reid became one of the most celebrated war correspondents in the North, especially for his dispatches from Shiloh and Gettysburg. Prior to this assignment, he had edited the Xenia (Ohio) *News*, was an enthusiastic Republican, and reported from Ohio's capital for several Ohio papers. After the war, he published a two-volume history of *Ohio in the War*; he published his account of a trip through the South in 1866, *After the War*; and ultimately succeeded Horace Greeley as editor of the New York *Tribune*. Late in the nineteenth century he served as ambassador to France and then to Great Britain. A perceptive reporter, his columns from western Virginia illustrate the boredom of camp life, the revulsion of war, and the criticism of military leadership.

storm," he wrote. We "are waiting, waiting, waiting." To while away the long hours, the soldiers practiced the sport of "eyeballing," Reid reported. Players in the game "mysteriously spirit away everything from a pistol to a camp-stool, the moment it is left for an instant beyond the range of your own eye." So fine an art did the Ohio soldiers make it, that "the old saying about the Ohio volunteers in Mexico, that if they couldn't take a town they could always steal it, applies with literal truthfulness to the camps here."

Reid complained that "this war is to be conducted on peace principles," but the army in Western Virginia's mountains slowly began to move. McClellan led one column and Morris another in an effort to trap the Confederates at Laurel Hill, near Philippi. Morris's column moved swiftly into position, but McClellan's wing was delayed, and Reid complained of "more warfare on the peaceable system." Reid's fears that the Confederates would escape proved correct when, at dawn on a warm July day, a reconnaissance mission revealed that Confederate General Robert S. Garnett had pulled out in order to escape the obvious trap.

The ensuing drama was characteristic of green troops on both sides in many other episodes in many other places throughout the war. The pursuing soldiers of Morris's column stalled immediately in the recent rebel campsite. They beheld in great disarray "camp stools, tables, camp cots, camp chests, underclothing, uniforms, overcoats, bundles of books, drawers, shirts, knapsacks, valises. . . . axes, . . . bowie knives, shovels, inkstands, love-letters, spurs, boots," and many other items. "The accumulation of bottles was amazing. . . . And of playing cards, what *shall* I say? . . . The whole camp was sown broadcast with cards and whisky bottles," Reid observed, "not a single one [bottle] found with anything save the memory of departed spirits." The Union troops worked "like beavers" accumulating all they could carry. Looting the camp delayed the pursuit longer and more effectively than did the obstacles the retreating Confederates placed in the road.

The chase continued into the next day, this time in mud and rain. Unable to catch the Confederates, the Union soldiers took to calling them the F.F.V., the fleet-footed Virginians. At Carrick's Ford, Garnett himself directed a short but hard-fought rearguard action when a portion of McClellan's advance party stumbled upon them. Garnett, the first Confederate general to fall in battle, died on a bluff above the ford. Reid arrived shortly thereafter, and chronicled what he saw. "Along the brink of that bluff lay ten bodies, stiffening in their own gore. Others were gasping in the last agonies, and still others were writhing with horrible but not mortal wounds." Sickened by his first battle, Reid wrote: "Never before had I so ghastly a realization of the horrid nature of this fraternal struggle." Sadly, he realized that "these men were all Americans." Reid's reaction at Carrick's Ford to the horror of death and the irony of Americans fighting Americans was not unlike the same reaction of thousands of others in similar circumstances. The glamor of war faded as Reid exclaimed: "May I never see another field like that!" He lived to see worse, at Shiloh and Gettysburg.

The skirmishes at Laurel Hill were not very important in themselves. Yet Reid, the experienced newsman, described much that was relevant. The waiting, the delays, the missed signals, the looting of the enemy camp, and the disillusion and sickness after battle marked nearly every campaign, major and minor, in the years to come.

McClellan's reputation soared, for when the campaigns were over western Virginia rested securely in Union hands. The savior acclaimed by most of the press was the stocky, red-haired general from Ohio; but McClellan's reputation foundered on the point of Reid's pen. Reid wrote that the plan had been "to *catch* the [Confederate] army, instead of driving it. *That has failed. . . . he didn't catch them!*" McClellan gave the rebels "ample time to see the trap closing. . . . Of course they escaped. . . . This," wrote Reid acidly, "is the culmination of the brilliant generalship, of which the journals of the sensational persuasion have been besmearing with such nauseous flattery."

The "flattery" won McClellan the command of the Eastern armies, but McClellan did not disappoint Reid's expectations. After the war, Reid observed that "the historian who shall seek to trace in detail the steps to the strange torpor that subsequently befell the Army of the Potomac may indeed find in . . . [the West Virginia campaign] suggestive hints."

General William S. Rosecrans succeeded McClellan in western Virginia and was ordered to mop up and to force Confederate General Robert E. Lee out of the mountains, a task Rosecrans completed largely because Lee's forces were inadequate to the contest. Lee's ill fortune in western Virginia stained his reputation with the

Confederacy until his defense of Richmond the next year bleached the stains away.

Missouri

"Missouri . . . will in my opinion best consult her own interest, and the interest of the whole country," Governor Claiborne Fox Jackson exclaimed in his inaugural address in January 1861, "by a timely declaration of her determination to stand by her sister slave-holding States, . . . with whose institutions and people she sympathizes." Jackson, who had supported Douglas in the 1860 elections, left no doubt where he stood on the matter of secession. The new session of the Missouri legislature called for a state convention to examine the question, with the promise that if an ordinance of secession resulted it would be subject to a plebiscite. The convention adjourned March 22 having expressed itself in favor of the Union and compromise.

Attention focused on St. Louis, its United States arsenal, and the 60,000 stand of arms located within. Secessionists coveted the arsenal, which was under the command of a Southern sympathizer. But early in February a company of United States Army regulars arrived in St. Louis, headed by young, red-bearded Captain Nathaniel Lyon. Lyon, a Yankee from Connecticut and an antislavery Unionist, had observed the activities of Missourians in Kansas in the 1850s from his station at Fort Riley. He was determined to prevent the arms in the St. Louis arsenal from falling into the hands of secessionists. Francis P. Blair, an old Jacksonian who had been Senator Thomas Hart Benton's right-hand man, who had organized the Republican party in Missouri, and who was an intimate of Lincoln, shared Lyon's aim. (Blair's brother had been named to Lincoln's cabinet.) Blair and Lyon hit it off famously, and together were as responsible as any two persons could be for keeping Missouri in the Union.

Lyon commanded the men stationed at the arsenal, but the physical plant and stores remained under the control of Major Peter V. Hager, an officer of secessionist proclivities. Shortly after Sumter, Lincoln set Missouri's quota of volunteers at 4,000. Governor Jackson refused to provide any troops, claiming that the call self was illegal. Public meetings in Missouri supported the governor's stand. Blair, meanwhile, had received permission from Washington to muster the St. Louis Home Guards into federal service in order to fill Missouri's quota, and shortly after that Lyon received full command of all forces around St. Louis.

Around midnight on April 25 Lyon secretly transferred the weapons from the arsenal to Illinois and safety. Within a few days he received additional orders to enlist up to 10,000 men to protect Missouri and to declare martial law in St. Louis if necessary. Blair had been instrumental in getting Lyon this authority.

Governor Jackson, on his part, had mobilized the militia and sent to the Confederacy for assistance, which arrived early in May in the form of light artillery. Lyon determined that it would be necessary to prevent those arms from being used by the state militia at nearby Camp Jackson. Thus on May 10 Lyon's forces surrounded the camp and demanded its surrender. Their commander complied; Lyon arrested the militia, but someone started shooting and before the smoke cleared twenty-eight persons lay dead and many others wounded. As a result of the Camp Jackson affair, riots broke out in St. Louis, lasting overnight.

The governor had called the legislature into session at Jefferson City on May 2, but Unionists had immobilized it. Then came news of the shooting at Camp Jackson. The legislature passed immediate measures for financing the militia, then panicked when rumors spread that Blair was about to descend upon them with three regiments of soldiers recruited from among the German population. The rumor proved false, but the whole Camp Jackson affair drove many borderline Unionists into the governor's camp, including Sterling Price, a former governor who had chaired the recent state convention. Jackson appointed Price to command the Missouri State Guard and ordered the enrollment of militia. Over a thousand men had already gathered at Jefferson City.

An agreement on May 21 between General William S. Harney, Lyon's superior, and Sterling Price in effect brought a truce. Harney agreed to respect the neutrality of the state, and both men agreed to maintain peace. Yet there were indications that Unionists were still harassed by the Missouri government; and Blair, not satisfied with the truce in any case, secured Harney's removal by the end of May. Lyon was promoted to brigadier general of Missouri volunteers by the War Department and assumed command of the Department of the West and Missouri. To Price this meant the agreement with Harney had been abrogated, so he stepped up recruiting.

Conservatives still hoped to avert conflict within the state, and a meeting was called in St. Louis early in June to work out another compromise. After a futile four-hour discussion Lyon adjourned the meeting with the words, "this means war." The state officials fled to Jefferson City, burning bridges after them to thwart pursuit. Jackson called for 50,000 volunteers to fill the ranks of the state guard and joined Price at Boonville where state troops were supposed to rendezvous. On June 14 Lyon occupied the capital without opposition, and three days later his forces drove the state troops from Boonville. Jackson now headed a government-in-exile. A new state convention soon deposed Jackson and his government, establishing a Union government for Missouri. The Union prevailed, and though Missouri became a guerrilla battleground it remained in the Union.

Kentucky and Maryland

Kentucky was in a dilemma. Secessionists called for an assembly to take the state out of the Union, Unionists demanded that the secessionists be hanged. The legislature vacillated, then finally on May 20 resolved to be neutral. Governor Beriah Magoffin, though secessionist oriented, issued a neutrality proclamation. The citizens were too divided emotionally to remain neutral, and secessionists drilled the state militia in southern Kentucky. The Unionists, in turn, formed companies of home guards. President Lincoln remained cautious, aware that neutrality kept the state from seceding. Jefferson Davis, however, grew increasingly sensitive about Union troops gathering in southern Illinois near Columbus, Kentucky, a point Davis hoped to make into a stronghold, one of the anchors of the Ohio River defense line.

In late June elections for Congress and for the state legislature resulted in Unionist victories and increased Confederate uneasiness about the fate of Kentucky. Before the summer was over, the Confederacy sent General Leonidas Polk to seize Columbus and another force to secure Louisville. In effect, the Confederacy invaded Kentucky. The Kentucky legislature asked the Confederate troops to leave, vaulting their bill over the veto of Governor Magoffin. The legislature called out the home guard, and asked for help from the

United States. Illinois troops commanded by General Ulysses S. Grant crossed the Ohio and occupied Paducah. Kentucky's neutrality ended; officially the state threw its lot in with the Union, though another year would pass before Union armies secured it.

Maryland, too, was divided, but so far as the Union government was concerned, Maryland was vital. The national capital lay cradled on the banks of the Potomac, with Maryland astride its communications with the North. Both "Dixie" and the "Star Spangled Banner" could be heard in the streets of Baltimore. When the Sixth Massachusetts Volunteers marched through on their way to Washington, D.C., April 19, 1861, they were attacked by a hostile crowd that forced the soldiers to open fire and clear the way to their train with bayonets. A few soldiers were killed in the melee as were a somewhat larger number of their assailants. After the troops left, rioters destroyed bridges, burned railroad stations, and cut the telegraph to Washington. The capital was in near panic, but additional troops arrived in short order and the expected Confederate attack failed to materialize. The Maryland legislature made cautious overtures to the Confederacy, although Governor Thomas Hicks attempted to block outright secession. Union forces occupied Baltimore. The transit of other Union troops to the capital continued unhindered. Some members of the Maryland legislature were placed under arrest; a closely supervised election in November brought a Unionist government into power. Maryland, too, was secured for the Union.

Major Campaigns of 1861 and 1862

First Bull Run

A major factor in the Eastern Theater of operations was the continuous Union search for a successful commander. One after another, from the outbreak of the war until March 1864, six commanders unsuccessfully attempted to bring the war in the East to a conclusion. In contrast, the Confederates enjoyed excellent leadership from the beginning. Their first commander, General Joseph E. Johnston, served with distinction until he was wounded; then Robert E. Lee, the superb field general, assumed command.

General Irvin McDowell was first to lead the Union's Eastern armies. A career officer, he fought a well-planned battle at Bull

Run and lost through no direct fault of his own. His object was Manassas Junction, a station on the best overland and rail route to Richmond. The Manassas Gap Railroad joined the Orange and Alexandria line at the junction, winding westward from there through the gap of the same name into the rich Shenandoah Valley. Recognizing Manassas' strategic value, the Confederates seized and fortified the junction in May 1861. On June 1, 1861, the hero of Sumter, General Pierre G. T. Beauregard took command. A few hours away down the Manassas Gap Railroad General Joseph E. Johnston's command rested in the valley.

The Confederate activity in Virginia distressed Washington, and the public demanded an immediate stroke against Beauregard's forces. McDowell resisted the pressure as long as he could, for no one knew better than he that his army, composed for the most part of ninety-day volunteers, lacked adequate training. But at the same time, unless he made use of these volunteers, their term of service would expire, and the process of training a new army would delay operations even longer. On July 16, 1861, McDowell reluctantly put the army in motion. Moving out of the defenses of Washington, his forces successfully invested Fairfax Courthouse, moved on to Centerville, and by noon of the eighteenth gathered there ready to strike.

Members of Congress and their ladies climbed into their carriages and rode to Centerville to watch the battle as if they were going for a Sunday picnic. McDowell struck at Manassas at dawn on Sunday, July 21. His army quickly turned the Confederate left, but Thomas J. Jackson rallied his men, made his stand on Henry House Hill (earning the nickname "Stonewall"), and prevented the Union forces from driving the Confederates from the field. Johnston and Beauregard arrived on the scene shortly before noon, giving a boost to Confederate morale. The Union forces kept up the pressure, and the battle raged with considerable intensity between 2:00 and 3:00 P.M.

At about 3:45, just as it appeared the Union army would win the day, Johnston's army arrived from the valley and delivered a determined attack on the Union left. The Union position was a strong one, but the untrained troops in their baptism of fire had had enough. It had been a long day, and morale plummeted when they saw Johnston's fresh troops join the battle. They broke and fled.

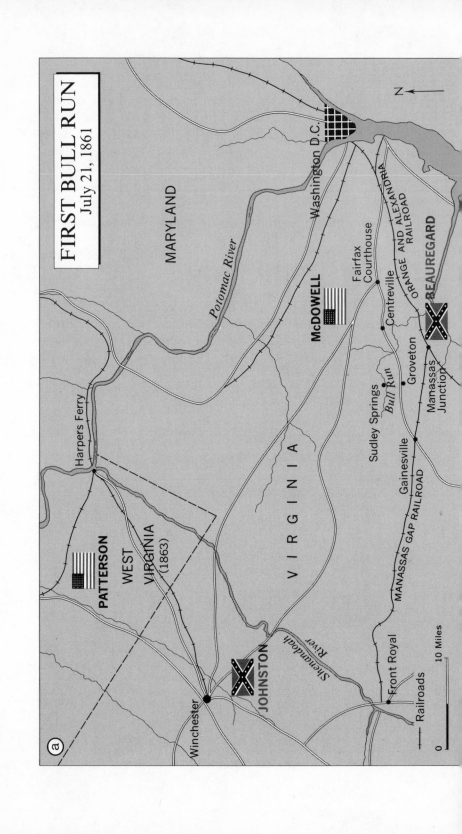

FIRST BULL RUN
July 21, 1861

MARYLAND

Potomac River

Washington D.C.

N ←

VIRGINIA

WEST
VIRGINIA
(1863)

Harpers Ferry

Winchester

Shenandoah
River

Front Royal

PATTERSON

JOHNSTON

MANASSAS GAP RAILROAD

Gainesville

Groveton

Sudley Springs

Bull Run

Manassas
Junction

McDOWELL

Centreville

Fairfax
Courthouse

BEAUREGARD

ORANGE AND ALEXANDRIA
RAILROAD

ⓐ

0   10 Miles

━━━ Railroads

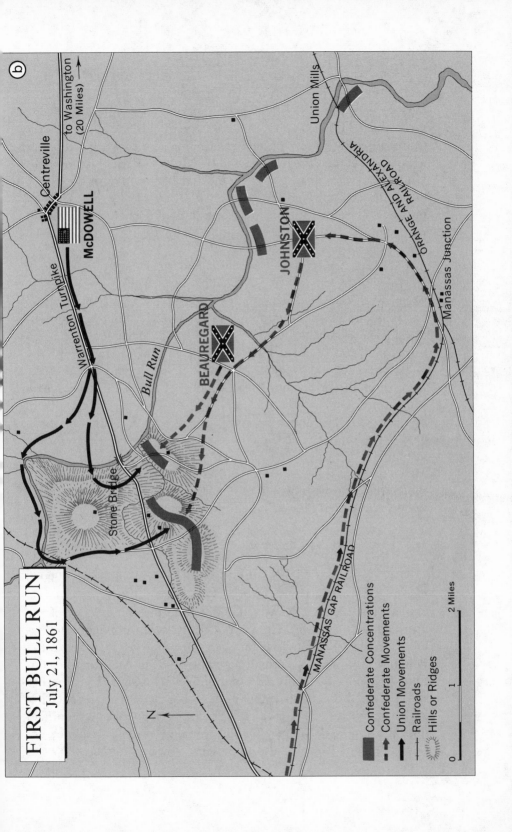

FIRST BULL RUN
July 21, 1861

N

to Washington
(20 Miles)

Centreville

McDOWELL

Warrenton Turnpike

Bull Run

Stone Bridge

JOHNSTON

BEAUREGARD

Union Mills

ORANGE AND ALEXANDRIA
RAILROAD

Manassas Junction

MANASSAS GAP RAILROAD

Confederate Concentrations
Confederate Movements
Union Movements
Railroads
Hills or Ridges

0   1   2 Miles

The Union rear was a scene of incredible disorder. Confused soldiers clogged the roads to Washington; panic-stricken civilians, their picnic a disaster, joined in the muddle; wagon masters tried to save their supplies; ambulances attempted to evacuate the wounded; and artillery pushed rapidly into the crowd. Fortunately a battalion of regulars commanded by Major George Sykes held the Union rear with great discipline and terrible losses until the Union army crossed Bull Run. Fortunately also, no effective Confederate pursuit followed, for the green, exhausted Confederate soldiers wasted much time and energy looting Union camps and gawking at Union prisoners.

His prestige damaged by the defeat, McDowell was replaced on July 27 by George B. McClellan, fresh from his victories in western Virginia. McClellan had an ability to buoy up the spirits of his troops, and his unusual talent as an organizer quickly improved the efficiency of the army. On the other hand, McClellan was a sensitive man and resented interference from others. He continually quarreled with old General Winfield Scott, nominally the commander of the army, until on October 31, 1861, Scott resigned. McClellan openly criticized the War Department for its political appointments and made powerful enemies in Washington. As a field commander, McClellan distressingly overestimated the strength of his opponents on nearly every occasion. In politics, McClellan was a Democrat, and that, coupled with his criticism of the War Department, won him the open hostility of Stanton, one of the most powerful figures in Lincoln's cabinet.

The Peninsular Campaign

By the end of October 1861 McClellan commanded 138,000 men in training in the vicinity of Washington. Once more public opinion favored an advance; but this time the commander of the army refused to give in. He was not ready for a campaign. On October 21 McClellan had incautiously thrown 2,000 men across the Potomac at Ball's Bluff, only to lose half of them. After that he continued training the army and planning a campaign. The weather stayed clear through November and most of December, yet McClellan's army waited. McClellan fell ill with typhoid and was confined until the middle of January. Public opinion clamored for Union action. President Lincoln, also impatient, issued an order on Washington's birthday for the advance of all armies, East and West. Obviously the order was not practical; McClellan ignored it. By that time, however, he had perfected his plan.

The general proposed to take the army by water to Fort Monroe and to move from there toward Richmond via the peninsula between the York and the James rivers. His flanks would be protected by the navy, which would also keep his lines of communications open. The government immediately objected to this plan, warning that the move would expose Washington, D.C., to the Confederate army. McClellan pointed out that so long as his army moved on Richmond, the Confederates would be too busy to think about the capital. Lincoln remained cool to the plan, but consented to it provided that enough troops stayed near to defend Washington. McClellan set out, then discovered that McDowell and 40,000 troops on whom he had counted would be retained on the Potomac in front of Washington. McClellan complained, but Lincoln would not yield.

By early April 1862 McClellan had gathered 100,000 men at Fort Monroe and cautiously begun his advance. At Yorktown the Confederates threw a defensive line across the peninsula, only thirteen miles wide at that point. McClellan's advance ground to a halt, even though the line could easily have been carried. McClellan believed it required siege operations, and he delayed a month bringing up heavy guns and constructing entrenchments of his own. When McClellan was finally ready to lay siege, the Confederates quietly withdrew. McClellan followed, on occasion engaging the Confederate rear guard. Meanwhile the fleet moved up the York River and seized White House Landing, twenty miles from Richmond. McClellan made the landing a supply base for his army, and by May 16 was only ten miles from Richmond.

In the face of the Union advance up the peninsula, the Confederates evacuated the Norfolk Naval Yard and destroyed the ram *Virginia* (the old *Merrimac*), which they could not remove. That operation left the Union fleet free to operate on the James River as well as the York, and they ascended as far as Drewry's Bluff, eight miles from Richmond, where a strong artillery battery held them back.

Since the Confederates had failed to move on Washington, Lincoln allowed McDowell to move to Fredericksburg, from which location he could easily march to support McClellan. But on May 24

Lincoln recalled McDowell because of a Confederate threat to the capital from the Shenandoah Valley.

McClellan's approach to Richmond prompted Stonewall Jackson to create a diversion in the Shenandoah Valley, in hopes of creating enough panic in Washington either to draw McClellan back or at least to dilute his forces. The Shenandoah Valley offered a sheltered approach to Harpers Ferry, located sixty miles from Washington and seventy-five miles from Baltimore. Stonewall Jackson had an army of 18,000 men in the southwestern part of the valley, while Union General Nathaniel P. Banks kept tabs on him with a force of perhaps 15,000 in the valley near Strasburg. Another Union force of about 15,000, commanded by General John C. Frémont, lurked in the mountains to the west. A third Yankee force, led by Robert H. Milroy, one of Frémont's officers, was stationed west of Staunton, so that if Jackson should close on Banks, Milroy's troops could cut off Jackson's retreat.

Jackson soon proved his superiority by giving the Union generals a lesson in how to handle a divided enemy with an inferior force. Jackson unexpectedly hit Milroy first, defeating him and pursuing him northward. Stunned by Milroy's defeat, Frémont recovered too slowly to be effective. Marching rapidly back into the valley, Jackson turned on Banks at Strasburg. Banks had just turned 10,000 of his troops over to McDowell, to take to McClellan's aid. When he discovered Jackson nearly upon him and closing rapidly, he put the remainder of his weak army in flight. Nipping at Banks's heels all the way, Jackson caught him at Winchester on May 25 and sent his forces reeling for the Potomac. The pursuit ended at Harpers Ferry.

Jackson's unexpected and successful action stirred great concern in Washington, which the administration guessed was Jackson's objective. At this point, the president recalled McDowell from Fredericksburg and sent him into the valley south of Jackson, hoping to cut the Confederates off. Frémont also received orders to move into the valley, where he was to cooperate with McDowell and capture Jackson. Jackson, however, had accomplished his mission. Aware of his danger, he about-faced and marched rapidly south to escape the trap. With luck and hard marching, he avoided encirclement, turned on his tormentors, hurt them in two sharp engagements, took a number of Union prisoners, and captured rich supply trains.

Near Richmond, McClellan had remained perfectly safe without McDowell. He commanded 120,000 men—nearly twice Johnston's 63,000—and his scouts were in sight of the Confederate capital. Back at Williamsburg McClellan had directed two corps of the Union army south of the Chickahominy River and the three others north of it to protect the supply route and to keep the way open for McDowell. Swollen by spring rains, the high river by the end of May isolated the two corps to the south from the main body of the army. Johnston seized the opportunity on May 31 to engage this segment of the Union forces at Seven Pines. Johnston fought hard, but the Union forces, though driven back, were not beaten. Another Union corps successfully reinforced the beleaguered units in the afternoon, and still other troops arrived by the next morning. By evening of June 1 Johnston's army had been pushed back to its original position. Johnston himself had been wounded late on the first day, and when his troops arrived within the defenses of Richmond they were under a new commander, General Robert E. Lee. Lee set the army to work at once refining the defenses of Richmond to withstand an attack by McClellan. He once again had an ally in the spring rains, for the dirt roads had turned to mud and were impassable to the Union army artillery.

McClellan, however, did not plan to follow the affair at Seven Pines with an attack on Richmond. Rather, he intended to approach the city slowly, lay siege, and blast the defenses with his superior numbers of cannon. Lee—and Confederate President Davis—preferred not to stand and wait for an attack, since McClellan's strength would give him too great an advantage.

Lee ordered Jackson to outrun the Union forces in the valley and march rapidly to a position on McClellan's north flank, where Lee would join him. Swiftly they would cut McClellan's communications, knock his army off balance, and send it fleeing in disorder back to the York River. Jackson responded quickly and moved into position on June 26, facing the only Union corps still north of the Chickahominy. Lee detached three divisions from Richmond to join Jackson. On June 26 the Confederate troops slammed into the Union corps at Mechanicsville, but their communications had broken down: Lee's three divisions had arrived on the scene in the morning and commenced the action, but Jackson did not arrive until late afternoon. The Union corps, commanded by Fitz-John Porter, repulsed the Confederates who, with 55,000 troops to the Union's 25,000, planned to renew the attack the following morning.

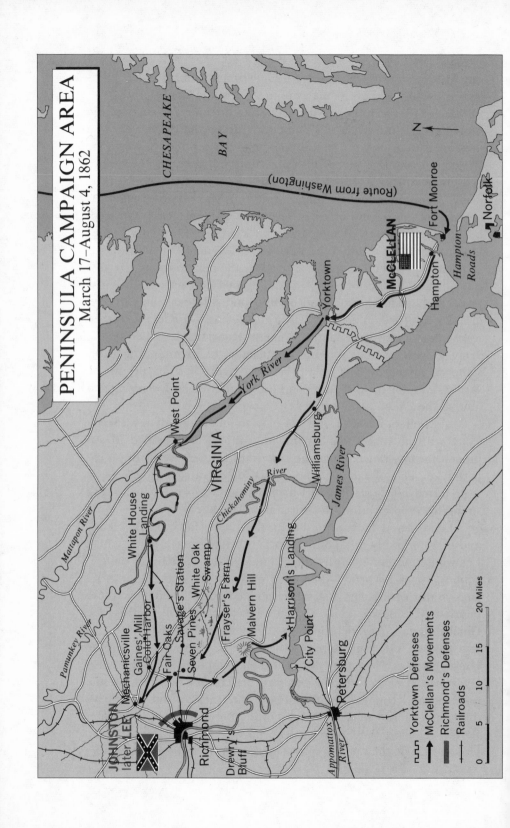

PENINSULA CAMPAIGN AREA
March 17–August 4, 1862

CHESAPEAKE

BAY

N

(Route from Washington)

McCLELLAN

Fort Monroe

Hampton

Hampton Roads

Norfolk

Yorktown

Williamsburg

York River

West Point

James River

VIRGINIA

River

Chickahominy

White House Landing

Savage's Station

White Oak Swamp

Frayser's Farm

Harrison's Landing

Malvern Hill

Mattapon River

Pamunkey River

Mechanicsville

Gaines' Mill

Cold Harbor

Fair Oaks

Seven Pines

City Point

JOHNSTON
later LEE

Richmond

Drewry's Bluff

Petersburg

Appomattox River

꘍꘍꘍꘍ Yorktown Defenses

▮ McClellan's Movements

▮ Richmond's Defenses

─── Railroads

0   5   10   15   20 Miles

During the night Porter fell back to a position at Gaines' Mill, where the Confederates found him in the morning. He checked their second attack but, overwhelmingly outnumbered, retreated across the river in late afternoon. At this point, McClellan still had 60,000 men facing Richmond, while Lee had reduced his forces within the city to only 25,000. McClellan could have struck the Confederate capital with every chance of success; he did not because intelligence reports convinced him that Lee still had a 100,000 man force within. McClellan refused to listen to his quartermaster, whose estimates of Confederate strength were more realistic.

Having cut the Union line of communications, Lee thought McClellan would either fight his way back to the York River to reopen the line or retreat down the peninsula to Fort Monroe. McClellan instead shifted his communications line to the James River. Lee misinterpreted the ensuing movement of Union forces as the beginning of a retreat down the peninsula, and he made plans to follow McClellan at a safe distance. Unwittingly, Lee gave McClellan the time he needed to shift his base without losing a single supply wagon. When Lee discovered McClellan's actual move, he marched quickly but ran into a strong Union force at Savage's Station on June 29, and another at Frayser's Farm on June 30. By July 1 McClellan had his army safe on the banks of the James River and was busily establishing his new base at Harrison's Landing.

Still expecting Lee to fall upon his army, McClellan established a strong cover position at Malvern Hill. Lee hesitated to attack for a time. But believing that he had shaken the Union army's confidence in the fighting from Gaines' Mill to Frayser's Farm, he incautiously soon hurled his troops against the new Union positions. McClellan awaited the assault with his infantry well dug in, and his artillery set to sweep the field with a murderous cross fire. The Confederate attack ended abruptly in unexpected slaughter.

The Seven Days' Battles, from June 26 to July 1, cost McClellan almost 16,000 casualties and Lee nearly 20,000. The fighting was fierce, but McClellan held Harrison's Landing twenty miles from Richmond. McClellan had not sustained a clear battlefield defeat; he had cleverly changed his base of operations, and his army remained ready and capable of taking the field at any time. Lee, though his losses had been costly, had ended the immediate threat to Richmond.

If the army's confidence was not shaken, McClellan's was. He asked Lincoln for reinforcements, complained of McDowell's withdrawal, and planned to remain at Harrison's Landing until reinforcements came and he could move out against Richmond with a numerically superior force. Lincoln and his cabinet had other plans. They refused to send more troops to the peninsula; they called John Pope east in July and early in August sent orders for McClellan to return to Washington. Discouraged and bitter, McClellan lashed out at Lincoln, the government, the rest of the army, and John Pope.

Second Bull Run

When Pope arrived in Washington early in July 1862, he was put in command of the troops under Frémont, Banks, and McDowell—about 45,000 men in all. In mid-July, he moved his army southward toward Culpepper Courthouse, threatening Gordonsville, a junction on the Virginia Central Railroad that runs north and west from Richmond. Pope's idea was to cut Richmond's communications from the west, catching Lee between his army and McClellan's on the peninsula. But Henry W. Halleck, who was general-in-chief in Washington, undermined the plan with his inefficiency. If he grasped the significance of the situation, Halleck showed no evidence of it. Rather, he forwarded orders for McClellan's withdrawal and for McClellan's corps to join Pope's army.

When Lee observed McClellan preparing to embark his army from the peninsula, he quickly detached Jackson with 24,000 men to delay Pope. On August 8 Jackson fell upon Banks, with Pope's advance, at Cedar Mountain. Already defeated once by Jackson in the valley, Banks now fought bravely, with only 8,000 men. He refused to be routed, and held on until reinforced late in the afternoon. Jackson then halted and awaited the rest of Lee's army. Lee's scouts reported that McClellan continued to embark troops, and with this information, Lee rushed most of the remainder of his army to Jackson.

Pope discovered Lee's plan from a captured document. Aware that it would be impossible to pen Lee up in Richmond and that the bulk of Lee's army would soon face him at Culpepper, Pope fell back to the north bank of the Rappahannock River. Only thirty-five miles away, elements of McClellan's army disembarked at Aquia Landing, moving to reinforce Pope. Lee's opportunity, as he saw it, was to engage Pope's army before McClellan could reinforce it. Daringly, Lee divided his own army, sending Jackson on another quick march to Pope's rear to cut Pope's communications at Manassas. If the plan succeeded, Jackson would be in the rear before Pope discovered him, and by the time Pope could fall back, Lee would have sent the rest of his army to join Jackson; he would thus force battle on Pope before Union reinforcements could arrive. Lee's plan worked almost perfectly.

On August 25 Jackson swung west of the Bull Run Mountains and suddenly appeared at Manassas, burning storehouses and supply wagons, and cutting the telegraph. Pope searched out Jackson, but by the time he found him, the remainder of Lee's army was coming on the field. Without a firm grasp of the situation, he ordered Porter's corps (a part of McClellan's army, which had reached him) to attack Jackson's right; but Porter found Longstreet in his way and refused to sacrifice his men in what he believed to be a futile attack. Pope, believing Longstreet still beyond the Bull Run Mountains, again ordered Porter to attack, and again Porter refused. For his action, or lack of it, Porter was later court-martialed and removed from command. Many years after the war, Congress exonerated and reinstated him. Though Pope attacked without Porter on August 29, his assault on the center of the Confederate position was repulsed.

Rather than retreat, Pope renewed the battle on August 30. Porter, stung by criticism of his action the previous day, fought hard but to no avail. Lee took the offensive, forcing the Union army back upon the old Bull Run battlefield, where it made a desperate stand to protect its comrades as they withdrew. When the army had safely removed across the creek, it blew up the old stone bridge and retreated in good order to the defenses of Washington.

As Pope's army tramped back to Washington, Lee sent Jackson in pursuit. Pope had foreseen the possibility, and waiting for Jackson at Chantilly were Union troops commanded by Phil Kearny and Isaac Stevens. They stopped Jackson on September 1 in a hard fight during which they both lost their lives.

Pope, believing himself still in command of the army, sent cavalry patrols out to watch Lee and planned the reorganization of the

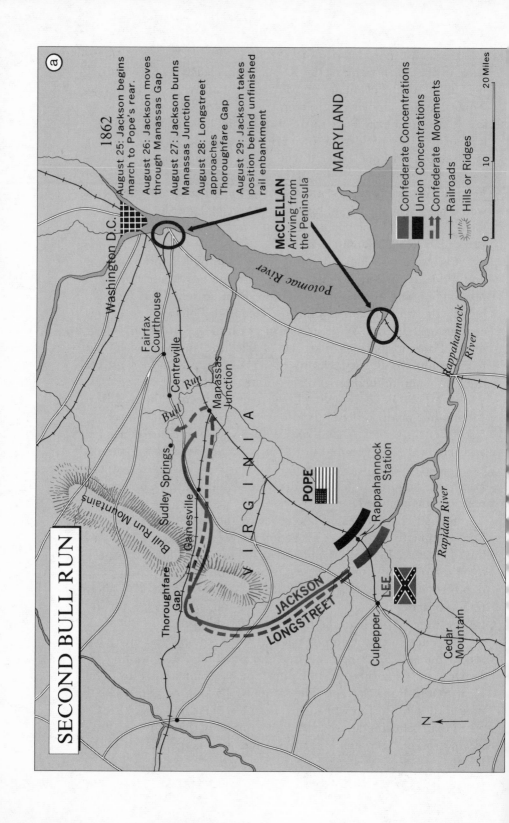

SECOND BULL RUN

1862

August 25: Jackson begins march to Pope's rear.

August 26: Jackson moves through Manassas Gap

August 27: Jackson burns Manassas Junction

August 28: Longstreet approaches Thoroughfare Gap

August 29: Jackson takes position behind unfinished rail enbankment

McCLELLAN Arriving from the Peninsula

Washington D.C.

Fairfax Courthouse

Centreville

Bull Run

Manassas Junction

Sudley Springs

Gainesville

Thoroughfare Gap

Bull Run Mountains

VIRGINIA

POPE

Rappahannock Station

Rappahannock River

JACKSON

LONGSTREET

LEE

Culpepper

Cedar Mountain

Rapidan River

MARYLAND

Potomac River

Rappahannock River

Confederate Concentrations

Union Concentrations

Confederate Movements

Railroads

Hills or Ridges

0   10   20 Miles

N

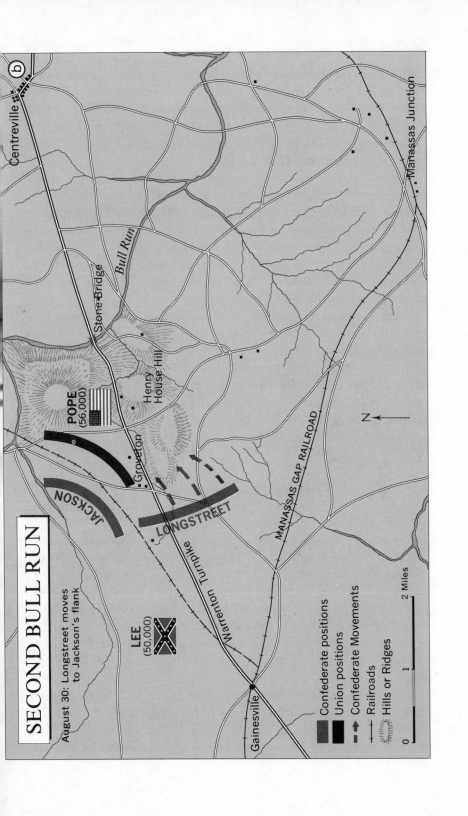

SECOND BULL RUN

August 30: Longstreet moves
to Jackson's flank

Centreville

Bull Run

Stone Bridge

POPE
(56,000)

Henry
House Hill

Groveton

JACKSON

LONGSTREET

LEE
(50,000)

Warrenton Turnpike

Gainesville

MANASSAS GAP RAILROAD

Manassas Junction

N

- Confederate positions
- Union positions
- Confederate Movements
- Railroads
- Hills or Ridges

0   1   2 Miles

army. Lee saw no advantage in butting up against the defenses of Washington nor in remaining at Manassas awaiting another Union attack. He decided immediately to move into Maryland, to recruit and feed his army, and then to invade Pennsylvania, perhaps threatening Harrisburg or Baltimore, or both. Shadowed by Union cavalry, Lee began to cross the Potomac.

McClellan, meanwhile, had impeded the movement of troops to Pope's aid. "Leave Pope get out of his own scrape," McClellan groused. With Pope's defeat at Second Bull Run, Lincoln made McClellan commander of the defenses of Washington. A grinning McClellan was thus on hand to grant Pope permission to enter the defenses of the city. Ironically, Pope returned to Washington in the company of McDowell, one of his officers, who had made this same return journey from Bull Run once before.

In Washington, Pope was much criticized for his failure at Second Bull Run. In turn, he ungraciously blamed his subordinates and threatened to publicize an unflattering report in an effort to vindicate himself. He had lost Lincoln's confidence and more importantly the faith of the troops. Lincoln wanted no further dissension in Washington, so he transferred Pope to Minnesota, where a serious uprising of the Sioux Indians kept him occupied. Once more, McClellan took command of the army.

Antietam

Lee's march into Maryland had diplomatic as well as military repercussions. In Kentucky, pro-Confederates Kirby Smith and Braxton Bragg began an operation to secure that state; President Davis hoped that Lee's invasion and the Kentucky campaign would impress Europe, particularly England, enough to recognize the Confederacy as a nation. By September 7 Lee's entire army of about 60,000 men, including troops he had previously left at Richmond, had crossed the Potomac. To Lee's chagrin, Maryland farmers refused to sell their grain and drove off their cattle, forcing Lee to open a supply line through the Shenandoah Valley. The cork in the bottle was Harpers Ferry, garrisoned by over 12,000 Union soldiers.

In order to open the supply line, Lee sent Jackson against Harpers Ferry. Lee gambled again in dividing his army in the face of the enemy, but he was confident that his opponents would close on him slowly and felt he faced little risk. Jackson's march was rapid, and on September 14 he occupied the hills surrounding the ferry. The garrison surrendered without a fight.

Meanwhile, the morale of the Union army rose under McClellan's leadership. By Steptember 10 he had completed his reorganization and set out in pursuit of Lee. On the twelfth McClellan reached Frederick, a few days behind Jackson's troops. On the thirteenth a Union private found a dispatch that showed Lee had divided his army. McClellan decided to follow the book and place his own army between the two parts of Lee's.

Had McClellan marched swiftly at that point, he could have slipped through the passes of the South Mountains only twelve miles away and succeeded in positioning his forces between Lee's two groups. But he moved slowly, and by the time he reached the passes the Confederates had occupied them. It took hard fighting to clear the way, but McClellan managed by September 14. Lee had learned of the lost dispatch by then and rapidly fell back from his advance toward Hagerstown. At Sharpsburg he stopped, dug in, and in a strong position with Antietam Creek at his front, awaited Jackson. After taking Harpers Ferry and opening the road south, Jackson turned around and immediately moved to join Lee. If McClellan had forced battle on the fifteenth, while Jackson was at Harpers Ferry, he would still have had Lee at his mercy with only half an army. But McClellan seldom moved fast. Before he moved to Antietam, he held up to let his army recover from the sharp skirmish in the mountains. The Union army remained idle on the sixteenth except for minor skirmishes, and Jackson's force closed fast.

Three Union corps did approach Lee's left on the sixteenth, and Lee strengthened his position. On the morning of the seventeenth, the Union forces attacked. "Fighting Joe" Hooker, commanding one corps, was wounded; and Joseph Mansfield, commanding another, was killed; the Union attack was repulsed. McClellan then ordered an assault on the right, where Confederate lines had been thinned to meet the attack on the left. This Union strike was at first successful, but at a critical moment part of Jackson's army arrived, went directly into battle, and drove the Union attackers back to their starting point. Then the sun set, darkness covered the field, and the battle of Antietam ended. Lee suffered over 10,000 casualties, McClellan over 12,000.

When dawn came on the eighteenth, both armies remained in position, each expecting a counter blow. But McClellan failed to renew the battle, and Lee prepared to slip back across the Potomac. On the nineteenth Lee's army moved away, unimpeded. The North considered Antietam a victory, even though the action on the field resulted in a draw. Lee's invasion had been stopped, and the Confederates had retreated back south of the Potomac. However, McClellan's shortcomings, including his failure to contest Lee's retreat, cost him the command of the Army of the Potomac. On November 5 the new commander, Ambrose Burnside, the officer with the luxurious side whiskers, took over.

Fredericksburg

Burnside, who did not relish taking command of the army, knew that the situation called for an advance against Richmond. Two railroads ran southward from the Potomac, one by way of Manassas through rolling country and across narrow rivers, the other from Aquia Creek through Fredericksburg to Richmond, over slightly rougher country and across wider rivers. McDowell in 1861 and Pope in 1862 had tried the first way. Burnside chose the second. When he was ready to put his army in motion, Lee and Longstreet were in camp at Culpepper Courthouse and Jackson was stationed in the Shenandoah Valley. Burnside's engineers busily constructed pontoons for a bridge that could be thrown across the Rappahannock at Fredericksburg.

Burnside maneuvered the army to the north bank of the river before Lee caught on, but the pontoons were late in arriving. Burnside's thrust was blunted, and he could not cross the river to occupy the heights south of the town before Lee arrived on the scene. By the time Burnside finally bridged the river, Longstreet was in position on the southern heights and Jackson was marching to his aid. The Army of the Potomac numbered about 113,000 men; Lee faced it with approximately 78,000.

On the heights Longstreet held the left flank and Jackson, when he arrived, the right. Burnside divided his army into three segments; one commanded by Hooker was held in reserve on the north bank, and two others, under William B. Franklin and Edwin V. Sumner, crossed the river. Protected by the streets of Fredericksburg, Sumner faced Longstreet, and Franklin confronted Jackson. Burnside was indecisive, knowing he faced an ominous situation should he decide to assault Lee's strong position. Early on December 13, he sent an order to Franklin worded so ambiguously that

Franklin did not know if he should attack or just make a reconnaissance that tested Jackson's strength. Burnside seems to have intended that Franklin attack, but in doubt, Franklin merely sent a division forward to penetrate Jackson's line; it was not well supported, and fell back with heavy losses.

Next it was Sumner's turn. His forces moved out of the town toward Marye's Heights, which Longstreet defended. Artillery bristled along the crest, and at the foot of the hill Confederate infantrymen crouched behind a stone wall. A canal bisected the plain which Sumner had to cross—a difficult barrier in the open. Moreover, Longstreet's artillery enjoyed a clear field of fire across the plain. Six times Sumner's men charged across the field, virtually unprotected when the artillery opened up. Each time they took great losses. Hooker came across the river, sized up the situation as impossible, and returned to urge Burnside to give up the senseless slaughter. Burnside instead continued until 8,000 of his men lay dead on the slopes. Casualties totaled over 12,500 for the Union and over 5,300 for the Confederacy.

On December 15 a violent storm raked the field, and under cover of darkness, Burnside's men withdrew to the north bank. The troops were dispirited; the nation mourned their defeat. Burnside's officers quarreled openly with him, until he asked the government either to dismiss them or to accept his resignation. On January 26, 1863, the government accepted his resignation. Hooker, Burnside's chief critic, assumed command.

The Campaigns of 1863

Chancellorsville

The men respected Hooker, and his appointment restored the soldiers' confidence. By spring the Army of the Potomac was eager to test Lee again. With new additions its forces numbered 122,000. Lee, who had remained in Fredericksburg, counted barely 60,000. In April Hooker broke camp and sent three corps upriver thirty miles, where they crossed and turned back toward Chancellorsville, less than ten miles from Fredericksburg. A fourth Union corps soon joined them. By clever marching, the Army of the Potomac had moved into good position south of the river, on Lee's flank, with over 40,000 men. Another 20,000 soldiers crossed the river south of Lee's position and threatened his rear.

On May 1, 1863, Hooker's army suddenly met Lee's troops coming toward him. He stopped, uncertain, and fell back on Chancellorsville. There he chose a position with his back to the river and dug in—awaiting attack. Hooker's staff advised against the move, pointing out that with his numerical strength Hooker should have attacked rather than suddenly assume the defensive. A part of Hooker's line was anchored in the Wilderness, a region of thick undergrowth difficult to move troops through and impassable for artillery.

In spite of his smaller force, Lee poised, ready for the attack on May 2. While the Confederate line feinted against the Union front, Jackson detoured and fell unexpectedly on Hooker's extreme right, routing one corps and demoralizing the corps in position next to it. Then darkness fell; Hooker awaited morning and a renewed assault by the terrible Jackson. Yet Jackson did not appear the next day: At dusk he had ridden out with some of his staff to reconnoiter, and when the Jackson horsemen returned, a Confederate volley had greeted them; Jackson fell wounded, was transported to a hospital, and died the next week.

On May 3 the battle flared again, and by mid-morning the field belonged to Lee. Hooker seemed incapable of making decisions, dazed as he was by a cannonball that had struck a column of the porch against which he had been leaning. All Hooker could think of was retreat, and he moved his army back toward the river ford.

Meanwhile, behind Lee came the other wing of the federal army, driving before it the men whom Lee had left at Fredericksburg. Turning his back on the retreating Hooker, Lee confronted the new menace, forcing that wing of the Union army to slip away to safety across the Rappahannock on the night of the fourth. Once more Lee wheeled around, hoping to confront Hooker again; but by the evening of May 6 Hooker had crossed the river. The three days of fighting at Chancellorsville cost Hooker and Lee over 10,000 men each. Lee had scored another big victory.

Gettysburg

Conditions now made a Confederate offensive necessary. Vicksburg, under siege, would clearly fall, and Lee needed another victory to offset the loss. He in fact needed a victory as decisive as the capture of Harrisburg, or Philadelphia, or Baltimore, or even

Washington. Another victory in Virginia would solve little and would only inflict battle wounds on that state, which had suffered enough. Lee further calculated that a great victory would convince the North, already tired of defeat, that it was useless to continue the war. The enlistment terms of many of the Union soldiers were due to expire that summer, and the Union would thus be short of veteran soldiers. So an invasion of the North at this point might convince the North to make peace on Southern terms—to accept the independence of the South.

Calling up Longstreet, who was no longer at Chancellorsville but involved in the West, Lee boosted his troops to about 76,000. The Army of the Potomac could count few more until new levies could be assembled. Longstreet commanded a third of Lee's army, Richard S. Ewell now led Jackson's third, and the other third marched under Ambrose P. Hill. Jackson's old foot cavalry took the lead, starting out for the Potomac via the Shenandoah Valley on June 10. Ewell easily cleared the valley of Union troops, crossed the Potomac on June 15, and marched on to Hagerstown. Hill's corps followed a few days behind, and Longstreet brought up the rear. Lee's cavalry busied themselves screening the movement and did the job so effectively that his intentions were not apparent to Hooker until Lee was well underway. James E. B. Stuart, in command of Lee's cavalry, actually passed into Pennsylvania between Washington and the bulk of the Union army, via York and Carlisle, and arrived at Gettysburg on July 2. By then his horses were too exhausted to contribute much to that encounter. At Hanover, Stuart's cavalry fought a rough skirmish with Union cavalry, a branch of the army that Hooker had much improved. Stuart's absence from in front of Lee allowed the Union army to observe the Confederate forces more closely, and it was thus able to initiate a more rapid pursuit and engagement than Lee expected.

Simultaneously Ewell moved swiftly toward Harrisburg with Jackson's troops. On June 27 he reached Carlisle and sent a division east to York, forcing that town to pay ransom. A Pennsylvania militia regiment prudently burned a bridge across the Susquehanna River, thereby preventing the division at York from moving on Harrisburg from the east. At Carlisle Ewell prepared to attack Harrisburg with his main force.

Hooker now led the Army of the Potomac across the Potomac to Frederick. But Halleck and he disagreed over the campaign so seriously that Hooker offered to resign rather than tolerate Halleck's meddling. Washington accepted his resignation, and on June 27 General George C. Meade took over. By now the Union forces numbered 115,000. Meade marched north to put his army between Lee and Baltimore, crossing the line into Pennsylvania on June 30. Having learned of the Union pursuit, Lee sent Hill at once to Gettysburg, ordered Longstreet to follow, and on June 29 directed Ewell to rendezvous at the same place. The Confederate movements convinced Meade that Lee expected to fight, and Meade did not wish to disappoint him; but the Union commander was determined to pick the time and place. He selected Pipe Creek, just south of the Maryland line, about thirteen miles from Gettysburg. To slow Lee while he made preparations, Meade sent three corps under John F. Reynolds ahead to Gettysburg, with orders to fall back as they were pressed. Ahead of Reynolds rode Napoleon B. Buford's Union cavalry; the entire contingent arrived in Gettysburg during the evening of June 30.

On July 1, Hill and Longstreet were tramping along the Chambersburg Pike to Gettysburg. Ewell proceeded over the road from Carlisle to Gettysburg. Over the roads from the south marched Reynolds. Early in the morning Buford distributed his cavalry across the approaches to Gettysburg north of the town: on Seminary Ridge, a wooded area commanding the Chambersburg Pike. About 9:00 A.M. Hill's leading regiments came into sight, formed a battle line, and began the skirmish. Buford's regulars held until about eleven o'clock and were about to fall back when Reynolds' troops arrived. Both Confederate and Union soldiers moved into new battle lines, and the fight continued. Reynolds fell, dead, about noon. Still the Union troops held the line, until mid-afternoon when Ewell's vanguard approached from the north, threatening the Union flank. The Union line fell back, Ewell took Seminary Ridge and pushed his soldiers on through the town of Gettysburg. Retreating Union soldiers gathered on Cemetery Hill, south of the town, in some confusion. Had Ewell continued his advance at that time, Meade's original plan to fight it out at Pipe Creek would have followed. But Ewell halted; and Winfield S. Hancock, who arrived to take Reynolds' command, quickly sized up the situation, observed the strength of the position, ordered the army to dig in, put his artillery in position, and sent messengers to Meade, urging him to bring up the rest of the army and fight at Gettysburg.

As he rode up Cemetery Hill, Hancock observed how well the high ground there gave artillery excellent play, how a ridge runs away from the hill southward for a mile or more, ending at another hill, Little Round Top, with a still larger hill, Big Round Top, beyond it. East of the cemetery on top of the hill was a gully, beyond that, Culp's Hill. Hancock recognized the excellence of the position for an army fighting on the defensive. The slopes away from the position were ideal for artillery. Stone walls and large rocks furnished cover for infantry. The horseshoe shape of the position gave it the advantage of short interior lines, and the hills at each extremity provided, excellent protection against flanking movements. Meade took Hancock's advice, and by nightfall the remainder of the Army of the Potomac marched up. Meade himself arrived after midnight, agreed with Hancock's estimate, and by dawn, July 2, the position was well defended.

The two armies kept up a brisk fusillade all morning. Opposite the Union position, Hill's corps occupied Seminary Ridge. On Hill's left, Ewell's line stretched as far as Culp's Hill. Longstreet, ordered to move from Hill's right and take Little Round Top at dawn, hesitated, because he understood the strength of the Union position and opposed forcing a battle against the Union defenses at Gettysburg. He suggested that Meade be flanked out. But Lee remained firm in his determination to assault the Union army, and Longstreet finally attacked in the afternoon.

Meade's staff, meanwhile, had proposed attacking the Confederate center, but Meade had refused, anticipating an assault just as Lee had ordered. When it failed to materialize in the morning, Meade ordered Daniel E. Sickles' corps out to probe Confederate preparataions. About four o'clock in the afternoon, Longstreet's corps charged, but reeled back when struck by a barrage from Union artillery. Another charge formed, again the Union artillery opened fire, and Confederate cannon replied. After two hours, Sickles was pushed back to the Union lines, which held firm. Longstreet failed to occupy Little Round Top. At dusk Ewell attacked the Union right, carrying all before him as darkness fell, ending the July 2 battle.

At a staff meeting that night, Meade told his officers that the losses had been heavy, that the army had been pushed back on both wings, but that he intended to stand and fight another day, to the finish if necessary. Turning to John Gibbon, Meade remarked that

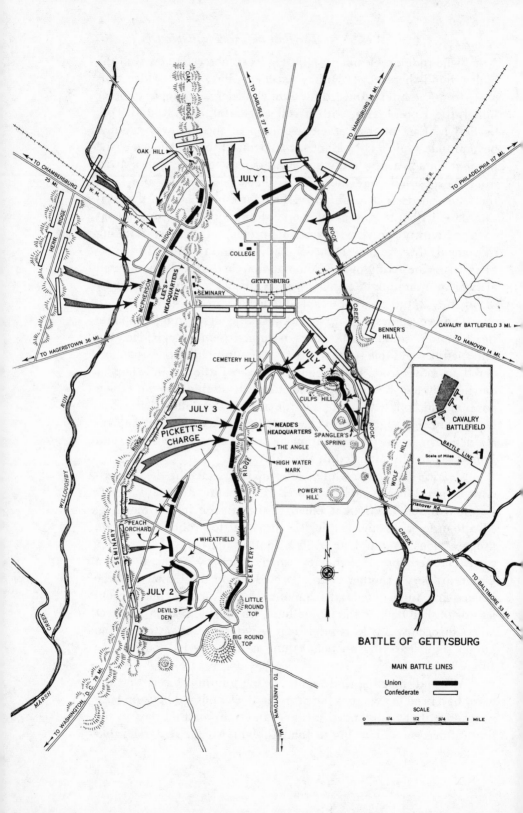

BATTLE OF GETTYSBURG

MAIN BATTLE LINES

Union
Confederate

CAVALRY BATTLEFIELD

SCALE

0   1/4   1/2   3/4   1 MILE

it would be his turn tomorrow, for Lee had struck the flanks and would next hit the center. Meade guessed correctly.

The firing renewed at dawn, July 3, as both sides attempted to readjust their positions. Lee prepared for his all-out assault on Meade's center. At one o'clock 250 Confederate cannon opened on the Union positions, and Union artillery replied. The great artillery duel lasted for about an hour, when the Union artillery ceased fire to conserve ammunition. As if that were the signal, Confederate guns slowed their barrage as well. George E. Pickett's division of 5,400 men faced the Union lines on Cemetery Hill, with orders to penetrate. Hill's corps readied another 10,000 men for support.

Pickett's division began their move across the mile that separated the lines. "Down came the rebel lines . . . as if for a parade. . . . They were well up to our front," wrote correspondent White-law Reid, when the opposing Union corps "sprang up and poured out their sheet of flame and smoke, and swiftly-flying death." The Union batteries opened up again when Pickett's men were six hundred yards away. "The solid lines broke," leaving great holes in the advancing columns, which bravely continued without wavering. At closer range the cannon fell silent, and the thick ranks of Union infantrymen crouching behind the batteries rose up and charged. But the advance did not break until it had caught the Union infantry and carried it back behind the batteries, where yet another solid Union rank rose to oppose the gray lines.

"In some places," Reid observed, "they literally lifted up and pushed back our lines," but as they stormed the Union position "enfilading fires . . . swept away their columns." The Confederate "line literally melted away, but there came a second. . . . Up to the rifle-pits, across them, over the barricades—the momentum of their charge . . . swept them on. . . . They were upon the guns," Reid recalled, "were bayoneting the gunners, were waving their flags above our pieces." Then "the enfilading fire of the guns on the western slope of Cemetery Hill" hit them. "The line reeled back . . . in an instant in fragments. Our men . . . leaped forward upon the disordered mass; but there was little fighting now. A [Confederate] regiment threw down its arms," and the battle was over.

Pickett's gallant charge had been "such a sight as few men may ever hope to see twice in a lifetime. . . . it was a sensation for a century!" exclaimed the reporter. Hancock, though severely wounded, personally directed the Union struggle, throwing out regiments to take the Confederate charge in the flank. For a time, as Pickett's men actually passed the Union artillery, the battle hung in the balance. But the charge was in vain, for the attackers either died, were captured, or retreated back across the deadly plain, now literally carpeted with bodies. Lee's army, badly shaken, prepared to receive the countercharge it felt would come; but Meade's plans were defensive, and the Army of the Potomac remained at its lines.

Night fell, and soldiers from both sides slept in their places, exhausted. All the next day, the Confederate army remained undisturbed by the Union forces, and on July 5 they began their withdrawal southward. Meade made no real effort to impede their crossing of the Potomac on July 13. Three days of the battle cost Lee over 28,000 casualties, and Meade, about 23,000. The victory, wrote Reid, had been "a clean, honest, acknowledged victory." Yet it had been a narrow one, for "there stood in the rear just one single [Union] brigade that constituted the entire reserve." Reid criticized Meade for not following up the victory.

From Lee's standpoint, the battle of Gettysburg had been a hazardous undertaking. With his army of about 76,000 he had invaded enemy territory to fight an aggressive engagement with an entrenched and well-placed army of over 88,000. The only justification for the attack was Lee's confidence that he could beat the Union army, an assurance born of his experience with Pope, Burnside, and Hooker. In Meade, Lee faced a more competent commander. Meade was not a brilliant man, but at Gettysburg he showed no serious faults; he had the confidence of his army and the War Department, advantages his predecessors in command had not. The victory at Gettysburg was made all the sweeter for the Union, as news arrived from Vicksburg on the Mississippi River that the Confederate garrison had ended the two-month seige by surrendering to Grant on July 4. Union armies, east and west, had won two great victories to be celebrated on Independence Day.

After Gettysburg the two armies remained inactive in Virginia. Lee maneuvered some to keep Meade in the northern part of the state, but neither side in the eastern theater risked battle during the fall. This was the autumn that Bragg faced Rosecrans and Grant in the vicinity of Chattanooga, and neither North nor South wished to complicate that campaign with another. On November 18, 1863, Lincoln spoke at the ceremony to dedicate the Union cemetery at Gettysburg.

The Campaigns of 1864 and 1865

Grant Takes Command

In March 1864 Grant came east, was promoted to lieutenant general, and assumed command of all Union armies, east and west. He joined the headquarters of the Army of the Potomac, and although Meade remained actual commander of that army, Grant directed its movements from then on. Short, grizzly faced, and round-shouldered, in a wrinkled plain blue uniform, cigar clenched between his teeth, Grant contrasted sharply with the splendidly outfitted officers riding desk chairs in the capital.

Grant's strategy was simple, as it always had been: move on the enemy with everything available, and if he doesn't move, try again. He told Sherman that he wanted to "work all parts of the army together," that is, to apply constant pressure on the Confederacy, both east and west, making use of the North's superior manpower. He informed Sherman that he intended to hound Lee's army "wherever it may be found," and he instructed him to break up Johnston's army and "get into the interior of the enemy's country as far as you can, inflicting all the damage you can against their war resources. . . ." Grant brought to the Union armies, for the first time, a unified command, and with it the single objective of destroying the enemy forces.

Grant completed the reorganization of the cavalry, making it a separate and more effective arm, and placed it under the command of Philip H. Sheridan. He ordered much of the garrison of Washington, heavy artillery, cavalry escorts, and the like, into the field. He sent inspectors general through the hospitals, paring down the staffs and putting convalescents back with their units. His officers toured the military departments west of the Mississippi, cutting their garrisons to the bone. He reorganized the Army of the Potomac, turning five army corps into four, three for offensive operations and one to guard communications. By May the Army of the Potomac, reorganized, well-drilled and well-equipped, numbered around 102,000 men, in camp just north of the Rapidan River, on the railroad that ran through Manassas. Just south of the same river Lee camped, with about 61,000 men, also well-drilled but lacking many of the necessities of war.

On May 3 Grant crossed the Rapidan, moving by his left into the Wilderness area of the Chancellorsville campaign. The vigilant Lee confronted the Union army on May 5 in this area his men knew so well. Although Grant threw his army at Lee, his superior firepower proved of little use, and in two days of hard fighting, Lee checked him. When Lee did not fall back as Grant expected, Grant marched off to the left again. Lee anticipated Grant and on May 8 faced him, dug in in a strong position at Spottsylvania Courthouse. Grant assaulted Lee at once but failed to break the Confederate line. On May 12 Grant took 8,500 casualties; still Lee repulsed him. Giving up his attempt to break through Lee's army, Grant flanked to the left again. From May 5 through May 21, Grant's losses numbered 34,000 men.

Grant stopped at the north bank of the North Anna River on May 23, only to find Lee ahead of him on the other bank, well dug in. Without bothering to attack, Grant marched off to the left flank yet again—with Lee anticipating the maneuver. By these encounters—in some ways similar to Sherman's moves against Johnston— the two armies maneuvered ever closer to Richmond, facing one another at Cold Harbor on June 2, six miles from Richmond. Lee's army now included an additional 14,000 men. Grant, hoping to crush Lee before he could further improve the defenses of Richmond, ordered an attack all along the line. At dawn, June 3, the grand assault came, involving 80,000 Union soldiers. In the face of tremendously heavy fire, the assault failed within twenty minutes, with a federal loss of 7,000 to a Confederate loss of 600. Grant was severely criticized for the useless loss of life; later he admitted the assault had been an error. But the results of Cold Harbor convinced him that he could not crush Lee in battle; so he moved across the James River in order to lay siege to Richmond. From Wilderness to Cold Harbor, Union losses mounted to 55,000 to Lee's 39,000.

On June 14 Grant crossed the James River at City Point, linking up with troops commanded by Ben Butler. Butler's army of 30,000 had been landed on the banks of the James two months earlier, with orders to move in and take Petersburg, thus cutting Richmond off from communication with the South. But with a small force, Beauregard had managed to thwart Butler's move. Grant now ordered Butler to attack Petersburg at once, but Butler failed to move promptly. The next day Grant's own advance corps received the same order, took the outer works, and halted. Since

Petersburg was weakly defended, they might have been successful if they had pushed on. But the next day Lee's army arrived to defend the city, and the opportunity was lost. By June 18 Lee discovered that all of Grant's army had marched south of the James, so he prepared to defend Petersburg.

The Last Siege

Grant now settled down to siege operations. On July 30 his engineers exploded a great mine under the Confederate works, momentarily opening a road to the rear. But the assault troops hesitated and were driven back, with great slaughter inflicted by the defenders. The affair of the "Crater" cost almost 4,000 lives and brought no recognizable gain. Grant's costly campaign, and his failure to destroy Lee or capture Richmond outraged the public. Yet Grant had accomplished something: Lee had been greatly weakened in manpower and supplies, and the Confederate government had not been able to forward replacements or supplies in adequate amounts. Grant's army numbered almost 125,000; Lee's, 60,000.

The siege of Petersburg continued throughout the summer, the fall, and the winter with the same inevitability that characterized the ultimate success at Vicksburg. Lee could not—would not—wait for the end to come without making a serious attempt to break the siege. While the operation at Petersburg was in its early stages, Lee attempted a diversion on July 1. He sent Jubal E. Early with 13,000 men into the Shenandoah Valley to threaten Washington. The objective was to cause Grant to fall back to defend Washington and abandon his Petersburg operation.

Early moved quickly, driving Union opposition before him. He crossed the Potomac and turned east, and by the afternoon of July 11 he paused at the gates of the capital. Had he marched that afternoon, he could have taken the city. But he went into camp and planned to enter the city the next morning, by which time it was too late. When he made his move in the morning he found before him reinforcements from Grant's army that had arrived during the night. Repulsed, Early fell back and retreated into the valley. He turned around at Strasburg, Virginia, four days later and marched north into Pennsylvania, burning Chambersburg.

As determined as Lee was to create a diversion that would move Grant from his front, so was Grant determined to put an end to the sort of raid that Early carried out. Grant sent Sheridan with 50,000 men, half cavalry and half infantry, to drive Early from the valley. Confederate reinforcements helped stall Sheridan, but Lee had to recall them in the face of Grant's pressure at Petersburg. Sheridan then took the offensive. In two sharp battles, at Winchester on September 19 and at Fisher's Hill on September 22, he drove Early southward with high losses on both sides. Following Grant's orders, Sheridan adopted a policy of destruction. All structures, mills, barns, houses, and fences were put to the torch; grain and other crops, cattle, horses, mules, agricultural implements, and tools were taken or destroyed; and the rich Shenandoah Valley was left so empty of supplies that Sheridan could remark with accuracy that "a crow flying over the country would need to carry his rations." The object of the destruction was, of course, to seal off the valley, to prevent Lee from using it again to operate against Washington.

The South cried for vengeance, and Lee again sent help to Early. That audacious general followed Sheridan, coming upon his army at Cedar Creek on October 19 when Sheridan himself was absent. Early attacked at dawn, routing Sheridan's army in complete surprise. Sheridan had spent the night at Winchester, twenty miles to the rear, and had been riding leisurely toward the scene when news of the attack reached him. He galloped forward, by noon had joined the one corps of his army that had not been routed—although it had fallen back some four miles—helped them rally the fugitives, and turned his army to face Early. Early, who believed he had won, was in turn taken by surprise as his troops hungrily looted the Union camp. He fought courageously, but his army, swept off the field, fled before Sheridan's cavalry. In November Early again moved into the valley, but this time without verve, without success. Amazing as it seems, Early had actually kept Sheridan in the valley from summer until the middle of December; by doing so he had very probably prolonged Lee's ability to resist at Petersburg.

As 1865 opened, the Confederate military fortunes rapidly ebbed. The Confederacy faced imminent danger of collapse. Hood's army was shattered on the Rock of Chickamauga in Tennessee. Early lost the Shenandoah Valley. Federal cavalry rode at will through all of Virginia north of the James River and through very nearly all of Mississippi, Georgia, and Alabama. Dire want plagued Lee's slowly melting army around Richmond, and Joe Johnston sought in vain to check Sherman in North Carolina. A Confederate defeat appeared inevitable; it seemed imperative for the Confederate government to make peace.

Under the circumstances, private citizens arranged a meeting of peace commissioners at Hampton Roads, Virginia, on February 3, 1865. The president himself represented the Union. Lincoln offered to stop the war if the Confederate states would accept emancipation and return to the authority of the Union. The president even offered to ask Congress to pay slaveholders compensation for their slaves, although he must have known that Congress would not have agreed. Jefferson Davis, on the other hand, shortsightedly asked, indeed demanded, that the independence of the South should be the basis for peace. Had he been less bullheaded, Davis would have known that that was an impossible precondition for an armistice. The peace negotiations came to nothing.

As spring arrived, Grant stretched his lines farther and farther to the west, threatening the Petersburg and Lynchburg Railroad, one of two lines still open to the Confederates. To check Grant, Lee had to stretch his own lines, and with far fewer troops his lines grew thinner and thinner. On April 1 Sheridan successfully attacked Lee's right wing at Five Forks. As soon as Grant learned of the success, he ordered a general assault all along the front. This too proved successful; the Confederate line was broken in two places. On April 3 Grant extended his lines even farther west, threatening Lee with complete encirclement.

Victory in the East

Lee could not wait for that move, choosing instead to evacuate Petersburg, concentrate his army southwest of Richmond, and try to flee along the line of the railroad to Danville. In mid-morning April 2 Lee gave Davis and the Confederate government notice of his plans so that they might escape. On April 3 his army trudged along the four roads that converged on Amelia Courthouse, on the railroad to Danville, thirty-five miles southwest of Richmond. Lee hoped to link up with Joe Johnston, who had received orders at Raleigh to concentrate at Greensboro, fifty miles south of Danville.

Although Grant sent troops to occupy Richmond and Petersburg, he wasted no time celebrating. He intended to bag Lee before Lee could reach Johnston. He marched after Lee by every road available, often fighting Lee's rear guard. Early on April 4 Lee reached Amelia Courthouse, expecting supplies to have been collected for him, but none were on hand, and he lost a precious day collecting necessities. On April 5 Sheridan seized the railroad to Danville, turning Lee toward Lynchburg. Lee's army, many ill, all dispirited and on short rations, disappeared in squads. On the evening of April 8 Sheridan swept in front of Lee at Appomattox Courthouse. A large body of infantry, commanded by General Edward O. C. Ord, also slipped around Lee and took up a position behind Sheridan. On April 9 Lee ordered his infantry to brush aside the Union cavalry and march for Lynchburg. As the Confederate soldiers moved forward, Sheridan's troopers wheeled off, revealing Ord's infantry in a solid formation. Lee's men stopped, their part in the war ended.

Lee asked for a truce and met Grant at the McLean House in Appomattox Village. Ironically, Wilmer McLean had moved to Appomattox after First Bull Run to get away from the war; now the war ended in his living room. Lee, impeccably dressed in a splendid gray uniform and sword, posed a sharp contrast to Grant in his rough and dusty blue uniform without ornamentation except for the shoulder rank insignia. After the preliminaries of conversation, Lee asked Grant on what terms the surrender would be received. Grant wrote out the conditions, which Lee accepted: officers and men would be paroled not to fight again, in consideration of which they would not be disturbed by the federal government so long as they observed the law; officers kept their side arms and horses, if they owned them, and their own baggage. Lee, hesitating a moment, asked Grant if his cavalrymen and artillerymen might not keep their horses for "the spring plowing" since many of them owned their own beasts. Grant agreed. Grant also allowed Lee to keep his sword, a courtesy on Grant's part toward a worthy adversary. Lee departed, made a touching farewell to his army, which had been reduced by hardship and desertion to under 28,000 men, and then rode back to Richmond. The Confederate troops surrendered their arms, took mess in Union kitchens, and returned to their homes. Grant marched his army back to the James River and embarked it for Washington. The North celebrated Appomattox as if it in fact ended the war.

10
The Western Theater
of Operations

If one of the main factors in the Eastern Theater was the search for a successful commander, a second was the army's inability to penetrate Confederate defenses and link up with the Union armies of the West at the foot of the Appalachian Mountain chain, as originally planned. The Union armies in the West, on the other hand, were successful in carrying out their assignment, even turning eastward to help conclude the war.

The Campaigns of 1862

Forts Henry and Donelson

The successful campaigns by the Western armies of the Union began in 1862, after the preliminaries in western Virginia and Kentucky had set the stage. The Confederates, who had hoped to make the Ohio River their primary line of defense, had too few troops to hold Kentucky. Grant had taken Paducah in September 1861, and had rendered the river defensive line insecure for the Confederates.

Albert Sidney Johnston took command of the Confederate forces in the West that month, and immediately set about recruiting and arming troops for the defense of the region, and sending reinforcements to Kentucky. His task was complicated by a lack of arms, but Johnston nevertheless created a new line of defense in Kentucky that ran eastward from Island No. 10 in the Mississippi River (near New Madrid, Missouri) to Forts Henry and Donelson on the Tennessee and Cumberland Rivers, and thence to Bowling Green, Kentucky. A small Confederate force occupied eastern and central Kentucky, where Union feelings were the strongest, but a determined federal army drove it back in January 1862.

Grant, at Paducah, planned to strike at the heart of the new Confederate line by knocking out the defenses at Fort Henry and Fort Donelson, located twelve miles apart. With over 17,000 men and seven gunboats, Grant moved south from Paducah up the Tennessee River. The outnumbered Confederate forces withdrew to Fort Donelson, surrendering Fort Henry. Grant immediately wheeled for Fort Donelson sending his gunboats back down the Tennessee to the Ohio and then up the Cumberland to meet him. Fort Donelson artillery repulsed the first attack of the gunboats, which then retired for repair. Grant, meanwhile, had hemmed in the fort from the land side. He had the option of waiting for the defenders to starve and surrender, or attempting to storm the place. The Confederates gave Grant little time to think over his alternatives as they attacked the Union right wing at dawn on February 15, in an effort to open up an escape route.

Grant reacted by ordering his troops to attack all along the line, and they responded enthusiastically, ending any Confederate hope of escape. That evening the three Confederate generals in charge, John B. Floyd, Gideon G. Pillow, and Simon B. Buckner, concluded that they must surrender the fort. Floyd, who was once secretary of war under Buchanan, wanted at all costs to avoid capture; he handed over command of the fort and escaped on a small boat under cover of darkness. Near dawn, two small Confederate steamers arrived, and Pillow and a few troops also escaped up river on them. A troop of cavalry led by Nathan B. Forrest slipped away along the river bank about the same time. That left Buckner to ask Grant for surrender terms. Grant replied that "no terms except an unconditional immediate surrender" would be acceptable. Buckner, who thought the terms "ungenerous," surrendered about 12,000 men later that morning.

Shiloh

With the fall of Forts Henry and Donelson, Johnston withdrew the Confederate force from Bowling Green, Kentucky, to Nashville, Tennessee. Don Carlos Buell and the Union command that had been watching Bowling Green followed the Confederates to Nashville. Fearing a sequel to Fort Donelson if Buell and Grant united forces, Johnston evacuated Nashville, moving southeastward to Murfreesboro, and then swinging rapidly southwestward in a broad arc through Decatur, Alabama, to Corinth, Mississippi. The Southern press soundly criticized Johnston for leaving Nashville, but Corinth was an important railroad junction on the line from Memphis to Chattanooga and south to Mobile. Johnston hurriedly collected supplies and reinforcements, while Grant and Buell overran western Tennessee.

By the middle of March 1862 Grant's army, following the Tennessee River, camped in haphazard fashion around Pittsburgh Landing. Grant set up his headquarters at Savannah, a few miles to the north. There he awaited Buell, now leisurely crossing Tennessee and heading southwest from Columbia. They planned to join their armies, Grant's 40,000 men and Buell's 50,000 men, to crush Johnston. Reinforcements from Arkansas and Florida rushed to join Johnston at Corinth, bringing his force up to 57,000.

Although Grant seemed to expect no attack, the Confederates were massing troops. Grant had five divisions sprawled out between Shiloh Church and Pittsburgh Landing, and a sixth division four or five miles away to the northwest. The main body was only twenty miles from the Confederate positions, yet except for posting a few guards, Grant erected no defensive perimeter. An occasional skirmish between Grant's guards and Confederate patrols took place very early in April. Johnston was aware of the defenselessness of the Union position and was determined to strike at Grant before Buell arrived. He ordered the Confederates to attack the Union camps at dawn on April 6.

The assault took Grant's troops by surprise. Confederate soldiers, running, yelling, firing at random, broke into the camps on the heels of the guards they chased before them. Some of the Union officers had not yet risen, others were dressing, washing, or eating

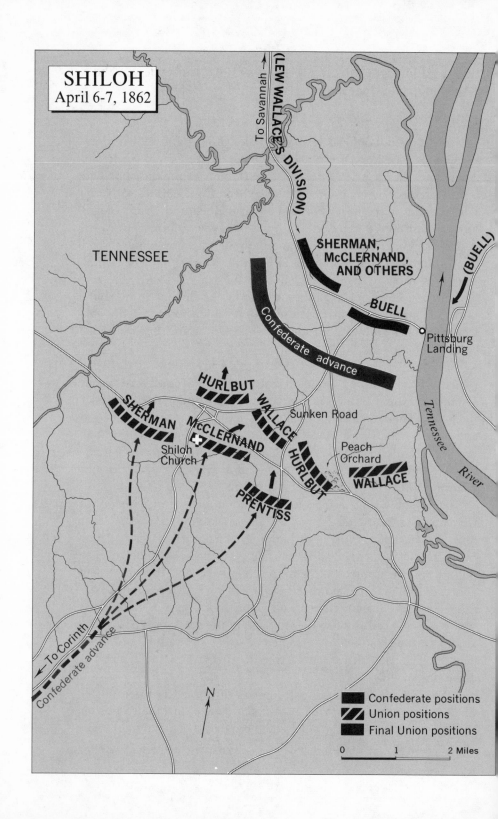

SHILOH
April 6-7, 1862

TENNESSEE

To Savannah

(LEW WALLACE'S DIVISION)

SHERMAN,
McCLERNAND,
AND OTHERS

(BUELL)

BUELL

Confederate advance

Pittsburg
Landing

HURLBUT

SHERMAN

WALLACE

Sunken Road

McCLERNAND

Shiloh
Church

HURLBUT

Peach
Orchard

WALLACE

Tennessee River

PRENTISS

N

To Corinth

Confederate advance

Confederate positions
Union positions
Final Union positions

0   1   2 Miles

breakfast. Some of the Union troops died in their beds, others fell as they tried to ward off bayonets, or were shot down as they fled, often without weapons, often undressed, toward the river. Some did the best they could, falling back, trying to form a line of battle.

One Union brigade fell back to a sunken road, a ready made trench. Led by General Benjamin Prentiss, an Illinois politician who was a veteran of the Mexican War, the brigade withstood repeated charges, even though they were outflanked. They held their ground until late afternoon, when sixty Confederate artillery pieces converged on them, and they were forced to surrender. One of their number fired the shot that wounded Johnston, causing him to bleed to death that day. Another Union force made a desperate stand in a peach orchard. But for the most part chaos reigned.

Alerted by the sound of battle at dawn, Grant had boarded the steamer *Tigress* and made his way to Pittsburgh Landing. By the time he arrived, hundreds of fugitives lined the west bank of the river trying to flee. They shouted that the Union army was "clean cut to pieces." Yet Union officers kept trying to rally the army. General William T. Sherman rode fearlessly along the lines exposing himself to the same risk of death as his soldiers. Generals Edward J. McClernand and Irvin McDowell proved very stubborn, but still the Union army was forced back. When dusk came, part of Grant's force crouched with their backs to the river, part lay dead on the field, and part had been marched off as captives. The Confederate advance had been weakened by green troops who stopped to loot the Union camps and by others who ran off to gawk at the Union prisoners, who were supposed to be cutthroats and murderers enlisted from the slums of Northern cities sent south to rape and pillage.

That evening at Pittsburgh Landing, Grant told his staff, "we can hold them off till tomorrow, when they'll be exhausted, and we'll go at them with fresh troops." From the opposite bank of the river a body of Buell's cavalry shouted for transportation across and said Buell's infantry was close behind. Grant's officers set up their remaining artillery, twenty-two pieces, in a semi-circle to protect the landing. General Lew Wallace's division, lost in the maze of roads between Crump's Landing and Pittsburgh Landing, arrived too late to be of much help during the day, but they took up positions on the Union right. Buell's divisions spent the night crossing the river, and Grant's hastily reorganized troops made up the remainder of the battle line. The Union gunboats, *Tyler* and the *Lexington*, kept up a steady, probing cannonade on the Confederate positions all night. About midnight a drenching thunderstorm swept the field.

In the morning, Lew Wallace's batteries opened on the Confederates, and the battle was on again. Grant now had the advantage of both numbers and fresh troops. The Union forces drove the Confederates back, but slowly, as they valiantly contested the field. After a day of hard and costly fighting, the Confederates called retreat; the Union army pursued them as far as their old camp grounds; and the battle of Shiloh was over. More than 13,000 Union casualties and 10,500 Confederate casualties made it a very costly two days in April.

Beauregard, who assumed command when Johnston died, took the Confederate army to Corinth, and Grant ordered no general pursuit. The Union army learned a valuable lesson at Shiloh: never again would it encamp without digging in. Henry Halleck arrived to take command of Grant's and Buell's armies. The press had praised Grant for his "great coolness under fire," but condemned him for his failure to take proper precautions.

Unable to stop the Union movement through western Tennessee at Shiloh, the Confederates fortified Corinth. Halleck rested the army, brought its numbers up to about 100,000, and then cautiously moved toward the new Confederate position. Expecting a hard campaign, he took elaborate precautions against surprise attack, and prepared to besiege Corinth. But the Confederates, unwilling to be bottled up by so superior a force, evacuated the town without a fight.

The campaign on the Tennessee River left Confederate positions along the Mississippi exposed in the interim. They abandoned Columbus, Kentucky, on March 4 and a Union army under General Pope invested New Madrid, Missouri, on March 14. Below New Madrid, fortified Confederate-held Island No. 10 nestled in a bend of the Mississippi prohibiting Union navigation of the river below that point. On the west bank of the river, Pope needed boats to ferry his army across in order to attack Island No. 10 from the rear or to outflank it entirely. After an abortive effort to dig a canal that would bypass the island, Union gunboats made a spectacular dash past the batteries, ferried Pope's army across the Mississippi, and enabled the general to capture that post. All together, Pope took more than 7,000 prisoners. After Corinth fell into Union hands, Fort Pillow and then Memphis followed early in June. Meanwhile, Admiral David G. Farragut led a naval expedition with the object of capturing New Orleans. Stalled at first by the forts on the river below the town, Farragut with great bravery rushed past them. On April 25 New Orleans fell to Farragut and was occupied by a garrison commanded by Benjamin Franklin Butler. The forts on the river below New Orleans, now cut off, surrendered to Admiral David D. Porter.

Tennessee

After the evacuation of Corinth, the Union army, still commanded by Halleck, remained inactive. The Confederates, however, worked to build up their strength and prepared for another major campaign in the western theater. At Chattanooga, the key to southeastern Tennessee, the Confederate army under Braxton Bragg was brought up to 35,000 men in strength. Buell, back in Nashville, was now ordered to protect the city from Bragg. Buell collected his forces at Murfreesboro, thirty-five miles southeast of Nashville. Before he could move on Bragg, Bragg outflanked him and moved into Kentucky. Bragg's seizure of Lexington threw the cities of Louisville and Cincinnati into a state of panic lest they be captured or ravaged before help could arrive. Buell turned around and headed for Louisville. Bragg, ahead of Buell, probably could have taken the town, but his invasion had not quite worked out as he had planned. The people of Kentucky had not flocked to his standard. Somewhat discouraged, he allowed Buell to reach Louisville with an army numbering over 58,000.

On October 6, 1862, Bragg and Buell's forces clashed at Perryville, Kentucky, sixty-five miles southeast of Louisville. The battle did not seem decisive for either side, but at dusk Bragg withdrew his army and returned safely to Chattanooga. Union casualties at Perryville totalled 4,200, on the Confederate side 3,400. Buell received orders to follow Bragg and hold east Tennessee, but he instead took up position at Nashville since he did not believe he could maintain his army far from its base. For disobeying orders, Buell lost his command to Rosecrans.

Rosecrans received the same order Buell had balked at, to take and hold eastern Tennessee. Like Buell, he refused to try. Rosecrans stayed in Nashville. Bragg, meanwhile, slipped back to Murfreesboro and entrenched his troops. On December 26, 1862, Rosecrans moved his army against Bragg, and on December 31 they fought at Stone's River, three miles from Murfreesboro. Confederate General William J. Hardee led a vicious attack on the Union right at dawn, and the Union right wing crumpled back on the center. There, with determination, General George H. Thomas held firm until finally the struggle stopped at nightfall. Rosecrans seemed beaten, but he would not retreat. Both armies lay on their arms January 1; Bragg renewed the attack on January 2, but he was unable to dislodge his opponent. He broke off the action and once more retired safely to Chattanooga. In the two days of fighting, the Union lost 13,000 out of an army of 43,000 men, while the Confederacy lost 10,000 out of their forces of 38,000. Bragg's army captured twenty-eight artillery pieces and claimed victory, but it was they who left the field, it was they who failed to wrest central Tennessee from the control of the Union.

The Union had fared well in the Western Theater during 1862. All of Kentucky, western and central Tennessee, New Orleans and vicinity, and much of the Mississippi River had passed to Union control.

The 1863 Campaigns

Vicksburg

After Memphis and New Orleans fell to the Union, the Confederates carefully fortified Vicksburg, making it the one great strong point along the Mississippi River. Should Vicksburg fall, the trans-Mississippi West would be cut off from the Confederacy, the link with Texas beef and the supply route from Mexico would be lost. At Corinth, Grant resumed command of the army in the summer of 1862 when Lincoln called Halleck east to make him general-in-chief of the army. Grant remained inactive, and the press criticized him unmercifully, for his incaution at Shiloh, his inaction at Corinth, and his alleged intemperate drinking. Through it all, Lincoln doggedly supported the general.

Lincoln's confidence paid off in the campaign against Vicksburg. Late in 1862 Sherman took 30,000 men and a fleet of gunboats down river from Memphis, while Grant, with a similar force, started south along the railroad to Jackson, Mississippi, intending to approach Vicksburg from the east. Grant's advance stalled when the Confederates cut his communications line at Holly Springs. Sherman's force reached Vicksburg, but the defenders beat off his attempt to cross the Yazoo bottoms and approach the city from the north.

Regrouping his armies during the winter, Grant determined to approach Vicksburg from the south. He moved his army down river in early spring and had his engineers work to build a canal to by-pass Vicksburg. He hoped in this way to get his supply ships past the batteries that commanded the river and to use them to ferry his army across to the east bank. When a March storm destroyed his canal, Grant had no choice but to order his ships to run past the batteries. They did in the night, with slight loss, and on April 30, 1863, the boats ferried the Union army of 44,000 across the river. Grand Gulf, below Vicksburg, fell that day: the Confederates had not expected operations in this quarter, and the area was not strongly defended. Meanwhile, Grant continued to enlarge his army—reinforcements arrived in a steady stream.

While this operation was underway, Grant ordered Colonel Benjamin H. Grierson, with three regiments of cavalry, to move south from Cairo, Illinois, roughly along the line of the Mississippi Central Railroad, to cut communications, confuse the enemy, and generally screen Grant's march to the south of Vicksburg. Grierson, the Illinois music teacher, effectively completed his mission and arrived safely at Baton Rouge.

General Nathaniel P. Banks was ordered to move north from New Orleans to take Port Hudson—the only other Confederate strong point on the Mississippi—and then join Grant in the assault on Vicksburg. Banks' conquest of Port Hudson would also allow supply vessels from that quarter to supply Grant's army unhindered. Banks' advance stalled, however, leaving Grant without help from that quarter. At the same time Grant learned that Confederate soldiers were concentrating at Jackson, Mississippi. Should John C. Pemberton's Vicksburg garrison of nearly 30,000 be joined by Joseph E. Johnston's 15,000 that were reportedly moving up to Jackson, Grant's army could be in trouble. Grant acted quickly. Abandoning his base at Grand Gulf, he moved to seize Jackson before Johnston could reach it, placing his entire army between Pemberton and Johnston. The cautious Pemberton remained in Vicksburg, despite Johnston's order to move out and link up. When

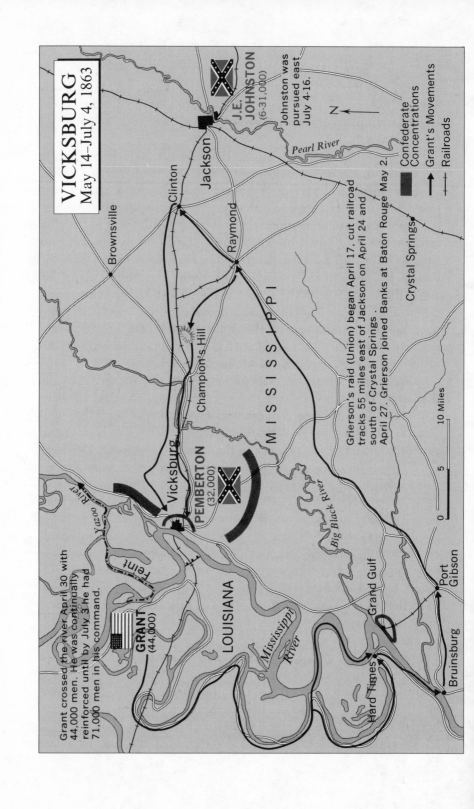

VICKSBURG
May 14–July 4, 1863

Johnston was
pursued east
July 4-16.

J.E. JOHNSTON
(6-31,000)

Pearl River

Jackson

Clinton

Brownsville

Raymond

Champion's Hill

MISSISSIPPI

Vicksburg

PEMBERTON
(32,000)

Crystal Springs

Big Black River

Grierson's raid (Union) began April 17, cut railroad
tracks 55 miles east of Jackson on April 24 and
south of Crystal Springs .
April 27. Grierson joined Banks at Baton Rouge May 2

Yazoo River

Feint

GRANT
(44,000)

LOUISIANA

Mississippi River

Grand Gulf

Port Gibson

Hard Times

Bruinsburg

Grant crossed the river April 30 with
44,000 men. He was continually
reinforced until by July 3 he had
71,000 men in his command.

Confederate
Concentrations
Grant's Movements
Railroads

0   5   10 Miles

Pemberton did move, he moved to the south with about 20,000 men, seeking to cut Grant's lines of communication. At the same time Johnston swung northward to get into Vicksburg. Pemberton soon discovered that Grant maintained no communication lines, but by that time it was too late to turn north and link up with Johnston.

Johnston could not risk battle with Grant then nor could he reach Vicksburg, and he had no choice but to leave Pemberton to his fate. Pemberton stood Grant in battle, first at Champion's Hill, then at the Big Black River, suffering defeat both times. On May 18 he retired within the defenses of Vicksburg. Grant followed him, established siege lines from the high banks of the Yazoo to the Mississippi south of Vicksburg, and once more contacted his supply ships. Reinforcements poured in, and Grant soon counted over 71,000 men—enough to besiege Vicksburg and simultaneously repulse any rescue force the Confederates could raise in the vicinity.

After beating off two determined attempts to storm their position, the Confederates settled down to withstand the siege. Grant brought cannon and mortars and put sappers and miners to work, edging his lines ever tighter. Hunger played a key role at Vicksburg. Confederate authorities, who needed every man to hold Chattanooga in the face of Rosecrans' threat, could offer no assistance to the beleaguered garrison on the Mississippi. By June the food supply had nearly failed inside the city. Confederate defenders were deserting, and on the twenty-eighth the garrison suggested that its commander capitulate. On July 3 Pemberton held an interview with Grant, and on July 4 the siege ended. The garrison, now numbering a little over 29,000, surrendered. They gave up 170 cannons and 50,000 small arms.

The surrender at Vicksburg came the day after the victory in the Eastern Theater at Gettysburg. July 4, 1863, was a day of wild celebration throughout the North. Shortly after Vicksburg capitulated, Port Hudson fell, opening the entire Mississippi to the Union and cutting the Confederacy off from the trans-Mississippi west. The Vicksburg operation made Grant a national hero, overshadowing the Shiloh criticism and the persistent rumors about the bottle.

Chickamauga and Lookout Mountain

As Grant campaigned against Vicksburg, Rosecrans sat in Nashville, his army totalling 70,000, keeping an eye on Bragg in

Chattanooga. Rosecrans was unwilling to campaign against Bragg while the Vicksburg affair remained in doubt. Bragg's forces moved out to Shelbyville, and in June, with the Vicksburg episode near successful conclusion, Rosecrans moved out of Nashville. He flanked Bragg back into Chattanooga without a battle. Bragg's position at Chattanooga was strong: the city faced the east bank of the Tennessee River, a bold waterway at that point; it was surrounded by mountain ridges, making it defensible; in addition, the country southwest of Chattanooga was quite rough, and the best military approach was from the northeast. Bragg expected Rosecrans to come against him from that direction, and his guess seemed accurate when Ambrose E. Burnside moved a column from Kentucky into eastern Tennessee, stopping at Knoxville. Burnside took an obvious position from which to support Rosecrans. But when the Burnside column failed to leave Knoxville, Bragg decided the attack would not come in the near future. He was mistaken.

Rosecrans approached Chattanooga from the southwest, not the northeast. He knew the move would be hazardous, but he guessed—correctly—that it would not be expected; besides, the movement threatened Bragg's communications. Yet Rosecrans was unfamiliar with the country, and once he launched the campaign the various wings of his army, wending their way through disconnected valleys, were often several days march from one another. An alert Bragg could have demolished Rosecrans' army piece by piece. When Bragg came to his senses, he had to face Rosecrans' entire force at Chickamauga Creek, about a dozen miles south of Chattanooga.

Bragg, nevertheless, had help at hand. All was quiet for a while in the Eastern Theater, and James Longstreet had been detached to the west. In addition, Buckner's small army, which Burnside had driven from Kentucky, had joined Bragg. The strength of the Union and the Confederate armies was nearly equal at Chickamauga—65,000 for Rosecrans and 62,000 for Bragg. In joining their forces, the Confederates moved in such a direction that Rosecrans actually stood between them and Chattanooga: Rossville Gap, through which the Chattanooga Road ran, was located behind Rosecrans' position.

In an effort to seize the Gap and isolate Rosecrans, Bragg lashed out hard at the Union left, commanded by Thomas. Thomas held firm, but Rosecrans weakened the rest of his line to shift reinforcements to Thomas. About noon, September 20, 1863, in a disastrous error, a Union division pulled out of the center of the line to move to the left. Longstreet, waiting opposite, took advantage of the move and sent eight brigades hurtling through the gap, crushing the Union center and throwing the Union right into confusion. Both parts of the line fell back in disorder and followed Rosecrans through Rossville Gap. Failing to rally his troops, Rosecrans ordered Thomas to hold the rear and protect the retreat. Thomas successfully beat off attacks from three sides until night fell, when he retired to the gap and held it until the order came to join Rosecrans in Chattanooga. Fought on September 19 and 20, 1863, Chickamauga cost Rosecrans 16,000 casualties, and Bragg 18,000. Thomas' great stand kept the Union army from a sound beating and won him the title, "the Rock of Chickamauga."

Bragg pursued the Union army and penned them in Chattanooga by fortifying Missionary Ridge and Lookout Mountain, east and south of the city. His Lookout Mountain position covered the railroad, closing that route to Rosecrans' supplies. As a result, Rosecrans depended upon a circuitous wagon route of over sixty miles, a nearly impossible situation. Within a month, the Union forces faced the alternatives of starving or retreating.

Alarmed, Lincoln sent in 16,000 men from Virginia under Joseph Hooker, ordered Sherman up from Vicksburg with an even larger contingent, removed Rosecrans from command and replaced him with Thomas, put Grant in command of all the Western armies except the garrison at New Orleans, and directed Grant to Chattanooga as well. When Grant arrived in late October, he sent Hooker across the river to open up the railroad within four miles of town and built a new, short wagon road; he thus averted the danger of starvation.

Grant next determined to drive Bragg from Missionary Ridge and Lookout Mountain. Bragg, believing he had a very strong position and still not thinking an early attack likely, withdrew Longstreet from his center and sent him to annoy Burnside at Knoxville. Bragg thought Longstreet would be back long before he would be needed at Chattanooga, but he underestimated Grant. So Longstreet was out of reach on November 24, 1863, when the battle began.

Grant sent Sherman to turn the Confederate right at Missionary Ridge, keeping Bragg in position by feinting with Thomas in

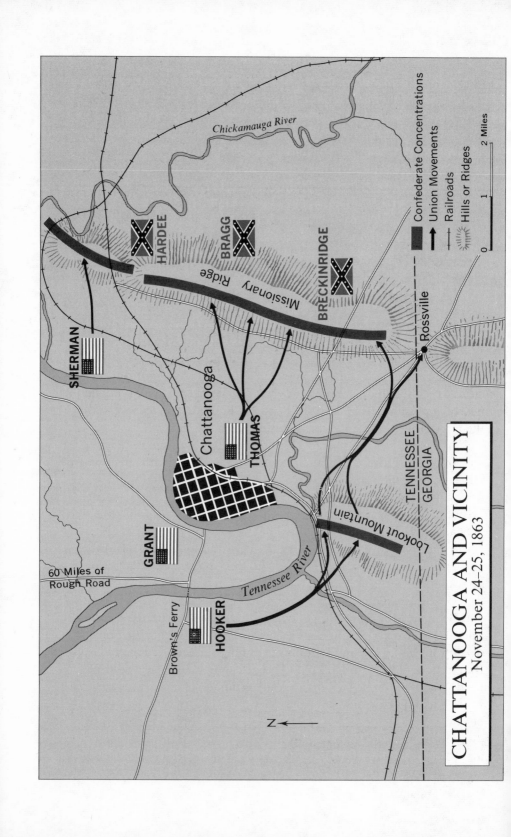

CHATTANOOGA AND VICINITY
November 24–25, 1863

Chickamauga River

HARDEE

BRAGG

BRECKINRIDGE

Missionary Ridge

SHERMAN

Chattanooga

THOMAS

Rossville

GRANT

Lookout Mountain

60 Miles of
Rough Road

Tennessee River

Brown's Ferry

HOOKER

TENNESSEE
GEORGIA

N

Confederate Concentrations
Union Movements
Railroads
Hills or Ridges

0   1   2 Miles

the center and Hooker on the right. As Sherman drove the Confederates along the ridge, Thomas approached the base of the ridge at the center, and Hooker's troops carried the crest of Lookout Mountain. This unexpected achievement greatly boosted the morale of the Union army. On November 25, Sherman renewed hard fighting along the ridge, and to help him, Grant ordered Thomas to take the Confederate works on the lower slopes. Thomas' soldiers found their new position exposed to heavy fire from above, and without orders they swept up to the crest of the ridge, four hundred feet above them.

Viewing the course of the battle, Grant asked Thomas by whose orders his troops began their move up the ridge. Thomas coolly replied, "By their own." They watched in fascination as Thomas' army progressed upwards, struggled furiously at the top, and scored a victory. Bragg fell quickly back to northern Georgia. In this encounter Bragg lost 6,500 men, Grant 5,500. Exhausted, both armies went into winter quarters, Grant's in Chattanooga, Bragg's in Dalton, Georgia.

The Campaigns of 1864 and 1865

The Atlanta Campaign

Bragg faced severe criticism in the South and remained in command only because of his close friendship with Jefferson Davis. After the loss above the clouds on Lookout Mountain and Missionary Ridge, even that friendship could not save him. Bragg was replaced by Joseph E. Johnston. Johnston, a very capable officer, nevertheless did not have the full confidence of Davis—the two men in fact disliked each other thoroughly. Grant, however, respected Johnston's ability, remarking at one time that he feared him more than any other Confederate commander. Johnston's obvious task was to defend Atlanta by keeping the Union army out of Georgia. Reinforcements trickled into his camps until his troops totaled some 60,000 men.

Early in 1864 Congress promoted Grant to the rank of lieutenant general, making him by virtue of this rank commander of all Union armies. The second American officer to hold this permanent rank—the other was George Washington—Grant departed for Virginia and assumed charge of operations in the Eastern Theater.

The army in Chattanooga, brought up to a strength of 100,000, was placed under William Sherman. Under Sherman, Thomas still commanded Rosecrans' former army; James B. McPherson commanded the troops Sherman had brought up from Vicksburg; and John M. Schofield took charge of the Burnside forces from Knoxville. Sherman's army at Chattanooga was a superior force. The troops were seasoned veterans, most of them with two years' experience. The rigors of battle and long marches had weeded out the weak officers, the political appointees, and the cowards. Experienced and trusted officers occupied responsible positions at all levels.

The men knew Atlanta was their goal; they knew they had a formidable opponent in Johnston, who would make the best possible use of the hill country through which they must fight. The route of attack was no secret—it would be the line of the railroad from Chattanooga to Atlanta, which would serve as a communications and supply link for either army. Sherman's engineers were experienced enough to repair the railroad as fast as, or faster than, Johnston could destroy it; they replaced track and rebuilt bridges so efficiently that the Confederate rear guard could often hear the whistle of Sherman's locomotive.

Early in May Sherman marched his veteran army to Dalton. He found Johnston waiting, entrenched along a range of hills before the town. After sending Thomas and Schofield to test the strength of the position, Sherman sent McPherson and his Army of the Tennessee off to the right in a rapid flanking movement. Not waiting to be trapped, Johnston moved his army south to Resaca just in time to dig in and face Sherman again. Once more, after testing the position, the Army of the Tennessee swung wide to the right flank. Every day there was contact, Thomas' veterans keeping up a hot skirmish line while McPherson moved out on the flank, avoiding head-on collision.

Johnston, always retreating to meet the new threat, and Sherman, sidestepping and flanking, repeated this awesome dance in a kind of frenzied slow motion, progressing ever southward through Georgia. Johnston never could make a formal stand, being always a little off balance, and Sherman never could force a decision of arms.

At the end of June, twenty-five miles north of Atlanta, Sherman found Johnston dug in on Kenesaw Mountain, a strong defensive position. Sherman chose to slug it out, and he delivered a

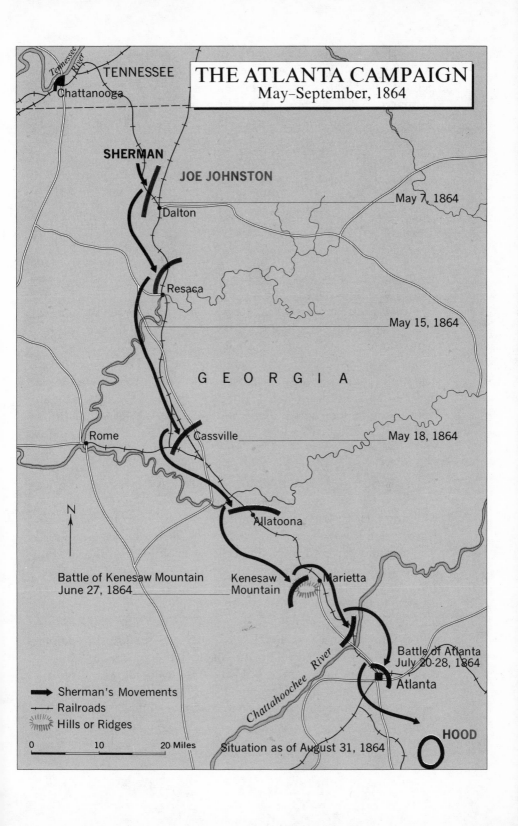

THE ATLANTA CAMPAIGN
May–September, 1864

TENNESSEE

Chattanooga

Tennessee River

SHERMAN

JOE JOHNSTON

May 7, 1864

Dalton

Resaca

May 15, 1864

G E O R G I A

Rome

Cassville

May 18, 1864

N

Allatoona

Battle of Kenesaw Mountain
June 27, 1864

Kenesaw
Mountain

Marietta

Battle of Atlanta
July 20-28, 1864

Chattahoochee River

Atlanta

➤ Sherman's Movements
┼ Railroads
⋔ Hills or Ridges

0   10   20 Miles   Situation as of August 31, 1864

HOOD

powerful assault against what he believed to be Johnston's weakest point. Over 2,500 Union soldiers fell on the slopes of the mountain compared to 800 defenders, but Sherman failed to dent the Confederate position. Sherman asked Thomas if he should continue the assault, and Thomas replied that a few more assaults like the last one would use up the entire army. McPherson called upon the Army of the Tennessee once more, and his veterans, whom he knew would rather march than die, swung out on the flank again. On July 9 Sherman's army reached the north bank of the Chattahoochee River, six miles from Atlanta, with Johnston facing him on the south bank. For two months the armies had contested from Dalton to the Chattahoochee, continuously skirmishing, fighting only a few sharp engagements like Kenesaw Mountain, all of which had resulted in a loss of over 16,000 for Sherman and 14,000 for Johnston.

In his retreat to Atlanta, Johnston fell back much as Lee fell back before Grant in Virginia. If the losses were lighter, it was because Sherman campaigned more cautiously than did Grant. Johnston, however, was under heavy fire from the Southern press. Davis, also under great pressure to save a Confederacy that seemed to be dissolving before him, believed Johnston should have been able to stop Sherman somewhere along the line. Davis queried Johnston about his next move, and Johnston replied that he would fight Sherman any time he could do so with advantage. That was not quite what Davis wanted to hear; he replaced Johnston with General John B. Hood. Hood, his arm crippled at Gettysburg and his leg lost at Chickamauga, assumed command on July 17. Schofield, who knew Hood from West Point days, told Sherman that while Hood was not very smart, he would fight like hell. And so he did.

Sherman crossed the Chattahoochee July 17, and within eleven days engaged Hood in three battles—Peach Tree Creek, July 20; Atlanta, July 22; and Ezra Church, July 28. Hood lost nearly 11,000 men to Sherman's 10,000, but he kept Atlanta from his foe. Sherman spent the better part of August in an effort to surround the city and pen up Hood. The Northern press despaired that Atlanta would ever fall and likened the process to Grant's costly campaign in Virginia. But unlike the campaign in Virginia, Hood would not let himself be besieged. He evacuated Atlanta on September 2, and Sherman occupied it the following day. The North celebrated, for the fall of Atlanta was the first great victory of

1864—among other factors, it smoothed the way for Lincoln's victory in the upcoming elections.

Hood's Defeat

Yet Sherman, though he now had Atlanta, faced a relatively insecure situation. He was deep in the heart of hostile country; his communications line stretched out like a long, vulnerable thread from Chattanooga, likely to be clipped at any point by a large and determined force. Much valuable strength had to be spent in keeping garrisons along the line. Recognizing Sherman's touchy situation, Hood swung in a great arc westward, falling upon Allatoona, a railroad station about 45 miles north of Atlanta. The Union garrison beat off the attack, but had it been a success, Sherman would have been forced north to recover the station. Hood then turned west again, stopping at Decatur, Alabama, on the Tennessee River, 110 miles south on the railroad from Nashville. Hood hoped to draw Sherman after him, but Sherman did not rise to the bait.

Sherman instead sent Thomas to Nashville, and Grant hurried reinforcements to him, bringing his forces up to about 60,000—quite enough to handle Hood's 54,000. Sherman, meanwhile, asked permission to head east for the seacoast with his veteran army. Grant reluctantly consented, because although the campaign would be risky—Sherman would be out of touch with the North the whole time—nothing could better demonstrate the weakness of the Confederacy than to divide the Union Western army into two wings, either of which would be larger than anything the Confederacy could put in the field. Sherman knew he would face no serious opposition, so long as Grant kept the pressure on Lee in the East, and he was confident that Thomas could handle anything Hood might throw at him.

Hood had many problems. After Johnston left and Atlanta fell, the morale of his troops was very low. Hood had few supplies, which gave his opponents time to prepare for him. Schofield and a force of over 20,000 men waited across his line of march to Tennessee with orders to impede Hood's advance and fall back. Hood knew he had to surround and destroy Schofield, but the opportunity never quite materialized. Yet Schofield was hard pressed when he arrived at Franklin on November 30 to find the bridge over the Harpeth River partially destroyed. Pursued by Hood, Schofield dug in hurriedly, while attempting to fix the bridge. Hood arrived late in the afternoon and assaulted Schofield at once. The battle raged until dark, Schofield holding firm, and by morning Schofield had slipped away across the repaired bridge to Nashville, twenty miles away. Schofield lost about 2,300 men to Hood's 6,000. Hood could ill afford to lose so many.

Hood followed slowly and occupied the hills south of Nashville. His army, in tatters, numbered now about 23,000, reduced by fighting and marching. Thomas and Schofield mustered over 50,000 men in Nashville. But Thomas was in no hurry to march out and destroy Hood. The days fled by, and still Thomas waited. Lincoln, Grant, and the North feared that Hood would slip away and that Thomas would lose the opportunity to end the last major resistance in the Western Theater. Grant sent a telegram to Thomas, but the Rock of Chickamauga did not budge; so Grant ordered Schofield to replace him, but at the last moment, that order was canceled.

By December 15 Thomas was ready. He moved out against Hood and drove him back about four miles with bitter fighting. The next day Thomas tore into Hood again. Determined to stand for a life-and-death battle, the Confederates made a fight of it until, nearly surrounded, all hope gone, they broke and fled south in whatever formation they could keep. Fewer than 15,000 infantrymen made the crossing of the Tennessee River on the seventeenth. The rest had been killed or captured, or had headed for home, believing the war had ended. Later, about 9,000 survivors joined Johnston in North Carolina in his futile effort to stop Sherman. With Thomas' victory and the destruction of Hood's army, the objectives of the Union forces in the Western Theater of Operations had been accomplished. Nowhere between the Ohio River and the Gulf of Mexico could Yankee arms be resisted. Only a few Confederate posts like Mobile held out.

The March to the Sea

On November 15, 1864, Sherman began his march to the sea. Before the army left Atlanta, they destroyed the railroad to Chattanooga and cut the telegraph wires. As the army tramped out on the first leg of its march, they fired the machine shops in the city. Marching on parallel roads, Sherman's army covered a zone about sixty miles wide. They carried supplies for about three weeks but were ordered to forage liberally along the way.

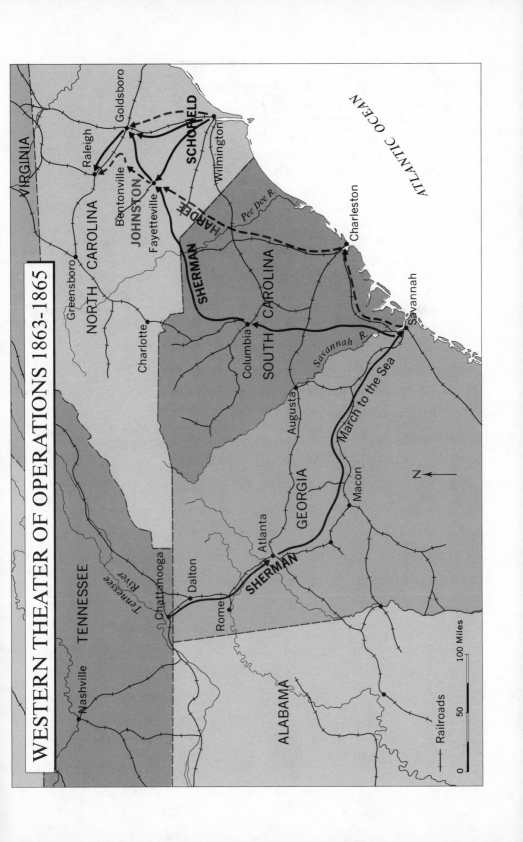

WESTERN THEATER OF OPERATIONS 1863-1865

The march to the sea was a campaign unlike any before or since. The troops were not hunting an enemy force: the only foe that could give them a scrap—Hood's army—was hundreds of miles away, heading in a different direction. The army moved at a leisurely pace, only about fifteen miles a day, considerably less than they could easily make. The soldiers all knew that their mission was to destroy an economy and to demolish morale. Their orders directed them to destroy all railway lines, repair shops, depots, and industrial installations.

Each day the routine followed the same pattern. Every brigade sent out a party of foragers in the morning, led by an officer and followed by wagons. They did not return to their unit until evening. According to the orders, they were to stay out of inhabited dwellings and seize no more food than necessary. Yet they were not tightly controlled, and they were joined or followed by a steadily growing mob of armed skulkers, called bummers, who knew no restraint. Plantations that loomed in the army's path were treated roughly by both groups. A fertile land, Georgia yielded an abundance of food from its barns and cellars and smokehouses for Sherman's soldiers.

Near Milledgeville, a former state capital, a few thousand Georgian militiamen and a troop or two of regular Confederate cavalry stood bravely to oppose Sherman's advance. Sherman sent one brigade of veterans from one of his four corps to deal with the situation, and the brigade cleared the way with ease. The Union soldiers were horrified to discover they had been up against old men and young boys. On occasion Southerners felled trees across the roads or burned bridges. The usual Yankee reprisal was to burn all barns or houses within a set radius of the obstruction. As the army moved on, plantations were looted outright—not just hams, chickens, and horses, but silver, heirlooms, and other valuables as well.

Although crowds of fugitive slaves trailed Sherman's army, he did his best to discourage them. In fact, there was very little the army could do. Sherman's columns, feinting at Macon and then Augusta, confused the Confederates. Judson Kilpatrick's Union cavalry, a very rough, seasoned group, reached out beyond the line of march, further adding to the confusion. The followers, the bummers, and fugitive slaves gave the kite a long and dangerous tail.

The effect of the march was devastating. The very fact that an army of 60,000 men could walk straight through the heartland of the South, feasting every evening, destroying resources, without meeting resistance enough to delay them even one day, was clear evidence that the end of the war was near. The morale of Confederate soldiers in Virginia sank to a new low as they received letters from home describing how Sherman was pillaging everything and leaving starvation in his wake. The rate of desertion from Confederate service, high since Vicksburg and Gettysburg, increased. Confederate soldiers in Virginia, short on the necessities of war and desperate for food and clothing, saw as their commanders did how inadequate the Southern transportation system was: in Georgia, Sherman's men feasted, while they tightened their belts. Sherman's march caused the North—Lincoln, the War Department, and Grant—many anxious moments, for his troops slipped from view when they left Atlanta. Confederate newspapers optimistically reported time after time that Sherman had been cut off or would be wiped out. As November drew to a close, no one up North knew just where the army was or what its fate held. But the Georgians knew. They followed its progress by the light of burning railroad ties, twisted and useless rails, pillars of smoke from burning buildings, vacant pastures, and the long line of bummers and slaves.

Sherman said, as he set out after leaving a third of Atlanta in ashes, that he would "make Georgia howl." Later, in his official report, he estimated that his men damaged the state of Georgia to the sum of $100,000,000.

On December 10 Sherman confronted Savannah, his march of 360 miles all but complete. Hardee, who led a Confederate garrison of 15,000 men at Savannah, refused to allow Sherman to besiege him and withdrew on December 20. Sherman remained in Savannah from December 20 until February 1, when he put his troops back on the march, this time headed north. During his stay, he linked up with the navy, bringing the news of his safety to a cheering North.

Sherman and the Carolinas

The march north was slowed by severe storms and bad roads, but Hardee could offer no effective opposition. Moving out from Savannah, Sherman's army entered South Carolina, the state his soldiers blamed for starting the war by being the first to secede. Pillaging was consequently even more severe than it had been in Georgia. The troops thought it their particular duty to wreak vengeance upon South Carolina and its inhabitants. Sherman gave new orders to prevent plundering of private dwellings, but he found it impossible to enforce them.

When his army reached Columbia, the capital of South Carolina, advance units found the remains of a great bonfire of cotton—destroyed to prevent it from falling into Union hands. The first patrols in town also stumbled on liquor stores; they broke from the control of their officers and apparently put the torch to Columbia. By morning the city lay in ruins. The business district was completely destroyed, fine homes of the residential district smoldered for blocks around, and even the old shade trees appeared to be little more than stumps of charcoal.

With Columbia occupied, Hardee, who had fled to Charleston, was forced to evacuate that port city. He marched his army rapidly north to position it before Sherman arrived. By March 11, 1865, Sherman's legions reached Fayetteville, North Carolina. They destroyed an arsenal, but the town itself did not suffer. North Carolina, the last state to secede, fared much better than had South Carolina. Still, despite greater efforts to control pillaging, Sherman exercised little control over the bummers and some of the soldiers.

By the time Sherman reached Fayetteville, Johnston had been restored to command. Gathering all the strength he could muster, he made a stand 30 miles north of the town. Sherman's well-fed veterans beat off Johnston, but the determined general made yet another stand three days later at Bentonville. The result was the same. On March 23 Sherman arrived at Goldsboro, only 160 miles south of Richmond. At the time Grant was concluding his operations against Lee. Strategically, it was necessary for Sherman to keep enough pressure on Johnston to prevent him from slipping north to aid Lee, while Grant had to keep Lee so occupied that he could not detach any of his army to rush south and slap at Sherman.

Upon his arrival in Goldsboro, Sherman was greeted by Schofield, who had led an army of 20,000 into town two days earlier. Schofield had made the journey from Tennessee to Virginia by rail, then by water to Wilmington, which had fallen to the Union in January. Sherman thus received substantial reinforcement, even though it was not necessary. After a couple of weeks' rest in Goldsboro, Sherman learned that Lee had evacuated Petersburg and Richmond and turned west to the mountains, perhaps to join with Johnston. Sherman's men swung out on the road again, heading west toward Raleigh. Johnston retired in front of him.

The news of Lee's surrender to Grant at Appomattox, April 9, came to both Johnston and Sherman in short order. Commanding the only army still in the field, Johnston knew he was no match for Sherman. He also knew that the Confederacy was dead, even though Jefferson Davis, now a fugitive, had ordered him to fight on. For over a week Johnston hesitated, but on April 17 and 18, 1865, he met with Sherman at Durham, North Carolina, just two days after Lincoln had died at the hands of an assassin. The two generals agreed upon an armistice pending reference of surrender terms to the president. The terms included recognition by the Union of the states of the Confederacy, the reestablishment of federal courts in the South, and the parole of Confederate armies still in resistance. Sherman agreed because he felt that it would be difficult to bag Johnston and fighting would have needlessly prolonged the war.* With that armistice and subsequent surrender, the work of the Western armies came to an end. They had already successfully concluded affairs in the Western Theater of Operations, and although some of their battles ended in a draw, they never experienced a serious setback. From Forts Henry and Donelson to Atlanta, they had done their work. After Atlanta they had turned east and played a role in the conclusion of affairs in that theater. The fighting done, they had one more duty to perform.

The Grand Review

Victory celebrations were interrupted by the death of the president on April 15, the flurry of activity that resulted in the roundup of the conspirators and the death of the assassin, and the swift trial of the principals in the plot. The black bunting of mourning had scarcely disappeared from the streets of the capital, when gay flags and banners replaced it as the city prepared two days of celebration and welcome for the victorious Union armies.

May 23, 1865, dawned clear and bright, as great crowds of spectators gathered along Pennsylvania Avenue. A reviewing stand, covered with flowers and evergreens, stood in front of the White House. President Andrew Johnson, Grant, the cabinet, important diplomats and guests, the Supreme Court, and other dignitaries

* The terms dealt with civil matters, which were not within Sherman's power to discuss and were disapproved. On April 26 Johnston accepted the same terms Lee had and disbanded his army of about 37,000.

took their places shortly before nine o'clock. Then a signal gun boomed, and the last great march of the Union armies began.

Meade, astride a horse covered with flowers, led the first units of the Army of the Potomac onto the avenue. The roadway trembled under the cadence of soldiers' boots as steady lines of men, sixty abreast, marched smartly by. Military bands accompanied the steady step of the infantry with "When Johnny Comes Marching Home" and "Tramp, Tramp, Tramp," but were nearly drowned out by the crowd's enthusiastic cheers. Sheridan's cavalry clattered by, sabers rattling and bugles sounding, a cavalcade of color, the officers and their horses covered with flowers. Blossoms decked the caissons and cannon of the artillery as well. The crowds roared time and again as the endless rows of men marched by in tight blue coats, jaunty hats, rifles and bayonets glinting in the sun. All day they paraded, the Eastern armies, until late in the afternoon when spectators, hoarse from hollering, saluted the last units.

The next day, ever curious, the crowds returned to Pennsylvania Avenue to welcome strangers, the armies of the West. When the signal cannon boomed again, Sherman raised his sword and led the Western troops down the avenue. A band struck up "Marching Through Georgia," and the spectators broke into cheers. They noted the different look of the Westerners, who wore their travel-marked, stained, and patched field uniforms, and carried faded and tattered, occasionally bullet-marked standards. Foragers pulled their loaded pack-trains, and the pioneer corps, composed of black soldiers, carried axes, spades, and shovels. Sherman's army was equipped just as it had been for any field march, contrasting vividly with the spit, polish, glitter, and precision of the Eastern army's full dress parade of the previous day. The Easterners had so impressed Sherman with their drill proficiency that he had exclaimed, "we cannot beat those fellows" in parade. So he had accepted a suggestion that they of the West pass in review just as they had marched through Georgia. They appeared to stroll rather than march, and they seemed rough and aggressive rather than smooth and polished. Washingtonians showered them with flowers and applauded as they read the streamers on the battle flags: Shiloh, Vicksburg, and Atlanta. When the sun again moved far to the west, and once more the crowds had worn their voices thin, the last soldiers paraded by. The Grand Review was over; the soldiers of the Eastern and Western armies were going home.

11
The War in the
Trans-Mississippi West

The Civil War affected the sparsely settled two-thirds of the United States located between the Mississippi River and the Pacific Ocean much less intensely than the more densely populated areas east of the river. The vast far western region of flat grassy prairies, rugged mountains, quiet valleys, and arid deserts contained four free and four slave states, and huge territories in various stages of civilization. The free states of Iowa and Minnesota clung to the banks of the Mississippi, while California and Oregon hugged the Pacific shore. Older than all the free states that had come into being since the Wilmot Proviso, the four slave states of Missouri, Arkansas, Louisiana, and Texas clustered west of the lower Mississippi. All except Missouri joined their fellow slaveholders in the Confederacy. The vast inland empire between the Missouri River and California, between British North America and Mexico, contained the territories of Dakota, Washington, Nebraska, Kansas, Utah, Colorado, Nevada, New Mexico, and Indian Territory.

Most of the territories were unknown except by name to the Easterners, with Kansas most recently in the news, born in 1854

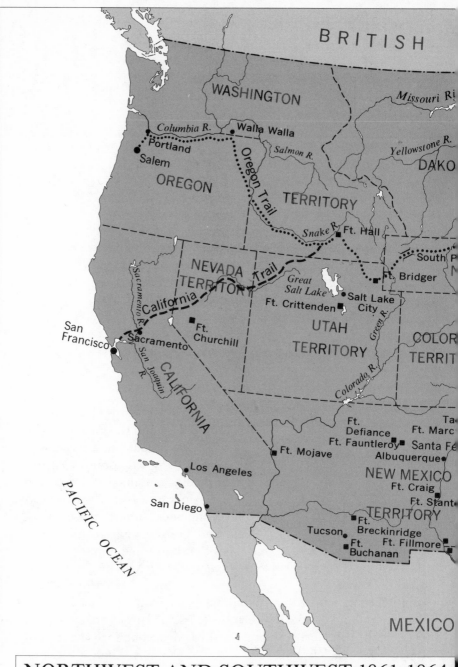

NORTHWEST AND SOUTHWEST 1861-1864
Showing military posts at the outbreak of the civil war

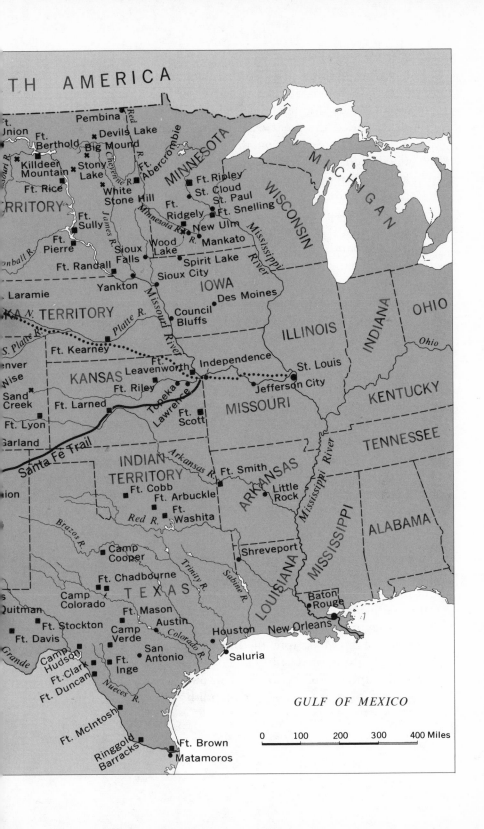

and christened in blood as Northern emigrants struggled in the violent decade before Sumter to carry out Whittier's command to make the West "the homestead of the free!" The trans-Mississippi West straddled the great overland trails that followed the Platte and North Platte rivers on their course from Independence and Council Bluffs to Oregon and California via Fort Bridger and Salt Lake City. Proud Indians, who cared little for the Union or the Confederacy, roamed the prairies, occupied the mountains and deserts, and feared for their way of life as frontiersmen intruded on their domain. The powerful Sioux and Cheyenne guarded their hunting grounds in the Dakotas and Nebraska, as the Arapaho, Kiowa, Comanche, and Apache tribes prepared to contest the white man for title to Kansas, Utah, New Mexico, and western Texas.

Sharing the land with emigrants on the trails and often hostile Indians, a few white men had carved out settlements in the great interior. The old and the new thrived, like Santa Fé on the banks of the Rio Grande, one of the oldest settlements in the United States, and Salt Lake City, new by comparison and the Mormon haven. Some were tiny former fur trading posts like Fort Hall on the banks of the Snake River; others were originally military outposts like Fort Laramie. A few had mushroomed in the wake of the discovery of precious metals as had Denver and Virginia City. Yet this frontier region of drifting whites and restless Indians was drawn into the maelstrom as the sections clashed, just as the remainder of the nation was. Both the Union and the Confederacy claimed a share of the West, and as a result several far-flung engagements of the Civil War took place there.

But the war west of the Mississippi was disturbed by a third element, the Indians. Just as they had historically been an important factor in the other wars of the United States, allied with the French or the British a century earlier as those great nations fought to win the continent, allied with the British during the Revolution, and only grudgingly giving way before the pressure of American expansion east of the Mississippi, the Indians again were an element to be reckoned with in the Civil War. For the most part, western Indians turned distraction of the war to their own benefit and remained immune to Union or Confederate blandishments.

New Mexico

In 1861 the Territory of New Mexico included the present states of New Mexico, Arizona, and southern Nevada, covering 250,000 square miles and some of the most rugged and arid terrain in North America. Roads were few and crude, no railroads yet crossed the territory, and both travel and communications were difficult and hazardous because of nature and the attitude of the Indians. On June 30, 1861, 2,466 officers and men of the Union army were garrisoned in the area. They had carried on continuous but ineffective warfare against determined nomadic Indians for years and were scattered in small forts across the territory in an effort to keep the main routes to California open.

New Mexico's strategic location interested the Confederate government. Control of the territory would limit Union communication with California and slow the flow of gold to the North. Confederate officials believed that the secessionist element in Southern California was strong enough to wrest that area from the Union if New Mexico should fall. Acquisition of California would divert badly needed gold and specie to the South, as well as provide the Confederacy with Pacific seaports. Even if those ends should fail, warfare in New Mexico and California would open a second front and divert Union strength from its concentration east of the Mississippi. Confederate officers further speculated that the Mormons in Utah, who had no firm attachment to the Union, would join the Confederacy if New Mexico were secured. Then Colorado, whose gold fields were worked by many Southerners, could be invaded from two sides. Moreover, since the Texans coveted the north Mexican states of Chihuahua and Sonora as a likely area in which to expand slavery, they anticipated minimal opposition from north Mexico either to conquest or to purchase should New Mexico fall.

New Mexico, then, appeared to be the key to a much enlarged Confederacy that would stretch from sea to sea, bringing the nation great prestige abroad, and perhaps the recognition and aid it sought. New Mexico, furthermore, looked like a plum ripe and ready for plucking. The Union force there was scattered and small; it had not enough artillery to equip a single fort properly; its stock of ammunition was low; the weapons were antiques; cavalry remounts were not available; and because they had not been paid for six months, the soldiers' morale was low.

Confederate military intelligence regarding New Mexico was excellent, for a number of famous officers went into Southern service from New Mexico's garrisons—including Major James Longstreet, Captain Richard S. Ewell, and Lieutenant Joseph Wheeler. Entrusted with the conquest of New Mexico was Major Henry H. Sibley, who received orders from Richmond in July 1861 to recruit troops in Texas and sweep the Union army from New Mexico. On July 23 Sibley led a force of about 400 Texas Mounted Rifles into Mesilla, and soon captured a Union force at nearby Fort Fillmore. Sibley made Mesilla capital of the Confederate Territory of Arizona.

Colonel Edward R. S. Canby, ranking Union officer in New Mexico, abandoned all outlying posts and concentrated his forces at Fort Craig and Fort Union. But at Mesilla, Sibley found the situation intolerable. The apathetic Spanish-American natives refused him assistance, Indians harassed his troops, bandits from Sonora plundered at will, and Sibley heard rumors of Union troops moving east from California to reinforce Canby. Sibley abandoned Mesilla and returned to Fort Bliss, Texas, to assume command of the Army of New Mexico recently created for him by Richmond. By January 1862 Sibley's new army numbered 2,500; although the soldiers were poorly supplied and equipped, Sibley once again advanced into New Mexico, determined to capture Union stores as he drove out the Union forces. Indian raids slowed Sibley's advance toward Fort Craig, and in particular the Chiricahua Apaches picked off his scouts and messengers.

Rather than attack Fort Craig, Sibley decided to bypass it. Canby anticipated this move, and attempted to head Sibley off at the Val Verde crossing of the Rio Grande. Canby's force included about 3,800 men, infantry, cavalry, and artillery, with a regiment of New Mexico Volunteers led by Colonel Christopher "Kit" Carson, and a handful of Colorado volunteers. Sibley, with perhaps 2,000 cavalry, sent his Texans into hot fire to capture the Union batteries, and force Canby into retreat. Both sides took heavy losses.

Victorious but weakened, Sibley marched north for Albuquerque and Santa Fé, where he expected to find supplies. But the Union troops had already removed all military stores from those towns to Fort Union, destroying what they could not carry. Canby now proposed to hold Fort Union at all costs and stoutly defend Fort Craig in order to cut off any supply line Sibley might try to establish with Texas. Without supplies, Sibley would have no choice but to retreat. Meanwhile, Canby's command was strengthened by the arrival at Fort Union of the First Colorado Volunteer Regiment under Colonel John B. Slough. From the West, Colonel James H. Carleton led 2,300 troops from southern California slowly into New Mexico.

Slough, ordered to defend Fort Union, interpreted the order to mean he should seek out and harass Sibley. Sibley, desperate because he found no supplies at Albuquerque or Santa Fé, decided to try to plunder Fort Union, although he was unaware of Slough's arrival. On the way to Fort Union, Sibley's vanguard ran head on into Slough's volunteers in Apache Canyon in the Sangre de Christo Mountains. The Texans retreated but turned and faced their pursuers two days later, March 28, 1862, at Glorietta Pass.

Slough gained the victory by sending Major John M. Chivington around the Confederate flank to destroy Sibley's wagon train and livestock. Sibley retreated back to Santa Fé and Albuquerque; Slough returned to Fort Union. Canby then marched to Albuquerque, where Sibley's position was so precarious he had to retreat. Canby pursued him at leisure, stirring later accusations that he had allowed Sibley to escape because Sibley was his brother-in-law. In fact Canby could not have fed nor guarded the Confederate force had he captured it, so he allowed Sibley to depart. On April 17, Sibley abandoned all the equipment he could not carry and struck off across some of the worst country in New Mexico to elude Canby. Without guides or a trail, Sibley reached Fort Bliss the first week in May, his command straggling along behind him for fifty miles. Canby returned to Fort Craig.

At Fort Bliss Sibley learned of Carleton's approach from the west and rode to San Antonio to find help. Sibley left his ragged Army of New Mexico to shift "every man for himself"; he had lost 1,700 men, and the army was in fact nothing more than a band of fugitives. Carleton had overcome great hardship to cross the southwestern desert and to reach the Texas border, only to find hostile Indians and no Confederates. Carleton subsequently sent patrols hundreds of miles into Texas, but seldom encountered armed resistance. Yet he had not strength enough to occupy the country because of the Indians. In August 1862 Canby was promoted and ordered east, and Carleton took command of New Mexico. He dealt mostly with the Navajos and Apaches for the remainder of the war, since the Confederate threat to New Mexico, key to a dream of a greatly expanded Southern nation, had collapsed.

Guerrilla Warfare

In Missouri in 1861 Union forces occupied the capital and drove the deposed Governor Jackson's troops from Boonville. Jackson soon rallied his troops at Carthage, and successfully beat off a Union attack led by Franz Sigel, a subordinate of General Lyon. Sterling Price then received reinforcements from Arkansas, bringing his Confederate forces up to 10,000 men. Though Lyon commanded only 6,000 Union troops, he met Price in battle at Wilson's Creek on August 10, 1861. Price routed Lyon, who died on the battlefield. After both sides rested and recruited during the fall and winter, Samuel R. Curtis forced Price to retreat to Arkansas. Then Earl Van Dorn assumed command of the Confederate army, and met Curtis in a showdown at Pea Ridge, Arkansas, March 7 and 8, 1862. Curtis drubbed Van Doren, even though the Confederates outnumbered the Union troops 16,000 to 10,000. Thereafter many of Van Doren's troops were transferred to Tennessee, and the Confederates were unable to prevent Curtis from occupying much of Arkansas.

The war in Arkansas, Kansas, Missouri, and southern Iowa turned into a guerrilla war, often difficult to separate from ordinary frontier banditry. Kansans, still smarting from their own bloody civil war, mistrusted the Missourians who had meddled in their affairs. Missourians in turn hated the "Jayhawkers" of Kansas and were themselves deeply divided on the question of union. More sparsely settled than the other two, Arkansas was in many respects more of a frontier but it was filled with Confederate partisans who longed to get at Missouri and Kansas Unionists. Southern Iowa counties felt the repercussions and formed a special militia organization to protect themselves from Missouri marauders.

Private violence mixed with guerrilla war to the extent that grudge battles were inseparable from military clashes. Union and Confederate guerrillas raided each other's territory, murdering, raping, burning, and looting. Union military commanders charged with keeping the peace in Missouri and Kansas found it nearly impossible to keep the civilian population from destroying itself.

Kansans welcomed the opportunity to wipe out Confederate sympathizers in Missouri. Led by James H. Lane, the militant free-state leader who had become one of the state's first senators after it joined the Union in 1861, the "Jayhawkers" ravaged the Missouri border, cleaning out "everything disloyal." Ironically the tables had turned: in the 1850s Missouri Senator Atchison had led armed Missourians into Kansas; now in the early 1860s a Kansas senator wrought revenge on Missouri. That spirit only kindled opposition and further divided the people.

Although the Confederate government early refused to recognize guerrilla companies as a part of their military organization, the companies existed anyway. William C. Quantrill in August 1863 led a band of over 300 men on a raid into Kansas. They surprised Lawrence on August 21, met no resistance, robbed most of the stores and banks, burned about a quarter of the town, and murdered 140 unarmed citizens. Quantrill was pursued vigorously, and nearby Missouri counties were partly devastated in revenge. Kansas rose to arms, protesting to Lincoln that federal forces, commanded by General John M. Schofield, were unable to protect Kansas. Rather than concentrating on Quantrill's capture, Schofield continued to devote much of his strength to policing the border between Kansas and Missouri. In an effort to put an end to the raids, Union officials decreed that prisoners identified as guerrillas would be hanged. The guerrillas replied that they would lay waste to the areas in which they operated, burning houses and killing civilians in retaliation.

The irregular activity along the border served little useful military purpose. Psychopathic killers like Quantrill and "Bloody" Bill Anderson, his lieutenant, used the Civil War as an excuse; border roughnecks used the war as a cover for theft and banditry. Quantrill's raiders included members of the James and Younger families, who learned their murderous postwar trade from their wartime actions.

In the fall of 1864, Sterling Price reappeared on the scene with an army of 15,000 and struck boldly into Missouri. His goal was St. Louis, but finding it too strongly defended, he turned west to Jefferson City. Union forces reacted promptly, and Price fought nothing more than several small engagements as he moved rapidly to avoid being encircled. After a month of semiguerrilla activity, and without seriously hurting his enemies, Price returned to Arkansas. With him went a number of irregular guerrilla bands, bringing a measure of relief to southern Missouri. His invasion represented the last Confederate threat to the state.

Indians and the Civil War

The Indians of the Northwest

Western Indians grew restless in the 1860s partly in response to the war, but not, as was widely believed, because of Confederate activity. In the Indian Country west of Arkansas a Confederate Indian Office was established to take over from the Union's Bureau of Indian Affairs, since the Confederacy claimed the territory. Union agents were forced out, and the inhabitants entered into treaties with Richmond. Confederate activities hurt the tribes in the long run, for the United States considered them defectors. As a result, after the war the Five Civilized Tribes lost half their territory, which the United States used to resettle some of the Plains Indians. The Five Civilized Tribes were in fact divided over the issue of support for the Confederacy, with those who supported the Union forced to flee to Union-held western military posts for protection. Some Indians soldiered for the Confederacy; Cherokee troops were present at the battle of Pea Ridge, while Colonel Stand Watie distinguished himself as a Confederate officer. Another Indian leader, John Ross, used his influence for the Union.

Outside of Confederate operations in Indian Territory, no evidence existed to connect Richmond with other Indian difficulties. It was simply easier to blame the Confederacy for Indian problems than to blame United States Indian policy. One of the greatest Indian massacres of white settlers in the history of the nation occurred in the Minnesota Valley in August 1862, when Minnesota Sioux rose up in arms and slaughtered hundreds of settlers. It could not have come at a worse time for the Union, following as it did on the heels of the defeat at Second Bull Run.

Over 6,600 Minnesota Sioux had been compressed into a reserve ten miles wide and 150 miles long on the south bank of the Minnesota River between Fort Ridgely and Lake Traverse. Their cousins, another 3,000 Yanktonai Sioux, roamed neighboring Dakota Territory. Proud of their heritage and way of life, the Sioux resisted efforts to turn them into farmers or to Christianize them, "to make white men of them," as an Indian agent put it. They mistrusted the white man who stole their land, hated the traders who cheated them out of their annuities and treated them as inferiors, and protested the Lincoln administration's appointments of both agents and the district superintendents. They came to regard the relaxed military strength on the frontier as an opportunity to drive out the whites. They needed no enticement from the Confederacy.

Rumors circulated in Minnesota that the Sioux had made common cause with their ancient enemies, the Chippewa, and with the Winnebago as well, to get rid of the white man. The rumor was false, though a simultaneous uprising of the Chippewa was narrowly averted at the time of the Sioux massacre. The secretary of the interior in Washington feared that nearly all of the tribes were involved in a giant conspiracy. He had word that the Shoshoni in Utah and all the other tribes west of the Missouri—the Mandan, Assiniboin, Blackfoot, Teton Sioux, and others on the northern plains—were ready to go on the warpath. The commissioner of Indian affairs publicly warned against travel on the plains.

For the Minnesota Sioux, the "spark of fire, upon a mass of discontent" fell on August 17, 1862. A few braves murdered several settlers, then the Sioux, afraid of retaliation, apparently decided to wage a preventive war. They swept violently down upon the Minnesota frontier, with no specific campaign tactic other than to erase Fort Ridgely and New Ulm and push the whites back across the Mississippi. Their hopes were thwarted by stubborn resistance at both places, as well as by their own lack of organization. Along the entire frontier, from Wisconsin west through Minnesota, Iowa, Dakota, and Nebraska settlers trembled. Frontiersmen abandoned outlying settlements and hastened to safer ground. The Minnesota Valley emptied of whites and furious Indians plundered and burned homes and settlements.

The army maintained four posts in the area, Forts Abercrombie and Randall in Dakota Territory and Ridgely and Ripley in Minnesota. Usually they employed about fourteen companies of the regular army, but by the time of the Sioux uprising only seven companies were on duty, all men who had volunteered to fight the Confederacy, all untrained. Fort Snelling, Minnesota, had recently been reactivated for the state to use to gather its volunteers. With the news of the outbreak, Dakota mobilized its militia; Iowans es-

tablished the Northern Border Brigade to man a chain of block-
houses along the Minnesota line; Wisconsin distributed arms along
the frontier; and Nebraska appealed to the federal government for
help.

Minnesota's governor commissioned Colonel Henry H. Sibley
(unrelated to the Confederate officer of the same name) to lead an
expedition against the Sioux. Using the volunteers assembled at
Fort Snelling, Sibley soon raised the siege of New Ulm and shortly
thereafter, Fort Ridgely. The governor appealed also to the federal
government, and the War Department responded by creating the
military Department of the Northwest on September 6. General
John Pope, recently defeated at Second Bull Run and an embarrassment to the Lincoln administration, took command. By the
time he arrived in St. Paul on September 16, Sibley had the situation well in hand. On September 23 Sibley defeated the Sioux in a
pitched battle at Wood Lake, and the Sioux either surrendered as
Sibley directed them or fled to the Dakotas.

The Sioux who surrendered or who were apprehended by various scouting parties after Wood Lake were tried for a variety of
crimes by a military commission. Over 1,600 were held in custody
at Fort Snelling, and another 346 at Mankato. The commission
tried 425 for murder and participation in the outbreak, found 321
guilty, and sentenced 303 to death by hanging. Cautious, Pope sent
the trial transcripts to Lincoln, who subsequently approved the
death sentence for only 38, and ordered the remainder held. On
December 26, 1862, the 38 died on a mass scaffold at Mankato. The
others were removed to a military prison near Davenport, Iowa.
The Indians at Fort Snelling, partly to protect them from vengeance at the hands of irate Minnesotans and partly because Congress had revoked their treaty and closed their reservation in Minnesota, were removed along with the Winnebago to a new
reservation at Crow Creek, on the Missouri River above Fort Randall.

The Minnesota Sioux had taken between 200 and 800 lives
(the exact number is unknown) in August and September of 1862.
Their power in Minnesota was broken, but not outside of the state.
The Uncpapa, Blackfoot, Yanktonai, and renegade Minnesota
Sioux announced that they considered the Upper Missouri Valley
closed to whites. According to rumor, Little Crow, who had led the
Minnesota Sioux in their outbreak and who remained a fugitive,

had mobilized 500 to 1,000 warriors for a spring campaign. Other intelligence reports seemed to confirm the rumor. Pope sent two columns into the field in the summer of 1863, one led by Sibley to sweep up the Minnesota and into Dakota to the vicinity of Devil's Lake, then westward to the Missouri River. A second column, led by General Alfred Sully, was to march north up the Missouri and join there with Sibley. They hoped to catch the Sioux between them, and cut off their escape across the Missouri River.

Sibley's column moved as planned, and met 1,000 to 1,500 Sioux in battle at Big Mound, Dakota Territory, on July 24, but the Indians escaped westward. In pursuit, Sibley fought another engagement at Dead Buffalo Lake two days later. Then, on July 28 the Sioux "in numbers that seemed almost incredible" attacked him at Stony Lake. Sibley routed them, but they escaped, without their equipage, across the Missouri. Unfortunately Sully arrived at the rendezvous a month late, and then turned back down the Missouri. One of his patrols ran into a Sioux encampment and were surrounded, as a group led by Inkpaduta, the notorious renegade who had led the Spirit Lake, Iowa, massacre in 1857, prepared for a slow, ceremonial slaughter of the troopers. In a Hollywood-style finish, Sully's main force galloped to their rescue at dusk. "The fight took place," Sully reported, on September 3 "near a hill called by the Indians White Stone Hill." Although there had been much fighting, the Sirocco Campaign of 1863 in the Dakotas did not accomplish its objective.

No sooner were Sibley and Sully back in camp when new reports filtered in of Sioux determination to block the Missouri, close the trails, and perhaps strike at white settlements. In May 1864 Sioux raiding parties harassed the Minnesota-Iowa border, struck details of soldiers along the Missouri above Fort Randall, and in June stole forty cavalry horses from Fort Randall itself. Pope's plan to build a string of forts up the Missouri and northeastward to Devil's Lake was approved by the War Department. Sully led an expedition up the Missouri to locate the new posts and chastize the Sioux, and while engaged in the construction of Fort Rice, received reports of a concentration of Sioux at Killdeer Mountain. Sully rapidly closed on that place, and on July 28 Sully's 2,200 soldiers defeated a large body of Sioux in a sharp fight. Sully then chased them westward across the Bad Lands of Dakota to rendezvous with steamers sent to pick him up on the Yellowstone. Back at Fort Rice after tramping down the Yellowstone to the Missouri and down the Missouri to the fort, Sully dispatched 900 men to rescue a wagon train besieged by the Sioux between the Little Missouri and the Cannonball rivers. Sully thought the Bad Lands Campaign of 1864 a success.

Yet the Sioux refused to settle down and leave the frontier quiet. Still another federal expedition searched them out in the Dakota Territory in 1865. By then the Sioux hostilities had ceased to be a part of the Union's Civil War burden and had launched instead into the prolonged war between the Sioux and the United States that never really concluded until the battle of Wounded Knee, two weeks after Sitting Bull's death in 1890.

The Indians of the Southwest

As Congress debated the creation of Colorado Territory in 1861, the Arapaho and Cheyenne negotiated a treaty at Fort Wise according them as a reservation a triangular tract of land where Big Sandy Creek and the Arkansas River meet in southwestern Colorado. Fort Lyon, near that junction, became their agency. Although they ceded the remainder of their range to the United States, they retained the right to hunt over it until it should be disposed of and settled. The Sandy Creek reserve failed because it contained some of the driest, most desolate parts of the original Indian range; it had been allotted in the first place only because it was removed from the main routes of travel. The Indians never lived on the reserve but continued to wander over their old lands, growing more and more upset as they watched the traffic increase on the stage lines and more and more whites file into their country. White settlements sprang up across the Indian hunting grounds at every place there was a water hole. The Indians remained patient for three years, but in the summer of 1864 they attacked the stage line along its entire length from Fort Kearny to Denver.

Reports of their intentions had led the governor to ask friendly Indians to collect around the agencies and to warn that those who did not would be treated as hostile and killed. The Arapaho and Cheyenne ignored the warning and instead destroyed the stage line. Casualties were few, but property damage was huge. By September, communication with Missouri was uncertain; every stagecoach needed a military escort; and wagon trains traveled in tight groups for mutual protection.

Later in the fall, Arapaho and Cheyenne groups began arriving at Fort Lyon, professing their friendship. On September 28 Black Kettle told Governor John Evans "we want . . . our people . . . [to] sleep in peace." Evans replied that he could not make a new treaty then; he had heard, he said, that because "the whites are at war among themselves, you think you can now drive the whites from this country," but that was a false hope. Soon the war among the whites will end, Evans told the Indians, and then "the Great Father will not know what to do with all his soldiers, except to send them after the Indians." The governor advised them to make their peace as best they could with the military.

Colonel Chivington, of Glorietta Pass fame, had accompanied the governor to the council, and told the Indians the soldiers were under his command. He warned that his rule of war was to fight the enemy "until they lay down their arms and submit." The council ended on that note, and that same evening, Chivington received a dispatch from General Samuel R. Curtis at Fort Leavenworth, departmental headquarters. Curtis wanted "no peace till the Indians suffer more," he said, and in any event, there could be no peace "without my directions."

The Arapaho and Cheyenne, without any assurances, continued to gather at Fort Lyon hoping to come to terms with the military. They made their camp at Sandy Creek, and convinced the Indian agent of their good intentions. Authorities at Fort Lyon gave them permission to camp peacefully under the watchful eye of the garrison. But Colorado authorities, including Governor Evans, believed the only way to lasting peace was through a punitive winter campaign. Colonel Chivington agreed, and stationed two regiments of volunteers at Fort Lyon early in November. After dark on November 28, Chivington led his force to Sandy Creek, surrounded the slumbering encampment, and ordered his men to attack at dawn.

As the sun rose on November 29, Chivington's men opened fire. Black Kettle raised both an American and a white flag to stop the slaughter, to no avail. The Colorado troops destroyed the camp and indiscriminately killed braves, squaws, and children. In a vicious massacre, some Indians "were scalped, their brains knocked out; the men used their knives, ripped open women, clubbed little children," and "mutilated their bodies in every sense of the word." Colorado authorities called it a punitive campaign. The Commissioner of Indian Affairs, horrified, described it as a massacre "in cold blood by troops in the service of the United States."

Remaining Arapaho and Cheyenne took to the plains again and remained on the move until October 1865. Then, at a conference attended not only by the Arapaho and Cheyenne, but also by some Apache, Kiowa, and Comanche, they accepted a temporary peace. The Senate never confirmed the treaty they signed. Not until 1867 were they provided a new home, and then it was land in Indian Territory taken from the Five Civilized Tribes.

Indian Problems and the Civil War

Neither the conflict in Texas and New Mexico between soldiers in blue and soldiers in gray, nor the conflicts in the northwest and southwest between red and white men affected the outcome of the Civil War. Rather, the Civil War affected the frontier. The weakened state of frontier defenses, as regulars were withdrawn to participate in the major war and untrained volunteers took their place, provided both the Sioux and the Cheyenne with opportunities for war. Moreover, war stories excited the Indians, and continued white migration into the west gave them motivation. Still, the impact of the war went much deeper.

Not only were regulars withdrawn from the frontier and replaced by volunteers and militia, but the manpower demands of the larger war continuously wreaked havoc with even the skeleton protection. Records of the Civil War era contain uncounted pleas from the frontier to the War Department and the president for men and weapons. The governors of Dakota Territory, Iowa, Kansas, Nebraska, and Wisconsin pleaded for help following each Sioux uprising. The governor of Minnesota had the greatest need, with perhaps 800 settlers dead, 2,000 wounded, and 30,000 refugees. He used the Minnesota volunteers being mustered into federal service at Fort Snelling, and then wondered how the state could possibly fill its Civil War quotas. He tried to get Lincoln to postpone the draft, but the president refused as had the War Department before him.

When the War Department created the military Department of the Northwest, it merely recognized the frontier's problem, nothing more. The department included "the troops raised, and to be raised" in Wisconsin, Minnesota, Iowa, and Nebraska and Dakota territories. Yet Pope had little control over those levies. Of the one

Iowa, seven Minnesota, and six Wisconsin regiments he ordered into the field, he received only the seven Minnesota (already chasing Little Crow) and one of the Wisconsin regiments. The others were earmarked for service against the Confederacy. Pope had even worse luck trying to use troops captured by the Confederates and paroled—only one such regiment joined him.

The commander had similar troubles in mounting his troops. He felt at a distinct disadvantage using infantry against mounted Indians, but his efforts to buy mounts met with only minimum success. The insatiable demand of the Civil War for both men and horses scooped up available stock. The same pertained with regard to wagons and harness. Requisitions on the War Department met with cold replies such as "your requisitions cannot be filled without taking supplies from other troops now in the field," or else simply, "not approved." The need for transport to move supplies for frontier troops was graphically demonstrated when Sibley's soldiers dug potatoes from Indian fields "in order to subsist."

Neither were there enough arms to go around. At one time Pope had 5,600 men, 1,200 of whom were unarmed. Many carried whatever weapons they were able to find, even preferring them to obsolete Belgian muskets and other castoffs that ultimately found their way to the frontier. For the most part the Sioux were better armed, having long since discarded their bows, arrows, and lances for double-barreled guns that fired either buckshot or large caliber "traders balls," supplied for hunting by the Interior Department under the annuity clause of their treaties.

Frontier departments also faced considerable difficulty retaining their troops. The War Department time and again ordered this regiment or that to service elsewhere, putting frontier commanders in a dilemma over protection of the frontier. For example, the War Department removed one regiment for service in the South on the eve of the Bad Lands Campaign, nearly upsetting those plans. The War Department never trusted the number of troops reported by frontier commanders as in service, and frequently sent investigators to ascertain the actual count. Frontier commanders, on the other hand, often did report fewer men in service than they actually had, lest the War Department strip them of manpower they felt they needed. In almost every way, operations on the frontier were minimized by the war in the east.

Louisiana

One of the strongest Confederate military centers west of the Mississippi was located in the Red River Valley of Louisiana. Kirby Smith and a Confederate force of about 25,000 men occupied the area, affording protection for the large stores of cotton located there. Federal authorities hoped to seize the cotton and ordered General Nathaniel Banks to move up river from New Orleans to try. Banks refused in 1863, complaining that the water level in the river was too low to permit his army to be supplied by water. Early in 1864 he marched out with 27,000 men and a fleet of gunboats. He moved slowly toward Shreveport, his objective, but was intercepted on April 8 by Kirby Smith's forces at Sabine Crossroads, just two days' march from the city. Banks failed to complete his mission, and returned to New Orleans.

Kirby Smith, commander of the Confederate Trans-Mississippi Department, and Edward R. S. Canby, then commander of the Union Department of the Gulf, shared honors for the final surrender of Confederate forces. Lee surrendered at Appomattox on April 9; Canby completed a successful campaign against Mobile, the last Confederate stronghold on the Gulf, and accepted its surrender on April 12, which included all Confederate forces in Alabama and Mississippi; and Johnston surrendered to Sherman on April 18. That left only Kirby Smith's troops in western Louisiana and Texas. Smith had called on his troops to remain at arms and had fostered meetings in Texas that resolved never to give up to the United States. It was all in vain, and reluctantly about a month later, on May 26, Smith closed out the last Confederate land resistance by surrendering to Canby. It was a source of satisfaction to Canby to have had presided over some of the earliest engagements in the war in New Mexico and then to be the one to take the final surrender.

12
Naval Operations

For nearly twenty years prior to Sumter, the graceful and speedy clipper ships of the American merchant marine dominated the seas, carrying the cream of the world's commerce and penetrating to every part of the globe. Alongside these hundreds of fine American clippers, the United States Navy suffered in comparison. At the time of Sumter it had forty-two ships in commission, including storeships and tenders. Six ships rode at anchor in Northern ports, four nestled in Pensacola harbor, another cruised the Great Lakes. The remainder bobbed on station or sailed the seas, in the East Indies, in the Mediterranean, off the slave coasts of Africa, near Brazil, at Vera Cruz, and in the Pacific. Some of the vessels, like the *Congress*, represented the best ships of war of their class under sail; yet in 1861 they already belonged to the past. The era of steam had dawned on the navies of the world, an era that heralded the demise of the peaceful clippers as well.

The U.S. Navy listed about forty vessels of this modern sort, but not all in commission. Fourteen were laid up or were not fit for service. Seventeen remained on foreign station. Some were only tenders for sailing vessels. Six, built in 1855, were screw-driven frigates that were the pride of the navy; another twelve, much smaller sloops-of-war built in 1858, promised to be very useful. The screw frigates were not able to operate in shallow coastal waters, but the screw sloops-of-war became the mainstay of the Gulf Squadron.

Congress neglected the navy in the decade before the Civil War, reluctantly appropriating funds sufficient to keep the fleet little more than a national gesture. That was traditionally the fate of a peacetime navy in the United States. Congressman Owen Lovejoy of Illinois, during a session of Buchanan's congress full of secession talk and war threats, roundly condemned a naval appropriations bill. He was tired of spending money on the army and navy, he said, when "they are of no use whatever." He wanted to "strike a blow" at naval expenditure "and let the navy go out of existence." Lovejoy, staunch abolitionist that he was, proved distressingly shortsighted; like others at the time, including Ohio's John Sherman, he truly believed war to be out of the question. No wonder Gideon Welles, charged by Lincoln with administering the navy, should lament shortly after Sumter in an understatement typical of his Yankee background, that the navy was "not as powerful or in numbers as extensive as I wished."

The Confederacy, of course, had not even that much at the outset. On April 17, 1861, Davis issued a proclamation inviting prospective privateers to apply for letters of marque, and the Confederate Congress complied with the necessary legislation the following month. Although the Union seized a number of excellent Southern owned ships in Northern ports, a few privateers put to sea. The schooner *Savannah* was one, but it was taken by the Union navy within a few weeks off the coast of South Carolina. The initial activities of the Southern vessels aroused Yankee ship-owners and merchants. The Atlantic and Pacific Steamship Company of New York sought permission to arm its vessels; the Pacific Mail Steamship Company, insistently echoed by insurance firms, asked for protection; and Northern commercial interests in general demanded that the South be promptly and tightly blockaded.

The Union Blockade

A week after Sumter and two days after Davis' privateers proclamation, Lincoln promulgated his blockade. Because a "combina-

tion of persons" in insurrection "have threatened to grant pretended letters of marque" against the property and commerce of the
United States, and for other reasons, such as the inability to enforce
revenue laws of the United States, and in order to protect "the public peace," Lincoln "deemed it advisable to set on foot a blockade of
the ports" of the seceded states. He did so "in pursuance of the laws
of the United States, and of the law of Nations." Lincoln warned
that any "person" apprehended molesting a vessel of the United
States with a letter of marque would be held accountable under federal piracy laws.

Lincoln claimed the proclamation was based both on United
States law and the law of nations, yet the United States had refused
to join nearly every other major commercial nation in signing the
Declaration of Paris in 1856.* Secretary of State Seward moved
quickly on April 24 to get the U.S. to adhere to the treaty, but after
more than a year of negotiations, the venture failed. Had Seward
succeeded, the European nations would have been obliged to treat
Confederate privateers as pirates, and neither Britain nor France
were prepared to do that. The problem was that by the time the
U.S. entered negotiations, Britain had declared neutrality, in effect
recognizing the belligerent rights of the South. As a belligerent, the
Confederacy had the right to arm privateers, which under international law would then have to be treated like any other armed vessels of a belligerent. The United States did not recognize the belligerent status of the Confederacy, Washington claimed, and thus held
that Confederate privateers were pirates; as a signatory to the Declaration of Paris, the U.S. would have insisted that other party
nations also treat Southern vessels as pirates. Since the Union and
Europe differed on the nature of the conflict in America, mutual
adherence to the declaration would have been meaningless and
have only led to friction.

Immediately after Lincoln's statement, Welles began to purchase or lease vessels for the navy to implement the blockade, as the
Union was determined to carry it out regardless of foreign reactions
to Seward's negotiations. The blockade was an important factor in

---

* The Declaration of Paris on maritime warfare included these points: 1) privateering was
abolished; 2) a neutral flag protects enemy goods, except for contraband; 3) neutral goods,
except for contraband, are safe under the enemy's flag; and 4) blockades if they are to be considered binding must be effective, that is, upheld by a naval force sufficient to actually block
the enemy's coast.

Union military strategy. While the armies on land sought to divide and conquer the Confederacy, the blockade at sea was designed to strangle the South, not just to prevent privateering. Thus Confederate ports from Chesapeake Bay to Key West were to be closed by Louis M. Goldsborough's North Atlantic Squadron and Samuel F. Du Pont's South Atlantic Squadron. The Gulf Squadron assumed responsibility for ports in that area. Before spring had turned to summer, the Union navy had ships on station and had seized several privateers and detained several British vessels. Secretary of the Navy Welles was aware how imperfect the blockade was at first, but Northerners hurried to build and convert ships for the duty, confident they would be able to increase the effectiveness of the blockade.

Southerners meanwhile took advantage of their 3,500-mile coastline, secure in the knowledge that the Union navy could not hermetically seal it off even with vastly greater resources than they had at hand. The deep sea ports were more or less closed from the beginning, but the Confederacy exploited small coasting vessels of limited cargo capacities using alternate ports with second-rate facilities. Many ships entered and departed from the Confederacy. Northern yachts, ferries, freighters, and the like were rapidly converted for blockade duty, and the problem of running the federal blockade became increasingly complex. By mid-1864 the effort was mostly confined to fast steamers and specially-built, low-silhouette, light-draft craft. Yet no matter how speculative blockade running became, the Union navy never succeeded in making it an unprofitable venture.

The Union navy was forced to occupy several Confederate coastal ports, not only to close them effectively, but also to provide service bases for its own often unusual, occasionally unseaworthy blockaders. Moreover, Union ships could spend more time on station if they had to spend less time in transit to supply bases. One of the first Union efforts to this end was the capture of Hatteras Inlet, the principal sea entrance to the North Carolina Sounds, in August 1861. They followed with the capture of Roanoke Island, which lay between the Sounds, in a joint army-navy operation in February 1862. Burnside, commanding the army force, next took New Berne, North Carolina's second most important port, in March. In April federal forces reduced Fort Macon, which overlooked the channel to Beaufort, North Carolina. These actions established the Union in command over much of the North Carolina coast, and with the acquisition of Beaufort, the navy obtained a good base for its blockaders.

A similar operation was launched in South Carolina. Just as the North Atlantic Squadron needed a base on North Carolina's coast, the South Atlantic Squadron sought a base in South Carolina. Port Royal, about midway between Charleston and Savannah, looked like a good target to Welles. Du Pont led an expedition of 12,000 men, many transports, and 45 naval vessels of all types, which on November 7, 1861, reduced Forts Walker and Beauregard, and took Port Royal. The next day one of the warships sailed up the Beaufort River as far as Beaufort, reporting that citizens had set the cotton afire and fled. In April 1862 another expedition took Fort Pulaski, closing the entrance to Savannah. Du Pont then controlled the two best harbors in his area, Charleston and Savannah.

The Confederate Navy Department concluded that wooden vessels would not suffice to sweep the Yankee navy from the seas and open commerce with foreign powers. Stephen R. Mallory, the Confederate navy secretary who before the war had chaired the Senate Committee on Naval Affairs, was enamored of ironclads. He knew that the French had used armored batteries in the Crimean War and that the French and British were both building armored frigates and battleships. In the *Merrimac*, a screw frigate burned and sunk by the Union navy when they evacuated Norfolk, Mallory had a suitable hull. On the restored body the Confederates put a long, sloping casemate, covering it with two feet of timber over which four inches of iron, from railroad rails, was fixed. They mounted ten heavy guns behind this protection, and fixed a cast iron ram to her bow. The *Merrimac*, rechristened the *Virginia*, posed a powerful threat to the wooden Union navy, despite serious drawbacks. The Confederacy could not build a marine engine, and the one aboard the *Merrimac* had been condemned after her last voyage; it could deliver no more than five knots speed and would not run reliably for more than six hours at a stretch. A heavy vessel, she drew twenty feet of water and was very cumbersome to steer, taking the better part of an hour to turn about.

Even so, when the *Merrimac* appeared at Hampton Roads on March 8, 1862, she was able to destroy the Union ships *Congress* and *Cumberland*, without any damage to herself except the loss of her ram. In spite of the *Merrimac*'s shortcomings, she proved an effective war machine in action against the wooden blockaders. Elated Confederate officials awaited her reappearance on March 9, when she was expected to finish off the Union flagship *Minnesota*. In Washington, Union officials reacted in near panic. What would prevent the *Merrimac* from steaming up the Potomac and reducing the capital?

Union naval officials had come to an appreciation of the possibilities of ironclad warships more slowly. They had allowed the Confederacy to get the jump on them, then upon learning about the *Merrimac*, had raced to catch up. Three ironclad designs were quickly approved and begun. The first to be launched was designed by Captain John Ericsson, a Swedish-born marine engineer who had developed and patented a screw propeller. Ericsson's *Monitor* was an original design, unlike any warship afloat. It looked like a long raft with a turret mounted on top and was familiarly known as "a cheesebox on a raft." It was over 170 feet long, had a draft of just over 10 feet. Only 2 feet of the hull remained above water, protected by 5 inches of iron. The revolving turret was a cylinder of 8-inch thick wrought iron that stood 9 feet high, carried two 11-inch smoothbore guns, and revolved in a full circle. The bridge or pilot house rode forward, with a speaking tube for communication with the turret. The *Monitor* had a speed of about six knots, but with less draft and of shorter length than the *Merrimac*, it was easier to handle.

Launched January 30, 1862, commissioned February 25, the *Monitor* left New York under tow March 6, for Hampton Roads. She arrived about 9:00 P.M. on March 8, too late to participate in the *Merrimac*'s party that day. About 7:00 A.M. on March 9, a Sunday, Union officials observed the *Merrimac* steaming toward the *Minnesota*, which had gone aground the day before. The *Monitor* quickly got under way and made for the *Merrimac*. The two vessels drew side by side and exchanged fire. "The battle continued at close quarters," the *Monitor*'s executive officer reported, "without apparent damage to either side."

After a time, a shell from the *Merrimac* struck the pilot house and injured the *Monitor*'s captain, creating confusion and causing the *Monitor* to break off action temporarily. By the time the executive officer had made his way from the turret to the pilot house, the *Merrimac*'s commander concluded the *Monitor* had quit and ordered the *Merrimac* back to her base. The *Monitor* fired a few parting shots, then returned to her own anchorage near the *Minnesota*. The two iron monsters had shelled each other at close range, with small damage to either; they had tried to ram each other, without success. The fight had been a draw, though in a tactical sense the victory was the *Monitor*'s. She had prevented the destruction of the *Minnesota* or any other blockaders of the wooden navy after her arrival and thus saved the blockade.

Like two wary antagonists on a chessboard, the *Monitor* and *Merrimac* cautiously watched each other. Twice the *Merrimac* steamed out on the Elizabeth River, unable to attack the *Monitor*, sheltered as it was by the guns of the federal batteries, or lure her into a showdown, for the *Monitor* was ordered only to fight if the *Merrimac* attacked the blockaders. The *Merrimac* kept the Union fleet out of the James River just as the *Monitor* kept her out of Chesapeake Bay.

Ultimately the Confederates evacuated Norfolk and had to destroy the *Merrimac*, whose deep draft prevented her from crossing the James River bar and escaping upstream. With the James River thus open, the *Monitor* and other ironclads steamed up the river to protect McClellan's flank during the peninsular campaign. Toward the end of December, after McClellan had withdrawn from the peninsula, the *Monitor* was ordered to Beaufort, North Carolina. Under tow, she perished on New Year's Eve 1862 in a gale off Cape Hatteras.

The Confederacy built other ironclads of the *Merrimac* type, but none successfully emulated the original. Toward the end of January 1863 two of these ironclads fought with blockaders off Charleston for a couple of hours in the pre-dawn haze, damaging the two Union vessels but failing to raise the blockade. A third ironclad engaged two monitors off Savannah in June 1863 but took a terrible beating from them. The Union navy built a number of ships of the *Monitor* class, usually larger and heavier, which were effective against Confederate ironclads but not against shore batteries. The Confederates manned an early type of submarine off Charleston, which successfully sank a blockader before it went to the bottom itself.

The *Albemarle*, a Southern ironclad of the *Merrimac* type built on the Roanoke River, successfully regained control of that river mouth for the Confederacy in mid-April 1864. It contributed to the surrender of the Union garrison at Plymouth and early in May took on the Union squadron in Albemarle Sound. The Union could field no monitors in the sound, for they could not cross Hatteras bar. In October 1864 Lieutenant William B. Cushing led a commando-like raid against the *Albemarle* and succeeded in exploding a torpedo against her. She sank, but Cushing's vessel was also destroyed and his crew captured; Cushing alone escaped. Albemarle Sound again fell to the Union navy, and Plymouth was recaptured.

The River War

The contest for control of the inland waterways erupted early. By November 1861 three river steamers had been converted into gunboats for service on the Mississippi, with five inches of solid oak as armor. By January 1862 seven ironclads, built by James Buchanan Eads, an engineer from Indiana, joined the river fleet. Partially protected by armor and designed to carry thirteen guns, these vessels accompanied the wooden gunboats that aided Grant's campaign against Fort Henry and Fort Donelson on the Tennessee and Cumberland rivers. When those Confederate strongholds fell, the navy controlled the Tennessee River as far as Florence, Alabama, and the Cumberland to Nashville. The ironclads next assisted Pope in the capture of Island No. 10, the Confederate strongpoint whose batteries commanded the Mississippi River. The distinction of being the first gunboat to run past heavy enemy batteries fell to the *Carondelet*, which made a dramatic nighttime dash past the guns of Island No. 10 to cut off Confederate reinforcements from downstream, facilitate the crossing of Pope's army, and make possible the capture of the batteries and some 7,000 prisoners.

The fleet continued down the Mississippi, now in company with another class of river warship, rams designed by Colonel Charles R. Ellet, an engineer from Pennsylvania. Ellet had picked seven river steamers for their speed and strength and had added solid timber bulkheads, with two feet of oak to protect their boilers. Unable to oppose the federal fleet on the Tennessee and the Cumberland, the Confederacy hastily turned fourteen river steamers at New Orleans into rams and sent eight of them up to Memphis to defend the river. On May 10, 1862, the Confederate rams sank one federal gunboat and drove another ashore off Fort Pillow, about eighty miles below Island No. 10. Both federal ships were quickly repaired and ready for action by June.

On June 6 the fleets clashed near Memphis. Flag Officer

Charles Henry Davis, Harvard educated and an experienced and knowledgeable naval officer, commanded the Union flotilla. The tiny Confederate fleet fought under Commodore J. E. Montgomery, a former steamboat pilot. In a short but hard fight, watched from a high bluff by the citizens of Memphis, the Union flotilla destroyed the Confederate fleet—only one of the eight escaped, and not before it too had been damaged. The Union ram *Queen of the West* sliced the Confederate flagship in two, while other Confederate vessels sank, ran aground, or were disabled. Memphis had little to cheer about that day, and on the next, the city surrendered. Within a month just above Vicksburg Davis' squadron met another group of federal ships that had come up river from New Orleans.

"The most important event of the War of the Rebellion," wrote Admiral David D. Porter of the U.S. Navy, "with the exception of the fall of Richmond, was the capture of New Orleans." Porter planned the expedition and picked his friend, David G. Farragut, to command it. Confederate officials expected the assault and prepared feverishly for it. They strengthened Fort Jackson and Fort St. Philip, which guarded the river below New Orleans, and constructed several powerful rams. The *Manassas*, complete, was ready for action; the *Louisiana*, nearly complete, but with defective engines, was moored as a floating battery just above the forts; and the largest of all, the *Mississippi*, was abuilding. A number of other vessels, ranging in size from ocean-going steamers to tugs, brought to forty the number of Confederate naval guns poised to repulse the attack.

At midnight, April 18, 1862, federal mortar ships began to pound Fort Jackson. Despite the terrible noise and din, the sturdy old fort sustained little damage in the next five days of constant bombardment. Farragut despaired of reducing the forts and proposed to run past them. By three in the morning of April 24, Farragut's ships were underway. The frigates swept the forts with grape and canister as they passed by and engaged in a hot fire fight with the Confederate flotilla. The Confederates fought valiantly, but Farragut's fleet successfully disabled or destroyed many of them and pressed on to New Orleans. The *Manassas* was put out of action, and the *Louisiana* was set afire by her commander to prevent capture. Farragut arrived at New Orleans about noon on April 25. Nearly all Confederate troops had been sent north to Shiloh, so city officials had little choice but to surrender. On May 1 federal troops occupied New Orleans. The mighty Mississippi had been unlocked; only Vicksburg remained. On June 28 Farragut's ships ran past Vicksburg's batteries and joined Davis.

Lurking up the Yazoo River was the recently completed *Arkansas*, a Confederate ironclad commanded by Lieutenant Isaac N. Brown of Kentucky, who had supervised construction of the ship except for the hull. On July 12, Brown set out downstream to engage the combined fleets of Farragut and Davis. The *Arkansas* put a Union naval patrol to flight and fought her way through the astonished Union fleet to the safety of Vicksburg, though she suffered some damage and about sixty casualties. The daring exploit cheered the people of Vicksburg, and infuriated Farragut.

That evening at dusk, Farragut again ran the batteries at Vicksburg, hoping to destroy the *Arkansas*. The mission aborted even though his fleet again passed the town with few casualties. Farragut sent two vessels out to ram and sink the *Arkansas* five days later, on July 26, but they, too, were unsuccessful. Low on fuel, fearing that the river would fall too low for his deep-water vessels to navigate, Farragut retired downstream and left to the Confederates the stretch of river between Port Hudson and Vicksburg. The strip of water had a special strategic significance for the Confederacy, for it left in their hands the mouth of the Red River, the highway through Louisiana that funneled supplies from the trans-Mississippi region eastward. Along with grain and cattle from Texas, a steady trickle of supplies hauled overland from Matamoros, Mexico, came in via the Red River. The Confederates immediately strengthened the batteries at Vicksburg and installed new ones at Port Hudson in order to hold the position. They then mounted an attack on Baton Rouge, below Port Hudson, using the *Arkansas* in a supportive role. Since the *Arkansas* had persistent engine trouble, she was thrust hard aground, set afire, and left to explode in order to prevent capture by a Union gunboat on August 5, 1862, thus ending her career of less than one month. Baton Rouge held in that assault, but the Union forces abandoned the city a short time later.

On March 14, 1863, Farragut's ships ran past the batteries at Port Hudson once again. This time, of four sloops and three gunboats, only his flagship, the *Hartford*, and one gunboat escaped serious harm. Yet the two successfully closed the Red River and roamed as far north as Vicksburg. Meanwhile, Grant launched his campaign against that city, marching down the western bank of the river. He needed ships to ferry his men across, and on April 16 in the dark of night seven ironclads, with coal barges lashed alongside, escorted three transports laden with stores past the Vicksburg batteries, losing only one transport and one barge. They then brought Grant's army across the river below Vicksburg, assuring the fall of the city after a land campaign of several months. Port Hudson fell shortly after, and the Union took full control of the Mississippi.

Tightening the Blockade

After the fall of New Orleans in 1862 and the Confederate evacuation of Pensacola, Mobile remained as the only important Confederate-held Gulf coast port. Back in command of the Gulf Squadron early in 1864, Farragut made plans to take Mobile Bay. The situation became urgent when the Union learned that the Confederates had ironclads under construction up river from the town. The geography of the bay itself and the location of Confederate forts made the task more complicated than the New Orleans operation. Mobile City would not fall to naval power alone as New Orleans had; the forts, unless reduced by a land force, would make untenable any effort to sustain the fleet in Mobile Bay if Farragut should run past them. Farragut estimated he needed at least a brigade of troops and an ironclad fleet of his own, but the government offered him neither.

The Confederates worked feverishly to complete the powerful ironclad ram, the *Tennessee*, before Farragut made his move. She was over two hundred feet long, had a draft of fourteen feet, was well armored with five inches of armor over two feet of wood, mounted six heavy guns, and wore a powerful ram. She was much more of a threat than the *Merrimac*, better constructed, larger, and better protected. Yet she was underpowered, with engines taken from a river steamer, and her steering mechanism was exposed and thus subject to damage by enemy fire. The Confederates hoped to take Farragut's fleet by surprise in May 1864, but the vessel stuck as she tried to cross a bar and the element of surprise was lost. The *Tennessee* anchored near Fort Morgan and did not take the offensive.

In the interim Farragut had received a division of troops and four monitors, two from Mississippi river duty and two from the Atlantic. On August 4 the troops landed to lay siege to the forts, and on August 5 Farragut stormed into Mobile Bay. The fight began about 7:00 A.M. and lasted for nearly three hours. The Union monitor *Tecumseh*, leading the squadron, pursued the *Tennessee*, whose fire was raking the Union fleet from a position above a minefield in the channel. In her eagerness to get at the *Tennessee*, the *Tecumseh* turned into the minefield, struck a mine, and sank. Farragut also passed into the minefield in order to race past his own lead ship, and made it safely into Mobile Bay. The *Tennessee* attempted to ram the *Hartford*, Farragut's flagship, but the more agile *Hartford* eluded her and dashed on to pursue Confederate gunboats. The *Tennessee* then turned to the Union fleet, and ran past it, exchanging broadsides and ultimately taking shelter under the guns of Fort Morgan. Now inside Mobile Bay, Farragut's fleet expected the *Tennessee* to remain close by the fort. She did not, and returned instead to attack the Union squadron. Farragut ordered two of his speediest vessels to ram the *Tennessee*, but she was well protected and inflicted more damage than she received. Farragut tried once to ram the *Tennessee*, unsuccessfully, then on making a turn to try again, collided with one of his own vessels also attempting to ram the Confederate ironclad. Meanwhile the Union monitor *Chickasaw* had come up on the *Tennessee*'s stern, blasting her again and again with eleven-inch guns. Already the *Tennessee* had taken considerable damage—her stack was shot away, her speed reduced to four knots, her two heaviest guns put out of action, and her captain severely wounded—when the *Chickasaw* disabled her steering. As Union vessels prepared to ram, the *Tennessee*, battered and helpless, surrendered. It was 10:00 A.M., and the battle of Mobile Bay ended. The three forts soon surrendered, two of them within days and the third before the end of the month. Mobile Bay was under Union control.

With the fall of Mobile Bay, nearly all the important Confederate ports had been neutralized or captured except for Charleston and Wilmington on the Atlantic coast. Military strategy now called for Wilmington's capture, as Grant determined it would open an avenue to supply or reinforce Sherman, then marching north from Savannah. Wilmington, about thirty miles up the Cape Fear River, was protected on the seaside by Fort Fisher's fifty guns, and capture of the fort would close the port as a blockade-runner station and provide a beachhead for operations against the city itself. In December 1864 Butler had made an abortive effort to take the fort, but his own ego had made cooperation between the army and navy difficult, and the attempt failed. Admiral Porter, however, reported that with the proper collaboration the fort could be taken.

The second attack on Fort Fisher came in mid-January. Porter himself commanded the largest fleet ever assembled up until then under one United States naval officer, boasting some sixty ships with more than six hundred guns as well as four monitors. Two divisions of soldiers plus part of a third division under the command of Bull Run veteran General Alfred H. Terry made up the landing force. For the better part of three days the fleet pounded Fort Fisher with such accuracy that when Terry's infantry attacked on January 15, only one heavy gun remained in service to confront them.

A contingent of sailors and marines tried to take the fort from the seaside but were repulsed. Even with its batteries silenced, the fort provided excellent cover for its defenders. The fleet renewed its bombardment and drove the defenders out. By the end of February Wilmington itself fell to Union hands, virtually completing the seal on the Confederate coast, and providing Sherman a contact with the sea should he need it, which he did not.

The Confederate Raiders

In June 1861 Captain James D. Bulloch of the Confederate navy arrived in England to contract with the Laird shipbuilding organization of Birkenhead for six stern-propeller ships, capable of high speeds and long cruises, to be used as commerce destroyers. Bulloch had the authority to spend a million dollars for their construction. The most famous of the vessels was the *Alabama*, which alone cost about $250,000. Often referred to by the Laird's designation "290," it was first called the *Enrica* while still building. The United States protested the building of the cruiser, furnishing evidence that it was to be a Confederate warship and charging that the contract violated Britain's neutrality. Under pressure the British foreign office ordered the ship detained, but before the order could be delivered the *Enrica* had sailed on a trial run, putting out of Liverpool on July 26, 1862. She never returned, but instead steamed for the Azores where she took on arms, munitions, and a crew. Captain Raphael Semmes, who had recently commanded the *Sumter*, then bottled up at Gibraltar, took command. On August 24 the *Enrica* was christened the *Alabama*, which, with Semmes at her helm, cruised for nearly two years and took nearly seventy prizes.

The *Alabama*'s two 300 horsepower engines drove her at a speed of 13 knots, though she was rigged for sail and used steam only when necessary to conserve fuel. Semmes began by capturing a fleet of Union whalers near the Azores, another fleet of corn transports off Newfoundland, and a mail steamer off Haiti. Hearing of an attempt to take Galveston by sea, Semmes sailed for Texas, intending to destroy troop transports. But geared for speed and not naval battle, the *Alabama* turned away from a naval squadron off Galveston, with the *Hatteras*, a converted river boat, in pursuit. After a few miles, the *Alabama* turned, made short work of her pursuer, and sailed for the Atlantic.

Semmes took about two dozen prizes between Africa and Brazil, stopped off at Capetown, and meandered into the Indian Ocean and the China Sea. But the Far Eastern waters yielded few prizes, and the *Alabama* soon returned to the Atlantic, sailing northward and ultimately putting into Cherbourg, France, for refitting on June 11, 1864. The *Kearsarge*, a Union warship under the command of Captain John A. Winslow, arrived off Cherbourg within a few days, determined to prevent the *Alabama*'s escape.

Although the *Alabama*'s policy was to avoid naval conflict, Semmes had little choice. He challenged the *Kearsarge*, perhaps to frighten her off, but Winslow was a naval veteran of forty years and eager for the opportunity to fight the famous raider. The two vessels nearly equalled each other in size, speed, armament, and crew. The ship's company of the *Kearsarge* numbered 163, that of the *Alabama* about 150. The *Kearsarge* mounted seven guns: two 11-inch smoothbore pivots, a 30-pounder rifle, and four light 32-pounders. The *Alabama* carried eight guns: a 68-pounder smoothbore pivot, a 100-pounder pivot rifle, and six heavy 32-pounders. Both vessels made thirteen knots under steam. While neither was armored, the *Kearsarge* carried a plating of sheet chain over her engines.

On Sunday morning, June 19, with an estimated 15,000 spectators "upon the heights of Cherbourg, the breakwater, and rigging of men-of-war," the *Alabama*, escorted by a French naval vessel as far as the three-mile limit, steamed straight for the *Kearsarge*. Winslow immediately put to sea, having assured the French that the engagement would not take place in French waters and wanting to draw the *Alabama* far enough away so that she could not take refuge in French waters should she be crippled.

The *Alabama* pursued the *Kearsarge* for about seven miles, when

Winslow wheeled about and sailed straight at her. The *Alabama*'s gunners opened fire at about 1800 yards, but the *Kearsarge* withheld fire until it could come round broadside at about 900 yards. The two vessels ran at full steam, broadside to broadside, in a large circle at distances of from a quarter- to a half-mile. The *Alabama*'s gunners, less practiced than Winslow's, fired rapidly and often wildly, the *Kearsarge*'s gunners, slowly and deliberately. Early on they shot the *Alabama*'s flag away and effectively raked her with the *Kearsarge*'s 11-inch guns. She began to settle by the stern. After seven full circles, the *Alabama* crowded on sail and attempted to break for the French coast. The *Kearsarge* pursued, but before she could come across the *Alabama*'s bow to deliver the *coup de grâce*, the *Alabama* struck her colors. The battle lasted two minutes over an hour.

The *Alabama* lowered her boats, as the ship now settled rapidly. To Winslow's chagrin, the yacht *Deerhound*, of the English Royal Mersey Yacht Club, rescued Semmes and about forty of the crew, while the *Kearsarge* picked up about seventy, and two French pilot boats another dozen. The *Deerhound* sped Semmes and the others to Southampton.

The *Florida*, another successful Confederate raider, was also English-built. She left Liverpool in March 1862 and was armed in the West Indies. She then ran into Mobile to complete her outfitting and gather a crew, spending nearly four months at anchor— unlike the *Alabama*, which never put into a Confederate port. She burst through the blockade in January 1863 and cruised between Brazil and the United States, taking nearly forty prizes before putting into the port of Bahia, Brazil. The U.S.S. *Wachusett* was also in Bahia harbor, but her commander could not lure the *Florida* out. In violation of Brazilian neutrality, early in the morning of October 10, 1864, the *Wachusett* tried unsuccessfully to ram her, then sent a crew to board her, took her surrender (the captain and half of the crew were ashore), made fast a tow line, and, with a full head of steam, towed her to sea. Brazilian authorities gave chase but were too slow. The *Wachusett* brought the *Florida* to Hampton Roads, Virginia, where she sank a few days later after a collision.

That same October, Bulloch secured for the South the steamer *Sea King*, originally built for the Indian trade. Rechristened the *Shenandoah*, she left Britain for Madeira, was fitted out by the tender *Laurel*, and headed for the Pacific to destroy the whaling fleet. In need of more crew, she stopped at Melbourne, Australia, for a month. She reached the Bering Sea in June 1865 and took over two dozen prizes, unaware of the war's end. On August 2, 1865, the *Shenandoah* learned from a captain of a British ship that Lee and Johnston had surrendered, that Davis was a prisoner, and that the war had ended. Disappointed, the captain and crew sailed slowly back to Liverpool.

The *Alabama*, the *Florida*, the *Shenandoah*, and other Confederate raiders hastened the demise of the American merchant marine, although they had no direct effect on the outcome of the war. The virtual disappearance of the United States merchant marine fleet resulted from the excuse the war provided for British insurance companies to boost premiums and discriminate against American owners in favor of the British—a compelling factor since British companies wrote most of the marine insurance sold in the United States. American shipowners transferred their registry to British or other foreign flags in order to avoid the soaring insurance rates as well as to gain foreign protection from the Confederate cruisers.

The blockade by Union vessels, on the other hand, had a definite effect on the war, even if small ships could penetrate it. The policy had two major aims: to stop the exportation of cotton which would bring the Confederacy specie and credit to finance the war; and to prevent the importation of military supplies from abroad. It was estimated that the first object could be accomplished with the closing of only seven Southern ports,* namely Norfolk, Virginia; Wilmington, North Carolina; Charleston, South Carolina; Savannah, Georgia; Mobile, Alabama; New Orleans, Louisiana; and Galveston, Texas. Only at those harbors could deep-draft ocean-going freighters load massive cargoes of bulky cotton. Lesser ports had not the warehouses, docks, and facilities for handling such vessels. And while blockade runners could carry out cotton from almost any port, they did not have the capacity to carry substantial amounts. The Union blockade shut off most of the deep water ports from the first, though some, like Mobile and Wilmington, had to be occupied militarily before the seal was totally effective. Very little cotton leaked through the blockade. The same blockade that prevented the shipment of cotton also prevented the importation of significant quantities of military stores—for much the same reasons.

* See Ephraim D. Adams, *Great Britain and the American Civil War* (New York: Russell and Russell, 1958 edition), vol. I, p. 253.

With the seizure of Mobile Bay in 1864 and the fall of Wilmington in 1865, the Union navy climaxed its task of strangulation of the South at about the same moment the Union armies concluded their job of conquest. The Confederate war effort was seriously constricted. Isolated from the sea, occupied on land, the Confederacy saw its hopes for independence sicken and die.

13

Anglo-American Diplomacy

When William H. Seward accepted the office of secretary of state in 1861, most Americans still thought of foreign relations in the same confident terms as John L. O'Sullivan had fifteen years earlier. "Armed with the plough and the rifle, and marking its trail with schools and colleges, courts and representative halls, mills and meeting-houses," Americans had followed their manifest destiny to fill out the continent from coast to coast. It had been their mission. If it meant removing foreign influence or foreign governments from the continent, then so be it, and the continent included Canada and Spanish America. "Away, then, with all idle . . . talk of *balances of power* on the American continent," O'Sullivan wrote, for even if all of Europe should stand against America's destiny, America would prevail.

Americans looked to their foreign policy not only to free their own continent of foreign influences, but also to bring the blessing of freedom to the young nations of Europe. Prussia's effort to unify Germany, Garibaldi's redshirts in the vanguard as Italy strove for union, Ireland's revolt against British rule, and the Hungarian patriots' stand for freedom from the Hapsburgs—all attracted attention and sympathy in the American press. Webster summed up American attitudes when he observed that although the United States had no business interfering in the Hungarian revolution, still when Americans beheld peoples "moving toward the adoption of institutions like their own, it surely cannot be expected of them to remain wholly indifferent spectators."

Yet, while Americans in 1851 welcomed Louis Kossuth, the Hungarian revolutionary, while they sympathized with Senator Lewis Cass when he urged the United States to exert its influence in Europe against the suppression following the abortive revolutions of 1848, and while their embassies entertained Hungarian, Russian, and Italian liberals abroad, American policy stopped with expressions of sympathy and never included actual intervention in European affairs. The American mission to bring its version of democracy and freedom to all of North America had not yet gathered sufficient determination to extend itself to the old world through more than verbal encouragement.

In North America manifest destiny was as virile as ever. Through the Clayton-Bulwer Treaty of 1850, the United States prevented Britain from exercising exclusive control over any future Central American canal, a subject of great importance because of the area's value as a link to the newly discovered gold fields of California. Cuba, coveted since Jefferson's time, was still an enticing prize as Polk tried to purchase it in 1848 and Pierce bid on it in 1854; in the Ostend Manifesto of 1854 Pierce's ministers in Madrid, London, and Paris went so far as to urge him to seize the island if Spain refused to sell.

Manifest destiny received no bolder expression than that manifesto, unless one takes into account private American filibustering in Cuba, Nicaragua, and Lower Mexico. The government of the United States drew the line on filibustering, however, and even helped check the adventure in Nicaragua. For one reason, abolitionists widely believed filibusterers were working to implement the South's alleged plot to extend the boundaries of slavery.

By the 1850s it was clear that manifest destiny was caught in the web of suspicion that the sectional quarrels wove. If the South approved expansion, Northerners denounced it as a slaveholder's scheme to add slave territory. If the North approved expansion, Southerners saw it as a means to add free states that would increase the North's growing majority in Congress and further threaten the South's weakening political influence in the nation. Even after the rupture of the Union, the Confederacy embraced manifest destiny in its chimerical desire to add the American Southwest and the northern tier of Mexican states to the Confederacy.

Coincident with manifest destiny, which included the removal of foreign influence already in North America, was the effort to keep foreign influence and power from the Western Hemisphere; and its most powerful statement was in the Monroe Doctrine of 1823. Napoleon III's foray into Mexico during the Civil War obviously violated that doctrine. While the Confederacy would have traded the Monroe Doctrine for a French treaty of alliance,* public opinion in the North strongly opposed French intervention. Only the Civil War delayed Union efforts to squelch the French bid for empire.

Manifest destiny and the American mission were expressed in still other ways. In a real sense, Northerners who sought to keep the territories free desired to extend their concept of democracy and freedom, the American mission as they saw it, to the remainder of the continent, and ultimately to the slave states as well. And Southerners sought to extend their system, in order to keep the institution of slavery viable. Thus two conflicting ideas of mission clashed in the new territories.

Many of these American attitudes found their way, then, into the foreign policy concepts of the protagonists in the Civil War. The Union made every effort to prevent foreign governments from intervening in the war, which would have bolstered Confederate independence. Two American nations would have made it possible for Europeans to play one against the other, and thus have opened the American heartland to foreign influence. That threat had surfaced during the brief existence of the Texas republic, had been one excuse for Polk's desire to acquire California, and was constantly in the minds of many Americans because of Canada. Foreign intervention would pose a real threat to the ultimate success of both manifest destiny and the American mission, something Northern politicians understood. Lincoln had good reason for insisting the South was in insurrection and not in rebellion, for insurrection was a domestic affair, whereas rebellion had international overtones.

* An alliance with France would have meant Confederate repudiation of still another major American foreign policy rule, that against a permanent alliance with a foreign power.

On April 1, 1861, Seward told the president: "We are at the end of a month's administration and yet without a policy either domestic or foreign." Seward warned further delay was dangerous. Regarding domestic policy he proposed changing the "question before the Public" and shifting from "Slavery" to a "question . . . [of] Union or Disunion." In foreign policy he would "demand explanations" from Spain and France "at once" and "seek explanations from Great Britain and Russia." He would "send agents into Canada, Mexico, and Central America to rouse a vigorous continental *spirit of independence* . . . against European intervention." If "satisfactory explanations" failed to come from Spain and France, Seward recommended war.

France and England had been regularly dunning Mexico for debt payments; in 1838 France had collected Mexican debts by force and might be moved to do so again. Spain had recently been involved in Santo Domingo. By fanning America's desire to rid the Western hemisphere of foreign influence, Seward hoped to overshadow the domestic controversy and reunify the nation behind a foreign war. Seward's suggestions reflected his own notion that he, and not the bewhiskered politician from Illinois, would actually run the administration.

Lincoln quietly dismissed the idea, but Europe had good reason to distrust Seward. He had told the duke of Newcastle in 1860 that should the secretary of state's job fall to him, he would insult England if he felt he had to. So far as the English were concerned, that indicated Seward's belief that a foreign war would be beneficial to the United States. The English feared Seward would go so far as to provoke war. As late as December 1861 Charles Francis Adams, Union minister to England, reported that Britons saw Seward as an "ogre fully resolved to eat all Englishmen raw."

In spite of their mistrust of Seward, Britain's relations with the Union throughout the war remained viable though rocky. Adams earned the respect of the British Foreign Office, and as a team Adams and Seward worked well together. Once the initial diplomatic storms of 1861 and 1862 blew over, Britain and the United States drew closer together.

Britain and the Union: Myth and Reality

Immediately after Sumter, the English press sympathized with the Union. For years many Englishmen had sought worldwide emancipation of slaves, and they naturally supposed that the struggle in the United States concerned that end. Yet official Northern spokesmen ignored the moral question because they wanted to keep the border slave states from seceding. Lincoln claimed again and again that the sole object of his administration was to maintain the Union, and he managed to convince the English. If that were so, Englishmen reasoned, and the Union had no intention of eliminating slavery, then the South's fight was indeed for independence as it claimed, and the North's motives were not so lofty.

This may have helped propagate the myth in the United States that the British upper classes were repelled by the North. The main tenets of this view were that Southern gentlemen plantation owners and the English landed gentry had more in common with each other than either had with the obnoxious Yankees; that the English gentleman held democracy in contempt and fully expected mob rule to destroy the United States; that a Union victory would discredit aristocracy and cause political unrest in Britain, perhaps ending in a broadened franchise. British aristocrats, it was assumed, therefore favored the Confederacy because a Southern victory would humiliate democracy.

That the British upper classes in 1860 yearned to see the Union shattered was nonsense. Aside from the pro-Southern feelings of Lord Robert Cecil and Seymour Fitzgerald, the Conservative party was divided. As the opposition party they worked to discredit the administration of the Palmerston-Russell Liberal coalition ministry, but their opposition stopped short of violating the official policy of neutrality. Lord Derby (Edward Stanley) opposed any British non-neutral activity unless Britain was prepared to go to war with the North, which he thought foolish. Benjamin Disraeli agreed. In fact, the Conservatives were not overly concerned with the Civil War in America, and very little evidence exists to sustain the belief that they desired the dissolution of the United States. As a result, the "South received only the most illusory solace from British aristocrats . . . which was quickly lost amid practical concerns." *

If aristocrats in England failed to take the question of democracy versus aristocracy very seriously, and if the bond with Southern

* Wilbur Devereux Jones, "The British Conservatives and the American Civil War," *American Historical Review*, LVIII (April, 1953), p. 543. This is a careful and convincing study of Conservative opinion in Britain.

plantation owners proved feeble, English gentlemen still had no difficulty seeing the United States as a serious economic threat. Merchants opposed the high tariff enacted by the North in 1861 as a threat to Britain's free trade policy. On the other hand, although the South offered to trade manufactured goods without a meddlesome tariff, the Confederacy would need British help for that trade to become a reality.

To those merchants who flirted with intervening on the side of the South, others speculated on how American privateers would hurt business and trade more than any tariff or blockade. But if Britain remained aloof from the struggle in America, Confederate cruisers could take their toll of Yankee merchantmen, reducing competition from that quarter, and British industrialists and manufacturers could sell to both sides with attractive profits. As the Yankee merchant marine suffered, Britain's sea trade would prosper, enhancing her prosperity. And should the South separate successfully, as many Britons believed inevitable, then Britain would be able to trade with both nations without either having a claim to injury or advantage. The industrial and commercial aristocrats of Britain were thus divided; they neither spurned the cause of the North nor championed the cause of the South in any collective way. (Moreover, British officials had warned that a war to obtain Southern cotton for the mills would be far more expensive than relief for the unemployed.)

Another myth also breaks down under examination: The pro-Northern British working classes in no way seem responsible for holding in check the pro-Southern sympathies of the aristocrats. The influence of working-class opinion upon the government was questionable in any case since it sent no members to Parliament. Primarily antiaristocratic in outlook, the workers aimed more to embarrass the ruling classes by taking a democratic stand than to support the North. Furthermore, what support the working class did lend to the Union stemmed from its own self-interest, an effort to exert pressure for franchise reform, among other things.

Some officials of the British government, especially those closely connected with American affairs, believed the North had the power to triumph in the long run. W. Douglas Irvine, secretary of the British legation in the United States, told the Foreign Office in July 1860 that in the event of American disunion "the people of the North . . . would probably gain the upper hand." He speculated that the South might attempt to reopen the slave trade, which the British had been trying to close for decades, and might thus create a situation that would bring the Confederacy into conflict with Britain, "civilized Europe," and the United States. Lord Lyons, the British minister to the United States, feared that "we shall have very considerable difficulty in placing our relations, commercial or political, on a satisfactory footing with a people imbued with such sentiments [as the South]." After the firing on Sumter in April 1861, Lyons found that "abhorrence of slavery; respect for law; more complete community of race and language, enlist his [the Englishman's] sympathies on the side of the North."

Lyons also touched on the question of "respect for law." To him, the Lincoln government stood for law, order, and stability, and the Southern separatists for rebellion. With possessions all over the world, it would be a mistake for the British to foster revolution anywhere. Other officials seldom made that point.

A most important consideration to British policy was the fact that European difficulties attracted more of England's attention than did American problems. "The dominant anxiety in [Prime Minister Viscount Henry] Palmerston's mind during the whole period" was fear of a war in Europe.* Under the circumstances it certainly would not do to risk an overseas war with the Union through pro-Southernism or non-neutrality. The Liberal party advanced economic arguments for nonintervention as a part of their platform, not just for America but for Denmark and Poland as well. The Conservative party adopted the same line.

One argument or another served to pull the British toward an official neutrality. Peace, prosperity, and neutrality were synonyms to many Englishmen, who found the advantages of a neutral position far more compelling than arguments for intervention, recognition of the Confederacy, or any partisan position. In the case of America, a practical military matter underlaid the economic concerns: Canada could not be properly defended in the event of a collision with the United States.

The Policy of Neutrality

Abreast of the secession crisis in the United States, the British foreign office had kept its activities in America coolly correct. Al-

* Max Beloff, "Great Britain and the American Civil War," *History*, XXXVII (February, 1952), p. 42. This is a thoughtful survey of British attitudes.

though Foreign Minister Lord John Russell hoped Lincoln had "the prudence and good sense" to prevent a rupture, he instructed Lyons (as South Carolina prepared to secede) to refrain from appearing to favor one party or the other.

George M. Dallas, Buchanan's minister to England, told Russell in March 1861 that the president viewed secession as illegal and unconstitutional. Russell replied that Britain would be "very reluctant to take any step which might encourage or sanction" secession. In April, after Lincoln had taken office, Russell instructed Lyons to recommend conciliation if anyone in America asked him for an opinion, but not to offer any advice unasked. Shortly thereafter, Russell advised Dallas that American problems were not for the British to decide and that Britain was "in no hurry to recognize the separation as complete and final."

On May 1 Russell cautiously strengthened Britain's naval squadrons in America and ordered them to remain carefully impartial. On May 3 in a policy review for Parliament Russell proclaimed that the government "felt that it was its duty to use every possible means to avoid taking part in the . . . contest now raging in the American states." He concluded with the exclamation: "For God's sake, let us, if possible, keep out of it!" The lawmakers cheered their approval.

A week later Russell reported that he had visited with Confederate agents William L. Yancey, Pierre A. Rost, and A. Dudley Mann "at my house," but that he refused to deal with them officially, which would have meant recognition of their government. Then on May 13, 1861, the climax came. Queen Victoria officially proclaimed Britain's neutrality in the conflict in the United States. Her proclamation reflected the policy of both political parties; it recognized that a civil war raged in the United States and not merely a domestic insurrection as Lincoln's government claimed. According to international law, the queen's proclamation recognized the belligerent status but not the government of the Confederacy. The proclamation logically extended the cautious and impartial policy that Russell had followed since the advent of secession in the United States. That proclamation also invoked the Act of 59 George III, "An Act to Prevent the Enlisting or Engagement of His Majesty's Subjects to Serve in a Foreign Service. . . ."

The law made it a misdemeanor for "any person, within any part of the United Kingdom" to "equip, furnish, fit out, or arm" or cause or attempt to do so, "any ship or vessel, with intent . . . that such . . . shall be employed in the service of any foreign . . . state . . . or province, or any part of any province or people" as a transport or store-ship or cruiser, or to enlist in any foreign service "with whom His Majesty shall not then be at war." The act sounded clear, but conflicting interpretations of the statute and the difficulty of enforcement combined to allow Englishmen to evade the intent of the law on occasion.

The Lincoln government maintained that the Southerners were insurgents and not rebels in order to prevent legitimate foreign aid or assistance from reaching the Confederacy. According to international law, insurgents were not entitled to seek nor were foreign governments allowed to provide aid, for insurgencies were domestic affairs. Yet the reverse applied to rebels, who were considered full-fledged belligerents. Thus the queen's proclamation disturbed the Lincoln government because Britain was prepared to extend the Confederacy belligerent status that the Union denied. So far as Britain was concerned, the Confederacy could issue letters of marque and put privateers as well as naval vessels on the seas, seek financial assistance and other aid, and perhaps succeed in broadening the war. The Confederacy welcomed the queen's proclamation as a sign that Britain would soon follow with recognition for their government.

Irate Northerners looked upon the British neutrality proclamation as a decidedly unfriendly act; the British on the other hand believed it equitable and just and found the Union's reaction amazing. The British government felt the queen's proclamation had only formalized its previous policy; it still had no intention of appearing to encourage the Confederacy, even though both North and South believed it had. Once the policy of neutrality had been fixed by the proclamation, the government never altered it. Both political parties wished Britain to stand firm in its impartiality. Under the circumstances, Englishmen never completely understood the Union's aversion to British neutrality. As Union feedback reached the foreign office, Russell hastened to assure the United States that Britain had no intention of giving either spiritual assistance or hope of recognition to the Confederacy. "We had no thoughts of doing so," Russell told Adams; moreover, "the sympathies of this country were rather with the North than with the South, but we wished to live on amicable terms with both parties."

To clarify further the British position, Russell notified the Admiralty, the Colonial, War, and India offices that the government would "interdict the armed ships, and also the privateers of both parties, from carrying prizes . . . into the Ports, Harbours, Roadsteads, or Waters of the United Kingdom, or any of Her Majesty's Colonies or Possessions abroad." While the directive applied to North and South alike, Confederate interests suffered the most. Yankee privateers were unnecessary because the Confederacy had no merchant marine to attack, but Confederate privateers or cruisers were prohibited from taking prizes into British ports, and the Union blockade made it difficult for them to use their own.

Adams and Seward nevertheless continued to protest the neutrality policy, and Russell and Lyons constantly tried to convince Seward of its propriety. On June 21, 1861, Russell observed that "the question of belligerent rights is one, not of principle, but of fact." A month later he pointed to the decision made by Judge James Dunlop in the United States District of Columbia Court in the case of the *United States* v. *the Schooner Tropic Wind and Cargo*. The judge ruled that on the basis of American law, civil war existed in the United States with the same belligerent rights for civil as for foreign war. Seward insisted that the British neutrality policy improperly bestowed belligerent rights on the South. Russell reminded Seward that the British policy also accorded the United States full rights as a belligerent. At the same time Russell refused to communicate officially with the Confederate mission in England, telling it Britain would continue to observe her neutrality. If that made any impression on Seward, Russell was unable to discover it. "Mr. Seward never chooses to understand the position of Her Majesty's government," he lamented.

In January 1862 Russell directed Lyons to inform Seward "that an insurrection extending over nine states in space and ten months in duration, can only be considered as a civil war. . . ." In February 1862 Russell, in a continued effort to placate the Union, revised his interdict on belligerent ships, specifically mentioning the Bahamas. Should any belligerent vessel enter a British port, it would have twenty-four hours to depart and would not be provisioned. Although no explanation of the neutrality policy by Russell or Lyons would satisfy Seward, Russell tried his best to clarify Britain's position for the Union.

The British and the Union Blockade

A source of British amazement over the Union's reaction to the queen's neutrality proclamation and its grant of belligerent rights to the Confederacy arose from Lincoln's earlier proclamation of a blockade of the ports of the seceded states. According to the tenets of international law, Lincoln's blockade proclamation served notice that the situation in the United States had changed from mere insurrection to civil rebellion. Although Lincoln refused to acknowledge the Confederate government's existence, according to international law he had recognized the belligerent status of the Confederacy by claiming for the Union the right of blockade. The imposition of the blockade tacitly admitted that the Confederates controlled a large coastal area and had sufficient organization to resist the Union. To foreign observers, Lincoln confessed that he needed to use measures of war to combat the revolt.

Britain, followed by other nations, recognized this fact, and to protect themselves against the possible consequences of belligerency, they declared their neutrality. The recognition of belligerency by foreign states served as a warning to their citizens that a war existed in America and that they had a duty to observe the restrictions neutrality placed upon them. The nation that imposed a blockade also had regulations placed upon it; the first rule of a blockade was that it had to be physically effective, as formally required by the Declaration of Paris (1856).*

At first the British attempted to determine if the Union might interpret the blockade liberally, perhaps excepting the British; the Union refused. As a major sea power Britain then considered it in her best interest to observe the blockade officially, so long as it was a de facto blockade. The British feared for a time that the Union would erect a "paper blockade," and Congress gave point to such fears in July 1861 with a bill empowering the president to close ports of entry, or in other words, to limit foreign trade to Northern ports. In peacetime, nations could restrict foreign trade to specified ports, but in wartime they could not prohibit trade with ports not under their control. Both the British and the French protested Con-

---

* See discussion of the Declaration of Paris in Chapter 12. The Union refused to admit that the blockade proclamation granted belligerent rights to the South and that the rebellion was anything more than a domestic insurrection.

gress' effort to authorize the president to impose a "paper block-ade." Seward, however, assured them that Lincoln had no intention of exercising the power.

The British also learned of a Union attempt to seal Southern harbors by sinking hulks laden with stones across the approaches. Russell angrily denounced the plan as a "plot against the commerce of nations, . . . a project . . . of barbarism." Lyons first protested this sort of activity in November 1861, but was rebuffed by Seward. Later, when a Union fleet tried to seal Charleston harbor, Lyons stalked into Seward's office with an indignant protest, only to have Seward calmly reply that the obstructions were temporary and would be removed after the war; that the Confederates had done the same thing to keep the Union navy out of Southern ports; and that in any event no port had yet been closed. When Lyons produced a copy of a *National Intelligencer* report that Charleston had been barricaded, Seward admitted the effort had failed since "a British steamer laden with contraband of war had just succeeded in getting in."

The blockade prompted a continuous exchange between Britain and the United States, with American complaints of violations and British charges of irregularities. Through it all, Her Majesty's government remained steadfast in its recognition of the blockade. Russell observed to Parliament on February 10, 1862: "It was an evil on the one hand if the blockade were ineffective, and therefore invalid; and on the other hand if we were to run the risk of a dispute with the United States without having strong ground for it, it would be a great[er] evil."

Had they wished to invoke them, the British could have found grounds for declaring the blockade ineffective. Confederate emissaries in England sent Russell list after list of vessels that entered Southern ports. In addition, the British North American Squadron patrolled the Confederacy's Atlantic shore and frequently reported no Union blockaders in sight. Nevertheless, the blockade was effective enough to make Britain's contact with the consuls in the Confederacy difficult. The commander of the British West Indian Squadron received instructions on one occasion to send communications to these consuls "under cover . . . as may be most convenient," that is, through the blockade if necessary.

Russell, however, had no intention of admitting the blockade was anything but effective so long as the Union seriously attempted to maintain it. He became especially impatient with Confederate emissary James M. Mason's continued reference to it as a "paper blockade." To quiet Mason Russell lectured him on February 10, 1863:

> The Declaration of Paris could not be intended to mean that a port must be so blockaded as to really prevent access in all winds . . . in a dark night . . . by means of low steamers or coasting craft creeping along the shore. . . . Certainly the manner in which it [the blockade] has since been enforced gives to neutral governments no excuse for asserting that the blockade has not been efficiently maintained.

Britain's official observance of the blockade remained an obvious advantage for the Union. Few British ocean-going freighters tried to run the blockade directly, though many carried cargoes to the Caribbean and then either ran the blockade or transshipped their cargoes to blockade runners.

The Declaration of Paris failed to deal with transshipment in any practical way. The United States applied the doctrine of "continuous voyage," a solution previously used by the British.* The doctrine meant that ships destined for the Confederacy could be stopped on the high seas and the cargo confiscated. The chief difference between the Union's application of "continuous voyage" and that of the British over a century earlier was the distinction between the destination of the vessel itself and the cargo. Cargoes transshipped from Cuba, for example, came to be known as "continuous transports," and the Union used the doctrine of "ultimate destination" against them. In the case of the *Springbok*, a British ship taken enroute from London to Nassau, the United States Supreme Court condemned the ship's cargo because the court believed the cargo to be on a continuous voyage to the Confederacy even though the *Springbok* was not. Although the application of the doctrine troubled the British and other nations, the British reluctantly acceded because it was a useful precedent for them.

---

* The reference is to the Rule of 1756, when Britain forbade neutrals to trade in wartime between enemy colonial ports and the enemy's mother country. An American vessel, the *William*, had been captured and its cargo condemned on the ground that, although it had not made a direct journey, its cargo was actually on a continuous voyage of the prohibited nature. Neutrals protested the Union's application of the doctrine during the Civil War as a means of extending the blockade from enemy ports to neutral ports as well, and the practice was condemned in the Declaration of London (1909). But the Declaration went unratified, and the British used continuous voyage to their advantage in 1914.

The Trent Affair

Although the British officially observed the blockade and followed their declared policy of neutrality as they sought to remain correctly impartial, a single Union naval officer nearly destroyed their achievements. The Confederate government decided to replace Yancey, Rost, and Mann in Europe with new commissioners, James M. Mason and John Slidell. Mason was sent to London, Slidell to Paris. Together, they made their way through the blockade to Havana and booked passage to London on the *Trent*, a British mail ship. Captain Charles Wilkes, commander of the Union warship *San Jacinto*, intercepted the *Trent* in the Bahama Channel on November 8, captured Mason, Slidell, and their secretaries, and then released the *Trent*.

In so doing Wilkes raised the issue of impressment.* Many diplomatic historians agree that this was a major cause of the War of 1812. Wilkes had the right to search a ship suspected of carrying contraband, but he had no right to make a judgment that Mason and Slidell were contraband. Only a prize court could make that determination, a highly questionable one at best. Yet Wilkes ignored the technical questions and seized the two commissioners. Northerners expressed little concern over a possible violation of international law and made Wilkes a hero. The House of Representatives gave Wilkes a gold medal; the navy promoted him; Northern newspapers lauded him.

When the British received the news on November 28 they reacted angrily. Wilkes had insulted the flag. Talk of war flared. The British government feared, among other things, that the incident had been designed by Seward to promote war. As a precaution, Britain alerted its navy and readied troops for transfer to Canada. The British demanded, at the very least, an apology.

The cabinet drafted a strong note to the United States demanding the release of Mason and Slidell as well as "a suitable apology for the aggression." Prince Albert tempered the language of the note by suggesting that Wilkes had acted without instructions, thus leaving the United States an honorable way out. The cabinet

---

* During the Napoleonic Wars Britain, in an effort to increase her naval manpower, frequently stopped American ships and impressed American citizens into her service.

ordered Russell to transmit two sets of instructions, dated November 30, to Lyons. The first included requests for the release of the prisoners and an apology; the second gave the first the quality of an ultimatum. Should Seward ask for a delay in replying, Lyons was to give him only seven days, and if no suitable answer came within that time, Lyons was to break off diplomatic relations.

Russell added his own instructions to the orders of the cabinet. These despatches, he wrote, "impose upon you a disagreeable task." At your first interview with Seward "you should not take any despatch with you," but tell him the story, and "ask him to settle with the President and Cabinet what course they would propose." The next time you meet with Seward, Russell cautioned, "bring him my despatch and read it to him fully." Should he ask the consequences of a refusal to apologize and free Mason and Slidell, tell him "that you wish to leave him and the president quite free to take their own course, and that you desire to abstain from anything like menace."

Thus Lyons was to take a firm but cautious line with Seward, avoiding the ultimatum if possible. The British government still mistrusted Seward, so it readied its diplomatic weapons to force a peaceful conclusion. The transfer of troops to Canada was a show of force to punctuate the seriousness of the situation. Lyons could present the ultimatum and rupture relations if necessary. But a hard line proved unnecessary. Seward realized his difficulty. If he upheld Wilkes, he discarded principles of neutrality the United States fought for in 1812. If he upheld the principles, he had to admit Britain had been wronged.

By coincidence or design, Lyons received Seward's reply exactly seven days after meeting with him. On behalf of the cabinet, Seward explained that Wilkes had stopped the *Trent* without orders, that Mason and Slidell were contraband of war, but that Wilkes should have made the *Trent* a prize, which he had not. "For this error the British government has a right to expect the same reparation that we . . . should expect from Great Britain . . . in a similar case." Seward added that it pleased him to know the British government now accepted a principle long argued by the United States because it removed difficulties that had "alienated the two countries from each other" for over fifty years. He asked for instructions concerning the return of the captives.

Even before Lyons received the official reply, Seward had informed Adams that Wilkes had acted on his own, and he had expressed hope that the British would not take the situation too seriously. Through Adams, Russell learned of Seward's intentions before the official reply arrived, easing tension and preparing the way for acceptance of the apology. The British government considered the official reply adequate.

The crisis left a bad impression on the North, for Northerners felt the British had risked war over a practice they had deemed acceptable in the past. On the other hand, the British public seemed to be relieved by the solution. The fact that the United States had done "the right thing" may even have strengthened sympathy for the North.

Cotton Is King

Southerners believed that by withholding cotton from British mills, they would force the mills to close, throw great numbers of cotton operatives out of work, and seriously damage Britain's economy. That would encourage Great Britain to break the Union blockade and recognize the Confederacy.* They thought that cotton was so important to Britain's prosperity that "cotton was king." But Englishmen disagreed. In July 1860 the secretary of the British legation in Washington observed that Southerners "exaggerated" the situation, and that British help in return for cotton would not follow automatically.

Lord Lyons became so irritated by constant Southern repetition of the King Cotton argument that he wrote Russell in December 1860:

> Great as is the importance of their staple, their own notions of the influence it will secure to them have become so much exaggerated as to be preposterous. They seem to think that the [need for cotton] . . . will oblige all Europe, and especially Great Britain, to treat with them on any terms they may dictate. They talk of withholding their cotton . . . forgetting that their own prosperity depends much more upon selling it than that of the Northern States and Europe can ever depend upon buying it. They do not choose to remember the lesson so often taught by experience, that stopping the supply . . . results

* In 1860 slightly more than 80 percent of the raw cotton that the British textile industry used was imported from the United States. Also, about 20 percent of Britain's labor force depended either directly or indirectly on the textile industry for their living.

in stimulating . . . [the production of] it elsewhere. . . .
In answer to all arguments they are apt to repeat their
senseless cry that 'Cotton is King."

Even had the British government seriously believed that cotton
was king, they would have been set straight by British merchants
who, at the onset of the war, had on hand heavy inventories of both
raw cotton and manufactured cotton goods. The Southern withholding of cotton and the Northern blockade actually helped British merchants and manufacturers avoid an impending depression in
the satiated cotton market, enabling them to turn an anticipated
loss into a profit. It took nearly two years for British mills to absorb
the raw material stocks on hand in 1861. When the "cotton famine"

Total Raw Cotton Imported into the United Kingdom (in pounds)

YEAR	FROM U.S.A. (000)	FROM ALL SOURCES (000)	PERCETNAGE FROM U.S.A.	PRICE PER CWT. (SELECTED YEARS)
1850	493,000	663,000	74.35	
1851	596,000	757,000	78.74	
1852	765,000	929,000	82.34	
1853	658,000	895,000	73.52	
1854	722,000	887,000	81.39	
1855	681,000	891,000	76.43	£ 2.15.5
1856	780,000	1,023,000	76.24	
1857	654,000	969,000	67.49	£ 3.13.9
1858	833,000	1,034,000	80.56	
1859	961,000	1,225,000	78.44	
1860	1,115,000	1,390,000	80.21	£ 3.00.4
1861	819,000	1,256,000	65.46	£ 3.12.5
1862	13,000	523,000	2.48	£10.02.4
1863	6,000	669,000	.89	£11.05.8
1864	14,000	893,000	1.56	£13.11.0
1865	135,000	977,000	13.88	£ 9.18.6
1866	520,057	1,377,000	37.76	£ 7.10.8
1867	528,162	1,263,000	41.81	
1868	574,445	1,328,000	43.25	£ 5.05.4
1869	457,359	1,221,000	37.45	
1870	716,245	1,338,000	53.53	

The figures are from Tables II and IV in Robert H. Jones, "Long Live the King?"
Agricultural History, Vol. 37 (August 1963), pp. 166–169. The source for the figures are
statistical abstract tables in the *British Sessional Papers*, 1865, 1866, and 1871.

did come, it had a limited effect since discharged workers found other employment in war industries. An investigator for the Poor Law Board reported that in light of "the predictions of disaster and the cry of distress which accompanied the first alarm of the cotton famine," it satisfied him to report "that the manufacturers have passed the climax . . . without much difficulty" and that in one Lancashire district "fully 60,000 operatives have found other employment."

Total Wheat, Wheat Meal and Flour, and Maize Imported into the United Kingdom
Percentages from the United States

YEAR	PERCENTAGE	PRICE (PER QUARTER*) SELECTED YEARS
1850	16.75	
1851	15.64	
1852	23.21	
1853	21.93	
1854	34.98	£4.03.9
1855	24.92	
1856	43.52	£3.10.0
1857	27.50	£2.18.9
1858	20.29	£2.03.1
1859	1.48	
1860	27.51	£2.17.8
1861	44.67	£2.15.2
1862	45.30	£2.10.2
1863	37.29	£2.03.9
1864	29.22	£2.00.5
1865	10.01	£2.01.8
1866	18.39	£2.11.2
1867	20.76	
1868	22.44	£3.04.3
1869	26.73	
1870	27.72	

* Price per quarter, an eight-bushel measure.

These figures are from Tables I and IV in Robert H. Jones, "Long Live the King?" *Agricultural History*, Vol. 37 (August, 1963), pp. 166–169. The source for the figures are the statistical abstract tables in the *British Sessional Papers*, 1865, 1866, and 1871.

Lyons predicted that cotton production would be stimulated elsewhere, and in fact India and Egypt grew more cotton expressly for the British market than ever before, though not in quantities such as America had been producing. Not only that, trade with the United States boomed without cotton. America, the Commissioners of the Customs in Britain reported in 1862, "has increased [her] supply of British produce and manufactures, as compared with 1861." Though British exports to the United States fell in 1861, they have "again advanced," the Commissioners noted. Their statistics proved, to their surprise, that even without the South, the North was Britain's best customer.

That fact may have had something to do with the now discredited notion that "King Corn" dethroned "King Cotton" during the war. The English used the word "corn" to denote wheat and other grains, including maize, which to Americans is corn. According to the theory, the English, suffering from a decline in wheat production, depended upon Northern wheat during the critical war years. If England broke the blockade to get cotton, then the North would have cut off her wheat supply, bringing starvation to the island. In fact American wheat could be purchased and shipped more cheaply than wheat from any other source. The North never supplied more than half of Britain's wheat imports, in any case, the largest amount approaching 45 percent in 1862. Britain's other sources were never closed to her; the British could have acquired wheat from Eastern Europe had they chose. Thus King Corn had very little to do with discrediting King Cotton, because wheat never became a factor in the diplomatic situation.*

Mediation

After General Pope's failure at Second Bull Run in the last days of August 1862, Englishmen who watched the American scene felt that the best the Union could achieve on the battlefield was a draw. The British respected the Union navy, especially after the *Monitor-Merrimac* struggle in March 1862, and when the Union had captured New Orleans in April Southern sympathizers in Britain

* See Robert H. Jones, "Long Live the King?" *Agricultural History*, Vol. 37 (August 1963), for statistics on the King Cotton/King Corn controversy.

despaired of the Confederacy's chances. But after McClellan failed to take Richmond and Lee chastized Pope, the English viewed the situation as a standoff.

Debate in the House of Commons on a resolution to recognize the Confederacy elated Southerners. Some members of Parliament favored the resolution because they felt that the division of the Union was inevitable. Though the resolution failed, the debate had a serious impact on English public opinion. In France, Napoleon III concluded that the Confederacy could maintain its independence and offered to recognize the Confederacy provided the British would do the same. Edouard A. Thouvenel, Napoleon's secretary for foreign affairs, had other ideas. He cautiously advised his government to do nothing before the 1864 fall elections in America. He foresaw the possibility that Lincoln and Seward might be "set aside" by those in America who desired peace. In any event he thought that not just England and France, but all the European powers should participate in peace efforts or recognition of the Confederacy, even though Russia had already rebuffed the idea. He felt that there was "less public pressure" in France than in England for recognition. In spite of the failure of the resolution in the House, Russell wrote Palmerston that he agreed on the tactic of proposing an armistic in America, perhaps taking the action in October when he would return from the continent and after the vacations of other cabinet members.

In the critical period, July through October 1862, both Palmerston and Russell considered some form of mediation aimed at ending the war and pondered the recognition of the Confederacy. Within the cabinet, Sir George Cornewall Lewis strongly opposed any meddling in American affairs, and the opposition party, led by Derby, likewise resisted intervention. In September Palmerston contemplated the Union defeat at Second Bull Run and speculated that Washington or Baltimore might fall to the Confederates. And that, he thought, might force the Union to accept mediation by France and England.

By the end of September, however, neither Washington nor Baltimore had succumbed to Confederate arms, and Lee had been stopped at Antietam and forced back to Virginia. Moreover, though Palmerston received steady encouragement from Russell, he had met opposition from Earl Granville, who thought it "premature to depart from the policy which has hitherto been adopted," that is, neutrality. Neutrality had "general approval from Parliament, the press, and the public" in spite of "antipathy" for the North and "strong sympathy" with the South. Involvement might also mean war, Granville cautioned. Influenced by Granville and by military events across the Atlantic, Palmerston on October 2 urged delay of any mediation effort.

On October 7 William E. Gladstone, Chancellor of the Exchequer, observed that Southern leaders had "made an army, they are making . . . a navy; and . . . they have made a nation." Gladstone predicted their successful separation from the North. Because of the reference by a cabinet member to a Confederate "nation" he appeared to forecast a policy of intervention and recognition of the Confederacy. Russell, a leader in the mediation effort, circulated a memorandum to other cabinet members calling for an attempt to seek an armistice in America. His effort drew countermemoranda from both Lewis and Palmerston. The latter indicated he would not proceed unless he had evidence that the North planned to abandon its struggle. Northern success at Antietam, plus news of Lincoln's preliminary Emancipation Proclamation, gave no sign of the North's willingness to quit. Those factors combined with the opposition of cabinet members and of Conservative party leader Derby were apparently decisive in the prime minister's determination.

Although sympathetic with the cause of the South, Napoleon III hesitated to intervene alone. He feared the attempt might bring war with America and that other European powers, including England, might be pleased to see France so involved. He proposed joint action for a six-month armistice, which upset Palmerston but which Russell insisted upon airing. After the cabinet discussed Napoleon's proposal early in November, Russell "turned tail," as Gladstone put it. Russell reluctantly accepted Palmerston's position, finally agreeing that Britain should remain out of American affairs. The cabinet told Napoleon that mediation was impossible because the North opposed it.

From his vantage point in Washington, Lyons echoed Palmerston's view. Mediation would preface recognition of the Confederacy, Lyons said, and "I do not clearly understand what advantage is expected to result from a simple recognition . . . and I presume that the European powers do not contemplate breaking up the blockade by force . . . or engaging in hostilities with the United States. . . ." Lyons concluded that war certainly would result from a mediation effort that included recognition.

Just before the cabinet meeting on November 11, which apparently decided the issue, Russell learned that Russia had flatly rejected joint mediation. Russell had indicated in September that no mediation should occur without Russian support, because that would "ensure the rejection of our proposal." On November 11 the Russian government published its decision, holding "the foreign powers have no right to impose their mediation upon the country [the United States]." Neutrality was the safest and most profitable course for the British to pursue.*

Though the British decision had not been greatly influenced by Union pressure, Seward had steadfastly opposed all mediation efforts from abroad. He convinced Henri Mercier, the French minister in Washington, that intervention could mean war, and Mercier reported that conviction to Thouvenal. Seward made the same point with Lyons, and instructed Adams to make it clear in London. After Lee defeated Burnside at Fredericksburg in December, Napoleon made a final proposal to Lincoln's administration in January 1863. Congress followed Lincoln's rejection by passing a resolution that declared mediation proposals "unfriendly" acts. Congress' resolution came after the fact, but it gave teeth to Seward's work. "Europe's final refusal to involve itself in the American struggle was nothing less than a total vindication of Seward's diplomacy," one historian wrote.** If Seward's efforts were not of primary importance in Europe's decision, they certainly were a factor.

The Emancipation Proclamation

Britain's thoughts on mediation may have also been influenced by the Emancipation Proclamation. In July 1862 Lincoln showed a draft of the document to his cabinet. The members received the

* The last move in the direction of recognition of the Confederacy came in June 1863, when John A. Roebuck introduced a motion to that effect in Parliament. A Southern sympathizer and amateur diplomat, Roebuck had been in unofficial contact with Napoleon III. He received little support in the ensuing debate, and was flayed by Palmerston for his unauthorized fling at diplomacy. Chastened, Roebuck withdrew his motion on July 13.

** Norman A. Graebner, "Northern Diplomacy and European Neutrality," in David Donald (ed.), *Why the North Won the Civil War* (Baton Rouge: Louisiana State University Press, 1960), p. 74. In this excellent brief survey, Graebner accords Seward a primary position in preserving European neutrality.

idea with some enthusiasm, but Seward cautioned Lincoln to think of the question of timing. He believed Lincoln should wait for a battlefield victory before issuing the document lest it seem that the Union sought only to incite a slave insurrection as a last ditch effort to salvage victory.

Lincoln used the battle of Antietam as his springboard for emancipation; and on September 23, 1862, he announced that as of January 1, 1863, "all persons held as slaves" in those places then "in rebellion against the United States shall be then, thenceforward, and forever free." Lincoln failed to emancipate any slaves held in the Union, either in the border states or in occupied areas. He hoped that with Congress' aid emancipation might come to those places as well. The immediate reaction in the United States was propitious. Abolitionists Henry Ward Beecher and Charles Sumner voiced their approval. "The skies are brighter and the air is purer," said Sumner. Frederick Douglass believed that now "England was morally bound to hold aloof from the Confederacy." The press lauded Lincoln for the most part, though all were not as enthusiastic as Greeley, who exclaimed: "God bless Abraham Lincoln."

The Emancipation Proclamation probably stiffened the Confederacy's will to resist rather than provided a stimulus to end the rebellion. Abolitionists, though not unhappy with the step, nevertheless felt it was a half a loaf and continued to seek complete emancipation. The proclamation failed to help the Republicans in the fall elections, since the Democrats made significant gains. Confederate sympathizers abroad saw it as only a war measure, a tacit admission that the North, near failure, was grasping at straws.

In Britain, Palmerston called it "trash" and thought it should not be taken seriously, while Union observers in England saw no immediate gains for the United States. The Manchester *Guardian* considered it " 'bunkum' on a grand scale with the swaggering bravado so conspicuous throughout the present war." The London *Times* was so hostile that it sounded like Southern papers. The business community in Britain, especially the cotton barons, regarded it suspiciously, if for no other reason than emancipation threatened the future of the labor force that produced their raw material.

The most consistent supporters of emancipation were the workers. Birmingham working men praised Lincoln's "steady advance . . . along the path of emancipation." They prayed, they said, for the Union's realization of "brotherhood, freedom, and the equality of all men." The mayor of Manchester forwarded an address to the president from "the working men and others of this city," who admitted they had been unhappy with the United States because of slavery, but now that Lincoln would "strike off the fetters of the slave," the Union's cause had their "warm and earnest sympathy." They "joyfully" honored Lincoln, they said, for living the belief of the Union's founders that " 'all men are created free and equal.' " They admired the president for firmly "upholding the proclamation of freedom."

Influenced by the hostile press, some of the workers initially reacted unsympathetically to the proclamation. But then, few Englishmen except the British and Foreign Antislavery Society expressed enthusiasm at the outset. When the final version was issued on January 1, it became clear that emancipation was a war aim, and British views changed. The constitutional goal of preserving the Union had now been joined with a moral one to end slavery. Despite the proclamation's defects, that affected British opinion. Even the London *Times*, so hostile earlier, conceded that point in mid-January 1863. Favorable reaction ballooned during the first quarter of the year, when, according to one estimate, resolutions from over fifty public meetings endorsed the Northern cause and emancipation. Henry Adams, son of the American minister in London, asserted that the proclamation "has done more for us here than all our former victories. . . . It is creating an almost convulsive reaction in our favor. . . ." In that sense, the Emancipation Proclamation proved to be an effective diplomatic act on Lincoln's part. Sentiment shifted from initial hostility to favorable acceptance in Europe as well.*

British-built Confederate Warships

Another storm on the sea of Anglo-American diplomacy brewed over English-built Confederate commerce destroyers and rams. Lacking the means to build warships themselves, the Confed-

---

* John Hope Franklin, *The Emancipation Proclamation* (Garden City, N.Y.: Doubleday and Company, 1963), pp. 139–140 writes: "Her Majesty's Government . . . began to take cognizance of the pressures of the rank and file of the British people. . . . The Emancipation Proclamation had played an important role in achieving this signal diplomatic victory." On pp. 123–128 Franklin surveys European reaction.

erates sought them abroad. As British companies undertook to provide such vessels, the Union protested. Palmerston's government found itself in a difficult position as it earnestly tried to enforce neutrality, for although British law forbade such ship construction, the interpretation of the law and the machinery of Britain's bureaucracy seriously hampered compliance. On June 23, 1862, Charles Francis Adams warned the British Foreign Office that a Confederate cruiser was under construction at Birkenhead. Adams' evidence went to the customs officers at Liverpool, who promised to remain alert but took no action. Work continued on the vessel, variously called the "290" or the *Enrica*, and later renamed the *Alabama*, while the United States consul at Liverpool collected affidavits describing the ship's true character.

Even the respected attorney whom Adams hired to present the case to the authorities, though himself convinced the Act of 59 George III was being violated, had little success with his presentation. Rather than ordering the *Alabama* detained, Russell sent the evidence to the queen's law officers, who delayed action. Once the attorney general finally saw the papers, he ordered the *Alabama* held, but it was July 29 and she had put to sea on her trial run, never again to be seen in Britain. When Russell learned "what a fearful blunder he had made" he ordered the ship seized if it touched any British port, but that order also came too late.

Adams subsequently harassed Russell with demands for payment for every victim the *Alabama* and her sister built-in-Britain cruisers sent to the bottom, and the amount pyramided as those ships accomplished their task. Russell and other Englishmen felt it was a dangerous precedent as well as an obvious embarrassment of neutrality to allow the construction of the vessels. At some future time the Union might construct commerce destroyers for Britain's enemies; in fact, in March 1863 Congress authorized Lincoln to issue letters of marque, an obvious threat to Britain since Union privateers had no Confederate merchant marine to prey on. The *Alabama* situation thus put the Palmerston-Russell government on the defensive, as Russell later admitted.

Russell, that same month, in conversation with Adams disclaimed any responsibility for the activities of the *Alabama* but confessed "that the cases of the *Alabama* and the *Oreto* [the *Florida*] were a scandal, and in some degree a reproach to our laws." Thirty-one shipowners of Liverpool, who feared the Yankees would launch privateers after their trade in retaliation for British vessel construction, petitioned the government in June for an amendment to the Foreign Enlistment Act effective enough to stop the building. Under great pressure, the British government employed various legal tactics to so delay the departure of the *Alexandra* that she arrived in American waters only at the war's end.

Still, Confederate commerce destroyers *per se* failed to drive the Union merchant marine from the seas, although they destroyed or disabled over two hundred Union vessels. Instead, a combination of the cruisers plus soaring insurance rates drove over seven hundred American ships to seek shelter under British registry. Yet the crisis in diplomacy that led to the decline of the Union merchant marine came not over the transfer of registry but over the violation of neutrality seen in Britain's construction of warships for the Confederacy.

Lyons considered the question nearly as serious a threat to peace as the *Trent* affair had been. He advised Russell that if war resulted he hoped it would be "upon some better ground" than building ships for the South. And indeed, as the petition from the Liverpool shipowners showed, many Englishmen doubted the wisdom of allowing the shipbuilding. On March 26, 1863, a large trade union meeting in London expressed its opposition. Russell advised Palmerston that he could declare in Parliament that the government disapproved "of all such attempts to elude our laws," but Palmerston instead merely defended the government's action in regard to the *Alabama*.

At that point, a second factor complicated the picture. Powerful, ironclad, steam-propelled warships equipped with seven-foot spikes attached to their prows were under construction by the same firm that had built the *Alabama*. When afloat, the spike would be three feet under water, excellent for use against wooden ships blockading a port but nearly useless in sea battles. The British press dubbed them "new *Alabamas*," but they doubtless had a much different purpose. Seward threatened to commission Union privateers for purposes other than engaging Confederate cruisers or assisting the blockaders if the British did not end construction of both the cruisers and the rams. Russell ordered Lyons to protest the privateer plan, but by the time the instructions had been received and carried out, the situation had moderated.

On April 3, 1863, Russell told Palmerston that he "thought it necessary to direct" that the ironclads "should be detained." It would satisfy "the opinion which prevails here as well as in America that this kind of neutral hostility should not be allowed to go on without some attempt to stop it." Two days later he detained the *Alexandra* as a test case, an act supported by a mass meeting in Manchester. On April 7 Russell explained to Lyons that he had given orders to "stop when evidence can be procured, vessels apparently intended for Confederate service. . . ."

The crisis over Confederate cruisers and rams in fact ended before the rams were seized in September. In August Seward had made public appearances with Lyons, demonstrating the good will that existed between the two governments. Officially, Union protests continued down to Adams' "this is war" note to Russell two days after Russell had secretly ordered the rams seized. The fact remained that the British government had made its decision in April and had given its pledge, though its delay in seizing the rams caused continued uneasiness in the United States and raised doubts that the British intended to keep their word.*

Confederate Collapse

Many lesser problems figured in Anglo-American diplomacy, including the arbitrary arrest of British nationals by the Union government, or alleged federal recruiting in Ireland, but none proved serious enough to break the structure of neutrality. By 1863 Confederate hopes for diplomatic intervention or recognition by England collapsed. The Confederacy recalled Mason from England and expelled the British consuls from Confederate cities where they had remained since 1861, still accredited to the Lincoln government. England's attention turned to the continent: Bismarck of Germany spoke of blood and iron, and after a three-month crisis in 1864 the Danish War ensued.

Britain and the Union drew closer together after the diplomatic storms of 1861 and 1862. "Finality John" Russell admitted his friendship for both Adams and the United States. "Mr. Adams . . . [has] always laboured for peace between our two nations, nor,

---

* Ephraim D. Adams, *Great Britain and the American Civil War* (New York: Russell & Russell, c.1958), Vol. II, pp. 116–150, treats the subject in considerable detail, including the intricacies of ficticious ownership of the rams and the court cases that followed the seizure of the *Alexandra*.

I trust, will his efforts and those of the two governments fail of success." For the North, the importance of British neutrality was its continuity, or at least Britain's determination to maintain it as best it could. With that as a base policy, neither recognition of the Confederacy nor violation of the blockade was likely to follow. With all of its imperfections, neutrality was a positive benefit not only to the English but also to the North. English neutrality, despite its grant of belligerent rights, was not of much use to the Confederacy. Recognition was not just around the corner; cotton was not king; the British closed their ports to Confederate cruisers and their prizes, and made it difficult for the South to use British shipyards. Only by defeating the Union on the field of battle could the Confederacy have brought those things to pass.

14
Diplomacy and War: Europe

Except for France, the great nations of the continent paid little attention to the American Civil War. Napoleon III favored intervention on the side of the South, but was stymied without the support of Britain and her navy. France ran afoul of the Monroe Doctrine with her adventure in Mexico. Austria threatened to stand by the Hapsburg puppet on Mexico's throne, but the menace proved empty. Russia used the Union as a safe port for portions of her fleet in the event a European war broke out over the czar's effort to put down rebellion in Poland. The Dutch accorded the Confederacy belligerent rights, following England's lead and causing Seward some anxious moments, but they remained neutral. Spain proclaimed her neutrality, although blockade running from Cuba and a violation of the Monroe Doctrine in the Dominican Republic drew Union protests. On its side, the Union expended little diplomatic energy on the continent.

France and the Monroe Doctrine

Relations between the United States and Mexico had been unsatisfactory since the Mexican War. Mexico felt the full impact of American manifest destiny, as Buchanan bullishly sought to purchase parts of Northern Mexico and even suggested sending an army to collect an indemnity for Mexican expressions of hostility toward the United States. Europeans suspected that the United States wanted to swallow Mexico whole. In July 1861, just before First Bull Run, the Mexican legislature temporarily deferred payment on the nation's foreign debt, inaugurating the chain of events that involved the United States, Mexico, and France in a conflict over the Monroe Doctrine.

Mexico's act aroused Britain, Spain, and France, all of whom had large investments there. In October 1861 the three nations decided to collect by force the amounts due them. About 10,000 British, French, and Spanish troops landed in Mexico, aiming to occupy the customs houses and control that revenue until their claims were satisfied. The European powers both negotiated with and recognized the government of Benito Juarez and by the spring of 1862 had received Juarez' assurance that Mexico would respect its obligations. Satisfied, England and Spain withdrew. France remained and landed additional forces, simultaneously making new and heavy demands upon the Juarez government.

In part to bolster his waning popularity at home, Napoleon III sought to create a satellite state in Mexico. In so doing, he violated the pledges that he, along with Britain and Spain, had given before they began their original expedition: all had promised to seek no territory and exercise no political control over Mexico. Napoleon soon put nearly 35,000 troops ashore in an attempt to overrun the Juarez government. The emperor knew that the United States, engaged in its own titanic struggle, could not implement the Monroe Doctrine. From that time on he paraded his Southern sympathies, for a divided Union was to his advantage.

The French conquest of Mexico proceeded vigorously. Juarez capably managed a guerrilla resistance, the only resistance Mexico could offer against the better trained and better equipped French forces. It was not enough. The French entered Mexico City on June 7, 1863, but failed either to capture or destroy Juarez. French sympathizers from the clergy and royalist groups that opposed Juarez formed an Assembly of Notables which, at Napoleon's suggestion, offered the Mexican throne to Archduke Ferdinand Maximilian of Austria.

The offer came as no surprise to Maximilian, for the young Austrian nobleman and his beautiful wife, Carlotta, daughter of Leopold I of Belgium, supported Napoleon's overtures. Ambitious Carlotta, bored with life in the Hapsburg palace, wanted to be an empress in her own right. Though Maximilian at first had reservations, the couple accepted the offer from Mexico, along with a military alliance with France. Maximilian mistakenly believed that he had considerable Mexican support. When the royal couple arrived in Mexico late in May, a stage-managed demonstration greeted them. Napoleon believed he had virtually completed the task of creating a puppet government in potentially wealthy but weak Mexico, a satellite country that would provide a stronger Latin barrier to further United States expansion.

Americans remembered Napoleon III as the man who had overturned the French Republic in 1852 and assumed the throne as emperor. Since Americans despised monarchies, they had little fondness for Napoleon. Yet Americans had at first been indifferent to the French venture. Immersed in their own problems, those in the United States who even considered the Mexican situation tended to feel the country deserved to be punished for defaulting on its foreign debt. As French designs became clearer by 1863, and as the Union's military position improved, people in the North expressed unhappiness with the French escapade more frequently.

In September 1863 Seward admonished France that the American republics ought to be free from foreign domination. The warning went unheeded. In January 1864 a New York newspaper speculated that with the end of the Civil War 50,000 Union and 50,000 Confederate veterans would drive the French out of Mexico because America would not tolerate "a French monarchy" on its borders. In April, the House of Representatives resolved that the French venture violated the Monroe Doctrine, and in May and June Republican gatherings endorsed similar statements. Yet Seward walked softly, for he realized the folly of driving France into an alliance with the Confederacy.

Confederate leaders exploited the Mexican situation as best they could. Judah P. Benjamin, Confederate secretary of state, argued that the French would fail in Mexico unless the Confederates won their war for independence. He offered Maximilian Confederate support in return for French recognition of the Confederacy. Some evidence suggests that Maximilian desired both English and French recognition of the Confederacy prior to taking the throne of Mexico, but Napoleon apparently convinced him otherwise. Napoleon even prevented Slidell from meeting with Maximilian in France. Expediency forced the Confederacy to depart from two traditional American policies: it turned its back on the Monroe Doctrine and it sought a permanent alliance with France.

As the Civil War drew to an end, American public opinion demanded that France withdraw from Mexico. After accepting the Republican nomination for vice president in 1864, Andrew Johnson promised that once the rebellion ended, the United States would "attend to the Mexican affair. . . . An expedition to Mexico would be a sort of recreation to the brave soldiers who are now fighting the battles of the Union. . . ." While visiting Richmond in January 1865, Francis P. Blair, Sr., proposed an armistice to Jefferson Davis to allow the North and South to unite for the purpose of reestablishing the Juarez government in Mexico. Seward also took a firmer stance with France, asking Napoleon when the United States could expect the French army to depart. At the war's end Grant dispatched 50,000 men to Texas and prepared to order Schofield to Mexico to assemble Union and Confederate veterans to assist Juarez. But Seward, who wanted no bloodshed, sent Schofield to France to ask Napoleon to leave Mexico. American newspapers hammered away on the theme, and the London *Times* assured the English that Americans would go to war with France rather than allow her to remain in Mexico. "That is their own language," the *Times* warned, "used at every public meeting and at every dinner table, and in every paper, from Maine to California."

Growing impatient, Seward in February 1866 demanded an answer from Napoleon concerning a timetable for the French departure. In April France answered that her army would leave by November 1867. On the heels of that reply, the United States learned that Austria sought to raise 4,000 volunteers for duty in Mexico to keep the archduke on his new throne. Seward protested to Austria, threatening to break off relations. But Austria had enough trouble in Europe, and no volunteers materialized.

The last of the French troops embarked for home in February

1867. However, Maximilian remained behind, throwing away his chance to escape. Apparently he hoped to negotiate for leniency for those Mexicans who had supported him, but Juarez allowed no clemency. He captured Maximilian, sentenced him to death, and refused to listen to pleas for his life from foreigners. On June 19, 1867, Maximilian died before a firing squad.

An important result of the French fling in Mexico was that for the first time the Monroe Doctrine achieved respectability. Backed with the sort of power Europe could understand, it became a policy to be respected. For years to come, France found few champions in the United States, and when the Franco-Prussian War erupted in 1870, Americans sympathized with the Prussian invaders.

Russia and the Union

By 1860 Russia's czarist government took vicarious pleasure in the commercial rivalry the United States offered Britain in the world of trade. When fighting broke out in America, Russia feared that Britain would be able to assume world commercial dominance and perhaps even bring two weak American nations into her orbit. Baron de Brunow, Russian minister to England, warned Prince Alexander Gorchakov on January 1, 1861, that the English wanted America divided, for then Great Britain "on terms of peace and commerce with both . . . would dominate them."

In an attempt to head off British influence in America, Edward de Stoeckl, Russian minister to the United States, tried to mediate the quarrel before Sumter. Called the "jovial gambler" by Washington society, de Stoeckl had married Elizabeth Howard, a clever and charming girl from a socially prominent Washington family. Through her, he became more intimately acquainted with Washington society than were other foreign diplomats. He considered both Seward and Jefferson Davis, whom he knew and liked, superior to most other American politicians. He believed that the economic needs of the two sections would ultimately lead to conciliation. He rejected slavery as an issue. Gorchakov suggested compromise before blood was shed and the sections driven farther asunder.

Through his contacts in Washington, de Stoeckl found the Confederates willing to negotiate. Then he convinced Seward to attend a clandestine meeting at the Russian Embassy. Unfortunately for de Stoeckl, who prematurely saw himself as the peacemaker in

America, Seward changed his mind and refused to attend. The Russian-sponsored peace conference never occurred.

Meanwhile, Lincoln, whom de Stoeckl found unimpressive, had difficulty finding a minister to Russia. Cassius Marcellus Clay of Kentucky reluctantly accepted the post, asked to be recalled, and was replaced with Simon Cameron who remained only a short time. Clay meanwhile had become disenchanted with life as a general, and returned to Russia and the ballet girls he found so attractive, to serve out the Lincoln-Johnson period in St. Petersburg. If the continual changes ruffled the Russians, they did not show it. They continued to express sympathy for the Northern cause, as demonstrated by their refusal to become involved with British and French mediation efforts. De Stoeckl reported from Washington that no foreign intervention would meet with success, thus reinforcing his government's decision. In turn, the United States refused to join with European powers in an effort to mediate the rebellion in Poland, which Russia subsequently squelched without interference.

In the summer and fall of 1863, Russian naval vessels began arriving in Union ports. A Baltic squadron rendezvoused in New York, and a Pacific squadron anchored in San Francisco. Warmly welcomed and entertained, they remained throughout the winter of 1863–1864. Northerners realized that if England or France became involved in the war Russia could be a useful ally. According to the myth surrounding the Russian fleet, the czar ordered the visit to express his sympathy for the Union cause. By sending naval units to America, he hoped to block European meddling in the Civil War, reciprocating for the Union stand on Poland. The myth also presumed that Americans and Russians had much in common, especially Alexander's liberation of the serfs and Lincoln's emancipation of the slaves, as well as internal insurrections both wished to handle without foreign interference.

Yet knowledgeable Americans recognized that other reasons impelled the czar to send his squadrons to America. Gideon Welles, Charles Sumner, and Thurlow Weed all commented that the czar really intended to prevent his entire navy from being bottled up in Baltic or Pacific ports if a European war should erupt over the Polish rebellion. Russian military planners, informed Americans realized, simply chose to deploy some of their strength for possible action against enemy commerce. American harbors were a natural choice because of the friendly relations of the two powers. The Rus-

sian men-of-war had been ordered to remain in America until a political settlement had been worked out for Poland. In any case, the
spirit of friendship between the nations fostered the purchase of
Alaska by Seward a few years later.

Spain

American ministers came and went from Madrid with much
the same frequency as from St. Petersburg. Carl Schurz spent five
months there, and Gustave Koerner of Illinois about a year and a
half. For much of the Civil War period no American minister attended to diplomatic duties in the Spanish capital, but the chargé
d'affaires, Horatio J. Perry, proved a capable substitute.

Because of American designs on Cuba, expressed most recently
in the 1854 Ostend Manifesto, relations between the two nations
prior to the Civil War were tenuous. Though the Spanish upper
classes tended to side with the South, Perry convinced them that it
had been Southerners who filibustered in Cuba; that Northern
trade with Spain was more important than any prospective Southern trade might be; and that revolt and secession were bad examples for a colonial nation to support.

Spain followed Britain's lead and proclaimed her neutrality on
June 17, 1861. Pierre A. Rost, a Confederate emissary, conferred
with Calderon Collantes, Spain's foreign minister, on an unofficial
basis for about six weeks in the spring of 1862, without accom-
plishing a thing. Spain refused to recognize the Confederacy unless
Britain and France did so first. In February 1863 Francisco Serrano, former governor of Cuba and an open Southern sympathizer,
replaced Collantes. Sensing an opportunity, the Confederacy appointed John Slidell as a special commissioner to Spain in March.
But by the time Slidell arrived in Madrid, Serrano had been forced
out of the cabinet, and Slidell could only report, like Rost, that the
Confederate cause in Madrid was hopeless.

Most of the diplomatic interchanges between the Union and
Spain dealt with Cuba. In July 1861 the South appointed Charles
J. Helm as commissioner to the West Indies largely to take advantage of then-Cuban Governor Serrano's friendship. Helm succeeded
in keeping Cuba's harbors open to the Confederacy, for Serrano ignored the brisk Confederate trade. By 1863 a ship a day departed
Havana for a Confederate port. Serrano also disregarded Madrid's

insistence that the trade violated Queen Isabella II's neutrality proclamation.

The Union reacted by stationing warships on the sea lanes that converged on Havana and ignoring Spanish protests. In October 1862 the *Montgomery* intercepted the blockade runner *Blanche*, which ran aground east of Havana. Shells from the *Montgomery* set her afire and completed her destruction. As it happened, the *Blanche* claimed British registry and the *Montgomery* demolished her in Cuban waters over Spanish protest. When Spain demanded both an apology and an indemnity, Seward impressed Madrid with his speedy compliance. Later, when the Confederacy tried to secure the indemnity from Spain by claiming that the *Blanche* was really the Confederate ship *General Turk*, Madrid ignored the claim.

In July 1861 the Confederate cruiser *Sumter* herded six prizes into Cienfuegos harbor, took on coal, and departed, in apparent violation of Spanish neutrality. The *Florida* stopped over in Havana in January 1863. Serrano violated a rule, patterned after British practice, to insist upon twenty-four hours between the departure of belligerent ships. He allowed the *Florida* to depart within twenty hours after the Union dispatch boat *Reaney* sailed from Havana presumably to warn the Union navy. Union protests came to naught.

Spain proved more circumspect in her home waters. Early in January 1862 the *Sumter* sailed into Cadiz harbor, requesting permission to remain for extensive repairs. Spanish officials allowed only those repairs necessary to make her seaworthy and forced her departure in less than two weeks. Spain also released over forty American sailors the *Sumter* had taken prisoner. In defiance, the *Sumter* then burned the Union merchant ship *Neapolitan* within Spanish waters off Gibralter.

In February 1865 the powerful ironclad ram C.S.S. *Stonewall* arrived in Corunna Bay. The United States requested that the Spanish seize her, for the Union did not want her forced to sea. Using the French detention of the *Rappahannock* as a precedent, the Spanish interned the ship. However, the Spanish government later reversed itself and after permitting repairs allowed the ship to depart. Union naval vessels *Niagara* and *Sacramento* had shadowed the *Stonewall* to Corunna Bay but, outclassed, made no attempt to stop her when she sailed late in March. The *Stonewall* coaled at the Canary Islands and arrived in Havana May 11, 1865. With the war over, the United States demanded the vessel be seized and turned over to Union authorities. After initial hesitation, the ship's commander surrendered it to the Spanish, who then allowed the Union to claim it.

Spain's annexation of the Dominican Republic also involved her in a diplomatic exchange with the United States. A self-proclaimed dictator of the Dominican Republic invited Spain to reannex the island, and Spain complied in May 1861. Madrid ignored Seward's protest of this violation of the Monroe Doctrine. Then in 1863 a new revolution broke out on the island, and although the Union maintained strict neutrality, the Spanish feared American intervention. With the end of the Civil War, they voluntarily evacuated the island on June 30, 1865, ending their challenge to the Monroe Doctrine.

Other problems arose between Spain and the Union, such as Spain's refusal to let the United States arbitrate her conflict with Peru over the Chincha Islands and General Benjamin F. Butler's thirty-day internment of Spanish vessels in New Orleans. The fact remained that no matter who won the Civil War, Spain wanted to be on amicable terms with the power that controlled the Caribbean and the Gulf. That consideration overrode any contrary desires of Spanish aristocrats or liberals and forced Spain to observe as strict a neutrality as she was able to enforce. As a result the nations maintained generally correct, if not always cordial, relations.

The Netherlands

James S. Pike, a Radical Republican from Maine, accepted Lincoln's nomination as minister to the Netherlands. In 1861 slavery still existed in the Dutch colonies, but in July 1862 the Dutch government announced the emancipation of the 36,000 slaves under its jurisdiction as of one year later. Even so, the Civil War in the United States failed to interest the Dutch, who focused their interest instead on the activities of Garibaldi in Italy.

For the most part the Dutch maintained a strict neutrality, instructing their consuls in America not to intervene in the nation's internal affairs. On June 16, 1861, the Dutch followed the English and declared their neutrality. Aware of the Union's reaction to Britain's proclamation of neutrality, King William III sought out Pike at a ball to impress upon him Dutch friendship for the United States.

Dutch policy concerning the use of their ports by belligerents remained more liberal than England's, as the case of the *Sumter* illustrated. That Confederate raider visited Curaçao, Netherlands West Indies, in July 1861 for coal and supplies, and the next month coaled again at Paramaibo. Seward unsuccessfully protested, but as it turned out the Union reaped most of the benefits of the Dutch policy. The *Kearsarge* had just been repaired at the Royal Dutch Naval Yard at Flushing before she intercepted and sank the *Alabama* in 1864.

Besides the case of the *Sumter* and the one Dutch merchantman seized as a blockade runner late in 1864, the major incident that marked diplomatic relations between the nations came in 1862. After occupying New Orleans, General Butler suspected that Confederate specie had been hidden in the Netherlands consulate. Butler's troops invaded the office and seized $800,000 in silver, plus Dutch files, from the consul's vault. After a protest by the Dutch and an investigation, the money, property of a Dutch firm, was returned and the United States apologized for Butler's disregard of international law. Generally, relations between the United States and the Netherlands remained stable. The Dutch never considered recognizing the Confederacy, nor did any Confederate agent visit the Netherlands.

Austria

The historian John Lothrop Motley represented the United States in Austria. In 1856 he had published the *Rise of the Dutch Republic*, and had sought an appointment to The Hague in order to continue his work. Disappointed in that endeavor, he accepted the post at Vienna since he also contemplated writing a history of the Thirty Years' War. Motley had strong connections in Germanic circles that dated from his student days at the University of Berlin where he had roomed with Otto von Bismarck. He believed that his connections might be useful in Germanic Europe.

Like the Netherlands, Austria remained largely unconcerned with the Civil War in America. She focused her attention on Europe, as she had lost most of her Italian possessions in 1859, and in 1861 faced the threat of Hungarian secession. Basically agricultural, Austria found it difficult to keep pace with her rapidly industrializing neighbors, particularly Prussia. Virtually ignoring

America, Austria never declared her neutrality, and firmly continued to express official sympathy with the Union cause. But since the Austrians had not recognized the belligerency of the Confederacy, Motley explained to Seward, Austria could not recognize the Union blockade as legal.

In regard to Maximilian, younger brother of Emperor Franz Josef, the Imperial government took the position that the Mexican throne was the archduke's personal business, and, as Motley explained, the "government had not the means nor the inclination to send out forces . . . to maintain the new empire." Motley explained to his mother that Maximilian's venture was "exceedingly unpopular in Austria. That a Prince of the House of Hapsburg should become a satrap of the Bonaparte dynasty, and should sit on an American throne which could not exist a moment but for French bayonets . . . is most galling to most classes of Austrians."

In the end Austria could not stand idle as Maximilian's throne crumbled. Vienna concluded an agreement with France to recruit volunteers for service in Mexico, but few signed up and those who did never sailed. Seward's protest had been sharp and had included instructions to Motley to break off diplomatic relations if the volunteers embarked. Seward's protest as well as the unpopularity of the Maximilian affair and the threat of war with Prussia combined to avert a possible Austro-American crisis.

Italy and the Garibaldi Affair

In March 1861 Lincoln appointed George P. Marsh minister to the Kingdom of Sardinia. Soldier-king Victor Emmanuel had nearly completed the unification of Italy, with the aid of his premier, the astute Count Camillo di Cavour, and patriots Giuseppe Garibaldi and Giuseppe Mazzini. Sardinia, busy with conquests, plebiscites, and politics, paid little attention to the American Civil War.

In 1861 Garibaldi presented his conquest of the Two Sicilies (southern Italy) to his king, completing his work. In 1862 he embarked upon an abortive attempt to conquer the Papal states. Meanwhile, a United States consul in Vienna suggested that Garibaldi might be interested in a Union command. The recommendation received publicity in Europe, and when the consul reported his idea to Seward, Seward fired him.

Garibaldi seemed fascinated with the thought, and in the summer of 1861 indicated a willingness to participate if his king no longer needed him. Both circumstances and illness forced Garibaldi to tell Marsh that he could not consider going to his "second country" for some months, yet in the future he would not hesitate to join the "Holy battle" against slavery. It seems clear that Garibaldi believed he would become commander-in-chief of the Union armies and not just another general. The matter never came to a head, for by the time he recovered from his illness the Union had no need of him. It would have shocked him to learn that his participation had never been taken seriously.

The Germanies

During the time of the American Civil War, Bismarck of Prussia maneuvered to unite the Germanic Confederation. Lincoln sent his friend and campaign manager, Norman B. Judd, to Berlin as minister. The outlook in official German circles favored the Union, as Bismarck told Judd, and outside of Prussia the South German states also generally favored the Union cause. As with Italy, however, Germany's own destiny involved the Germans too deeply for them to give much thought to a remote America.

Neither the Germanies nor Sardinia could have influenced the war in America in any meaningful way. If Americans engaged in war, so did the Italians, and in 1866, so did the Germans. So it was that the Union's diplomacy focused on Britain, and occasionally on France, Russia, and Spain. Even for Britain, under the circumstances, the primary diplomatic concern during the war years remained Europe, not America.

PART FOUR

THE TRIALS
OF REUNION

O people-chosen! are ye not
    Likewise the chosen of the Lord,
    To do his will and speak his word?

Make all men peers before the law,
    Take hands from off the negro's throat,
    Give black and white an equal vote.

Keep all your forfeit lives and lands,
    But give the common law's redress
    To labor's utter nakedness.

Then shall the Union's mother-heart
    Her lost and wandering ones recall,
    Forgiving and restoring all,—

And Freedom break her marble trance
    Above the Capitolian dome,
    Stretch hands, and bid ye welcome home!

JOHN GREENLEAF WHITTIER,
"To the Thirty-Ninth Congress," 1865

15
Lincoln, Johnson, and Reconstruction

As Union armies recovered parts of the Confederacy, military officers preserved order in those localities. To relieve field officers of that improper function, Lincoln appointed military governors for parts of Tennessee, Arkansas, and Louisiana as early as 1862. They opened courts and appointed officers who carried out police duties. Lincoln's authority as commander-in-chief was the justification for appointing them, so he could remove them at his whim. They were, in his mind, only temporary, for he disliked military government. Lincoln aimed to replace military governors with civilian authority as soon as practicable. Francis H. Pierpoint's bobtail government at Alexandria functioned for the Union-held portions of that state, obviating the need to appoint a military governor there.

Lincoln set forth a tentative plan of reconstruction December 8, 1863, with his Proclamation of Amnesty and Reconstruction. In it Lincoln said that he wanted it known "to all persons who have . . . participated in the existing rebellion" with certain specific exceptions, "that a full pardon is hereby granted to them," provided they take and keep an oath of allegiance to the Constitution and the Union, as well as to all the laws of the United States, especially those passed during the rebellion regarding the institution of slavery, and to presidential proclamations on the subject. The amnesty did not apply to those who were "civil or diplomatic officers or agents" of the Confederacy, who "left judicial stations under the United States to aid the rebellion," who were military or naval officers of the Confederacy "above the rank of colonel in the army or of lieutenant in the navy," who "resigned commissions in the army or navy of the United States" to take part in the rebellion, or any who had treated either black or white persons other "than lawfully as prisoners of war" when those persons were in the United States armed forces.

Lincoln further proclaimed "that whenever, in any of the States of Arkansas, Texas, Louisiana, Mississippi, Tennessee, Alabama, Georgia, Florida, South Carolina, and North Carolina" no less than one-tenth of the number of qualified voters who voted in the 1860 presidential elections had taken the oath, they could "reestablish a State government." That government would receive the benefits of that section of the Constitution which guaranteed a republican form of government to the states and protected them from invasion or, under the proper circumstances, domestic violence.*

The proclamation continued: "the national Executive" would not object to "any provision" of a new state government "which shall recognize and declare . . . permanent freedom [for former slaves], provide for their education" as might "be consistent, as a temporary arrangement, with their present condition as a laboring, landless, and homeless class." Lincoln apparently foresaw a need for a transition period, during which time the freedmen would be educated to the responsibilities of citizenship.

Lincoln recognized that his reconstruction plan had limits. The proclamation read: "it may be proper to further say" that the question of whether members sent to Congress from the states reconstructed under his plan "shall be admitted to seats, constitutionally rests exclusively with the respective Houses, and not to any extent with the Executive." Not only did Lincoln raise the possibility that Congress might refuse to seat congressmen chosen under his plan, he further warned that while he thought "the mode presented is the best the Executive can suggest, with his present impressions, it

* Article IV, Section 4.

must not be understood that no other possible mode would be acceptable."

His proclamation, Lincoln said, "is intended to present" to the people of the former Confederacy a means "by which the national authority and loyal State governments may be re-established" in the South. He regarded his plan as a temporary expedient, necessary in the circumstances, and not a final plan of reconstruction. The date of the proclamation coincided with the day of his 1863 annual message to Congress, and in that message, Lincoln made clear the reasons for proclaiming a temporary plan of reconstruction.*

He told Congress: "the proposed acquiescence of the national Executive in any reasonable temporary state arrangement for the freed people is made with the view of possibly modifying the confusion and destitution which must, at best, attend all classes by a total revolution of labor throughout whole States." He hoped the proclamation would "avoid great confusion" in the South. He acknowledged that the question of reconstruction was "beset with conflicting views that the step might be delayed too long or be taken too soon." He felt a need for a plan by which Southerners could organize and bring order to their governmental affairs. He asked them to accept his plan "as a rallying point" and presumed they would thus "act sooner than they otherwise would." Lincoln implied that the rebellion and confusion in the Confederacy would dissipate more quickly if Southerners knew they had a reasonable direction to follow.

Yet Lincoln wanted to avoid "the danger of committals on points which could be more safely left to further developments. Care has been taken," he assured Congress, "to so shape the document as to avoid embarrassments from this source. . . . Saying that reconstruction will be accepted if presented in a specified way, it is not said it will never be accepted in any other way." Reemphasizing the temporary nature of his plan, he also failed to exclude the possibility that it might be the only plan. The central idea, Lincoln told Congress, was "to give confidence to the people in the contested regions, that the insurgent power will not again overrun them. Until that confidence shall be established," he warned, "little can be done anywhere for what is called reconstruction." In looking for

---

* Historians have too often made Lincoln's plan of reconstruction appear as the only standard by which he would accept reconstruction. Yet he took pains to make it clear the plan was, in fact, subject to possible modification.

Southerners themselves to reestablish loyal governments, Lincoln remained consistent with his past efforts to encourage them to come to their senses and return to the Union.

Lincoln had already partially implemented his plan in Louisiana. Thirteen parishes in Union hands had been placed under a military governor in August 1862. Just before the proclamation in December 1863, two districts in Louisiana had elected representatives whom the House seated.* After the proclamation was issued, Lincoln encouraged Banks, the commanding general in Louisiana, to hold an election for state officials in February 1864.

At that time, Hahn swept to victory in the gubernatorial race at the head of a pro-Union ticket. Yet the Hahn party scarcely represented white Louisiana and was dismissed by one observer as "Northern flunkeyism." Other factions protested Hahn's election on the grounds of military interference. In the House of Representatives, late in February, a joint resolution recognizing Louisiana's new government as "legitimate" faced opposition on the floor from most Democrats and a small but determined band of Radical Republicans led by Sumner. Although a clear majority favored the resolution, Sumner managed, according to Trumbull, to "browbeat the Senate" into defeating it by not allowing it to come up for a vote. As a result, Hahn's senators and representatives were not seated.

Undaunted, Hahn's group continued with their program in Louisiana. They called a state convention that met in April and changed the Louisiana constitution by abolishing slavery and providing male citizens with equal civil status regardless of race. Louisianans ratified the new constitution by a six-to-one vote. Yet black suffrage was not included, which doomed the efforts in the eyes of many Radical Republicans.

Those Louisiana blacks who had appealed for the vote comprised over 18,000 free blacks who in 1860 had owned New Orleans property worth about $15,000,000. Many were educated, many were "acknowledged kinsmen" of Louisiana's leading white families. Failing in appeals to the military governors, they went directly to Lincoln. Perhaps as a result of their appeal and certainly as a consequence of anticipated Radical Republican reaction to the new

---

* They were Michael Hahn and Benjamin F. Flanders, who served from February 9, 1863, to the end of the session in March.

Louisiana constitution, Lincoln delicately warned Governor Hahn: "You are about to have a Convention which, among other things, will probably define the elective franchise. I barely suggest for your private consideration whether some of the colored people may not be let in—as, for instance, the very intelligent, and especially those who have fought gallantly in our ranks."

Lincoln's suggestion—or warning—to Hahn reflected the development of Lincoln's own views on black suffrage. The president had written to General James S. Wadsworth in January that he had studied seriously and carefully the question of the "condition of the colored race." In reply to Wadsworth's query whether "universal amnesty should not be accompanied with universal suffrage" in a defeated South, the president wrote: "I cannot see, . . . how . . . I can avoid exacting in return universal suffrage, or, at least, suffrage on the basis of intelligence and military service." It was this "least" that he advocated for Louisiana.

Nor did Hahn miss the point. A convention resolution forbidding blacks from ever voting was replaced by another authorizing the Louisiana legislature to allow suffrage to those "citizens of the United States, as by military service, by taxation to support the government, or by intellectual fitness, may be deemed entitled thereto." The resolution was tabled by the convention and blacks still remained without the franchise.

Lincoln believed he had done all he could and that imperfect as the Louisiana constitution was on the matter of black suffrage, a great deal had been gained for the blacks on other fronts like equal civil status. In November 1864 Lincoln wrote that the people of Louisiana had made "an excellent new constitution—better for the poor black man than we have done in Illinois." He admitted that it was accomplished "under military protection, directed by me" in the sincere belief that "with such a nucleus around which to build we could get the State into position again sooner than otherwise." As a temporary expedient, he implied, it would do until future events determined otherwise; in the meantime a loyal government would be established in Louisiana.

Arkansas followed the example of Louisiana in 1864, constructing a "free state" government with a new constitution. The state suffered the same fate as Louisiana, when Congress refused to seat its representatives in June. Tennessee held conventions in 1864 and 1865, amended its constitution, chose a government and elected officials to Congress, but Congress refused to recognize these officials in December 1865. In both Arkansas and Tennessee, constitutional proceedings were irregular and unsupported by large majorities, so that even holding meaningful elections was difficult. As a result, Lincoln never managed to put his plan of reconstruction, no matter how temporary or how expedient, into full effect.

On July 2, 1864, the Wade-Davis bill passed Congress, embodying the thought of Radical Republicans who opposed Lincoln's plan. They rejected Lincoln's loyal 10 percent as a basis for action and substituted instead a majority taken from among all white male citizens enrolled by the provisional governor, provided they had taken a loyalty oath. These voters could then hold a constitutional convention, but all Confederate state and national officials and all who voluntarily bore arms in Confederate service were excluded. The state governments so established had to prohibit slavery and repudiate Confederate debts; with few exceptions, state and national Confederate officials were barred from service in the legislatures or the state executive offices. Lincoln pocket-vetoed the bill but explained his reasons in an unusual proclamation of July 8.

The president admitted that the Wade-Davis bill expressed "the sense of Congress" on the subject of reconstruction. But, he said, he was "unprepared, by a formal approval of this Bill, to be inflexibly committed to any single plan of restoration" and "unprepared to declare" that the constitutions and governments already adopted in Louisiana and Arkansas "shall be set aside" and come to nothing since it would discourage the "loyal citizens" in those states from "further effort." Constitutionally he believed that Congress had not the authority "to abolish slavery in the states," though he hoped that a constitutional amendment to that end would soon come to pass. Yet, he admitted: "I am fully satisfied with the system for restoration contained in the Bill, as one very proper plan for the loyal people of any State choosing to adopt it," and he maintained he would help those people who chose that path to reconstruction to implement it.

The Wade-Davis bill anticipated the passage of the Thirteenth Amendment through the House by six months, even though the amendment was then under consideration. In a strict constitutional sense, Lincoln correctly offered that as one reason for the veto. The Wade-Davis bill on those grounds alone faced a dubious future in the courts. More important to Lincoln was the ex-post-facto effect the bill would have had upon the Louisiana and Arkansas governments and the consequent demoralizing effect it would have had upon "loyalists" in those states. Their efforts had been uncertain enough as it was, and the Wade-Davis bill would probably have thoroughly discredited them and abruptly ended their activities. Lincoln clearly preferred to accept their immediate attempts to restore a loyal government rather than face a more traumatic experience later. He was enough of a political realist, however, to welcome the congressional plan as viable for any subsequent reconstruction movements. It was Congress that proved inflexible, not the president.

Lincoln discussed reconstruction at length in his last public address on April 11, 1865. Reconstruction, he reported, "which has had a large share of our thought from the first, is pressed much more closely upon our attention. It is fraught with great difficulty." Unlike a war between nations, "there is no authorized organ for us to treat with." It is necessary for us to "begin with, and mould from, disorganized and discordant elements." And it is no small "embarrassment" that we "differ among ourselves as to the mode, manner, and means of reconstruction." He knew, he said, that he was "much censured" for "setting up, and seeking to sustain, the new State Government of Louisiana." He reviewed his message of December 8, 1863, and the proclamation of the same date in which he presented *"a plan"* of reconstruction and promised to sustain any state that followed it. He reiterated that it was "not the only plan."

Lincoln argued forcefully for acceptance of what he had done in Louisiana, then added: "as to sustaining it, my promise is out. . . . But as bad promises are better broken than kept, I shall treat this as a bad promise and break it" if ever convinced that it might be "adverse to the public interest." He was not "yet" convinced that that was true. There was, however, much that was unsatisfactory about things in Louisiana, especially "that the elective franchise is not given to the colored man. I would myself prefer that it were now conferred on the very intelligent, and on those who serve our cause as soldiers," he announced. His open statement on this matter was probably intended to help force that modification in Louisiana.

The president reminded his listeners that Louisiana's constitution empowered the legislature "to confer the elective franchise upon the colored man." After all, he said, that legislature had voted to ratify the Thirteenth Amendment. He asked that the government of Louisiana not be demolished under his plan but that it be encouraged "to adhere to their work, and argue for it, and proselyte for it, and fight for it, and feed it, and grow it, and ripen it to a complete success." Granting that the black man desired the "elective franchise, will he not attain it sooner by saving the already advanced steps toward it, than by running backward over them?"

"What has been said of Louisiana will apply generally to other states," Lincoln lectured, thinking of Arkansas and Tennessee. "No exclusive, and inflexible plan can safely be prescribed" for varying conditions in different areas. "Important principles may, and must, be inflexible," he admonished, implying, though, that these principles could be fit into flexible plans. If black suffrage was such an "inflexible" yet "important principle," it could and should be a part of any reconstruction plan. "In the present *'situation'* as the phrase goes," Lincoln concluded, "it may be my duty to make some new announcement to the people of the South. I am considering, and shall not fail to act, when satisfied that action will be proper." The "present situation" was the deadlock between Lincoln and Congress on the matter of reconstruction. With its ability to block the acceptance of new state governments in the South by failing to seat their elected representatives, Congress held the upper hand. Lincoln had alluded to his willingness to break a "bad promise"; he had warned the South to include a black franchise in their new constitutions; it is not farfetched to believe that his "new announcement" would have contained a mandate for some sort of black franchise. Yet within a week Lincoln was shot, and the "new announcement" he was "considering" died with him.

Lincoln's last address answered at least partly a letter from Chief Justice Chase, advocating "securing suffrage to all citizens" in the "rebel States." Chase believed the way was open for this to be accomplished in Louisiana, as Lincoln pointed out, and even in Arkansas and other states. In another letter after Lincoln's speech, Chase told Lincoln how he had worked to get Louisiana leaders, including Banks, to extend suffrage to freedmen. He urged Lincoln to cause "every proper representation to be made to the Louisiana legislature" for including black suffrage. Chase, however, wanted to include more than just black soldiers and the black intelligentsia. He asked for "universal suffrage" and indicated to Lincoln that the president's plan, if so modified, would satisfy him. Lincoln may have intended to hold out for a modified suffrage along the lines he mentioned, for it was not outside the realm of possibility that he would trade universal suffrage for Radical acceptance of the remainder of the plan.

The Assassination

Lee had surrendered to Grant on April 9, two days before Lincoln appeared in a window of the White House to deliver his address of April 11. On April 10, in the evening, a group had come to serenade him, but he had' declined to speak to them, asking them back the next night when he would have something serious to say. If the crowd expected a victory speech, they got only a few lines, and heard him instead analyze reconstruction. With the group on the White House lawn stood John Wilkes Booth, who had already hatched a plot to kill the president.

Washington was in a festive mood. April 13 had been a day of especial celebration, with the city decked out in flags and bunting and entertained by a fireworks display in the evening. Everyone expected Sherman to take Johnston's surrender momentarily. The president, as his April 11 speech showed, and his cabinet had turned to the work of peace. For three hours on the morning of Good Friday, April 14, Lincoln and the cabinet, with Grant in attendance, discussed reconstruction.

Since Grant was the hero of the hour, Lincoln had asked the general and his wife to accompany him and Mrs. Lincoln to Ford's Theater at the invitation of the management. Grant accepted, but later excused himself. On the bill was Tom Taylor's play, *Our American Cousin*, starring Laura Keene, Harry Hawk, and John Dyott. The play had begun by the time the Lincolns arrived, accompanied by Major Henry R. Rathbone and his fiancée, Clara Harris, daughter of the senator from New York. Charles Forbes, Lincoln's personal attendant, joined the party a little later, while John F. Parker, a patrolman from the Metropolitan Police Force and Lincoln's only bodyguard, sat for a time outside the door to the president's box.

The play moved smoothly along until the middle of the second scene of the third act. Then, at a few minutes after ten o'clock, John Wilkes Booth entered the presidential box, put a small pistol to the president's head, and fired. After stabbing Major Rathbone, who tried to capture him, Booth leaped to the stage below, brandishing his knife and shouting *"Sic semper tyrannis."* In spite of fracturing a bone in his right leg, Booth escaped across the stage and out the back where a colleague waited with a horse for his getaway. It all happened in the space of perhaps thirty seconds, in front of an audience so stunned the people scarcely realized what was happening.

Booth's bullet entered Lincoln's brain, immediately rendering him unconscious. The president was carried across the street to the Petersen House, where he died at 7:22 A.M., April 15. "About the same time this murder was being committed at the theater," wrote Stanton the next day, "another assassin presented himself at the door of Mr. Seward's residence," where Seward lay abed, recovering from an accident. The intruder attacked Seward's son Frederick and a male nurse as well as Seward himself, then fought his way past another of Seward's sons and another attendant, and also escaped. Unknown at the time, a third conspirator had been assigned to the vice president, and a fourth to General Grant.

On Saturday morning the nation learned of the death of Lincoln and the attack on Seward. Washington was sealed off, and a roundup of suspicious characters began. Cavalry and mounted police clattered over the roads in nearby Virginia and Maryland, seeking Booth and his comrades. Inspired by the memory of Confederate schemes to incite revolt in northern cities, to free prisoners of war, or to put the torch to Union towns, the press construed the assassination as a Confederate plot and charged Davis and other Confederate officials with its inception. Even formerly anti-Lincoln papers took up the cry for revenge.

With the president dead, the vice president preparing to take the oath of office so tragically thrust upon him, and Seward lying wounded, weak, and speechless in his bed, Stanton loomed as the avenger, determined to capture, try, and execute the assassins. He had already expressed his firm views on the need to impose a harsh policy on the South as retribution for the war. Orders went out from the War Department for the arrest and confinement of leading Confederate officials and certain rebel officers.

The state funeral occupied the public in Washington for the next several days. Few found much joy in the celebration of the risen Christ that Easter Sunday. The wake began in the darkened East Room of the White House on Monday, and on Wednesday it moved in a great procession to the rotunda of the Capitol. Thousands paid their last respects before the body was taken aboard the funeral train on Friday; perhaps 7,000,000 more saluted the slain leader as the train made a slow, circuitous twelve-day journey to Springfield, Illinois.

On May 3 President Johnson proclaimed that Davis and other Confederates had connived in the assassination and offered rewards for their arrest. The price on Davis' head alone was set at $100,000. The manhunt continued; the Metropolitan Police were assisted by detectives from other cities and the full strength of the military. They filled the jails with suspects and witnesses, and friends and relatives of the suspects and witnesses. Ella Turner, Booth's blonde mistress, unsuccessfully attempted suicide and was jailed, along with the girls from a house of ill-fame run by Booth's sister. The Ford brothers, their employees, and members of the cast were detained.

One by one, the conspirators were apprehended. Mrs. Mary E. Surrat, operator of the boardinghouse that had harbored the plotters, was arrested. Michael O'Laughlin, who supposedly had lain in wait to assassinate Grant, was found in Baltimore on April 17. That same day Lewis Payne, who made the attempt on Seward's life, was arrested as he returned to the Surrat house after hiding in the woods. Samuel B. Arnold, who had been part of an earlier plot to kidnap Lincoln, was taken in custody at Fort Monroe. Edward Spangler, a Ford's Theater stagehand, though not a conspirator, had helped Booth with his horse at the theater and was jailed. George Atzerodt, whose mark had been Johnson, was found at a relative's home in Maryland. Arnold, Atzerodt, Payne, and Spangler, in double irons, were kept in the hold of a ship in the navy yard.

Booth, traveling with David E. Herold, had his broken leg treated by Dr. Samuel Mudd, an acquaintance. Suspicious, Mudd told his cousin of the visit and suggested that he alert Lieutenant David A. Dana, whose cavalry detachment was searching the district. Dana relayed Mudd's message to detectives from the provost marshal's office, who investigated and arrested Dr. Mudd. Booth and Herold, meanwhile, hid out in southern Maryland for days before crossing the Potomac into Virginia. That Booth was not captured before he left Maryland can be blamed on the confusion of the manhunt. His pursuers failed to cooperate with one another.

Soldiers, police, detectives, and others conducted independent expeditions and kept clues to themselves. By April 20 rewards totaled $50,000 for Booth and $25,000 for Herold.

Colonel Lafayette C. Baker, who headed the War Department's Secret Service, had arrived in Washington on April 16 and taken command of the army's pursuit. Once he learned that Provost Marshal Major James R. O'Beirne was close on Booth's trail in Virginia, Baker took the field himself with a detachment of the Sixteenth New York Cavalry. They closed in shortly after midnight, April 26, at William Garrett's farm, near Port Royal, Virginia, where Booth and Herold had hidden in the tobacco shed. The soldiers surrounded the shed and sent Garrett, a paroled Confederate cavalryman, to get the fugitives' weapons—he was unsuccessful. Shortly, Herold surrendered, but Booth refused. The soldiers set the shed on fire to force him out; as he moved toward the door, a shot rang out, and Booth fell. He died on the porch of the Garrett house at sunrise.

Herold was put in irons with the rest, and Booth's body was carefully hidden in Washington for a time before being buried secretly to keep it from being used by some sort of feared resistance group. The other prisoners came to trial before a military commission on May 10. The seven generals and two colonels who heard the case sentenced Mrs. Surrat, Atzerodt, Herold, and Payne to hang, and sentenced Arnold, Mudd, O'Laughlin, and Spangler to prison in the Dry Tortugas for various periods of time. The trial had gone as Stanton felt it should, and the murderers of Lincoln paid the price. Justice proved swift and harsh, marked more by vengeance than equity.

Lincoln's assassination had at least two obvious effects. One was the birth of the "Lincoln legend," which elevated the murdered president to the status of a folk hero. Abraham Lincoln became the man who had come from the backwoods of the American West; who, unrecognized and maligned, became president at the crucial moment in United States history; who soared to heights of greatness by preserving the Union; who led the emancipation movement, was charitable even toward his enemies, and was crucified at the peak of success. Following the assassination Lincoln appeared as the Christ-like president who had taken the nation's burdens on his broad shoulders and redeemed both the nation and its people. Americans treasured the vision of the rail-splitter, the self-made man, the patron saint of honesty, charity, and homely wit who studied by flickering firelight and who walked miles to return a few cents or borrow a book. Lincoln, the practical politician, receded in the mist of myth.

The second effect of the assassination was its immediate impact on the temper of the North. The act outraged Northerners as a vicious murder as well as a senseless, revengeful act on the part of a vanquished foe. It did not matter that the enemy had not been responsible for the deed of a demented actor and his fellow conspirators. The public seemed to agree with the press and with Johnson's proclamation. Even Sherman, when he accepted the surrender of Johnston, was denounced as a traitor in the pay of the enemy. Public anger paved the way in the North for a strict and stern peace with the South. Lincoln's charitable approach to reconstruction had been the generous act of a folk hero; the public was ready to exact a much more stern settlement.

Johnson Takes Over

At ten o'clock on the morning of April 15, Chief Justice Chase, accompanied by Hugh McCulloch of Indiana, the new secretary of the treasury, James Speed of Kentucky, attorney general since the past December, and several others, called upon Johnson at Kirkwood House; there Chase administered the presidential oath of office. Born in North Carolina, Johnson had moved to Tennessee as a young man. Self-educated, he followed a tailor's trade but soon became involved in politics, serving as mayor of Greenville, state legislator, representative to Congress for a decade, governor of Tennessee, and United States senator. A slaveholder and a Democrat, he had been a firm defender of the Union and was the only Southern senator who refused to resign when his state seceded. After the Union recovered western Tennessee, Lincoln appointed Johnson as the military governor, and by 1864 he had organized a new state government along the lines Lincoln suggested in his plan. That accomplishment, along with practical political considerations, had won him the vice presidency on the 1864 Union party ticket. As Lincoln's successor, Johnson became the seventeenth president.

Though a Unionist, and one who at the very least mistrusted the old Southern power structure on whom he blamed the war, Johnson was not anti-Southern, a fact at first misunderstood by the

Radical Republicans. As one whose own state stood to benefit from Lincoln's plan of reconstruction, he sympathized with Lincoln's approach. Almost immediately a parade of congressmen, including Sumner, arrived to inform Johnson that black suffrage was "essential." Thaddeus Stevens, master of the House, felt disturbed that Johnson failed to agree that the Southern states had committed suicide, for, as he told Johnson, he could not see how states that were in the Union could be remodeled. Stevens suggested that Johnson suspend reconstruction until Congress could act on the matter.

Seward, recovering from the assassin's attack, asked Johnson to continue Lincoln's policies, with a few modifications. Southerners, who normally would have had nothing to do with Johnson socially, indicated that they were willing to cooperate under the presidential plan. Democrats camped on his doorstep in an effort to woo him back into the fold, convincing him he had bipartisan support.

That Johnson kept Lincoln's cabinet indicated that he planned no radical departure from Lincoln's policies. Yet the cabinet was itself divided on reconstruction. Stanton headed the radical faction, and Johnson found himself in sympathy with Stanton's determination to bring the former rulers of the South to book. Johnson talked about the odiousness of treason and offered large rewards for Confederate officials on the grounds that they had been involved in the conspiracy to kill Lincoln. The Radicals also called for the arrest and punishment of Lee and other paroled Confederate generals, holding that their paroles expired with the end of hostilities. Only Grant's firm intervention prevented such a move. Seward headed the moderate faction in the cabinet and, once back on the job, brought a more moderate influence to bear upon the president. However he might feel toward the South's former leaders, Johnson still favored Lincoln's plan of reconstruction.

On May 9, 1865, Johnson recognized the Pierpoint government of Virginia; twenty days later he issued his Proclamation of Amnesty, which paralleled Lincoln's in general terms but differed from it on specifics. Former Confederates would be pardoned upon taking a loyalty oath to the Union, but Johnson excepted Confederate civil and diplomatic officers, Confederate army officers above the rank of colonel, navy officers above the rank of lieutenant, Confederate governors, former United States officials who resigned to serve the Confederacy, and all persons whose taxable property exceeded an estimated $20,000. This last category was new, and illustrated Johnson's effort to punish the wealthy men who he felt had brought on the war. Any in the excepted classifications could make special application for pardon directly to Johnson, who promised he would "liberally" extend clemency.

Also on May 29, Johnson appointed William W. Holden provisional governor of North Carolina and directed him to hold a constitutional convention. As provisional governor, Holden was granted whatever powers were necessary to enable North Carolinians to restore the state to the Union. No person was eligible to serve either as a delegate to or elector for delegates unless he had been a qualified elector before the war and had taken the loyalty oath. Stanton had tried to get Johnson to include all freemen, white and black, but Johnson agreed with Seward and limited the franchise. Even so, according to the proclamation, the convention, once elected, controlled both the franchise and eligibility for office in the state, "a power," Johnson claimed, "the people of the several states" had "rightfully exercised" since the formation of the Union.

As it emerged, Johnson's plan of reconstruction followed neither Lincoln's 10 percent policy nor the stiffer requirements of Congress in the Wade-Davis bill. Johnson required only that a loyal "portion" of the people write a constitution and form a government. In this respect he opened the door wider than Lincoln had. Johnson omitted any reference to the franchise, except to permit whatever state conventions might decide. He showed that he had learned little from Lincoln's struggle with Congress by making no move toward, and even backing farther away from, compromise with the legislative branch. If he misinterpreted the amount of political support he thought he had, he nevertheless showed himself to be less than the politician necessary to overcome the deadlock between the two branches of government. While black suffrage had not been required by the Wade-Davis bill, or in any other vote of Congress, and although it was denied in all but six Northern states,* Lincoln had come to see the necessity of at least a modified black franchise. Leading Radicals, including the great powers in the Senate and House, Sumner and Stevens, had in fact made no secret of their own view—freedmen had to have the vote in order to protect themselves and their free status.

* Northern states that permitted a black to vote were Maine, Massachusetts, New Hampshire, New York, Rhode Island, and Vermont.

Within the next month and a half, Johnson issued proclamations similar to North Carolina's for South Carolina, Georgia,
Florida, Alabama, Mississippi, and Texas. Anxious Southerners,
relieved that neither black enfranchisement, confiscation, nor other
dreaded disabilities had been pressed upon them, went busily to
work reestablishing their governments and social and economic systems. They hoped that the North would no longer dare trample the
rights of sovereign states; they believed that by the time Congress
met in December it would not dare overturn their efforts as sanctioned by the president of the United States.

By mid-autumn 1865 all of the states under Johnson's plan, except Texas, had held their state conventions. Texas convened in the
spring of 1866. Together they repealed secession and abolished slavery and, except for South Carolina, they repudiated state debts incurred because of the war. Johnson insisted on those steps. When
the new state legislatures met, the Thirteenth Amendment came to
them for ratification. Johnson intervened again, and every Southern
state but Mississippi ratified it.

The State of the Nation

Meanwhile, Union soldiers returned home to their Northern
states to find the comparative prosperity that flourished during the
war. Some of the veterans returned to farms to find and use the new
machinery that speeded planting and harvests, increasing their
yields. Others returned to cities that continued to build and grow,
or to factories that increased their output, or to railroads that had
added many miles of new track. Wartime savings poured out to
finance the continued expansion, and it seemed as if Americans in
the North had never had it so good.

Going home after the war, Confederate veterans found little
glory in the South. Perhaps that was why they searched for meaning and honor in the antebellum days of heady optimism and in the
vain triumphs of the war years. In 1865 observers in the South
found discouraged men, eager to sell their property and move elsewhere. Advertisements of plantations for sale at far below their prewar value filled the newspapers. As little as $2.00 an acre would
buy prime Virginia land that commanded fifty times that price before the war. The figures differed, but the facts remained the same
all over the South. The South's economic system had broken down.

Southerners found hunger, desolation, and decay, as they contemplated the wreckage of four years of savage war. Not just the economic system had caved in, but also the social system, as 4,000,000 slaves were now 4,000,000 freedmen.

The upper Shenandoah Valley, traversed again and again by both armies, was a melancholy waste. Between Winchester and Harrisonburg not a horse, cow, pig, or chicken, or a crop or a fence, could be found. Beyond Harrisonburg, toward Staunton, was the region desolated by Sheridan, and there, within a five-mile radius, scarcely any building stood. Destitution prevailed in the valley. Able-bodied blacks had left. Travelers described the area between Richmond and Washington as a desert, with burned farmhouses, untilled land, and no cattle. In Richmond itself, the army fed the starving: thousands of Lee's men on their way home and 25,000 women and children of all colors. In hundreds of other Southern towns and villages, the story repeated itself. In Atlanta, during one week in June 1865, the army distributed 45,000 pounds of meat, 45,000 pounds of meal, and 10,000 pounds of flour.

In the track of Sherman's army, across Georgia and South Carolina, the distress was enormous. Reports told of women and children who had walked miles in search of bread; of others who were found crouching half-naked beside old brick chimneys, all that remained of their homes; of ten counties in northern Georgia that produced less food than could be found on any ordinary Northern farm. Families of Union volunteers in southern Tennessee and northern Georgia, whose homes had been ruined by rebel armies and guerrilla warfare, were among the worst sufferers. In Missouri, even after Kirby Smith's surrender, guerrilla bands remained restless, and some, including the James and Younger brothers, turned to crime and terror.

A visitor to Charleston, South Carolina, described the city as one "of ruins, of deserted streets, of vacant houses, of widowed women, of deserted warehouses, of weed-wild gardens, of miles of grass-grown streets." Once admired for its broad avenues, shaded by beautiful trees and flanked by fine lawns and gardens, the capital city of South Carolina had become a wilderness of ruins. As the birthplace of secession, the city had been methodically destroyed by Sherman's soldiers. The heart of the city was no more than blackened chimneys and crumbling walls, with not a store standing in the business district. For the better part of a mile along each of twelve streets nearby, not a building remained. In place of shade trees, stark rows of stumps remained. Not a railroad line reached within twelve miles of town, and some had been destroyed for as far as fifty miles.

Not many Southern cities were as devastated as Charleston. Vicksburg had succumbed to a hard siege, but by the time newsman Whitelaw Reid visited in late 1865 it "had already lost most of the traces of the siege. . . . Few of the houses showed much serious damage. . . . Stores had been reopened; ox-teams, bringing in cotton, filled the streets" and in general the city showed signs of eagerness to get on with business.

By November 1865, even Richmond strove to revitalize itself. "The burnt district," Reid wrote, "comprising nearly all the business portion of the city . . . was beginning to rise from its ruins. Between a fourth and a third of it would soon be better than before the conflagration" set by the Confederates to signal their retreat. Yet Virginians, Reid found, mistrusted the Yankee dollar. "Men who had been declaring for four years that the United States Government was overthrown, could not at once convince themselves that its money was good. . . . Whoever wanted to trade with the Virginians in the rural districts, must prepare himself with gold."

Knoxville, Tennessee, had suffered, too. "Burnt houses and solitary chimneys over one whole quarter of the city, showed that the heart of East Tennessee loyalty had not been without its sufferings," Reid reported. Yet "the best part . . . of the little city seemed to be saved." Between Knoxville and Atlanta, especially from Dalton south, "solitary chimneys and the debris of burnt buildings everywhere tell the old, old story" of Sherman's persistent push against Johnston's determined resistance.

Atlanta, while clearly stamped with the signs of Sherman, "his mark," as Reid put it, "was adapting itself with remarkable rapidity, to the new order of things." Reid observed "gaping windows and roofless houses, heaps of ruins on the principal corners and traces of unsparing destruction everywhere." Yet "Richmond was not half so far rebuilt as Atlanta" even though Northern capital flowed into Richmond. Atlantans "were bringing a city out of this desert of shattered brick," rebuilding warehouses, "hastily establishing stores in houses half finished and unroofed," taking lessons "from Chicago." At least 4,000 construction workers labored feverishly, and had enough building materials been available, twice as many might have been employed. "Drays and wagons" filled the streets, the railroads labored "to their utmost capacity," and "the trade of the city was a third greater than it had ever been, in its most prosperous days."

Atlanta shone as a monument to its inhabitants' determination, but not all cities recovered so fast. "Selma bore rough marks of the Yankee General [James H.] Wilson," who raided it before the last gun sounded. A third of the city lay in ruins, and the Confederate army's machine shops and foundries had been "thoroughly destroyed." By the time Reid reached Mobile, though, he found that port city a hive of activity, much like Atlanta. "When I had last seen Mobile," he explained, in the spring of 1865, "it was a city of ruins" and of disheartened people. But by the following fall "one rubbed his eyes" as one came from the "chaotic interior," for as he "whirled through the bustling streets" the change struck him. "Warehouses were rising, torpedoes had been removed from the harbor, and a fleet of sail and steam vessels lined the repaired wharves. The main thoroughfares resounded with the rush of business . . . the hotels were overflowing. The 'new blood of the South'" leaped "in right riotous pulsations" through the city.

Reid found Memphis, which in June had been "full of returning . . . soldiers" to be full of businessmen in the fall. Perhaps the volume of business did not match the successes of New Orleans, but next to New Orleans, Memphis "seemed to be doing the heaviest business of any Southern city. The streets were filled with drays, and the levee was crowded with freight." New Orleans, of course, had come into Union hands early and had not suffered in battle. The "city itself showed no traces of war" even in June 1865.

The urban areas of the South revived quickly in contrast to the rural areas. Plantation owners in Alabama, as in Virginia, hoped to sell or rent their lands. Reid told of one treasury agent in Alabama who went into the "land agency" business, and within a day or two "had twelve plantations . . . to be sold at fixed prices, ranging from seven to fourteen dollars per acre. Before the war these lands were valued at from fifty to a hundred dollars." Many Northerners, ex-soldiers in particular, leased or bought plantations. "I should judge it a splendid opening," commented Reid, "for careless men to lose money." Reid knew that working a plantation depended upon "skillful management," and that much Northern speculation was doomed by inexperience.

The "straits to which the people had been reduced" in the
South showed in other ways, even where military demolition was
not involved. "The pianos all jangled, and the legs of the parlor
chairs were out of tune quite as badly," wrote Reid. "Sofas had
grown dangerous places for any but the most slow-motioned and se-
date. Missing bits of veneering from the furniture illustrated the absence of Yankee prepared glue." Window curtains had departed,
along with carpets. "We saw rough earthen mugs, that looked as if
they had been dug out of Pompeii. . . . These were specimens of
home manufacture" and had cost many Confederate dollars. The
decrepit glasses, dishes, and household necessities would have been
unusual even in poor households.

The Southern railroad system had collapsed. The Confederates
had stripped short lines to keep the major ones in repair. Locomo-
tives stood idle for want of parts. Passenger coach windows sported
wood coverings for want of glass. Where trains ran, passengers often
rode in boxcars. Stage coaches frequently connected gaps in the
war-ravaged railway system. Reid found "not a platform or water-
tank" left on one Virginia line and rails "in the worst possible condition." Even twelve miles an hour seemed too fast for the condition
of the roadbed. Yet the conductors told of great improvements over
conditions six months earlier, and Reid saw, every few miles, gangs
of men at work.

Southerners wasted little time turning to rebuilding, according
to Reid. The prices of plantation lands, for lease or sale, had begun
to recover by the first of the year, 1866. Not only whites, but blacks,
too, had made considerable progress. Blacks worked at "fitting
themselves" for the responsibilities of citizenship "with a zeal and
rapidity never equalled by any similar class." Correctly, Reid felt
that "the only guaranty" for the return of prosperity to the South
was the "order and industry" of the black citizens. And in the reorganization then facing Southern states, Reid warned that "the Nation can not longer afford" a policy of ignoring the black people.

Economic conditions in the North appeared very good in contrast with the South. The number of manufacturing establishments
nearly doubled from 1860 to 1870; the railway mileage and the
labor force both doubled. In iron, steel, oil refining, textiles, and
shoes, Northern industry leaped ahead. The tremendous American
domestic market continued to grow as the population expanded
from 31,443,000 in 1860, to 38,558,000 in 1870, to 50,155,800 in

1880—of whom only about 5,000,000 had come as immigrants during those two decades. By 1869 steel rails spanned the nation from coast to coast, and the rapid rail growth unlocked at the same time more natural resources and more markets. From the end of the war for a period of seven or eight years the industrial machine and financial system of the North exploded in a frenzied, inflated expansion. The economic collapse of 1873 brought an interim of depression and readjustment, but was followed by yet another period of spectacular growth in the 1880s.

The South, by contrast, missed out on the industrial and financial growth of the late 1860s and early 1870s. Aside from their frantic rebuilding of destroyed and damaged rail lines, very little new construction extended the Southern rail network. Manufacturing plants that had bloomed in the hothouse atmosphere of the South at war died afterwards, and little new industrialization took place. Southern agriculture took decades for its slow and painful comeback. The traumatic experience of political and social reconstruction, following on the heels of the equally frustrating experience of the war, left a deep scar on the South and compounded the economic burden of its people.

The South and Presidential Reconstruction

The humorist Petroleum V. Nasby (David Ross Locke), in his letter entitled "The Assassination," dated April 20, 1865, wrote "didst think that Linkin's death wood help the South? Linkin's hand wuz velvet—Johnson's may be, to the eye, but to the feel it will be found iron. Where Linkin switched" Nasby wrote in his own unique way, "Johnson will flay. Where Linkin banished, Johnson will hang. . . . In common with all troo Dimekrats, I weep."

Nasby expressed the mixed emotions of many Southerners. At first they felt uneasy about Johnson, but his actions reassured them. His hand, like "Linkin's," turned out to be velvet. States' rights appeared safe. Johnson seemed even more attractive when he chose a former Confederate colonel to process the requests for pardon that poured into the executive office. Because wealthy Southerners could not reclaim their property without a pardon, getting that pardon became a volume business, with over a hundred a day being granted by the fall of 1865. Over six hundred North Carolinians

were cleared before November 1865, including some very prominent individuals. Other Confederate leaders, from Semmes, the
Alabama's commander, to Stephens, Reagan, and Memminger were
pardoned within a year. Within less than a year after Johnson's amnesty proclamation nearly 15,000 persons had received a clean bill,
nearly half of those in the $20,000 category. Not only was the vol-
ume heavy, the fees charged by the sharp lawyers and pardon brokers ranged up to $500.

Southerners found the pardon situation and state building in
the South hopeful. Careful Southern observers further noted that
federal armies stationed in the South were rapidly melting away.
By the fall of 1865 the War Department observed that the re-crea-
tion of civil government in the South made possible a great reduction of the military establishment. There had been well over
200,000 troops in the states of the former Confederacy in June 1865
(probably nearer 250,000, but the exact number is unknown), yet
the number dropped to just under 39,000 by April 1866, and to just
over 9,000 by October 1870 * and it continued to decrease. There
were fewer federal troops in the South after October 1869 than a
normal peacetime constabulary would have demanded.

In spite of the reduction of federal troops, Southerners complained of their presence, particularly of the black regiments. Yet
they, too, were soon gone from every state except Louisiana and
Texas; they remained in Texas, even after military reconstruction
ended, only because they shared frontier duty with the rest of the
regular army. Southern complaints of a large occupation force consisting of many black troops were not substantiated by the facts. Yet
Confederate veterans deeply resented the presence of even the few
that remained as visible evidence of the recent defeat and of the
radically changed social structure. Moreover, the Union military,
though diminishing, was highly visible at election time and thus un-
welcome. Despite all Southern protests to the contrary, the quick
removal of the troops—considering the many insults to the national
government and the appearance of armed citizens and Ku-Kluxers
—was a positive indication of federal generosity. The army returned smoothly to a peacetime footing.

---

* War Department figures showed 20,000 troops stationed in Arkansas, Alabama, Florida,
Georgia, Louisiana, Mississippi, the Carolinas, Tennessee, Texas, and Virginia in October
1867; 17,500 in October 1868; 11,000 in October 1869; 9,000 in October 1870; 8,000 in Oc-
tober 1871; 7,300 in October 1872; 7,700 in October 1874; and 6,000 in October 1876.

On March 3, 1865, Congress created the Freedmen's Bureau,* entrusting to it the care of Southern refugees and displaced persons, black and white alike. Organized in every Southern state, the bureau supervised the labor and employment of the freedmen, set their wages and terms of labor, found them jobs, helped some establish themselves on public land under the homestead law, and provided hospitals and schools for them. The bureau had a semimilitary structure, with General Oliver O. Howard as bureau chief or commissioner and other army officers as assistant commissioners in charge of each state.

As the labor arbiter in the South, the bureau's courts and boards arbitrated disputes between freedmen and planters, and handled civil and some criminal matters as well when an involved party was a freedman. Confederates resented these activities and considered the bureau a troublesome meddler in labor problems. Johnson opposed the bureau's judicial functions, especially after the extension of the bureau in 1866 over his veto; Southerners objected to bureau courts as unnecessary since regular civil and criminal courts had reopened.

Although the bureau faced great hostility on labor and race-relations problems, it proved eminently successful in education. By 1870, when this phase of the bureau's work ended, it reported having spent over $5,000,000 on educational programs; that year alone the bureau had enrolled about 250,000 freedmen in over 4,000 schools. In contrast, the bureau's other work became less and less effective after 1866 because of persistent Southern hostility to the bureau as an outside, irregular, and most unwelcome Yankee agency. Johnson further contributed to its demise with his refusal to fix regulations for the handling of racial discrimination cases as provided by law.

Southerners also objected to the activities of the Treasury Department. Even before the war ended, scores of agents were entrusted with seizing abandoned property; and in the spring of 1865 cotton that belonged to the Confederate government was added to the list of confiscated goods. Agents also collected the 25 percent federal sales tax levied on property sales in the South, plus other duties Congress levied on the former Confederacy. After May 1865 the sales tax was modified to include only goods that had been pro-

---

* The Bureau of Refugees, Freedmen, and Abandoned Lands.

duced by slave labor. Agents received a 25 percent commission on seizures and collections, which made the job so profitable that one agent reportedly sold an assistantship for $25,000. The corruption of the Treasury agents, along with the discriminatory nature of the taxes and seizures, appalled people in the South.

Outraged by Freedmen's Bureau workers and Yankee Treasury agents, encouraged by Johnson's leniency, and optimistic about their own future, Southern leaders ignored all suggestions to include freedmen in the franchise. In August 1865 Johnson asked Mississippi's governor to include black suffrage along the lines of Lincoln's suggestion to the governor of Louisiana. Such a move, Johnson said, "would . . . disarm the adversary" and provide an example for other Southern states to follow. His plea fell on deaf ears. First Lincoln, then Johnson, relied on vain efforts to persuade rather than demand. If he truly desired to foster black suffrage of any degree, Johnson had already forfeited the opportunity with his omission of the question from his May 9 proclamation. The South failed to take seriously anything less than an enforceable requirement. That would be their undoing, as both Lincoln and Johnson suspected, for Northern organizations and Northern activists increasingly advocated full black suffrage for the protection of freedmen in the South. Southern whites stubbornly held to their position that blacks were neither educated for the franchise, nor fit for it racially, and they had no intention of extending it to any blacks.

Former Confederates were predominant in the new state governments and made up a large proportion of those elected to the Thirty-ninth Congress, scheduled to meet in December 1865. Among the congressmen-elect were Stephens, former Confederate vice-president; several of the former Confederate cabinet officers; a handful of ranking Confederate military men; and a large number of former members of the Confederate Congress. Many of those elected had not even been pardoned. Johnson was clearly upset by the lack of diplomacy and tact on the part of the new governments. He told the governor of North Carolina that the number of former Confederate officials chosen for office seriously damaged the South's chances with Congress; he insisted that Confederate officials not take office until they were pardoned, and he enforced that rule as best he could.

The new Southern legislatures proceeded to define the legal relationships of white and black citizens through a series of laws known as the "black codes." Not precisely alike in all the Southern states, the black codes had certain features in common. They granted blacks the right to hold property, to sue and be sued, to contract legal marriages with their own race (but made it a felony to intermarry with whites), and to be witnesses in court—but only when at least one party in the case was also black. The Mississippi code, one of the first to be enacted, specified that as of November 1865 freedmen must carry licenses naming their homes and employment, that their labor contracts for more than a month in duration be in writing, and that they must forfeit their wages if they violated such a contract. If a freedman were adjudged to have no employment, then he was defined as a vagrant and subject to fine. The freedman was also subject to fine if he were found guilty of trespass, rioting, seditious speeches, insulting gestures, selling intoxicating liquor, or preaching without a license.

According to the Mississippi code, a freedman who could not pay his fine ($50 for vagrancy) would be remanded to the custody of a white man who would pay it and take him for labor until the freedman had worked it off. Minors—orphans or children whose parents failed to support them—were to be bound to a white man until they came of age. The laws did not conflict with the Thirteenth Amendment, which only prohibited involuntary servitude when not inflicted for a crime. They did, however, define a large area as "crime." The laws were not much different from older Mississippi laws on vagrancy and apprenticeship, but they were specifically aimed at reestablishing white supremacy. Some of the black codes prohibited the use or possession of firearms by blacks, imposed curfews, established a condition of semislavery for all violators, and together put blacks in a position of inferiority to whites. The South would be a white man's country. The sentiment echoed all across the South, as in a Jackson, Mississippi, newspaper headline of fall 1865: "This is a white man's country—President Johnson."

Southerners intended to make certain that the black remained "in his place." To this end they opposed black education and the Freedmen's Bureau. The Southern states that did enact free public education laws—South Carolina, Georgia, Texas, Florida, and Arkansas—limited the schools to white only. If blacks were categorized as "ignorant" and unfit for the duties of citizenship, Southern whites were determined to keep them that way.

Northerners, meanwhile, watched developments in the South

with mounting dismay. They believed that black codes and educational discrimination were open devices to keep the blacks in de facto slavery. Republican politicians saw any basis for a Southern Republican party being swept away. The Chicago *Tribune* wrathfully suggested that Mississippi be turned into a frog pond before the disgraceful black codes be allowed to undo the sacrifice of Northern soldiers and desecrate the "flag of freedom." Greeley's New York *Tribune* suggested that the North plow under everything the newly reconstructed states had done and start again. The Southern states seemed to taunt Congress deliberately: they refused even the most modest black suffrage; they filled their governments with former Confederate leaders; they passed laws to keep the black man a second-class citizen.

Toward Congressional Reconstruction

> I'm glad I fought agin her, I only wish we'd won,
> And I ain't axed any pardon for anything I've done.
> And I don't want no pardon for what I was or am,
> I won't be reconstructed and I don't give a damn.

Those defiant sentiments from a reconstruction era song of the South echoed widespread Southern feelings. "Official" and unofficial tourists from the North who visited Southern states in 1865 and 1866 concurred. Reid commented that Southerners "were 'loyal' in May 1865 in the sense of enforced submission to the Government, and," he said, "they are loyal in the same sense in May 1866. At neither time has the loyalty of the most had any wider meaning." All that had been gained, Reid emphasized, was that the notion of secession had been effectively stamped out. Southerners would unite "with whatever party at the North favors the fewest possible changes from the old order of things" and would leave them most free to handle their own domestic problems "in their own way." Real hope for the kind of loyalty to the Union that Northerners looked for in the South, Reid found only in the blacks. "Their devotion to the Union," he remarked, "may prove one of the strongest guarantees for the speedy return of loyalty to the South."

The Nation, a new weekly magazine appearing for the first time in New York in July 1865, centered part of its attention on the black American and his problems. The magazine immediately dispatched New England-reared and Harvard-educated John R. Dennett to report on Southern attitudes. Dennett's qualifications for the job included a stint as a plantation supervisor in the Port Royal experiment, where free blacks had been resettled on land in the Sea Islands of South Carolina. He began his tour in July 1865 and wrapped it up nine months later, concluding that the North had muffed its opportunity to impose its will on the South by not being ready to act promptly at the war's end. Southerners knew then that "their army and all their cause was lost," and they "expected to take the law from their conqueror." Dennett felt that Southerners would have accepted even universal suffrage right then. "Not willingly," he admitted, "but with far less resistance" than later, even a year later.

Southerners he talked with during his tour were "but little inclined to accept" the "natural results of the war." They knew that slavery was dead, they repealed the ordinances of secession, and they conceded that civil war had failed them. But that was as far as they were willing to go. Southerners were sorry "for nothing but their ill-success." Politically, Dennett wrote, "for some time to come the South will be a unit on all questions of Federal politics." He believed that if "the few Union men in each State had been supported" firmly by the might of the United States, if treason "had been made odious," the "Union party" might have made some headway "against its opponents. But that opportunity," he concluded, "has been lost." The Union had not acted promptly and firmly, nor had it insisted upon political equality for the freedman.

As a result, Dennett predicted, the future of the freed black was "anything but bright." He conceded that some freedmen might not have been ready for instant citizenship, but he thought they were quite capable of learning quickly. Freedmen "are of the Union party," Dennett acknowledged, because they know the fate of their own welfare. "But I hesitate to apply the name of loyalty to their feeling towards the Government. They have never had a country." In the mind of the black man "there is always a secret distrust of the white man," particularly of the Southern white, Dennett remarked. He thus questioned even the loyalty of the blacks, yet he reckoned that they would be a powerful force in aiding "the loyal people to retain what has been won by war," especially as military occupation drew to a close.

Interestingly, both Reid and Dennett concluded that a "solid South" would arise politically when the opportunity presented itself. Both agreed that there was little evidence of white "loyalty" to the federal government, and both agreed that the freedman was an essential element in rebuilding the South. They saw the future of the freedman as dim if left to the Southerners. A third traveler who also agreed was Carl Schurz, sent out on tour in 1865 by President Johnson.

Schurz found the South in "passive submission." Southerners, he wrote, had not taken well to the "new labor system" and were "unquestionably thinking of subjecting the negroes to some kind of slavery again after the restoration of civil government and the withdrawal of our troops." From South Carolina Schurz wrote his wife in July 1865 that he was firmly convinced "that the policy of the government is the worst that could be hit upon. At this moment it is impossible to calculate the results." Schurz referred, of course, to presidential reconstruction. He hoped that the president would change his policies as a result of the report, for he found presidential reconstruction "a false course" given the disposition and attitudes of Southerners.

If Reid, Dennett, and Schurz quickly came to the conclusion that presidential reconstruction was a mistake and that black franchise was the best means of protecting the freedman, most Northerners still shied away from that view. Even the intense Garrison had remarked in 1864 that he saw no "permanent advantage" in black suffrage. Southerners would only alter the franchise as soon as they could, he believed, to exclude the freedmen. In early 1866 Sumner advocated black suffrage with educational qualifications; Greeley agreed and might have added tax and trade stipulations; the head of the Freedmen's Bureau would have established educational qualifications at the minimum. It would appear that they all agreed with Lincoln and Johnson.

Only six of the Northern states permitted black voting, and proposals to allow a black franchise in Wisconsin, Minnesota, and Connecticut failed in 1865. Nebraska's 1866 constitution excluded blacks. In 1867 New Jersey and Ohio and in 1868 Michigan and Pennsylvania refused to include black voters. Stevens, master of the House of Representatives, remarked in December 1865 that Southern blacks under slavery had no education and no understanding of the law, and he was unwilling to see immediate black enfranchisement. In four or five years, he thought, when the freedmen became really free, when their political education had progressed enough for them not to be under the guidance of their old masters, then they would be ready for the vote.

Stevens hoped to place Southern whites in an awkward position with his proposed Fourteenth Amendment to the Constitution. Under its terms Southern whites could exclude blacks from the franchise, but this would reduce Southern representation in Congress proportionately; or they could enfranchise blacks and increase Southern representation, but at the expense of giving control of Southern politics to the Republicans, assuming the Republicans organized the blacks. Stevens proposed that the amendment be adopted by three-fourths of the states that had remained in the Union, but his fellow Republicans turned down that move. As Stevens expected, when the amendment became a reality Southern states turned it down.

Stevens tried another approach, still short of universal black suffrage, in December 1866. In a measure for the reconstruction of North Carolina, he advocated confining the ballot to those of both races who could read and write, or those who owned a certain amount of real property; certain classes of Confederates would be disfranchised. When that failed, Stevens advocated full enfranchisement of the blacks and heavy disfranchisement of former Confederates, along with military rule to insure the objective.

By 1867 Stevens and other Republican leaders in the North faced some harsh political realities. Under presidential reconstruction, Southern representation in the House would have increased over antebellum Southern representation by thirteen because all blacks, rather than just three-fifths, would be counted in apportionment. Unless the blacks voted, and voted Republican, the Southern delegation would increase Democratic strength. This increased Democratic voice in the House would include perhaps thirty-six Southern seats accounted for by the black population, but held by opponents not only of the Republicans but also of black freedom. Even conservative Republicans could not stand by and watch their party commit political suicide.

If the Southern states sent a solid Democratic delegation to Congress, "they, along with their kindred Copperheads of the North, would always elect the President and control Congress." To Stevens, that was an intolerable situation for any Republican to face. Roscoe Conkling of New York agreed. "Shall the death of slavery add two-fifths to the entire power which slavery had" when it was in full bloom? "Not if I can help it," he answered his own question. Stevens and Conkling had more than just political ends in view, for they represented their sections of the North. The manufacturers and businessmen had cast their lot with the Republican party years before when it became evident that the agrarian South had consistently blocked their tariffs and other economic benefits. A rejuvenated Democratic party with a strong Southern agrarian base almost certainly would resume that obstructionism, and perhaps even overturn the orderly progress businessmen felt had come during the years of Republican control. The tariff, the National Bank Act, railroad and other subsidies would certainly become objects of Democratic attention. The Republican party, which had courted business support in 1860, needed that support more than ever after the war. Political and practical business objectives thus clearly came together on the question of reconstruction. Republican conservatives moved closer to their Radical brothers and became susceptible to the influences of Reid, Schurz, and Dennett, who came to view black franchise as the only means of protecting the freedmen and who had forecast the appearance of a solid, Democratic front in the South.

Men like Reid and Schurz, as well as mounting dissatisfaction with the progress of presidential reconstruction, provided the Republican party with arguments necessary to convince the North that the freedmen needed more positive protection than that provided by the president. The political possibility of Democratic dominance, the business fear of renewed agrarian power, and the practical evidence of impaired civil liberty motivated Republicans to turn reconstruction over to Congress and take it from the hands of the president.

16
The Second Phase
of Reconstruction

Before the First Session of the Thirty-ninth Congress met on December 4, 1865, Thaddeus Stevens and the House leadership had already decided not to seat any representatives from any of the seceded states and to create a Joint Committee on Reconstruction to oversee that task. Clerk of the House Edward McPherson dutifully omitted the names of the members elected by the presidentially reconstructed states from the roll call, including some like Horace Maynard of Tennessee whose Unionist credentials were impeccable. President Johnson had believed Congress could not leave out Maynard, but he was mistaken. The House ban was complete.

After Schuyler Colfax of Indiana was reelected Speaker, Stevens moved to create a Joint Committee on Reconstruction to be composed of nine representatives and six senators. Ostensibly the committee's purpose was to inquire into "the condition" of the former Confederate states, to determine whether any of them were "entitled" to representation in either house. According to Stevens' resolution, no representative from the Southern states would be seated until the committee reported "by bill or otherwise." All communications and "all papers" relating to the matter were to be referred to the Joint Committee "without debate." The resolution was adopted overwhelmingly (133 to 36) with virtually no debate and without amendments, with the support of the moderates as well as the Radicals. "It would be wrong to suppose," wrote one historian, ". . . that Congress in December, 1865, was abandoned to radical madness." *

The Senate, acting with greater deliberation than the House, approved the idea although they amended the resolution. They refused to exclude Southern representatives categorically until the committee reported, and they thought it unnecessary for all papers pertinent to the subject to be turned over to the committee without debate. They also selected its members with care, casting a distinct conservative shadow across the group. Senator William P. Fessenden of Maine chaired the committee.**

Johnson delivered his first annual message to Congress on December 5. Written primarily by the president and Seward, polished brightly by historian George Bancroft, the speech glittered with appeal to moderates in both sections. Johnson expounded the theory of presidential reconstruction, saw the Thirteenth Amendment as the climax to it, and detailed the gradual, quiet, and "almost imperceptible" steps for restoring the states and avoiding the necessity of military government. Since the states had carried out the task as required by the president, and since the Thirteenth Amendment had passed, Johnson told the congressmen it was then up to them to "judge" both the election returns in the South and the "qualifications of your own members."

The first reaction to Johnson's address was praise for its moderate tone and apparent recognition that Congress would play a role in reconstruction. Unfortunately, the Copperheads played into the Radicals' hands by lavishing praise upon Johnson. The reception accorded the president's speech worried the Radicals, who recognized it as a clear attempt to rally the nation's moderates of both

* Eric L. McKitrick, *Andrew Johnson and Reconstruction* (Chicago: The University of Chicago Press, 1960), p. 259. McKitrick discusses the entire situation in considerable depth.

** Members of the committee from the House were: John A. Bingham (R., Ohio), Henry T. Blow (R., Mo.), George S. Boutwell (R., Mass.), Roscoe Conkling (R., N.Y.), Henry Grider (D., Ky.), Justin S. Morrill (R., Vt.), Andrew Rogers (D., N.J.), Thaddeus Stevens (R., Pa.), and Elihu B. Washburne (R., Ill.). Senate members were: the chairman, Fessenden (R., Me.), James Grimes (R., Ia.), Ira Harris (R., N.Y.), Jacob Howard (R., Mich.), Reverdy Johnson (D., Md.), and George Williams (R., Ore.).

parties. They also chafed under Johnson's admonition to let the two races in the South seek their own relationships, which Johnson claimed would prove that the freedmen "will receive the kindest usage from some of those on whom they have hitherto most closely depended."

Determined to play a primary role in reconstruction, many Republicans also hoped to avoid a split with the executive. Fessenden observed that he was inclined to support Johnson "in good faith and with kind feelings." Fessenden and many of his fellows in Congress hoped that Johnson would agree that presidential reconstruction was the temporary expedient Lincoln had claimed it was. Such a view would not prevent Congress from taking part and would preserve a measure of harmony between the branches of government. In a practical sense it would circumvent the danger to party unity inherent in an executive-legislative split.

Fessenden also made it clear that Johnson would have to work with Congress, and not force policy upon that body, in order to have his support. That moderate requirement echoed what many others believed to be a harmonious minimum. That same sort of moderation was reflected in the composition of the Joint Committee that Fessenden chaired. He had, for example, purposely excluded Sumner from it because of the senator's "ultra views." Years later, James G. Blaine wrote that the make-up of the committee "gave universal satisfaction" to the Republican party, conveniently forgetting Sumner's chagrin at being omitted.

Fessenden, Senator James M. Grimes of Iowa, and Representative John A. Bingham of Ohio led the moderate group, while Stevens, Representative George S. Boutwell, and Senator Jacob Howard represented the Radical leaders. Since neither Grimes nor Fessenden cared much for the sarcastic Stevens, the House leader was unable to manipulate the committee as he could the House. If Johnson heeded moderate sentiment in Congress he would probably be able to preserve much of presidential reconstruction, head off Radical control, and preserve a degree of leadership in the Republican party; if he chose to pursue some other course, he would certainly lose any chance of congressional cooperation and perhaps see presidential reconstruction entirely upset.

On January 5, 1866, Lyman Trumbull of Illinois, an old friend of Lincoln's and now the conservative chairman of the Senate Judiciary Committee, reported out the Freedmen's Bureau bill of 1866.

The bill enlarged the power of the Bureau and continued its existence at the pleasure of Congress. The bill also provided for the president to extend military law, administered by Freedmen's Bureau officials, over any state whose laws discriminated against the freedmen, a reaction to the enactment of the black codes by Southern states. The bill applied only to states that had seceded and would automatically cease to apply when a seceded state had been reconstructed.

At the same time Trumbull's committee reported out the Civil Rights bill, which declared that all persons born in the United States, except untaxed Indians and foreign subjects, were citizens of the United States. As such they were guaranteed equal rights, regardless of "race and color" and without regard to previous slavery or involuntary servitude, to make contracts, sue, give evidence, hold and dispose of property, and generally have the same rights "enjoyed by white citizens." Federal courts were given jurisdiction.

The Freedmen's Bureau bill cleared the House and Senate without difficulty and went to the president for his signature on February 6. Between that time and Johnson's veto two weeks later, Fessenden and others tried to convince him that it was necessary for him to accept the bill in order for Congressional moderates to back him. Johnson was noncommittal, but clearly disturbed about the Joint Committee on Reconstruction's failure to readmit Tennessee. When he told his cabinet he intended to veto the Freedmen's Bureau bill, he also informed them that in his view the Joint Committee was nothing more than part of a Radical plot to dictate policy to the administration.

In the veto message on February 19, Johnson claimed that the bill violently invaded the powers of the states and was unconstitutional. The message went beyond the veto, however, as Johnson complained that no states that the bill would affect had representatives in Congress to take part in creating the legislation. Since Congress failed to represent the people of those eleven states, Johnson claimed that it was his duty to represent them. As far as he was concerned, those states had been fully restored and were entitled to "enjoy their constitutional rights" as full members of the Union. Johnson served notice that he intended to stand by and support the results of presidential reconstruction and that he would oppose any effort by Congress to change the state of affairs unless it admitted elected representatives from his reconstructed states. Lincoln's idea of avoiding inflexibility, of possibly accepting reconstruction under other terms, and the indication that Lincoln might have called presidential reconstruction a "bad promise," evaporated. Johnson's hope of avoiding a rift with Congress and preserving his program intact diminished greatly.

Johnson versus Congress

Indignant over the veto, Northerners attacked Johnson both in Congress and out of it. Republicans portrayed him as a renegade whose Democratic proclivities had returned to the fore. Others called him a Southern sympathizer, a Copperhead, who was disloyal to the Unionists who had suffered greatly in the war by demanding that states filled with rebellion and hatred for the Union should resume representation. Stevens proposed that Congress immediately pass a concurrent resolution excluding any state of the former Confederacy from resuming representation until Congress specifically approved. In the Senate, Trumbull defended the Freedmen's Bureau bill against Johnson's objections. It *was* constitutional, Trumbull replied, and necessary to keep the freedmen from being reenslaved. He claimed that the bill had been designed to be "in harmony" with the president's views as previously understood, and that he regretted "the antagonism" the president had for the views of Congress. He asked the Senate to pass the bill over Johnson's veto, but that effort failed. Meanwhile, the House passed Stevens' concurrent resolution by a wide margin.

Johnson's fury at the reaction to his veto manifested itself on Washington's Birthday, when a crowd gathered to serenade him. He spoke in an East Tennessee stump manner, hitting hard and naming names in frontier style, a performance in marked contrast to his almost eloquent annual message of nearly two months before; he shocked even some of his best friends. One rebellion was finished, said he, but another had sprung up. A few men now sought to defy the Constitution and take over the government. Their motives were as treasonous as those of Davis, Toombs, and other former Confederate leaders whom he, Johnson, had fought. When pressed for their names, the president blurted out: "I say Thaddeus Stevens . . . I say Charles Sumner . . . I say Wendell Phillips and others of the same stripe. . . ." Each name was greeted by a burst of applause from the audience. Johnson attempted to repudiate Stevens' allegation that King Charles had lost his head under conditions similar to Johnson's usurpations. Johnson recited his public record, proclaiming that he had always stood loyal to the people and that the purpose of the plotters was to bring about his assassination and get him out of their way. In view of the horrible war and the murder of Lincoln, "Do they still want more blood?" Johnson asked. If that is what they want, he shouted, then they could sacrifice him on "an altar to the Union" and in so doing they would create in him a martyr to the purity and preservation of the Union. Then he appeared to calm down, speaking of himself as a defender of the Constitution and the people. "I have not deserted the people," he told them, "and I believe they will not desert me."

Johnson's behavior left many Republicans stunned. He had not acted as most other presidents had, but then most other presidents had neither his emotional makeup (or had successfully controlled it) nor his political background. Johnson had also romanticized the powers of the presidency, feeling them to be greater than they were. He threw away, in an hour and ten minutes, political leadership that was commonly based upon oratorical finesse and semantic care. He committed a great political blunder by calling attention in no uncertain terms to the wide gulf between the executive and the legislative branches, rather than playing it down. By singling out certain of his opponents by name and charging them with plotting against the very government they were a part of (except for Phillips), he guaranteed them fame and recognition they could have attained in no other way. Statesmanship deserted the executive.

Yet the door to Congress had not slammed shut on the president. Fessenden and others still retained an admittedly slim hope that the party could work with Johnson. Along with Fessenden, Senator John Sherman from Ohio, brother of the famous general (a staunch Johnson man) and one whose party supporters back home worried about the effect of the Johnson-Congress split, worked to heal the wound. In a very temperate Senate talk on February 26, Sherman acknowledged Johnson's mistake in both his veto and the Washington's Birthday speech, but attempted to defend the president and smooth out the division. Reaction to these efforts were mixed, and when it came to voting on Stevens' concurrent resolution, Sherman supported it. The resolution passed the Senate.

Johnson's supporters now urged him to accept the Civil Rights bill; Sherman and others firmly believed that he would. Oliver P. Morton, a Johnson supporter from Indiana, interviewed Johnson early in March. Dismayed to find Johnson unwilling to support the bill, he warned that if Johnson vetoed the Civil Rights bill, he would lose the Republican party. In reply, Johnson told Morton of his plan to build a new, moderate party, to which Morton replied that the attempt would fail. Others also urged Johnson to uphold the Civil Rights bill. In the cabinet, only Welles continued to oppose it. Even Seward seemed unable to influence Johnson. The only organized support Johnson had for a veto came from the Democrats. There was no question that Johnson knew the likely consequences of his veto.

On March 27 Johnson claimed that the Civil Rights bill set standards for black security far beyond any "ever provided for the white race." He held the bill unconstitutional because the bill's provisions interfered with the relations between the people of a state and their state government, as well as between the inhabitants of the same state. The bill destroyed the concept of federalism, and he had no choice but to veto it, he said. Johnson's course of action left the Republican party with virtually no choice but to repudiate him. Fessenden, Sherman, Morton, Trumbull, and all Republican conservatives and moderates no longer could hope to compromise with the man who was titular head of the party. The gulf between them was so clear, obvious, and deep that no Republican could seriously entertain any further thoughts of bridging it.

Trumbull coldly grumbled that Johnson's "facts are as bad as his law," and he demolished Johnson's objections one by one. He further observed that the bill contained what he, in consultation with the president, took to be Johnson's own views, intimating that Johnson had acted in bad faith with those who had drafted it. On April 6 the Senate overrode the veto by a margin of one vote. The House followed suit by a more comfortable margin three days later.

Both the Freedmen's Bureau bill and the Civil Rights bill had been hatched in the Senate; both were mild bills compared to what Radical Republicans in the House might have concocted. The moderate and conservative Republicans had been the key; had they supported Johnson his policy would have prevailed. They clearly would have backed him had he accepted their bills, but his refusal to do so alienated them. They could not accept turning the South back to local control, and their efforts were aimed at preserving justice, protecting the freedmen, and nullifying the black codes.

The bitter debate on the two bills, in Congress and out, contained many references to violence perpetrated by Southern whites on blacks and Union supporters. Southern whites, for their part, resented congressional efforts to overturn or circumscribe presidential reconstruction. The Freedmen's Bureau itself, as well as the attempted broadening of its powers, irritated them, and their opposition occasionally expressed itself in open conflict with either white or black men who defended the proposed new order. The intransigence of the South, often exaggerated in the Northern press, showed to the satisfaction of many Northerners that the area was still rebellious and determined to preserve white supremacy. Southerners thus helped bring congressional reconstruction upon themselves.

The Fourteenth Amendment

The Joint Committee on Reconstruction began hearings in January 1866 to find out how Southern whites viewed the United States government and how they in fact treated Northerners and Southern blacks, hoping to determine the utility of both the Freedmen's Bureau and military garrisons. Those who testified included a number of Union army officers, many of them generals; Freedmen's Bureau officers, many of them military men; about seventy Southerners, including a handful of blacks and a baker's dozen admitted ex-Confederates; perhaps twice that many Southern Unionists; plus a few others, such as a dozen Northerners who had made Southern journeys.

The preponderance of testimony showed the existence of widespread hostility toward the Union and a need for both the bureau and the army. Inhumane treatment of blacks and abuse of bureau officials, soldiers, and Union men filled over seven hundred pages. Committee members concluded that presidential reconstruction only served to foster the rule of former Confederates and intensify abuses of freedmen and Unionists. Protection of those groups would have to be insured before the Southern states resumed their place in the Union, and the question before the committee quickly became one of determining how to provide the necessary safeguards. Johnson's veto of the Freedmen's Bureau bill, which Congress had sustained, and his veto of the Civil Rights bill, which Congress repassed over the veto, along with the public testimony before the Joint Committee, had convinced congressmen that protection was not only necessary but vital.

Although Republicans came to general agreement on the need for safeguards, they differed on the allied question of black suffrage. Sumner and his friends adamantly favored guaranteed voting rights for the freedmen, but many Republican congressmen wavered and hoped to dodge the issue, fearing political consequences at home. Stevens and most Midwesterners advocated a device that based Southern representation on suffrage: the more blacks enfranchised in a state, the greater the representation from that state. The plan avoided a direct stand on black suffrage, but it would in effect force the Southern states to allow it, to allow some degree of it, or to suffer the consequences of reduced representation. New Englanders, however, remained cool to the scheme, for they knew it might reduce their representation since they had fewer voters per capita than western states had.

Still other uncertain areas emerged among Republicans. Stevens and his followers wanted to disfranchise as many former Confederates as possible, reducing, they believed, Southern political power. Others favored exclusion of only the most famous rebels, and still others held views that fell between the extremes. Another problem failed to surface openly at this time, yet it too troubled Republicans. Should they attempt a reconstruction solution of a permanent nature, or one that was temporary and flexible? Stevens and his group, along with Sumner, hoped to postpone a permanent settlement until they felt the nation would accept something as radical as universal suffrage. They appeared to be in the minority on that question—widespread sentiment favored offering the South a definitive package that it could accept or refuse. As Congress hammered out the Fourteenth Amendment, most Republicans looked upon it as just that sort of a package.

The evolution of the amendment began as early as December 5, 1865, when Stevens offered to the House a resolution to apportion representation among the states according to their "legal voters." The committee considered the resolution in January. Conkling supported Stevens, and Conkling's famous adversary, James G. Blaine of Maine, virtually killed it with his announcement of New England's opposition. On January 22 Fessenden introduced to the Senate and Stevens to the House a resolution that the Joint Committee had worked out. Representation was to be based upon the whole number of persons in a state, except when the franchise had been abridged or denied "on account of race or color," in which case all such persons would be excluded from the basis of representation. The resolution passed the House but failed in the Senate largely due to Sumner's opposition. Sumner still stood for equal civil and political rights for all, would accept nothing less, and told the Senate that drawing race or color lines or bribing the South with such a resolution would defile the Constitution in the first instance and lead to circumvention in the second.

Other resolutions were debated to no avail. After Johnson's veto of the Civil Rights bill, Republicans sought more than ever a general framework for settling their problems and finding a compromise. Public opinion, as reflected in the press, had grown impatient with a Congress that seemed unable to formulate a policy. The Joint Committee and Congress worked harder than ever, settling on the idea of a constitutional amendment.

Work on the Fourteenth Amendment took place under yet another sort of pressure. Presidential reconstruction came under attack as riots broke out in Memphis and New Orleans. Between April 30 and May 2 white mobs and white police indiscriminately attacked Memphis' black population. By the time the army restored order, nearly fifty black men, women, and children had been killed and almost twice that number wounded; black churches and school buildings had been burned. One white man was hurt. As a result, state commissioners took over the city's government, and investigators from the army, the Freedmen's Bureau, and the House of Representatives moved in. The House committee concluded that violence had occurred because of white hatred of blacks.

On the day the Memphis riots broke out Fessenden and Stevens introduced a proposed constitutional amendment and two bills. The proposed amendment forbade a state to make laws that would abridge the privileges or immunities of United States citizens or deprive them of life, liberty, or property without due process of law, or deny them the equal protection of its laws; representation would be apportioned in a manner not unlike that of the January 22 resolution; ex-Confederates would be excluded from the franchise in national elections until July 4, 1870; Confederate debts would be repudiated; and Congress would have the power to enforce the amendment.

The first bill set down adoption of the amendment as a condition for readmission and required the former Confederate states to pay the direct tax levied August 5, 1861, but suspended payment of it for ten years. The other bill declared that the president, vice president, and cabinet members of the Confederacy were not eligible to hold federal office, along with Confederate agents abroad, former U.S. officeholders who served the Confederacy, and various Confederate army and navy officers.

The package was received with little enthusiasm, though most congressmen appeared willing to support it. Johnson, of course, denounced the whole plan openly. The amendment passed the House May 10; House action on the two bills was delayed until the Senate voted on the amendment. The Senate debated the amendment between May 23 and May 29, until the Republican Senate caucus presented a revised draft. The Senate passed this version on June 8; the House concurred on June 13.

The Fourteenth Amendment as it finally appeared consisted of five sections. Section 1 defined "all persons born or naturalized in the United States" as citizens of both the United States and their state. No state should make any law which would "abridge the privileges or immunities" of those citizens, nor deprive them of life, liberty, or property without due process of law, nor deny them "equal protection of the laws." Section 2 apportioned representation among the states on the basis of total population. In the vote for president, vice president, Congress, or the executive or judicial officers of a state, the basis of representation was reduced if any males over twenty-one were denied the franchise, excepting those excluded for participation in rebellion, in direct proportion to the ratio of the disfranchised to the whole population of a state. Section 3 excluded former Confederates who had once held state or federal office from holding any federal or state office except as Congress by a two-thirds vote chose to remove that disability. Section 4 held the validity of the national debt inviolate but renounced any Confederate debt, including claims for the emancipation of slaves. Section 5 gave Congress the right to pass legislation to enforce the amendment.

Even Sumner voted for it. It was a compromise, clear and simple, and the public accepted it as such. Newspapers, including the pro-Johnson papers, generally thought it reasonable. The New York *Times* speculated that the president would accept it, as did the New York *Herald. Harper's Weekly* thought it would reunite Johnson with the Union party—but *Harper's* was mistaken. Johnson denounced the amendment on June 22 and opined that the Southern states had no obligation to accept it.

Another race riot broke out on July 30, this time in New Orleans. Unionists there had attempted to disfranchise some Confederates and apparently intended to extend the franchise to certain freedmen. In the ensuing turmoil over thirty blacks were killed, and another two hundred injured. Four whites died, ten policemen were hurt. The federal military reported that the police as well as white citizens had participated in the "massacre." Northerners felt that the Fourteenth Amendment was even more necessary to protect the freedmen, and they now had Memphis and New Orleans to prove it.

Shortly after the New Orleans riot, Johnson organized a "National Union" party convention with a view to defeating in the fall elections those who opposed him. He thus continued his opposition and gave heart to the presidentially reconstructed governments. Of those governments, only one, Tennessee, ratified the amendment and was readmitted to the Union. The others all rejected it in the fall and winter of 1866–1867. Filled with former Confederates, their legislatures resented the disfranchisement of their late comrades and the effort to abridge their representation in Congress. They refused what they considered an attempt to humiliate them; Northerners thought them unreasonable. Congress, meanwhile, passed another Freedmen's Bureau bill and then repassed it over the president's veto.

Johnson's campaign against the amendment began with his "swing around the circle" tour in late August–early September. Along with Seward, Grant, and others, he traveled through Baltimore, Philadelphia, New York, Albany, Buffalo, Erie, Cleveland, Detroit, Chicago, St. Louis, Indianapolis, Harrisburg, and many points in between, and returned to Washington. He openly criticized Congress, attacking the Civil Rights Act and the Fourteenth Amendment. The legislation meant another civil war, he told his audiences. Much in the style of his Washington's Birthday speech, he launched into harangues on several occasions, intemperately raged at hecklers, found stiff opposition in Chicago, and was booed from the platform in Pittsburgh and Indianapolis. He played into the hands of the Radicals, hurting his own cause. Political prognosticators predicted that it was the Johnson forces that would take a beating in November.

While Radical Republicans failed to win the elections decisively, Johnson's efforts to build a "National Union" party fell even flatter. The Radicals made strong showings in Indiana and New York, and the regular Republican organization swept the North. The Republicans won every contested governorship, took every state legislature, and had a majority in every Northern congressional delegation. Johnson had been shot down along with the Democrats. No doubt existed that the Radicals were in a stronger position than before and that with other sympathetic Republicans they would demand ratification of the Fourteenth Amendment by the Southern states. Since some—especially the Radicals—in Congress considered the amendment just a beginning and not a final solution, it appeared that Congress would demand even more of the South. In his second annual address to Congress, Johnson belabored the tired theme of admitting Southern members, and he castigated Congress for not having done so. White Southerners who saw the elections as ill omens for themselves took what solace they could in the president's firm stand, and those states in the South that had not yet rejected the amendment did so.

The Reconstruction Acts of 1867

Congressmen like Stevens and Sumner, who thought the freedman could only be protected by giving him the ballot, were ready to demand full enfranchisement and now believed that the country would back their move. The feeling of many Northern congressmen was summed up in a speech by Ohio's James A. Garfield. In its attitude toward the former Confederacy, Garfield observed, Congress had been generous. Congress might have insisted that "every rebel traitor" be hanged for his part in the "bloody conspiracy," or it might have confiscated all rebel property, but it had not. Congress' offer to bring the Southern states back into the Union with only the Fourteenth Amendment as a qualification had been rejected, and, Garfield observed, "it is now our turn to act. . . . We must remove the rubbish and rebuild from the bottom." The "rubbish," of course, referred to Southern governments erected on Johnson's plan. By rebuilding from the bottom, Garfield meant that freedmen must participate.

In that spirit, Northern states that had delayed consideration of the Fourteenth Amendment—and perhaps in so doing had encouraged the Southerners—moved to ratify it. Connecticut and New Hampshire had quickly approved it in the summer of 1866; during the winter and spring of 1867 the other Northern states belatedly followed the example of their small New England brothers.

When the lame-duck session of the Thirty-ninth Congress met in December 1866, Sumner introduced a bill that provided for black suffrage in the District of Columbia. Although it encountered considerable debate, it passed both houses; it was then vetoed by Johnson. Congress promptly repassed the bill over his veto. On January 3, 1867, Stevens called up a bill he had previously introduced but had not pressed in the earlier session. In spite of opposition, it was referred to the Joint Committee on Reconstruction, which reported it out in a slightly modified form a month later.

Stevens' bill abolished Southern governments and established military rule in the former Confederacy, except for Tennessee. The bill passed the House but faced stiffer opposition in the Senate where a point of disagreement centered around the appointment of military governors. The House version gave that power to Grant, as ranking general; senators believed that this bypassed the president, who constitutionally was the commander-in-chief. The House version also failed to specify a deadline for an end to military rule, leaving that to the discretion of Congress. Generally the Senate had its way; the revised bill passed both houses and vaulted over Johnson's veto on March 2, 1867.

The bill divided the South into five military districts: the first, Virginia; the second, North and South Carolina; the third, Alabama, Florida, and Georgia; the fourth, Arkansas and Mississippi; and the fifth, Louisiana and Texas. It further provided for a military governor, appointed by the president with the Senate's consent, to rule each district. The military governor's task was to preserve order; he had the option of doing this through local civil officers or through military tribunals. All citizens of a state, regardless of race or color, except disfranchised rebels, would choose delegates for a constitutional convention; after the constitutional convention presented a revised constitution that accepted the specified franchise, and after a legislature so elected ratified the Fourteenth Amendment and the amendment became a part of the United States Constitution, then that state would be readmitted to the Union and military government would end.

Along with that act another, introduced by Stevens the previous December, also became law. The Tenure of Office Act was designed to keep Johnson from dismissing cabinet officers, like Stanton, who agreed with Radical aims, and to keep the president from using some of his patronage powers. It was a direct slap at Johnson. Another act designed to circumscribe the executive, the Command of the Army Act, became law on March 2. It limited Johnson's military powers by requiring him to issue orders through Grant. Both acts were constructed to minimize Johnson's interference with the Reconstruction Act. Congress usurped still another presidential prerogative in January: it provided that the first session of the next Congress, the Fortieth, would begin in March rather than December.

The Fortieth Congress carried on the task of reconstruction eagerly, allowing virtually no lapse in time following the adjournment of the Thirty-ninth. On March 23 it established machinery for putting into effect the earlier Reconstruction Act: It provided for registration of voters who would take the "ironclad oath"; the election of delegates to the conventions; the meeting of the conventions; and the machinery for adopting constitutions. Congress required that a constitution acceptable to the Union must also meet the approval of a majority of the registered voters in the state. The last stipulation represented a gesture to those in Congress who objected that otherwise the proceedings would be nothing more than minority legislation. As usual, Johnson vetoed the bill, and as usual, Congress repassed it over his veto.

Though opposed to the reconstruction acts, Johnson considered it his duty to enforce the law. He appointed the military governors, all of whom were prominent generals.* They, in turn, ordered voter registration and called for elections as the acts required. Southerners were stunned. Congress ignored the president and refused to listen to either him or his arguments. The South's last hope of avoiding congressional reconstruction seemed to lie with the courts.

* The officers, in order of their districts, were generals Schofield, Sickles, Pope, Ord, and Sheridan.

The South and the Courts

Alabamans found a weak point in the laws with the aid of Attorney General Henry Stanbery of Ohio, who had assumed the cabinet post on July 23, 1866. The law allowed all to register who had not served the Confederacy voluntarily. Had registration officials the authority to determine what "voluntarily" meant? Stanbery held that the officials did not have the power to make that decision and would therefore have to register all who presented themselves. Alabamans thus registered in large numbers and then defeated the revised constitution by not voting on it, depriving it of the majority approval necessary. Alarmed, the Radicals, on July 19, 1867, passed a third Reconstruction Act that specifically gave the registration officials the power that Stanbery had denied them. It also made a majority of the votes cast at the constitutional referendum the determining factor in approval, rather than a majority of the registered voters as previously specified.

Southerners had still not exhausted their legal maneuvers. They took heart from three decisions the Supreme Court handed down in 1866 and early 1867, although the decisions failed to bear directly on reconstruction. In *Ex Parte Milligan*, which dealt with a military commission's sentence of death in 1864, the Supreme Court ruled that neither the president nor Congress could use military tribunals to try civilians in places where the civil courts were open. Such a decision might impede the Radicals who operated through military law. In *Cummings* v. *Missouri* the Court held that a Missouri law refusing licenses to former Confederates in certain professions was ex post facto, and thus forbidden by the Constitution. In *Ex Parte Garland* it struck down a similar law in Arkansas, also as ex post facto. Stevens and the Radicals proceeded with the three Reconstruction Acts even after the Supreme Court rendered those verdicts.

In April 1867 the state of Mississippi attempted to get an injunction to block reconstruction. The actual effort was aimed at keeping the president from executing the law. If Mississippians thought they could count on Johnson because of his opposition to the law, they were mistaken. Johnson resisted the injunction through Stanbery, who argued that the president could be tried only by impeachment, that the matter was a political one, and not one for the courts. In *Mississippi* v. *Johnson* that April, the Court agreed and declined to interfere.

Not willing to drop the matter on the basis of a single test, Georgia took the initiative and applied for a similar injunction against Stanton, thus keeping the president out of it. In *Georgia* v. *Stanton* the Supreme Court again declined to act, holding that a writ which might not be served on the president could not be served on his agent, a member of his cabinet. Yet a third test followed. A Mississippi editor arrested by the new military government appealed to the Supreme Court under the Civil Rights Act of 1866 for a writ of habeas corpus. The Radicals in Congress were alarmed, for it appeared that according to *Ex Parte Milligan*, concerning the inoperability of military law in peacetime, the editor must be set free. Congress hastily sped through a law that denied the Supreme Court the right to issue a writ of habeas corpus, relieving the court from a difficult confrontation with the Radicals. The Court then declined jurisdiction in the pending case of *Ex Parte McCardle*. The South thus lost its appeal to the courts.

Impeachment

Johnson still looked for vindication at the ballot box, and the fall elections of 1867 were at hand. Perhaps now, with congressional reconstruction a reality and with black suffrage operating in the South, Northerners would react in his favor. The Democratic party did make a small comeback, winning the legislatures in Connecticut, Ohio, Pennsylvania, and New York, and cutting into Republican majorities in other Northern states. Ohio and New Jersey rejected black suffrage proposals, while Maryland's new voting law conferred that right on whites only. These political facts encouraged Johnson to blast black suffrage in his December 1867 message to Congress. Blacks knew nothing of politics, he told Congress, nor had they any regard for property rights. He saw the greatest danger to the United States yet in the attempt "to Africanize" half the nation. Johnson, in this manner, announced his continued opposition to Congress.

Perhaps this was the last straw, this never-ending opposition. The man refused to be humble. Congress had discarded presidential reconstruction and adopted its own plan. It had little to fear from his opposition or his vetoes; it had little to fear from the Supreme

Court. Yet the Democrats were gaining strength, and it was not in-conceivable that Johnson might return to his own party, his prestige enhanced by his firm opposition to congressional reconstruction and, more importantly, to a black franchise that many Northerners found difficult to accept—in their own Northern states. Republi-cans, however, could not risk either a renegade Johnson or an inde-pendent Republican Johnson, or a Johnson who headed a third party of "National Unionists" that might cost them their political base in the North. If they lost that, then any new political strength built up in the South would quickly dissipate.

Along with Stanbery's aid to the Alabamans, Johnson's re-newed attack on Congress and his removal of military commanders who were too zealous in carrying out the reconstruction laws seemed to put him in concert with the South in blocking congres-sional reconstruction. To some congressmen, the time had come to pull this last thorn: Johnson would have to be removed. Con-gressmen had for some time considered impeachment. Back in Jan-uary 1867 the House had ordered its judiciary committee to see if evidence existed to support the move.

That committee had investigated, found no evidence, but ad-vised that further investigation be made. The judiciary committee of the next Congress continued the task and also reported against impeachment. They were instructed to continue their work. In the meantime, Johnson had suspended Stanton from the War Depart-ment in August, pending a report to the Senate demanded by the Tenure of Office Act; Grant had taken the job on a temporary basis. Over Grant's objections, Johnson also removed Sheridan as a military governor, and then removed Sickles. Northern Con-gressmen and many of their constituents felt the removals were un-just. Shortly after the November elections in 1867 with their Demo-cratic gains, Johnson told a crowd that the public backed him. Then on November 20, 1867, the House committee recommended impeachment by a 5 to 4 vote.

Undaunted, Johnson renewed his attack on Congress in his an-nual message on December 2; on December 7 the House refused the impeachment recommendation. That might have ended the effort, but Johnson had not finished. December 12 he sent the Senate the required statement on Stanton's suspension and also asked the House to vote a resolution of thanks to General Hancock, who had replaced Sheridan. Hancock, a Democrat who disapproved of the reconstruction acts, had published an order that expressed his view that civil government was superior to military government. That order was inconsistent with the Third Reconstruction Act he was supposed to be following. Doubtless Johnson asked for the resolution of thanks to nettle Congress, for he could not have expected to be taken seriously—especially since Congress had passed similar resolutions the previous summer for its darlings, Pope, Sheridan, and Sickles. On December 28 Johnson removed Ord, Pope, and the Alabama Freedmen's Bureau chief, General Wager Swayne.

Johnson informed Congress that Stanton had been suspended because he had refused to resign when requested to do so and because as president he could not execute laws through a department head in whom he had no confidence. On January 10, 1868, the Senate Military Affairs Committee rejected Johnson's reasoning, and on January 13 the Senate refused to concur with Stanton's suspension. Grant, uneasy on the tightrope Johnson wished him to walk, vacated the War Department office which Stanton then quickly reoccupied. Johnson had hoped to persuade Grant to remain since it appeared the Tenure of Office Act would be tested in the courts. He mistakenly believed that Grant had agreed, but the general had no stomach for political acrobatics. Johnson retaliated by attempting to humiliate Grant and by publicly calling him a liar. In the process Johnson drew more adverse reaction to himself than he was able to turn on Grant and managed to alienate the general in the process.

Still determined to test the Tenure of Office Act, Johnson sought another general to take up the fight. After Sherman and George H. Thomas, among others, had turned him down he finally persuaded old Lorenzo Thomas, the former adjutant general, to make the effort and appointed him ad interim secretary of war on February 21. Thomas called on Stanton that very day with his letter of appointment fresh in his hand, but Stanton turned him away. He awoke the following day as a marshal rousted him out with a warrant Stanton had issued for his arrest. After he made bail he visited Johnson who told him to go and occupy his office. Once more at the War Department, Thomas found Stanton determined to remain, so he retreated.

On that same day the House wing of the Reconstruction Committee submitted a resolution for the impeachment of the president for high crimes and misdemeanors. The House voted in favor of the resolution, thereby impeaching Johnson on February 24. According to the Constitution, the president could be arraigned for "treason, bribery, or other high crimes and misdemeanors." No one could allege treason or bribery in Johnson's case, but congressmen believed that he had committed high crimes and misdemeanors in opposing them. The eleven articles of impeachment reflected by their very flimsiness how cocksure most House Republicans were of their case and its prospects. Conservative congressmen believed that the conditions of impeachment applied not to political acts, which made up the substance of the indictment in Johnson's case, but only to the violation of specific laws or the commission of felonies of which Johnson was innocent.

Yet in a trial of impeachment the senators, who sit as judges, need not be bound by ordinary rules of evidence. They hear testimony and the arguments of both sides and rule as they think proper. Under those circumstances and considering the strong feelings of the time, few could expect that the Johnson trial would be unbiased or that political accusations would fail to carry considerable weight. Conviction by the Senate demanded a two-thirds vote. The Democrats would oppose conviction, and very likely conservative Republicans would, too, unless the case was a strong one. And Congress had to consider public opinion as well. The prestige of the office of the president was at stake, and it was questionable whether the nation would tolerate degrading the president because of his political disagreements with Congress. Public opinion would demand an overt act.

The overt act that had driven congressmen to act on February 22 and 24 had come, they believed, on February 21, when Johnson had in effect dismissed Stanton with the executive order that appointed Thomas to the post of secretary of war ad interim. As far as Congress was concerned, the president had openly violated the Tenure of Office Act.

On March 4, 1868, seven managers chosen by the House appeared before the Senate bearing the eleven charges against Johnson and demanding that the president be tried. The Senate convened the next day as a court of impeachment, with Chief Justice Salmon P. Chase presiding. Johnson was allowed ten days to prepare his case, and the House appointed a committee to conduct the prosecution. The prosecutors included Stevens, Butler, and Boutwell, the last two men having been strong advocates of impeachment since early 1867; all were better known as politicians than constitutional lawyers. Numbered among Johnson's team of attorneys were some of the most distinguished legal minds in the country, including William M. Evarts, head of the New York Bar Association, former Supreme Court Justice Benjamin R. Curtis, and Attorney General Stanbery.

Johnson's alleged high crimes and misdemeanors broke down into four categories. First, he had dismissed Stanton contrary to the Tenure of Office Act; second, he had declared several laws unconstitutional; third, he had maliciously criticized Congress in the "swing around the circle" campaign of 1866; and fourth, he had opposed congressional reconstruction in general. The last two categories, in reality the tenth and eleventh articles, were largely the work of Butler and Stevens, who thought that they might help convince senators who might have some qualms about the other charges. The first category, the overt act, was the substance of the first eight articles. Of the fifty-four senators, House prosecutors had to secure thirty-six votes for conviction.

The question soon arose, should the Senate act as a judicial or as a political body? If it acted as a judicial body, then House prosecutors would be forced to submit evidence that would have weight in a law court. If it acted as a political group, then House prosecutors had the somewhat simpler task of convincing senators that Johnson ought to be removed. The House team of course took the political view and addressed Justice Chase as "Mr. President," while the defense called him "Mr. Chief Justice." Chase viewed the Senate as a court and ruled on evidence as though he actually sat on a bench. But by agreement with the Senate, he submitted his rulings to them, and they usually overruled him by a simple majority vote. The Radicals soon repudiated Chase, who they had thought was a reliable friend.

The crux of Johnson's defense was that he had removed Stanton to test the legality of the Tenure of Office Act because he believed the act to be unconstitutional. Since he held that view, he thought it both his privilege and duty to see the matter decided in court. Johnson's attorneys attempted to show that the entire cabinet, including Stanton, thought that the law was unconstitutional when it was first enacted. Chase agreed to admit this as evidence, but the Senate overruled him. The defense then urged that the actual removal of Stanton did not violate the act, since it specified that a cabinet member should hold office during the term of the president who made his appointment and for one month after that. Stanton had been appointed by Lincoln and had, in fact, served the time specified; besides, since Congress could not enact an ex post facto law, the act did not apply to Lincoln's appointees in the first place. Curtis made these arguments so well that it became clear that conviction of Johnson would have to come on political grounds.

A political conviction worried cautious Republicans, lest the party suffer an adverse public reaction in the 1868 elections. Also, if Johnson were convicted, the presidency would pass to Wade, the president of the Senate. Wade had been such a violent partisan that few conservatives and moderates wanted to see him in the White House, even for a year. The longer the articles of impeachment were debated, the less of a case there appeared to be. And while the trial was underway, Johnson adroitly named Schofield to the war secretary's job. Schofield had sufficient stature in the country to weaken the Radical argument that a presidential puppet would be placed over the War Department, an area vital to the success of congressional reconstruction. Even the hostile press moderated its tone, and public opinion seemed to favor letting Johnson fill out the remainder of his term.

By May 16 the Senate was ready to vote. The House prosecutors felt their best chance for conviction was on the last article, and they determined to take the vote on it first. Chase called the roll of senators alphabetically, and down the line Republicans voted "guilty," and Democrats, "not guilty," until Chase came to Fessenden. Fessenden remarked that it was the duty of "those on whom a judicial task is imposed to meet reproach and not court popularity"; he added that he had taken an oath to do impartial justice according to the Constitution and the laws and therefore voted "not guilty." Four other Republicans agreed with Fessenden, including Trumbull. Only three more Republicans, plus those four, were necessary for acquittal along with the twelve Democrats. One by one they appeared until, with West Virginia's Peter G. Van Winkle, Radical hearts sank, and impeachment was not sustained.

The Senate adjourned for ten days, while the Radicals frantically attempted to find that "improper or corrupt" means had been used to influence the senators who voted for acquittal. Butler, especially, used every means at the disposal of the House to find evidence of bribery or other pressure, but he found none. When the

Senate reconvened on May 26, the vote on the first and second articles remained the same, 35 guilty, 19 not guilty, still insufficient by one vote for conviction. The prosecution had been defeated; Stanton yielded his office to Schofield; Johnson remained president; and the Senate adjourned without voting on the remainder of the articles. The seven Republicans who saved Johnson with their "not guilty" votes* endured some continued harassment by the others, but public opinion supported them. In later years Blaine, who had voted for conviction, reviewed the situation and declared that the result satisfied him.

Trumbull summed it up adequately when he remarked that, had impeachment been successful, "no future President will be safe" who quarrels with a majority of the House and two-thirds of the Senate. Had they succeeded, the Radicals might well have upset the constitutional system of checks and balances, as well as the independence of the executive office. Presidents historically had been interpreters of the Constitution, most especially Andrew Jackson and most recently Lincoln, and had Johnson's impeachment been sustained that function would certainly have been removed from them. Johnson served out the remainder of his term, returned to Tennessee in March 1869, and ironically five years later returned to the Senate that had so nearly convicted him. He had never given up his fight against congressional reconstruction, a fact he made clear in a Senate speech in March 1875, when he castigated the Radicals as violators of the Constitution. He died a few months after that last blast.

The Radicals had been checked and were disappointed, but they had not been stopped. Their accomplishments were still impressive. They had substituted congressional for presidential reconstruction and proceeded to execute their program. They had made black suffrage a needed protection for the success of their programs in the states of the former Confederacy. And, though they had to suffer with Johnson for the remainder of his term, the Republican National Convention had met before the final Senate vote had been taken and had nominated Ulysses S. Grant for president.

* The Republican senators for acquittal were: Fessenden (Me.), Joseph S. Fowler (Tenn.), James W. Grimes (Ia.), John B. Henderson (Mo.), Edmund G. Ross (Kan.), Trumbull (Ill.), and Van Winkle (W. Va.).

17

Congressional Reconstruction in Operation

Southerners viewed military defeat at the hands of the Union army as an unfortunate but unavoidable fact. Reconstruction would have been easy if, with Lee's surrender and the flight of the Davis government, Southerners had been able to resume their old relationship with the rest of the Union. But a great deal had changed. Union success brought social and political upheaval that Southerners could scarcely comprehend because of their background and history, that thrust them into controversies more difficult than those that had brought them to war.

White Southerners firmly believed in white superiority and thought it more than sufficient that the war had freed the black man from bondage. They clung as tightly as ever to the notion of state sovereignty, a concept that the war had altered more profoundly than men, even in the North, cared to admit. Under the circumstances, Southerners were in no hurry to accept Northern demands for equal civil status for blacks or congressional attempts to dictate the contents of their state constitutions. They had seen their cotton prosperity swept away, many of their number reduced to poverty, and their labor force disorganized. When Congress imposed military rule, white Southerners felt that few greater calamities could befall them. They had no intention of compromising that which remained, that which they called their honor.

Northerners, on the other hand, were constantly surprised at Southern resistance. They were amazed that the South, defeated on the battlefield, should refuse to yield to each effort to protect the freedmen and should continuously demand the right to rule themselves. Northerners forgot that they had claimed secession was impossible and had fought a war to prove it, and perhaps they should not have been so surprised when Southerners claimed they had never left the Union. The views of Lincoln and Johnson on reconstruction seemed all the more logical to Southerners, since the presidents accepted the fact that the states existed and only the governments needed revision for them to resume their prewar status. When Northerners talked about "state suicide" or "conquered provinces" it made no sense to Southerners. If secession had been illegal, then in fact the states had not left the Union, and if Congress could not impose conditions on the internal affairs of Northern states, then how could that same Congress meddle in the internal affairs of the Southern states?

From that point of view, the interlude of presidential reconstruction may well have been a most serious mistake; the knowledge that the president stood with the Southern states against Congress and its alleged unconstitutional activities gave them courage. At the very moment of Lee's surrender Southerners might have accepted black suffrage, as Dennett later speculated in *The Nation*—as unwillingly as they had accepted the Thirteenth Amendment perhaps, but "with far less resistance" than afterward. Few Northern statesmen had the understanding that came with Dennett's hindsight.

The Freedman and the Republican Party

Most Southern whites had been exposed to military rule as soldiers, so military rule did not frighten them. But white Southerners had been humiliated by war, by postwar chaos and poverty, by the overturn of presidential reconstruction, and by the imposition of military government. Thus they were convinced that subverting the activities of the hated Radical Republican Congress justified any means, including violence and fraud. This conviction formed the basis for the white "solid South" that both Reid and Dennett had predicted and inspired white Southern contempt for anything associated with the Republican party.

Thus the future held a minimum of promise for the freedman. He was caught in a torrent that was not only not of his making but also far beyond his control. He played no real part in the Republican party decisions that affected him deeply. Even if the Republicans had his interests at heart, as in fact some few really did, their program smacked of paternalism. That was the least of it. The Southern black became an instrument of party necessity and sectional business requirements, which bore little relation to his real needs or actual welfare. If it happened that those party needs or business aims could be fulfilled without him, he would be alone again in the South. The Democrats, his major political opposition, had no commitment to black political, social, economic, or civil equality. When the white Southern Democratic party regained control, the Southern black could expect nothing. Despite these political realities the freedmen focused their attention on their opportunity to participate in the remaking of Southern states.

A Southern Republican party emerged quickly, composed of several elements including white Northerners new to the South. These were former Yankee soldiers who had become aware of the physical potential of the area, or businessmen who sought new opportunities, or humanitarians who came to assist the freedmen. Most were not wealthy and carried their belongings in the inexpensive bags that led to the derisive Southern term for them, "carpetbaggers." They ranged from serious emigrants to unscrupulous opportunists, but white Southerners lumped them all together under the one label. A second element of the Southern Republican party comprised old Unionists native to the South, former Whigs attracted by the economic goals of the Republican party, and other Southerners who had never been happy with the rule of the planters. They accepted congressional reconstruction for a variety of political and economic reasons, and were referred to time and again in Northern reports as "truly loyal" Southerners. Most Southern whites regarded them as traitors, despised them even more than they did the carpetbaggers, and scornfully called them "scalawags."

The bulk of the Southern Republican party was made up of blacks. While many were new to politics, a few were well-educated and capable, and proved to be responsible, dedicated leaders. By and large they were moderate in their goals and untouched with a desire for revenge against their former white masters—which, after nearly two and a half centuries of bondage, was in itself a remarkable fact. Among the black leaders who served in Congress were Massachusetts-born Robert B. Elliott, educated at Eton in England, and sent to Congress from South Carolina; Richard H. Gleaves who also went to Congress from South Carolina; and Hiram Revels, a Mississippian who was elected to the United States Senate; all had better than average educations. Self-educated Robert Smalls, from South Carolina, John R. Lynch of Mississippi, and Jefferson Long of Georgia were also elected congressmen. Many of the blacks, like Francis L. Cardozo, who studied in Scotland and England, were also ministers; others were federal employees, especially of the Freedmen's Bureau, or school teachers, and of course farmers.

The Southern Republican party—no more than any other political party in any section of the nation in an age of public corruption—was not free from corruption. Those few freedmen who might be tagged as unscrupulous emerged as amateurs compared to the white professionals elsewhere; and nowhere in the South did black Southern Republicans occupy all the offices or even control the legislatures. The one exception was in South Carolina where blacks held a majority in the lower house. Only three blacks were elected to the Forty-first Congress; no black held a governorship; but they served in almost every other capacity. The fact that they were not predominant is startling, given the size of the black population and their potential voting strength as a bloc. Since nearly all black politicians were inexperienced, many made mistakes that were grotesquely exaggerated by the hostile white population. Coming from a background of poverty in both education and finance, their performance was impressive.

Operation of Congressional Reconstruction

In March 1867 Johnson appointed the military governors provided for by the act of March 2. In their district they were supreme, answerable only to the president, the Constitution, and the laws of Congress. They attempted to keep existing state officials in office and to operate through them, but they showed no hesitation in removing those officeholders who obstructed directives such as registration of the freedmen. Schofield blocked implementation of a proposal to remove all local officials by noting that there would not be enough loyal whites to fill the vacancies. Yet removal of officials became more frequent in 1868 as congressional reconstruction proceeded more rapidly, although of those removed only two were governors (from Georgia and Mississippi).

The laws of the states continued in force except as they conflicted with reconstruction acts. Nevertheless, military courts frequently ruled on various types of crime. Soldiers replaced sheriffs in making arrests and executing judgment, and in some places, military governors put blacks on juries, an obvious innovation in Southern civil government. The success of the military governors depended largely upon their personality and politics, but even those most sympathetic to the South fell into disfavor with Southern whites as they carried out the will of Congress. They faced both violent and passive resistance from those who opposed reconstruction. However, even as the number of federal troops in the South melted away, the military governors who remained were able to preserve an uneasy peace.

By the spring of 1868 most Southern states had held new conventions and adopted new constitutions. The new laws accepted black suffrage, as Congress demanded; six states temporarily restricted the franchise of ex-Confederates. Most instituted public school systems, a distinct advance in Southern education. The conventions generally extended a measure of poor relief through tax exemptions and the abolition of imprisonment for debt. They established orphan homes, insane asylums, and provided for the aged and handicapped. Except for black suffrage, every new provision was debated and strongly opposed, often on the grounds of cost, but also for its implied racial overtones.

Some delegates refused to sign the new documents and walked out. Others, like the Texas Republicans, condemned the results as a conservative victory and in so doing divided the Republican party in their state. The bitter debates and speeches of the delegates themselves clearly revealed that Southern Republicans could not take full credit for the new constitutions anywhere. Southern conservatives in both parties organized across the South to prevent the ratification of the documents. Their technique of boycotting the elections in Alabama failed when Congress enacted the Third Reconstruction Act. In Mississippi conservatives mounted a relentless campaign to reject the constitution and succeeded. Votes in other states were close, and hostility, violence, and fraud were in some measure more than mere spectators on either side. After the elections, Alabama, Arkansas, the Carolinas, Florida, Georgia, and Louisiana returned to the Union, having fulfilled Congress' requirements.

Mississippi, Texas, and Virginia remained unreconstructed by the time Grant took office in March 1869. Mississippi had rejected her constitution outright, while Texas and Virginia were impaled on a provision that disfranchised ex-Confederates. Grant suggested in April that those two states take separate votes on the constitution with and without disfranchisement; they did so and promptly ratified the constitutions without. Congress stepped in in the case of Mississippi, making ratification of the Fifteenth Amendment a new condition, along with resubmission of the constitution to the people. Mississippians now ratified, but like Texas and Virginia they threw out disfranchisement provisions. Those states were readmitted in 1870. As the new governments took over, the military governors retired and left affairs in the hands of the new legislatures. Federal troops, though continually decreasing in number, remained for a time.

The new state officials quickly realized that the reduction of federal forces left them virtually at the mercy of their opponents and without the power to raise militias of their own, an authority Congress denied all of the former Confederate states. Arkansas, among others, begged Congress to repeal the law, and Congress obliged after some debate. In March 1869 Alabama, Arkansas, the Carolinas, Florida, and Louisiana were once more granted the power to establish militias. In 1870 Congress extended the privilege to Georgia, Mississippi, Texas, and Virginia. Virginia and Georgia never took advantage of the opportunity, Florida actually used it before congressional approval, and between 1870 and 1877 the Carolinas, Louisiana, Mississippi, Tennessee, and Texas used militias to a greater or less degree depending upon the circumstances. While most militiamen were black, the organizations also included many whites as officers and in the ranks. Yet Southerners commonly labeled them all "the Negro militia."

The new governments used the militia to prevent conservatives from hatching plots against the reconstruction regimes, to protect the polls from conservative intimidation, and to keep the peace during periods of Ku Klux Klan activity. Their appearance during political campaigns often provoked violence as the conservatives strove to capture state governments.

Radical Republicans in the South faced the task of molding an essentially nonpolitical black population into the mainstay of their organization. To do so they had to convince the black man that they were his only friends and that black power was politically vital to the success of the new order in the South. Conservatives also wooed the black vote in various locales, making the new Radical regimes still more afraid for their future. However, Radical Republicans had machinery available to secure black support, in the form of the Freedman's Bureau and the Union League. Immediately after Lee's surrender, Union Leaguers, whose organization had been founded several years earlier to win support for the Union, began educating blacks for the new cause. They set up many branches of the League and carefully propagandized among freedmen, urging them to support the Republican party as the party responsible for their freedom. Between the League and the Bureau, and sometimes one was indistinguishable from the other, they succeeded.

Once the Southern states were readmitted to the Union, the conservatives organized as Democrats or Conservative Unionists and launched attacks against the new governments. In Georgia they wasted no time in expelling black members from the legislature. They held that while the new constitution allowed black suffrage, it failed to grant blacks the right to hold office. After an investigation by the Reconstruction Committee, the U.S. Senate refused a Georgia senator his seat. Then, when Georgia vented its displeasure at congressional reconstruction by refusing to ratify the Fifteenth Amendment, Congress returned the state to military rule and stipulated that it must ratify the amendment before being readmitted. The military governor expelled two dozen Democrats from the state legislature, holding that they were disfranchised by the Fourteenth Amendment; he restored the blacks and filled the vacant Democratic seats with Republicans. Georgia finally ratified the Fifteenth Amendment, accepted the black legislators, and for the second time, in January 1870, was readmitted to the Union. The rash action of Georgia's conservatives convinced Northerners that the South would evade reconstruction whenever it could.

Not until the presidential election of 1868 had safely passed did the promise of guaranteed black suffrage come to fruition, with the submission of the Fifteenth Amendment to the states on February 27, 1869. It read, "the right of citizens of the United States to vote shall not be denied or abridged by the United States or by any state on account of color, race, or previous condition of servitude." The amendment went into effect on March 30, 1870, a little over a year after it had been proposed. Not all Radicals were satisfied with the wording; some had attempted to add education and property-holding after "previous condition of servitude." Indiana's Senator Morton predicted that the time would come when Southern blacks would be disfranchised with the imposition of just such qualifications.

By 1870, however, Radical Republicans in Congress were running out of steam. On August 11, 1868, seventy-seven-year-old Stevens died. Fessenden and Stanton followed him to the grave in 1869, and Sumner, Schurz, Trumbull, and other leaders were diverted by other problems of the Grant administration. Sumner and Schurz broke with Grant, and the president's allies restricted Sumner's power in the Senate. Ben Wade lost his seat in Congress in 1869. By 1870, with the war now over for five years, the North's attention focused on Grant's activities and the business boom. The "Southern problem," an eternal source of irritating news, had begun to bore them; it was no longer directly relevant to their main preoccupations.

The Ku Klux Klan

Many white Southerners viewed the Klan as a legitimate organization designed to counteract the Union League and the Freedmen's Bureau. Southerners also found the Klan a convenient tool to use against the black militia in their struggle for control of the reconstructed governments. The Klan was not the only group of its type, and the term often encompassed organizations such as "The Knights of the White Camelia" in the Gulf states, the "Association of '76," "Constitutional Union Guards," "Pale Faces," "White Brotherhood," "White League," "Council of Safety," "Knights of the Rising Sun" in Texas, and the "White Line" in Mississippi.

The Ku Klux Klan originated as a fraternity of young white men in Pulaski, Tennessee, in 1866. The "Ku Klux" part of the name came from the Greek "Kuklos," for circle, and "Klan" was

added for alliteration. The young men soon discovered that their in-
itiation ceremonies frightened local blacks; to heighten the effect
they spread the rumor that the antics were performed by ghosts of
dead Confederates, disturbed by the activities of their freed slaves.
To scare aggressive blacks, that is, blacks who participated in civic
activities, the Klansmen paraded on horseback at night disguised in
white robes and face masks. Whites widely accepted any method of
keeping blacks out of politics and away from the polls, and other
communities quickly organized klans for that purpose. The original
fraternal objectives of the group disappeared.

By the time the reconstruction acts were passed in 1867, the
movement had spread across the South. Prominent Southern leaders became associated with it, and in a secret meeting at Nashville,
Tennessee, in April 1867 they established the "Invisible Empire," to
be held together by military obedience. The "Empire" was presided
over by the "Grand Wizard" and his ten "Genii." Each state became a "Realm" ruled by a "Grand Dragon" and his eight "Hy-
dras." Each congressional district in a state was a "Dominion" controlled by a "Grand Titan" and his six "Furies," while the local
groups were "Dens" led by the "Grand Cyclops" and his two
"Nighthawks." The "Den" carried out the work of the "Invisible
Empire," and the local members were sworn to march at any time
"of the moon."

Usually meeting in the woods at night, they decided whom
they would visit. Sometimes they honored the directive to visit no
person without first sending him a warning to change his conduct.
Their notices were delivered in the night, and the physical violence
often, but not always, came then. Since the disguises masked the
identities of the white men who wore them, none but the initiated
knew who was and who was not a Klansman. Absolute secrecy, loyalty, and obedience was demanded from members. The secrecy and
disguise was so perfect in many communities that concerned persons
hesitated to complain, lest they complain to a Klansman. In court,
one never knew how many members of a jury might be Klansmen.

As blacks learned that Klansmen were not ghosts and no
longer reacted with fear, the Klan resorted to increased physical violence, including whipping, tar-and-feathering, and even maiming,
to instill another sort of terror. They aimed to punish no one without careful deliberation, but turbulent Klansmen were frequently
carried away by their emotions. The Klan also pressured white men

with influence in the black community, often ordering them out of the area or physically punishing them, or both.

Allegedly organized "to act purely in self-defense," by 1868 the Klan had turned its "defense" vigorously against blacks and white Republicans who possessed any measure of political power. Blacks were punished for alleged offenses that ranged from "insolence" to the much more serious charges of voting or officeholding. Whites were punished for association with blacks or for participation in Radical governments. The Klan moved quickly to excess, as gangs of psychopathic killers roamed one countryside or another wearing the mantle of the Klan. One gang in Mississippi killed 116 blacks; North Carolinian Klansmen murdered 7 and whipped over 140 blacks and half that number of whites. In one South Carolina county 6 murders and over 300 whippings took place in the first half of 1870. Aimed to intimidate the victim, some of the whippings and other indignities were public ceremonies.

Union League officials were whipped, threatened, and murdered, as were officials of the Freedmen's Bureau, even after the bureau was dissolved. Members of the black militia were singled out for personal violence, and militia officers were special targets for killers. The Klan burnt homes and destroyed other property.

The Grand Wizard of the Klan in 1869 was former Confederate General Nathan Bedford Forrest. He denounced the excesses of certain groups and attempted to disassociate the Klan from them. Although other moderates in the Klan supported him, their public statements had little effect other than providing an excuse for moderates and conservatives to leave their local units without being branded as traitors. Klan leaders such as former Confederate generals John B. Gordon, Albert Pike, and John T. Morgan may have agreed with Forrest, but they either wielded remarkably little restraining influence or in fact simply winked at the bloodshed.

The elections of 1870 sparked more Klan activity, and stories of outrage after outrage were published in the North. The reconstructed states themselves, beginning with Tennessee in 1868, sought protection for their citizens in a series of acts designed to end the lawlessness of the Klan. The laws specified stiff penalties and sometimes included declarations of martial law, but they generally failed. Martial law occasionally resulted in mass arrests of Klan suspects, and in North Carolina a few were even hanged. Yet Klan activities continued almost unabated.

In April 1871 Congress passed the Ku Klux Act in an attempt to come to the rescue of the Southern Republican party, Northern business interests, and the tottering reconstruction governments. It gave the president power to suspend habeas corpus in dealing with conspiracies, and it enlarged the power of federal courts by allowing them to hold individuals responsible for the consequences if they made no attempt to end a known conspiracy. Grant, who had asked for a strong act, warned that he would use it wherever necessary. The law resulted in hundreds of arrests and a few convictions, but it had little more effect than state laws on the subject.

Along with the Ku Klux Act, Congress set up a joint House-Senate committee to investigate conditions "in the late insurrectionary states." One subcommittee held hearings in Washington, three others in the South. The final report, published in a dozen large volumes, represented one of the most extensive investigations ever undertaken by a congressional committee. Testimony from former Confederate leaders, including Grand Wizard Forrest, Wade Hampton of South Carolina, and ex-Governor Joseph Brown of Georgia, showed that white Southerners still refused to bow to federal control or to comply with Congress' attempt to reconstruct the South. Forrest had publicly dissolved the Klan in 1869, in a subterfuge enabling witnesses to testify that they knew nothing of Klan activities. The report clearly indicated that white resistance to the reconstructed governments had grown so strong that they could not endure without federal aid. The Fourteenth and Fifteenth Amendments and the Ku Klux Act failed to protect the freedmen. Black voters remained away from the polls in direct proportion to the decline in supervision by the army.

The Success of Southern Counterreconstruction

The Klan and its violence, as well as the tactics of the ex-Confederate white leaders, represented a strong counterreconstruction movement that in the end challenged congressional reconstruction and won. Only a strong and vigorous military occupation could prop up the reconstruction governments for any length of time, and federal military forces in the South were decreasing.* The Northern

* Affairs in the South had very little to do with the decrease of the military. An act of March 3, 1869, reduced the size of the army and few congressmen even mentioned the South

public no longer gave the South its undivided attention, particularly after the election of Grant. Too many other factors drew their energies away from the seemingly eternal problem of the South: e.g., Northern political graft and the corruption that extended from the cities to the nation's capital; alleged corruption of the reconstruction regimes in the South; internal quarrels within the Republican party that led to the Liberal Republican split in 1872; and a serious economic depression after 1873.

In the main conservatives of the Southern Democratic party were men of property while the Republican reconstruction administrations were not. Failure to provide the black man with an independent economic base through land reform or other means left the freedmen without economic power sufficient to maintain their legal civil status. Politically and legally oriented congressmen had little concept of the economic principles that might have been involved in making the freedman truly free. A few Radical Republicans had thought in terms of chastizing Confederates by confiscating plantations and parceling them out to blacks or by purchasing plantations for that purpose, but ordinarily it was an era when legislators considered social reform legislation out of their purview. If lawmakers thought in terms of economics, it had little to do with individual welfare, except so far as aid to business might improve the individual's status. That left the Southern black without a substantial economic base; and that put the economic power that ultimately meant political power in the South in the hands of conservative Southern Democrats.

The Radical reconstruction regimes succumbed to white Southern Democratic assault one by one. Georgia Democrats won the legislature in 1870 and discussed the impeachment of Radical Republican governor Rufus Bulloch, whom many Georgians considered a carpetbagger even though he had lived in the state since 1859 and had been a Confederate officer. His position untenable, Bulloch resigned and left the state. The Democrats chose Bulloch's successor, and the Radical Republican period of reconstruction ended in Georgia in January 1872.

North Carolina also elected a Democratic legislature in 1870. William W. Holden, appointed provisional governor by Johnson in

---

in the debate; they were concerned with finances and cutting an unwieldy officer corps. See James E. Sefton, *The United States Army and Reconstruction, 1865–1877* (Baton Rouge: Louisiana State University Press, 1967), pp. 207–208.

1865 and elected by the Radicals in 1868, was impeached and removed by the Democrats in March 1871, partly in reaction against the Ku Klux Act in that state. By 1871 North Carolina had been redeemed from Radical Republican rule by white conservative Democrats.

Because of the delayed ratification of her new constitution, Virginia held her first election under reconstruction in 1869 and chose a conservative governor, Gilbert C. Walker. The conservatives carried Tennessee in 1870 and Texas in 1872. White majorities of the population made "redemption" by the conservatives easier in Georgia, North Carolina, Virginia, Tennessee, and Texas than in other Southern states. It took longer in Alabama, Arkansas, and Mississippi for conservatives to achieve their goal. Alabama and Arkansas were redeemed in 1874 and Mississippi in 1875.

The struggle in Mississippi was not easy. After much violence during the course of which many blacks lost their lives, Mississippi Radical Republicans appealed to Grant to send troops to police the 1874 elections. He refused, remarking that the public was tired "of these annual autumnal outbreaks." Left to themselves, the Democrats carried out a successful program of violence and intimidation designed to make Mississippi a "white man's country"; they swept the elections of 1875. As the presidential election of 1876 approached, only South Carolina, Florida, and Louisiana remained in Radical hands, and their position was not secure. Democrats mounted vigorous campaigns in 1876, and once the last federal troops were withdrawn in 1877, the final vestiges of Radical Republican rule disappeared from the South.

The period of Radical rule had been, after all, brief in most Southern states and for practical purposes nonexistent in others. Tennessee, readmitted early and not formally under congressional reconstruction at all, and Virginia, where conservatives delayed ratification of the constitution for two years and then chose a conservative governor, escaped Radical Republican rule; Georgia and North Carolina had a minimum of it. In only three states was there even one decade of congressional control.

Reconstruction and the Grant Regime

When Stevens died in 1868, leadership on Southern affairs passed to Butler. Butler, however, displayed little of the driving purpose that had directed Stevens. He was primarily a party man who valued the South for whatever Republican votes it would bring, and to that end he sought to perpetuate Republican control. Though Butler had followers, liberal reformers like Schurz and Trumbull soon broke with the political hacks surrounding Grant—including Butler—and as a result seldom supported his goals. Sumner never ceased to urge strong measures in support of the freedmen until his death in 1874, but his support in the Senate had been damaged by his breech with Grant. Grant wanted only peace and order and usually supported measures to this end.

During Grant's presidency, a number of acts were designed to support Radical Republican rule. To enforce the Fourteenth and Fifteenth amendments the Enforcement Act of 1870 provided that if a state abridged suffrage on the grounds of race, color, or previous servitude, the federal government could correct the situation. But in 1875 the Supreme Court struck the act down, holding that the amendments only restricted the states from passing laws and left to the states the power to protect individual rights. A second type of enforcement act was the Ku Klux Act of 1871 which the Supreme Court virtually nullified in 1882.

In 1875 Congress passed a Civil Rights Act designed to insure blacks equal privileges in theaters, hotels, railroad cars, and other public utilities. Sumner, before he died, had advocated including schools, churches, and cemeteries, but Congress stopped short of this. The Supreme Court in 1883 cut much of the ground from under that act by claiming that it dealt with social, not civil, rights. A force bill tailored to enforce the law in Alabama, Arkansas, Louisiana, and Mississippi passed the House but failed in the Senate in 1874. The Enforcement Act, the KKK Act, the Civil Rights Act, and the force bill were the work of Butler and House Radicals who sought to continue vigorous enforcement of congressional reconstruction. They came to grief at the hands of a Supreme Court determined to maintain state authority in its interpretations of the Constitution.

Congressional reconstructionists fared better in their effort to control elections. A Second Enforcement Act was passed in 1871, placing elections to Congress under federal jurisdiction, allowing federal judges to appoint election supervisors under certain conditions, and authorizing federal marshals and their deputies to police the polls. It was a part of congressional reaction to Ku Klux activity.

Meanwhile, criticism of continued disfranchisement of Southerners mounted within the Republican party, particularly among the liberal Republicans who challenged Grant's party leadership. Since 1868 Congress had reenfranchised nearly 5,000 persons, although at least 150,000 more remained under the ban. In 1871 Grant asked that a general amnesty be provided for all but prominent Confederate leaders. Sumner blocked implementation of a bill to that end unless his civil rights bill became a part of it. In May 1872 the House killed Sumner's amendment and passed the amnesty bill, which then moved successfully through the Senate. One estimate concluded that not more than 500 Southerners remained excluded from the franchise after passage. Certainly "redemption" of Southern states became easier with the new law.

The Supreme Court and Reconstruction

The Court, unwilling to intervene in the struggle between the legislature and executive over reconstruction, became a factor in interpreting the amendments to the Constitution. The Thirteenth Amendment caused little controversy, unequivocally abolishing slavery. The Fifteenth Amendment, which concerned suffrage, also inspired little argument. The second, third, fourth, and fifth sections of the Fourteenth Amendment, that dealt with apportionment, disfranchisement, the Confederate debt, and the power to enforce the amendment, evoked little legal interest. The first section of the Fourteenth Amendment, however, soon drew the Supreme Court's attention.*

In line with other activities of the Reconstruction Era, many who approved of the amendment believed that it secured blacks' rights and immunities under the protection of the national government. Other acts of Congress had tended to centralization, and a reading of that section of the amendment appeared to justify a gen-

---

* This section of the Fourteenth Amendment read: "All persons born or naturalized in the United States, and subject to the jurisdiction thereof, are citizens of the United States and of the State wherein they reside. No State shall make or enforce any law which shall abridge the privileges or immunities of citizens of the United States; nor shall any State deprive any person of life, liberty, or property, without due process of law; nor deny to any person within its jurisdiction the equal protection of the laws."

eral belief that it was another step toward strong federalism. The Supreme Court opposed the trend in several decisions and restricted its application, enhancing state autonomy.

The first such decision came in 1873 in the Slaughterhouse Cases. Louisiana had issued a charter to one New Orleans company making it the only slaughterhouse licensed to kill and dress livestock in that city. Other New Orleans butchers were required to use that plant for fees not to exceed a specified maximum. Several butchers claimed that the Louisiana law violated the Fourteenth Amendment by depriving them of their business through the establishment of a monopoly. Their arguments failed in state courts, and the appeal went to the Supreme Court.

By a five to four vote, the Court announced that the Fourteenth Amendment was intended to protect the individual freedmen, not businessmen. The Court also claimed that the amendment recognized two distinct types of citizenship, state and federal, each with different privileges. A state, the Court continued, could not infringe on federal citizenship, but since the privileges under state citizenship were broad prior to the adoption of the amendment, they remained that way except so far as the amendment transferred them to the nation. The law did not intend the Supreme Court to be "a perpetual censor upon all legislation of the states" that concerned the civil rights of the state's citizens. Regulation of the slaughterhouses was a state privilege subject to state control. The Court would not then define the privileges of federal citizenship, but it noted that among them were those that grew out of the nature of the federal government and were specifically granted in the Constitution. Since most civil rights stemmed from state citizenship, the Fourteenth Amendment failed to protect individuals against state laws that regulated their rights or deprived them of their rights altogether. Only if a state discriminated against blacks as a class, or because of their race, would the amendment apply. "It is so clearly a provision for that race and that emergency, that a strong case would be necessary for its application to any other."

Those who opposed the concentration of power in federal hands rejoiced in the decision. The Court announced that it intended to preserve for the states "powers for domestic and local government, including the regulation of civil rights, the rights of person and property." It was the purpose of the Court to maintain "with a steady and even hand the balance between state and federal power," the Court proclaimed, apparently marking an end to federal assumption of power at the expense of the states.

The narrow interpretation of the first clause of the Fourteenth Amendment came as close to nullifying the intent of the amendment as possible. Congress had intended to place civil and private rights under the protection of the federal government against state action, but the Court's idea of dual citizenship denied that the federal government had any such power over the states. The majority of the Court acknowledged simply that the amendment protected the freedmen and extended no further, and specifically did not include any limitation on the states over private property rights.

Seven years later the Supreme Court again interpreted the first section of the Fourteenth Amendment in three decisions that concerned the right of blacks to serve on juries. This political right, necessary to insure a black defendant a trial by his peers, depended upon the clause that forbade a state to deny equality before the law. The Court held that if a state excluded blacks from the jury, then that state violated the amendment. Or, if the officers who made up jury lists refused to include blacks among them, then the amendment was also violated. But if state law admitted blacks to jury duty, and if a black defendant was convicted by a white jury, then the conviction stood and the amendment had not been violated. Exclusion of blacks from the jury had been one of the reasons for the passage of the amendment, and the Court, essentially, advised that the amendment provided the remedy intended simply by including blacks in the pool from which the jurors would be selected.

Following the 1880 jury cases, came the Civil Rights Cases. These cases dealt not with the Fourteenth Amendment but with the Civil Rights Act of 1875. That act guaranteed to blacks equal privileges in inns, theaters, and public conveyances. Several cases came before the Court at once, and it decided to handle them together. Black petitioners urged that the Civil Rights Act had been violated but the Court could not see that any state was guilty, which would have been contrary to the Fourteenth Amendment, and indeed no state action had been alleged. The Court also held that Congress had no authority over private individual rights in inns, theaters, or public conveyances, that no such authority had been conferred on Congress in any amendment or in the Constitution, and that Congress could not legislate on such matters. The Civil Rights Act was therefore void in the clauses concerned. Very likely those clauses were applicable in the District of Columbia and the territories, and Congress might also regulate black accommodations in interstate travel. But the heart of the act was destroyed.

So the Court contributed, along with Southern white conservatives, to the undoing of reconstruction. Black civil and social disfranchisement proceeded along a path that led to white supremacy in the states of the former Confederacy, culminating with Court recognition of the separate but equal doctrine in the *Plessy* v. *Ferguson* decision of 1896. The breakdown of congressional reconstruction, in intent as well as in fact, was complete by the turn of the century. The war aims of preserving the Union and destroying slavery had been met successfully, but the reconstruction goals of protecting the freedmen failed abjectly.

18
The Grant Era
and Postwar Politics

As the Civil War ended and the nation grappled with the problems of reconstruction, the major political parties sought new identities. They had changed in the cauldron of war as had their goals. Neither party recognized itself from its antebellum portrait. The debris of war had buried the platform on which the Republican party had been founded: opposition to the spread of slavery into the territories. Subsequent issues, such as preservation of the Union and the death of slavery as an institution, evaporated at Appomattox. Radical Republicans in Congress clung to the new, but temporary issue of reconstruction, but they had not the firm support of the entire party.

If the wartime coalition, the Union party of Republicans and War Democrats, was to continue as a viable peacetime coalition, it needed firm and enlightened leadership that the president would normally have been expected to supply. Although moderate Republicans gave Johnson every opportunity to work with them and save presidential reconstruction, Johnson blindly and inflexibly refused to cooperate, alienating them and forcing them into an alliance with the Radicals. Still the Republicans could not easily shed the mantle of Unionism, nor did many of them really desire to do so until events proved that both Unionism and Johnson were no longer assets to the party.

Tied to the quarrels between Johnson's reconstruction and Congress' opposition were the four political meetings of 1866. The first of these, the "National Union" party meeting, was an August 14 gathering in Philadelphia of Johnson's followers, including Seward and other presidential advisors. Johnson hoped to mobilize support in order to bring defeat to his opponents in the fall elections. Essentially an effort to show how the sections could unite peacefully under the president, the convention failed to arouse much enthusiasm. Johnson's "swinging around the circle" tour only documented his unpopularity. On September 3 Philadelphia hosted a gathering of Southern Unionists and a few Northerners—who sought to convince the nation that presidential reconstruction was a mistake. At Cleveland on September 17 Johnson's friends tried again to convince the nation, as well as the gathering of veterans on hand, that they owed their true loyalty to the president. Finally at Pittsburgh on September 25 a Republican meeting, controlled by the Radicals, endorsed the work of Congress. All the meetings had been calculated to influence the electorate, but in November the Democrats gained only seven seats in the House and one in the Senate. The Radical Republicans, undaunted, seized their party banner and shed Johnson's leadership.

The Republican quest for a new identity narrowed as Northern business interests renewed their prewar alliance on the re-emerging tariff and currency questions. Partner of the protected manufacturers, friend of the commercial interests, the Republican party soon became the darling of finance. The association provided them with an ideological base more durable than the temporary question of reconstruction and carried them into the last third of the century with added cohesion.

Had it not been for the solid opposition in the South to Radical Republican reconstruction and its implications for white supremacy, the Democratic party would have been in a desperate condition in 1866. The peace Democrats were effectively held up to ridicule by the Republicans. The war Democrats, who supported Johnson's reconstruction policy, were speedily drummed out of the wartime coalition with the Republicans as the Union party disap-

peared. Radical Republicans castigated war Democrats as untrust-
worthy supporters of unreconstructed rebels, little different in heart
from their brothers the peace Democrats, and kin to traitors, the
Southern Democrats. Scarred and leaderless, the Democrats nevertheless continued to espouse the local autonomy they called states'
rights as they upheld presidential reconstruction. They vigorously
adopted other expedient issues to oppose the Republicans at local
levels, and this solid opposition kept them together and in contention as a major political force. They showed their strength in 1867
as they carried local elections in New York and Pennsylvania and
made considerable gains in Ohio. They made the Republicans ap-
prehensive about the presidential-year elections of 1868, particularly since Democratic gains came so shortly after the inauguration
of congressional reconstruction.

The Election of 1868

Although they had firm control of the party, the Radical
Republicans were politicians enough to continue the fiction that
they still represented the wartime alliance. They met under the title
"National Union Republican Party" in Chicago on May 20, 1868.
Their convention met between the two votes on impeachment, and
if that venture caused some misgivings among the party members,
most of them anticipated with great political pleasure the nomination of Grant and victory in November.

As with other popular generals in American history, Grant's
politics were unknown enough for him to have been a candidate for
either party, and his public image strong enough to assure his election under any label. Grant himself had cast but one vote for a presidential candidate, and that had been for Buchanan, a Democrat,
in 1856. Had he met Illinois residence requirements in 1860, he
would have voted for Douglas, he later revealed in his memoirs.
Following the war his movement into the Republican camp had
been due largely to his somewhat less than cordial relations with
President Johnson, because of his involvement in the Tenure of
Office affair.

Radical Republicans, unsure of Grant's position on reconstruction, had favored the nomination of Chase. Wade had remarked
that Grant "may be all right on horses and all wrong on politics,"
an insight that went far beyond Wade's usual sagaciousness. Most

Republican leaders were convinced that Grant would "take the game at a swoop," and John Sherman remarked that he saw nothing to block Grant's election "unless he is foolish enough to connect his future with the Democratic Party." Grant chose the Republicans, and won nomination on their ticket unanimously. Speaker of the House Schuyler Colfax of Indiana, whom Edwin L. Godkin of *The Nation* claimed had "the White House on the brain," nosed out Wade for the second spot on the ticket.

The Republican platform endorsed congressional reconstruction, and reflected the Republican connection with business by strongly denouncing any effort to repay war bonds with anything but gold. The Republicans considered, they said, payment of interest on the war bonds in greenbacks to be a repudiation of the debt. Their platform contained no surprises.

When the Democrats met in New York City on July 4, a date chosen to illustrate their patriotism, two Ohioans were the frontrunners: Chief Justice Salmon Chase, a former Republican, and ex-representative George H. "Gentleman George" Pendleton, a War Democrat. Chase, who coveted the presidency, had concluded during the winter of 1868 that his chances for the Republican nomination were slim. Even while he presided over the impeachment proceedings, he corresponded privately with leading Democrats and Democratic newsmen like Greeley, Halstead, Bennett, and Manton Marble. By June, Chase's eagerness was obvious to the Democratic party, and even Godkin remarked that Chase had not a craving, but a "lust," for the office. If Chase switched parties in an effort to capture the prize he sought, he still had not changed his mind on the question of black suffrage. Other issues were negotiable, but not that.

Pendleton, an accomplished debater with an aristocratic bearing, had been an early advocate of the "Ohio Idea," essentially the notion that the principal on Civil War 5-20 bonds should be paid in greenbacks rather than gold, an idea the Republicans labelled "a national crime." His slogan, "the same currency for the bond-holder and the plow-holder," had catapulted him to the leadership of the Democratic party in the West and had contributed to the party's success in 1867.

The point of dispute over the method of payment of the Civil War 5-20 bonds stemmed from the act providing for their issue. The same act of Congress that had authorized greenbacks also authorized the issue of the bonds. The interest was to be paid in gold, according to the law, but the principal was to be repaid in "dollars." As greenbacks were legal tender and were much cheaper than gold, and as most of the bonds had been purchased with greenbacks, Pendleton argued that it would be extravagant of the government to retire them in gold. To do so would assure the bond-holders an additional profit, the cost of which would be borne by the taxpayer. In other words, wealthy holders of bonds would get wealthier at the expense of the public. Yet in order to pay bond-holders in greenbacks, a new and large issue of that currency would be necessary. The outstanding 5-20s were worth about $1,600,000,000 and the total greenback issue stood in 1868 at about $356,000,000. The attractiveness of the "Ohio Idea" then lay in the inexpensive way of reducing the debt as well as in inflating the currency, a combination appealing to Western debtors.

Secretary of the Treasury Hugh McCullough had been authorized by the Funding Act of 1866 to convert various short-term notes into 5-20s and to retire greenbacks from circulation at the rate of $10,000,000 within the first six months and $4,000,000 a month thereafter. As a result the number of 5-20s had increased at precisely the same time the number of greenbacks decreased. Coincidentally with McCulloch's implementation of the law, poor crops and a business panic in Britain caused a recession and a sharp drop in prices in the United States. The economic troubles were blamed on the contraction of the greenback issue, and the Funding Act of 1866 was repealed early in 1868. For the moment the currency situation was static. But those who had suffered from the price skid and recession advocated inflation.

They were joined by certain Democrats who saw the "Ohio Idea" as a means of getting back at those who had both incurred the Civil War debt for their own profit and had waged an unnecessary war. As a means of putting the wealthy businessmen who backed the Republican party in their proper place, the "Ohio Idea" had obvious political as well as economic overtones. Yet most Democrats and Republicans who sympathized with the "Ohio Idea" saw it simply as an expedient means of paying debts without granting the wealthy an unnecessary profit at the taxpayer's expense.

To Westerners, contraction of greenbacks represented a disaster, for it had been the best currency they had known. Although gold and silver had always been the standards, very little actually circulated except for silver coin. The primary medium of exchange had been bank notes, issued by the various national and state banks. These always evoked unpleasant memories of wildcat banking days; in contrast the greenbacks circulated everywhere, had the same value in any part of the country, and were difficult to counterfeit. Greenbacks were safe and reliable. If they were also cheap, it became easier to repay debts. So Pendleton and the "Ohio Idea" struck a popular note, and the man was a formidable contender as the Democratic convention opened.

The Pendleton forces successfully influenced the platform by incorporating the "Ohio Idea." The platform went even further by advocating taxation of government bonds as well as their payment in "lawful money." The "greenback plank," as it was called, drew great enthusiasm from the delegates. They also expressed their firm opposition to congressional reconstruction, calling the process "unconstitutional, revolutionary, and void."

The Pendleton forces had less success nominating their candidate. Eastern Democrats were willing to accept the "Ohio Idea" in the platform, but were unwilling to accept Pendleton as a candidate. They hoped to avoid a campaign on the sole issue of finance. Pendleton led the field on the early ballots, followed closely by Indiana Senator Thomas A. Hendricks and General Winfield Scott Hancock, and more distantly by Chase. After the second day of balloting, with no clear choice in sight, Horatio Seymour, former governor of New York, attempted to activate a Chase boom. On the third day of voting, Pendleton's name was withdrawn, but Hancock and Hendricks held their own. When neither could acquire the support necessary, delegates turned to Chase and to the convention's chairman, Seymour. On the twenty-second ballot, with Pendleton's support, the Ohio delegation proposed Seymour, who won the bid.

For all their frenzied efforts to find a leader, the Democrats probably made as good a choice as possible. Pendleton would have committed the campaign to an inflationary issue; Chase would have drawn sharp fire as a renegade Republican. Though the Republicans attacked Seymour for his wartime opposition to the Emancipation Proclamation and the draft, he had prestige within his party as well as experience as governor of one of the nation's largest states. Missouri's Francis P. Blair won the second spot. If Seymour proved a reasonable choice, Blair represented the other extreme. On the eve of the convention, the former Free-Soiler, Lincoln backer, Union general, and renegade Republican congressman, had openly expressed his opposition to congressional reconstruction. He had opined that the carpetbag governments in the South ought to be dispersed by the president with bayonets. Under the circumstances, his nomination was indiscreet at best. Republicans pointed to Blair as evidence that the Democrats would violently undo congressional reconstruction.

The campaign of 1868 took place amid various phases of congressional reconstruction in operation. At the end of July, the Fourteenth Amendment was ratified. By the same time seven states had been reconstructed by Congress and had resumed representation in that body. The Ku Klux Klan was riding high. In August 1868 conservative white Democrats expelled black members from Georgia's legislature, creating a crisis in that state with repercussions for the North that lasted well past the November elections. On the eve of the election came the riot at Camilla, Georgia, in which local civil officers and townspeople physically discouraged several hundred Republicans, mostly black, from holding a mass meeting. Under the circumstances, the "southern question" was a prime issue in the campaign.

Seymour followed a moderate course, assuring the nation that a Democratic victory would not mean "sudden or violent" changes in reconstruction, but would mean a check against those "extreme measures" that have been "deplored by the best men of both organizations." Grant's simple declaration, "let us have peace," caught the public fancy much more than Seymour's cautious statements. Republicans parlayed that into the slogan, "Grant and Peace," and coupled it with the denunciation "Blair and Revolution." Although Pendleton and Fessenden fought the "greenback issue" out in Maine's September elections, the financial question subsided into the shadow of the southern problem. Godkin supposed, he wrote, "that hundreds of thousands of meetings are held every evening— that thousands of bands of 'Boys in Blue' . . . march . . . in the towns and villages every night" presumably to get their mates to vote as they shot.

In spite of Grant's sure popularity, Democratic enthusiasm, moderation, and their contention that the nation was tired of eight years of Republican rule made the contest exciting and close. They made prodigious efforts to carry state elections in Indiana, Ohio, and Pennsylvania in October. In Indiana, Hendricks lost his bid for the governor's job by less than a thousand votes; Pennsylvania went Republican by less than 10,000; and the Republican candidate in Ohio won with only a 17,000 majority in the state which was thought the most certain of the three to go Republican. As usual, those Republican victories forecast the outcome in November. Seymour took to the stump in vain, and in November Grant swept into office with an electoral majority of 214 to Seymour's 80, and with better than 52 percent of the popular vote.*

Grant the President

Although the Democrats had made the campaign an energetic one, they had not directed it against Grant personally, just against Republican policy. Grant's stature as a national hero and his "let us have peace" policy endeared him to citizens of all political persuasions. Few other American men faced inauguration as president as universally well regarded as Grant. On March 4, 1869, the only unusual note in the tranquil ceremony was Grant's refusal to bow to custom and ride to the Capitol alongside Johnson. They rode in separate carriages.

In the manner of a general rather than a politician, as might have been expected, Grant nominated a cabinet of his own choosing without consulting party leaders, public opinion, or the merits of men so honored. As a result, most of his choices came as a complete surprise to the party, the press, the nation, and even, perhaps, to a few of those included. He chose Elihu B. Washburne for secretary of state. Washburne, former representative from Illinois, was a friend of both his and Lincoln's, but without any qualifications for the job. Washburne soon resigned and became minister to France, and Hamilton Fish of New York took the post. Fish, head of a wealthy and socially prominent family, had served in New York both as a legislator and as governor of the state and in Washington in both houses. He took the post with "misgivings and at the sacrifice of personal ease," he said, but he proved to be an able secretary of state.

---

* Statistics were: Grant, 214 electoral votes, 3,013,313 popular votes, for 52.7 percent of the popular total; Seymour, 80 electoral, 2,703,933 popular for 47.3 percent of the popular total. Seymour carried eight states, Georgia, Louisiana, Delaware, Maryland, Kentucky, Oregon, New Jersey, and New York. Grant carried the rest, twenty-six states, including Alabama, Arkansas, the Carolinas, Florida, and Tennessee of the former Confederacy. Unreconstructed Virginia, Mississippi, and Texas took no part in the election.

Grant asked Alexander T. Stewart, one of the richest merchants in the country, to be secretary of the treasury, but uneasy congressmen pointed out a 1789 law that forbade one who engaged in trade or commerce to hold that post. Disgruntled, Grant unsuccessfully tried to get Stewart excepted from the law, and then appointed George S. Boutwell of Massachusetts in his stead. A Radical Republican, a scrupulously honest man, former governor, and dedicated representative, Boutwell had little working knowledge of the job and only reluctantly accepted it.

With the appointment of Ohioan Jacob D. Cox to the Interior Department post, Grant scored a goal for excellence. A man who had fought with distinction in the late war, a man who was well-read, honest, vigorous, and a former governor of Ohio, Cox brought both dedication and intelligence to the post. Yet American blacks could not forget that Cox had opposed black suffrage in Ohio, and that Cox opposed it in the South as unworkable.

Grant scored a second time with the nomination of Ebenezer Rockwood Hoar, a Massachusetts supreme court judge, for attorney general. In 1846 Hoar had opined that he would rather be a "Conscience Whig" than a "Cotton Whig," bringing that terminology into the antislavery arena. Hoar was widely respected for his stability, courage, and integrity, and soon became fast friends with Cox.

Grant's other appointments failed to rise above mediocrity. John A. Rawlins, former city attorney of Galena, Illinois, and the president's friend, had served on Grant's staff during the war and become a major general in the regular army in April 1865. Grant appointed him secretary of war. John A. J. Creswell of Maryland was appointed postmaster general. Though he had served a term in the House of Representatives and two years in the United States Senate, he was relatively unknown.*

The most important of Grant's advisors, however, inhabited not the official cabinet, but the "kitchen cabinet." General Horace Porter, who served as Grant's military aide during the war, became his private secretary. Colonel Orville E. Babcock, another former aide, controlled access to Grant as an assistant secretary, and thus wielded great power. Their friends included Benjamin F. Butler,

---

* Unknown or not, Creswell blossomed in the job. He reorganized the Post Office, introduced the penny postcard, reduced the cost of overseas mail, extended free delivery, limited the franking privilege, revised postal treaties, and recodified postal laws. He advocated the creation of postal savings banks and a postal telegraph system.

Roscoe Conkling, Simon Cameron, and Zachariah Chandler, all radical political bosses who had been among Grant's strongest backers for the nomination. Grant felt most at east with these men, trusted them, often sought and followed their advice, and thought them his friends. Critics felt that Grant and his "kitchen cabinet" brought the "atmosphere of the headquarters tent" to the White House; it in fact gave the Radical political bosses an inside track with the president.

If many of Grant's major appointments shocked people, his minor appointments were even worse, "evangelists and cranks at home and abroad. At one time, forty-two of Grant's relatives were on the federal pay roll." * Grant seemed to view the presidency as an opportunity to pay personal debts and build a sort of disciplined hierarchy from whom he expected unquestioned loyalty. Opposition became disloyalty in his mind, an attitude his cronies exploited without Grant's realizing it.

If the Radical Republican bosses had the ear of the president almost to the exclusion of other Republicans, especially those interested in civil service reform, so did certain groups of businessmen. Grant admired successful businessmen, perhaps because he had been a business failure, perhaps because he felt they were partly responsible for winning the war. At any rate, he socialized in Washington with Henry D. Cooke, brother of financier Jay Cooke; he dined publicly in New York with both James Fisk and Jay Gould, the Erie Railroad tycoons, and rode on "Admiral" Fisk's boats; and he enjoyed the use of Commodore Vanderbilt's private railroad car.

The general had been used to deferential treatment by the wealthy, and it flattered him. Stewart, his nominee for the treasury secretaryship, had headed a group of millionaires that made available for his use a fully equipped house in Philadelphia. Hamilton Fish, among others, had raised funds to pay off the mortgage on Grant's Washington, D.C., house. That businessmen should have joined political bosses in the president's immediate circle illustrated another facet of American life in the postwar decades—the new primacy of industrialism in the United States. Not only were business leaders courting the president, their representatives wooed Congress as well. Their agents—the lobbyists—maintained full-time offices in

---

* Avery Craven, *Reconstruction: The Ending of the Civil War* (New York: Holt, Rinehart and Winston, c. 1969), p. 280.

the nation's capital in order to protect industry's wartime gains and seek new favors. John L. Hayes of the National Association of Wool Manufacturers and James M. Swank of the American Iron and Steel Association led the way. Even Congressman Oakes Ames worked for the Union Pacific Railroad and its construction company, the Crédit Mobilier.

Industrialists found Americans willing enough to follow *laissez-faire* American style, with the government aiding industry without regulating it. As nineteenth-century America moved toward the zenith of the industrial revolution, the dislocations hurt the farmers, exploited the working men, and intensified the growth of slums in the cities. Yet most Americans, clinging to their ever-present optimism where American destiny was concerned, had shed their prewar humanitarian idealism in favor of a new materialism that they believed would bring to the nation a utopia of peace, security, and comfort. Conditioned to fend for themselves, they ignored industrial selfishness, government graft, and social ills in order to develop a vibrant system of national production that in fact increased the standard of living measurably.

Grant, the soldier, like many of the men in Congress, understood little of the change in America, and uncritically accepted the new industrial order. Unlike most congressmen, Grant also understood little of the demands or workings of politics and government. Once he made up his mind on a matter, he had only the soldier's desire to be obeyed. Initially inclined to follow a moderate course with the South, his friends in that instance convinced him of the section's continuing disloyalty. As commander-in-chief of the army, Grant was largely responsible for the military support of the Republican regimes in the Southern states, just as his Radical Republican chums had known he would be if he followed their advice. Their counsel to Grant had little to do with protecting the lot of the black man, and a great deal to do with protecting the lot of the Republican party.

Grant magnified his ineptitude in appointing men and judging the character and motives of his friends with his equal ineptitude for diplomacy and politics. Witness his effort to annex Santo Domingo. Battling constant revolution, one of the leaders of the former Spanish colony that pretended to be a republic conceived the idea of annexing it to the United States, for a price. Some of the money would remain with leader Buenaventura Baez's faction, and some would find its way to Americans who facilitated annexation. Grant was impressed with Santo Domingo's potential—a land of sparse population that could support millions; plus an attractive harbor (the Bay of Samana) that would make, in the president's estimation, a fine coaling station for the navy.

In a flush of enthusiasm, Grant sent Babcock in July 1869 to look the situation over in Santo Domingo. Babcock returned with a treaty of annexation, which Grant presented to an astonished cabinet. Grant admitted Babcock had no diplomatic authority, and proposed to send him back to Santo Domingo to have the treaty signed by the U.S. consul, which, in Grant's opinion, would make the treaty legal. The dumbfounded cabinet replied with silence, until Cox asked the president if it had been decided that the United States wanted to annex Santo Domingo.

Fish later asked if Grant wanted his resignation, in view of the fact that the treaty had been negotiated without his knowledge. Grant refused it, but sent Babcock back to the island republic. With a properly executed treaty in hand, that provided for annexation of Santo Domingo for $1,500,000, Babcock returned to the United States and turned the document over to Grant. Grant sent it to the Senate.

Sumner, chairman of the Senate Foreign Relations Committee, opposed the treaty. Sumner assailed the irregular manner of the treaty's negotiation, and cries of fraud and corruption were raised. It appeared that Baez was being maintained in power by American speculators and the U.S. Navy. On June 30, 1870, the Senate refused to ratify the treaty. Grant blamed Sumner for the failure, and since he could not strike at Sumner in any other way, he had Sumner's friend, John L. Motley, recalled the very next day from his post as minister to England. Grant's action enraged Sumner, and the press carried a full account of their mutual recriminations.

Grant continued to press on with his project. He managed to get Congress, against Sumner's will, to create a commission to investigate the controversial subject. The commission ultimately reported in favor of annexation, whereupon Grant urged annexation either by treaty, which needed a two-thirds Senate vote, or by joint resolution of both houses, which required only a majority of each. Support for annexation was not to be found in Congress, and there the matter ended, though Grant continued to preach on its benefits. Grant and Sumner continued to feud, and as the attorney general remarked: "Each looked with a blood-shotten eye at the conduct of the other." Sumner would have been a valuable man for Grant to have had in his corner, but the useless quarrel made them enemies instead.

As Grant scratched for votes to pass the Santo Domingo Treaty, he appealed to Southern senators. Sumner, however, rated very high with them since he was a strong supporter of Radical reconstruction. If they were to support Grant against Sumner, they observed, they would need something tangible in return, such as Southern representation in the cabinet, perhaps the attorney generalship. Hoar had told Grant that his resignation was at Grant's disposal at any time, so Grant requested it on June 15, 1870. Grant replaced Hoar with Amos T. Akerman, a Georgia lawyer whom Hoar had proposed as a circuit court judge. The Southern senators had their way; Grant sacrificed one of his best cabinet appointments and lost the Santo Domingo Treaty as well.

Almost as if he were determined to rid his cabinet of its best minds, Grant next dismissed Cox. Cox's only mistake was his attempt to reform the Interior Department. Not only had Cox distressed the kitchen cabinet by shooting down an attempt of its friends to acquire certain California mining lands, thus preventing "a swindle," according to *The Nation*, but he had also tried to introduce civil service examinations and a merit system into the department, as well as to protect its clerks from political assessments. His actions ran directly counter to the needs of spoilsmen for patronage, and they attacked him bitterly. Cameron and Chandler denounced Cox to Grant, so when Cox offered to resign in October 1870, Grant snapped up the offer so rapidly there was no doubt that his sympathy was with the spoilsmen. Small wonder that Hoar, upon his resignation and while Cox was under attack, should have told Fish "to hold fast. You are the bulwark now standing between the country and destruction."

The press considered it "intolerable" the way Grant summarily dismissed first Motley, then Hoar, and then Cox. *The Nation* intimated that Hoar, who had "given a back-handed blow to many an impudent and arrogant disposer of patronage," could well return home proud of the enemies he had made. Grant's name became more and more associated with spoils and seamy politics. When he confronted the civil service reformers, it only served to put a seal on the rumors.

Carl Schurz and Lyman Trumbull, among others, had early convinced Grant to honor an 1871 bill empowering him to establish an advisory civil service commission to establish rules for hiring civil servants. Grant followed through by appointing George W. Curtis (of *Harper's Weekly*) as commission chairman. The machine politicians resented the civil service movement on the one hand, while reformers berated Grant for not strongly supporting them on the other. Grant, impatient with the bickering, accepted the resignation tendered to him by Curtis, who felt that he could expect no cooperation from the government. The civil service reformers now wholly mistrusted Grant, and almost to a man supported the liberal Republican movement in an effort to dump him. That only convinced Grant that they could not be trusted either, and he joined his spoilsmen cronies in denouncing civil service reform.

While upsetting to reformers and moderates, Grant's juggling showed only his lack of political finesse and the influence of the machine politicians on his administration. The outrageous scandals that marked his administration from the beginning, such as the "Black Friday" speculations of James Fisk, Jr., and Jay Gould, were much more disturbing. The pair owned the Erie Railroad primarily for their manipulations in its stock. They were quite a team: small, dark, clever, and quiet Gould, the brains of the operation, and Fisk, who was a large, florid, loud, man-about-town type. Gould, in 1869, figured that if he and Fisk could force the price of gold up, then Europeans who paid gold for wheat would buy more American wheat. This would stimulate the demand for Western wheat, as farmers would take advantage of the favorable market. Wheat would have to be carried to the East for shipment overseas, and the Erie Railroad, a large grain carrier, would reap the benefits.

The success of the plan hinged on their ability to boost the price of gold in New York: there was only about $20,000,000 of the metal available there, which changed hands continually as foreign trade balances and customs duties were settled in gold. Gould and Fisk felt confident the gold could be cornered if they could keep the government from selling its gold for bonds when the price of gold rose, something Boutwell did frequently. So Gould undertook to induce the president to restrain Boutwell from selling government gold for a time, which would make it possible for the pair to buy gold and drive the price up without fear of jeopardizing their operation.

Working through Grant's brother-in-law, Abel R. Corbin of New York, Gould and Fisk at length convinced Grant of the need to allow gold to rise in order to create a demand for Western wheat. Early in September, Grant ordered Boutwell to stop selling government gold, and Gould and Fisk at once began to buy. Gould bought large quantities for Corbin and others associated with the president. As the price of gold reached $140 (it had previously been at about $132 before the pair plunged into the market), businessmen who needed gold suffered greatly in their efforts to obtain it. They frantically urged Grant to sell government gold and drive the price down. Gould learned of the pleas to Grant, and knew that the president, under pressure, would soon order the sale of government gold again, so he began to sell out. Fisk, however, continued to stampede the price—on "Black Friday," September 24, it zoomed from $145 to $162 by noontime. Fisk, who saw himself as "the Napoleon of Wall Street," boasted he would drive the price above $200, and many feared he might have the power to do just that.

Gold had reached about $163 when the news came that government gold was selling again; by the close of trading that Friday the price had plummeted to $135. Boutwell had consulted with Grant that morning, pointing out that the gold corner was causing a severe business panic and threatened to disrupt the nation's economy. Grant had approved the decision to sell government gold, and Boutwell's telegram had reached New York a little after noon, bursting Fisk's bubble. Gould had sold enough to be able to honor his financial obligations; Fisk, who was caught with purchase orders at high levels, had no choice but to declare bankruptcy and forfeit his contracts. Fisk's brokers failed, as did many other businessmen who had bought gold at high prices on credit.

Grant had not financially benefited from the operation, and technically was not involved. Yet he had been used by Gould and Fisk in their unscrupulous operation. They had openly paraded their acquaintance with Grant and had let it be inferred they had the backing of the government. And they had had the connivance of Grant's own brother-in-law. Grant's personal innocence in the affair mattered little since, without the ability to manipulate him, "Black Friday" could not have occurred.

Grant had been made president by a Republican party that used him: used him to win an election that otherwise might have been in doubt; and used him as a figurehead to maintain the party

in power in order successfully to carry out their programs of reconstruction and finance. Grant had no policy of his own as president,
except for the popularly expressed notion of restoring peace to the
nation. When he sought to follow an expansionist course that he recalled had thrilled Americans several decades earlier, he bungled
the job. By not seeking advice on appointments, by siding with the
spoilsmen, and by allowing unscrupulous businessmen to use him,
Grant too spurned the moderates in his own party. He alienated
those who supported civil service reform and who were shocked by
scandal. Grant opened the door for the liberal Republican movement that threatened the party in 1872.

Unfinished Business Abroad

The expansionist or manifest destiny tendencies of American
foreign policy continued unabated at the conclusion of the Civil
War, as Seward enforced the Monroe Doctrine in Mexico and
jumped at the opportunity to purchase Alaska. Russia had found
Alaska to be more of a burden than an asset, and her encounter
with British naval power in the Crimean War persuaded her that
Britain, her neighbor in North America, could pluck Alaska whenever she thought it ripe. Russia concluded that this indefensible
burden should be disposed of, preferably to the United States, with
whom Russia had friendlier relations. Alaska in possession of the
United States would keep Britain from expanding her North American holdings to the very doorstep of Siberia. And in the hands of
the United States, Alaska would not be nearly so vulnerable to British power. The czar's plans were stalled by the war.

In 1867 Russia finally made her offer, and Seward accepted at
a price of $7,200,000. Yet a number of obstacles stood in the way of
ratification of the purchase treaty. Sumner's Senate Foreign Relations Committee had not been informed of the negotiations, and
Sumner, like other congressional Radicals, balked at any undertaking of Johnson's or Seward's, since Seward was clearly a Johnson
man. Also the treaty would have to be accepted by the House, since
that body would have to provide the appropriation. Seward argued
that rejection would estrange the United States from Russia, which
had unwaveringly supported the Union during the war. He convinced Sumner, whose committee reported favorably, bringing Senate ratification in April 1867. The treaty had a more difficult time

in the House, as the Radicals delayed it. Nevertheless the representatives subsequently approved the appropriation, and the United States took over Alaska in October. Lashing out at the Johnson administration, Republican papers called the purchase "Seward's Folly" and refused to recognize the price as a bargain for a land with great potential.

Seward was less successful in his effort to acquire the Virgin Islands. He steered a treaty through the proper Danish channels, but the Senate balked. On the other hand, Anson Burlingame, who had been minister to China since 1861, concluded a treaty of amity between the two nations, and successfully implemented a nineteenth century version of the "open door" policy. Burlingame also acted as an emissary for China in her negotiations with European powers.*

The United States had a minor diplomatic conflict with Britain after the war over Fenian activities,** but the major dispute concerned the *Alabama* claims. During the Civil War, Charles Francis Adams had presented the British with a bill for every vessel damaged by the *Alabama* and other British-built Confederate commerce destroyers. Adams had pressed for damages, including the value of the vessel and its cargo, as reparations for Britain's lax enforcement of her neutrality laws.

In 1868 Adams resigned as minister to England and was replaced by Reverdy Johnson, a Unionist Democrat from Maryland. The seventy-two-year-old lawyer's warm and courtly manners contrasted with the cool aloofness of Adams, and he found a warm welcome in London. By 1868, wartime passions had cooled and the English, the greatest commercial nation at sea, looked with perspective and interest on the vital question of neutral commerce in time of war. The British wanted to settle the *Alabama* claims, for if they engaged in some future war, the United States might very well let loose commerce destroyers against Britain in retaliation. So the question in fact revolved not around whether to settle but around how much they were willing to pay and the mechanics of settlement.

* Reference is to the Burlingame Treaty of 1868. Among other things, it recognized China's territorial integrity and pledged American noninterference in China's domestic affairs.
** Johnson quashed an attempted invasion of Canada from Maine by members of the Fenian Brotherhood which clamored for Irish independence, in April 1866. He also managed in 1870 to free Irish-American veterans taken prisoner by the British for their activities on behalf of Irish liberty.

Seward and President Johnson both eagerly sought a settlement that would bring credit to the Johnson administration and perhaps bolster its political stock. For the same reason, Stevens, Sumner, and the Radicals, busy with their plans to discredit Johnson, hoped the negotiations would fail. The Radical Republicans, in an effort to neutralize Reverdy Johnson's efforts, scored him for courting Englishmen who had not been friendly to the Union cause and accused him of discrediting Adams and thereby impairing national honor.

Even so, Reverdy Johnson concluded an agreement known as the Johnson-Clarendon Convention of 1869. It provided for a commission of two Englishmen and two Americans who would select an arbiter. All disputed claims would be referred to the arbiter, whose decision would be final. The agreement was fair enough, but it came at the wrong time to be acceptable to Americans. First of all, the political climate in the United States made it nearly impossible for a Radical-controlled Congress to accept an agreement made by an appointee of the Johnson administration, particularly at a time when the Radical Republicans still smoldered over their failure to impeach the president. And second, American confidence that they could have their way in foreign affairs was at a peak, especially following the successful conclusion of the Maximilian affair in Mexico.

The Johnson-Clarendon Convention came to a vote in the Senate in mid-April 1869, shortly after Grant had been inaugurated. Sumner spoke against the convention. He demanded reparations for all losses the United States suffered due to England's recognition of Confederate belligerency as well as for all losses that resulted from the activities of the commerce destroyers, and also for prolonging the war because of the South's continued hope that England would assist her. He went far beyond the original concept of settlement for the *Alabama* claims. His estimate of damages amounted to $2,115,000,000. He told the Senate he believed England would not pay that amount, but he felt it should be stated to make England realize the tremendous wrong she had done the United States.

Sumner's speech helped defeat the Convention by a vote of 54 to 1, and proved unwise in other ways. It raised American hopes for a settlement figure beyond what was practical or possible, and it became quite clear that if Americans insisted on such a figure, further negotiations were out of the question. No immediate overtures followed the defeat of the Johnson-Clarendon Convention, which allowed time to heal Sumner's sharp slash at the British.

It remained, then, for Secretary of State Hamilton Fish to re-open the subject. Fish considered a settlement of the *Alabama* claims very important, so he swallowed his distaste for Grant's opportunism in the Santo Domingo affair, supported Grant, and won a free hand in the negotiations with Britain. Fish carefully laid the groundwork, and in January 1871 Sir John Rose arrived in the United States with authority to conclude a treaty that would settle all matters in dispute between the two nations. In addition to the *Alabama* claims, this included fishing rights on the Newfoundland Banks, and the boundary between the United States and Canada in the Puget Sound area.

The agreement that resulted from the Fish-Rose talks, called the Treaty of Washington, provided for the *Alabama* claims and the boundary question to be settled by arbitration, and the fishing rights issue to be concluded by a joint commission. The treaty opened the way for *Alabama* claims settlement with a formal expression of England's regret over the escape of the *Alabama* and other vessels as well as the losses they had inflicted. It also attempted to define the role of neutral powers in future instances of a similar nature. Both assertions appeared to be advantageous to the American position if a tribunal considered them in making an award.

The *Alabama* claims case went to an arbitration tribunal made up of very distinguished statesmen and jurists, one each selected from the United States (Charles Francis Adams), England, Italy, Brazil, and Switzerland. The tribunal met in Geneva in 1871, and after some debate and the presentation of the case for both England and the United States, the judges ruled that England had had the responsibility to prevent the departure of the commerce destroyers. They awarded damages of $15,500,000 to the United States.

After taking into consideration certain British claims against America, Britain was awarded $1,900,000; and later, when the fisheries commission settled that question, Britain was awarded another $5,500,000 for American infringement on the Banks. In all, the United States owed about $7,500,000 to Britain, making the American return a total of about $8,000,000. The German emperor satisfactorily resolved the Puget Sound boundary. Americans were resentful that the *Alabama* claims had been whittled down, but it was perhaps the greatest victory in world history for arbitration. It thoroughly cleared the air between Britain and America by removing every important dispute between the two nations. And certainly, for the Grant administration it represented one very solid accomplishment in an era of few.

The Campaign of 1872

Serious political opposition to Grant from within his own party surfaced first in Missouri, when Missouri Senator Carl Schurz agreed to head a group of Republicans who desired a more liberal Southern policy. Within the state, Republicans divided on the question of reenfranchising Missouri Confederates. Schurz led those in favor, and with the support of Missouri Democrats, in 1870 elected as governor Benjamin Gratz Brown, former Free-Soiler, senator, and a founder of the Republican party in Missouri. They defeated Missouri's Radical Republicans.

Riding on their momentum, the Schurz-Gratz Brown group took the name of Liberal Republicans, met in convention in Jefferson City in January 1872, and invited all Republicans who opposed the Grant administration to join them in another meeting at Cincinnati in May. They received enthusiastic response from segments of the press, including the powerful Chicago *Tribune* and Cincinnati *Commercial*, plus cautious approval from *The Nation* and the New York *Evening Post*. Democratic journals, such as the Louisville *Courier-Journal* and the New York *World* expressed considerable interest, while Greeley's New York *Tribune* endorsed the movement with reservations about the Liberal Republican call for tariff reform.

The Liberal Republicans attracted a number of nationally known figures to their ranks. Former Interior Secretary Cox, Illinois Senator Trumbull, Supreme Court Justice Davis, and ailing Senator Charles Sumner joined. It seemed clear to these men that the Republican party, in its search for identity, had to face the future with a renewed moral cause, and they were willing to settle for government reform and an end to corruption and the spoils system. In addition, they felt the party must heal over the running sore of an outmoded Southern policy, and they must begin by ousting Grant.

The Liberal Republicans nevertheless had to overcome a serious handicap. It had been the Democrats who had been calling for reform and who had insisted upon such policies as a moderate tariff and a speedy reconstruction of Southern states. The image the

Republicans had fostered was that of a Democratic party of Copperheads and traitors. They could not now simply embrace Democratic views without opening themselves to severe criticism and providing the Democrats with fresh ammunition. Neither could they close their eyes to graft and corruption as Grant seemed to do. They had to face the fact that the general remained popular in spite of the scandals, because the scandals did not taint his reputation as a war hero. Moreover, they had to face the fact that the orientation of most Republicans on an emotional level was still toward past glory, toward saving the Union, destroying slavery, and winning the holy war: Republicans looked to the past. On the practical level, the Republican party orientation favored business, which brought in campaign funds and financial support in return for government favors. Liberal Republicans had to deal with the problems of how to appear as a reform group without inviting Democratic attacks, and how to reorient the party on the emotional level and get it to look to the future.

A course of action which few Republicans considered was to bolt the party and lead a revolt to set up a new party. Since that was not practical, the Liberal Republicans had little recourse but to try to assume control of the Republican party. To accomplish that, they needed votes. They knew they could not count on support from the regular party organization. The solution seemed to be to appeal to rank and file Republicans by openly breaking with Grant, by accusing him of having betrayed Republican principles with his blindness to graft and corruption, and by announcing they wanted a return to honest old Republican ideals. In this way they could steer clear of the Democrats and make the strongest appeal to their own party. Liberal Republicans thus continued to denounce Democrats as a collection of unprincipled scoundrels, who might redeem themselves if they wished by voting with the Liberal Republicans for those principles they had paid lip service to in recent years.

The Democrats should disband, chorused the Horaces, Greeley of New York and White of the Chicago *Tribune*, as they left for Cincinnati to support the Liberal Republican movement. Greeley, White, and other newsmen played a major role in the convention. They were able to do so because the men who attended the convention were not formally chosen delegates, were split into factions, and never really achieved unity.

Schurz was chosen permanent president of the convention,

which removed him from the floor leadership where his talents might have been better used for shaping a realistic platform and choosing a candidate. The platform included a demand for the removal of "all disabilities" imposed on Southerners because of the war and a similar demand for the states to govern themselves without federal interference. Civil service reform was a prominent feature, but the platform equivocated on the tariff, remanding the subject to Congress. While the tariff stand was a compromise to insure the support of Greeley and the New York *Tribune*, nearly any Liberal Republican could support the platform.

Charles Francis Adams and Horace Greeley emerged as the leading contenders for the nomination, with Trumbull, Gratz Brown, David Davis, and a few others trailing. Gratz Brown threw his support to Greeley, and on the sixth ballot 8,000 boisterous conventioneers cheered the newsman's nomination, with 482 votes to Adams' 187. Gratz Brown won the vice presidential nomination. Reid, Brown, and the Greeleyites—New Yorkers, New Jerseymen, and Southerners—were of course elated. Adams supporters, including Schurz, Halstead, Bowles, Watterson, and White, were disappointed. Greeley would appeal to former Democrats and perhaps to regular Democrats, but long-time Republicans would have preferred Adams to the vain editor.

On June 5 the regular Republican convention met in Philadelphia, with blacks and Southern white Republicans very conspicuous among the delegates. A North Carolina judge became president of the convention. The platform endorsed Grant and the work of the Republican Congress. The convention unanimously renominated Grant and with little difficulty picked as his running mate Henry Wilson, a Radical Republican Senator from Massachusetts.

On July 9 the Democrats held their meeting in Baltimore. Southerners, indifferent to civil service reform and wanting home rule more than they did a lower tariff, still remembered that it was Greeley who had signed Jefferson Davis' bail bond; they were determined to back the editor. Northern Democrats generally opposed Greeley, but knew full well that the party's hope for success was to support and concentrate the opposition to Grant. The convention was a curious one, wrote *The Nation*, full of "the old politicians who have so long been absent from national conventions, famous warhorses and eaters of fire" who had been leaders "before the deluge," and "who have since been statesmen in the Confederacy, emigrants to Brazil, [and] residents in Canada." *The Nation* considered the convention "intellectually" inferior to the Republican gathering at Philadelphia and filled with "negro-hating and office-seeking" hypocrites. The Democrats dutifully accepted the Liberal Republican platform, and nominated Greeley and Gratz Brown.

The ensuing campaign quickly became personal. On the one side loomed Grant the hero, perhaps all the more popular because his errors made him seem human. The Grant campaign managers worked hard to discredit Greeley. They presented the editor as a tariff protectionist who headed a party of tariff reformers, as the Democrats historically had been. They castigated him as an opponent of civil service reform leading the civil service reformers, as the Liberal Republicans certainly were. Thomas Nast, the great political cartoonist, furiously scratched out anti-Greeley cartoons with a sharp pen dipped in the ink of ridicule.

Businessmen supported Grant because business was good and they feared change. Greeley was an uncertain quantity to them. Rank and file Republicans remained with the man who, with Lincoln, had saved the nation in the war. The Democrats knew the campaign was all but over and Grant back in the White House when their candidates failed by substantial margins in the October elections in Pennsylvania and Ohio. Their narrow victory in the Indiana gubernatorial contest was no consolation, since Hoosiers chose a Republican legislature.

On November 5 the Liberal Republicans, Democrats, and Greeley went down to a crushing defeat. Greeley carried six states— Georgia, Kentucky, Maryland, Missouri, Tennessee, and Texas— for 66 electoral votes. Grant carried the remainder, including Greeley's home state of New York, for 286 electoral votes,* and over 55 percent of the popular vote. It seemed clear that the nation was not yet inclined to accept either reform or change.

The vicissitudes of the campaign wounded thin-skinned and vain Greeley, but his sorrow multiplied as his wife died October 30. On November 5 he lost the election, and on November 29, he too died. After the death of his wife and his defeat, Greeley admitted: "I have been assailed so bitterly that I hardly knew whether I was

---

* Grant, 286 electoral votes, 3,597,375 popular votes, for 55.6 percent. Greeley, who died before the electoral votes were counted, won 2,833,711 popular votes for 43.8 percent of the total. His electoral votes were scattered between Thomas A. Hendricks (42), an Indiana Democrat, B. Gratz Brown (18), and other candidates, with 17 electoral votes not cast.

running for President or Penitentiary. . . . Well I am used up." Yet the despairing Greeley had served a purpose. In supporting the Liberal Republicans the Democrats had pledged to "maintain" the Union, to bury controversy over the Thirteenth, Fourteenth, and Fifteenth Amendments, to preserve public credit and "denounce repudiation," all of which put the party once more on a positive track. It also gave status to the party's claim for reform, and provided Americans with food for thought in the reaction against corruption. Perhaps Americans weren't ready for reform or political change, but the effort to get Americans to put the past behind them and look to the future had influenced a large portion of the voters.

Grant's Second Term

During the campaign, the New York *Sun* broke the Crédit Mobilier story, with the allegation that the Union Pacific Railroad operated a construction ring that had distributed $9,000,000 worth or 30,000 shares of Crédit Mobilier stock (Crédit Mobilier was the company, headed by Union Pacific officials, that built the transcontinental railroad) as bribes to government officials, mostly members of Congress. Vice President Schuyler Colfax, Secretary of the Treasury George S. Boutwell, a couple of senators and former senators, the Speaker of the House and six other House members, and a couple of former representatives were all included. The Greeley campaigners crowed about it, Republican campaigners branded it a lie, and the issue had virtually no influence on the campaign.

James G. Blaine, Speaker of the House, resented the allegations that tied him into the Crédit Mobilier, and asked for an investigation. House and Senate committees complied. They found that the Crédit Mobilier made a $23,000,000 profit on its activities, and in 1868 had begun to divide its earnings among its shareholders. Shareholders received dividends consisting of a small amount of cash, a larger amount of first mortgage bonds, and a still larger amount of railroad stock. Distribution of stock was in violation of the charter, which required all stock to be issued for cash only. In addition, Oakes Ames, a wealthy congressman from Massachusetts, had in fact distributed stock at par value—even though it was worth twice that amount—to congressmen, even lending them the money to purchase the stock if they otherwise could not afford it. Ames had done so to head off a congressional investigation that would perhaps uncover the charter violation. Initially successful, Ames was unable to shortcircuit the subsequent investigation. The House censured both Ames and a New York congressman; Colfax might well have been impeached except that he was about to leave office. The scandal wrecked his career. The Senate committee recommended expulsion of a New Hampshire senator, but as his term was nearly over, they simply allowed him to depart. Others were acquitted, including many prominent figures in Congress. The situation left a markedly bad impression on the nation.

No sooner was the Crédit Mobilier affair fading from the news, than the public was incensed by the congressional "Salary Grab" Act passed March 3, 1873. As the lame duck Forty-second Congress closed its deliberations, it passed a law increasing the salaries of government officials, including senators and representatives. It increased congressmen's salaries by $2500* and made the increase retroactive. The following Congress repealed the law as it related to legislators, but even so the "salary grab" aroused voters enough to make the 1874 congressional elections a disaster for many incumbents.

Two months after the "Salary Grab" Act a House committee uncovered yet another scandal. John D. Sanborn, a protégé of Benjamin F. Butler of Massachusetts, had received a federal contract to collect overdue internal revenue claims at a 50 percent commission. He managed to recover $427,000, for which he received $213,500 in fees. He claimed to have paid out $156,000 in expenses, which was interpreted as a kickback to the Butler machine in Massachusetts. The contract was legal enough, if ridiculous, and Sanborn was not indicted. William A. Richardson, of Massachusetts, the secretary of the treasury who had approved the contracts, escaped a vote of censure only by resigning. Congress amended the situation after the fact by passing a law outlawing similar contracts in the future.

The Crash of 1873

On the business front in the summer of 1873, everything looked encouraging. Railroads in 1872 alone had built 6,000 miles of track, a vivid jump over the annual 2,000-mile average during the years 1865 through 1868. Agriculture continued to expand dramatically, with nearly 20,000,000 new acres brought under the plow between

* Congressmen's paychecks rose from $5000 annually to $7500.

1867 and 1873. The amount of capital invested in business, from both foreign and domestic sources, more than doubled in the decade from 1860 to 1870. Credit expanded as the establishment of national banks, the sale of war bonds, and the expansion of currency provided much of the base; the sale of both government and industrial securities further increased the inward flow of capital. The prosperity of the late 1860s and early 1870s fostered a confidence in business affairs that boosted the price of land, bonds, and stocks to highly speculative levels.

Hidden in the scramble for speculative profit were an increasing number of economic danger signals. The inflationary price rises in the iron and steel that railroads used in huge quantities meant that banking houses like Jay Cooke and Company were needed to finance railroad construction. Jay Cooke and Company carried the Northern Pacific, for example, while Fisk and Hatch supported the Chesapeake and Ohio. Even they had to offer their own bonds at speculative rates in order to attract buyers, and they, by mid-1873, found their needs outstripping the money supply. Eager European buyers of American securities turned cautious when the Vienna market suffered a financial panic in May 1873, and Europeans began to dispose of or cease to purchase American stocks and bonds. That meant that rapidly expanding American industry placed overwhelming demands on domestic capital.

Railroad and agricultural expansion consumed tremendous amounts of credit, and natural disaster had already weakened the amount of money available. On Sunday, October 8, 1871, a fire levelled over 2,000 acres of Chicago, causing a property loss of over $200,000,000. On November 9, 1872, a fire destroyed about 65 acres of Boston, for another loss of $73,000,000. As insurance companies strove to meet their commitments, some failed, and others had to liquidate investments and call in loans in order to break even. The financial substructure of the domestic economy suffered just at the time when it had to bear the brunt of expansion by itself.

On September 18, 1873, Jay Cooke and Company could no longer find the necessary funds to sustain the Northern Pacific, and announced that they were bankrupt. Their announcement was greeted with "derisive incredulity on the part of the mercantile public," at first, but on the exchange leading stocks promptly fell twenty to thirty points. On the next day the banking house of Fisk and Hatch fell, and panic reigned in the market. On September 20 the exchange closed for eight days. Money became so scarce that people began to withdraw it from the banks to hoard, producing more bank failures. When the financiers failed or could no longer supply money, railroad building stopped. Manufacturers found themselves with heavy inventories and cancelled orders, so plants closed down. Laborers on the railroads and factory workers were thrown out of work, decreasing purchasing power. That, in turn, caused manufacturers of general merchandise either to close down or cut back, further aggravating the situation. The panic of 1873 gave way to a bleak depression that lasted for several years.

The financial collapse and the steady revelation of scandal in government meant that there was no way in which the Republicans could escape a public expression of displeasure in the elections of 1874. Yet few expected so deep a reaction as that which followed. The Republican party lost eighty-nine seats in the House and four in the Senate. For the first time since the Civil War the Democrats won a majority in the lower house of Congress. At the same time, Samuel J. Tilden, who had become famous for prosecuting the Tweed Ring in New York City and for putting boss William Marcy Tweed behind bars, was elected Democratic governor of New York.*

Scandal was all the more shocking to people struggling with a depression. Reformer Benjamin H. Bristow of Kentucky, who followed Richardson into the Treasury, in 1875 uncovered yet another mess within his department. A group of distillers in St. Louis had defrauded the government out of millions of dollars in whisky taxes with the connivance of a supervisor of internal revenue. Grant's own private secretary, Babcock, was intimately connected with the Whisky Ring. Grant intervened in the trials and successfully got Babcock acquitted, while the internal revenue supervisor went to prison along with several of his fellow conspirators. But the outcry against Babcock was so great that even Grant could not keep him in the White House for very long. The Whisky Ring case dragged on in the press for over a year, with freely aired suspicions that Grant was also involved. Faithfulness and trust for his friends was one of Grant's best traits, but his poor judgment of character in this case betrayed him. Grant became so hostile to the treasury secretary

* The Tweed Ring had bilked New York City of over $30,000,000 in municipal building funds. Tweed had controlled the Tammany Hall Democratic organization.

who had uncovered the whole affair that Bristow resigned in June 1876.

While the Whisky Ring scandal was winding down in the spring of 1876, a congressional committee in March "found . . . uncontradicted evidence of the malfeasance in office by General William W. Belknap," the secretary of war. Belknap, of Iowa, directly received payments from an Indian agent at Fort Sill, Indian Territory, in order that the agent might keep his appointment. Payments of $6,000 a year first went to Mrs. Belknap, and upon her death, directly to Belknap himself. Another $6,000 a year went to a friend of Mrs. Belknap provided that he would not seek the appointment.

The committee recommended that Belknap be impeached, and the House passed a resolution to that effect. Belknap promptly sent his resignation to his long-time friend, Grant, who accepted it immediately, thwarting impeachment. Belknap's guilt was as clear as Grant's move to save him from trial. Scandal after scandal had marked Grant's administration, singeing his very whiskers several times. And the depression had begun after Grant's last election. In 1876, the nation faced the next presidential contest.

The Election of 1876

Grant's supporters continued to urge his renomination and candidacy for a third term. Grant, himself, was not especially unwilling, but the House of Representatives in an unprecedented move resolved that "it would be unwise, unpatriotic, and fraught with perils" for the president to seek a third term. This resolution passed the House in December 1875 by the overwhelming vote of 234 to 18. The resolution, along with the Democratic gains of 1874, the scandals, and the depression, combined to make Grant widely unacceptable. Grant men turned to Roscoe Conkling of New York and Oliver P. Morton of Indiana as possible candidates.

The rank and file, however, preferred James G. Blaine. When the Republican convention opened in Cincinnati on June 14 and got down to the business of nominations, Robert G. Ingersoll, the great orator from Illinois, nominated Blaine. "Like a plumed knight . . . Blaine marched down the halls of . . . Congress and threw his shining lance full and fair against the brazen forehead of every traitor." It would not do, he reminded the delegates, "to desert that gallant man" now. Blaine led the field in the early balloting, but his own indiscretions had already come back to roost, and a stop-Blaine movement dashed his chances. Blaine had been suspected of improper relations with an Arkansas railroad, and only weeks before the convention had defended himself by reading to the House the "Mulligan letters," his correspondence with an officer of the railroad. One James Mulligan had told a House committee that the letters incriminated Blaine, detailing his investment in Little Rock and Fort Smith Railroad securities and the use of his position in Congress to profit from it. Although Blaine's defense had been clever and apparently successful, his opponents in the convention felt the party should not take the chance of nominating one who had even flirted with scandal. The same group opposed Conkling and Morton, and in a reform spirit backed Bristow, the former treasury secretary who had uncovered the Whisky Ring.

Yet on the fifth ballot in the convention, Blaine still held first place and was within 70 votes of the nomination. Blaine's opposition, fearing that he might win, engineered a shift to Ohio's favorite son, Rutherford B. Hayes. Conkling, Morton, and Bristow withdrew in favor of Hayes, and on the seventh ballot Hayes nosed out Blaine 384 to 351. The nomination lost, a Blaine lieutenant moved that it be made unanimous for Hayes, and the convention responded. Curiously enough, it was the spoilsmen, Conkling and Morton and their group, who cooperated with the reformers, many of them former Liberal Republicans, to defeat Blaine. Hayes was acceptable to the reformers because of his unblemished character and his regard for civil service reform; he was acceptable, too, to the spoilsmen, who feared Blaine as too independent. Besides, Conkling and Blaine had been open enemies for years, their personal vendetta delighting congressmen whenever they tangled. The convention chose William A. Wheeler, of New York, for second spot on the ticket.

On June 28, the Democrats assembled in St. Louis. They naturally attacked both Grant and the Republican party, and made out a strong case for across-the-board reform. They also in their platform called for "home rule" in the South: an end to reconstruction. The Democrats chose the leading contender for the nomination, New York Governor Samuel J. Tilden. For vice president they selected Thomas A. Hendricks of Indiana. Tilden, the wealthy corporation lawyer and New York City reformer, was well known nationally for his anti-corruption activities.

Basically a conservative, Tilden had made his money in railroads and in speculation. He fought Pendleton in 1868 because he felt the "Ohio Idea" was financially unsound. Democratic liberals were aware of this, and were not overjoyed with his nomination. Neither was a large bloc of the Democratic party for, being the party out of power for so long, they lusted after their share of the spoils and eschewed reform. Western and Southern Democrats were not pleased with Eastern leadership, which partly explained the presence of Westerner Hendricks on the ticket. Yet the White House, as the Democrats well knew, was in reach only if the strongest reformer headed the ticket. And that was Tilden.

The Republican platform, like the Democratic platform, was reform-oriented and general. With little choice in policy, the main issue shifted again to sectional discord. The House of Representatives had before it an amnesty bill that would have exempted those former Confederates still under civil disability. Blaine moved to exempt Jefferson Davis from it, charging him with the responsibility for Andersonville. This waving of the bloody shirt brought forth a warm reply from Southern legislators, reviving the sectional issue and in fact making it a campaign question. Blaine, of course, hoped it would offset Grant's record of corruption and the depression.

Federal officials, products of the spoils system, swung into line behind Hayes. Morton and even Conkling delivered speeches, realizing that victory would blot out previous scandal and continue their influence in Washington. Blaine chastized Copperheads as traitors, and implored veterans to vote "as they shot." He told audiences that a Democratic victory would cost faithful patriots the fruits of the peace.

Democrats emphasized harmony for the nation and the tradition of local self government, exaggerated Carpetbagger and Scalawag graft and corruption in the South, and pointed out how congressional reconstruction had failed. They boasted of their reform candidates in contrast to Grant's grafters. Republicans in turn displayed Hayes's open honesty and pointed to Republican accomplishments. They played up Southern riots in order to prey upon Northern fears that Southerners intended to keep the freedmen in bondage by one means or another. Although both Hayes and Tilden kept out of it personally, their managers resorted to the usual mud-slinging.

On election night, November 7, it appeared as if Tilden had scored a victory. On the basis of incomplete returns he had won 184 of the 185 electoral votes needed for victory, and he clearly led in the popular vote. Both Democratic and Republican headquarters proclaimed victory, but in the next few days as the results became clearer, Tilden still had his 184 electoral votes, Hayes claimed 165, and 20 electoral votes were in dispute. Tilden still had the better of it in popular totals, with 4,287,670 and 50.9 percent of the vote to Hayes's 4,035,924, or 47.9 percent of the vote. Greenbacker Peter Cooper polled over 82,000 votes, and a prohibition candidate nearly another 10,000. But the fact remained that Tilden needed one more electoral vote, and Hayes needed 20 before either could be declared elected. The disputed returns included one from Oregon, four from Florida, seven from South Carolina, and eight from Louisiana.

In Oregon, the three Hayes electors won a thousand more votes than their Democratic counterparts. One of the Hayes electors, however, was a postmaster and as such was constitutionally barred from serving in the Electoral College. The Democratic governor of Oregon appointed a Democrat to replace the unlawful Republican elector, which resulted in two sets of returns from Oregon, one with three votes for Hayes and another with two for Hayes and one for Tilden. No Republican and very few Democrats thought there was much room for argument over the clearly Republican vote in that state. The focal point was the contested returns in Florida, Louisiana, and South Carolina. Had those three states been in the hands of Southern redeemers as were the eight other Southern states that gave their vote solidly to Tilden, there would have been no contest over the election. Although the Democrats used every means at their disposal to hold down the black vote and get out the white vote, the returning boards were still controlled by Republicans.

Both parties sent delegations to Florida, Louisiana, and South Carolina to oversee the count, and, apparently, to watch each other. In Florida, where the returning board consisted of one Democrat and two Republicans, it certified four electoral votes for Hayes and declared the Republican candidate elected governor. The Democrats, with clear majorities in both houses of the Florida legislature, demanded a recount and got it with an order from the Republican state Supreme Court. The recount put the Democratic gubernatorial candidate in office by a slim margin, and Democrats returned four electoral votes for Tilden. Both the original Hayes set of electoral votes and the alternate set of Tilden electoral votes were forwarded to the United States Senate.

If the South Carolina returns were taken at face value, the Democrats were victorious all along the line, including seven electoral votes for Tilden. The Republican-controlled returning board, however, observed more votes than registered voters in many precincts, and certified the election of Hayes electors. Both the Republican and Democratic candidates for governor claimed election, and both were inaugurated, with federal troops protecting the Republican. And, like Florida, two sets of electoral returns reached the United States Senate.

In Louisiana, Democratic electors apparently had secured substantial victories over their Republican opponents. But the Republican returning board noted the illegal activities of the whites in intimidating black voters, observed that counties which had black voters outnumbering whites had returned large white majorities, and threw out the returns. They certified the election of eight Hayes electors. Democrats forwarded the eight Tilden votes to the Senate. Therefore, the Senate had two sets of electoral returns from the three Southern states.

Both Republicans and Democrats claimed they had been victims of fraud in the three contested states, and doubtless both had been. Each had practiced ballot box stuffing and intimidation. Both had tried to bribe the returning boards, but in that contest the Republicans had more to offer, and subsequently did tender federal jobs to Republican officials. Democrats indignantly shouted, "Tilden or fight!" and the Republicans seemed quite willing to take them up on it. Tempers flared as the two sets of returns came in. Both Houses of Congress sent investigating committees to the Southern states. No one had yet been elected president.

With the returns disputed, the question of how the electoral vote would be counted became critical. Neither the Constitution, nor the law, nor the rules of Congress, nor precedent, nor custom offered a solution acceptable to both parties. The Twelfth Amendment to the Constitution stated that "the President of the Senate shall, in the presence of the Senate and the House of Representa-

tives, open all the certificates, and the votes shall then be counted."
But it does not designate who shall actually count. Republicans believed the Republican president of the Senate should do the job,
while Democrats thought the Democratic Speaker of the House
should.* In the one case, Republican returns would be counted, in
the other, the Democratic ones. If done by some joint House-Senate
arrangement, the Democrats would win.

Since neither candidate had a clear majority of the electoral
votes, the Democrats demanded the election be thrown into the
House, as another section of the Twelfth Amendment provided, but
the Republicans refused to consider that alternative. Other disturbing questions arose as well. Must the state returns be accepted on
their face, or could Congress go behind the official state returns in
an effort to determine who in fact had won the election? The Republicans claimed Congress could not; the Democrats believed Congress could. If Congress could come to no solution by inauguration
day, March 4, 1877, who would be the President of the United
States? Would Grant remain in office? And if the dilemma resulted
in another appeal to arms, where was the advantage? The Republicans controlled the scattered units of the regular army, but Democratic governors controlled the state militia.

The Compromise of 1877

The year 1876 drew to a close with no prospect of a solution.
The debate on Capitol Hill became angrier and members came to
the sessions of Congress armed, reminding observers of antebellum
days. Behind the scenes, meanwhile, Ohio Congressman James A.
Garfield proposed to Hayes a means of dividing the Democrats.
Democratic businessmen, he felt, were "more anxious for quiet than
Tilden." Southerners in Congress, Garfield believed, particularly
those who were formerly Whigs, had seen trouble enough and were
not eager to "follow the lead of their Northern associates who were
invincible in peace and invisible in war." If Republicans could win
over the ex-Whig Southern Democrats and in so doing split the
Democratic party, they could put Hayes in the White House.

---

* The 44th Congress, elected in 1874, was composed of 45 Republicans and 29 Democrats
in the Senate, and 169 Democrats and 109 Republicans in the House; the Senate had 2 of
neither party, the House 14. The 44th Congress, meeting in lame duck session, faced the dilemma above, for the new Congress, the 45th, would not convene until 1877. But it would
have made little difference. The line-up in the 45th Congress was: Senate—39 Republican,
36 Democrat, 1 other; House—153 Democrat, 140 Republican.

The idea was not new to Hayes, who had been approached by other Republican leaders with the same idea. Garfield told Hayes the idea might work if it were quietly pursued and if Southerners, who were disgruntled with Northern leadership and with Tilden, knew Hayes would treat them well. He had heard from Southerners the opinion that they would be better treated by Republicans on questions of internal improvements, which the South badly needed, than by Democrats pledged to reform. Besides, Garfield believed, many of the former Whigs were still distressed at the need to be in the Democratic party at all. Garfield urged Hayes to move rapidly to implement the plan. Hayes had, in fact, made it known to certain Southern leaders that he believed congressional reconstruction had been unsuccessful and that black justice would best be achieved by entrusting Southern government to honorable and influential Southern whites. Certain Southerners had been impressed with this attitude, but at the same time it could spell trouble for Hayes within his own party. Rapprochement with Southern white, ex-Whig leaders would have to be carried out as inconspiciously as possible.

A willing group that could act quietly, behind the scenes, existed. They were the officers and correspondents of the Western Associated Press, men like Halstead, of the Cincinnati *Commercial*, president of the organization; Joseph Medill of the Chicago *Tribune*; Andrew J. Kellar of the Memphis *Avalanche*; William H. Smith, the chief WAP correspondent in Chicago; Henry Boynton, WAP Washington correspondent; and others. Garfield, Kellar, a former Douglas Democrat who had followed Tennessee out of the Union, and Boynton, a Union veteran from Massachusetts, son of an abolitionist, critic of Grant, and a reformer, began to sound out the situation in Washington.

Kellar knew, for example, that prior to 1856 Southerners were fairly equally divided between Whigs and Democrats, and that after the disappearance of the Whig party many ex-Whigs, who were reluctant to follow the lead of their old political foes, the Democrats, had cast their lot instead for American or Constitutional Union Party candidates. During reconstruction, the white supremacy issue produced temporary alliances of former secessionists and Unionists, ex-Whigs and Democrats, as they sought together to control the destiny of their own states and oppose congressional reconstruction. The labels "Bourbons" and "Redeemers" only reflected the effort to oust carpetbag reconstruction state governments, and failed to take into account the existence of the old and more enduring division on the philosophical lines that had been represented by the Whig party. It was that seam in the South that Kellar wanted to exploit; that Garfield believed still existed; and that Hayes and other Republicans saw as a way to gain the White House.*

Characteristic of the conservative, business-oriented, former Whig group within the Democratic party were aging ex-Whigs, ex-Unionists, ex-non-Democrats of all sorts who desired both federal economic assistance and strong state control of state affairs. They sought black votes so long as black votes strengthened their position. Many of them bore famous names in the South: governors Vance of North Carolina, Augustus H. Garland of Arkansas, George F. Drew of Florida, John C. Brown and subsequently James D. Porter of Tennessee were all former Whigs. In the House of Representatives, twenty-six former Whigs, including Benjamin Hill and Alexander Stephens of Georgia, chafed at the leadership of Northern Democrats.

Some of these same individuals and other leading Southerners had important business connections as well. The Texas and Pacific Railroad employed a former governor of Tennessee as a vice president, as well as a former governor of Texas. Colonel Arthur S. Colyar, Democratic boss in Tennessee, was a leading official in the Tennessee Iron and Coal Company. The Southern Pacific Railroad wooed General John B. Gordon of Georgia, as they did Zachary Taylor's only son, Louisiana General Richard C. Taylor. An Alabama governor linked his political and economic fortunes with the Louisville and Nashville Railroad. And so it went.

In the natural course of events, these Southern Whig-Democrats (as distinguished from "regular" Democrats) reacted much the same in politics as some Northern Republicans and some former Southern Republican regimes, in using public office for personal gain. They did not hesitate to vote lucrative franchises or dispose of natural resources to business interests, and they actively opposed any restraint on free enterprise. Their goals and objectives, subtracting reconstruction and Civil War-bred emotions, paralleled those of Northern Republicans.

* See, for example, the detailed account in C. Vann Woodward, *Reunion and Reaction* (2nd edn., revised, Garden City: Doubleday and Company, 1956); and also Rembert W. Patrick, *The Reconstruction of the Nation* (New York: Oxford University Press, 1967), Ch. XI.

In order to be effective and win political leadership in their section, Southern Whig-Democrats needed issues that brought in the votes. Federal patronage, internal improvements, rebuilding and expanding railroads and industry were not enough. Home rule had the mass appeal necessary. If the Southern Whig-Democrats could use the present presidential election controversy to rid the South of the last vestige of Republican reconstruction governments, of federal troops, and win an end to federal interference in the South, they felt they could secure the ballot-power to entrench themselves in firm control. And they could see possibilities in Hayes that they failed to find in Tilden. Tilden had spoken of federal reform, of an end to graft-tinged patronage, of an end to federal subsidy to business such as the land grants, which probably meant an end to internal improvements. But Hayes, though pledged to reform, represented the national party of business. Most encouraging, this Republican candidate had not himself invoked the bloody-shirt; he said he was willing to put the black man in the hands of Southern whites, for he trusted their sense of honor and justice. If Southern Whig-Democrats cooperated with Hayes, and saw him into the White House, Hayes would owe them a debt. Repayment could very well include a final end to reconstruction—home rule for the South—and the door would still be open on patronage and internal improvements.

Results of the election so far as the composition of Congress was concerned were not lost on either Republican leaders or Hayes. The Democrats had maintained their control of the House (153–140) and cut the Republican majority in the Senate dramatically (39 Republicans, 36 Democrats, 1 other). Democrats could have ended appropriations for an army used to maintain reconstruction in the South, so removal of the last federal troops was possible without a presidential directive. Anyway, only a few remained: in October 1876, on the eve of the election, they totalled just over 6,000, down from the 20,000 of a decade before. For all practical purposes, Democrats had in fact won control of all the Southern states. What then, was left to compromise about on that score?

Obviously, even the small occupational force could be effective in protecting black voters in those areas where intimidation of blacks was thought necessary to insure white victories. Hayes' expressed sympathy for Southern whites represented no guarantee the troops would not in the future be used again. He might very well be subjected to Northern pressure for protection of the blacks. So Southern Whig-Democrats wanted concrete assurances of an end to military occupation. And, if they could also gain patronage or federal assistance in addition, they stood to make very real gains from Hayes.

Unwilling to overlook any device that might help deliver Whig-Democrat support for Hayes, Boynton made a case to Hayes for an exception to the new Republican policy that opposed federal subsidy to business. There were those in Arkansas, Western Tennessee, Kentucky, Louisiana, Texas, and Mississippi, he wrote, who wanted assistance for the Texas and Pacific Railroad. Thomas A. Scott, formerly Lincoln's railroad manager and at the time president of both the Pennyslvania Railroad and the Texas Pacific, could use his powerful lobby to get Whig-Democrat votes for Hayes if he were properly motivated to do so, Boynton told Hayes. Boynton pointed out that many Whig-Democrats stood to gain from the success of the Texas Pacific.

Democrat Montgomery Blair, through his paper, the Washington *Union*, claimed that the Texas Pacific interests had been enlisted to take the election away from Tilden, and condemned Southern Democrats, whom he felt were cooperating with Republicans, as men who would destroy the Democratic party. Actually, Blair's open accusation only widened the rift between the Whig-Democrats and the Northern Democrats. Kellar, from the pages of the Memphis *Avalanche*, called Blair's attack a journalistic "abortion."

While the action behind the scenes accelerated, Congress, after a month of deliberation, established a bipartisan Electoral Commission on January 18, 1877. The commission was to include fifteen members, five each from the House, Senate, and Supreme Court. It would be composed of three House Democrats and two House Republicans, two Senate Democrats and three Senate Republicans, and two Supreme Court Democrats and two Supreme Court Republicans, with the choice of the fifth Justice left to the Court. Everyone assumed the choice would be independent David Davis of Illinois. The Electoral Commission's decision on the disputed returns was to be final.

Democrats had been in favor of the commission in overwhelming numbers, while Republicans had been divided. Democrats felt they had won a significant victory, for they needed only one of the twenty contested votes to elect Tilden, and they felt their chances were very good. Their elation lasted only a week, for on January 25 the Illinois legislature elected David Davis to the United States Senate, and the judge immediately declared himself ineligible to serve on the commission. Yet the Democrats were firmly committed to the Electoral Commission, and could not very well change their minds. Elation gave way to uncertainty, for the remainder of the Supreme Court justices were all Republicans. The Court chose Justice Joseph Bradley who had spent years on the Southern Circuit, and who was trusted by many Southerners. Yet on February 8, when the Electoral Commission voted 8 to 7 to accept the Hayes electors from Florida, Democratic uncertainty became despair. Bradley had voted with the Republicans! Rumors circulated that Bradley was controlled by the Texas and Pacific interests, and his life was threatened.

The Democrats believed their strongest case was in Louisiana, and tensely awaited that decision. When the Commission also voted 8 to 7 to accept Louisiana's Hayes electors, Democrats raised the cry of conspiracy and accused the Republicans of not wanting to end corruption, of being willing to violate the Constitution, and of raping democracy by setting aside the choice of the people. Tempers flared both in and out of Congress; rumors circulated that armed men drilled in the South; someone fired a shot through a window of the Hayes home; a Democrat shot and wounded a Republican; and Democrats worked to organize a filibuster to prevent the Electoral Commission from reporting its findings to Congress. Republican charges that a filibuster would be a violation of the spirit of compromise failed to stop the Democrats.

That the Whig-Democrats at first backed their Northern colleagues in support of a filibuster was not as ominous as it seemed. The behind-the-scenes work went on as usual. Both Boynton and Kellar told Hayes that they would succeed in the end. The Washington *National Republican* reported that Hayes would maintain his determination to change the Republican Southern policy, and that meant, the paper commented, not just self-government for the South but also a liberal policy of internal improvement.

Whig-Democrats made it known that one of their conditions for breaking the filibuster and electing Hayes was a cabinet post, that of postmaster general—the patronage position. Republicans made it known that they wanted to elect the Speaker of the House in return for that favor. If those two conditions became a hard and fast bargain, then the Republicans would have gained two important things the electorate had apparently denied them in November, the House speakership and the presidency.

By a similar 8 to 7 vote, the Commission accepted the Hayes electors from South Carolina. By February 20, the filibuster threat was ended with the cooperation of the Whig-Democrats and Republicans, and the split in Democratic ranks was in the open. The Electoral Commission concluded its work on February 23, leaving only the official count to be made by a joint session of Congress. It appeared as if Hayes was finally to be declared the next president of the United States.

But on February 22 the *Ohio State Journal*, whose editor was a close personal friend of Hayes, waved the frayed bloody shirt again in an attack on Louisiana Democrats. Frightened Democrats assumed this represented Hayes' real policy, and Northern Democrats quickly circulated copies of the editorial among their colleagues. Furthermore, Whig-Democrats had been receiving mail from their constituents in support of Tilden and they found it difficult to explain to them how a cabinet post, railroad subsidies, and other internal improvements could have some connection with the electoral count. Practically overnight, the filibuster opened before the count could be reported. Then the filibuster faltered on February 24, and the Democratic Speaker of the House, Samuel J. Randall, ruled a motion to reconsider it out of order. Abram S. Hewitt, Democratic party chairman, denounced the Electoral Commission but asked for an end to the filibuster and completion of the count in order to keep the nation's peace.

Hewitt had been under pressure from business interests who warned him that the continuing crisis situation had hurt business, already staggering from the depression. Hewitt and Speaker Randall apparently felt that Hayes' election was less of a threat than renewed war might be. As a result, some Northeastern Democrats joined the ranks opposed to the filibuster, but at the same time some of the Whig-Democrats joined with the filibusterers. Confusion reigned in Congress. Once more the behind-the-scenes group went to work.

The climax of their activities came at the Wormley Hotel, in Washington, D.C., February 26 and 27. As a result of the editorial in the *Ohio State Journal*, Democrats at the meeting wanted concrete assurances that the troops would be removed from Louisiana when the electoral count was finished, which they apparently got from President Grant. They also wanted an official statement from Hayes that the Southern policy would, in fact, be changed when he took office. Republican leaders opposed an open statement, lest Radical Republicans like Morton, Conkling, and others somehow upset the bargain. Reluctantly, the Democrats concurred, and the filibuster again ended.

At 4:00 A.M. on the morning of March 2, the electoral tabulation was completed and Hayes was declared the victor over Tilden by an electoral vote of 185 to 184. Later that same day Grant ordered the troops from Louisiana. Also on that day, a Friday, Tom Scott's private railroad car sped Hayes to Washington. Since March 4 fell on a Sunday, Hayes privately took the oath of office on March 3, lest something else occur to intervene; on Monday, March 5, he was publicly inaugurated.

In a last blast at the Republicans, House Democrats resolved on March 3 that Tilden, not Hayes, was elected. That gesture of defiance might have provided some ammunition for Tilden had he been inclined to protest, but he was not. The Democrats, in a surly mood, blocked an army appropriations bill just before the session of Congress adjourned, with the result that the session ended with no money for the army.

The Aftermath

Many Americans felt relieved. Even though days, then weeks, then months had dragged by after the elections in November 1876 without a new president, the American political system had finally resolved the problem two days before the scheduled inauguration. Hayes, with opposition from his own party, initiated his new Southern policy with some success. He nominated former Confederate General David M. Key of Tennessee for postmaster general. Immediately, Radical Republicans, including Conkling and Cameron, attacked Key, as well as William M. Evarts of New York, Hayes's nomination for secretary of state, and Carl Schurz, his nomination for secretary of the interior. Radical Republican hopes of combining the attack on Key with the fight against the hated reformers, Schurz and Evarts, represented their effort to combine with Northern Democrats and defeat Hayes's entire cabinet. But the heyday of the Radicals had ended, and a combination of moderate Republicans and Whig-Democrats defeated them.

In both South Carolina and Louisiana rival governments still faced each other, and although Hayes delayed longer than the Democrats wished, by the end of April the president had neutralized the Carpetbag opposition and home rule was a reality. With the cabinet post and home rule settled, the questions of Southern internal improvements and Whig-Democrat pledges to let the Republicans organize the House remained. But Southern Democrats now reasoned that their chances for internal improvements were better with a Democratic-controlled House, and Garfield lost the speakership by nine votes.

That marked the first breach in the so-called Compromise of 1877. The second came when Hayes expressed doubt about a Texas Pacific bill in Congress, lest the situation create a new era of Crédit Mobilier type scandals. Hayes need not have worried. The Southern Pacific, to protect its west coast monopoly, illegally preempted the right of way to California that the Texas Pacific might have used. With that *fait accompli*, the Texas Pacific question was academic, and the railroad was destined never to reach the Pacific.

If, during the hectic winter months of 1876–1877, it still looked as if there might be a future in the Whig-Democrat and Republican courtship, based on a similarity of politico-economic interest, it was not to be. A powerful force was already at work to disrupt the alliance: Southern agrarianism. Southern farmers reacted to the depression of the 1870s like their Western counterparts, advocating greenbacks, free silver, antimonopoly policies, and other financial panaceas. Southern agrarians resented the way in which black-belt Whig-Democrats won their political power. They did not trust those who courted the business interests. Moreover, the internal improvements and subsidies to business that the Whig-Democrats promised never seemed to appear. Southern agrarians called for an alliance with Western agrarians, and moved to form third parties that threatened Whig-Democrat political control in various states.

If the Democratic party were to split and if the Whig-Democrats formed an alliance with Northern Republicans or even if they formed their own party, they would probably lose control of the South to the agrarians. The agrarians would attack tariffs, subsidies, bank laws, and other legal aids to business. The Whig-Democrats had no choice but to remain with the Democratic party for the political strength it gave them. Southern Democrats drew closer to the Eastern Democrats in order to make common cause within the party against the agrarian threat. There were times, in later years, when Southern Whig-Democrats and Eastern Democrats politely cooperated with the Republicans to defend business against the increasing populist clamor, but the Republicans, for many years to come, were unable to dent on election day the reconstruction-born, solid Democratic ranks in the South.

Although the two major parties bore the same names as in the antebellum era, they were different entities in the postwar years. Their base of support had changed, as had their ideals. The Democratic party, which once had a penchant for moderation, became a party of opportunism, an alliance of urban party machines of the North with the rural, white supremacist South. The once idealistic Republican party turned into a conservative protector of business. The years of war and reconstruction, of shifting issues and personnel, hammered the parties into new configurations.

Not only did political parties undergo great changes during the decades of disruption, but so did Americans. In the antebellum days, the North had been convulsed with surging tides of humanistic social reform, from the utopian communitarians of New Harmony and Brook Farm to Dorothea Dix and concern for the insane, Neal Dow and temperance, and of course, Frederick Douglass, Garrison, and the abolitionists. After the war, Americans seemed to lose their idealism to an equally energetic spirit of materialism, riding the roller coaster of optimistic expansion which crested in 1873, and plunged to the depths of depression in the following years. Although the voice of a social reformer cried out now and again, Americans were tuned to the industrial machine. Southerners, who so energetically turned to a defense of slavery prior to the war, equally energetically turned to the undoing of reconstruction, with civil and political disfranchisement of the blacks their first aim. The South remained primarily agrarian, with the sharecrop and tenant-farmer system serving to retard agricultural prosperity. The South was smothered under a blanket of poverty far into the next century.

The Civil War may have retarded Southern industrial development, but it encouraged Northern. Northern industry grew at a rapid pace in the decades before the war, perhaps slowed somewhat as the war oriented production toward war materials, and then burst forth with incredible renewed vigor by the end of the war. The impact of the Civil War on industrial and business growth was positive because of the needs of the war itself, and because the war situation centered that growth in the North to the virtual exclusion of the South. Republican-controlled Congresses saw to it that Northern business was well treated both during and after the war. Northern and Western agriculture, meanwhile, expanded mightily. Not only were many new acres brought under the plow, but mechanization spread as farm machinery found ready acceptance.

Few wars permanently settle any questions, but the Civil War in America did solve at least two previously insoluble issues. It determined the nature of the Union—the notion that a state could secede was buried forever, a fact confirmed by the Supreme Court in *Texas* v. *White* (1869). The Court ruled that the Union was indestructible, composed of indestructible states, and presided over by the Constitution. The question of the existence of slavery was also decided by the Thirteenth Amendment to the Constitution.

The war had demonstrated that the nation could fight a major war without impairing the basic rights of its citizens under the Constitution, even though the war greatly enhanced the powers of the executive. The war had in effect strengthened the centralization of power in the hands of the federal government at the expense of the states. The power of the federal government in a military sense—for the United States possessed trained military manpower that numbered in the millions—was unprecedented in American history. That power put teeth into the Monroe Doctrine, and lurked unmasked behind the effort to restore Mexico to the Mexicans.

The associationist tendencies of Americans continued undiminished from the antebellum period. Farmers joined together in Grange units that helped them to fight the abuses of railroad monopoly and to protect their collective welfare as the continued expansion of agriculture steadily depressed farm prices. The industrial machine accelerated the growth of labor organizations. The Knights of Labor attracted increasing numbers of workmen, who sometimes successfully, often unsuccessfully crusaded against the new giant business corporations. The plight of labor vis-à-vis business came home to Americans with astounding suddenness when President Hayes had to deal with the Great Strike of 1877, the first major labor disruption in American history. That strike heralded the thousands that were to follow before the century ended. Veterans by the millions joined the Grand Army of the Republic, a Union veterans' organization that grew into a potent lobbying force for veterans' benefits for the remainder of the century and often functioned as a powerful adjunct of the Republican party as well.

The debris of war in fact spawned a new America. The postwar era, from the late 1860s to the turn of the century, was a period of many beginnings. Industrialism had clearly replaced agriculture as the center of the American economy. New forms of business organization, including monopoly and giant corporations, characterized the new age. The results of the industrial economy and the American fascination with materialism gave some indication of what Americans might expect in the next century: from urban growth and sprawling slums to labor unions and their bloody war with the captains of industry.

Political parties by the 1870s were coalitions of many factions, and as a result during the late 1870s and 1880s, and after, in order to alienate as few as possible of their diverse supporters from different sections of the country, they became more and more conservative and less and less distinctive. By the 1880s their platforms were often difficult to tell apart. That, too, provided Americans with a glimpse of the twentieth century.

Yet the new, postwar America still suffered from its scars. The sorest of these was the position of the black man in American society. As Southerners regained the reins of state government, they systematically denied the black man political, social, and civil equality, a process nearly complete by 1900. Even in the North, where the black citizen usually won the franchise, though often with a struggle, a myriad of factors worked against real social and civil equality. What had happened to the black's antebellum friends who had so ardently sought abolition? A few continued to worry about his condition; but some died off and there were no new leaders to replace them; others turned to business; still others gave up when the "Southern problem" began to bore them. Like the other antebellum social crusades, the one for black political and civil equality was swallowed up in postwar materialism. In urban centers, a new black society, virtually invisible to white people, grew up with striking parallels to white society, yet isolated from it. Few blacks moved out of the South following the war, for the new agricultural arrangements held them rooted to the land in a semi-legal peonage. The reconstructors of the South had never sought to provide freedmen with land or any sort of economic base that might have guaranteed their political and social welfare.

In the postwar decades, the eyes of the nation focused not only on dramatic industrial growth, but on the rapid settlement and development of the Far West. By the turn of the century, the frontier in America had disappeared; new commonwealths had come into the Union, tied to the whole by steel rails. The Western economy thrived on vast wheatlands and great herds of cattle, as well as on the production of precious metals, and on the greatest commodity of all, more land. Civil War veterans from both North and South, and a few blacks, joined the boisterous crowd of immigrants who built the railroads, who prospected in the mountains, and who planted the wheat and raised the cattle. The romance of the Far West tantalized the Northeast and the South as dozens of writers turned westward expansion into one of the most legendary events in American folklore. In all of this the American Indian suffered severely, for the growth of the West was at his expense.

The Civil War marked the end of the older, adolescent days of agrarian America. The antebellum era had signs enough that America's youth was nearly over, but the war climaxed the end with sudden finality. The new era was symbolized by the Centennial Exhibition that opened in Philadelphia in the spring of 1876. This world's fair emphasized the material advance of America, bringing with it hope for the future, and it commemorated America's first century of independence. John Greenleaf Whittier summed it up when he prayed that future Americans might be "cast in some diviner mould." He implored: "Let the new cycle shame the old!" *

* The last two lines from Whittier's "Centennial Hymn." From *The Poetical Works of John Greenleaf Whitter*, Vol. IV (Boston and New York: Houghton, Mifflin and Company, 1892), p. 207.

For Further Reading:

A Select Bibliography

Those readers who may wish to study aspects of the era in more detail can begin with entries on this selective list. More detailed bibliographies are available in many of the volumes listed herein, but the student may also wish to consult Oscar Handlin et al., *The Harvard Guide to American History** (1955), or the *Goldentree Bibliographies in American History* series, especially David Donald, *The Nation in Crisis, 1861–1877* * (1969). Both offer more comprehensive collections, including source materials.

Important printed source materials for Congress include the *Congressional Globe, Containing the Debates and Proceedings, 1833–1873* (109 volumes, 1834–1873) and the *Congressional Record, Containing the Proceedings and Debates, 1873–* (1873–   ). Reports of the executive branch and House and Senate documents and committee reports can be found in the U. S. Serial Set. Military records are conveniently located in R. N. Scott et al., eds., *War of the Rebellion: A Compilation of the Official Records of the Union and Confederate Armies* (130 volumes, 1880–1901), and the parallel series for the navy. Chapter 5 in *The Harvard Guide*, above, provides a convenient key to other useful sources, government and otherwise.

In the following listing, many of the volumes under one subject heading might also be placed in another. The subject categories are in no way mutually exclusive. The publication date in parentheses indicates the edition the compiler believes most useful, not always the earliest publication date. An asterisk has been used to mark those works available in paperback.

General

Among the general works on the Civil War era are James Ford Rhodes, *History of the United States from the Compromise of 1850 to . . . 1877* (7 volumes, 1893–1900), dated, pro-Northern, yet scholarly; Allen Nevins, *Ordeal of the Union* (2 volumes, 1947), *The Emergence of Lincoln** (2 volumes, 1950), and *The War for the Union* (4 volumes, 1959–1971), a detailed, yet readable scholarly treatment; James G. Randall and David Donald, *The Civil War and Reconstruction* (2nd ed. revised, 1969), an updating of the work originally by Randall, the noted Lincoln scholar, comprehensive with an outstanding bibliography. Shorter works include Roy Nichols, *The Stakes of Power, 1845–1877* * (1961); Alan Barker, *The Civil War in America** (1961); Harry Hansen, *The Civil War** (1961); and Thomas H. O'Connor, *The Disunited States** (1972). Bruce Catton, *The Centennial History of the Civil War* (3 volumes, 1961–1965) is readable and popular. John Bach McMaster, *A History of the People of the United States during Lincoln's Administration* (1927) might better be put in another category, but its account, based often on contemporary newspapers, is unique. Thomas J. Pressly, *Americans Interpret their Civil War** (1964) is a look at the historical literature; while Edmund Wilson's *Patriotic Gore** is a study of the literature of the war. Arthur C. Cole's *The Irrepressible Conflict, 1850–1865* * (1934) and Avery Craven's *The Repressible Conflict* (1939) emphasize the 1850s.

Antebellum United States

Thomas C. Cochran and William Miller, *Age of Enterprise** (1940), George R. Taylor, *The Transportation Revolution, 1815–1860** (1951), Norman Ware, *The Industrial Worker, 1840–1860** (1924), and Joseph G. Rayback, *A History of American Labor** (1959) are useful treatments of industry and labor. Three excellent treatments of the immigration story are Oscar Handlin, *The Uprooted** (1951), Marcus L. Hansen, *The Atlantic Migration, 1607–1860** (1940), and Carl Wittke, *We Who Built America* (1939). Paul W. Gates, *The Farmer's Age** (1960) is a thorough treatment of agriculture from 1815 to 1860. Two volumes of the *New American Nation* series take up the far West: Francis S. Philbrick, *The Rise of the West, 1754–1830** (1965), and Ray A. Billington, *The Far Western Frontier, 1830–1860** (1956), the former thorough and old-fashioned, the latter excellent. Everett Dick, *The Dixie*

Frontier* (1948) concerns the southwest. Irving H. Bartlett, *The American Mind in the Mid-Nineteenth Century** (1967), Merle Curti, *The Growth of American Thought* (1943), Ralph H. Gabriel, *The Course of American Democratic Thought* (1940), and Vernon L. Parrington, *Main Currents in American Thought** (3 volumes, 1927-1930) are fine broad treatments, with Parrington unique among them. Ray A. Billington, *The Protestant Crusade, 1800–1860* (1938) is the standard study of nativism. Alice Felt Tyler, *Freedom's Ferment** (1944) and Gilbert Seldes, *The Stammering Century** (1928) make an interesting pair, with Tyler being a fine survey of reform movements and Seldes a social history of reformers and movements. Jerome Mushkat, *Tammany: The Evolution of a Political Machine, 1789–1865* (1971) is an example of urban politics in the antebellum and Civil War years.

The South. Clement Eaton, *A History of the Old South* (1966), Francis B. Simkins, *A History of the South* (1953), and Clement Eaton, *The Growth of Southern Civilization, 1790–1860* (1961) are useful tracts; Charles S. Sydnor, *The Development of Southern Sectionalism, 1819–1848** (1948) and David M. Potter's studies, *The South and the Sectional Conflict* (1968), are first rate. Three classics on the Old South, all worthy of attention, are Frederick L. Olmstead, *The Cotton Kingdom** (1953), Ulrich B. Phillips, *Life and Labor in the Old South** (1929), and Frank L. Owsley, *Plain Folk of the Old South** (1949). Eugene D. Genovese, *The Political Economy of Slavery** (1965) is reminiscent of economic interpretations of earlier decades, but with a modern outlook. W. J. Cash, *The Mind of the South** (1941), Clement Eaton, *The Mind of the Old South** (1967), William R. Taylor, *Cavalier and Yankee** (1961), and John H. Franklin, *The Militant South, 1800–1861** (1956) are all stimulating and scholarly treatments of the subject. Eugene D. Genovese's two essays in *The World the Slaveholders Made** (1969), are thought-provoking. Arthur C. Cole, *The Whig Party in the South* (1913), is especially helpful when supplemented with journal literature. Monroe L. Billington, *The American South** (1971) is a broad survey of Southern society from the colonial period to the present and provides perspective.

Slavery. John H. Franklin, *From Slavery to Freedom* (1967), is a standard account; August Meier and Eliott Rudwick, *From Plantation to Ghetto** (1966) is a brief account by white men; Benjamin Quarles, *The Negro in the Making of America** (1964) is a brief account by a black man; Lerone Bennett, *Before the Mayflower** (1966) is a journalistic account from the black viewpoint. Richard Bardolph, *The Negro Vanguard** (1959) examines black leadership. Ulrich B. Phillips, *American Negro Slavery** (1918) is an old standard that is enhanced in the 1966 edition with Eugene Genovese's introduction. Kenneth M. Stampp, *The Peculiar Institution** (1956) is another standard account. Carl N. Degler, *Neither Black Nor White: Slavery and Race Relations in Brazil and the United States** (1971) is a thoroughly modern comparison characterized by thoughtful scholarship, while Stanley M. Elkins,

Slavery: A Problem in American Institutional and Intellectual Life* (1959) is an interesting, provocative, and often controversial analysis of aspects of the institution. Richard C. Wade, *Slavery in the Cities, 1820–1860** (1964) and Robert S. Starobin, *Industrial Slavery in the Old South, 1790–1861* (1970) consider two different sides of the institution. On the slave trade see W. E. B. DuBois, *The Suppression of the African Slave Trade, 1683–1870* (1895), along with Daniel P. Mannix and Malcolm Cowley, *Black Cargoes** (1962), Peter Duignan and Clarence Clendenen, *The United States and the African Slave Trade* (1963), and Warren S. Howard, *American Slavers and Federal Law, 1837–1862* (1963).

Abolitionists. Louis Filler, *Crusade Against Slavery, 1830–1860** (1960) is a good general survey but often undigested; Dwight Dumond, *Antislavery: The Crusade for Freedom in America** (1966) is comprehensive; Gilbert H. Barnes, *The Antislavery Impulse, 1830–1844** (1964) is a reprint of the 1933 edition, old but useful. James M. McPherson, *The Struggle for Equality: Abolitionists and the Negro in the Civil War and Reconstruction** (1964) is a first-rate study of abolitionist ideals. Aileen Kraditor, *Means and Ends in American Abolition** (1969) is another good essay. Bertram Wyatt-Brown, *Lewis Tappan and the Evangelical War Against Slavery** (1969) is a thorough study of the evangelical aspect of abolition and antebellum reform. Russell B. Nye, *Fettered Freedom* (1949) explores civil liberties. Benjamin Quarles, *Black Abolitionists** (1969) presents an almost encyclopedic listing. Larry Gara, *The Liberty Line: The Legend of the Underground Railroad* (1961) is an up-to-date and thoughtful study, while Henrietta Buckmaster, *Let My People Go** (1941) is useful. Leon Litwack, *North of Slavery** (1961) is a study of Northern free blacks.

The 1850s. Holman Hamilton, *Prologue to Conflict** (1964) has become the standard scholarly work on the Compromise of 1850. Stanley W. Campbell, *The Slave Catchers: Enforcement of the Fugitive Slave Law, 1850–1860** (1972) is a well-done work on that subject. Philip Foner, *Business and Slavery* (1941) focuses on New York, while Thomas H. O'Connor, *Lords of the Loom* (1968) focuses on Massachusetts. Eric Foner, *Free Soil, Free Labor, Free Men** (1970) chronicles the antebellum Republican party. James C. Malin, *The Nebraska Question, 1852–1854* (1953) and Alice Nichols, *Bleeding Kansas* (1954), the former thorough, the latter short, deal with the Kansas-Nebraska issue. Paul W. Gates, *Fifty Million Acres** (1954) treats land policy in Kansas from the passage of the act in 1854 until 1890. Eugene H. Berwanger, *The Frontier Against Slavery* (1967) and James A. Rawley, *Race and Politics** (1969) deal with the extension of slavery and the race question on the frontier and Kansas. Robert W. Johannsen, *Frontier Politics and Sectional Conflict* (1955) is an excellent discussion of the subject. On Dred Scott see Vincent C. Hopkins, *Dred Scott's Case* (1951). Robert W. Johannsen edited a useful collection of documents on *The Lincoln-Douglas Debates of 1858**

(1965). A competent work on John Brown is J. C. Furnas, *The Road to Harper's Ferry* (1958). Roy F. Nichols analyzed the break-up of the Democratic Party in *The Disruption of American Democracy** (1948).

Secession. Emerson D. Fite, *The Presidential Campaign of 1860* (1911) and Ollinger Crenshaw, *The Slave States in the Presidential Election of 1860* (1945) together explore the ramifications of that crucial election. Southern viewpoints on secession are explained in Dwight L. Dumond, *The Secession Movement, 1860–1861* (1931) and Ralph A. Wooster, *The Secession Conventions of the South* (1962), the latter an analysis of their composition. Kenneth M. Stampp, *And the War Came* (1950) expresses Northern reaction to secession. Mary Scrugham, *The Peaceable Americans of 1860–1861* (1921) treats efforts at compromise. Robert G. Gunderson, *Old Gentlemen's Convention* (1961) deals with the Peace Convention at Washington, D.C., as does Jesse L. Keene, *The Peace Convention of 1861* (1961). David M. Potter, *Lincoln and his Party in the Secession Crisis** (1962) is an able study. Richard N. Current, *Lincoln and the First Shot** (1963) and Roy Meredith, *Storm over Sumter* (1957) both look at that crisis.

The War Years

Military. Short histories are R. E. and T. N. Dupuy, *The Compact History of the Civil War** (1960), Bruce Catton, *This Hallowed Ground** (1956), and Fletcher Pratt, *A Short History of the Civil War** (1952). Fred A. Shannon, *The Organization and Administration of the Union Army, 1861–1865* (2 volumes, 1928) is a prize-winning study of federal administration, while Kenneth P. Williams, *Lincoln Finds a General* (5 volumes, 1949–1959) examines Northern armies and commanders to 1864. Bruce Catton's three works on the Army of the Potomac, *Mr. Lincoln's Army** (1951), *Glory Road** (1952), and *A Stillness at Appomattox** (1953), look at the Eastern theater, as does Douglas S. Freeman, *Lee's Lieutenants* (3 volumes, 1942–1944). W. B. Wood and J. E. Edmonds, *A History of the Civil War in the United States, 1861–1865** (1905) is old, but excellent. Frank E. Vandiver, *Rebel Brass* (1956) considers the structure of Confederate command. Bell I. Wiley focuses on the soldier's life in *Johnny Reb* (1943) and *Billy Yank* (1952). Robert V. Bruce details Lincoln's relations with army ordnance in *Lincoln and the Tools of War.* Jack F. Leach deals with *Conscription in the United States* (1952), and Ella Lonn considers *Foreigners in the Army and Navy* (1951). Dudley T. Cornish, *The Sable Arm** (1956) tells the story of black soldiers in the Union service. The war in the West is treated by Jay Monaghan, *Civil War on the Western Border, 1854–1865* (1955), Richard S. Brownlee, *Gray Ghosts of the Confederacy: Guerilla Warfare in the West, 1861–1865* (1958), Ray C. Colton, *The Civil War in the Western Territories: Arizona, Colorado, New Mexico, and Utah* (1959), Robert H. Jones, *The Civil War in the Northwest: Nebraska, Wisconsin, Iowa, Minne-*

sota, and the Dakotas (1960), and Aurora Hunt, *The Army of the Pacific . . . 1860–1866* (1951). Two interesting books that deal with other aspects of military history are: Marcus Cunliffe, *Soldiers and Civilians: The Martial Spirit in America* (1968), which puts the Civil War in the perspective of United States military tradition; and Jay Luvaas, *The Military Legacy of the Civil War* (1959), which treats the Civil War's legacy for European military leaders.

There is a great amount of literature, often repetitious, on the battles. A very few of the better volumes are: Robert M. Johnston, *Bull Run* (1913); Clifford Dowdey, *The Seven Days: The Emergence of Lee* (1964); Edwin B. Coddington, *The Gettysburg Campaign* (1968); Clifford Dowdey, *Lee's Last Campaign* (1960); Frank E. Vandiver, *Jubal's Raid* (1960); Philip Van Doren Stern, *An End to Valor* (1958); Earl S. Miers, *Web of Victory* (1955); Thomas L. Connelly, *Army of the Heartland: The Army of Tennessee, 1861–1862* (1967); Dee A. Brown, *Grierson's Raid* (1954) and *The Bold Cavaliers* (1959). See also biographies of military figures. There also is a considerable literature of regimental histories. Two of the better ones are John J. Pullen, *The Twentieth Maine* (1957), and T. Harry Williams, who approached the subject through biography with *Hayes of the Twenty-third: The Civil War Volunteer Officer* (1965).

The Naval War. Virgil C. Jones, *The Civil War at Sea* (3 volumes, 1960–1962), and Bern Anderson, *By Sea and by River* (1962) are both excellent. Also useful are: Clarence E. Macartney, *Mr. Lincoln's Admirals* (1956); James M. Merrill, *The Rebel Shore* (1957); W. C. and Ruth White, *Tin Can on a Shingle* (1957); Edna and Frank Bradlow, *Here Comes the Alabama* (1958); William M. Robinson, Jr., *The Confederate Privateers* (1928); Hamilton Cochran, *Blockade Runners of the Confederacy* (1958); and John D. Milligan, *Gunboats down the Mississippi* (1965). A standard is H. Allen Gosnell, *Guns on the Western Waters* (1949). Philip Van Doren Stern, *The Confederate Navy* (1962) surveys that subject.

The North. T. Harry Williams, *Lincoln and the Radicals** (1941) takes up Lincoln's criticis, while W. B. Hesseltine considers *Lincoln and the War Governors* (1948). Burton Hendrick looks at *Lincoln's War Cabinet** (1946), and so does David Donald ed., *Inside Lincoln's Cabinet: The Civil War Diaries of Salmon P. Chase* (1954). Wood Gray, *The Hidden Civil War** (1942) and more recently, Frank L. Klement, *Copperheads in the Middle West* (1960) discuss Northern disaffection. David M. Silver, *Lincoln's Supreme Court* (1956) and James G. Randall's *Constitutional Problems Under Lincoln* (1951) are important studies of legal problems. Bert W. Rein, *An Analysis and Critique of the Union Financing of the Civil War* (1962), is short but sound, while the volume edited by David T. Gilchrist and W. David Lewis explores *Economic Change in the Civil War Era** (1965). G. E. Turner, *Victory Rode the Rails* (1953) discusses the Confederacy's railroads also. Norman J. Ware, *The Labor Move-*

ment in the United States, 1860–1895* (1929) follows Ware's *Industrial Worker*, cited above. Paul W. Gates, *Agriculture and the Civil War* (1965) discusses that aspect of life. George M. Frederickson probes *The Inner Civil War: Northern Intellectuals and the Crisis of the Union** (1965). The Union press is well treated in J. Cutler Andrews, *The North Reports the Civil War* (1955). James M. McPherson edited a unique volume on black reaction to the Civil War in *The Negro's Civil War** (1965), and Benjamin Quarles took a broader view in *The Negro in the Civil War** (1953). John Hope Franklin's *The Emancipation Proclamation** (1963) is a brief, but excellent study of that document and its impact. William F. Zornow, *Lincoln and the Party Divided* (1954) examines the election of 1864.

The South. Jefferson Davis, with an introduction by Earl S. Miers, *The Rise and Fall of the Confederate Government** (1961) tells Davis' side of the story. Three general studies are: Charles P. Roland, *The Confederacy** (1960); Clement Eaten, *A History of the Southern Confederacy** (1954); and E. Merton Coulter, *The Confederate States of America, 1861–1865* (1950). Emory Thomas views *The Confederacy as a Revolutionary Experience* (1971), and Frank Vandiver studies *Their Tattered Flags* (1970). Rembert W. Patrick studied *Jefferson Davis and His Cabinet* (1944), while Wilfred B. Yearns considered *The Confederate Congress* (1960). Federal relationships in the South are discussed by Curtis A. Amlund, *Federalism in the Southern Confederacy* (1966) and May S. Ringold, *The Role of the State Legislatures in the Confederacy* (1966). Confederate finances are explored by Richard C. Todd, *Confederate Finance* (1954), and John C. Schwab, *The Confederate States of America, 1861–1865* (1901), the latter a broader treatment. Opposition in the South is treated by Frank L. Owsley, *State Rights in the Confederacy* (1925) and by Georgia L. Tatum, *Disloyalty in the Confederacy* (1934). Mary E. Massey considers civilian hardship in *Ersatz in the Confederacy* (1952) and *Refugee Life in the Confederacy* (1964), while she surveys the women's role in *Bonnet Brigades: American Women in the Civil War* (1966). Bell I. Wiley Chronicles *Southern Negroes, 1861–1865* (1938). Robert C. Black looks at *Railroads of the Confederacy* (1952). J. Cutler Andrews, in a sequel to his earlier volume on the North, studies how *The South Reports the Civil War* (1970). Clement Eaton looks at *The Waning of the Old South Civilization** (1968).

Diplomacy

While there are no general studies, the standard work is that of Ephraim D. Adams, *Great Britain and the American Civil War* (2 volumes in one, reprinted c.1958). Also useful is H. C. Allen, *Great Britain and the United States* (1955). Two excellent Southern accounts are those by James M. Callahan, *Diplomatic History of the Southern Confederacy* (1901) and Frank L. Owsley, *King Cotton Diplomacy* (1959). Donaldson Jordan and Edwin J. Pratt,

Europe and the American Civil War (1926) along with Belle B. Sideman and Lillian Friedman, eds., *Europe Looks at the Civil War* (1960) show European responses. Lynn Case and Warren Spencer treat *The United States and France: Civil War Diplomacy* (1970). Both Benjamin P. Thomas, *Russo-American Relations, 1815–1867* (1930) and the more recent Albert A. Woldman, *Lincoln and the Russians* (1952) are excellent. Robin Winks produced a top-notch study of *Canada and the United States: The Civil War Years* (1960). Dexter Perkins, *The Monroe Doctrine, 1826–1867** (1933) is invaluable. On various aspects of diplomacy, the reader will have to consult the vast amount of periodical literature available.

Biographies

Biographical literature is profuse. A few worthy of consultation are: Martin B. Duberman, *Charles Francis Adams, 1806–1886** (1961); Henry Adams, *The Education of Henry Adams: An Autobiography** (1918); Fred H. Harrington, *Fighting Politician: Major General N. P. Banks* (1948); T. Harry Williams, *P. T. G. Beauregard: Napoleon in Gray* (1955); Betty Fladelander, *James Gillespie Birney: Slaveholder to Abolitionist* (1955); James C. Malin, *John Brown and the Legend of Fifty-Six* (1942); Hans L. Trefousse, *Ben Butler: The South Called Him Beast!* (1957); Richard N. Current, *John C. Calhoun* (1963); Thomas Graham and Marva R. Belden, *So Fell the Angels* (1956), a biography of Salmon P. Chase; Clement Eaton, *Henry Clay and the Art of American Politics** (1957); Hudson Strode, *Jefferson Davis* (3 volumes, 1955–1964); Gerald M. Capers, *Stephen A. Douglas, Defender of the Union* (1959); Benjamin Quarles, *Frederick Douglass** (1948); Charles A. Jellison, *Fessenden of Maine: Civil War Senator* (1962); Russel B. Nye, *William Lloyd Garrison and the Humanitarian Reformers** (1955); James B. Stewart, *Joshua R. Giddings and the Tactics of Radical Politics* (1970); Frank E. Vandiver, *Ploughshares into Swords: Josiah Gorgas and Confederate Ordnance* (1952); John F. C. Fuller, *The Generalship of Ulysses S. Grant* (1958); William B. Hesseltine, *Ulysses S. Grant, Politician* (1935); Glyndon G. Van Deusen, *Horace Greeley* (1953); Harold Schwartz, *Samuel Gridley Howe, Social Reformer, 1801–1876* (1956); Frank E. Vandiver, *Mighty Stonewall* (1957); Douglas S. Freeman, *R. E. Lee: A Biography* (4 volumes, 1934–1935); Earl S. Miers, *Robert E. Lee: A Great Life in Brief** (1956); Warren W. Hassler, Jr., *General George B. McClellan: Shield of the Union* (1957); Freeman Cleaves, *Meade of Gettysburg* (1960); Joseph Schafer, *Carl Schurz, Militant Liberal* (1930); Glyndon G. Van Deusen, *William Henry Seward* (1967); Earl S. Miers, *The General Who Marched to Hell: William Tecumseh Sherman and His March to Fame and Infamy** (1951); Benjamin P. Thomas and Harold M. Hyman, *Stanton: The Life and Times of Lincoln's Secretary of War* (1962); Richard N. Current, *Old Thad Stevens: A Story of Ambition* (1942); Burke Davis, *Jeb Stuart, the Last Cavalier* (1957); David

Donald, *Charles Sumner and the Coming of the Civil War* (1960); David Donald, *Charles Sumner and the Rights of Man* (1970); Richard O'Connor, *Thomas: Rock of Chickamauga* (1948); William Y. Thompson, *Robert Toombs of Georgia* (1966); Mark M. Krug, *Lyman Trumbull, Conservative Radical* (1965); Hans L. Trefousse, *Benjamin Franklin Wade: Radical Republican from Ohio* (1963).

Lincoln

There are many works that deal primarily with Lincoln. As with the previous section, only a few are listed here. One-volume biographies include: Benjamin P. Thomas, *Abraham Lincoln* (1952); R. H. Luthin, *The Real Abraham Lincoln* (1960); Lord Charnwood, *Abraham Lincoln** (1917). Multi-volume works include: J. G. Randall's scholarly *Lincoln the President** (4 volumes, with volume 4 concluded by Richard N. Current, 1945–1955); a sensitive biography by the great poet, Carl Sandburg, *Abraham Lincoln, The Prairie Years** (2 volumes, 1926) and *Abraham Lincoln, The War Years** (1939); and Albert J. Beveridge, *Abraham Lincoln, 1809–1858* (2 volumes, 1928), complete for Lincoln's earlier career. Benjamin P. Thomas, *Lincoln's New Salem* (1954) deals with his early life, while the following take up various segments of Lincoln's career: John J. Duff, *A. Lincoln, Prairie Lawyer* (1960); David Donald, *Lincoln's Herndon* (1948); Donald W. Riddle, *Lincoln Runs for Congress* (1948), and also *Congressman Abraham Lincoln* (1957); Don E. Fehrenbacher, *Prelude to Greatness* (1962); R. H. Luthin, *The First Lincoln Campaign* (1944); William E. Barringer, *A House Dividing* (1945). Other phases of Lincoln's life are explored by: Richard N. Current, *The Lincoln Nobody Knows** (1958); David Donald, *Lincoln Reconsidered** (1956); and J. G. Randall, *Lincoln the Liberal Statesman* (1947). Lincoln's relations with blacks can be found in Benjamin Quarles, *Lincoln and the Negro* (1962), and *Lincoln and the Politics of Slavery* (1970) by John S. Wright. David M. De-Witt, *The Assassination of Abraham Lincoln* (1909) is old but excellent, while Jim Bishop, *The Day Lincoln Was Shot** (1955) is popular and readable. Otto Eisenschiml asked *Why Was Lincoln Murdered?* (1937) and raised the question of Stanton's participation in the affair. Newspaperman Lloyd Lewis wrote a chatty book about the *Myths After Lincoln** (1929). Roy P. Basler et al. edited *The Collected Works of Abraham Lincoln* (9 volumes, 1953–1955), the source for Lincoln quotes in this volume. David M. Potter, *The Lincoln Theme and American National Historiography* (1948) examines the historical literature on Lincoln.

Reconstruction

General. William A. Dunning, *Reconstruction, Political and Economic** (1907) was the first major one-volume treatment that fathered a school of anti-Radical Republican studies. Among these are: Claude G. Bowers, *The Tragic Era** (1929); George Fort Milton, *The Age of Hate* (1930); and Hodding Carter, *The Angry Scar* (1959). More recent, and more moderate in nature, even occasionally revisionist, are: John Hope Franklin, *Reconstruction: After The Civil War** (1961); Rembert W. Patrick, *Reconstruction of the Nation** (1967); Allen W. Trelease, *Reconstruction: The Great Experiment** (1971); and Avery Craven, *Reconstruction: The Ending of the Civil War** (1969), which views Reconstruction as the last phase of the war. Kenneth M. Stampp in *The Era of Reconstruction, 1865-1877** (1965) has written an excellent revisionist synthesis. David Donald, *The Politics of Reconstruction, 1863-1867** (1965) and W. R. Brock, *An American Crisis: Congress and Reconstruction, 1865-1867** (1963) examine the politics of the presidential period. Eric L. McKitrick, *Andrew Johnson and Reconstruction** (1960) and John and La Wanda Cox, *Politics, Principles, and Prejudices** (1963) take President Johnson severely to task. A thoughtful account of Lincoln's approach to reconstruction that begins with the outbreak of the Civil War is William B. Hesseltine, *Lincoln's Plan of Reconstruction,** with an equally thoughtful introduction by Richard N. Current (1967). W. E. B. DuBois sets down a Marxist interpretation in *Black Reconstruction** (1935). Two black interpretations colored by a twentieth-century view are Henrietta Buckmaster, *Freedom Bound** (1965) and journalist Lerone Bennett's *Black Power, U.S.A.: The Human Side of Reconstruction, 1867-1877** (1967). James E. Sefton, *The United States Army and Reconstruction, 1865-1877* (1967) sheds light on the army's role.

The South. Among the accounts of visitors to the South after the war are: Whitelaw Reid, *After the War: A Tour of the Southern States, 1865-1866,** with an introduction by C. Vann Woodward (1965); and John R. Dennett, *The South As It Is, 1865-1866,** with an introduction by Henry M. Christman (1965). E. Merton Coulter, *The South During Reconstruction, 1865-1877* (1947) reflects a debt to Dunning. William B. Hesseltine, *Confederate Leaders in the New South* (1950), and William W. White, *The Confederate Veteran* (1962) explore the role of rebel leaders in the new South. Allen Trelease in *White Terror* (1971) examines the Ku Klux Klan. Vincent P. De Santis in *Republicans Face the Southern Question* (1959) along with Stanley P. Hirshson in *Farewell to the Bloody Shirt* (1962) consider the Republican party and the black man. On constitutional amendments see Jacobus ten Broek, *The Antislavery Origins of the Fourteenth Amendment* (1951) and William Gilette, *The Right to Vote: Politics and the Passage of the Fifteenth Amendment* (1970). Theodore B. Wilson, *The Black Codes of the South* (1965) treats one aspect of white supremacy, while Claude H. Nolen, *The Negro's Image in the South: The Anatomy of White Supremacy* (1967) deals more extensively with the subject, and Lawrence J. Friedman's *The White Savage: Racial Fantasies in the Postbellum South** (1970) takes the story up to World War I. C. Vann Woodward, *The Strange Career of Jim Crow** (2nd edition, 1966) deals with segregation from reconstruction through the 1960s. No study of the South would be complete without the fine, brief volume of C. Vann Woodward's essays, *The Burden of Southern History** (1968).

Robert Cruden, *The Negro in Reconstruction** (1969) is a survey of the black man's role, while Otis A. Singletary examines the aspect of the *Negro Militia and Reconstruction** (1957). George R. Bentley wrote *A History of the Freedmen's Bureau* (1955). Willie Lee Rose, *Rehearsal for Reconstruction: The Port Royal Experiment** (1964) is a brilliant study of a resettlement attempt. Samuel D. Smith, *The Negro in Congress, 1870–1901* (1966) looks at black politics.

Postwar Politics

In addition to the works listed under Reconstruction, see Hans L. Trefousse, *The Radical Republicans: Lincoln's Vanguard for Racial Justice* (1969), which views the Radicals in a favorable light. A good companion to ten Broek, above, is Joseph B. James, *The Framing of the Fourteenth Amendment* (1959), which provides a broader treatment of the affair. Stanley Kutler, *Judicial Power and Reconstruction Politics* (1968) ascribes a stronger role than usual to the courts during reconstruction. Old, but good is Charles H. Coleman, *The Election of 1868* (1933). Ari Hoogenboom's fine study *Outlawing the Spoils: A History of the Civil Service Reform Movement, 1865–1883* (1961) surveys a movement so important to the subjects of John G. Sproat's study of *"The Best Men": Liberal Reformers in the Gilded Age* (1968). Matthew Josephson takes a dim view of *The Politicos, 1865–1896** (1938). David Montgomery, *Beyond Equality: Labor and the Radical Republicans, 1862–1872* (1967) focuses on labor's connection with politics, while Gerald N. Grob, *Workers and Utopia . . . 1865–1900* (1961) surveys labor philosophy. Robert P. Sharkey in *Money, Class, and Party** (1959) examines the politics of finance, as does Irwin Unger in *The Greenback Era: A Social and Political History of American Finance, 1865–1879* (1964), an excellent work. Walter T. K. Nugent in *The Money Question during Reconstruction** (1967) provides a good summary of the problem.

C. Vann Woodward in two fine books—*Reunion and Reaction** (1956) and *Origins of the New South, 1877–1913** (1951)—discusses first the circumstances of the disputed election of 1876 and its settlement, and then the period of the undoing of reconstruction.

Index